CANADIAN EDITION

Operations & Supply Chain Management

THE CORE

F. Robert Jacobs
Indiana University

Richard B. Chase
University of Southern California

Jaydeep Balakrishnan
University of Calgary

McGraw-Hill
Ryerson
Connect. Learn. Succeed.

Operations & Supply Management: The Core
Canadian Edition

ISBN-13: 978-0-07-096907-0
ISBN-10: 0-07-096907-8

1 2 3 4 5 6 7 8 9 10 TCP 1 9 8 7 6 5 4 3 2 1 0

Printed and bound in Canada.

Care has been taken to trace ownership of copyright material contained in this text; however, the publisher will welcome any information that enables them to rectify any reference or credit for subsequent editions.

VICE PRESIDENT & EDITOR-IN-CHIEF: Joanna Cotton
SPONSORING EDITOR: Kimberley Redhead
DEVELOPMENTAL EDITOR: Suzanne Simpson/Sarah Fulton
MARKETING MANAGER: Cathie Lefebvre
Senior EDITORIAL ASSOCIATE: Stephanie Hess
SUPERVISING EDITOR: Graeme Powell
COPY EDITOR: Gillian Scobie
PRODUCTION COORDINATOR: Sharon Stefanowicz/Jennifer Hall
COMPOSITION: Aptara
INTERIOR DESIGN: Artplus Design & Formatting/Sarah Orr
COVER DESIGN: Artplus Design & Formatting/Sarah Orr
COVER IMAGE CREDIT: © Digital Vision
PRINTER: Transcontinental Gagne

Library and Archives Canada Cataloguing in Publication

Jacobs, F. Robert
    Operations and supply management: the core/F. Robert Jacobs, Richard B. Chase, Jaydeep Balakrishnan.—Canadian ed.

    ISBN 978-0-07-096907-0

    1. Production management—Textbooks.   I. Chase, Richard B.
    II. Balakrishnan, Jaydeep   III. Title.
TS155.J28 2009   658.5   C2009-903246-5

To our wives Jeanne, Harriet
and to our children Jennifer and Suzy
Laurie, Andy, Glenn, Rob, Christine, and Batsheva
F. Robert Jacobs & Richard B. Chase

To my wife, Vineetha, and my sons, Rohil and Aneesh
Jaydeep Balakrishnan

F. Robert Jacobs is Chase Faculty Fellow Professor of Operations Management at the Kelley School of Business, Indiana University. He received a B.S. in Industrial Engineering as well as Computer and Information Science, an MBA, and a Ph.D. in Operations Management all from The Ohio State University. He has also taught at the University of Houston and The Ohio State University. He has published 7 books and over 50 research articles on topics that include enterprise resource planning, inventory control, the design of manufacturing facilities, cellular manufacturing, and the scheduling of manufacturing operations. He is a fellow of the Decision Sciences Institute and past president and has received teaching honors such as MBA Teaching Award, Students Award for Teaching Excellence in International Business Issues, and Teaching Excellence in Operations Management. He now serves on the APICS E&R Foundation Board of Directors.

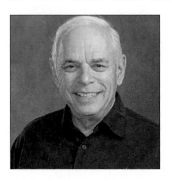

Richard B. Chase is Justin B. Dart Professor of Operations Management at the Marshall School of Business, University of Southern California. He received his Ph.D. in Operations Management, as well as an MBA and B.S. from UCLA. He has taught at the Harvard Business School, IMD (Switzerland), and the University of Arizona. His research examines service process design and service strategy. In 2006 he received a POMS Lifetime Achievement Award for his research in service operations and in 2004 received a Scholar of the Year Award by the Academy of Management. He is a Fellow of the Academy of Management, Production Operations Management Society, and the Decision Sciences Institute. He was also an Examiner for the Malcolm Baldrige National Quality Award. Dr. Chase has lectured/consulted recently on service and excellence to such organizations as Cisco Systems, Four Seasons Resorts, General Electric, and the Gartner Group.

Jaydeep Balakrishnan is Professor of Operations Management at the Haskayne School of Business, University of Calgary. He completed his doctorate in Operations Management from Indiana University. Prior to this he obtained an MBA at the University of Georgia, and an undergraduate degree in Mechanical Engineering from the Visvesvaraya National Institute of Technology, Nagpur University, India. Dr. Balakrishnan is certified in Production and Inventory Management by *APICS—The Association for Operations Management*. He has been a visiting, teaching, and research scholar in Hong Kong, Poland, Austria, Iran, and Singapore. Dr. Balakrishnan has served as the president of the Calgary Chapter of the *Canadian Operational Research Society* and the Calgary chapter of *APICS*.

Dr. Balakrishnan has been the recipient of several achievement awards including the *2007 Dean's Award for Outstanding Research Achievement*, an Honorable Mention from the *Decision Sciences Institute (DSI)* for Instructional Innovation in 2005, and the Best Operations Management Paper Award at the *Western DSI Meeting* in 1994. Dr. Balakrishnan has been a holder of Natural Sciences and Engineering Research Council (NSERC) grants and is listed in the *Who's Who in Canadian Business* published by the University of Toronto Press.

BRIEF TABLE OF CONTENTS

DETAILED TABLE OF CONTENTS

SECTION 2 PROCESSES

SECTION 4   MEDIUM- AND SHORT-RANGE OPERATIONS PLANNING

WHY YOU NEED THIS BOOK

The goal of this book is to provide you with the essential information that every manager needs to know about operations and supply-related activities in a business. Today's manager cannot ignore how the real work of the organization is done. This book is all about how to get the real work done effectively. **It makes little difference whether you are officially in finance, marketing, accounting, or operations:** The value-added work and the process of creating and delivering products need to be completed in a manner that is both high-quality and maximally efficient. Think of this course as preparing you to be your most productive.

We can consider the importance of the material in the book on many levels, but let's focus on three. **First, consider your role as a business unit manager with people working under your supervision.** The concepts in this text will be critical to your success in that role. One of your major duties will be to organize the way work is done. There needs to be some structure to the work process, including how information is captured and analyzed, as well as how decisions, changes, and improvements are made.

Designing efficient process flows is an important element of getting a group to work together. If your group is involved in creative activities such as designing cars, buildings, or even stock portfolios, the work to be done, who is responsible for what, and how progress is reported, need to be structured. The concepts of project management, manufacturing and service process design, capacity analysis, and quality in this text are all directly related to the knowledge you will need to be a great supervisor in your organization.

Next, think about becoming a senior executive. Making acquisitions, planning mergers, and buying and selling divisions will get your name and picture in business magazines. Deals are newsworthy and being a deal maker is consistent with the image of the modern executive as someone who focuses on grand strategy and leaves operations details to others. Unfortunately, the majority of deals are unsuccessful. The critical element of success, even with the grandest deals, can still be found most often in the operational details.

Real success happens when operational processes can be improved. Productivity improvements from things such as sharing customer service processes, purchasing systems, distribution and manufacturing systems, and other processes can lead to great synergies and success. Operations accounts for 60 to 80 percent of the direct expenses that limit the profit of most firms. Without these operations synergies, designed and implemented by executives with a keen understanding of the concepts in this book, companies are often left with expensive debt, disappointed customers and shareholders, and pressure on the bottom line—on earnings.

Finally, you may be interested in a career in operations. Well, you are not alone. Professional organizations such as APICS—The Association for Operations Management (an international organization active in Canada), the Purchasing Management Association of Canada (PMAC), and Supply Chain and Logistic Canada (SCL) have many members participating in regular monthly meetings, annual conferences, and certification programs. An entry-level job might be as a forecast strategist, operations (or supply chain) analyst, project manager, inventory control analyst, production supervisor, purchasing manager, logistics manager, transportation analyst, or warehouse specialist. In addition, top operations students may obtain their initial jobs with consulting firms, working as business process analysts and system design specialists.

A 2008 survey on supply-chain management employment conducted by PMAC found that even employees under the age of 25 working in supply chain functions **earned an average annual salary of over $50 000.** The authors' experience with students has been that initial offers for operations majors usually compare well with those in accounting, finance, and marketing. There are great opportunities for students who major in the field. For more information about careers in the field, visit the Web site of the Canadian Supply Chain Sector Council (www.supplychaincanada.org).

See pages xii–xvi for information about the tools in this text and online, which can help you to achieve success in this course.

About the Cover and Title

Operations and Supply Management: The Core derives its title from a combination of ideas and trends. In order to be lean and focused, the book presents the important core ideas. A review by Professor Jacobs of the syllabi of over a dozen representative American universities revealed that, as expected, there was a wide variety of topics covered, all of which would lead naturally to a comprehensive text such as *Operations Management for Competitive Advantage*. The topics covered in all of these sampled schools, i.e., the consistent or "core" topics, and only those is what this text includes.

Also, as is well known in the field, success for companies today requires successfully managing the entire supply flow, from the sources of the firm, through the value-added processes of the firm, and on to the customers of the firm.

The cover illustration is intended to represent the core as well as the supply flow. Just as lava flows from the core of the earth, operations and supply management is the core of business. Materials must flow through supply processes to create cash output and profits.

In *Operations and Supply Management: The Core,* we take students to the centre of the business and focus on the core concepts and tools needed to ensure that these processes run smoothly.

The first Canadian edition makes the textbook more relevant to students and instructors by incorporating appropriate material from this country through opening vignettes, discussion, Operations Management in Practice boxes, cases, and business examples interwoven throughout the text. Canadian organizations, such as EllisDon, RIM and Shouldice Hospital, are spotlighted as examples of operations and supply management in practice. Furthermore, material has been added on process management to enhance the student's understanding of the operations management field.

WALKTHROUGH

Chapter Opener

Each chapter begins with a set of learning objectives designed to provide a focus for the chapter. These objectives indicate what students should know after completing the chapter.

Opening Vignettes

Each chapter opens with a short vignette to set the stage and help pique students' interest in the material about to be studied. A few examples include:

- Arcelor Mittal Dofasco, Chapter 2,
- EllisDon, Chapter 3,
- GE, Chapter 7,
- Walmart, Chapter 11.

Operations and Supply Management in Practice Boxes

Operations and Supply Management in Practice boxes provide examples or expansions of the topics presented by highlighting leading companies practicing new, breakthrough ways to run their operations. Examples include:

- Zara Excels on Price, Speed, and Flexibility, Chapter 2.
- Supply Chain Services at DHL, Chapter 5
- J. D. Power and Associates Redefines Quality, Chapter 7
- Employee Suggestions Pay Off at Canada Post, Chapter 10

Examples with Solutions

Examples follow quantitative topics and demonstrate specific procedures and techniques. Clearly set off from the text, they help students understand the computations.

CHAPTER 4

STRATEGIC CAPACITY MANAGEMENT

Learning Objectives

1. Know what the concept of capacity is and how important it is to "manage" capacity over time.
2. Understand the impact of economies of scale on the capacity of a firm.
3. Understand what a learning curve is and how to analyze one.
4. Learn how to use decision trees to analyze alternatives when faced with the problem of adding capacity.
5. Know the differences in planning capacity between manufacturing firms and service firms.

SHOULDICE HOSPITAL: HERNIA SURGERY INNOVATION

During World War II, Dr. Edward Earle Shouldice, a major in the army, found that many young men willing to serve their country had to be denied enlistment because they needed surgical treatment to repair hernias before they could be pronounced physically fit for military training. In 1940, hospital space and doctors were scarce, especially for a nonemergency surgery that normally took three weeks of hospitalization. So, Dr. Shouldice resolved to do what he could to alleviate the problem. Contributing his services at no fee, he performed an innovative method of surgery on 70 of those men, speeding their induction into the army.

The recruits made their success stories known, and by the war's end, more than 200 civilians had contacted the doctor and were awaiting surgery. The limited availability of hospitals beds, however, created a major problem. There was only one solution: Dr. Shouldice decided to open his own hospital.

In July 1945, Shouldice Hospital, with a staff consisting of a nurse, a secretary, and a cook, opened its doors to its waiting patients. In a single operating room, Dr. Shouldice repaired two hernias per day. As requests for this surgery increased, he extended the facilities, located on Church Street in Toronto, by eventually buying three adjacent buildings and increasing the staff accordingly. In 1953, he purchased a country estate in Thornhill, where a second hospital was established.

Today all surgery takes place in Thornhill. Repeated development has culminated in the present 89-bed facility. Shouldice Hospital has been dedicated to the repair of hernias for over 60 years, using the "Shouldice Technique." The "formula,"

Operations and Supply Management in Practice

How IKEA Designs Its Attractive Prices

Competitive strategy is about being different. It means deliberately choosing a different set of activities to deliver a unique mix of value. IKEA, the Swedish retailer of home products, dominates markets in 43 countries, and is enjoying success in Canada too. One factor above all others accounts for IKEA's success: good quality at a low price. IKEA sells household items that are cheap but not cheapo, with prices that typically run 30 to 50 percent below those of the competition. While the price of other companies' products tends to rise over time, IKEA says it has reduced its retail prices by a total of about 20 percent during the last four years. At IKEA the process of driving down costs starts the moment a new item is conceived and continues relentlessly throughout the production run.

Consider IKEA's "Bang" mug, which has been redesigned three times so far, simply to maximize the number of mugs that can be stored on a pallet. Originally, only 864 mugs would fit.

A redesign added a rim such as you would find on a flowerpot so that each pallet could hold 1280 mugs. Last year, yet another redesign created a shorter mug with a new handle, allowing 2024 to squeeze onto a pallet. While the mug's sales price has remained the same shipping cost has been reduced by 60 percent, which is a significant savings, given that IKEA sells about 25 million mugs each year.

EXAMPLE 4.1: SAMPLE LEARNING CURVE PROBLEM

Captain Nemo, owner of the Suboptimum Underwater Boat Company (SUB), is puzzled. He has a contract for 11 boats and has completed 4 of them. He has observed that his production manager, young Mr. Overick, has been reassigning more and more people to torpedo assembly after the construction of the first four boats. The first boat, for example, required 225 workers, each working a 40-hour week, while 45 fewer workers were required for the second boat. Overick has told them that "this is just the beginning" and that he will complete the last boat in the current contract with only 100 workers!

Overick is banking on the learning curve, but has he gone overboard?

SOLUTION

Because the second boat required 180 workers, a simple exponential curve shows that the learning percentage is 80 percent ($180 \div 225$). To find out how many workers are required for the 11th boat, we look up unit 11 for an 80 percent improvement ratio in Appendix Exhibit B.1 and multiply this value by the number required for the first sub. By interpolating between Unit 10 and Unit 12 we find the improvement ratio is equal to 0.4629. This yields 104.15 workers (0.4269 interpolated from table $\times$ 225). Thus, Overick's estimate missed the boat by four people.

Global

Global icons identify international examples and text discussion.

Cross Functional

These icons highlight areas where operations management concepts "link" and integrate with other business functions. (i.e. marketing, finance, and accounting).

Supply Chain

These icons highlight areas with a direct link to supply-chain management.

Excel

These icons point out concepts where Excel templates are available on the text Web site.

Interactive Operations Management

These icons direct students to Interactive Operations Management Java applets that are available on the text Web site.

Photos and Exhibits

Over thirty photos and over one hundred fifty exhibits are included in the text to enhance visual appeal and clarify text discussions. Many of the photos illustrate additional examples of companies that use the operations and supply chain concepts in their business.

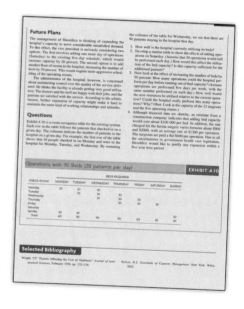

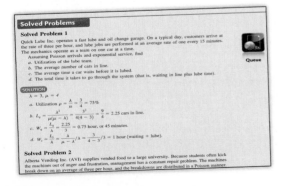

Solved Problems

Representative sample problems are placed at the end of appropriate chapters. Each includes a detailed, worked-out solution and provides another level of support for students before they try problems on their own.

Key Terms

The unique vocabulary of *Operations and Supply Management* is highlighted in the Key Terms section at the end of each chapter and includes definitions.

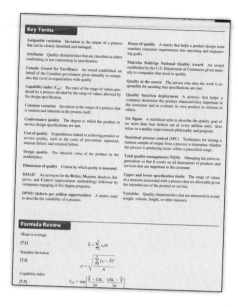

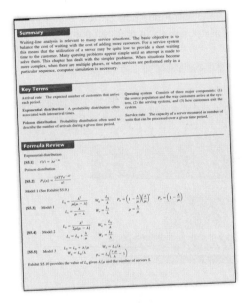

Formula Reviews

These lists at the end of chapters summarize formulas in one spot for easy student access and review.

Cases

Located at the end of all chapters, twenty-one cases allow students to think critically about issues discussed in the chapter. Cases include:

- Lasik Vision, Chapter 2
- Shouldice Hospital, Chapter 4
- Kristen's Cookie Company, Chapter 6
- Hewlett Packard, Chapter 13

Online Learning Centre

The Online Learning Centre, developed by Franca Giacomelli of Humber College, available at www.mcgrawhill.ca/olc/jacobs includes additional content, chapter summaries, multiple choice quizzes, key terms and formulas.

Connect* Operations Management:** www.connectom.ca. This innovative online study space helps students master the concepts with all of the learning tools they've come to expect, including multiple-choice and true/false quizzes, chapter-by-chapter learning goals, and key term reviews, plus OM interactivities, videos, and pre- and post-diagnostic assessments that point them to the concepts they need to focus on to improve their grades. Students can choose from all of these features to create their own personalized study plan—Connect*** offers the best, most convenient way to Learn, Interact, and Succeed!

OMC

The Operations Management Center Supersite at www.mhhe.com/pom offers a wealth of edited and organized OM resources including links to Operations Management *Business-Week* articles, OM Organizations, and virtual tours of operations in real companies.

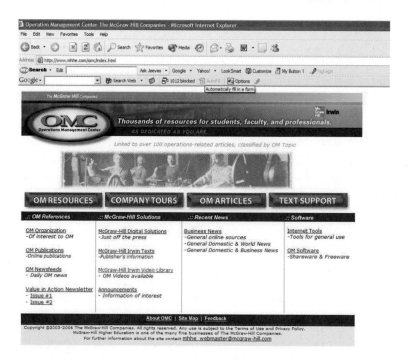

Instructor Resources

Instructor Online Learning Centre

The Online Learning Centre at www.mcgraw-hill.ca/olc/jacobs includes a password-protected Web site for instructors. The site offers downloadable supplements and customizable teaching aids.

Content cartridges are also available for course management systems, such as WebCT and Blackboard, to expand the reach of your course and open up distance-learning operations.

Instructor's Solutions Manual

This manual, prepared by the Canadian edition author Jaydeep Balakrishnan, contains the complete solutions to all exercises.

Downloadable Computerized Test Bank

Developed by Rob Shepherd of Niagara College, the EZ-Test test-generating engine is stocked with true/false, multiple choice, and short answer questions. Generating quizzes and tests is as easy as clicking a mouse. The Computerized Test Bank contains the answers to all questions, along with a difficulty rating and the relevant Learning Objective.

Microsoft® PowerPoint® Presentations

Microsoft® PowerPoint® Presentations, prepared by Michael Bozzo of Mohawk College, provide lecture outlines plus graphic material from the text to complement and customize lectures.

Image Library

The image library contains all of the illustrations, photographs, and tables from the text for use in multimedia presentations. Instructors can use these to create their own lecture presentations.

Acknowledgments

The author is thankful to colleagues Giovani da Silveira, Janice Eliasson, and Brent Snider, and Area Administrative Assistant, Ada Routly for their contributions to the book in different ways. The support of the Haskayne School of Business and other colleagues is also gratefully acknowledged.

The author also wishes to thank the following reviewers for their many thoughtful suggestions for this text:

Reviewers

Kirk L. Bailey, *Ryerson University*
Paul Callaghan, *Acadia University*
Liming Dai, *University of Regina*
Dr. Beverley Fretz, *University of Guelph*
David A. Johnston, *York University*
Binyamin Mantin, *University of British Columbia*
M. Abdur Rahim, *University of New Brunswick*
Saibal Ray, *McGill University*
Barry Cross, *Queen's University*
Randy Delorey, *St. Francis Xavier University*
Mary Drane, *Seneca College*
Donglei Du, *University of New Brunswick*
Alok Dua, *University of Manitoba*

Paul Gallagher, *Durham College*
Janet Porter, *Humber College*
Rob Shepherd, *Niagara College*
Edward R. Syme, *Georgian College*
Terry Hickey, *Loyalist College*
Linda Lakats, *York University*
David Laurentiu, *Centennial College of Applied Arts and Technology*
Sandi Findlay, *Mount Saint Vincent University*
Michael Bozzo, *Mohawk College*
Jackie Shemko, *Durham College*
Sam Lampropoulos, *George Brown College*
Cyril Foropon, *University of Manitoba*
Franca Giacomelli, *Humber College*
Kalinga Jagoda, *Mount Royal College*
David Slichter, *Conestoga College*

Twenty-First-Century Operations and Supply Management

Managing a modern supply chain, obviously, involves specialists in manufacturing, purchasing, and distribution. However, today it is also vital to the work of chief financial officers, chief information officers, operations and customer service executives, and chief executives. Changes in operations and supply management have been truly revolutionary, and the pace of progress shows no sign of moderating. In our increasingly interconnected and interdependent global economy, the process of delivering supplies and finished goods from one place to another is accomplished by means of mind-boggling technological innovation, clever new applications of old ideas, seemingly magical mathematics, powerful software, and old-fashioned concrete, steel, and muscle.

In the first section of *Operations and Supply Management: The Core*, we lay a foundation for understanding the dynamic field of operations and supply management. This book is about designing and operating processes that deliver a firm's goods and services in a way that matches customers' expectations. Really successful firms have a clear and unambiguous idea of how they intend to make money. Whether it is high-end goods or services tailored to the needs of a single customer or generic inexpensive commodities that are bought largely on the basis of cost, competitively producing and distributing these products is a great challenge.

INTRODUCTION TO OPERATIONS AND SUPPLY MANAGEMENT

Learning Objectives:

1. Understand what operations and supply management is.
2. Know why understanding operations and supply management is important to any manager.
3. Understand the meaning of efficient and effective operations.
4. Describe transformation processes.
5. Differentiate between goods and services.
6. Understand how operations and supply management got to where it is.
7. Discuss important current challenges facing operations and supply management.

EFFECTIVE BOARDING PROCESSES CAN INCREASE AIRLINE BOTTOM LINE

An important question for airlines is "What is the best way to board passengers?". Getting passengers on a plane quickly can greatly affect an airline's costs. Southwest says that if its boarding times increased by 10 minutes per flight, it would need 40 more planes at a cost of US$40 million each to run the same number of flights it runs now.

You have probably experienced waiting in line at the gate to board an airplane. You may also recall that the gate attendant, after first boarding passengers with special needs, probably boarded passengers depending on their seat numbers. Passengers seated at the back of the plane are boarded first so they will not get in the other passengers' way. Have you ever wondered whether there is a better way?

There definitely is, according to Clive Beddoe, former CEO of Calgary-based WestJet Airlines Ltd. After trying different methods, he was convinced that the best way to board passengers is to do so randomly. The reason, according to Mr. Beddoe, is that even when boarding is done by rows, it doesn't account for passengers with complications such as a big overcoat or big bag blocking others. Interestingly, WestJet hit upon this method when a boarding-gate attendant humorously decided to board passengers by the colour of their socks. This created a random order, which WestJet discovered to be the most effective.

On the other hand, Air Canada feels that the best way to ensure smooth boarding is to give priority to passengers at the back of the plane. United Airlines boards passengers in window seats first, then those seated in the middle, and finally passengers seated on the aisle. United feels that this method reduces boarding times by four to five minutes on average and saves US$1 million annually. America West uses what it calls a "reverse pyramid." The first economy-class passengers to get on the plane are those with window seats in the middle and rear of the plane. Then America West gradually fills in the plane, giving priority to those with window or rear seats, until it finally boards those seated along aisles in the front.

These examples show that while there may be more than one solution to a problem, what is important is that every organization has processes, and these processes should be frequently analyzed for improvements.

Creating Order

America West's reverse pyramid system boards coach-class passengers in back-row window seats first.

Order of boarding

First   Last

Source: *Interfaces*, May/June 2005, p. 194.

■ Sources: Brent Jang, "Best Boarding Rules are No Rules, Beddoe says," *The Globe and Mail*, November 4, 2005, B1.

Nicholas Zamiska, "Plane Geometry: Scientists Help Speed Boarding of Aircraft; America West Saves Minutes with 'Reverse Pyramid;' Link to Relativity Theory," *The Wall Street Journal*, November 2, 2005, A21.

Interfaces, May/June 2005, p. 194.

WHAT IS OPERATIONS AND SUPPLY MANAGEMENT?

Operations and supply management (OSM) is the design, operation, and improvement of the systems that create and deliver a firm's primary products (goods and services). Like marketing and finance, OSM is a functional area of business with clear line-management responsibilities. This point is important because operations and supply management is frequently confused with operations research and management science (OR/MS) and industrial engineering (IE). The essential difference is that OSM is a field of management, whereas OR/MS is the application of quantitative methods to decision making in all fields, and IE is an engineering discipline. Thus, while operations and supply managers use the decision-making tools of OR/MS (such as critical path scheduling) and are concerned with many of the same issues as IE (such as factory automation), OSM's distinct management role distinguishes it from these other disciplines.

As Exhibit 1.1 shows, OSM is concerned with the management of the entire system that produces a good or delivers a product. Producing a product such as a cell phone, or providing a service such as a cellular phone account, involves a complex series of transformation processes. Exhibit 1.1 is a simplified supply chain for an original equipment

Supply Chain of a Typical Original Equipment Manufacturer	EXHIBIT 1.1

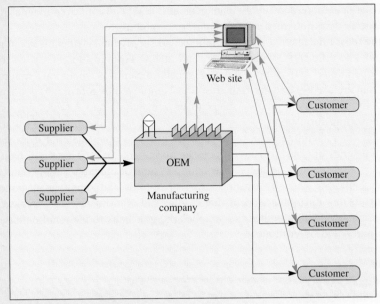

As this schematic suggests, a value chain is not a simple linear series of connections. It typically involves a complex series of business interactions and channel configurations. The Web is a key technology enabling efficient communication throughout the chain.

manufacturer (OEM), such as RIM, the Canadian maker of the famous Blackberry smart-phones (even U.S. President Barack Obama carries one!). A supply chain is a network of facilities that procures raw materials, transforms them into intermediate goods or services and then final goods or services, and delivers the goods or services to customers through a distribution system. To actually produce the phones and get them to the customer, many transformations must take place. For example, the suppliers (also called vendors) purchase raw materials and produce the parts for the phone. The RIM manufacturing plant takes these parts and assembles the various popular cell phone models. Orders for the phones are taken over the Internet from intermediate customers (all the distributor, dealer, and warehouse sites around the world). These intermediate customers work with their customers (local retailers), who in turn work directly with the end customer (the consumer) in setting up and managing the cell phone accounts. OSM is concerned with managing all of these individual processes as effectively as possible. A more detailed version of a supply chain is presented in Chapter 8. Chapter 2 discusses where OSM fits in the company's organization and strategy.

OPERATIONS AND SUPPLY MANAGEMENT: A CRITICAL RESPONSIBILITY OF EVERY MANAGER

If you are interested in becoming a great manager, the topics in this book are important for achieving this goal. Whether the economy is booming or in a recession, delivering a firm's goods and services in the most effective manner is critical to its survival. And if you think this book is just about manufacturing and relevant only for people working in a factory, you are in for some surprises about this fascinating field. The accompanying OSMP (operations and supply management in practice) with letters from MBA students shows that operations and supply management (OSM) is useful even in areas not traditionally associated with it, such as medicine or accounting.

At the most fundamental level, operations and supply management is about getting work done quickly, efficiently, without error, and at low cost. In the context of this book the terms "operations" and "supply" take on special meaning. "Operations" refers to the processes that are used to transform the resources employed by a firm into goods and services desired by customers. "Supply" refers to how materials and services are moved to and from those transformation processes. Take a simple manufacturing plant that makes golf balls. The manufacturing plant takes rubber, cork, and other material from suppliers, and through a series of transformation processes makes golf balls. These golf balls are sold to customers after moving through a distribution system designed to supply retail outlets with the golf balls. So when we use the term "operations and supply management," we are referring to this integrated system that at one end coordinates the purchase of material from suppliers and at the other end supplies the golf balls to the retail outlets, where they can be purchased by customers.

Supply Chain

Operations and Supply Management in Practice

Letters from Two MBA Students at the University of Calgary

. . . the ever-increasing cost of delivering health care along with government funding constraints has resulted in challenges in managing the tension between those administering care to patients i.e., doctors and nurses, and the managers running hospitals as organizations.

Among the many facets of health care delivery that requires [sic] a critical re-evaluation, the processes used to deliver care certainly come to mind. Why do some patients wait for up to 3–4 hours before seeing a doctor with whom they had an appointment? Why do some patients get laboratory or imaging results a week after the test is performed, when the results often are available the same day? Why do hospitals work full throttle from Monday to Friday, 8 a.m. to 5 p.m., and continue at half speed (if that) after 5 p.m. or on the weekend?

It would be too easy (and erroneous by the way) to blame the doctors and nurses for these inexplicable shortcomings. The challenge in how health care is delivered is a more fundamental one: doctors and nurses just work the best they can in the systems they are provided with. Operations management provides the tools to start analyzing and subsequently optimizing the fundamental structures upon which health care delivery is built. Concepts such as process selection, total quality management, statistical quality control, capacity planning, facility layout, and scheduling, just to name a few, have the potential to modernize health care delivery in a manner that will allow health care providers to provide true medical excellence, as expected by the public.

Max J. Coppes, MD, Ph.D.

I thought my management accounting background would be all I needed when I became a business analyst, but within weeks I found myself re-reading my old operations management textbook.

In order to understand how the business operated, I was forced to learn about the information system the business used. I was initially shocked at how much operations management stuff was in the software, and that it actually was being extensively used.

Working now as a business consultant, an understanding of operations management has proven invaluable in working with various product and service organizations. It seems that regardless of the type or size of business, some form of operations management is always a part of it.

Please share this with your current students—effort put into an operations management course will pay off regardless of what role they will eventually play in an organization. At the very least, it will prevent them from having to re-read their textbook like I did.

Brent Snider, BComm, CMA

The topics in this book include those that all managers should understand. We consider the topics included in this book as the foundation or "core" material. Many other topics could be included, but these are the most important. All managers should understand the basic principles that guide the design of transformation processes. These include understanding how different types of processes are organized, how to determine the capacity of a process, how long it should take a process to make a unit, and how the quality of a process is monitored. Oil refineries, automobile manufacturing, computer makers, and food products all use different types of manufacturing processes. Similarly, services such as insurance companies, fast food restaurants, and call centres are organized in unique ways. In addition to understanding how the processes within these operations are organized, another major set of topics relates to how the operations are supplied. Parts and other raw materials must be moved into and out of these operations. On the input side, suppliers' coordination is needed so that appropriate quantities of material and other items are made available. On the output or customer side, the finished goods are distributed, often through a complex network of distribution centres and retailers. These supply topics include where to locate the facilities, strategic sourcing and outsourcing of material and service, and managing the supply inventories.

Companies today have found how essential great operations and supply management is to the success of the firm. Saving a dollar in how a product is produced or distributed results directly in an extra dollar of profit. What other area can claim this? If Marketing sells an extra dollar worth of product, profit only sees a few percent of this amount. If Finance figures out a way to get an extra half percent on an investment, by the time the extra cost of procuring the investment, managing the transaction, and accounting for the investment is factored in, little return is left to show in added profit. Operations and supply management is focused on the actions of providing services and goods. Doing this at low cost and at a level of service that meets customer expectations is essential for business success.

EFFICIENCY, EFFECTIVENESS, AND VALUE

Compared with most of the other ways managers try to stimulate growth—technology investments, acquisitions, and major market campaigns, for example—innovations in operations are relatively reliable and low cost. As a business student, you are perfectly positioned to come up with innovative operations-related ideas. You understand the big picture of all the processes that generate the costs and support the cash flow essential to the firm's long-term viability.

Through this book you will become aware of the concepts and tools now being employed by companies around the world as they craft efficient and effective operations. **Efficiency** means doing something at the lowest possible cost. Later in the book we define this more thoroughly, but, roughly speaking, the goal of an efficient process is to produce a good or provide a service by using the smallest input of resources. **Effectiveness** means doing the right things to create the most value for the company. Often, maximizing effectiveness and efficiency at the same time creates conflict between the two goals. We see this trade-off every day in our lives. At the customer service counter at a local store or bank, being efficient means using the fewest people possible at the counter. Being effective, though, means minimizing the amount of time customers need to wait in line. Related to efficiency and effectiveness is the concept of **value**, which can be defined metaphorically as quality divided by price. If you can provide the customer with a better car without changing price, value has gone up. If you can give the customer a better car at a *lower* price, value goes way up. A major objective of this book is to show how smart management can achieve high levels of value.

Besides its importance to corporate competitiveness, the reasons for studying OSM are as follows:

1. **A business education is incomplete without an understanding of modern approaches to managing operations.** Every organization produces some product or service, so students must be exposed to modern approaches for doing this effectively. Moreover, hiring organizations now expect business graduates to speak knowledgeably about many issues in the field. While this has long been true in manufacturing, it is becoming equally important in services, both public and private. For example, "reinventing government" initiatives draw heavily on supply chain management, total quality management, business process reengineering, and just-in-time delivery—concepts that fall under the OSM umbrella.

2. **Operations and supply management provides a systematic way of looking at organizational processes.** OSM uses analytical thinking to deal with real-world problems. It sharpens our understanding of the world around us, whether we are talking about how to expand globally or how many lines to have at the bank teller's window.

3. **Operations and supply management presents interesting career opportunities.** These can be in direct supervision of operations or in staff positions in OSM specialties, such as supply chain management, purchasing, and quality assurance. In addition, consulting firms regularly recruit individuals with strong OSM capabilities to work in such areas as process reengineering and enterprise resource planning systems.

4. **The concepts and tools of OSM are widely used in managing other functions of a business.** All managers have to plan work, control quality, and ensure productivity of individuals under their supervision. Other employees must know how operations work to effectively perform their jobs.

Cross Functional

Global

SUPPLY CHAIN TRANSFORMATION PROCESSES[1]

Transformation processes are used in all types of businesses. A transformation process uses resources to convert inputs into some desired output. Inputs may be raw material, a customer, or a finished product from another system. Exhibit 1.2 shows examples of different types of transformation processes in such varied areas as health care, education, and retail stores. In general, transformation processes can be categorized as follows:

Physical (as in manufacturing).

Location (as in transportation).

Exchange (as in retailing).

Storage (as in warehousing).

Physiological (as in health care).

Informational (as in telecommunications).

These transformations are not mutually exclusive. For example, a department store can (1) allow shoppers to compare prices and quality (informational), (2) hold items in inventory until needed (storage), and (3) sell goods (exchange).

Operations and supply management is about learning how to design these transformation processes. In the context of supply chains, Exhibit 1.3 depicts sets of processes specialized for the various parts of the supply chain. Companies strive to learn the "best way" to perform each task, and these are often referred to as best practices.

				EXHIBIT 1.2
Input–Transformation–Output Relationships for Typical Systems				
SYSTEM	PRIMARY INPUTS	RESOURCES	PRIMARY TRANSFORMATION FUNCTION(S)	TYPICAL DESIRED OUTPUT
Hospital	Patients	MDs, nurses, medical supplies, equipment	Health care (physiological)	Healthy individuals
Restaurant	Hungry customers	Food, chef, wait staff, environment	Well-prepared, well-served food; agreeable environment (physical and exchange)	Satisfied customers
Automobile factory	Sheet steel, engine parts	Tools, equipment, workers	Fabrication and assembly of cars (physical)	High-quality cars
College or university	High school graduates	Teachers, books, classrooms	Imparting knowledge and skills (informational)	Educated individuals
Department store	Shoppers	Displays, stocks of goods, sales clerks	Attracting shoppers, Promoting products, Filling orders (exchange)	Sales to satisfied customers
Distribution centre	Stockkeeping units (SKUs)	Storage bins, stockpickers	Storage and redistribution	Fast delivery, availability of SKUs
Airline	Travelers	Airplanes, crews, scheduling/ ticketing systems	Moving destination	On-time, safe delivery to destination

	EXHIBIT 1.3
Operations and Supply Management Supply Chain Processes	

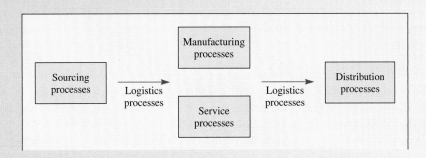

There are many ways that each function can be performed and significant performance related trade-offs that need consideration. Sourcing processes, for example, relate to how a firm purchases the raw materials and other goods needed to support manufacturing and service processes. Processes for sourcing (a fancy word for purchasing) vary, from putting the

Operations and Supply Management in Practice

Products and Processes Should be for People, Not the Other Way Around

Kim Vicente of the University of Toronto, in his book *The Human Factor,* emphasizes the importance of designing goods and services that fit the physical and psychological characteristics of humans rather than the other way around. Professor Vicente calls this the "Human-Tech" approach.

Often what we think of as "human error" is caused by people trying to adapt to a technology that was not designed with them in mind. For example, in the 1940s, many American military pilots were pulling up the wheels of their planes after landing rather than pulling up the wing flaps (as they should have done to slow down the plane). This, of course, was considered "pilot error." An investigation revealed that the real reason was that the two related controls were right beside each other on the instrument panel and almost identical in appearance. The control design was altered to give the wheel switch a rubberized disc (which made it look like a wheel) and the flap switch a wedge shape (which made it look like a wing flap). This eliminated the error because there was now a clear, intuitive relationship between the shape of the controls and their functions. The same con-

cepts apply to processes. Processes have to be designed with physical, psychological, team, organizational, and political considerations in mind. For example, how humans teams work within any setting should be a critical consideration in designing processes, especially those in which human life is concerned, such as an operating theatre, an aircraft cockpit, or utilities. Vicente cites the two examples of the Chernobyl nuclear disaster in 1986 and the Walkerton, Ontario, E. coli outbreak in 2000—tragedies resulting from processes that did not follow the Human-Tech approach.

On the positive side, Vicente cites the creation of the Aviation Safety Reporting System (ASRS) by U.S. government agencies in 1976 as an example of the success of Human-Tech-based systems. Under the ASRS, aviation professionals who are involved in near misses can voluntarily report such incidents without fear of being subject to legal action. These reports can then be used to improve aviation safety. The system works because it avoids the "shoot the messenger of bad news" syndrome that would have prevented the pilots from reporting near misses.

■   Source: Kim Vicente. *The Human Factor: Revolutionizing the Way People Live with Technology* (Toronto: Knopf Canada, 2003).

item out for bid to simply buying from a catalogue. The best process will depend on such factors as volume, cost, and speed of delivery.

Logistics processes are the various ways that material can he moved. Here, a variety of approaches is available, from the use of ships, trucks, and airplanes to the hand delivery of goods. Often combinations are used—for example, movement from China to Canada using a ship where the item is offloaded at Vancouver and moved to its final destination on a truck. The best process depends again on such factors as volume, cost, and speed of transit. Processes for moving material into the manufacturing and service processes are referred to as "inbound logistics," and movement to distribution centres as "outbound logistics."

Distribution processes relate to warehouse functions. These involve the storage of material, how material is picked and packed for delivery, and methods for moving material around in the warehouse. These functions can be simple manual procedures or highly computerized systems using robots and conveyor systems. The sourcing, logistics, and distribution processes link the elements of the supply chain and need to be tightly coordinated to be effective.

The manufacturing and service processes are involved with the actual production of the goods and services desired by different types of customers. The widely varying requirements for these result in many different types of processes, ranging, for example, from high volume assembly lines to very flexible work centres for making things. Similarly, for services, the processes vary from the work done in a small architect's office to the high-volume processes needed in a global call centre. As the OSMP on designing goods and services shows, it is important that we keep the users in mind while designing transformation processes.

DIFFERENCES BETWEEN SERVICES AND GOODS[2]

There are five essential differences between services and goods.

1. A service is an *intangible* process that cannot be weighed or measured, whereas a good is a tangible output of a process that has physical dimensions. This distinction has important business implications since a service innovation, unlike a product innovation, cannot be patented. Thus, a company with a new concept must expand rapidly before competitors copy its procedures. Service intangibility also presents a problem for customers, since, unlike with a physical product, they cannot try it out and test it before purchase.

2. Service requires some *degree of interaction with the customer* for it to be a service. The interaction may be brief, but it must exist for the service to be complete. Where face-to-face service is required, the service facility must be designed to handle the customer's presence. Goods, on the other hand, are generally produced in a facility separate from the customer. They can be made according to a production schedule that is efficient for the company.

3. Services, with the big exception of hard technologies such as ATMs and information technologies such as answering machines and automated Internet exchanges, are inherently *heterogeneous*—they vary from day to day and even hour to hour as a function of the attitudes of the customer and the servers. Thus, even highly scripted work such as that found in call centres can produce unpredictable outcomes. Goods, in contrast, can be produced to meet very tight specifications day in and day out, with essentially zero variability. In cases where a defective good is produced, it can be reworked or scrapped.

4. Services as a process are *perishable and time dependent* and, unlike goods, they can't be stored (inventoried). You cannot "come back last week" for a flight or a hotel room.

5. The specifications of a service are defined and evaluated as a *package of features* that affect the five senses. These features are

    -   Supporting facility (location, decoration, layout, architectural appropriateness, supporting equipment).
    -   Facilitating goods (variety, consistency, quantity of the physical goods that go with the service; for example, the food items that accompany an airline meal service).
    -   Explicit services (training of service personnel, consistency of service performance, availability and access to the service, and comprehensiveness of the service).
    -   Implicit services (attitude of the servers, atmosphere, waiting time, status, privacy and security, and convenience).

The Goods–Services Continuum

Most any product offering is a combination of goods and services. In Exhibit 1.4, we show this arrayed along a continuum of "pure goods" to "pure services." The continuum captures the main focus of the business and runs from firms that just produce goods to those that only provide services. Pure goods industries, such as those producing common chemicals, have become low margin commodity businesses, and in order to differentiate, they are often adding some services (called value-added services). Some examples are providing help with logistical aspects of stocking items, maintaining extensive information databases, and providing consulting advice. Xerox Canada, traditionally a manufacturer of copiers and printers, now calls itself the "document company." To improve its competitiveness, it has moved from providing hardware only to offering solutions that can improve the customer's processing of information, which involves a considerable value-added service aspect.

Core goods providers already provide a significant service component as part of their businesses. For example, automobile manufacturers provide extensive spare parts distribution services to support repair centres at dealers.

EXHIBIT 1.4	The Goods–Services Continuum

Pure Goods	Core Goods	Core Services	Pure Services
Food products	Appliances	Hotels	Teaching
Chemicals	Data storage systems	Airlines	Medical advice
Book publishing	Automobiles	Internet service providers	Financial consulting

Goods ◄───────────────────────────────────► Services

Source: Anders Gustofsson and Michael D. Johnson, *Competing in a Service Economy* (San Francisco: Jossey-Bass, 2003), p. 7.

Core service providers must integrate tangible goods. For example, your cable television company must provide cable hookup and repair services and also high-definition cable boxes. Pure services, such as those offered by a financial consulting firm, may need little in the way of facilitating goods, but what they do use—such as textbooks, professional references, and spreadsheets—are critical to their performance.

Growth of Services

In Canada, about 77 percent of the workforce is employed in service as opposed to 20 percent in manufacturing and less than 3 percent in agriculture.[3] The figure is similar for other developed economies such as those of the U.S., Germany, and Japan. This is a vast change from one hundred years ago when manufacturing and agriculture dominated our economy. However, in a developing nation such as China, only about 35 percent of the workforce is employed in services. Fifty percent of the workforce is still employed in agriculture. What the dominance of the service sector in Canada means is that companies must pay more attention to the effective and efficient management of services, as explained in the OSMP on service providers employing manufacturing principles. Henri De Castries, the CEO of French insurance giant AXA, illustrated how important operations and supply management has become in services when he said, "We have to increase productivity in our factories. The first to understand that financial services are an industrial business will be the winners"[4]

Operations and Supply Management in Practice

Service Providers Increase Operations Effectiveness and Profitability by Adopting Principles from Manufacturing

According to McKinsey, one of the leading global consulting companies, many executives in service companies are looking to adopt methods and tools used by manufacturers to increase the effectiveness of operations. One of these companies is AXA, the well-known French insurance giant. The insurance industry that traditionally relied on investments for profitability is realizing in these days of lower market returns that effective operations management is key in maintaining profitability.

Some of the manufacturing-originated tools that AXA uses include Six Sigma in quality and productivity improvement, benchmarking to compare processes against others within the company, and cost modelling. Just as in manufacturing, the goal is for employees to understand what a process is, how to analyze it, and improve it. This includes reducing the time required to develop a new insurance or financial product and launch it before AXA's competitors in order to gain an advantage.

Dr. Michael Rachlis, MD, a health policy analyst and faculty member at the University of Toronto, calls managing the health care system "supply chain management." He uses the following examples of the manufacturing concepts discussed in this textbook that are being used in health care delivery improvement:

- The Alberta Bone and Joint Institute reduced wait time for joint replacements from 19 months to 11 weeks using queueing theory.
- In other instances, using check lists as a quality tool reduced post-surgery complications by up to one-third.
- The Pan Am Clinic in Winnipeg used the concept of lot sizes and set-up time to reduce MRI wait lists.
- The UBC Hospital in Vancouver increased operating theatre utilization by using lean principles.
- Specialized clinics in the Toronto area, such as The Trillium Health Centre, use assembly-line techniques to schedule surgeries more efficiently.

■ Sources: Eric Monnoyer and Stefan Spang, "Manufacturing lessons for service industries: An interview with AXA's Claude Brunet," *The McKinsey Quarterly*, May 2005, www.mckinseyquarterly.com. *The Current*, CBC Radio, May 11, 2009 (http://www.cbc.ca/thecurrent/2009/200905/20090511.html)

THE EVOLUTION OF OPERATIONS AND SUPPLY MANAGEMENT FROM AN INTERNATIONAL AND CANADIAN PERSPECTIVE[5]

Unlike the United States, which evolved from an agricultural base, business in Canada began as a commodity-based colony. Fish, fur, and forests were harvested, then shipped back to France or the U.K. Manufacturing as we know it today did not exist. Items were usually custom-made by skilled artisans who spent many years in apprenticeship learning every facet of how to make a good or provide a service. No two products were ever the same. For many products, trades or guilds were established to provide a common basis of knowledge for these apprenticeship programs. This cottage industry approach to manufacturing began to change at the beginning of the nineteenth century with the introduction of the steam engine and other machines in the U.K., which allowed the Industrial Revolution to take place. In the nineteenth century, industrial development in Canada generally lagged behind that of its neighbour, the U.S., and its colonizer, the U.K., for a variety of reasons, such as slow population growth, tariffs, and poor transportation infrastructure.

Traditionally with cottage industry manufacturing, management has been an art rather than science. As seen in Exhibit 1.5 (where a historical summary of the developments in OSM are given) the introduction of scientific management developed by Frederick W. Taylor at the beginning of the twentieth century changed this. Taylor proposed that scientific laws govern how much a worker can produce per day and that it is the role of management to discover and use these laws in its production systems, while the worker just executed orders. Taylor's philosophy was not without controversy. Some unions resented scientific management since this idea ignored the fact that workers should be as important to the business as management. On the other hand, managers readily embraced Taylor's philosophy—time study, incentive plans, and so forth—but ignored their responsibility for the humane treatment of workers. Charlie Chaplin's famous satirical movie, *Modern Times*, provides a critique of the manufacturing management philosophy of that time. Other notable management scientists of the day include Frank and Lillian Gilbreth (motion study) and Henry L. Gantt (scheduling).

EXHIBIT 1.5	Historical Summary of OM

YEAR	CONCEPT	TOOL	ORIGINATOR
1910s	Principles of scientific management	Formalized time-study and work-study concepts	Frederick W. Taylor
	Industrial psychology	Motion study	Frank and Lillian Gilbreth
	Moving assembly line	Activity scheduling chart	Henry Ford and Henry L. Gantt
	Economic lot size	Economic Order Quantity (EOQ) applied to inventory control	F. W. Harris
1930s	Quality control	Sampling inspection and statistical tables for quality control	Walter Shewhart, H. F. Dodge, and H. G. Romig
	Hawthorne studies of worker motivation	Activity sampling for work analysis	Elton Mayo and L. H. C. Tippett
1940s–60s	Extensive development of operations research tools	Simulation, waiting-line theory, decision theory, mathematical programming, project scheduling techniques of PERT and CPM	Many researchers globally
1970s	Widespread use of computers in business	Shop scheduling, inventory control, forecasting, project management, MRP	Led by computer manufacturers, in particular, IBM; Joseph Orlicky and Oliver Wight were the major MRP innovators
	Service quality and productivity	Mass production in the service sector	McDonald's restaurants
1980s	Manufacturing strategy paradigm	Manufacturing as a competitive weapon	Harvard Business School faculty
	JIT, TQC, and factory automation	Kanban, poka-yokes, CIM, FMS, CAD/CAM, robots, etc.	Tai-Ichi Ohno of Toyota Motors, W.E. Deming and J. M. Juran and engineering disciplines
1990s	Total quality management	Canada Awards for Excellence, ISO 9000, quality function development, value and concurrent engineering, continuous improvement paradigm	National Quality Institute (NQI), American Society of Quality Control (ASQC), and International Organization for Standardization (ISO)
	Business process reengineering	Radical change paradigm	Michael Hammer and major consulting firms
	Electronic enterprise	Internet, World Wide Web	U.S. government, Netscape Communication Corporation, and Microsoft Corporation
	Supply chain management	SAP/R_3, client/server software	SAP, Oracle
2000s	E-commerce	Internet, World Wide Web	Amazon, eBay, Canadian banks

Source: Jacobs, F. Robert, Chase, Richard B., and Aquilano, Nicholas J., *Operations and Supply Management*, 12th ed. New York: Irwin McGraw Hill, 2009, p15.

In spite of economic disadvantages, by the early 1900s there were some notable Canadian industries, as mass manufacturing became more feasible due to the increasing population, availability of hydroelectricity, and reduced foreign tariffs, leading to exports.

In 1913, Henry Ford moved the factory into a new era by developing an assembly line to make the Model-T car in Detroit. The assembly line depended on a critical development—interchangeable (standardized) parts. For example, every piston (and every other component) that was manufactured for the Model-T was identical and thus could be assembled into any Model-T with non-artisan workers. Other modern aspects of manufacturing management were also evident. Quality was a critical prerequisite for Ford; the line could not run steadily at speed without consistently good components. On-time delivery was also critical; the desire to keep workers and machines busy with materials flowing constantly made scheduling important. Product, processes, material, logistics, and people were well integrated and balanced in the design and operation of the plant.[6] Canadian subsidiaries of U.S. factories also began to use assembly lines.

During World War I and World War II, Canada geared its manufacturing toward wartime production. After the end of World War II, Canada and the U.S. prospered because they were among the few industrialized countries whose infrastructure had not been destroyed. However, this had some negative consequences for operations. The high demand and the lack of international competition meant that companies did not think about operations strategically or as a competitive weapon. The operations function was assigned the responsibility of producing large quantities of standard products at minimum cost, regardless of the goals of the firm. Issues such as quality took a back seat. Later, when foreign manufacturers, especially the Japanese, entered the market with quality products, North American manufacturers were ill-equipped to respond quickly. This was foreseen by experts in operations, such as Wickham Skinner of the Harvard Business School, who suggested in the late 1960s that companies should place strategic emphasis on operations.[7] Today, of course, companies view operations as a competitive weapon and place great importance on operations management.

The last quarter of the twentieth century saw the rise of Japan and Germany as major economies. Following their lead, companies from Korea, Taiwan, and other Asian countries such as China and India, (though both are in the developing stage, they have aspects of developed economies) have also become formidable competitors. Other recent developments that affect international competition include the emergence of eastern Europe from Communism (particularly the re-emergence of Russia as a global economic force), and the transition of Latin America to democracy, with Brazil and Mexico being the major economic powers in the region.

A 1991 report by Professor Michael Porter of Harvard University and a follow-up report in 2004 by Porter and Professor Roger Martin, dean of the Rotman School of Management at the University of Toronto, studied Canadian products and their place in a globally competitive world. The study outlined how Canadian industry and government were doing on global issues. Topics of operational concern included Canadians' apparent reliance on raw materials, improving productivity, quality in manufacturing, and government protectionist policy.[8,9] Many experts emphasize that Canada should focus on innovative and value-added goods and services to alleviate these concerns and to be successful in the future. More information on operations and supply management in Canada can be found on Industry Canada's Web site (ic.gc.ca).

CURRENT ISSUES IN OPERATIONS AND SUPPLY MANAGEMENT

Operations and supply management is a dynamic area, and the challenges presented by global enterprise present exciting new issues for operations managers. It is important that Canadian mangers pay attention to these issues if Canada is to continue being a successful player in the world and if we are to maintain our standard of living. Looking forward to the future, we believe the major challenges in the area will be as follows:

1. Coordinating the relationships between mutually supportive but separate organizations. Recently there has been a dramatic surge in the outsourcing of parts and services that had previously been produced internally. This has been encouraged by the availability of fast, inexpensive communications. A whole new breed of *contract manufacturers* that specialize in performance-focused manufacturing activities now exists. The success of this kind of traditional outsourcing has led companies to consider outsourcing other major corporate functions such as information systems, product development and design, engineering services, packaging, testing, and distribution. The ability to coordinate these activities is a significant challenge for the operations manager of the future.

2. Optimizing global supplier, production, and distribution networks. The implementation of global enterprise resource planning systems (ERP), now common in large companies, has challenged managers to use all of this information. This requires a careful understanding of where control should be centralized and where autonomy is important, among other issues. Companies have only begun to truly take advantage of the information from these systems to optimally control such resources as inventory, transportation, and production equipment.

    With many companies from around the world becoming global (whether it is Magna in Canada or Acer, a computer maker, in Taiwan), managing operations will become more critical. Corporate head offices, marketing facilities, factories, and service centres may become geographically dispersed across different time zones. Each facility might manage the same process differently. Success will eventually depend upon the ability of the company to manage the global capital and human assets ethically and effectively in a multicultural environment and to provide goods and services efficiently. Other issues that managers will have to address when dealing with global operations are supply chain strategy, including location, currency fluctuation, the management of risk (including political), compensation, employment standards, vacations, religion, employees' attitudes toward work, local infrastructure, and other cultural diversity issues.

    In addition, there is the issue of ethics. For example, do we locate a facility in one country as opposed to another because the former has less stringent product labelling laws, leading to lower product cost? Or do we maintain high ethical standards, globally?

3. Increased co-production of goods and services. The Internet has opened new ways for the customer to interact directly with a firm. Simple direct entry and monitoring of orders is only the first step in the progression of value—added services made possible through information sharing. Intelligent use of information technology will allow the shedding of entire layers of inefficient customer-oriented functions within a firm, resulting in dramatic reductions in cost, while actually improving service to the customer.

4. Managing customer service points. As companies strive to become super-efficient, they often scrimp on customer support personnel (and training) required to effectively

staff service departments, help lines, and checkout counters. This leads to the frustrations we have all experienced, such as being placed in call-centre limbo, seemingly for hours, getting bad advice when we finally interact with a company rep, and so on. The issue here is to recognize that making resource utilization decisions must capture the implicit costs of lost customers as well as the direct costs of staffing.

5. Raising senior management awareness of operations as a significant competitive weapon. As we stated earlier, many senior executives entered the organization through finance, strategy, or marketing, and built their reputations on work in these areas. As a result, they often take operations for granted. As we will demonstrate in this book, this can be a critical mistake when we realize how profitable companies such as Toyota, Canadian Tire, Taco Bell, and WestJet are. These are companies where executives have creatively used operations management for competitive advantage.

6. Taking more environmental responsibility. It is clear consumers expect companies to significantly reduce their environmental footprint. This could involve using more recycled material, more environmentally friendly production and service processes, redesigning products, and processes to use less, or even eliminate, toxic processes. *The Globe and Mail* even gives annual awards to companies that are environmentally friendly. Many Canadian companies in so-called "dirty" industries such as oil, mining, and power generation are in the process of becoming more environmentally friendly, including attaining ISO 14000 environmental standards certification.

7. Corporate responsibility in supply chains. Consumers, nongovernmental organizations (NGOs), charities, and other similar organizations have been active in promoting fair trade practices. As a result, companies are also recognizing the importance of corporate responsibility, not only within their own organizations, but also in their supply chains. This helps ensure that companies that the organization deals with in the supply chain, especially in developing countries, follow environmentally conscious practices, offer acceptable working conditions, and respect human rights in issues such as child labour. Ten Thousand Villages, a non-profit chain with more than 40 stores across Canada, sells handicrafts purchased from all over the world that are produced using fair-trade and environmentally-friendly principles.

Summary

In this chapter, we have stressed the importance of operations and supply management to Canada. The topics in this book include ones that all managers should be familiar with. The operations and supply activities of the firm are part of the transformation process and include both manufacturing and service activities. Firms need to focus on efficiency, effectiveness, and value in managing operations. We also focused on the importance of services to Canada and the differences between manufacturing and services, since some aspects need to be managed differently. Further, we discussed the growth of globally-managed manufacturing, operations, and supply chain, with a special emphasis on Canada. Finally, we concluded with a discussion of the important issues that Canadian managers will be faced with as they compete in this increasingly global economy.

Key Terms

Effectiveness   Doing the right things to create the most value for the company.

Efficiency   Doing something at the lowest possible cost.

Operations and Supply Management (OSM)   Design, operation, and improvement of the systems that create and deliver a firm's primary goods and services.

Transformation Process   System by which resources are used to convert inputs into desired output.

Value   Ratio of quality to price paid. Competitive "happiness" is being able to increase quality and reduce price while maintaining or improving profit margins. (This is the way operations can directly increase customer retention and gain market share.)

Review and Discussion Questions

1. What factors account for the current resurgence of interest in OSM?
2. Look at the want ads in *The Globe and Mail* or your local newspaper and evaluate the opportunities for an OSM major with several years of experience. If there are limited opportunities, think about possible reasons for the lack of opportunities.
3. Using Exhibit 1.2 as a model, describe the input–transformation-output relationships in the following systems:
   a. An airline.
   b. A provincial penitentiary.
   c. A branch office of a bank.
   d. The home office of a major bank.
   e. A Blue Ray player manufacturer.
   f. A hospital.
   g. An automobile manufacturer.
4. Is the DVD accompanying a textbook a good or a service? Explain.
5. Define the service package of your college or university. What is its strongest element? Its weakest one?
6. Do universities offer goods or services or both? Give examples.
7. What service industry has impressed you the most with its innovativeness'?
8. What are value–added services and what are the benefits to external customers?
9. What is the difference between a service and a good?
10. Recent outsourcing of parts and services that had previously been produced internally is being addressed by which current issue facing operation management today?

Go to the Online Learning Centre (OLC) Web site at www.mcgrawhill.ca/olc/jacobs and visit the Web site of one of the companies that provide a virtual plant tour of their operations. Identify the company and describe the various operations presented in the tour. What do you think distinguishes this firm from its competition?

| CASE | Split Decision: How Back to Basics Supply Chain Management Can Save a Lot of Dough |

Often, simple improvements in the process can be leveraged for large cost savings and significantly better customer service. Consider the following real-life example in which a large baked goods company did exactly that to get control of its supply chain costs. This company produced baked products in Alberta that had a 10-day "shelf life" after production. When the product arrived at their store, customers expected at least another 7 days of shelf life, meaning that the product had to arrive within 3 days (72 hours) of production. Two cities the company shipped product to were Vancouver and Victoria, and 60 and 68 hours lead-time respectively were needed to ensure the product arrived at the distribution depots in time to be taken to grocery stores. Shipments occurred five days each week. For four of these days, two "double trailer" loads (two trucks hauling two trailers each) were sent to each city. Once a week, though, since demand dropped, the company sent only one double trailer to service both locations. The driver would then drop the rear trailer at a Vancouver depot and catch the ferry to Victoria.

This split trailer strategy worked well for a long period, because demand was consistent and the "split load" consistently took place on a given day. However, when market demands started to change, the system began to break down. As demand from the two cities began to fluctuate, split-loads would be assigned sporadically, as needed, with little or no warning. Sometimes, drivers accustomed to going to the Island would mistakenly take loads that were scheduled to split in Vancouver straight on to Victoria instead. Other times, drivers would divide loads that were not intended to be split in Vancouver and continue to Victoria, with only half the required stock.

Sometimes, drivers would even drop both trailers in Vancouver and return to Alberta, without splitting the load. All three mistakes resulted in excess stock in one location that would have to be discarded since it was past the due date, and produced dissatisfied customers who did not receive their product at the other location.

The resulting chaos cost the company hundreds of thousands of dollars annually due to lost product, extra shipping charges, and extra production to make up for shortfalls. As well, customers would fine the company when it didn't meet its contractual obligations. Worse yet, clients would sometimes switch to other suppliers. For years, the company had struggled to avoid these costs by hiring extra staff, opening a 24-hour hotline for customers, increasing safety stock in the depot to accommodate losses, and even hiring jet aircraft to "hotshot" the product when mistakes were made. The cumulative result was not only an exponential increase in shipping costs of around $400 000 annually, but also dissatisfied customers, strained production lines, and stressed-out managers, thus contributing other "soft costs" to the company (estimated at between $200 000 and $800 000 per year) as well as lost revenue. Many in the company were simply resigned to the fact that these additional costs were just part of doing business between Alberta and the West Coast.

The company hired a consultant to look at all areas to find the right solution. They suspected he might have to rework the shipping and distribution schedules, retrain the staff and drivers, and consider a different ordering system.

Questions:

1. What might be the root causes of this distribution problem?
2. What solution(s) would you suggest for this issue? (Be as creative as you like). How much might it/they cost?

Source: This case was written by Tim Sweet from Revolve Consulting in Calgary and Janice Eliasson of the Haskayne School of Business. It is based on a real situation.

Footnotes

[1] F. Robert Jacobs, Richard B. Chase, and Nicholas J. Aquilano, *Operations and Supply Management,* 12th ed. New York: Irwin McGraw Hill, 2009.

[2] Ibid.

[3] Bureau of Labor Statistics, U.S. Department of Labor (http://stats.bls.gov/fls/home.htm), retrieved May 8, 2008.

[4] Charles Fleming and Thomas Kamm, "AXA's CEO Set to Push Synergies," *The Wall Street Journal,* May 3, 2000.

[5] Parts of this section are based on information from the following sources: J. Balakrishnan, J.B. Eliasson, and T.R.C. Sweet, "Factors Affecting the Evolution of Manufacturing in Canada: An Historical Perspective," *Journal of Operations Management,* 25, 2, 2007, pp 260–283 and R. Pomfret, *The Economic Development of Canada,* Toronto, Ontario: Methuen, 1981.

[6]J. Wilson, "Henry Ford: A Just-in-Time Pioneer," *Production and Inventory Management Journal 37* (1996), pp. 26–31

[7]Wickham Skinner, "The Focused Factory," *Harvard Business Review* (May–June 1974): 113–121.

[8]Michael E. Porter and the Monitor Company. *Canada at the Crossroads: The New Reality of a New Competitive Environment.* A Report to the Business Council on National Issues and the Minister of Supply and Services. *Ottawa: Business Council on National Issues,* 1991, p. 4.

[9]Roger Martin and Michael E. Porter, 2001, "Canadian Competitiveness: A Decade after the Crossroads," www.rotman.utoronto.ca/research/competitive1.htm (accessed March 14, 2006).

Selected Bibliography

Hayes, Robert, Gary Pisano, David Upton, and Steven Wheelwright. *Operations, Strategy, and Technology: Pursuing the Competitive Edge.* New York: John Wiley & Sons, 2004.

Hill, T.J., *Manufacturing Strategy—Text* and *Cases.* Burr Ridge; IL: Irwin/McGraw-Hill, 2000.

Slack, N. and Lewis, M. *Operations Strategy.* Harlow, England, and New York: Prentice Hall, 2002.

Sower, Victor E., Motwani, Jaideep, and Savoie, Michael J. "Classics in Production and Operations Management," *International Journal of Operations & Production Management,* Vol. 17, no. 1 (1997), pp. 15–28.

OPERATIONS AND SUPPLY STRATEGY

1. Understand the competitive dimensions of operations and supply strategy.
2. Understand the notion of trade-offs.
3. Appreciate why it is important to fit operational activities to strategy.
4. Know what order winners and order qualifiers are.
5. Understand the notion of core capability.
6. Know what measures Bay Street analysts use to evaluate operations.

STEELMAKER DOFASCO DOES A TURNAROUND THROUGH STRATEGIC REFOCUSING

It is no secret that Canadian steelmakers are under pressure. The industry is facing increasing competition from steelmakers in developing countries such as Brazil, China, and India, where labour costs are low. While some other Canadian steelmakers struggle, Hamilton-based Dofasco (a unit of Luxembourg-based Arcelor and Mittal Steel Company), in business since 1912, has prospered through a revised strategy. The company also owns or has partial ownership in facilities in the United States and Mexico. Until the late 1980s, the company competed on price by producing as much steel as possible at the lowest possible prices. By the early 1990s, realizing that the current "competing on cost" strategy (cost leadership) was untenable given the competition from lower cost countries, Dofasco refocused its strategy to one of developing new and innovative products, and to providing its customers with solutions for high-quality and specialized applications (product differentiation). This business strategy was called Solutions in Steel and focused on operational excellence, technology and innovation, and intimate customer relationships. By 1999, Dofasco was the most profitable steel producer in North America (and still ranks among the most profitable). In 2000, it was ranked first in North America among thirty steel suppliers in an independent customer satisfaction survey, and was rated one of the best Canadian companies to work for by *Report on Business Magazine*.

What did it take to effect a successful transition from the old strategy to the new? Of course, this transformation did not come without effort, resources, or pain. Its workforce was reduced from about 13 000 to 7000 in order to become profitable

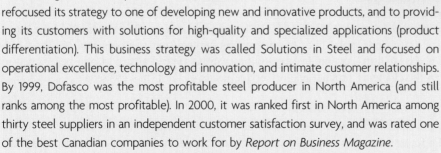

(as of the end of 2008 it stood at 5500). It spends considerable sums on research and development and facility upgrades in order to remain competitive. Dofasco recognized that employees would be critical to success in such a strategy. Thus, employees were provided a variety of training and development opportunities. In addition, the company invested in health, safety, and wellness in the workplace. In 2002, the National Quality Institute awarded Dofasco a Canadian Award for Excellence Healthy Workplace Trophy. Studies have shown that investing in health, safety, and wellness can improve productivity and lower costs. Quality at Dofasco has also meant paying attention to environmental concerns. In 2002, Dofasco's Hamilton facilities achieved ISO 14001 certification. This means that the company's environmental management systems comply with an international set of environmental standards (Chapter 6 discusses quality awards and ISO standards in detail). The Dofasco story provides an excellent example of the importance of formulating a successful business strategy and implementing supporting operations strategy decisions to ensure long-term survival.

■ Sources: Priya Ramu, "Report on Canada's Steel Industry," *World at Six*, CBC Radio, August 6, 2003. Gordon DiGiacomo, *Case Study: Dofasco's Healthy Lifestyles Program* (Canadian Labour and Business Centre, 2002), www.clbc.ca.
Dofasco Inc., www.dofasco.com.
National Quality Institute, www.nqi.com.

WHAT IS OPERATIONS AND SUPPLY STRATEGY?

Operations and supply strategy is concerned with setting broad policies and plans for using the resources of a firm to best support its long-term competitive strategy. A firm's operations and supply strategy is comprehensive when it integrates with corporate strategy. The strategy involves a long-term process that must foster inevitable change. An operations and supply strategy involves decisions that relate to the design of a process and the infrastructure needed to support the process. Process design includes the selection of appropriate technology, sizing the process over time, the role of inventory in the process, and locating the process. The infrastructure decisions involve the logic associated with the planning and control systems, quality assurance and control approaches, work payment structures, and organization of the operations function.

Operations and supply strategy can be viewed as part of a planning process that coordinates operational goals with those of the larger organization. Since the goals of the larger organization change over time, the operations strategy must be designed to anticipate future needs. A firm's operations capabilities can be viewed as a portfolio best suited to adapt to the changing product and/or service needs of the firm's customers.

Competitive Dimensions

Given the choices customers face today, how do they decide which product or service to buy? Different customers are attracted by different attributes. Some customers are interested primarily in the cost of a product or service. Correspondingly, some companies attempt to position themselves to offer the lowest prices. The major competitive dimensions that form the competitive position of a firm include the following.

Cost or Price: "Make the Product or Deliver the Service Cheap" Within every industry, there is usually a segment of the market that buys solely on the basis of low cost. To successfully compete in this niche, a firm must be the low-cost producer, but even this does not always guarantee profitability and success. Products and services sold strictly on the basis of cost are typically commodity-like; in other words, customers cannot distinguish the product or service of one firm from that of another. This segment of the market is frequently very large, and many companies are lured by the potential for significant profits, which they associate with the large unit volumes. As a consequence, however, competition in this segment is fierce—and so is the failure rate. After all, there can only be one low-cost producer, who usually establishes the selling price in the market.

Price, however, is not the only basis on which a firm can compete (although many economists appear to assume it is!). Other companies, such as BMW, seek to attract those who want *higher quality*—in terms of performance, appearance, or features—than that available in competing products and services, even though accompanied by a higher price.

Quality: "Make a Great Product or Deliver a Great Service" Two characteristics of a product or service define quality: design quality and process quality. Design quality relates to the set of features the product or service contains. This relates directly to the design of the product or service. Obviously, a child's first two-wheel bicycle is of significantly different quality than the bicycle of a world-class cyclist. The use of special aluminum alloys and special lightweight sprockets and chains is important to the performance needs of the advanced cyclist. These two types of bicycle are designed for different customers' needs. The higher-quality cyclist product commands a higher price in the marketplace due to its special features. The goal in establishing the proper level of design quality is to focus on the requirements of the customer. Overdesigned products and services with too many or inappropriate features will be viewed as prohibitively expensive. In comparison, underdesigned products and services will lose customers to products that cost a little more but are perceived by customers as offering greater value.

Process quality, the second characteristic of quality, is critical because it relates directly to the reliability of the product or service. Regardless of whether the product is a child's first two-wheeler or a bicycle for an international cyclist, customers want products without defects. Thus, the goal of process quality is to produce defect-free products and services. Product and service specifications, given in dimensional tolerances and/or service error rates, define how the product or service is to be made. Adherence to these specifications is critical to ensure the reliability of the product or service as defined by its intended use.

Delivery Speed: "Make the Product or Deliver the Service Quickly" In some markets, a firm's ability to deliver more quickly than its competitors is critical. A company that can offer an on-site repair service in only one or two hours has a significant advantage over a competing firm that guarantees service only within 24 hours.

Delivery Reliability: "Deliver It When Promised" This dimension relates to the firm's ability to supply the product or service on or before a promised delivery due date. For an automobile manufacturer, it is very important that its supplier of tires provide the needed quantity and types for each day's car production. If the tires needed for a particular car are not available when the car reaches the point on the assembly line where the tires are installed, the whole assembly line may have to be shut down until they arrive. For a service firm such as Federal Express, delivery reliability is the cornerstone of its strategy.

Coping with Changes in Demand: "Change Its Volume" In many markets, a company's ability to respond to increases and decreases in demand is important to its ability to compete. It is well known that a company with increasing demand can do little wrong. When demand is strong and increasing, costs are continuously reduced due to economies of scale, and investments in new technologies can be easily justified. But scaling back when demand decreases may require many difficult decisions about laying off employees and related reductions in assets. The ability to effectively deal with dynamic market demand over the long term is an essential element of operations strategy.

Flexibility and New-Product Introduction Speed: "Change It" Flexibility, from a strategic perspective, refers to the ability of a company to offer a wide variety of products to its customers. An important element of this ability to offer different products is the time required for a company to develop a new product and to convert its processes to offer the new product.

Other Product-Specific Criteria: "Support It" The competitive dimensions just described are certainly the most common. However, other dimensions often relate to specific products or situations. Notice that most of the dimensions listed next are primarily service in nature. Often special services are provided to augment the sales of manufactured products.

1. **Technical liaison and support.** A supplier may be expected to provide technical assistance for product development, particularly during the early stages of design and manufacturing.
2. **Meeting a launch date.** A firm may be required to coordinate with other firms on a complex project. In such cases, manufacturing may take place while development work is still being completed. Coordinating work between firms and working simultaneously on a project will reduce the total time required to complete the project.
3. **Supplier after-sale support.** An important competitive dimension may be the ability of a firm to support its product after the sale. This involves the availability of replacement parts and, possibly, modification of older, existing products to new performance levels. Speed of response to these after-sale needs is often important as well.
4. **Other dimensions.** These typically include such factors as available colours, size, weight, location of the fabrication site, customization available, and product mix options.

The Notion of Trade-Offs

Central to the concept of operations and supply strategy is the notion of operations focus and trade-offs. The underlying logic is that an operation cannot excel simultaneously on all competitive dimensions. Consequently, management has to decide which parameters of performance are critical to the firm's success and then concentrate the resources of the firm on these particular characteristics.

For example, if a company wants to focus on speed of delivery, it cannot be very flexible in its ability to offer a wide range of products. Similarly, a low-cost strategy is not compatible with either speed of delivery or flexibility. High quality is also viewed as a trade-off to low cost.

A strategic position is not sustainable unless there are compromises with other positions. Trade-offs occur when activities are incompatible—more of one thing necessitates less of another. An airline can choose to serve meals—adding cost and slowing turnaround time at the gate—or it can choose not to, but it cannot do both without bearing major inefficiencies.

Operations and Supply Management in Practice

Zara Excels on Price, Speed, and Flexibility

Zara, a retail chain of high-fashion boutique clothing stores, has grown rapidly since Amancio Ortega opened his first store in Spain in 1975. Headquartered in northern Spain, Zara, with more than 400 retail stores in 25 countries, now generates sales of more than $3 billion annually, primarily in Europe, but is now beginning to penetrate the Canadian market with 15 stores across the country. Zara's success is attributed to several factors, including low prices, speed of delivery, and flexibility. Merchandise is delivered to each Zara retail location twice a week. (Merchandise is airfreighted to its stores in Canada.) This fast and almost-continuous replenishment concept reduces the need for significant in-store inventories and the possibility of clothes going out of fashion. A major factor in Zara's ability to react quickly to changes in customer buying behaviour is its use of information and technology. Salespeople in each retail location use handheld computers to record buyer preferences and trends. This information, along with actual sales data, is transmitted daily through the Internet to Zara's headquarters in Spain.

In addition, unlike its major competitors, which outsource manufacturing, Zara produces most of its merchandise in its state-of-the-art factory in Spain. Products are designed, produced, and delivered to its stores in as little as two weeks, after appearing for the first time in a fashion show. By contrast, some competitors such as the GAP require up to nine months' lead time to fill orders from its retail operations. But some of Zara's competitors are not keeping quiet. H&M, a Swedish fashion chain that opened its first Canadian store in Toronto in 2004 and has since expanded, is very good at bringing out the latest fashions at very reasonable prices. In fact, H&M has compressed the time from design to store delivery to three weeks, only a little behind Zara.

■ Sources: Kerry Capell and Gerry Khermouch, "Hip H&M the Swedish Retailer Reinvents the World of Affordable Fashion," *Business Week* (Nov 11, 2002), p. 106.
William Echikson, "The Mark of Zara," *Business Week* (May 29, 2000), pp. 98–100.
Jane M. Folpe, "Zara Has a Made-to-Order Plan for Success," *Fortune* (September 4, 2000), p. 80.
Andy Georgiades, "Retailer H&M Is Set to Open Store in Canada," *The Wall Street Journal* (March 10, 2004), B.4B.
Richard Heller, "Galician Beauty," *Forbes* (May 28, 2001), p. 98.
Laurent Marchal, "In Their Own Words," *Space* (Winter 2003), p. 4.
Stryker McGuire, "Fast Fashion; How a Secretive Spanish Tycoon Has Defied the Postwar Tide of Globalization, Bringing Factory Jobs from Latin America and Asia back to Europe," *Newsweek*, International Edition
www.inditex.com (September 17, 2001), p. 36.

Though it is challenging, excellent companies are able to compete better on more competitive dimensions, as the OSMP on Zara shows. They can do this through better operations and supply management practices as well by using advanced manufacturing and information technology. However, trying to compete on multiple dimensions without actually being able to do so can result in failure, as the Continental Lite example below shows.

Straddling occurs when a company seeks to match the benefits of a successful position while maintaining its existing position. It adds new features, services, or technologies onto the activities it already performs. The risky nature of this strategy is shown by Continental Airlines' ill-fated attempt to compete with Southwest Airlines. While maintaining its position as a full-service airline, Continental set out to match Southwest on a number of point-to-point routes. The airline dubbed the new service Continental Lite. It eliminated meals and first-class service, increased departure frequency, lowered fares, and shortened gate turnaround time. Because Continental remained a full-service airline on other routes, it continued to use travel agents and its mixed fleet of planes, and to provide baggage checking and seat assignments.

Trade-offs ultimately grounded Continental Lite. The airline lost hundreds of millions of dollars, and the chief executive officer lost his job. Its planes were delayed leaving congested hub cities or slowed at the gate by baggage transfers. Late flights and cancellations generated a thousand complaints a day. Continental Lite could not afford to compete on price and still pay standard travel agent commissions, but neither could it do without agents for its full-service business. The airline compromised by cutting commissions for all Continental flights. Similarly, it could not afford to offer the same frequent-flier benefits to travellers paying the much lower ticket prices for Lite service. It compromised again by lowering the rewards of Continental's entire frequent-flier program. The results: angry travel agents and full-service customers. Continental tried to compete in two ways at once and paid an enormous straddling penalty.

Order Winners and Order Qualifiers: The Marketing–Operations Link

Cross Functional

An interface between marketing and operations is necessary to provide a business with an understanding of its markets from both perspectives. Terry Hill, a professor at Oxford University, has coined the terms *order winner* and *order qualifier* to describe marketing-oriented dimensions that are key to competitive success. An **order winner** is a criterion that differentiates the products or services of one firm from another. Depending on the situation, the order-winning criterion may be the cost of the product (price), product quality and reliability, or any of the other dimensions developed earlier. An **order qualifier** is a screening criterion that permits a firm's products to even be considered as possible candidates for purchase. Professor Hill states that a firm must "requalify the order qualifiers" every day it is in business.

It is important to remember that the order-winning and order-qualifying criteria may change over time. For example, when Japanese companies entered the world automobile markets in the 1970s, they changed the way these products won orders, from predominantly price to product quality and reliability. American automobile producers were losing orders through quality to the Japanese companies. By the late 1980s, product quality was raised by Ford, General Motors, and Chrysler today they are "qualified" to be in the market. Consumer groups continually monitor the quality and reliability criteria, thus requalifying the top-performing companies. Today, the order winners for automobiles vary greatly depending on the model. Customers know the set of features they want (such as reliability, design features, and gas mileage), and they want to purchase a particular combination at the lowest price, thus maximizing value.

Global

Similarly, even as recently as a few years ago, even an expensive hotel offering an Internet connection in its rooms would have used it as an order-winner. Today, however, almost all of these types of hotel chains offer in-room Internet connections. Thus, in-room Internet has become an order qualifier, since, if a hotel does not have this facility, many customers would choose another hotel. On the other hand, offering a high definition (HD) television set with 200 channels could be an order winner.

STRATEGIC FIT: FITTING OPERATIONAL ACTIVITIES TO STRATEGY

All the activities that make up a firm's operation relate to one another. To make these activities efficient, the firm must minimize its total cost without compromising customers' needs. Lululemon, of Vancouver, markets active wear for socially conscious customers. Thus, Lululemon has also chosen to perform activities differently from other clothing retailers who may sell cheaper active wear.

Clothing retailers who compete on cost may choose suppliers who use cheaper raw material and have low labour costs. While this does reduce cost, it does reduce the quality of the product, and the product might be less environmentally friendly, working conditions may not be up to standard, and market response may be slow. On the other hand, in some lines of Lululemon, at least 75 percent of the material is natural, organic, or sustainable.[1]

Operations and Supply Management in Practice

How IKEA Designs Its Attractive Prices

Competitive strategy is about being different. It means deliberately choosing a different set of activities to deliver a unique mix of value. IKEA, the Swedish retailer of home products, dominates markets in 43 countries, and is enjoying success in Canada too. One factor above all others accounts for IKEA's success: good quality at a low price. IKEA sells household items that are cheap but not cheapo, with prices that typically run 30 to 50 percent below those of the competition. While the price of other companies' products tends to rise over time, IKEA says it has reduced its retail prices by a total of about 20 percent during the last four years. At IKEA the process of driving down costs starts the moment a new item is conceived and continues relentlessly throughout the production run.

Consider IKEA's "Bang" mug, which has been redesigned three times so far, simply to maximize the number of mugs that can be stored on a pallet. Originally, only 864 mugs would fit.

A redesign added a rim such as you would find on a flowerpot so that each pallet could hold 1280 mugs. Last year, yet another redesign created a shorter mug with a new handle, allowing 2024 to squeeze onto a pallet. While the mug's sales price has remained the same shipping cost has been reduced by 60 percent, which is a significant savings, given that IKEA sells about 25 million mugs each year.

Naturally, this material is not going to be cheap. However, the target market for Lululemon is not expecting cheap apparel rather it is expecting environmentally sustainable apparel. While Lululemon does manufacture clothes in low labour-cost countries to increase cost effectiveness, it ensures that these factories are environmentally friendly and provide good working conditions. However, it does manufacture in North America (including Vancouver) to maintain speed of design and delivery for lines that value this as a competitive priority, i.e, those with short product life cycles, which are often common in higher-end apparel. Lululemon also offers additional services for customers such as showers in stores (to encourage activity) and classes on activity based themes. It even pays for employees to attend yoga classes, which helps retain knowledgeable employees. Having knowledgeable and satisfied employees will contribute toward better service. As mentioned, customers come to Lululemon not for its low prices but for its quality, service and environmental consciousness.

In order to succeed in the market place, a company's strategy must be delivered through a set of tailored activities. In companies with a clear strategy, a number of higher-order strategic themes can be identified and implemented through clusters of tightly linked activities. For example, Lululemon's strategic themes would include excellent customer service, responsive supply chain, and environmentally conscious production. Thus, in the retail clothing industry, both Lululemon as well as retailers selling cheaper apparel can be successful, but in either case the activities have to fit with and reinforce one another in line with the overall strategy. Competitive advantage comes from this fit.

A FRAMEWORK FOR OPERATIONS AND SUPPLY STRATEGY

Operations strategy cannot be designed in a vacuum. It must be linked vertically to the customer and horizontally to other parts of the enterprise. Exhibit 2.1 shows these linkages among customer needs, their performance priorities and requirements for manufacturing operations, and the operations-related decisions to satisfy those needs. Overlying this framework is senior management's strategic vision of the firm. The vision identifies, in general terms, the target market, the firm's product line, and its core capabilities.

EXHIBIT 2.1	The Operations Strategy Process

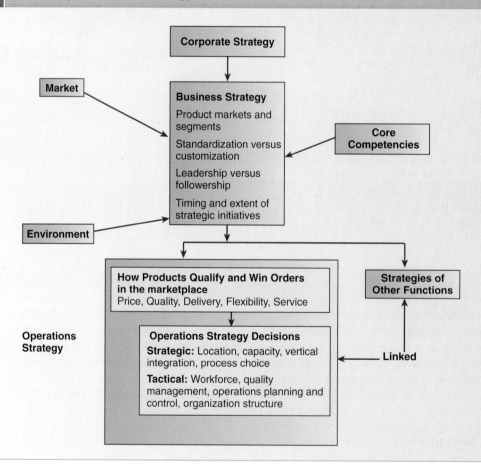

The choice of a target market can be difficult, but it must be made. Indeed, it may lead to turning away business—ruling out a customer segment that would simply be unprofitable or too hard to serve given the firm's capabilities. An example here is clothing manufacturers not making half-sizes in their dress lines. The environment is also important in formulating strategy. For example, the use of technology in manufacturing and services has increased greatly in recent years. Naturally, this affects the market choice (one might be able to provide the product globally as opposed to locally), and competitive priorities as well as operations strategy decisions.

Core capabilities (or competencies) are the distinctive skills or capabilities that the organization possesses. These often differentiate the service or manufacturing firm from its competitors and create a preference for its products in the marketplace. For example, Google's core capability is that it is able to create effective search algorithms that give useful results when a customer looks up a topic. Strategy is often based on core capabilities. For example, a company may decide to offer standardized goods rather than customized ones since its core capability may be in identifying high-volume low-cost suppliers.

Earlier, we discussed the fit of operations activities with the overall company strategy. It is important to note that the operations activities must be linked to the activities of the other functions of the firm. For example, if a competitive priority is quality then clearly the operations processes must ensure quality goods and services while the human resources activities must be geared toward hiring, training, and retaining skilled employees to support the processes required for high quality.

Possibly the most difficult thing for a firm to do is part with tradition. Top-level managers often make their mark based on innovations made 15 to 20 years ago. These managers are often too comfortable with just tinkering with the current system. All the new advanced technologies present themselves as quick fixes. It is easy to patch these technologies into the current system with great enthusiasm. But, while doing this might be exciting to managers and engineers working for the firm, they might not be creating a distinctive core competence—i.e., a competence that wins future customers. What companies need in this world of intense global competition is not more techniques but a way to structure a whole new product realization system differently and better than any competitor.

HOW DOES BAY STREET EVALUATE OPERATIONS PERFORMANCE?

Comparing firms from an operations view is important to investors since the relative cost of providing a good or service is essential to high earnings growth. When you think about it, earnings growth is largely a function of the firm's profitability, and profit can be increased through higher sales and/or reduced cost. Highly efficient firms usually shine when demand drops during recession periods since they can often continue to make a profit due to their low cost structure. These operations-savvy firms may even see a recession as an opportunity to gain market share as their less-efficient competitors struggle to remain in business.

One way to measure efficiency is to look at productivity measures. Productivity is defined as

$$Productivity = \frac{Outputs}{Inputs}$$

Take a look at the automobile industry, where efficiency has been such an important factor. Exhibit 2.2 shows a comparison of some of the major companies. As you can see, Toyota dominates the group. Toyota's net income per employee (where income is the output and employee is the input) is five times greater than that of Ford and DaimlerChrysler, truly an amazing accomplishment. Toyota also shines in receivables turnover, inventory turnover, and asset turnover. Ford and General Motors have worked hard at implementing the inventory management philosophy that was pioneered by Toyota in Japan. True efficiency goes beyond inventory management and requires an integrated product development, sales, manufacturing, and supply system. Toyota is very mature in its approach to these activities, and that clearly shows on its bottom line.

EXHIBIT 2.2 | Efficiency Measures Used by Bay Street

A COMPARISON OF AUTOMOBILE COMPANIES

MANAGEMENT EFFICIENCY MEASURE	TOYOTA	FORD	GENERAL MOTORS	DAIMLER CHRYSLER	INDUSTRY
Income per employee	$ 40 000	$ 8000	$ 10 000	$ 8000	$ 15 000
Revenue per employee	$663 000	$535 000	$597 000	$510 000	$568 000
Receivable turnover	4.0	1.5	1.0	2.2	2.1
Inventory turnover	12.0	11.5	11.7	5.9	11.0
Asset turnover	0.8	0.6	0.4	0.8	0.8

When evaluating the largest productivity winners and losers, it is important to look for unusual explanations. For example, energy companies have had big productivity gains due almost exclusively to higher oil prices, which boosted the companies' revenue without forcing them to add employees. Pharmaceutical companies such as Merck and Pfizer have not done well recently. Their productivity plunges were due primarily to one-time events, Merck because it spun off a company and Pfizer because it bought a company. Such one-time quirks create a lot of noise for anybody who wants to know how well companies are run. It is always best to examine multiyear productivity patterns.

Summary

In this chapter, we show how the overall strategy of the firm can be tied to operations and supply strategy. Important concepts are the operational competitive dimensions, order winner and qualifiers, and strategic fit. The ideas apply to virtually any business and are critical to the firm's ability to sustain a competitive advantage. For a firm to remain competitive, all of the operational activities must buttress the firm's strategy. Bay Street analysts are constantly monitoring how efficient companies are from an operations view. Companies that are strong operationally are able to generate more profit for each dollar of sales, thus making them attractive investments.

Key Terms

Competitive dimensions   One or more major attributes of a product or service that the company wishes to focus and compete on. Better companies are able to compete on more of these attributes.

Core capabilities   Skills that differentiate a manufacturing or service firm from its competitors.

Operations and supply strategy   Setting broad policies and plans for using the resources of a firm to best support the firm's long-term competitive strategy.

Order qualifier   A dimension used to screen a product or service as a candidate for purchase.

Order winner   A dimension that differentiates the products or services of one firm from those of another.

Straddling   Occurs when a firm seeks to match what a competitor is doing by adding new features, services, or technologies to existing activities. This often creates problems if certain trade-offs need to be made.

Review and Discussion Questions

1. Can a factory be fast, dependable, and flexible; produce high-quality products; and still provide poor service from a customer's perspective?
2. Why should a Canadian service organization worry about being world-class if it does not compete outside Canada? What impact does the Internet have on this?
3. What are the major priorities associated with operations and supply strategy? How do you think their relationship to one another has changed over the years? It might be best to think about this relative to a specific industry, for example, personal computers.
4. For each priority in question 3, describe the unique characteristics of the market niche with which it is most compatible.
5. Why does the "proper" operations and supply strategy keep changing for companies that are world-class competitors?
6. In your opinion, do business schools have competitive priorities?
7. What is meant by the expressions *order winners* and *order qualifiers*? What was the order winner for your last major purchase of a product or service?

Internet Exercise: Harley-Davidson Motorcycles

Harley-Davidson has developed a Web site that allows potential customers to customize their new motorcycles. Working from a "basic" model, the customer can choose from an assortment of bags, chrome covers, colour schemes, exhausts, foot controls, mirrors, and other accessories. The Web-based application is set up so that the customer is not only able to select from the extensive list of accessories but can also see exactly what the motorcycle will look like. These unique designs can be shared with friends and family by printing the final picture or transferring it via e-mail. What a slick way to sell motorcycles!

Go to the Harley-Davidson (HD) Web site (www.harley-davidson.com). From there select "Get on a Bike." After this you need to select "Customize Your Harley." This should get you into the application.

1. How many different bike configurations do you think are possible? Could every customer have a different bike? To make this a little simpler, what if HD had only two types of bikes, three handle bar choices, four saddlebag combinations, and two exhaust pipe choices? How many combinations are possible in this case?

2. To keep things simple, HD has the dealer install virtually all these options. What would the trade-off be if HD installed these options at the factory instead of having the dealers install them?

3. How important is this customization to HD's marketing strategy? What are HD's order winners and order qualifiers? Concisely describe HD's operations and supply strategy.

CASE | Lasik Vision Corp.

At its peak in late 2000, Lasik Vision Corporation had over 30 clinics operating in North America, second only to TLC Laser Eye Centers in Toronto, Ontario, which had 62 clinics. Dr. Hugo Sutton, an eye surgeon and a clinical associate professor at the University of British Columbia, and Michael Henderson founded Lasik Vision in 1997. Sutton had been operating his own eye clinic since 1978, initially specializing in cataract surgery. In the intervening years, technological advances such as the excimer laser had transformed refractive surgery (the process of correcting myopia, hyperopia, or astigmatism by altering the contours of the cornea) from a low-tech risky procedure using lathes and sutures into a viable proposition for patients who could spend $5000. After the surgery, they could discard their glasses or contacts. The efficient new procedure eventually allowed surgeons to reduce the fees for this service, making it even more attractive for patients. In 1991, in partnership with two other surgeons, Dr. Sutton set up his own refractive surgery clinic. By 1996, the Lasik technique became the vogue, sparing patients the months of healing that were the norm with older procedures.

It was at that time that Michael Henderson, a business executive and husband to one of Sutton's patients, approached him. Sutton remembers that "Henderson felt that this was a very powerful technology, a technology that he could take much further. He thought that we were rather pedestrian, slow, and old fashioned." Since Sutton was tiring of doing all the surgeries with little help, the proposal sounded very appealing. In June 1997, Michael Henderson joined Sutton's company, TMX Laser Vision Canada Inc., as vice president.

Soon it became clear that Henderson was on an efficiency drive. He felt that the way to fortune was to reengineer the traditional model of the refractive surgery process. To improve efficiency, he let a few employees go (increasing the workload for the remainder). To cut costs further he tried not to use expensive equipment. For example, he opposed installing an ultrasound scanner to measure the individual layers of each cornea. This scanner improves the Lasik technique's success ratio. Dr. Sutton overruled him on this idea, but many of Henderson's ideas were implemented.

The traditional model involved acquiring patients through optometrist referrals. The optometrists also provided the postoperative care and received a portion of the $4000 to $5000 fee. In the reengineered model, the optometrists were cut out of the loop. Also, every step in the care delivery system was standardized. Patients were attracted directly with aggressive advertising and a price well below competitors' price, initially $2995. Henderson's vision of mass volume with low margins was launched in February 1998. Traditionally, other competitors such as TLC ran higher-priced, lower-volume operations (TLC has continued with its model of including the optometrists).

At the same time, Sutton also believed in aggressive treatment. According to one of his colleagues, Dr. Dan Reinstein, "Hugo's nature is pioneering. And so, by definition, he is more likely to have less conservative, uh, outcomes." Unfortunately, many patients were not properly informed that they were less-than-ideal candidates for the surgery. In a competitive medical environment, patients emerging from surgery with poor outcomes lead to lawsuits. As a result, in August 1998, a rare public statement from the B.C. College of Physicians and Surgeons said that Sutton "has agreed to a modification of his practice and he has voluntarily agreed not to perform these surgical procedures on patients in the higher-risk categories."

In light of Sutton's troubles, Henderson became president and CEO in April 1999 and began pushing the company into massive expansion and a public offering. This expansion actually started in Toronto in September 1998, followed by Calgary two months later. Henderson continued expansion until eight more sites had been added by September 1999. Henderson insisted that pricing was the key. In TV advertisements, Henderson personally extolled the Lasik Vision message—Why pay more?—standing next to a large graphic proclaiming "$1475 per eye." By early 1999, the pricing was dropped to $1598 for both eyes, but Henderson preferred to see it even lower. One advertisement he initiated proclaimed a cost of $999 with an asterisk listing another $599 in additional fees in fine print. This prompted Advertising Standards Canada to demand a change.

In December 1999, Henderson announced his intention to step up the pace of expansion. Beginning March 2000, Lasik Vision would start expanding at the pace of one new site per week to open about 20 clinics in the United States. The whole delivery process would be standardized right from the décor of the waiting rooms to the approach in which patients were counselled and corneas were lasered. This was the only way large volumes of patients could be treated with a high level of care. The medical doctors involved responded to the challenge by devising a hiring and training system that Sutton and the other doctors felt would enable reliable quality across the country.

All this development and expansion was taking place while trouble was brewing between the doctors and Henderson over financial and managerial improprieties. Henderson was aggressively skimming off profits from the company for himself. The last straw came in the spring of 2000 when PriceWaterhouseCoopers grew concerned about Henderson's "unfettered" activities while auditing Lasik's financial statements. In June 2000, Henderson was fired from the company.

Epilogue

Henderson subsequently sued Lasik Vision and Sutton for negligence during an eye operation performed on his eyes in March 1998, which he claims damaged his vision. Reinstein admits that Henderson had a complication. Henderson's problem, Reinstein insists, is that he does not understand the difference between complication and negligence. "Well, maybe you shouldn't expect him to," he sniffs. "He is not a doctor." Still you have to hand it to him, says Reinstein, "He is an amazing guy. I did learn a lot about doing business from him."

By 2001, the industry was mired in the ugly price war initiated by Lasik Vision, in addition to an advertising war, with many companies spending 10 to 13 percent of revenue on advertising (TLC has even signed professional golfer Tiger Woods to a multi-year contract to endorse his surgery at TLC). Lasik's stock slid from $6 in April 1999 to about a tenth of that by December 2000. As a result of all this, a consolidation spree ensued.

The January 31, 2001 edition of *The Globe and Mail* reported that Lasik Vision had been acquired by another discounter, Icon Laser Eye Centers. At that time, Lasik called itself the Dell Computer of laser vision correction—"we offer a high-quality product direct to customers and we cut distribution costs without compromising patient care." However, TLC disagreed: "Clearly it's the utter failure of both their business and clinical models that has forced them into such dire financial circumstances and their marriage of desperation in the first place." At about the same time, Aris Vision of Los Angeles acquired control of Gimbel Vision International of Calgary.

The August 28, 2001 issue of *The Globe and Mail* reported that the two leading laser eye surgery companies, TLC Laser Centers and St. Louis-based Laser Vision Centers Inc., were merging. It also mentioned that these two companies had refused to participate in the price war initiated by Lasik Vision, which, ironically, had resulted in both Lasik Vision and its acquirer, Icon, going bankrupt. Lasik Vision is now called Lasik Eye Centres (http://lasikeyecentres.com).

Questions

1. What was Lasik Vision's competitive priority?
2. Is it an appropriate approach in this industry? What repercussions, actual or perceived, might occur with this priority?
3. What might be some of the external influences on strategy formulation?
4. Given that a company has chosen this priority, what would it have to do to achieve success?
5. What are the order-qualifiers and order-winners in this business?
6. Based on their Web site, do Lasik Eye Center's competitive priorities seem different from Lasik Vision's?

Source: This case was adapted by Jaydeep Balakrishnan from an article written by Trevor Cole in *ROB Magazine*, January 2001, and is for discussion purposes only. It is not intended to illustrate the proper or improper management of a situation. Richard B. Chase, F. Robert Jacobs, and Nicholas J. Aquilano, *Operations Management for Competitive Advantage*, 10th ed. (New York: Irwin McGraw-Hill, 2004).

Footnote

[1]www.lululemon.com

Selected Bibliography

Hayes, Robert; Gary Pisano; David Upton; and Steven Wheelwright. *Operations, Strategy, and Technology: Pursuing the Competitive Edge*. New York: John Wiley & Sons, 2004.

Hill, T. J. *Manufacturing Strategy—Text and Cases*. Burr Ridge; IL: Irwin/McGraw-Hill, 2000.

Slack, N., and M. Lewis. *Operations Strategy*. Harlow, England, and New York: Prentice Hall, 2002.

Sower, Victor E., Jaideep Motwani, and Michael J. Savoie. "Classics in Production and Operations Management," *International Journal of Operations & Production Management*, Vol. 17, no. 1 (1997), pp. 15–28.

CHAPTER 3

PROJECT MANAGEMENT

Learning Objectives:

1. Know what project management is and why it is important.
2. Understand the types of project organizations.
3. Learn how projects are organized into major subprojects (work breakdown structure).
4. Understand what is meant by project control.
5. Know how to determine the "critical path" for a project.
6. Know how to "crash," or reduce the length, of a project.

ELLISDON OFFERS TOTAL PROJECT MANAGEMENT

EllisDon is a leading, employee-owned, international construction company, completing more than $1 billion in industrial, commercial, institutional, civil, and multi-unit residential construction annually. Founded in London, Ontario in 1951, EllisDon has grown into one of Canada's premier builders, offering services in general contracting, construction management, project management, design-build, public/private partnerships (P3), and safety consulting.

EllisDon has successfully undertaken projects in Europe, the Middle East, Central America, the Caribbean, Malaysia, and the former Soviet Union. The company now has twelve offices across Canada and the United States and worked on projects in Greece for the 2004 Olympics.

In 2007 and 2008, *The Globe and Mail's* Report on Business named EllisDon the best company to work for in Canada, well ahead of its competition. The *National Post* also named EllisDon one of the 50 best managed companies in Canada.

Like other types of business, the construction industry has undergone many significant changes over the last few years. Traditionally a construction company, EllisDon had a reputation among both owners and subcontractors for being hard-nosed, which served it well for many years. By the late 1990s, the industry was changing; many clients had downsized and eliminated in-house experts. They began looking to contractors for more expertise and value-added services. EllisDon embraced this opportunity, changing its role from adversary to team player, and developed the "Client First" program. Under Client First, EllisDon offers guarantees in three aspects of a project that are critical to its clients: performance, price, and schedule.

Furthermore, not having found appropriate software to run all aspects of a successful construction project, EllisDon has developed an industry-leading project management software called EdgeBuilder. The EdgeBuilder system allows procurement durations to be reduced while maintaining (and even enhancing) business controls. This is accomplished through the use of online collaboration. The company also recognizes the value of its employees. EllisDon encourages employees to build their career within the firm, offering benefits such as a generous profit-sharing plan, training, career development, and tuition reimbursement.

■ Sources: Margot Gibb-Clark, "EllisDon Rebuilds How It Does Business," *The Globe and Mail*, May 1, 2000, M1.
EllisDon Corporation, www.ellisdon. com.

"The high-impact project is the gem . . . the fundamental nugget . . . the fundamental atomic particle from which the new white collar world will be constructed and/or reconstructed. Projects should be, well WOW!"
—Tom Peters, management guru and author

Although most of the material in this chapter focuses on the technical aspects of project management (structuring project networks and calculating the critical path), as we see in the opening vignette the management aspects are equally important. Success in project management is very much an activity that requires careful control of critical resources. We spend much of the time in this book focused on the management of nonhuman resources such as machines and material; for projects, however, the key resource is often our employees' time. Human resources are often the most expensive resources and those people involved in the projects critical to the success of the firm are often the most valuable managers, consultants, and engineers.

At the highest levels in an organization such as Waterloo-based Research in Motion (RIM), management often involves juggling a portfolio of projects. There are many different types of projects ranging from the development of totally new products, revisions to old products, new marketing plans, and a vast array of projects for better serving customers and reducing costs.

Most companies deal with projects individually—pushing each through the pipeline as quickly and cost-effectively as possible. Many of these same companies are very good at applying the techniques described in this chapter so that the myriad of tasks are executed flawlessly, but the projects just do not deliver the expected results. Worse, what often happens is that the projects consuming the most resources have the least connection to the firm's overall strategy.

The vital big-picture decision is what mix of projects is best for the organization. A firm should have the right mix of projects that best support a company's strategy. Projects should be selected from the following types: derivative (incremental changes such as new product packaging or no-frills versions), breakthrough (major changes that create entirely new markets), platform (fundamental improvements to existing products). This is certainly the case

EXHIBIT 3.1	Types of Development Projects

	More ←——— Change ———→ Less		
	Breakthrough Projects	Platform Projects	Derivative Projects
Product Change	New core product	Additional to product family	Product enhancement
Process Change	New core process	Process upgrade	Incremental change
Research & Development	New core technology	Technology upgrade	Incremental change
Alliance & Partnership	Outsource major activity	Select new partner	Incremental change

with RIM. Recently, RIM had to come up with a new platform product (the Blackberry Storm) as well having to make minor changes to existing models at the same time. It also has to do research and development into breakthrough projects to keep up in the rapidly developing smart-phone market. Projects can be categorized into four major areas: product change, process change, research and development, and alliance and partnership (see Exhibit 3.1).

In this chapter, we only scratch the surface in our introduction to the topic of project management. Professional project managers are individuals skilled not only at the technical aspects of calculating such things as early start and early finish time but, just as important, at the people skills related to motivation. In addition, the ability to resolve conflicts as key decision points occur in the project is a critical skill. Leading successful projects is the best way to prove your promotability to the people who make promotion decisions. Virtually all project work is team work and leading a project involves leading a team. Your success at leading a project will spread quickly through the individuals in the team. As organizations flatten (through reengineering, downsizing, outsourcing), more will depend on projects and project leaders to get work done, work that was previously handled within departments. As the OSMP on Apple shows, good project management can be an important ingredient in product success.

Why has studying project management becoming more important? According to Gray and Larson,[1] project management has taken on increased importance in recent years because of a) compression in the product life cycle, b) global competition, c) knowledge explosion, d) corporate downsizing, e) increased customer focus, f) rapid development of developing and formerly closed economies, and g) a multiple-project, more problematic environment.

Consider again the case of RIM. Its Blackberry smartphone certainly faces many of the seven factors listed in the previous paragraph. You have probably noticed that every time you visit an electronics store, there is probably a new model of cell phone, indicating how short product life cycles are. Thus, even a short delay in introducing a new model can mean ceding leadership in that model to a competitor like Nokia. Further, the competition is formidable. As a result, RIM had to respond quickly to Apple's introduction of the touch-sensitive iPhone in 2008 with its introduction of the comparable Storm model a few months later. Thus, RIM has to constantly bring out new products (often revolutionary, as

Apple's iPod Has Its Own Product Development Team

How does Apple develop the innovative products it sells? Apple has two separate product development teams, one organized around its Macintosh computer and the other focused on the iPod music player. By organizing this way, Apple can precisely focus resources on its amazingly successful products. The iPod has reinvigorated Apple and its bottom line over the past two years.

Much of the underlying iPod design was created by outside companies. Consumer electronics is a fast moving area, and, using established experts linked together in what could be called a design chain, Apple was able to quickly bring the iPod to market. Apple developed a layered project that relied on a platform created by a third party, PortalPlayer, of Santa Clara, California. PortalPlayer had developed a base platform for a variety of audio systems, including portable digital music devices, general audio systems, and streaming audio receivers.

Apple started with a vision of what the player should be and what it should look like. The subsequent design parameters were dictated by its appearance and form factor.

That outside-in perspective helped determine a number of the components, including the planar lithium battery from Sony and the 4.6-cm Toshiba hard drive. The essential units—battery, hard drive, and circuit board—are layered, one on top of the next. The rest of the device uses a dedicated MP3 decoder and controller chip from PortalPlayer, a Wolfson Microelectronics Ltd. stereo digital-to-analog converter, a flash memory chip from Sharp Electronics Corp., a Texas Instruments 1394 firewire interface controller, and a power management and battery charging integrated circuit from Linear Technologies, Inc.

Working with these partners, the iPod design project was completed in a few months of iterative loops. Managing activities among the multiple partners was extremely difficult since Apple needed to make sure that its suppliers' development schedules matched the product introduction schedule. No doubt, subsequent versions of the iPod will depend on this dynamic design chain as different components and optimizations are discovered. Apple's iPod product has been wildly successful, due in large part to successful project management efforts, the topic of this chapter.

when you move from a keypad to touch sensitive). Good project management can ensure that valuable time is not wasted in introducing new phones. And many products are very complex. No single company has the knowledge or resources to "do it all" (whether it is a cell phone or Bombardier aircraft). So RIM had to work with hardware providers like Synaptics (touch-interface technology) and Qualcomm (chipmaker), software providers like Google, and network providers such as Telus or Bell in order to make the product successful.[2] This often requires collaboration on a global scale. Project management principles can be very effective in managing this collaboration.

Companies have also realized that poor project management is costing millions, even billions of dollars, due to delays or customer dissatisfaction-related rework. This is particularly acute in the Canadian oil industry, where projects cost billions of dollars. Thus, more and more professional societies and consultants, including universities and colleges, are offering training seminars and courses related to project management to companies.

WHAT IS PROJECT MANAGEMENT?

A **project** may be defined as a series of related jobs usually directed toward some major output and requiring a significant period of time to perform. **Project management** can be defined as planning, directing, and controlling resources (people, equipment, material) to meet the technical, cost, and time constraints of the project.

Although projects are often thought to be one-time occurrences, the fact is that many projects can be repeated or transferred to other settings or products. The result will be another project output. A contractor building houses or a firm producing low-volume products such as supercomputers, locomotives, or linear accelerators can effectively consider these as projects.

TYPES OF PROJECT ORGANIZATION STRUCTURES

Before the project starts, senior management must decide which of three organizational structures will be used to tie the project to the parent firm: pure project, functional project, or matrix project. We next discuss the strengths and weaknesses of the three main forms.

Pure Project

Cross Functional

Tom Peters predicts that most of the world's work will be "brainwork," done in semipermanent networks of small project-oriented teams, each one an autonomous, entrepreneurial centre of opportunity, where the necessity for speed and flexibility dooms the hierarchical management structures we and our ancestors grew up with. Out of the three basic project organizational structures, Peters favours the **pure project** (nicknamed *skunkworks*), in which a self-contained team works full time on the project.

ADVANTAGES
- The project manager has full authority over the project.
- Team members report to one boss. They do not have to worry about dividing loyalty with a functional-area manager.
- Lines of communication are shortened. Decisions are made quickly.
- Team pride, motivation, and commitment are high.

DISADVANTAGES
- Duplication of resources. Equipment and people are not shared across projects.
- Organizational goals and policies are ignored, as team members are often both physically and psychologically removed from headquarters.
- The organization falls behind in its knowledge of new technology due to weakened functional divisions.
- Because team members have no functional-area home, they worry about life-after-project, and project termination is delayed.

Functional Project

At the other end of the project organization spectrum is the **functional project**, housing the project within a functional division.

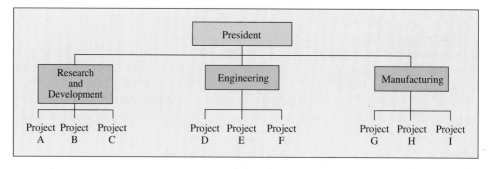

ADVANTAGES
- A team member can work on several projects.
- Technical expertise is maintained within the functional area even if individuals leave the project or organization.
- The functional area is a home after the project is completed. Functional specialists can advance vertically.
- A critical mass of specialized functional-area experts creates synergistic solutions to a project's technical problems.

- Aspects of the project that are not directly related to the functional area get short-changed.
- Motivation of team members is often weak.
- The needs of the client are secondary and are responded to slowly.

Matrix Project

The classic specialized organizational form, "the **matrix project**," attempts to blend properties of functional and pure project structures. Each project uses people from different functional areas. The project manager (PM) decides what tasks will be performed and when, but the functional managers control which people and technologies are used. If the matrix form is chosen, different projects (rows of the matrix) borrow resources from functional areas (columns). Senior management must then decide whether a weak, balanced, or strong form of a matrix is to be used. This establishes whether project managers have little, equal, or more authority than the functional managers with whom they negotiate for resources.

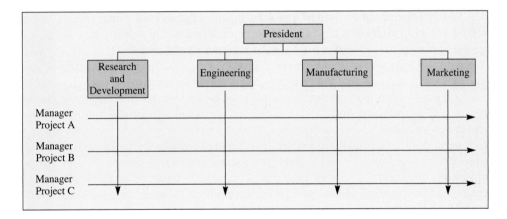

ADVANTAGES

- Communication between functional divisions is enhanced.
- A project manager is held responsible for successful completion of the project.
- Duplication of resources is minimized.
- Team members have a functional "home" after project completion, so they are less worried about life-after-project than if they were a pure project organization.
- Policies of the parent organization are followed. This increases support for the project.

DISADVANTAGES

- There are two bosses. Often the functional manager will be listened to before the project manager. After all, who can promote you or give you a raise?
- It is doomed to failure unless the PM has strong negotiating skills.
- Suboptimization is a danger, as PMs hoard resources for their own project, thus harming other projects.

Note that regardless of which of the three major organizational forms is used, the project manager is the primary contact point with the customer. Communication and flexibility are greatly enhanced because one person is responsible for successful completion of the project. With Canadian companies being involved today around the world it is also important to recognize that there can be significant cultural differences among countries. Besides, projects in Canada can involve multinational teams. For example, a recent major project, the Confederation Bridge linking Prince Edward Island to New Brunswick, was constructed by a consortium that included companies from France, the Netherlands, the U.S., and Canada. Similarly, Montreal-based SNC Lavalin does capital projects all over the world and has to take into account the diverse ways of doing business in countries such as Saudi Arabia, India, and China. So project teams may have to be managed with the cultural context in mind.

WORK BREAKDOWN STRUCTURE

A project starts out as a *statement of work* (SOW). The SOW may be a written description of the objectives to be achieved, with a brief statement of the work to be done and a proposed schedule specifying the start and completion dates. It could also contain performance measures that contain budget and completion steps (milestones) and the written reports to be supplied.

A *task* is a further subdivision of a project. It is usually not longer than several months in duration and is performed by one group or organization. A *subtask* may be used if needed to further subdivide the project into more meaningful pieces.

A *work package* is a group of activities combined to be assignable to a single organizational unit. It still falls into the format of all project management; the package provides a description of what is to be done, when it is to be started and completed, the budget, measures of performance, and specific events to be reached at points in time. These specific events are called **project milestones**. Typical milestones might be the completion of the design, the production of a prototype, the completed testing of the prototype, and the approval of a pilot run. The **work breakdown structure** (WBS) defines the hierarchy of project tasks, subtasks, and work packages. Completion of one or more work packages results in the completion of a subtask; completion of one or more subtasks results in the completion of a task; and finally, the completion of all tasks is required to complete the project. A representation of this structure is shown in Exhibit 3.2.

| EXHIBIT 3.2 | An Example of a Work Breakdown Structure |

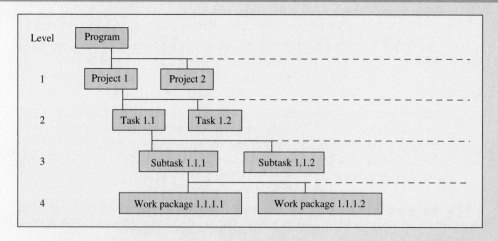

Work Breakdown Structure, Large Optical Scanner Design
(Tabular Format)

EXHIBIT 3.3

Level 1	2	3	4		
x				1	Optical simulator design
	x			1.1	Optical design
		x		1.1.1	Telescope design/fab
		x		1.1.2	Telescope/simulator optical interface
		x		1.1.3	Simulator zoom system design
		x		1.1.4	Ancillary simulator optical component specification
	x			1.2	System performance analysis
		x		1.2.1	Overall system firmware and software control
			x	1.2.1.1	Logic flow diagram generation and analysis
			x	1.2.1.2	Basic control algorithm design
		x		1.2.2	Far beam analyzer
		x		1.2.3	System inter- and intra-alignment method design
		x		1.2.4	Data recording and reduction requirements
	x			1.3	System integration
	x			1.4	Cost analysis
		x		1.4.1	Cost/system schedule analysis
		x		1.4.2	Cost/system performance analysis
	x			1.5	Management
		x		1.5.1	System design/engineering management
		x		1.5.2	Program management
	x			1.6	Long lead item procurement
		x		1.6.1	Large optics
		x		1.6.2	Target components
		x		1.6.3	Detectors

Exhibit 3.3 and 3.4 show the WBS for an optical scanner project in different formats. The WBS is important in organizing a project because it breaks the project down into manageable pieces. The number of levels will vary depending on the project. How much detail or how many levels to use depends on the following:

- The level at which a single individual or organization can be assigned responsibility and accountability for accomplishing the work package.
- The level at which budget and cost data will be collected during the project.

There is no single correct WBS for any project, and two different project teams might develop different WBSs for the same project. Some experts have referred to project management as an art rather than a science, because there are so many different ways to approach a project. Finding the correct way to organize a project depends on experience with the particular task.

Activities are defined within the context of the work breakdown structure and are pieces of work that consume time. Activities do not necessarily require the expenditure of effort by people, although they often do. For example, waiting for paint to dry may be an activity in a project. Activities are identified as part of the WBS. From our sample project in Exhibit 3.3, activities would include telescope design and fabrication (1.1.1), telescope/simulator optical interface (1.1.2), and data recording (1.2.4). Activities need to be defined in such a way that when they are all completed, the project is done.

EXHIBIT 3.4   Work Breakdown Structure, Large Optical Scanner Design
(Tree Format)

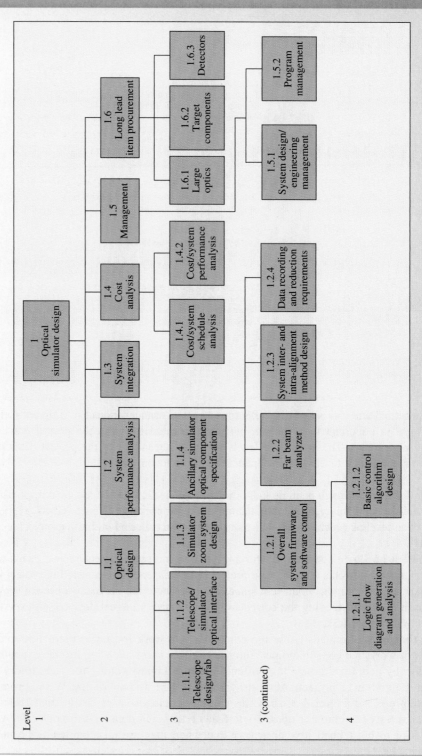

Operations Management in Practice

Every Project Needs to Manage Risks

Imagine what a disaster it would have been if the Vancouver 2010 Olympic Games had not started on time, some facilities could not be built for lack of funds, or the information system had crashed frequently during the games due to technical glitches.

Effective project management entails plans to manage financial, schedule, and technical risk. For example, the Vancouver 2010 Games had a project control and deficit avoidance plan as well as a risk management plan. These types of plans allow project managers to avoid occurrences that adversely affect the project as well as mitigate the adverse effects when they do occur so that the project is a success. Responding in fire-fighting mode to adverse occurrences is the least effective way of managing risk.

Effective risk management involves identifying the major risks as well as the minor ones. These risks (with a greater focus on high-effect, high-probability ones) then have to be mitigated: by avoiding them, transferring them, sharing them, or retaining them. For example, technical glitches can be avoided by building prototypes or doing test runs.

Companies can transfer project financial risk to suppliers by using fixed price contracts or through insurance. Boeing shares its product development risk by partnering with other aerospace companies. Any future losses are shared by all the partners. On the flip side, of course, the profits are also shared. So managing risk does come with a cost, but in most cases this cost is preferable to the disaster that might follow if no risk management is done.

Sometimes, companies retain risk and mitigate it through contingency plans. For example, the host city for an Olympics has to assume the risk of adverse weather and plan for it. In 1988, the Calgary Winter Olympics had to reschedule over 20 events (some even twice) because of balmy weather. In other cases, companies ignore minor risks with low probability of occurrence.

■ Sources: Clifford F. Gray and Erik W. Larson, *Project Management: The Managerial Approach* (New York: McGraw-Hill/Irwin, 2008), pp. 202–214.

http://www.vancouver2010.com/en/about-vanoc/business-plan-and-games-budget/-/32766/196rogx/index.html, retrieved June 17, 2009.

R.G. Holland, "The XV Olympic Games: A Case Study in Project Management," *PM Network*, (November 1989), 8–12.

PROJECT CONTROL CHARTS

The U.S. Department of Defense (one of the earliest large users of project management) has published a variety of helpful standard forms. Many are used directly or have been modified by firms engaged in project management. Computer programs are available to quickly generate the charts described in this section. Charts are useful because their visual presentation is easily understood. Exhibit 3.5 shows a sample of the available charts.

Exhibit 3.5A is a sample **Gantt chart**, sometimes referred to as a *bar chart,* showing both the amount of time involved and the sequence in which activities can be performed. The chart is named after an American, Henry L. Gantt, who won a presidential citation for his application of this type of chart to shipbuilding during World War I. In the example in Exhibit 3.5A, "long lead item procurement" and "manufacturing schedules" are independent activities and can occur simultaneously. All other activities must be done in the sequence from top to bottom. Exhibit 3.5B graphs the amounts of money spent on labour, material, and overhead. Its value is its clarity in identifying sources and amounts of cost.

Exhibit 3.5C shows the percentage of the project's labour hours that comes from the various areas of manufacturing, finance, and so on. These labour hours are related to the proportion of the project's total labour cost. For example, manufacturing is responsible for 50 percent of the project's labour hours, but this 50 percent has been allocated just 40 percent of the total labour dollars charged.

The top half of Exhibit 3.5D shows the degree of completion of these projects. The dotted vertical line signifies today. Project 1, therefore, is already late because it still has work to be done. Project 2 is not being worked on temporarily, so there is a space before the projected work. Project 3 continues to be worked on without interruption. The bottom of Exhibit 3.5D compares actual total costs and projected costs. As we see, two cost overruns occurred, and the current cumulative costs are over projected cumulative costs.

EXHIBIT 3.5   A Sample of Graphic Project Reports

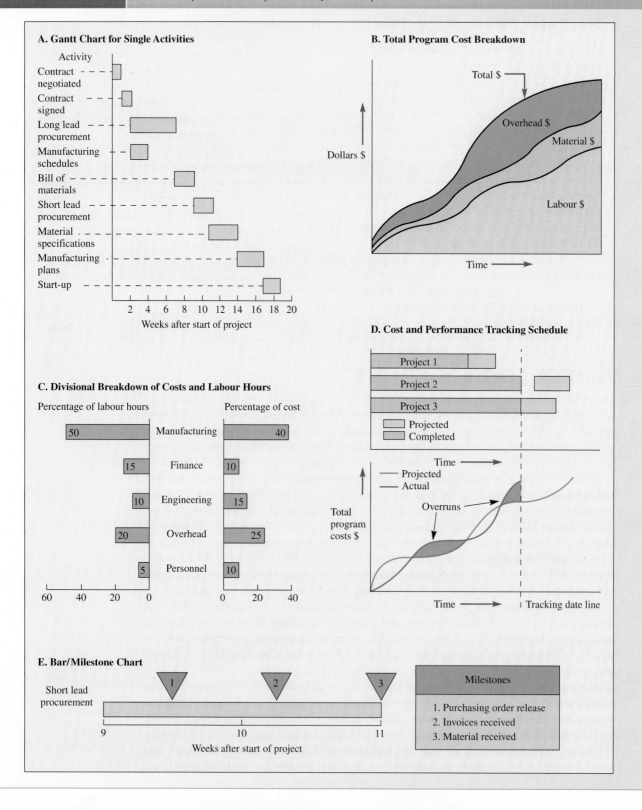

A. Gantt Chart for Single Activities

Activity

Contract negotiated
Contract signed
Long lead procurement
Manufacturing schedules
Bill of materials
Short lead procurement
Material specifications
Manufacturing plans
Start-up

Weeks after start of project

B. Total Program Cost Breakdown

Total $
Overhead $
Material $
Labour $
Dollars $
Time

C. Divisional Breakdown of Costs and Labour Hours

Percentage of labour hours   Percentage of cost

50	Manufacturing	40
15	Finance	10
10	Engineering	15
20	Overhead	25
5	Personnel	10

60 40 20 0   0 20 40

D. Cost and Performance Tracking Schedule

Project 1
Project 2
Project 3
Projected
Completed
Time

Time
Projected
Actual
Overruns
Total program costs $
Time   Tracking date line

E. Bar/Milestone Chart

Short lead procurement

1   2   3

9   10   11
Weeks after start of project

Milestones
1. Purchasing order release
2. Invoices received
3. Material received

Operations and Supply Management in Practice

Using Project Management Principles to Manage Your Group Term Paper

You might not have thought of it this way, but any group term paper that you do in university is a project. After all, it is expected to be a unique piece of work! In fact, one of the authors has student groups in his class use many of the project management principles you will see in this chapter. Students are expected to break down the project into its constituent parts (called the work breakdown structure or WBS). Furthermore, students are required to use Microsoft Project to come up with a project schedule and to assign responsibility for the various tasks to group members. The milestones (interim deliverables to be submitted to the instructor as well as any others determined by the group) of the project have to be identified in the schedule and the students are expected to meet their deadlines. Conflict in student groups (perhaps one of the project team is not pulling his or her weight), a fact of life in business and industry, is expected to be resolved as much as possible within the group.

Other project management principles are used implicitly. In order to meet a deadline, you might have to take over some of the work initially assigned to your friend because he fell ill. Furthermore, if your group realizes that the paper is behind schedule, you may speed up or "crash" your project by paying an outside party to do some tasks, such as proofreading. All this is part of project control—modifying aspects of the project to get it back on track.

Projects also involve trade-offs between time, cost, and scope. For example, if you hire a proofreader to speed up the project, your costs will go up. Furthermore, though you may have planned to interview someone from industry for this paper, due to lack of time you may have to give up this idea (i.e., reduce the scope of the project in order to avoid delays). Of course, this could result in lower customer (instructor) satisfaction and a lower grade!

Once, minutes before the start of the session in which the paper was due, one of the authors discovered three students from one group standing outside the classroom clutching papers. It turned out they were waiting for the fourth member of their group in order to submit his part, before stapling it and handing it in a few minutes later in class. Suffice to say their project was not one of the better ones the author had seen, a logical outcome for a paper written in four parts by four different people without much collaboration.

This is an important lesson in project management which companies have learned the hard way over the years: Projects have to be done in an integrated fashion. For example, if marketing, design, and manufacturing (and other functions in the firm) do not collaborate from the very beginning of a project, the result will be rework, delays, and additional costs before the customer gets a satisfactory product. In the worst case, the product will fail in the marketplace, in the same way that a badly planned and executed term paper will receive a poor grade.

Exhibit 3.5E is a milestone chart. The three milestones mark specific points in the project where checks can be made to see if the project is on time and where it should be. The best place to locate milestones is at the completion of a major activity. In this exhibit, the major activities completed were "purchase order release," "invoices received," and "material received."

Other standard reports can be used for a more detailed presentation comparing cost to progress (such as cost schedule status report—CSSR) or reports providing the basis for partial payment (such as the earned value report).

NETWORK-PLANNING MODELS

The two best-known network-planning models were developed in the 1950s. The Critical Path Method (CPM) was developed for scheduling maintenance shutdowns at chemical processing plants owned by Du Pont. Since maintenance projects are performed often in this industry, reasonably accurate time estimates for activities are available. CPM is based on the assumption that project activity times can be estimated accurately and that they do not vary. The Program Evaluation and Review Technique (PERT) was developed for the U.S. Navy's Polaris missile project. This was a massive project involving over 3000 contractors. Because most of the activities had never been done before, PERT was developed to handle uncertain time estimates. As years passed, features that distinguished CPM from PERT have diminished, so in our treatment here we just use the term CPM.

Interactive Operations Management

In a sense, the CPM techniques illustrated here owe their development to the widely used predecessor, the Gantt chart. Although the Gantt chart is able to relate activities to time in a usable fashion for small projects, the interrelationship of activities, when displayed in this form, becomes extremely difficult to visualize and to work with for projects that include more than 25 activities. Also, the Gantt chart provides no direct procedure for determining the critical path, which is of great practical value to identify.

The **critical path** of activities in a project is the sequence of activities that take the longest time to complete. If any one of the activities in the critical path is delayed, the entire project is delayed. Determining scheduling information about each activity in the project is the major goal of CPM techniques. The techniques calculate when an activity must start and end, together with whether the activity is part of the critical path. As we will see later, a project may have more than one critical path.

Critical Path Method (CPM)

Here is a procedure for scheduling a project. In this case, a single time estimate is used because we are assuming that the activity times are known. A very simple project will be scheduled to demonstrate the basic approach.

Consider that you have a group assignment that requires a decision on whether you should invest in a company. Your instructor has suggested that you perform the analysis in the following four steps:

A. Select a company.
B. Obtain the company's annual report and perform a ratio analysis.
C. Collect stock price data and do technical analysis.
D. Individually review the data and make a team decision on whether to buy the stock.

Your group of four people decides that the project can be divided into four activities as suggested by the instructor. You decide that all the team members should be involved in selecting the company and that it should take one week to complete this activity. You will meet at the end of the week to decide what company the group will consider. During this meeting you will divide your group: two people will be responsible for the annual report and ratio analysis, and the other two will collect the stock price data and do technical analysis. Your group expects it to take two weeks to get the annual report and perform the ratio analysis, and a week to collect the stock price data and do technical analysis. You agree that the two groups can work independently. Finally, you agree to meet as a team to make the purchase decision. Before you meet, you want to allow one week for each team member to review all the data.

This is a simple project, but it will serve to demonstrate the approach. The following are the appropriate steps.

1. **Identify each activity to be done in the project and estimate how long it will take to complete each activity.**   This is simple, given the information from your instructor. We identify the activities as follows: A(1), B(2), C(1), D(1). The number is the expected duration of the activity.

2. **Determine the required sequence of activities and construct a network reflecting the precedence relationships.**   An easy way to do this is to first identify the **immediate predecessors** associated with an activity. The immediate predecessors are the activities that need to be completed immediately before an activity. Activity A needs to be completed before activities B and C can start. B and C need to be completed before D can start. The following table reflects what we know so far:

ACTIVITY	DESIGNATION	IMMEDIATE PREDECESSORS	TIME (WEEKS)
Select company	A	None	1
Obtain annual report and perform ratio analysis	B	A	2
Collect stock price data and perform technical analysis	C	A	1
Review data and make a decision	D	B and C	1

Here is a diagram that depicts these precedence relationships:

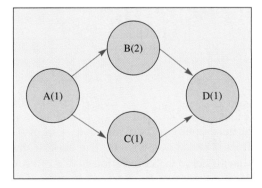

3. **Determine the critical path.**   Consider each sequence of activities that runs from the beginning to the end of the project. For our simple project there are two paths: A–B–D and A–C–D. The critical path is the path where the sum of the activity times is the longest. A–B–D has a duration of four weeks and A–C–D, a duration of three weeks. The critical path, therefore, is A–B–D. If any activity along the critical path is delayed, then the entire project will be delayed.

4. **Determine the early start/finish and late start/finish schedule.**   To schedule the project, find out when each activity needs to start and when it needs to finish. For some activities in a project there may be some leeway in when an activity can start and finish. This is called the **slack time** in an activity. For each activity in the project, we calculate four points in time: the early start, early finish, late start, and late finish times. The early start and early finish are the earliest times that the activity can start and be finished. Similarly, the late start and late finish are the latest times the activities can start and finish. The difference between the late start time and early start time is the slack time. To help keep all of this straight, we place these numbers in special places around the nodes that represent each activity in our network diagram, as shown here.

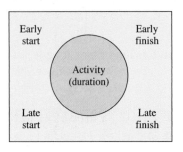

To calculate numbers, start from the beginning of the network and work to the end, calculating the early start and early finish numbers. Start counting with the current period, designated as period 0. Activity A has an early start of 0 and an early finish of 1. Activity B's early start is A's early finish or 1. Similarly, C's early start is 1. The early finish for B is 3, and the early finish for C is 2. Now consider activity D. D cannot start until both B and C are done. Because B cannot be done until 3, D cannot start until that time. The early start for D, therefore, is 3, and the early finish is 4. Our diagram now looks like this.

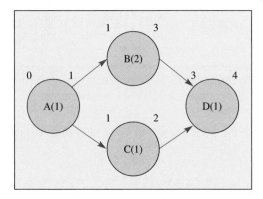

To calculate the late finish and late start times, start from the end of the network and work toward the front. Consider activity D. The earliest that it can be done is at time 4; if we do not want to delay the completion of the project, the late finish needs to be set to 4. With a duration of 1, the latest that D can start is 3. Now consider activity C. C must be done by time 3 so that D can start, so C's late finish time is 3 and its late start time is 2. Notice the difference between the early and late start and finish times: This activity has one week of slack time. Activity B must be done by time 3 so that D can start, so its late finish time is 3 and late start time is 1. There is no slack in B. Finally, activity A must be done so that B and C can start. Because B must start earlier than C, and A must get done in time for B to start, the late finish time for A is 1.

Finally, the late start time for A is 0. Notice there is no slack in activities A, B, and D. The final network looks like this. (Hopefully, the stock your investment team has chosen is a winner!)

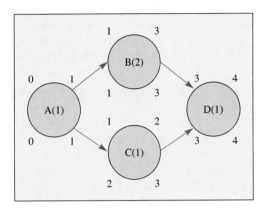

EXAMPLE 3.1:   CRITICAL PATH METHOD

Many firms that tried to enter the portable computer market have failed. Suppose your firm believes that there is a big demand in this market because existing products have not been designed correctly. They are either too heavy, too large, or too small to accommodate a standard-size keyboard. Your intended computer will be small enough to carry inside a jacket pocket if need be. The ideal size should be no larger than 8 cm × 20 cm, with a standard typewriter keyboard. It should weigh no more than 400 grams, have a 4- to 8-line × 80-character back-lit display, and have a micro disk drive and a micro printer. It should be aimed primarily toward word processing use but have plug-in ROMs to accommodate an assortment of computer languages and programs. These characteristics should appeal to travelling businesspeople, but could have a much wider market. If it can be priced to sell retail in the $175–$200 range, the computer should appeal to a wide market.

The project, then, is to design, develop, and produce a prototype of this portable computer. In the rapidly changing computer industry, it is crucial to hit the market with a product of this type in less than a year. Therefore, the project team has been allowed approximately eight months, or 35 weeks, to produce the prototype.

Project Management

SOLUTION

The first charge of the project team is to develop a project network chart and determine whether the prototype computer can be completed within 35 weeks. Let's follow the steps in the development of the network.

1. **Activity identification.** The project team decides that the following activities are the major components of the project: design of the computer, prototype construction, prototype testing, methods specification (summarized in a report), evaluation studies of automatic assembly equipment, an assembly equipment study report, and a final report summarizing all aspects of the design, equipment, and methods.

2. **Activity sequencing and network construction.** On the basis of discussion with staff, the project manager develops the precedence table and sequence network shown in Exhibit 3.6. When constructing a network, take care to ensure that the activities are in the proper order and that the logic of their relationships is maintained. For example, it would be illogical to have a situation where Event A precedes Event B, B precedes C, and C precedes A.

EXHIBIT 3.6	CPM Network for Computer Design Project

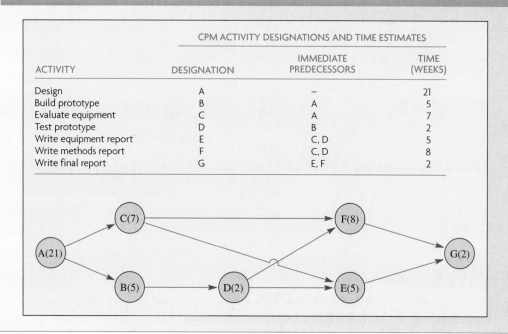

CPM ACTIVITY DESIGNATIONS AND TIME ESTIMATES

ACTIVITY	DESIGNATION	IMMEDIATE PREDECESSORS	TIME (WEEKS)
Design	A	–	21
Build prototype	B	A	5
Evaluate equipment	C	A	7
Test prototype	D	B	2
Write equipment report	E	C, D	5
Write methods report	F	C, D	8
Write final report	G	E, F	2

3. **Determine the critical path.**   The critical path is the longest sequence of connected activities throughout the network and is defined as the path with zero slack time. This network has four different paths: A–C–F–G, A–C–E–G, A–B–D–F–G, and A–B–D–E–G. The lengths of these paths are 38, 35, 38, and 35 weeks. This means that the project will take 38 weeks, so it cannot be completed in 35 weeks at the current pace. We will have to expedite some of the activities in the project to reduce the time to 35 weeks. The general procedure to do this is described later in this chapter. Note that this project has two different critical paths; this might indicate that this would be a fairly difficult project to manage. Calculating the early start and late start schedules gives additional insight into how difficult this project might be to complete on time.

Early Start and Late Start Schedules   An **early start schedule** is one that lists all of the activities by their early start times. For activities not on the critical path, there is slack time between the completion of each activity and the start of the next activity. The early start schedule completes the project and all its activities as soon as possible.

A **late start schedule** lists the activities to start as late as possible without delaying the completion date of the project. One motivation for using a late start schedule is that savings are realized by postponing purchases of materials, the use of labour, and other costs until necessary. These calculations are shown in Exhibit 3.7. From this we see that the only activity that has slack is activity E. This certainly would be a fairly difficult project to complete on time. As seen in the OSMP on slack times, this slack time represents flexibility in the project and should be used wisely.

CPM Network for Computer Design Project

EXHIBIT 3.7

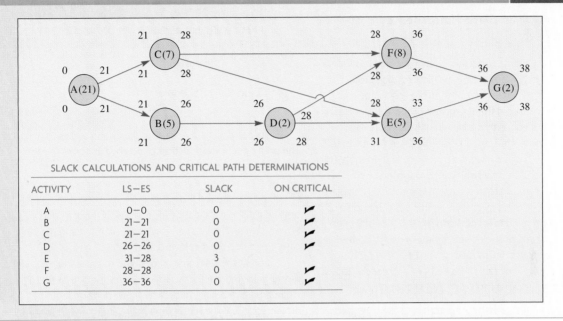

SLACK CALCULATIONS AND CRITICAL PATH DETERMINATIONS

ACTIVITY	LS−ES	SLACK	ON CRITICAL
A	0−0	0	✔
B	21−21	0	✔
C	21−21	0	✔
D	26−26	0	✔
E	31−28	3	
F	28−28	0	✔
G	36−36	0	✔

Time–Cost Models

In practice, project managers are as much concerned with the cost to complete a project as with the time to complete the project. For this reason, **time–cost models** have been devised. These models—extensions of the basic critical path method—attempt to develop a minimum-cost schedule for an entire project and to control expenditures during the project.

Minimum-Cost Scheduling (Time–Cost Trade-Off) The basic assumption in minimum-cost scheduling is that there is a relationship between activity completion time and the cost of a project. On the one hand, it costs money to expedite an activity, on the other, it costs money to sustain (or lengthen) the project. The costs associated with expediting activities are termed *activity direct costs* and add to the project direct cost. Some may be worker-related, such as overtime work, hiring more workers, and transferring workers from other jobs; others are resource-related, such as buying or leasing additional or more efficient equipment and drawing on additional support facilities.

The costs associated with sustaining the project are termed *project indirect costs:* overhead, facilities, and resource opportunity costs, and, under certain contractual situations, penalty costs or lost incentive payments. Because *activity direct costs* and *project indirect costs* are opposing costs dependent on time, the scheduling problem is essentially one of finding the project duration that minimizes their sum, or in other words, finding the optimum point in a time–cost trade-off.

The procedure for finding this point consists of the following five steps. It is explained by using the simple four-activity network shown in Exhibit 3.8. Assume that the indirect costs remain constant for eight days and then increase at the rate of $5 per day.

Operations and Supply Management in Practice

Everybody Uses Slack Time; the Key Is To Use It Wisely

Let us continue with our example from the previous Operations and Supply Management in Practice, using project management principles in your term paper. Assume that your project is due in the assignment dropoff box at noon today and it is currently 8 a. m. All paths in your project have been completed, except one. There are two tasks left on this path—proofreading the document and printing. This is a major paper worth a significant proportion of your grade. Thus, careful proofreading is essential. You calculate this task will take you two hours. Printing in colour on a laser jet printer will take another hour. So if you start now (the earliest time possible), you get the early start schedule, shown on the accompanying Gantt chart.

The proofreading task starts at 8 a.m. and ends at 10 a.m. The printing task starts at 10 a.m. and ends at 11 a.m.

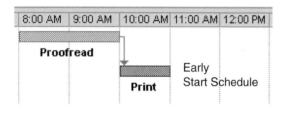

Now, let's say you had something else urgent to do now (at 8 a. m.). You figure you could work on that urgent task for an hour now and delay starting the proofreading until 9 a. m. at the latest and still complete both tasks by noon. This is called a late -start schedule. Here is what a Gantt chart of the schedule would look like:

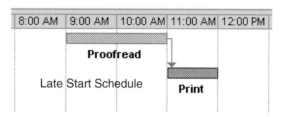

The proofreading task starts at 9 a.m. and ends at 11 a.m. The printing task starts at 11 a.m. and ends at noon. The project is still on time.

The maximum time you can delay an activity without affecting the required project completion time is the slack time. In other words, slack time is the difference in start times between the late and early start schedules. In this case, the tasks together have a slack time of one hour.

Note that the slack time allows you to reschedule activities to make more effective use of your time. This is useful when project team members may be working on multiple projects at the same time. Note, however, that with the late start schedule you cannot have any delays. For example, with the early start schedule, if your printer ran out of ink you would have time to fix it and still be on time. This will not be possible with the late start schedule. So good project managers use slack wisely, as a buffer against uncertainty. Perhaps it might be better to work on your other project for only 30 minutes. Then you could start the proofreading task at 8:30 a. m. and be done with the project at 11:30 a. m., leaving some time for delays.

■   Source: The authors are thankful to Brent Snider of the Haskayne School of Business, University of Calgary for suggesting that we use the paper submission deadline example to explain slack.

1. **Prepare a CPM-type network diagram.**   For each activity this diagram should list
   a. Normal cost (NC): the lowest expected activity costs. (These are the lesser of the cost figures shown under each node in Exhibit 3.8.)
   b. Normal time (NT): the time associated with each normal cost.
   c. Crash time (CT): the shortest possible activity time.
   d. Crash cost (CC): the cost associated with each crash time.
2. **Determine the cost per unit of time (assume days) to expedite each activity.**   The relationship between activity time and cost may be shown graphically by plotting CC and CT coordinates and connecting them to the NC and NT coordinates by a concave, convex, or straight line—or some other form, depending on the actual cost structure of activity performance, as in Exhibit 3.8. For activity A, we assume a linear relationship between time and cost. This assumption is common in practice and helps us

Example of Time–Cost Trade-Off Procedure

EXHIBIT 3.8

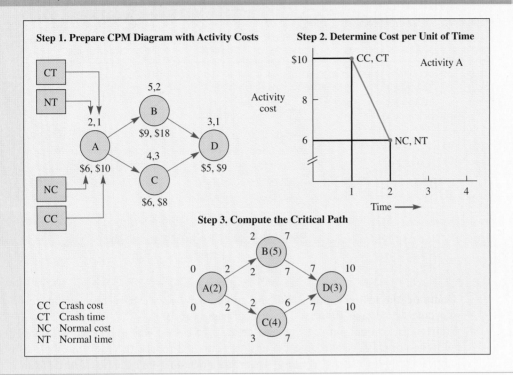

Step 1. Prepare CPM Diagram with Activity Costs

CT
NT

5,2
B

2,1
A
$9, $18

3,1
D

4,3
C
$5, $9

$6, $10

NC

CC

$6, $8

Step 2. Determine Cost per Unit of Time

Activity cost

$10 CC, CT   Activity A

8

6   NC, NT

1   2   3   4
Time →

Step 3. Compute the Critical Path

2   7
B (5)
2   7
0   2
A(2)
0   2
2   6
C(4)
3   7

7   10
D(3)
7   10

CC   Crash cost
CT   Crash time
NC   Normal cost
NT   Normal time

Project Management

Calculation of Cost per Day to Expedite Each Activity

EXHIBIT 3.9

ACTIVITY	CC − NC	NT − CT	$\dfrac{CC - NC}{NT - CT}$	COST PER DAY TO EXPEDITE	NUMBER OF DAYS ACTIVITY MAY BE SHORTENED
A	$10 − $6	2 − 1	$\dfrac{\$10 - \$6}{2 - 1}$	$4	1
B	$18 − $9	5 − 2	$\dfrac{\$18 - \$9}{5 - 2}$	$3	3
C	$8 − $6	4 − 3	$\dfrac{\$8 - \$6}{4 - 3}$	$2	1
D	$9 − $5	3 − 1	$\dfrac{\$9 - \$5}{3 - 1}$	$2	2

derive the cost per day to expedite because this value may be found directly by taking the slope of the line using the formula Slope = (CC − NC) ÷ (NT − CT). (When the assumption of linearity cannot be made, the cost of expediting must be determined graphically for each day the activity may be shortened.)

The calculations needed to obtain the cost of expediting the remaining activities are shown in Exhibit 3.9.

EXHIBIT 3.10	Reducing the Project Completion Time One Day at a Time

CURRENT CRITICAL PATH	REMAINING NUMBER OF DAYS ACTIVITY MAY BE SHORTENED	COST PER DAY TO EXPEDITE EACH ACTIVITY	LEAST-COST ACTIVITY TO EXPEDITE	TOTAL COST OF ALL ACTIVITIES IN NETWORK	PROJECT COMPLETION TIME
ABD	All activity times and costs are normal.			$26	10
ABD	A–1, B–3, D–2	A–4, B–3, D–2	D	28	9
ABD	A–1, B–3, D–1	A–4, B–3, D–2	D	30	8
ABD	A–1, B–3	A–4, B–3	B	33	7
ABD, ACD	A–1, B–2, C–1	A–4, B–3, C–2	A*	37	6
ABD, ACD	B–2, C–1	B–3, C–2	B&C†	42	5
ABD, ACD	B–1	B–3	B‡	45	5

*To reduce the critical path by one day, reduce either A alone or B and C together at the same time (either B or C by itself just modifies the critical path without shortening it).

† B&C must be crashed together to reduce the path by one day.

‡Crashing activity B does not reduce the length of the project, so this additional cost would not be incurred.

3. **Compute the critical path.** For the simple network we have been using, this schedule would take 10 days. The critical path is A–B–D.

4. **Shorten the critical path at the least cost.** The easiest way to proceed is to start with the normal schedule, find the critical path, and reduce the path time by one day using the lowest-cost activity. Then recompute and find the new critical path and reduce it too by one day. Repeat this procedure until the time of completion is satisfactory, or until there can be no further reduction in the project completion time. Exhibit 3.10 shows the reduction of the network one day at a time.

Working though Exhibit 3.10 might initially seem difficult. In the first line, all activities are at their normal time and costs are at their lowest value. The critical path is A–B–D, cost for completing the project is $26, and the project completion time is 10 days.

The goal in line two is to reduce the project completion time by one day. We know it is necessary to reduce the time for one or more of the activities on the critical path. In the second column we note that activity A can be reduced one day (from two to one day), activity B can be reduced three days (from five to two days), and activity D can be reduced two days (from three to one day). The next column tracks the cost to reduce each of the activities by a single day. For example, activity A normally costs $6 to complete in two days. It could be completed in one day at a cost of $10, a $4 increase. So we indicate that the cost to expedite activity A by one day is $4. For activity B, it normally costs $9 to complete in five days. It could be completed in two days at a cost of $18. Our cost to reduce B by three days is $9, or $3 per day. It normally costs $5 to complete C in three days. It could be completed in one day at a cost of $9; a two-day reduction would cost $4 ($2 per day). The least expensive alternative for a one-day reduction in time is to expedite activity D at a cost of $2. Total cost for the network goes up to $28 and the project completion time is reduced to nine days.

Our next iteration starts in line three, where the goal is to reduce the project completion time to eight days. The nine-day critical path is A–B–D. We could shorten activity A by one day, B by three days, and D by one day (note D has

Plot of Costs and Minimum-Cost Schedule   **EXHIBIT 3.11**

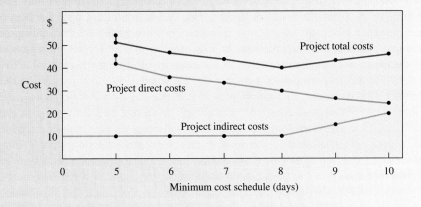

already been reduced from three to two days). Cost to reduce each activity by one day is the same as in line two. Again, the least expensive activity to reduce is D. Reducing activity D from two to one day results in the total cost for all activities in the network going up to $30 and the project completion time coming down to eight days.

Line four is similar to line three, but now only A and B are on the critical path and can be reduced. B is reduced, which takes our cost up $3 to $33 and reduces the project completion time to seven days.

In line five (actually our fifth iteration in solving the problem), activities A, B, C, and D are all critical. D cannot be reduced, so our only options are activities A, B, and C. Note that B and C are in parallel, so it does not help to reduce B without reducing C. Our options are to reduce A alone at a cost of $4 or B and C together at a cost of $5 ($3 for B and $2 for C), so we reduce A in this iteration.

In line six, we take the B and C option that was considered in line five. Finally, in line seven, our only option is to reduce activity B. Since B and C are in parallel and we cannot reduce C, there is no value in reducing B alone. We can reduce the project completion time no further.

5. **Plot project direct, indirect, and total-cost curves and find the minimum-cost schedule.** Exhibit 3.11 shows the indirect cost plotted as a constant $10 per day for eight days and increasing $5 per day thereafter. The direct costs are plotted from Exhibit 3.10, and the total project cost is shown as the total of the two costs.

Summing the values for direct and indirect costs for each day yields the project total cost curve. As you can see, this curve is at its minimum with an eight-day schedule, which costs $40 ($30 direct + $10 indirect).

CPM IN PRACTICE

As with many other methods, the basic CPM analysis may have to be modified to fit situations encountered in practice. Thus, management must be sure that the people charged with planning, monitoring, and controlling activities have a general understanding of how the CPM should be used in practice.

CPM assumes that project activities can be identified as entities (that is, there is a clear beginning and ending point for each activity). In practice, projects, especially complex ones, change in content over time, and therefore a network made at the beginning may be inaccurate later on. Also, activities can be conditional, i.e., be contingent upon the occurrence or non-occurrence of a previous activity. Therefore, monitoring the network during project progress and updating when appropriate are important aspects of project management and control (some project management software can actually incorporate conditional activities). Controlling the project is important not only for the schedule but also for cost and scope.

Though CPM focuses on the critical path, it is important to remember that delays and uncertainties in activities can cause the critical path to change during the project. For this reason, it has been suggested that a critical activity concept replace the critical path concept as a focus of managerial control. With this approach, attention would centre on activities that have a high potential variation and lie on a near-critical path. A near-critical path is one that, though it has slack, could become critical if one or a few activities along it were to be delayed. Obviously, the more parallelism in a network, the more likely that one or more near-critical paths exist. Conversely, the more a network approximates a single series of activities, the less likely it is to have near-critical paths.

Some of the available project management software packages can actually do a Monte Carlo computer simulation of the project to analyze uncertain events such as delays. In Monte Carlo simulation, the computer "does" the project virtually, thousands, if not tens of thousands, of times. Based on user assumptions regarding uncertainty, each time it "does the project" the computer generates a different activity completion time for each activity with uncertainty, and computes the project completion time based on the generated activity times. Thus, it is more flexible and provides more realistic and more detailed results than those that can be obtained by using CPM alone.

Gray and Larson[3] suggest that smaller projects (with less than 100 activities) can be effectively developed using Post-It type stickers, erasable markers, and a whiteboard. This is a flexible and visual way for the project team to create network diagrams.

MANAGING RESOURCES

Available resources is a further issue in using CPM in practice. In addition to scheduling each task, we must assign resources. Modern software quickly highlights overallocations—situations in which allocations exceed resources.

To resolve overallocations manually, you can either add resources or reschedule. Moving a task within its slack can free up resources.

Mid- to high-level project management information systems (PMIS) software can resolve overallocations through a "levelling" feature. Several rules of thumb can be used. You can specify that low-priority tasks should be delayed until higher-priority ones are complete, or that the project should end before or after the original deadline.

Tracking Progress

The real action starts after the project gets underway. Actual progress will differ from your original, or baseline, planned progress. Software can hold several different baseline plans, so you can compare monthly snapshots.

A *tracking Gantt chart* superimposes the current schedule onto a baseline plan so deviations are easily noticed. If you prefer, a spreadsheet view of the same information could be output. Deviations between planned start/finish and newly scheduled start/finish also appear, and a "slipping filter" can be applied to highlight or output only those tasks that are scheduled to finish at a later date than the planned baseline.

Operations and Supply Management in Practice

Project Management Information Systems

Interest in the techniques and concepts of project management has exploded in recent years. This has resulted in a parallel increase in project management software offerings. Now there are over 100 companies offering project management software. For the most up-to-date information about software available, check out the Web site of the Project Management Institute (www.pmi.org). The institute is a valuable source of knowledge for project management and also provides certification in project management. Two of the leading companies are Microsoft, with Microsoft Project, and Primavera, with Primavera Project Planner. The following is a brief review of these two programs:

The Microsoft Project program comes with an excellent online tutorial, which is one reason for its overwhelming popularity with project managers tracking midsized projects. This package is compatible with the Microsoft Office Suite, which opens all the communications and Internet integration capability that Microsoft offers. The program includes features for scheduling, allocating and levelling resources, as well as controlling costs and producing presentation-quality graphics and reports.

Finally, for managing very large projects or programs having several projects, Primavera Project Planner is often the choice. Primavera was the first major vendor of this type of software and has possibly the most sophisticated capability.

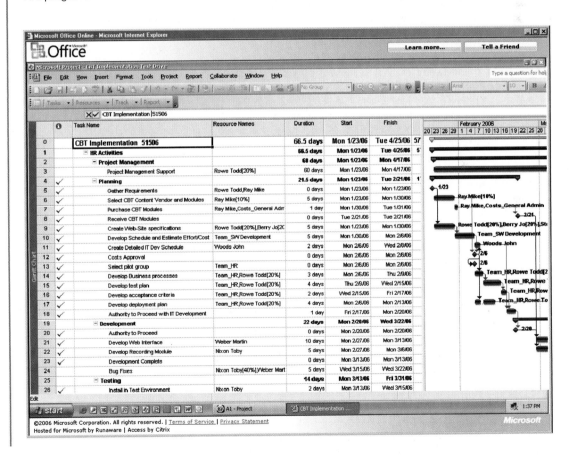

Management by exception can also be applied to find deviations between budgeted costs and actual costs. (See the Operations and Supply Management in Practice box above.)

Summary

This chapter provides a description of the basics of managing projects. The chapter first describes how the people involved with a project are organized from a management viewpoint. The scope of the project will help define the organization. This organization spans the use of a dedicated team to a largely undedicated matrix structure. Next, the chapter considers how project activities are organized into subprojects by using the work breakdown structure. Following this, the technical details of calculating the shortest time it should take to complete a project are covered. Finally, the chapter considers how projects can be shortened through the use of "crashing" concepts.

Key Terms

Activities   Pieces of work within a project that consume time. The completion of all the activities of a project marks the end of the project.

Critical path   The sequence of activities in a project that forms the longest chain in terms of their time to complete. This path contains zero slack time. Techniques used to find the critical path are called CPM or Critical Path Method techniques.

Early start schedule   A project schedule that lists all activities by their early start times.

Functional project   A structure where team members are assigned from the functional units of the organization. The team members remain a part of their functional units and typically are not dedicated to the project.

Gantt chart   Shows in a graphic manner the amount of time involved and the sequence in which activities can be performed. Often referred to as a *bar chart*.

Immediate predecessor   Activity that needs to be completed immediately before another activity.

Late start schedule   A project schedule that lists all activities by their late start times. This schedule may create savings by postponing purchases of material and other costs associated with the project.

Matrix project   A structure that blends the functional and pure project structures. Each project uses people from different functional areas. A dedicated project manager decides what tasks need to be performed and when, but the functional managers control which people to use.

Project   A series of related jobs usually directed toward some major output and requiring a significant period of time to perform.

Project management   Planning, directing, and controlling resources (people, equipment, material) to meet the technical, cost, and time constraints of a project.

Project milestone   A specific event in a project.

Pure project   A structure for organizing a project where a self-contained team works full time on the project.

Slack time   The time that an activity can be delayed; the difference between the late and early start times of an activity.

Time–cost (crash) models   Extension of the critical path models that considers the trade-off between the time required to complete an activity and cost. This is often referred to as "crashing" the project.

Work breakdown structure   The hierarchy of project tasks, subtasks, and work packages.

Solved Problems

Solved Problem 1

A project for Crowchild Avionics has been defined to contain the following list of activities, along with their required times for completion:

ACTIVITY	TIME (DAYS)	IMMEDIATE PREDECESSORS
A	1	—
B	4	A
C	3	A
D	7	A
E	6	B
F	2	C, D
G	7	E, F
H	9	D
I	4	G, H

Project Management_ Solved Problems

a. Draw the critical path diagram.
b. Show the early start, early finish, late start, and late finish times.
c. Show the critical path.
d. What would happen if activity F was revised to take four days instead of two?

SOLUTION

The answers to *a*, *b*, and *c* are shown in the following diagram.

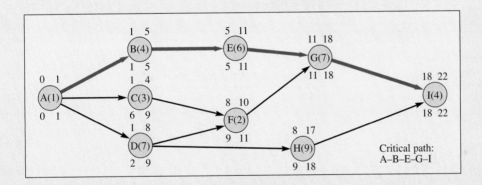

d. New critical path: A–D–F–G–I. Time of completion is 23 days.

Solved Problem 2

Here are the precedence requirements, normal and crash activity times, and normal and crash costs for a construction project:

Project Management_ Solved Problems

ACTIVITY	PRECEDING ACTIVITIES	REQUIRED TIME (WEEKS)		COST	
		NORMAL	CRASH	NORMAL	CRASH
A	—	4	2	$ 10 000	$ 11 000
B	A	3	2	6000	9000
C	A	2	1	4000	6000
D	B	5	3	14 000	18 000
E	B, C	1	1	9000	9000
F	C	3	2	7000	8000
G	E, F	4	2	13 000	25 000
H	D, E	4	1	11 000	18 000
I	H, G	6	5	20 000	29 000

a. What are the critical path and the estimated completion time?
b. To shorten the project by three weeks, which tasks would be shortened and what would the final total project cost be?

SOLUTION

The construction project network is shown below:

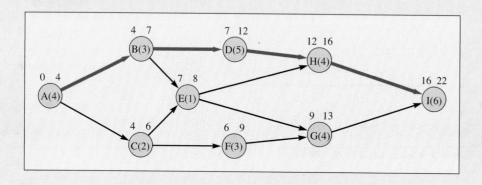

a. Critical path A–B–D–H–I.
   Normal completion time is 22 weeks.
b.

ACTIVITY	CRASH COST	NORMAL COST	NORMAL TIME	CRASH TIME	COST PER WEEK	WEEKS
A	$ 11 000	$10 000	4	2	$ 500	2
B	9000	6000	3	2	3000	1
C	6000	4000	2	1	2000	1
D	18 000	14 000	5	3	2000	2
E	9000	9000	1	1		0
F	8000	7000	3	2	1000	1
G	25 000	13 000	4	2	6000	2
H	18 000	11 000	4	1	2333	3
I	29 000	20 000	6	5	9000	1

(1) 1st week: CP = A–B–D–H–I. Cheapest is A at $500. Critical path stays the same.
(2) 2nd week: A is still the cheapest at $500. Critical path stays the same.
(3) 3rd week: Because A is no longer available, the choices are B (at $3000), D (at $2000),
    H (at $2333), or I (at $9000). Therefore, choose D at $2000.

Total project cost shortened three weeks is

A	$ 11 000
B	6000
C	4000
D	16 000
E	9000
F	7000
G	13 000
H	11 000
I	20 000
	$97 000

Review and Discussion Questions

1. What was the most complex project that you have been involved in? Give examples of the following as they pertain to the project: the work breakdown structure, tasks, subtasks, and work package. Were you on the critical path? Did it have a good project manager?
2. What are some reasons project scheduling is not done well?
3. Discuss the graphic presentations in Exhibit 3.5. Are there any other graphic outputs you would like to see if you were project manager?
4. Which characteristics must a project have for critical path scheduling to be applicable? What types of projects have been subjected to critical path analysis?
5. What are the underlying assumptions of minimum-cost scheduling? Are they equally realistic?
6. "Project control should always focus on the critical path." Comment.
7. Why would subcontractors for a government project want their activities on the critical path? Under what conditions would they try to avoid being on the critical path?
8. What are some of the challenges that personnel face while working on a project team? What are some of the challenges faced by the project manager?

Problems

1. The following activities are part of the TPJ project to be scheduled using CPM:

ACTIVITY	IMMEDIATE PREDECESSOR	TIME (WEEKS)
A	—	6
B	A	3
C	A	7
D	C	2
E	B, D	4
F	D	3
G	E, F	7

   a. Draw the network.
   b. What is the critical path?
   c. How many weeks will it take to complete the project?
   d. How much slack does activity B have?

2. Schedule the following activities for Abu Dubai Inc using CPM:

ACTIVITY	IMMEDIATE PREDECESSOR	TIME (WEEKS)
A	—	1
B	A	4
C	A	3
D	B	2
E	C, D	5
F	D	2
G	F	2
H	E, G	3

   a. Draw the network.
   b. What is the critical path?
   c. How many weeks will it take to complete the project?
   d. Which activities have slack, and how much?

3. The R&D department of Halifax Electronics is planning to bid on a large project for the development of a new communication system for commercial planes. The accompanying table shows the activities, times, and sequences required:

ACTIVITY	IMMEDIATE PREDECESSOR	TIME (WEEKS)
A	—	3
B	A	2
C	A	4
D	A	4
E	B	6
F	C, D	6
G	D, F	2
H	D	3
I	E, G, H	3

a. Draw the network diagram.
b. What is the critical path?
c. Suppose you want to shorten the completion time as much as possible, and you have the option of shortening any or all of B, C, D, and G each one week. Which would you shorten?
d. What is the new critical path and earliest completion time?

4. A construction project is broken down into the following 10 activities:

ACTIVITY	IMMEDIATE PREDECESSOR	TIME (WEEKS)
1	—	4
2	1	2
3	1	4
4	1	3
5	2, 3	5
6	3	6
7	4	2
8	5	3
9	6, 7	5
10	8, 9	7

a. Draw the network diagram.
b. Find the critical path.
c. If activities 1 and 10 cannot be shortened, but activities 2 through 9 can be shortened to a minimum of one week each at a cost of $10 000 per week, which activities would you shorten to cut the project by four weeks?

5. Here is a CPM network for Lau Architects with activity times in weeks:

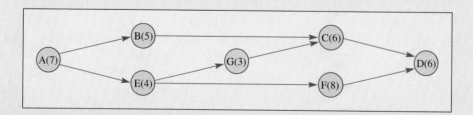

a. Determine the critical path.

b. How many weeks will the project take to complete?

c. Suppose F could be shortened by two weeks and B by one week. How would this affect the completion date?

6. Here is a network with the activity times shown in days:

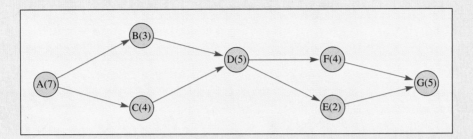

a. Find the critical path.

b. The following table shows the normal times and the crash times, along with the associated costs for each activity.

ACTIVITY	NORMAL TIME	CRASH TIME	NORMAL COST	CRASH COST
A	7	6	$7000	$ 8000
B	3	2	5000	7000
C	4	3	9000	10 200
D	5	4	3000	4500
E	2	1	2000	3000
F	4	2	4000	7000
G	5	4	5000	8000

If the project is to be shortened by four days, show which activities, in order of reduction, would be shortened and the resulting cost.

7. The home office billing department of Winnipeg Retailers Inc, a chain of department stores prepares monthly inventory reports for use by the stores' purchasing agents. Given the following information, use the critical path method to determine

a. How long the total process will take.

b. Which jobs can be delayed without delaying the early start of any subsequent activity.

JOB AND DESCRIPTION	IMMEDIATE PREDECESSORS	TIME (HOURS)
a Start	—	0
b Get computer printouts of customer purchases	a	10
c Get stock records for the month	a	20
d Reconcile purchase printouts and stock records	b, c	30
e Total stock records by department	b, c	20
f Determine reorder quantities for coming period	e	40
g Prepare stock reports for purchasing agents	d, f	20
h Finish	g	0

8. For the network shown:

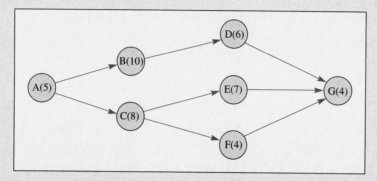

a. Determine the critical path and the early completion time in weeks for the project.
b. For the data shown, reduce the project completion time by three weeks. Assume a linear cost per week shortened, and show, step by step, how you arrived at your schedule.

ACTIVITY	NORMAL TIME	NORMAL COST	CRASH TIME	CRASH COST
A	5	$ 7000	3	$13 000
B	10	12 000	7	18 000
C	8	5000	7	7000
D	6	4000	5	5000
E	7	3000	6	6000
F	4	6000	3	7000
G	4	7000	3	9000

9. The following CPM network has estimates of the normal time in weeks listed for the activities:

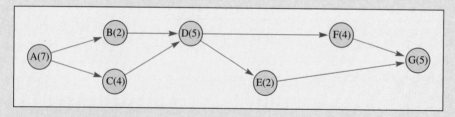

a. Identify the critical path.
b. What is the length of time to complete the project?
c. Which activities have slack, and how much?
d. Here is a table of normal and crash times and costs. Which activities would you shorten to cut two weeks from the schedule in a rational fashion? What would be the incremental cost? Is the critical path changed?

ACTIVITY	NORMAL TIME	CRASH TIME	NORMAL COST	CRASH COST
A	7	6	$7000	$ 8000
B	2	1	5000	7000
C	4	3	9000	10 200
D	5	4	3000	4500
E	2	1	2000	3000
F	4	2	4000	7000
G	5	4	5000	8000

10. Bragg's Bakery is building a new automated bakery in downtown Kelowna. Here are the activities that need to be completed to get the new bakery built and the equipment installed.

ACTIVITY	PREDECESSOR	NORMAL TIME (WEEKS)	CRASH TIME (WEEKS)	EXPEDITING COST/WEEK
A	—	9	6	$3000
B	A	8	5	$3500
C	A	15	10	$4000
D	B, C	5	3	$2000
E	C	10	6	$2500
F	D, E	2	1	$5000

a. Draw the project diagram.
b. What is the normal project length?
c. What is the project length if all activities are crashed to their minimum?
d. Bragg's loses $3500 in profit per week for every week the bakery is not completed. How many weeks will the project take if we are willing to pay crashing cost as long as it is less than $3500?

Advanced Problem

11. Assume the network and data that follow:

ACTIVITY	NORMAL TIME (WEEKS)	NORMAL COST	CRASH TIME (WEEKS)	CRASH COST	IMMEDIATE PREDECESSORS
A	2	$ 50	1	$ 70	—
B	4	80	2	160	A
C	8	70	4	110	A
D	6	60	5	80	A
E	7	100	6	130	B
F	4	40	3	100	D
G	5	100	4	150	E, F

a. Construct the network diagram.
b. Indicate the critical path when normal activity times are used.
c. Compute the minimum total direct cost for each project duration based on the cost associated with each activity. Consider durations of 13, 14, 15, 16, 17, and 18 weeks.
d. If the indirect costs for each project duration are $400 (18 weeks), $350 (17 weeks), $300 (16 weeks), $250 (15 weeks), $200 (14 weeks), and $150 (13 weeks), what is the total project cost for each duration? Indicate the minimum total project cost duration.

CASE | Cell Phone Design Project

You work for Research in Motion (RIM) in their global cell-phone group in Waterloo, Ontario. You have been made project manager for the design of a new cell phone model. Your supervisors have already scoped the project so you have a list showing the work breakdown structure and this includes major project activities. You must plan the project schedule and calculate project duration and project costs. Your boss wants the schedule and costs on his desk tomorrow morning!

You have been given the information in Exhibit 3.12. It includes all the activities required in the project and the duration of each activity. Also, precedence relationships between the activities have been identified. Remember that the preceding activity must be fully completed before work on the following activity can be started.

Your project is divided into five major tasks. Task "P" involves developing specifications for the new cell phone. Here

---

EXHIBIT 3.12 | Work Breakdown Structure and Activities for the Cell Phone Design Project

Cell Phone Design

MAJOR PROJECT TASKS/ACTIVITIES	ACTIVITY IDENTIFICATION	DEPENDENCY	DURATION (WEEKS)
Product specifications (P)			
Overall product specifications	P1	—	4
Hardware specifications	P2	P1	5
Software specifications	P3	P1	5
Market research	P4	P2, P3	2
Supplier specifications (S)			
Hardware	S1	P2	5
Software	S2	P3	6
Market research	S3	P4	1
Product design (D)			
Circuits	D1	S1, D7	3
Battery	D2	S1	1
Display	D3	S1	2
Outer cover	D4	S3	4
User interface	D5	S2	4
Camera	D6	S1, S2, S3	1
Functionality	D7	D5, D6	4
Product integration (I)			
Hardware	I1	D1, D2, D3, D4, D6	3
Software	I2	D7	5
Prototype Testing	I3	I1,I2	5
Subcontracting (V)			
Vendor selection	V1	D7	10
Contract negotiation	V2	I3, V1	2

decisions related to such things as battery life, size of the phone and features need to be determined. These details are based on how a customer uses the cell phone. These user specifications are redefined in terms that have meaning to the subcontractors that will actually make the new cell phone in Task "S" supplier specifications. These involve engineering details for how the product will perform. The individual components that make up the product are the focus of Task "D." Task "I" brings all the components together and a working prototype is built and tested. Finally in Task "V," vendors are selected and contracts are negotiated.

1. Draw a project network that includes all the activities.
2. Calculate the start and finish times for each activity and determine how many weeks is the minimum for completing the project. Find the critical set of activities for the project.
3. Identify slack in the activities not on the project critical path.
4. Your boss would like you to suggest changes that could be made to the project that would significantly shorten it. What would you suggest?

Footnotes

[1]Clifford F. Gray and Erik W. Larson, *Project Management: The Managerial Approach* (New York: McGraw-Hill/Irwin, 2008), p. 10–11.

[2]Arik Hesseldahl, "The Eye of the (BlackBerry) Storm," January 28, 2009, http://www.businessweek.com/technology/content/jan2009/tc20090128_050612.htm, retrieved February 4, 2009.

[3]*Project Management,* p. 153.

Selected Bibliography

Gray, C. *Agile Project Management: How to Succeed in the Face of Changing Project Requirements.* New York: American Management Association, 2004.

Gray, C.F., and E.W. Larson. *Project Management: The Managerial Process.* New York: Irwin/McGraw-Hill, 2002.

Kerzner, H. *Project Management: A Systems Approach to Planning, Scheduling, and Controlling.* 8th ed. New York: Wiley, 2002.

Lewis, James P. *The Project Manager's Desk Reference.* New York: McGraw-Hill Professional Publishing, 1999.

Processes

The second section of *Operations and Supply Management: The Core* centres on the design and analysis of business processes. Maybe becoming an efficiency expert is not your dream, but it is important to learn the fundamentals. Have you ever wondered why you always have to wait in line at one store but another one seems to be on top of the crowds? The key to serving customers well, whether with products or with services, is having a great process.

We use processes to do most things. You probably have a regular process that you use every morning. What are the tasks associated with your process? Do you brush your teeth, take a shower, dress, make coffee, and read the paper? Have you ever thought about how the tasks should be ordered or what the best way is to execute each task? In making these decisions you are allocating your own personal capacity.*

This section is about designing efficient processes and allocating capacity for all types of businesses. Companies also need to develop a quality philosophy and integrate it into their processes. Actually, quality and process efficiency are closely related. Have you ever done something but then had to do it again because it was not done properly the first time? This section considers these subjects in both manufacturing and service industries.

*The original version of the movie *Cheaper by the Dozen*, made in the 1950s, was based on the life of Frank Gilbreth, who invented motion study in the 1900s. Gilbreth was so concerned with personal efficiency that he did a study of whether it was faster and more accurate to button one's seven-button vest from the bottom up or the top down. (Answer: bottom up!)

STRATEGIC CAPACITY MANAGEMENT

1. Know what the concept of capacity is and how important it is to "manage" capacity over time.
2. Understand the impact of economies of scale on the capacity of a firm.
3. Understand what a learning curve is and how to analyze one.
4. Learn how to use decision trees to analyze alternatives when faced with the problem of adding capacity.
5. Know the differences in planning capacity between manufacturing firms and service firms.

SHOULDICE HOSPITAL: HERNIA SURGERY INNOVATION

During World War II, Dr. Edward Earle Shouldice, a major in the army, found that many young men willing to serve their country had to be denied enlistment because they needed surgical treatment to repair hernias before they could be pronounced physically fit for military training. In 1940, hospital space and doctors were scarce, especially for a nonemergency surgery that normally took three weeks of hospitalization. So, Dr. Shouldice resolved to do what he could to alleviate the problem. Contributing his services at no fee, he performed an innovative method of surgery on 70 of those men, speeding their induction into the army.

The recruits made their success stories known, and by the war's end, more than 200 civilians had contacted the doctor and were awaiting surgery. The limited availability of hospitals beds, however, created a major problem. There was only one solution: Dr. Shouldice decided to open his own hospital.

In July 1945, Shouldice Hospital, with a staff consisting of a nurse, a secretary, and a cook, opened its doors to its waiting patients. In a single operating room, Dr. Shouldice repaired two hernias per day. As requests for this surgery increased, he extended the facilities, located on Church Street in Toronto, by eventually buying three adjacent buildings and increasing the staff accordingly. In 1953, he purchased a country estate in Thornhill, where a second hospital was established.

Today all surgery takes place in Thornhill. Repeated development has culminated in the present 90-bed facility. Shouldice Hospital has been dedicated to the repair of hernias for over 60 years, using the "Shouldice Technique." The "formula," although not a secret, extends beyond the skill of surgeons and their ability to perform to the Shouldice standard. Shouldice Hospital is a total environment. Study the capacity problems with this special type of hospital in the case at the end of this chapter.

■ Source: Summarized from www.shouldice.com.

Manufacturing and service capacity investment decisions can be very complex. Consider some of the following difficult questions that need to be addressed:

- How long will it take to bring new capacity on stream? How does this match with the time that it takes to develop a new product?
- What will be the impact of not having sufficient capacity in the supply chain for a promising product?
- Should the firm use third-party contract manufacturers? How much of a premium will the contract manufacturer charge for providing flexibility in manufacturing volume?

In this chapter, we look at these tough strategic capacity decisions. We begin by discussing the nature of capacity from an OSM perspective.

CAPACITY MANAGEMENT IN OPERATIONS

A dictionary definition of **capacity** is "the ability to hold, receive, store, or accommodate." In a general business sense, it is most frequently viewed as the amount of output that a system is capable of achieving over a specific period of time. In a service setting, this might be the number of customers that can be handled between noon and 1:00 p.m. In manufacturing, this might be the number of automobiles that can be produced in a single shift.

When looking at capacity, operations managers need to look at both resource inputs *and* product outputs. The reason is that, for planning purposes, real (or effective) capacity depends on what is to be produced. For example, a firm that makes multiple products inevitably can produce more of one kind than of another with a given level of resource inputs. Thus, while the managers of an automobile factory may state that their facility has 6000 production hours available per year, they are also thinking that these hours can be used to make either 150 000 two-door models or 120 000 four-door models (or some mix of the two- and four-door models). This reflects their knowledge of what their current technology and labour force inputs can produce and the product mix that is to be demanded from these resources.

Cross Functional

An operations management view also emphasizes the time dimension of capacity. That is, capacity must also be stated relative to some period of time. This is evidenced in the common distinction drawn between long-range, intermediate-range, and short-range capacity planning.

Capacity planning is generally viewed in three time durations:

Long range—greater than one year. Where productive resources (such as buildings, equipment, or facilities) take a long time to acquire or dispose of, long-range capacity planning requires top management participation and approval.

Intermediate range—monthly or quarterly plans for the next 6 to 18 months. Here, capacity may be varied by such alternatives as hiring, layoffs, new tools, minor equipment purchases, and subcontracting. Different types of intermediate range capacity plans are discussed in Chapter 12.

Short range—less than one month. This is tied into the daily or weekly scheduling process and involves making adjustments to eliminate the variance between planned and actual output. This includes alternatives such as overtime, personnel transfers, and alternative production routings.

Although there is no one person with the job title "capacity manager," there are several managerial positions charged with the effective use of capacity. *Capacity* is a relative term; in an operations management context, it may be defined as *the amount of resource inputs available relative to output requirements over a particular period of time.* Note that this definition makes no distinction between efficient and inefficient use of capacity. In this respect, it is consistent with how the U.S. Bureau of Economic Analysis defines *maximum practical capacity* used in its surveys: "That output attained within the normal operating schedule of shifts per day and days per week including the use of high-cost inefficient facilities."

The objective of **strategic capacity planning** is to provide an approach for determining the overall capacity level of capital-intensive resources—facilities, equipment, and overall labour force size—that best supports the company's long-range competitive strategy. The capacity level selected has a critical impact on the firm's response rate, its cost structure, its inventory policies, and its management and staff support requirements. If capacity is inadequate, a company may lose customers through slow service or by allowing competitors to enter the market. If capacity is excessive, a company may have to reduce prices to stimulate demand; underutilize its workforce; carry excess inventory; or seek additional, less profitable products to stay in business.

CAPACITY PLANNING CONCEPTS

The term *capacity* implies an attainable rate of output, for example, 480 cars per day, but says nothing about how long that rate can be sustained. Thus, we do not know if this 480 cars per day figure is a one-day peak or a six-month average. To avoid this problem, the concept of **best operating level** is used. This is the level of capacity for which the process was designed and thus is the volume of output at which average unit cost is minimized. Determining this minimum is difficult because it involves a complex trade-off between the allocation of fixed overhead costs and the cost of overtime, equipment wear, defect rates, and other costs.

An important measure is the **capacity utilization rate**, which reveals how close a firm is to its best operating level:

$$Capacity\ utilization\ rate = \frac{Capacity\ used}{Best\ operating\ level}$$

So, for example, if our plant's *best operating level* were 500 cars per day and the plant was currently operating at 480 cars per day, the *capacity utilization rate* would be 96 percent.

$$Capacity\ utilization\ rate = \frac{480}{500} = 0.96\ or\ 96\%$$

The capacity utilization rate is expressed as a percentage and requires that the numerator and denominator be measured in the same units and time periods (such as machine hours/day, barrels of oil/day, dollars of output/day). If it is difficult to define a standard unit of output, as is the case in customized products or services, the capacity may be defined in terms of input, such as labour hours or machine hours available.

Economies and Diseconomies of Scale

The basic notion of economies of scale is that as a plant gets larger and volume increases, the average cost per unit of output drops. This is partially due to lower operating and capital cost, because a piece of equipment with twice the capacity of another piece typically does not cost twice as much to purchase or operate. Plants also gain efficiencies when they become large enough to fully utilize dedicated resources (people and equipment) for information technology, material handling, and administrative support.

Global

At some point, the size of a plant becomes too large and diseconomies of scale become a problem. These diseconomies may surface in many different ways. For example, maintaining the demand required to keep the large facility busy may require significant discounting of the product. Canadian automobile manufacturers continually face this problem. Another typical example involves using a few large-capacity pieces of equipment. Minimizing equipment downtime is essential in this type of operation. M&M Mars, for example, has highly automated, high-volume equipment to make M&Ms. A single packaging line moves 2.6 million M&Ms each hour. Even though direct labour to operate the equipment is very low, the labour required to maintain the equipment is high.

In many cases, the size of a plant may be influenced by factors other than the internal equipment, labour, and other capital expenditures. A major factor may be the cost to transport raw materials and finished product to and from the plant. A cement factory, for example, would have a difficult time serving customers more than a few hours from its plant. Analogously, automobile companies such as Ford, Honda, Nissan, and Toyota have found it advantageous to locate plants within specific international markets. The anticipated size of these intended markets will largely dictate the size and capacity of the plants.

Jaguar, the luxury automobile producer, recently found it had too many plants. Jaguar was employing 8560 workers in three plants that produced 126 122 cars, about 14 cars per employee. In comparison, Volvo's plant in Torslanda, Sweden, was more than twice as productive, building 158 466 cars with 5472 workers, or 29 cars per employee. By contrast, BMW AG's Mini unit made 174 000 vehicles at a single British plant with just 4500 workers (39 cars per employee).

Capacity Focus

The concept of the focused factory holds that a production facility works best when it focuses on a fairly limited set of production objectives. This means, for example, that a firm should not expect to excel in every aspect of manufacturing performance: cost, quality, delivery speed and reliability, changes in demand, and flexibility to adapt to new products. Rather, it should select a limited set of tasks that contribute the most to corporate objectives. However, given the breakthroughs in manufacturing technology, there is an evolution in factory objectives toward trying to do everything well. How do we deal with these apparent contradictions? One way is to say that if the firm does not have the technology to master multiple objectives, then a narrow focus is the logical choice. Another way is to recognize the practical reality that not all firms are in industries that require them to use their full range of capabilities to compete.

The **capacity focus** concept can also be operationalized through the mechanism of plants within plants—or *PWPs*. A focused plant may have several PWPs, each of which may have

The Xerox focused factory creates a flexible and efficient work environment where teams of employees are responsible for the end-to-end manufacturing of specific products. The factory was designed with input from the industrial staff, working in tandem with engineers and management.

separate suborganizations, equipment and process policies, workforce management policies, production control methods, and so forth for different products—even if they are made under the same roof. This, in effect, permits finding the best operating level for each department of the organization and thereby carries the focus concept down to the operating level.

Capacity Flexibility

Capacity flexibility means having the ability to rapidly increase or decrease production levels, or to shift production capacity quickly from one product or service to another. Such flexibility is achieved through flexible plants, processes, and workers, as well as through strategies that use the capacity of other organizations. Increasingly, companies are taking the idea of flexibility into account as they design their supply chains. Working with suppliers, they can build capacity into their whole systems. For example, some time ago the Detroit automakers realized that they were at a competitive disadvantage compared to their Japanese counter parts because their assembly lines were less flexible. Competitors like Honda were able to produce more models on the same line and thus were able to respond to demand changes much more rapidly whereas companies like Ford could not respond quickly since they would have had to set up the line for another model, a painstaking and slow process. In recent years, companies like Ford have made their factories more flexible in order to enhance competitiveness.

Flexible Plants Perhaps the ultimate in plant flexibility is the *zero-changeover-time* plant. Using movable equipment, knockdown walls, and easily accessible and reroutable utilities, such a plant can quickly adapt to change. An analogy to a familiar service business captures the flavour well: a plant with equipment "that is easy to install and easy to tear down and move—like the Ringling Bros Barnum and Bailey Circus in the old tent-circus days" (or like today's Quebec-based Cirque du Soleil).

Flexible Processes Flexible processes are epitomized by flexible manufacturing systems on the one hand and simple, easily set up equipment on the other. Both of these technological approaches permit rapid low-cost switching from one product to another, enabling what are sometimes referred to as economies of scope. (By definition, economies of scope exist when multiple products can be produced at a lower cost in combination than they can separately.)

Flexible Workers Flexible workers have multiple skills and the ability to switch easily from one kind of task to another. They require broader training than specialized workers and need managers and staff support to facilitate quick changes in their work assignments.

Lack of changeover flexibility can lead to jobs having to be done in batches to avoid wasting capacity. For example, at the Pan Am Clinic in Winnipeg, significant set-up times are required to change from a knee MRI to a shoulder MRI, because of the coil changeover time. The clinic realized that a first-come first-served policy, without taking into account the type of MRI required, resulted in the MRI equipment having to be set up too frequently and experiencing a lot of idle time (wasted capacity), leading to long wait times. Now the clinic does multiple jobs of the same type (knee MRIs, for example) before changing over to other jobs (such as shoulders). This change has increased capacity utilization and reduced overall wait times considerably. Batching and set-up are discussed further in Chapters 6 and 13.

THE LEARNING CURVE

A well-known concept is the learning curve. A **learning curve** is a line displaying the relationship between unit production and the cumulative number of units produced. As plants produce more, they gain experience in the best production methods, which reduce their costs of production in a predictable manner. Every time a plant's cumulative production doubles, its production costs decline by a specific percentage depending on the nature of the business. Exhibit 4.1 demonstrates the effect of a 90 percent learning curve on the production costs of a hypothetical product.

The learning curve percentage varies across industries. To apply this concept to the restaurant industry, consider a hypothetical fast-food chain that has produced 5 million hamburgers. Given a current variable cost of $0.55 per burger, what will the cost per burger be when cumulative production reaches 10 million burgers? If the firm has a 90 percent learning curve, costs will fall to 90 percent of $0.55, or $0.495, when accumulated production reaches 10 million. At 1 billion hamburgers, the variable cost drops to less than $0.25.

Note that sales volume becomes an important issue in achieving cost savings. If firm A serves twice as many hamburgers daily as firm B, it will accumulate "experience" twice as fast.

Learning curve theory is based on three assumptions:

1. The amount of time required to complete a given task or unit of a product will be less each time the task is undertaken.

EXHIBIT 4.1   The Learning Curve

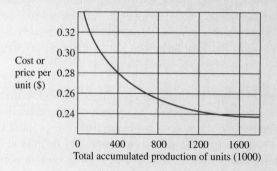

2. The time required per unit will decrease (although this rate of decrease will also be slowing).
3. The reduction in time will follow a predictable pattern.

Each of these assumptions was found to hold true in the airplane industry, where learning curves were first applied. In this application, it was observed that, as output doubled, there was a 20 percent reduction in direct production worker-hours per unit between doubled units. Thus, if it took 100 000 hours for Plane 1, it would take 80 000 hours for Plane 2, 64 000 hours for Plane 4, and so forth. Because the 20 percent reduction meant that, say, Unit 4 took only 80 percent of the production time required for Unit 2, the line connecting the coordinates of output and time was referred to as an "80 percent learning curve." (By convention, the percentage learning rate is used to denote any given exponential learning curve.)

A learning curve may be developed from an arithmetic tabulation, by logarithms, or by some other curve-fitting method, depending on the amount and form of the available data.

There are two ways to think about the improved performance that comes with learning curves: time per unit (as in Exhibit 4.2A) or units of output per time period (as in 4.2B). *Time per unit* shows the decrease in time required for each successive unit. *Cumulative average time* shows the cumulative average performance times as the total number of units increases. Time per unit and cumulative average times are also called *progress curves* or *product learning* and are useful for complex products or products with a longer cycle time. *Units of output per time period* is also called *industry learning* and is generally applied to high-volume production (short cycle time).

Note in Exhibit 4.2 A that the cumulative average curve does not decrease as fast as the time per unit because the time is being averaged. For example, if the time for Units 1, 2, 3, and 4 were 100, 80, 70, and 64, they would be plotted that way on the time per unit graph, but would be plotted as 100, 90, 83.3, and 78.5 on the cumulative average time graph.

Interactive Operations Management

Plotting Learning Curves

There are many ways to analyze past data to fit a useful trend line. We will use the simple exponential curve as an arithmetic procedure. In an arithmetical tabulation approach, a column for units is created by doubling, row by row, as 1, 2, 4, 8, 16. . . . The time for the first unit is multiplied by the learning percentage to obtain the time for the second unit.

Learning Curves Plotted as Times and Numbers of Units	EXHIBIT 4.2

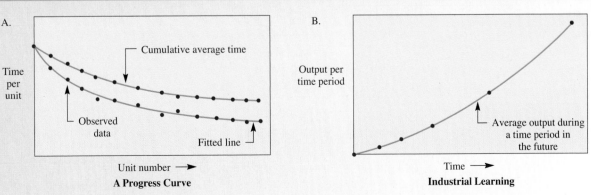

A.

Time per unit

Cumulative average time

Observed data

Fitted line

Unit number ⟶

A Progress Curve

B.

Output per time period

Average output during a time period in the future

Time ⟶

Industrial Learning

EXHIBIT 4.3	Unit, Cumulative, and Cumulative Average Direct Labour Worker-Hours Required for an 80 Percent Learning Curve

Learning Curves

(1) UNIT NUMBER	(2) UNIT DIRECT LABOUR HOURS	(3) CUMULATIVE DIRECT LABOUR HOURS	(4) CUMULATIVE AVERAGE DIRECT LABOUR HOURS
1	100 000	100 000	100 000
2	80 000	180 000	90 000
4	64 000	314 210	78 553
8	51 200	534 591	66 824
16	40 960	892 014	55 751
32	32 768	1 467 862	45 871
64	26 214	2 392 453	37 382
128	20 972	3 874 395	30 269
256	16 777	6 247 318	24 404

The second unit is multiplied by the learning percentage for the fourth unit, and so on. Thus, if we are developing an 80 percent learning curve, we would arrive at the figures listed in column 2 of Exhibit 4.3. Because it is often desirable for planning purposes to know the cumulative direct labour hours, column 3, which lists this information, is also provided. The calculation of these figures is straightforward; for example, for Unit 4, cumulative average direct labour hours would be found by dividing cumulative direct labour hours by 4, yielding the figure given in column 4.

Exhibit 4.4A shows three curves with different learning rates: 90 percent, 80 percent, and 70 percent. Note that if the cost of the first unit was $100, the 30th unit would cost $59.63 at the 90 percent rate and $17.37 at the 70 percent rate. Differences in learning rates can have dramatic effects.

EXHIBIT 4.4	4.4A—Arithmetic Plot of 70, 80, and 90 Percent Learning Curve 4.4B—Logarithmic Plot of an 80 Percent Learning Curves

Learning Curves

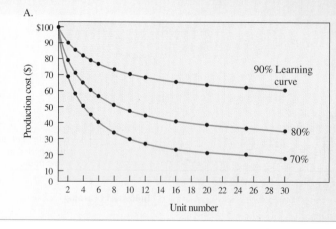

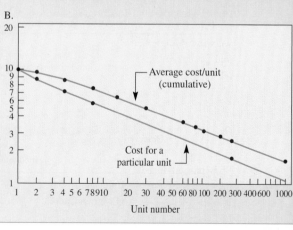

In practice, learning curves are often plotted using a graph with logarithmic scales (Exhibit 4.4B). The unit curves become linear throughout their entire range and the cumulative curve becomes linear after the first few units. The property of linearity is desirable because it facilitates extrapolation and permits a more accurate reading of the cumulative curve.

Learning Curve Tables

When the learning percentage is known, the tables in Appendix B can be easily used to calculate estimated labour hours for a specific unit or for cumulative groups of units. We need only multiply the initial unit labour hour figure by the appropriate tabled value.

To illustrate, suppose we want to double-check the figures in Exhibit 4.3 for unit and cumulative labour hours for Unit 16. From Appendix Exhibit B.1, the unit improvement factor for Unit 16 at 80 percent is 0.4096. This is multiplied by 100 000 (the hours for Unit 1) gives 40 960, the same as in Exhibit 4.3. From Appendix Exhibit B.2, the cumulative improvement factor for cumulative hours for the first 16 units is 8.920. When multiplied by 100 000, this gives 892 000, which is reasonably close to the exact value of 892 014 shown in Exhibit 4.3.

The following is a more involved example of the application of a learning curve to a production problem.

Learning Curves

EXAMPLE 4.1: SAMPLE LEARNING CURVE PROBLEM

Captain Nemo, owner of the Suboptimum Underwater Boat Company (SUB), is puzzled. He has a contract for 11 boats and has completed 4 of them. He has observed that his production manager, young Mr. Overick, has been reassigning more and more people to torpedo assembly after the construction of the first four boats. The first boat, for example, required 225 workers, each working a 40-hour week, while 45 fewer workers were required for the second boat. Overick has told them that "this is just the beginning" and that he will complete the last boat in the current contract with only 100 workers!

Overick is banking on the learning curve, but has he gone overboard?

SOLUTION

Because the second boat required 180 workers, a simple exponential curve shows that the learning percentage is 80 percent (180 ÷ 225). To find out how many workers are required for the 11th boat, we look up unit 11 for an 80 percent improvement ratio in Appendix Exhibit B.1 and multiply this value by the number required for the first sub. By interpolating between Unit 10 and Unit 12 we find the improvement ratio is equal to 0.4629. This yields 104.15 workers (0.4269 interpolated from table × 225). Thus, Overick's estimate missed the boat by four people.

EXAMPLE 4.2: ESTIMATING COST USING LEARNING CURVES

SUB has produced the first unit of a new line of minisubs at a cost of $500 000—$200 000 for materials and $300 000 for labour. It has agreed to accept a 10 percent profit, based on cost, and it is willing to contract on the basis of a 70 percent learning curve. What will be the contract price for three minisubs?

SOLUTION

Cost of first sub		$ 500 000
Cost of second sub		
Materials	$200 000	
Labour: $300 000 × 0.70	210 000	410 000
Cost of third sub		
Materials	200 000	
Labour: $300 000 × 0.5682	170 460	370 460
Total cost		1 280 460
Markup: $1 280 460 × 0.10		128 046
Selling price		$1 408 506

If the operation is interrupted, then some relearning must occur. How far to go back up the learning curve can be estimated in some cases.

CAPACITY PLANNING

Considerations in Adding Capacity

Many issues must be considered when adding capacity. Three important ones are maintaining system balance, frequency of capacity additions, and the use of external capacity.

Maintaining System Balance In a perfectly balanced plant, the output of stage 1 provides the exact input requirement for stage 2. Stage 2's output provides the exact input requirement for stage 3, and so on. In practice, however, achieving such a "perfect" design is usually both impossible and undesirable. One reason is that the best operating levels for each stage generally differ. For instance, department 1 may operate most efficiently over a range of 90 to 110 units per month, whereas department 2, the next stage in the process, is most efficient at 75 to 85 units per month, and department 3 works best over a range of 150 to 200 units per month. Another reason is that variability in product demand and the processes themselves generally leads to imbalance except in automated production lines, which, in essence, are just one big machine.

There are various ways of dealing with imbalance. One is to add capacity to stages that are bottlenecks. This can be done by temporary measures such as scheduling overtime, leasing equipment, or purchasing additional capacity through subcontracting. A second way is through the use of buffer inventories in front of the bottleneck stage to ensure that it always has something to work on. A third approach involves duplicating the facilities of one department on which another is dependent. All these approaches are increasingly being applied to supply chain design. This supply planning also helps reduce imbalances for supplier partners and customers.

Frequency of Capacity Additions There are two types of costs to consider when adding capacity: the cost of upgrading too frequently and that of upgrading too infrequently. Upgrading capacity too frequently is expensive. Direct costs include removing and replacing old equipment and training employees on the new equipment. In addition, the new equipment must be purchased, often for considerably more than the selling price of the old. Finally, there is the opportunity cost of idling the plant or service site during the changeover period.

Conversely, upgrading capacity too infrequently is also expensive. Infrequent expansion means that capacity is purchased in larger chunks. Any excess capacity that is purchased must be carried as overhead until it is utilized. (Exhibit 4.5 illustrates frequent versus infrequent capacity expansion.)

Supply Chain

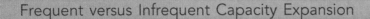

Frequent versus Infrequent Capacity Expansion   **EXHIBIT 4.5**

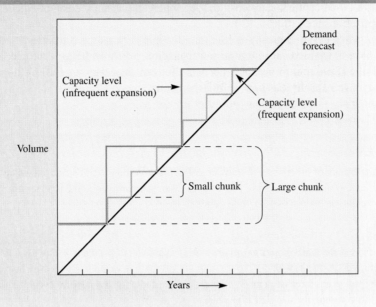

External Sources of Operations and Supply Capacity In some cases, it may be cheaper to not add capacity at all, but rather to use some existing external source of capacity. Two common strategies used by organizations are outsourcing and sharing capacity. An example of subcontracting is Air Canada subcontracting its ticketing, check-in, and ground services in a foreign destination to that country's national carrier. An example of sharing capacity is airlines sharing codes. For example, the same flight between Vancouver and Auckland may have an Air New Zealand flight number and an Air Canada flight number and each airline will be assigned seats on the flight that they can sell. Another interesting example of sharing capacity (and flexible processes) is the "night market" in the Kowloon area of Hong Kong. After business hours every day, the roads that are used by vehicles during business hours become an outdoor shopping centre with shops that can be erected and dismantled quickly (using scaffolding). Naturally, only products that can be moved and stored easily, such as clothing and jewellery, are sold in these shops. Outsourcing is covered in more depth in Chapter 8.

Determining Capacity Requirements

In determining capacity requirements, we must address the demands for individual product lines, individual plant capabilities, and allocation of production throughout the plant network. Typically this is done according to the following steps:

1. Use forecasting techniques (see Chapter 11) to predict sales for individual products within each product line.
2. Calculate equipment and labour requirements to meet product line forecasts.
3. Project labour and equipment availabilities over the planning horizon.

Often the firm then decides on some **capacity cushion** that will be maintained between the projected requirements and the actual capacity. A capacity cushion is an amount of capacity in excess of expected demand. For example, if the expected annual demand on a facility is $10 million in products per year and the design capacity is $12 million per year, it has a 20 percent capacity cushion. A 20 percent capacity cushion equates to an 83 percent utilization rate (100% / 120%).

When a firm's design capacity is less than the capacity required to meet its demand, it is said to have a negative capacity cushion (capacity shortfall). If, for example, a firm has a demand of $12 million in products per year but can produce only $10 million per year, it has a negative capacity cushion of 16.7 percent.

We now apply these three steps to an example.

EXAMPLE 4.3: DETERMINING CAPACITY REQUIREMENTS

The Stewart Company produces two flavours of salad dressings: Paul's and Newman's. Each is available in bottles and single-serving plastic bags. Management would like to determine equipment and labour requirements for the next five years.

SOLUTION

Step 1. Use forecasting techniques to predict sales for individual products within each product line. The marketing department, which is now running a promotional campaign for Newman's dressing, provided the following forecast demand values (in thousands) for the next five years. The campaign is expected to continue for the next two years.

	YEAR				
	1	2	3	4	5
PAUL'S					
Bottles (000s)	60	100	150	200	250
Plastic bags (000s)	100	200	300	400	500
NEWMAN'S					
Bottles (000s)	75	85	95	97	98
Plastic bags (000s)	200	400	600	650	680

Cross Functional

Step 2. Calculate equipment and labour requirements to meet product line forecasts. Currently, three machines that can package up to 150 000 bottles each per year are available. Each machine requires two operators and can produce bottles of both Newman's and Paul's dressings. Six bottle machine operators are available. Also, five machines that can package up to 250 000 plastic bags each per year are available. Three operators are required for each machine, which can produce plastic bags of both Newman's and Paul's dressings. Currently, 20 plastic bag machine operators are available.

Total product line forecasts can be calculated from the preceding table by adding the yearly demand for bottles and plastic bags as follows:

	YEAR				
	1	2	3	4	5
Bottles	135	185	245	297	348
Plastic bags	300	600	900	1050	1180

Capacity

We can now calculate equipment and labour requirements for the current year (year 1). Because the total available capacity for packaging bottles is 450 000/year (3 machines × 150 000 each), we will be using 135/450 = 0.3 of the available capacity for the current year, or 0.3 × 3 = 0.9 machine. Similarly, we will need 300/1250 = 0.24 of the available capacity for plastic bags for the current year, or 0.24 × 5 = 1.2 machines. The number of crew required to support our forecast demand for the first year will consist of the crew required for the bottle and the plastic bag machines.

The labour requirement for year 1's bottle operation is

$$0.9 \text{ bottle machine} \times 2 \text{ operators} = 1.8 \text{ operators}$$
$$1.2 \text{ bag machines} \times 3 \text{ operators} = 3.6 \text{ operators}$$

Step 3. Project labour and equipment availabilities over the planning horizon. We repeat the preceding calculations for the remaining years:

	YEAR				
	1	2	3	4	5
PLASTIC BAG OPERATION					
Percentage capacity utilized	24.0	48.0	72.0	84.0	94.0
Machine requirement	1.2	2.4	3.6	4.2	4.7
Labour requirement	3.6	7.2	10.8	12.6	14.1
BOTTLE OPERATION					
Percentage capacity utilized	30.0	41.0	54.0	66.0	77.0
Machine requirement	0.9	1.23	1.62	1.98	2.31
Labour requirement	1.8	2.46	3.24	3.96	4.62

A positive capacity cushion exists for all five years because the available capacity for both operations always exceeds the expected demand. The Stewart Company can now begin to develop the intermediate-range or sales and operations plan for the two production lines. (See Chapter 12 for a discussion of sales and operations planning.)

Using Decision Trees to Evaluate Capacity Alternatives

A convenient way to lay out the steps of a capacity problem is through the use of decision trees. The tree format helps not only in understanding the problem but also in finding a solution. A *decision tree* is a schematic model of the sequence of steps in a problem and the conditions and consequences of each step. In recent years, a few commercial software packages have been developed to assist in the construction and analysis of decision trees. These packages make the process quick and easy.

Decision trees are composed of decision nodes with branches to and from them. Usually squares represent decision points and circles represent chance events. Branches from decision points show the choices available to the decision maker; branches from chance events show the probabilities for their occurrence.

In solving decision tree problems, we work backward from the end of the tree to the start of the tree. As we work back, we calculate the expected values at each step. In calculating the expected value, the time value of money is important if the planning horizon is long.

Once the calculations are made, we prune the tree by eliminating from each decision point all branches except the one with the highest payoff. This process continues to the first decision point, and the decision problem is thereby solved.

We now demonstrate an application to capacity planning for Hackers Computer Store.

EXAMPLE 4.4: DECISION TREES

The owner of Hackers Computer Store is considering what to do with his business over the next five years. Sales growth over the past couple of years has been good, but sales could grow substantially if a major electronics firm is built in his area as proposed. Hackers' owner sees three options. The first is to enlarge his current store, the second is to locate at a new site, and the third is to simply wait and do nothing. The decision to expand or move would take little time, and, therefore, the store would not lose revenue. If nothing were done the first year and strong growth occurred, then the decision to expand would be reconsidered. Waiting longer than one year would allow competition to move in making expansion no longer feasible.

The assumptions and conditions are as follows:

1. Strong growth as a result of the increased population of computer fanatics from the new electronics firm has a 55 percent probability.

2. Strong growth with a new site would give annual returns of $195 000 per year. Weak growth with a new site would mean annual returns of $115 000.

3. Strong growth with an expansion would give annual returns of $190 000 per year. Weak growth with an expansion would mean annual returns of $100 000.

4. At the existing store with no changes, there would be returns of $170 000 per year if there is strong growth and $105 000 per year if growth is weak.

5. Expansion at the current site would cost $87 000.

6. The move to the new site would cost $210 000.

7. If growth is strong and the existing site is enlarged during the second year, the cost would still be $87 000.

8. Operating costs for all options are equal.

SOLUTION

We construct a decision tree to advise Hackers' owner on the best action. Exhibit 4.6 shows the decision tree for this problem. There are two decision points (square nodes) and three chance occurrences (round nodes).

EXHIBIT 4.6	Decision Tree for Hackers Computer Store Problem

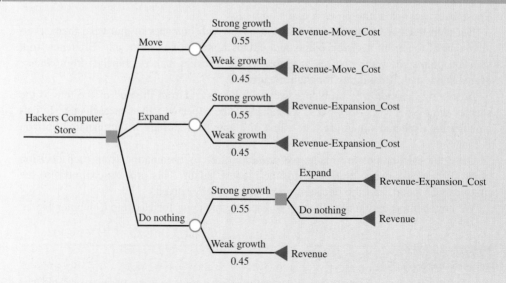

The values of each alternative outcome shown on the right of the diagram in Exhibit 4.7 are calculated as follows:

ALTERNATIVE	REVENUE	COST	VALUE
Move to new location, strong growth	$195 000 × 5 yrs	$210 000	$765 000
Move to new location, weak growth	$115 000 × 5 yrs	$210 000	$365 000
Expand store, strong growth	$190 000 × 5 yrs	$ 87 000	$863 000
Expand store, weak growth	$100 000 × 5 yrs	$ 87 000	$413 000
Do nothing now, strong growth, expand next year	$170 000 × 1 yr + $190 000 × 4 yrs	$ 87 000	$843 000
Do nothing now, strong growth, do not expand next year	$170 000 × 5 yrs	$0	$850 000
Do nothing now, weak growth	$105 000 × 5 yrs	$0	$525 000

Capacity

Decision Trees

Decision Tree Analysis

EXHIBIT 4.7

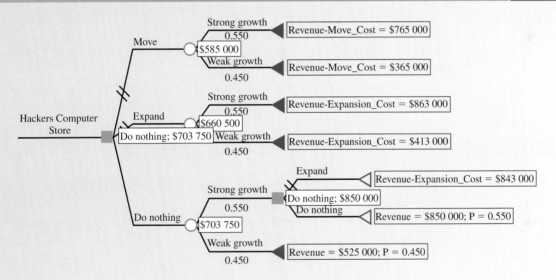

Working from the rightmost alternatives, which are associated with the decision of whether to expand, we see that the alternative of doing nothing has a higher value than the expansion alternative. We therefore eliminate the expansion in the second year alternatives. What this means is that if we do nothing in the first year and we experience strong growth, then in the second year it makes no sense to expand.

Now we can calculate the expected values associated with our current decision alternatives. We simply multiply the value of the alternative by its probability and sum the values. The expected value for the alternative of moving now is $585 000. The expansion alternative has an expected value of $660 500, and doing nothing now has an expected value of $703 750. Our analysis indicates that our best decision is to do nothing (both now and next year)!

Due to the five-year time horizon, it may be useful to consider the time value of the revenue and cost streams when solving this problem. If we assume a 16 percent interest rate, the first alternative outcome (move now, strong growth) has a discounted revenue valued at $428 487 (195 000 × 3.274293654) minus the $210 000 cost to move immediately. Exhibit 4.8 shows the analysis considering the discounted flows. Details of the calculations are given below. The present value table in Appendix C can be used to look up the discount factors. In order to make our calculations agree with those completed by Excel, we have used discount factors that are calculated to 10 digits of precision. The only calculation that is a little tricky is the one for revenue when we do nothing now and expand at the beginning of next year. In this case, we have a revenue stream of $170 000 the first year, followed by four years at $190 000. The first part of the calculation (170 000 × 0.862068966) discounts the first-year revenue to present. The next part (190 000 × 2.798180638) discounts the next four years to the start of year two. We then discount this four-year stream to present value.

Decision Trees

ALTERNATIVE	REVENUE	COST	VALUE
Move to new location, strong growth	$195 000 × 3.274293654	$210 000	$428 487
Move to new location, weak growth	$115 000 × 3.274293654	$210 000	$166 544
Expand store, strong growth	$190 000 × 3.274293654	$87 000	$535 116
Expand store, weak growth	$100 000 × 3.274203654	$87 000	$240 429
Do nothing now, strong growth, expand next year	$170 000 × 0.862068966 + $190 000 × 2.798180638 × 0.862068966	$87 000 × 0.862068966	$529 874
Do nothing now, strong growth, do not expand next year	$170 000 × 3.274293654	$0	$556 630
Do nothing now, weak growth	$105 000 × 3.274293654	$0	$343 801

EXHIBIT 4.8   Decision Tree Analysis Using Net Present Value Calculations

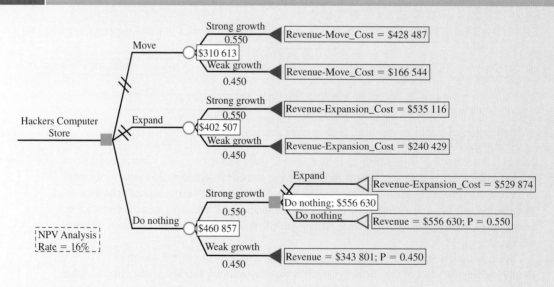

Based on this analysis, it appears that the best capacity strategy for Hackers is to not expand or move now. This is due to the fact there is a significant probability (0.45) that growth will be weak. This adversely affects the benefits if they expand or move.

PLANNING SERVICE CAPACITY

Capacity Planning in Service versus Manufacturing

Although capacity planning in services is subject to many of the same issues as manufacturing capacity planning, and facility sizing can be done in much the same way, there are several important differences. Service capacity is more time- and location-dependent, it is subject to more volatile demand fluctuations, and utilization directly impacts service quality.

Time Unlike goods, services cannot be stored for later use. As such, in services managers must consider time as one of their supplies. The capacity must be available to produce a service when it is needed. For example, a customer cannot be given a seat that went unoccupied on a previous airline flight if the current flight is full. Nor could the customer purchase a seat on a particular day's flight and take it home to be used at some later date.

Location In face-to-face settings, the service capacity must be located near the customer. In manufacturing, production takes place, and then the goods are distributed to the customer. With services, however, the opposite is true. The capacity to deliver the service must first be distributed to the customer (either physically or through some communications medium such as the telephone); then the service can be produced. A hotel room or rental car that is available in another city is not much use to the customer—it must be where the customer is when that customer needs it. Location is discussed in more detail in Chapter 9.

Volatility of Demand The volatility of demand on a service delivery system is much higher than that on a manufacturing production system for three reasons. First, as just mentioned, services cannot be stored. This means that inventory cannot smooth the demand as in manufacturing. The second reason is that the customers interact directly with the production system—and these customers often have different needs, will have different levels of experience with the process, and may require different numbers of transactions. This contributes to greater variability in the processing time required for each customer and hence greater variability in the minimum capacity needed. The third reason for the greater volatility in service demand is that it is directly affected by consumer behaviour. Influences on customer behaviour ranging from the weather to a major event can directly affect demand for different services. Go to any restaurant near your campus during spring break and it will probably be almost empty. This behavioural effect can be seen over even shorter time frames such as the lunch-hour rush at a bank's drive-through window. Because of this volatility, service capacity is often planned in increments as small as 10 to 30 minutes, as opposed to the one-week increments more common in manufacturing.

Capacity Utilization and Service Quality

Planning capacity levels for services must consider the day-to-day relationship between service utilization and service quality. Exhibit 4.9 shows a service situation cast in waiting line terms (arrival rates and service rates). The best operating point is near 70 percent of the maximum capacity. This is enough to keep servers busy but allows enough time to serve customers individually and keep enough capacity in reserve so as not to create too many managerial headaches. In the critical zone, customers are processed through the system, but service quality declines. Above the critical zone, the queue builds up and it is likely that many customers may never be served.

| EXHIBIT 4.9 | Relationship between the Rate of Service Utilization (ρ) and Service Quality |

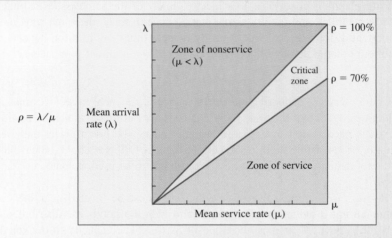

$\rho = \lambda / \mu$

Source: J. Haywood-Farmer and J. Nollet, *Services Plus: Effective Service Management* (Boucherville, Quebec, Canada: G. Morin Publisher Ltd., 1991), p. 59.

The optimal utilization rate is very context specific. Low rates are appropriate when both the degree of uncertainty and the stakes are high. For example, hospital emergency rooms and fire departments should aim for low utilization because of the high level of uncertainty and the life-or-death nature of their activities. Relatively predictable services such as commuter trains or service facilities without customer contact, such as postal sorting operations, can plan to operate much nearer 100 percent utilization. Interestingly, there is a third group for which high utilization is desirable. All sports teams like sellouts, not only because of the virtually 100 percent contribution margin of each customer, but because a full house creates an atmosphere that pleases customers, motivates the home team to perform better, and boosts future ticket sales. Stage performances and bars share this phenomenon. On the other hand, many airline passengers feel that a flight is too crowded when the seat next to theirs is occupied. Airlines capitalize on this response to sell more business-class seats. Note that this capacity utilization and service quality tradeoff can be applied to manufacturing situations also. For example, if a factory has high utilization, there will queues of parts at workcentres. This will naturally delay the completion of a customer order because of higher wait times at the workcentres, which results in poorer service.

Summary

Strategic capacity planning involves an investment decision that must match resource capabilities to a long-term demand forecast. As discussed in this chapter, factors to be taken into account in selecting capacity additions for both manufacturing and services include

- The likely effects of economies of scale.
- The effects of learning curves and how to analyze them.

- The impact of changing facility focus and balance among production stages.
- The degree of flexibility of facilities and the workforce in the operation and its supply system.

For services in particular, a key consideration is the effect of capacity changes on the quality of the service offering.

Key Terms

Best operating level   The level of capacity for which the process was designed and the volume of output at which average unit cost is minimized.

Capacity   The amount of output that a system is capable of achieving over a specific period of time.

Capacity cushion   Capacity in excess of expected demand.

Capacity focus   Can be operationalized through the plants-within-plants concept, where a plant has several suborganizations specialized for different products—even though they are under the same roof. This permits finding the best operating level for each suborganization.

Capacity utilization rate   Measures how close a firm is to its best operating level.

Economies of scope   Exist when multiple products can be produced at a lower cost in combination than they can separately.

Learning curve   A line displaying the relationship between unit production time and the cumulative number of units produced.

Strategic capacity planning   Determining the overall capacity level of capital-intensive resources that best supports the company's long-range competitive strategy.

Solved Problems

Solved Problem 1

A job applicant is being tested for an assembly line position. Management feels that steady-state times have been reached after approximately 1000 performances. Regular assembly line workers are expected to perform the task within four minutes.

a. If the job applicant performed the first test operation in 10 minutes and the second one in 9 minutes, should this applicant be hired?
b. What is the expected time that the job applicant would take to finish the 10th unit?
c. What is a significant limitation of this analysis?

SOLUTION

a. Learning rate = 9 minutes/10 minutes = 90%
   From Appendix Exhibit B.1, the time for the 1000th unit is 0.3499 × 10 minutes = 3.499 minutes. Yes, hire the person.
b. From Appendix Exhibit B.1, unit 10 at 90% is 0.7047. Therefore, the time for the 10th unit = 0.7047 × 10 = 7.047 minutes.
c. Extrapolating based on just the first two units is unrealistic. More data should be collected to evaluate the job applicant's performance.

Solved Problem 2

Boeing Aircraft collected the following cost data on the first 8 units of their new business jet.

UNIT NUMBER	COST ($ MILLIONS)	UNIT NUMBER	COST ($ MILLIONS)
1	$100	5	60
2	83	6	57
3	73	7	53
4	62	8	51

Learning Curves

a. Estimate the learning curve for the new business jet.
b. Estimate the average cost for the first 1000 units of the jet.
c. Estimate the cost to produce the 1000th jet.

SOLUTION

a. First, estimate the learning curve rate by calculating the average learning rate with each doubling of production.

$$\text{Units 1 to 2} = 83/100 = 83\%$$

$$\text{Units 2 to 4} = 62/83 = 74.7\%$$

$$\text{Units 4 to 8} = 51/62 = 82.26\%$$

$$\text{Average} = (83 + 74.4 + 82.6)/3 = 80\%$$

b. The average cost of the first 1000 units can be estimated using Appendix Exhibit B.2. The cumulative improvement factor for the 1000th unit at 80 percent learning is 158.7. The cost to produce the first 1000 units is

$$\$100\text{M} \times 158.7 = \$15\ 870\text{M}$$

The average cost for each of the first 1000 units is

$$\$15\ 870\text{M}/1000 = \$15.9\text{M}$$

c. To estimate the cost to produce the 1000th unit use Appendix Exhibit B.1. The unit improvement factor for the 1000th unit at 80 percent is 0.1082. The cost to produce the 1000th unit is

$$\$100\text{M} \times 0.1082 = \$10.82\text{M}$$

Solved Problem 3

E-Education is a new start-up that develops and markets MBA courses offered over the Internet. The company is currently located in Edmonton and employs 150 people. Due to strong growth, the company needs additional office space. The company has the option of leasing additional space at its current location in Edmonton for the next two years, but after that will need to move to a new building. Another option the company is considering is moving the entire operation to the nearby small town of Wetaskiwin immediately. A third option is for the company to immediately lease a new building in Edmonton. If the company chooses the first option and leases new space at its current location, it can, at the end of two years, either lease a new building in Edmonton or move to Wetaskiwin

The following are some additional facts about the alternatives and current situation:

1. The company has a 75 percent chance of surviving the next two years.
2. Leasing the new space for two years at the current location in Edmonton would cost $750 000 per year.

3. Moving the entire operation to Wetaskiwin would cost $1 million. Leasing space would run only $500 000 per year.
4. Moving to a new building in Edmonton would cost $200 000, and leasing the new building's space would cost $650 000 per year.
5. The company can cancel the lease at any time.
6. The company will build its own building in five years, if it survives.
7. Assume all other costs and revenues are the same no matter where the company is located.

What should E-Education do?

SOLUTION

Step 1: Construct a decision tree that considers all of E-Education's alternatives. The following shows the tree that has decision points (with the square nodes) followed by chance occurrences (round nodes). In the case of the first decision point, if the company survives, two additional decision points need consideration.

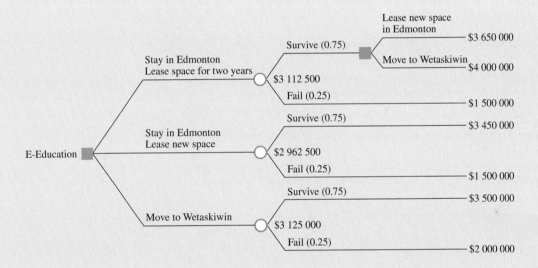

Step 2: Calculate the values of each alternative as follows:

ALTERNATIVE	CALCULATION	VALUE
Stay in Edmonton, lease space for two years, survive, lease new building in Edmonton	(750 000) × 2 + 200 000 + (650 000) × 3 =	$3 650 000
Stay in Edmonton, lease space for two years, survive, move to Wetaskiwin	(750 000) × 2 + 1 000 000 + (500 000) × 3 =	$4 000 000
Stay in Edmonton, lease space for two years, fail	(750 000) × 2 =	$1 500 000
Stay in Edmonton, lease new building in Edmonton, survive	200 000 + (650 000) × 5 =	$3 450 000
Stay in Edmonton, lease new building in Edmonton, fail	200 000 + (650 000) × 2 =	$1 500 000
Move to Wetaskiwin, survive	1 000 000 + (500 000) × 5 =	$3 500 000
Move to Wetaskiwin, fail	1 000 000 + (500 000) × 2 =	$2 000 000

Working from our rightmost alternatives, the first two alternatives end in decision nodes. Because the first option, staying in Edmonton and leasing space for two years, is the lowest cost, this is what we would do if we decide to stay in Edmonton for the first two years. If we fail after the first two years, represented by the third alternative, the cost is only $1 500 000. The expected value of the first option of staying in Edmonton and leasing space for the first two years is $0.75 \times 3\,650\,000 + 0.25 \times 1\,500\,000 = \$3\,112\,500$.

The second option, staying in Edmonton and leasing a new building now, has an expected value of $0.75 \times 3\,450\,000 + 0.25 \times 1\,500\,000 = \$2\,962\,500$.

Finally, the third option of moving to Wetaskiwin immediately has an expected value of $0.75 \times 3\,500\,000 + 0.25 \times 2\,000\,000 = \$3\,125\,000$.

From this, it looks like the best alternative is to stay in Edmonton and lease a new building immediately.

Review and Discussion Questions

1. What capacity problems are encountered when a new drug is introduced to the market?
2. List some practical limits to economies of scale; that is, when should a plant stop growing?
3. What are some capacity balance problems faced by the following organizations or facilities?
    a. An airline terminal.
    b. A university computing lab.
    c. A clothing manufacturer.
4. What are some major capacity considerations in a hospital? How do they differ from those of a factory?
5. Management may choose to build up capacity in anticipation of demand or in response to developing demand. Cite the advantages and disadvantages of both approaches.
6. What is capacity balance? Why is it hard to achieve? What methods are used to deal with capacity imbalances?
7. What are some reasons for a plant to maintain a capacity cushion? How about a negative capacity cushion?
8. Consider the concepts of the focused factory and capacity flexibility. In what way are these two concepts in agreement, even though at first glance they seem to contradict each other?

Problems

1. A time standard was set as 0.20 hour per unit based on the 50th unit produced. If the task has a 90 percent learning curve, what would be the expected time of the 100th, 200th, and 400th units?
2. You have just received 10 units of a special subassembly from an electronics manufacturer at a price of $250 per unit. A new order has also just come in for your company's product that uses these subassemblies, and you wish to purchase 40 more to be shipped in lots of 10 units each. (The subassemblies are bulky, and you need only 10 a month to fill your new order.)
    a. Assuming a 70 percent learning curve by your supplier on a similar product last year, how much should you pay for each lot? Assume that the learning rate of 70 percent applies to each lot of 10 units, not each unit.
    b. Suppose you are the supplier and can produce 20 units now but cannot start production on the second 20 units for two months. What price would you try to negotiate for the last 20 units?
3. Choudhary Industries received a contract to develop and produce four high-intensity long-distance receiver/transmitters for cellular telephones. The first took 2000 labour hours and $39\,000 worth of purchased and manufactured parts; the second took 1500 labour hours and $37\,050 in parts; the third took 1450 labour hours and $31\,000 in parts; and the fourth took 1275 labour hours and $31\,492 in parts.

    Choudhary was asked to bid on a follow-on contract for another dozen receiver/transmitter units. Ignoring any forgetting factor effects, what should Choudhary estimate time and parts costs to be for the dozen units? (Hint: There are two learning curves—one for labour and one for parts.)

4. Lambda Computer Products competed for and won a contract to produce two prototype units of a new type of computer that is based on laser optics rather than on electronic binary bits.

   The first unit produced by Lambda took 5000 hours to produce and required $250 000 worth of material, equipment usage, and supplies. The second unit took 3500 hours and used $200 000 worth of materials, equipment usage, and supplies. Labour is $30 per hour.

   a. Lambda was asked to present a bid for 10 additional units as soon as the second unit was completed. Production would start immediately. What would this bid be?

   b. Suppose there was a significant delay between the contracts. During this time, personnel and equipment were reassigned to other projects. Explain how this would affect the subsequent bid.

5. Zambrotta Inc. has just completed a pilot run of 10 units of a major product and found the processing time for each unit was as follows:

UNIT NUMBER	TIME (HOURS)
1	970
2	640
3	420
4	380
5	320
6	250
7	220
8	207
9	190
10	190

   a. According to the pilot run, what would you estimate the learning rate to be?

   b. Based on a, how much time would it take for the next 190 units, assuming no loss of learning?

   c. How much time would it take to make the 1000th unit?

6. Lazer Technologies Inc. (LTI) has produced a total of 20 high-power laser systems that could be used to destroy any approaching enemy missiles or aircraft. The 20 units have been produced, funded in part as private research within the research and development arm of LTI, but the bulk of the funding came from a contract with the Defence Department (DD).

   Testing of the laser units has shown that they are effective defense weapons, and through redesign to add portability and easier field maintenance, the units could be truck-mounted.

   DD has asked LTI to submit a bid for 100 units.

   The 20 units that LTI has built so far cost the following amounts and are listed in the order in which they were produced:

UNIT NUMBER	COST ($ MILLIONS)	UNIT NUMBER	COST ($ MILLIONS)
1	$12.0	11	$3.9
2	10.0	12	3.5
3	6.0	13	3.0
4	6.5	14	2.8
5	5.8	15	2.7
6	6.0	16	2.7
7	5.0	17	2.3
8	3.6	18	3.0
9	3.6	19	2.9
10	4.1	20	2.6

   a. Based on past experience, what is the learning rate?

   b. What bid should LTI submit for the total order of 100 units, assuming that learning continues?

   c. What is the cost expected to be for the last unit under the learning rate you estimated?

7. Jack Kalantzis, contract negotiator for Nebula Airframe Company, is currently involved in bid-ding on a follow-up government contract. In gathering cost data from the first three units, which Nebula produced under a research and development contract, he found that the first unit took 2000 labour hours, the second took 1800 labour hours, and the third took 1692 hours.

   In a contract for three more units, how many labour hours should Jack plan for?

8. Honda Motor Company has discovered a problem in the exhaust system of one of its automobile lines and has voluntarily agreed to make the necessary modifications to conform with govern-ment safety requirements. Standard procedure is for the firm to pay a flat fee to dealers for each modification completed.

   Honda is trying to establish a fair amount of compensation to pay dealers and has decided to choose a number of randomly selected mechanics and observe their performance and learning rate. Analysis demonstrated that the average learning rate was 90 percent, and Honda then decided to pay a $60 fee for each repair (3 hours × $20 per flat-rate hour).

   Southwest Honda, Inc., has complained to Honda Motor Company about the fee. Six mechan-ics, working independently, have completed two modifications each. All took 9 hours on the average to do the first unit and 6.3 hours to do the second. Southwest refuses to do any more unless Honda allows at least 4.5 hours. The dealership expects to perform the modification to approximately 300 vehicles.

   What is your opinion of Honda's allowed rate and the mechanics' performance?

9. United Research Associates (URA) had received a contract to produce two units of a new cruise missile guidance control. The first unit took 4000 hours to complete and cost $30000 in mate-rials and equipment usage. The second took 3200 hours and cost $21000 in materials and equipment usage. Labour cost is charged at $18 per hour.

   The prime contractor has now approached URA and asked to submit a bid for the cost of producing another 20 guidance controls.

   a. What will the last unit cost to build?

   b. What will be the average time for the 20 missile guidance controls?

   c. What will the average cost be for guidance control for the 20 in the contract?

10. AlwaysRain Irrigation, Inc., would like to determine capacity requirements for the next four years. Currently, two production lines are in place for bronze and plastic sprinklers. Three types of sprinklers are available in both bronze and plastic: 90-degree nozzle sprinklers, 180-degree nozzle sprinklers, and 360-degree nozzle sprinklers. Management has forecast demand for the next four years as follows:

| | YEARLY DEMAND | | | |
	1 (IN 000s)	2 (IN 000s)	3 (IN 000s)	4 (IN 000s)
Plastic 90	32	44	55	56
Plastic 180	15	16	17	18
Plastic 360	50	55	64	67
Bronze 90	7	8	9	10
Bronze 180	3	4	5	6
Bronze 360	11	12	15	18

Both production lines can produce all the different types of nozzles. Each bronze machine requires two operators and can produce up to 12000 sprinklers. The plastic injection molding machine requires four operators and can produce up to 200000 sprinklers. Three bronze machines and only one injection molding machine are available. What are the capacity requirements for the next four years? (Assume that there is no learning.)

11. Suppose that AlwaysRain Irrigation's marketing department will undertake an intense ad cam-paign for the bronze sprinklers, which are more expensive but also more durable than the plastic ones. Forecast demand for the next four years is

YEARLY DEMAND

	1 (IN 000s)	2 (IN 000s)	3 (IN 000s)	4 (IN 000s)
Plastic 90	32	44	55	56
Plastic 180	15	16	17	18
Plastic 360	50	55	64	67
Bronze 90	11	15	18	23
Bronze 180	6	5	6	9
Bronze 360	15	16	17	20

What are the capacity implications of the marketing campaign (assume no learning)?

12. In anticipation of the ad campaign, AlwaysRain bought an additional bronze machine. Will this be enough to ensure that enough capacity is available?

13. Suppose that operators have enough training to operate both the bronze machines and the injection molding machine for the plastic sprinklers. Currently, AlwaysRain has 10 such employees. In anticipation of the ad campaign described in Problem 11, management approved the purchase of two additional bronze machines. What are the labour requirement implications?

14. Expando, Inc., is considering the possibility of building an additional factory that would produce a new addition to their product line. The company is currently considering two options. The first is a small facility that it could build at a cost of $6 million. If demand for new products is low, the company expects to receive $10 million in discounted revenues (present value of future revenues) with the small facility. On the other hand, if demand is high, it expects $12 million in discounted revenues using the small facility. The second option is to build a large factory at a cost of $9 million. Were demand to be low, the company would expect $10 million in discounted revenues with the large plant. If demand is high, the company estimates that the discounted revenues would be $14 million. In either case, the probability of demand being high is 0.40, and the probability of it being low is 0.60. Not constructing a new factory would result in no additional revenue being generated because the current factories cannot produce these new products. Construct a decision tree to help Expando make the best decision.

15. A builder has located a piece of property that she would like to buy and eventually build on. The land is currently zoned for four homes per acre, but she is planning to request new zoning. What she builds depends on approval of zoning requests and your analysis of this problem to advise her. With her input and your help, the decision process has been reduced to the following costs, alternatives, and probabilities:

Cost of land: $2 million.

Probability of rezoning: 0.60.

If the land is rezoned, there will be additional costs for new roads, lighting, and so on, of $1 million.

If the land is rezoned, the contractor must decide whether to build a shopping centre or 1500 apartments that the tentative plan shows would be possible. If she builds a shopping centre, there is a 70 percent chance that she can sell the shopping centre to a large department chain for $4 million over her construction cost, which excludes the land; and there is a 30 percent chance that she can sell it to an insurance company for $5 million over her construction cost (also excluding the land). If, instead of the shopping centre, she decides to build the 1500 apartments, she places probabilities on the profits as follows: There is a 60 percent chance that she can sell the apartments to a real estate investment corporation for $3000 each over her construction cost; there is a 40 percent chance that she can get only $2000 each over her construction cost. (Both exclude the land cost.)

If the land is not rezoned, she will comply with the existing zoning restrictions and simply build 600 homes, on which she expects to make $4000 over the construction cost on each one (excluding the cost of land).

Draw a decision tree of the problem and determine the best solution and the expected net profit.

CASE | Shouldice Hospital—A Cut Above

"Shouldice Hospital, the house that hernias built, is a converted country estate which gives the hospital 'a country club' appeal."

American Medical News

Shouldice Hospital is widely known for one thing—hernia repair! In fact, that is the only operation it performs, and it performs a great many of them. Over the past two decades this small 90-bed hospital has averaged 7000 operations annually. Patients' ties to Shouldice do not end when they leave the hospital. Every year the gala Hernia Reunion dinner (with complimentary hernia inspection) draws more than 1000 former patients, some of whom have been attending the event for over 30 years.

A number of notable features in Shouldice's service delivery system contribute to its success. (1) Shouldice accepts only patients with the uncomplicated external hernias, and it uses a superior technique developed for this type of hernia by Dr. Shouldice during World War II. (2) Patients are subject to early ambulation, which promotes healing. (Patients literally walk off the operating table and engage in light exercise throughout their stay, which lasts only three days.) (3) Its country club atmosphere, gregarious nursing staff, and built-in socializing make a surprisingly pleasant experience out of an inherently unpleasant medical problem. Regular times are set aside for tea, cookies, and socializing. All patients are paired up with a roommate with similar background and interests.

The Production System

The medical facilities at Shouldice consist of five operating rooms, a patient recovery room, a laboratory, and six examination rooms. Shouldice performs, on average, 150 operations per week, with patients generally staying at the hospital for three days. Although operations are performed only five days a week, the remainder of the hospital is in operation continuously to attend to recovering patients.

An operation at Shouldice Hospital is performed by one of the 12 full-time surgeons, assisted by one of seven part-time assistant surgeons. Surgeons generally take about one hour to prepare for and perform each hernia operation, and they operate on four patients per day. The surgeons' day ends at 4 p.m., although they can expect to be on call every 14th night and every 10th weekend.

The Shouldice Experience

Each patient undergoes a screening exam prior to setting a date for his or her operation. Patients in the Toronto area are encouraged to walk in for the diagnosis. Examinations are done between 9 a.m. and 3:30 p.m. Monday through Friday, and between 10 a.m. and 2 p.m.. on Saturday. Out-of-town patients are mailed a medical information questionnaire (also available over the Internet), which is used for the diagnosis. A small percentage of patients who are overweight or otherwise represent an undue medical risk are refused treatment. The remaining patients receive confirmation cards with the scheduled dates for their operations. A patient's folder is transferred to the reception desk once an arrival date is confirmed.

Patients arrive at the clinic between 1 and 3 p.m. the day before their surgery. After a short wait, they receive a brief preoperative examination. They are then sent to an admissions clerk to complete any necessary paperwork. Patients are next directed to one of the two nurses' stations for blood and urine tests and then are shown to their rooms. They spend the remaining time before orientation getting settled and acquainting themselves with their roommates.

Orientation begins at 5 p.m., followed by dinner in the common dining room. Later in the evening, at 9 p.m., patients gather in the lounge area for tea and cookies. Here new patients can talk with patients who have already had their surgery. Bedtime is between 9:30 and 10 p.m.

On the day of the operation, patients with early operations are awakened at 5:30 a.m. for preoperative sedation. The first operations begin at 7:30 a.m. Shortly before an operation starts, the patient is administered a local anesthetic, leaving him or her alert and fully aware of the proceedings. At the conclusion of the operation, the patient is invited to walk from the operating table to a nearby wheelchair, which is waiting to return the patient to his or her room. After a brief period of rest, the patient is encouraged to get up and start exercising. By 9 p.m. that day, he or she is in the lounge having cookies and tea and talking with new, incoming patients.

The skin clips holding the incision together are loosened, and some are removed, the next day. The remainder are removed the following morning just before the patient is discharged.

When Shouldice Hospital started, the average hospital stay for hernia surgery was three weeks. Today, many institutions push "same day surgery" for a variety of reasons. Shouldice Hospital firmly believes that this is not in the best interests of patients, and is committed to its three-day process. Shouldice's postoperative rehabilitation program is designed to enable the patient to resume normal activities with minimal interruption and discomfort. Shouldice patients frequently return to work in a few days; the average total time off is eight days.

It is interesting to note that approximately 1 out of every 100 Shouldice patients is a medical doctor.

Shouldice Hospital

Future Plans

The management of Shouldice is thinking of expanding the hospital's capacity to serve considerable unsatisfied demand. To this effect, the vice president is seriously considering two options. The first involves adding one more day of operations (Saturday) to the existing five-day schedule, which would increase capacity by 20 percent. The second option is to add another floor of rooms to the hospital, increasing the number of beds by 50 percent. This would require more aggressive scheduling of the operating rooms.

The administrator of the hospital, however, is concerned about maintaining control over the quality of the service delivered. He thinks the facility is already getting very good utilization. The doctors and the staff are happy with their jobs, and the patients are satisfied with the service. According to the administrator, further expansion of capacity might make it hard to maintain the same kind of working relationships and attitudes.

Questions

Exhibit 4.10 is a room-occupancy table for the existing system. Each row in the table follows the patients that checked in on a given day. The columns indicate the number of patients in the hospital on a given day. For example, the first row of the table shows that 30 people checked in on Monday and were in the hospital for Monday, Tuesday, and Wednesday. By summing the columns of the table for Wednesday, we see that there are 90 patients staying in the hospital that day.

1. How well is the hospital currently utilizing its beds?
2. Develop a similar table to show the effects of adding operations on Saturday. (Assume that 30 operations would still be performed each day.) How would this affect the utilization of the bed capacity? Is this capacity sufficient for the additional patients?
3. Now look at the effect of increasing the number of beds by 50 percent. How many operations could the hospital perform per day before running out of bed capacity? (Assume operations are performed five days per week, with the same number performed on each day.) How well would the new resources be utilized relative to the current operation? Could the hospital really perform this many operations? Why? (Hint: Look at the capacity of the 12 surgeons and the five operating rooms.)
4. Although financial data are sketchy, an estimate from a construction company indicates that adding bed capacity would cost about $100 000 per bed. In addition, the rate charged for the hernia surgery varies between about $900 and $2000, with an average rate of $1300 per operation. The surgeons are paid a flat $600 per operation. Due to all the uncertainties in government health care legislation, Shouldice would like to justify any expansion within a five-year time period.

Operations with 90 Beds (30 patients per day) | EXHIBIT 4.10

CHECK-IN DAY	BEDS REQUIRED						
	MONDAY	TUESDAY	WEDNESDAY	THURSDAY	FRIDAY	SATURDAY	SUNDAY
Monday	30	30	30				
Tuesday		30	30	30			
Wednesday			30	30	30		
Thursday				30	30	30	
Friday							
Saturday							
Sunday	30	30					30
Total	60	90	90	90	60	30	30

Selected Bibliography

Wright, T.P. "Factors Affecting the Cost of Airplanes," *Journal of Aeronautical Sciences,* February 1936, pp. 122–128.

Yu-Lee, R.T. *Essentials of Capacity Management.* New York: Wiley, 2002.

STRATEGIC PROCESS DESIGN

Learning Objectives:

1. Know how production processes are organized.
2. Understand the product-process matrix.
3. Understand how break-even analysis is just as important in operations and supply-chain analysis as it is in other areas.
4. Be able to classify service processes.
5. Understand the service-system design matrix.
6. Understand the design of layouts for assembly lines and workcentres.

TOSHIBA: PRODUCER OF THE FIRST NOTEBOOK COMPUTER

Tokyo Shibaura Denki (Tokyo Shibaura Electric Co. Ltd) was formed in 1939 by a merger of two highly innovative Japanese companies: Shibaura Seisaku-sho (Shibaura Engineering Works), which manufactured transformers, electrical motors, hydroelectric generators, and x-ray tubes, and Tokyo Electric Company, which produced lightbulbs, radio receivers, and cathode-ray tubes. Soon after, the company was known as "Toshiba," which became its official name in 1978. Toshiba became the first company in Japan to make fluorescent lamps (1940), radar (1942), broadcasting equipment (1952), and digital computers (1954). Toshiba also became the first in the world to produce the powerful 1-megabit DRAM chip and the first laptop computer, the T3100, both in 1985.

Toshiba has built its strength in the notebook PC market by beating its competitors to the market with aggressively priced, technologically innovative products. Competition in the notebook PC market is fierce, and Toshiba can retain its position as a market leader only by relentlessly improving its manufacturing processes and lowering its costs.

Dell Computer is a formidable competitor and seeks to minimize its costs by assembling to order and selling directly to customers (though this is changing as PCs are becoming commodities and Dell has started selling through retailers). Toshiba has some significant advantages over Dell that stem largely from huge investments in technologies such as thin-film transistor (TFT) colour displays, hard-disk drives, lithium-ion batteries, and DVD drives. In addition, by forming partnerships and joint ventures with other industry giants, Toshiba can share the risk of developing expensive new technologies.

Put yourself in the position of Toshihiro Nakamura, the production supervisor at Toshiba's Ome Works. Production of Toshiba's latest subnotebook computer is scheduled to begin in only 10 days. As he wends his way through a maze of desks, heading to the factory floor, he wonders if it is really feasible to get the line designed in time.

Read the details related to designing the new assembly line in the case at the end of this chapter titled "Designing Toshiba's Notebook Computer Line."

Adapted from: *Toshiba: Ome Works*, Harvard Business School (9-696-059) and www.toshiba.co.jp/worldwide/about/history.html.

Global

HOW PRODUCTION PROCESSES ARE ORGANIZED

Process selection refers to the strategic decision of selecting which kind of processes to use to produce a product or provide a service. For example, in the case of Toshiba notebook computers, if the volume is very low, we may just have a worker manually assemble each computer by hand. In contrast, if the volume is higher, setting up an assembly line is appropriate. As we will discuss later, process design has to be linked to our competitive priorities. A mismatch between these can result in a process ill-suited to serve the customer.

The formats by which a facility is arranged are defined by the general pattern of work flow; there are five basic structures (project, workcentre, manufacturing cell, assembly line, and continuous process).

In a **project layout**, the product (by virtue of its bulk or weight) remains in a fixed location. Manufacturing equipment is moved to the product rather than vice versa. Construction sites (houses and roads) and movie shooting lots are examples of this format. Items produced with this type of layout are typically managed using the project management techniques described in Chapter 3. Areas on the site will be designated for various purposes, such as material staging, subassembly construction, site access for heavy equipment, and a management area.

In a **workcentre**, similar equipment or functions are grouped together, such as all drilling machines in one area and all stamping machines in another. A part being worked on then travels, according to the established sequence of operations, from workcentre to workcentre, where the proper machines are located for each operation. This type of layout is sometimes referred to as a job shop layout, functional layout, or a process layout (since equipment is grouped together by function or by process).

A **manufacturing cell** is a dedicated area where products that are similar in processing requirements are produced. These cells are designed to perform a specific set of processes, and the cells are dedicated to a limited range of products. A firm may have many different cells in a production area, each set up to produce a single product or a similar group of products efficiently. These cells are typically scheduled to produce "as needed" in response to current customer demand.

An **assembly line** is where work processes are arranged according to the progressive steps by which the product is made. The path for each part is, in effect, a straight line. Discrete parts are made by moving from workstation to workstation at a controlled rate, following the sequence needed to build the product. Examples include the assembly of toys, appliances, and automobiles.

A **continuous process** is similar to an assembly line in that production follows a pre-determined sequence of steps, but the flow is continuous rather than discrete. Such structures are usually highly automated and, in effect, constitute one integrated "machine" that may be operated 24 hours a day to avoid expensive shutdowns and start-ups. Conversion and processing of undifferentiated materials such as petroleum, chemicals, and drugs are good examples.

The relationship between layout structures is often depicted on a **product–process matrix** similar to the one shown in Exhibit 5.1. Two dimensions are shown. The first dimension relates to the volume of product produced. This refers to the volume of a particular product or group of standardized products. Standardization is shown on the vertical axis and refers to variations in the product. These variations are measured in terms of geometric differences, material differences, and so on. From a manufacturing processing point of view, standardized products are very similar, whereas low standardized products require different processes.

EXHIBIT 5.1   Product–Process Matrix: Framework Describing Layout Strategies

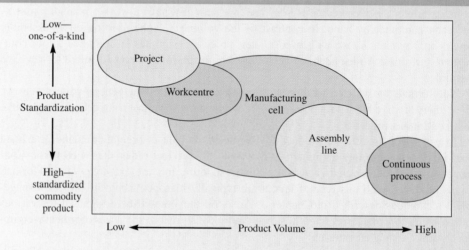

Exhibit 5.1 shows the processes approximately on a diagonal. In general, it can be argued that it is desirable to design facilities along the diagonal. For example, if we produce nonstandard products at relatively low volume, workcentres should be used. A highly standardized product (commodity) produced at high volume should be produced using an assembly line or a continuous process, if possible. As a result of the advanced manufacturing technology available today, we see that some of the layout structures span relatively large areas of the product–process matrix. For example, manufacturing cells can be used for a very wide range of applications, and this has become a popular layout structure that often is employed by manufacturing engineers.

Thus, it is clear that the processes are linked to the competitive priorities of a company discussed in Chapter 2. A competitive focus on cost is usually associated with high volume production, but low customization, to reduce cost. This necessitates a process that is highly standardized and relatively automated, i.e., an assembly line or continuous process. On the other hand, a competitive focus on flexibility is associated with customization but low volume. This would necessitate a workcentre or project type of process where volumes are low but the product can be customized to the client's exact needs. Projects and workcentres are associated with relatively less automation and more labour, since labour is more flexible (in general, trained labour is better at customization than automation is).

Matching strategy and process requires being on the diagonal of the product process matrix. What happens if there is a mismatch between the process design and strategy, i.e., the company is away from the diagonal? For example, what if your competitive focus was cost, for which, naturally, you need high volumes? If you tried to achieve this using a project type process (with flexible but more expensive labour instead of automation, i.e., top right corner of Exhibit 5.1) your unit costs would be abnormally high and you would not be cost competitive. On the other hand, if your competitive focus was flexibility, and you had relatively high level of automation and less flexible labour capacity (bottom left corner of Exhibit 5.1), you will find that your machinery would not be able to customize the product for the client (since machines in general are not flexible), leading to customer dissatisfaction.

BREAK-EVEN ANALYSIS

Often, the choice of which specific equipment to use in a process can be based on an analysis of cost trade-offs. In the product–process matrix (Exhibit 5.1) there is often a trade-off between more and less specialized equipment. Less specialized equipment is referred to as "general-purpose," meaning that it can be used easily in many different ways if it is set up in the proper way. More specialized equipment, referred to as "special-purpose," is often available as an alternative to a general-purpose machine. For example, if we need to drill holes in a piece of metal, the general-purpose option may be to use a simple hand drill. An alternative special-purpose drill is a drill press. Given the proper set-up, the drill press can drill holes much quicker than the hand drill can. The trade-offs involve the cost of the equipment (the manual drill is inexpensive, and the drill press expensive), the set-up time (the manual drill is quick, and the drill press takes some time), and the time per unit (the manual drill is slow, and the drill press quick).

A standard approach to choosing among alternative processes or equipment is *break-even analysis*. A break-even chart visually presents alternative profits and losses due to the number of units produced or sold. The choice obviously depends on anticipated demand. The method is most suitable when processes and equipment entail a large initial investment and fixed cost, and when variable costs are reasonably proportional to the number of units produced.

**Interactive
Operations
Management**

EXAMPLE 5.1:   BREAK-EVEN ANALYSIS

Suppose a manufacturer has identified the following options for obtaining a machined part: It can buy the part at $200 per unit (including materials); it can make the part on a numerically controlled semiautomatic lathe at $75 per unit (including materials); or it can make the part on a machining centre at $15 per unit (including materials). There is negligible fixed cost if the item is purchased; a semiautomatic lathe costs $80 000; and a machining centre costs $200 000.

The total cost for each option is

$$\text{Purchase cost} = \$200 \times \text{Demand}$$

$$\text{Produce-using-lathe cost} = \$80\,000 + \$75 \times \text{Demand}$$

$$\text{Produce-using-machining-centre cost} = \$200\,000 + \$15 \times \text{Demand}$$

SOLUTION

Whether we approach the solution to this problem as cost minimization or profit maximization really makes no difference as long as the relationships remain linear: that is, variable costs and revenue are the same for each incremental unit. Exhibit 5.2 shows the break-even point for each process. If demand is expected to be more than 2000 units (point A), the machine centre is the best choice because this would result in the lowest total cost. If demand is between 640 (point B) and 2000 units, the semiautomatic lathe is the cheapest. If demand is less than 640 (between 0 and point B), the most economical course is to buy the product.

The break-even point A calculation is

$$\$80\,000 + \$75 \times \text{Demand} = \$200\,000 + \$15 \times \text{Demand}$$
$$\text{Demand (point A)} = 120\,000/60 = 2000 \text{ units}$$

EXHIBIT 5.2   Break-Even Chart of Alternative Processes

Break-Even Analysis

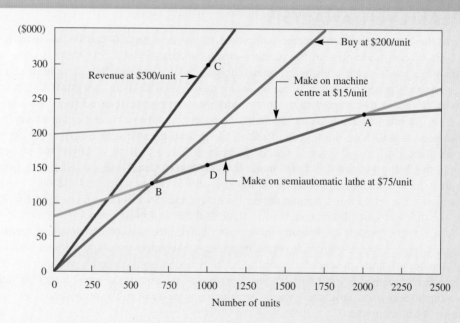

The break-even point B calculation is

$$\$200 \times \text{Demand} = \$80\,000 + \$75 \times \text{Demand}$$
$$\text{Demand (point B)} = 80\,000/125 = 640 \text{ units}$$

Consider the effect of revenue, assuming the parts sell for $300 each. As Exhibit 5.2 shows, profit (or loss) is the distance between the revenue line and the alternative process cost. At 1000 units, for example, maximum profit is the difference between the $300 000 revenue (point C) and the semiautomatic lathe cost of $155 000 (point D). For this quantity, the semiautomatic lathe is the cheapest alternative available. The optimal choices for both minimizing cost and maximizing profit are the lowest segments of the lines: origin to B, to A, and to the right side of Exhibit 5.2, as shown in green.

DESIGNING A PRODUCTION SYSTEM

There are many techniques available to determine the actual layouts of the production process. This section gives a quick overview of how the problems are addressed. For each of the layout types, descriptions are given of how the layouts are represented and the main criteria used. Later, we take an in-depth look at the assembly line balancing problem and the workcentre layout problem.

Project Layout

In developing a project layout, visualize the product as the hub of a wheel, with materials and equipment arranged concentrically around the production point in the order of use and movement difficulty (see photograph of a building under construction in the opening vignette of Chapter 3). Thus, in building custom yachts, for example, rivets that are used throughout construction would be placed close to or in the hull; heavy engine parts, which must travel to the hull only once, would be placed at a more distant location; and cranes would be set up close to the hull because of their constant use.

In a project layout, a high degree of task ordering is common. To the extent that this precedence determines production stages, a project layout may be developed by arranging materials according to their technological priority. This procedure would be expected in making a layout for a large machine tool, such as a stamping machine, where manufacture follows a rigid sequence; assembly is performed from the ground up, with parts being added to the base in almost a building-block fashion.

Workcentres

The most common approach to developing this type of layout is to arrange workcentres in a way that optimizes the movement of material. A workcentre is sometimes referred to as a department and is focused on a particular type of operation. Examples include a workcentre for drilling holes, one for performing grinding operations, and a heat-treating area (see Exhibit 5.3A). The workcentres in a low-volume toy factory might consist of shipping and receiving, plastic molding and stamping, metal forming, sewing, and painting. Parts for the toys are fabricated in these workcentres and then sent to the assembly workcentre, where they are put together. In many installations, optimal placement often means placing workcentres with large amounts of interdepartmental traffic adjacent to each other. Since workcentre layouts are common in small and medium-scale manufacturing and services, we will discuss this layout in more detail later.

Manufacturing Cell

A manufacturing cell is formed by allocating dissimilar machines to cells that are designed to work on products that have similar shapes and processing requirements. Manufacturing cells are widely used in metal fabricating, computer chip manufacture, and assembly work.

The process used to develop a manufacturing cell is depicted in Exhibit 5.3. It can be broken down into three distinct steps:

1. Group parts with common machine requirements (often having common material and dimension requirements also), into families. This requires classifying parts by

Manufacturing cells at Standard Aero, Winnipeg. The cells are clearly delineated and areas are clearly labelled. The board shown inside each cell is used to post the status of each cell, allowing problems and bottlenecks to be identified.

using some type of coding system. In practice, this can often be quite complex and can require a computerized system. For the purpose of the example shown in Exhibit 5.3A, four "part families" have already been defined and are identified by unique arrow designs. This part of the exhibit shows the routing of parts when a conventional workcentre-based layout is used. Here parts are routed through the individual workcentres to be produced.

2. Next, dominant flow patterns are identified for each part family. This will be used as the basis for reallocating equipment to the manufacturing cells (see Exhibit 5.3B).

3. Finally, machines and the associated processes are physically regrouped into cells (see Exhibit 5.3C). Often, there will be parts that cannot be associated with a family, and specialized machinery that cannot be placed in any single cell because of its general use. These unattached parts and machinery are placed in a "remainder cell."

Assembly Line and Continuous Process Layouts

An assembly line is a layout design for the special purpose of building a product by going through a progressive set of steps. The assembly steps are done in areas referred to as "stations." Typically, the stations are linked by some form of material-handling device. In addition, there is usually some form of pacing by which the amount of time allowed at each station is managed. Rather than develop the process for designing assembly at this time, we will devote an entire section of this chapter to the topic of assembly-line design since these designs are used so often by manufacturing and service firms around the world. A continuous or flow process is similar to an assembly line except that the product moves continuously through the process. Often, the item being produced by the continuous

Development of Manufacturing Cell

EXHIBIT 5.3

A. Original workcentre layout

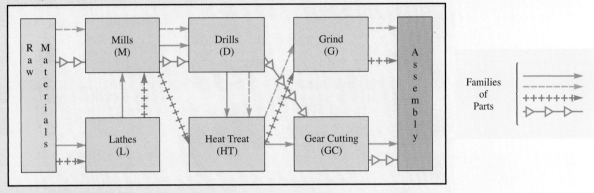

Adapted from D. Fogarty and T. Hoffman, *Production and Inventory Management* (Cincinnati: South-Western Publishing, 1983), p. 472.

B. Routing matrix based upon flow of parts

Raw Materials	Part Family	Lathes	Mills	Drills	Heat Treating	Grinders	Gear Cutting	To	Assembly
	- - - →		X	X	X	X		- - - →	
	→-▷-▷		X	X			X	→-▷-▷	
	——→	X	X	X	X		X	——→	
	+++▶	X	X		X	X		+++▶	

C. Reallocating machines to form cells according to part family processing requirements

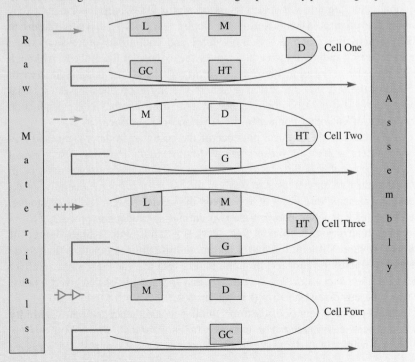

An automobile assembly line. The vehicles are transported on an underchassis conveyor. At each station, different parts such as dashboards are installed, or some other assembly work is done by workers or machines.

process is a liquid or chemical that actually "flows" through the system; this is the origin of the term. A gasoline refinery is a good example of a flow process.

AN OPERATIONAL CLASSIFICATION OF SERVICES

Service organizations are generally classified according to who the customer is, for example individuals or other businesses, and to the service they provide (financial services, health services, transportation services, and so on). These groupings, though useful in presenting aggregate economic data, are not particularly appropriate for OSM purposes because they tell us little about the process. Manufacturing, by contrast, has fairly evocative terms to classify production activities (such as assembly lines and continuous processes); when applied to a manufacturing setting, they readily convey the essence of the process. Although it is possible to describe services in these same terms, we need one additional item of information to reflect the fact that the customer is involved in the production system. That item, which we believe distinguishes one service system from another in its production function, is the extent of customer contact in the creation of the service.

Customer contact refers to the physical presence of the customer in the system, and *creation of the service* refers to the work process involved in providing the service itself. *Extent of contact* here may be roughly defined as the percentage of time the customer must be in the system relative to the total time it takes to perform the customer service. Generally speaking, the greater the percentage of contact time between the service system and the customer, the greater the degree of interaction between the two during the production process.

From this conceptualization, it follows that service systems with a **high degree of customer contact** are more difficult to control and more difficult to rationalize than those with a **low degree of customer contact**. In high-contact systems, the customer can affect the time of demand, the exact nature of the service, and the quality, or perceived quality, of service because the customer is involved in the process.

There can be tremendous diversity of customer influence and, hence, system variability within high-contact service systems. For example, a bank branch offers both simple services such as cash withdrawals that take just a minute or so and complicated services,

Operations and Supply Management in Practice

Supply Chain Services at DHL

To entice people to buy their mainstream products, companies often offer extensive additional services to their customers. Consider DHL, a global delivery company owned by Deutsche Post World Net that ships everything from flowers to industrial freight all over the world. With over 6500 offices around the world, DHL operates a network with 240 gateways and more than 450 hubs, warehouses, and terminals. Using its fleet of over 420 aircraft and over 76 200 vehicles, DHL serves some 4.1 million customers worldwide.

DHL offers customers a variety of value-added supply chain–related services that extend beyond delivering packages, improving efficiencies, and reducing costs. These services allow DHL customers to outsource much of the work required to coordinate their supply chain processes. The following is a quick list of some of the services offered by DHL:

Order management: Receipt, management, execution, sequencing, and dispatch of orders in a timely manner.

Call centre management: Manages orders, monitors sales activities, provides customer services, and functions as a help desk.

Global inventory management: DHL gives the customer a global view of inventory, thus enabling informed decisions about the disposition of stock.

Consolidated billing services: The creation of a consolidated and categorized invoice, based on all services performed in a specific period by more than one service provider.

Freight and customs solutions: DHL's experience servicing over 220 countries and territories with international trade requirements and formalities, combined with the European Competence Centre and country expertise, gives customers a leading edge in service, quality, and management in cross-border transactions.

such as loan application preparation, that can take more than an hour. Moreover, these activities may range from being self-service through an ATM, to coproduction, where bank personnel and the customer work as a team to develop the loan application. Also, manufacturing companies often provide a variety of value-added services to customers, such as logistics (sometimes using partners; see OSMP on DHL, above).

DESIGNING SERVICE ORGANIZATIONS

In designing service organizations, we must remember one distinctive characteristic of services: We cannot inventory services. Unlike manufacturing, where we can build up inventory during slack periods for peak demand, and thus maintain a relatively stable level of employment and production planning, in services we must (with a few exceptions) meet demand as it arises. Consequently, in services, capacity becomes a dominant issue. Think about the many service situations you find yourself in—for example, eating in a restaurant or going to a Saturday night movie. Generally speaking, if the restaurant or the theatre is full, you will decide to go someplace else. So, an important design parameter in services is "What capacity should we aim for?" Too much capacity generates excessive costs. Insufficient capacity leads to lost customers. In these situations, of course, we seek the assistance of marketing. This is one reason we have discount airfares, hotel specials on weekends, and so on. This is also a good illustration of why it is difficult to separate the operations management functions from marketing in services.

Waiting-line models, which are discussed in this chapter's supplement, provide a powerful mathematical tool for analyzing many common service situations. Questions such as how many tellers we should have in a bank or how many computer servers we need in an Internet service operation can be analyzed with these models. These models can be easily implemented using spreadsheets.

Cross Functional

STRUCTURING THE SERVICE ENCOUNTER: SERVICE-SYSTEM DESIGN MATRIX

Service encounters can be configured in a number of different ways. The service-system design matrix in Exhibit 5.4 identifies six common alternatives.

EXHIBIT 5.4	Service-System Design Matrix

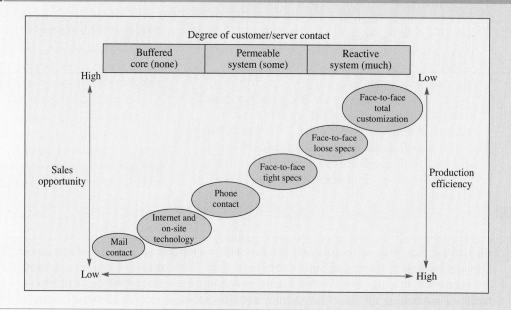

The top of the matrix shows the degree of customer/server contact: the *buffered core,* which is physically separated from the customer; the *permeable system,* which is penetrable by the customer via phone or face-to-face contact; and the *reactive system,* which is both penetrable and reactive to the customer's requirements. The left side of the matrix shows what we believe to be a logical marketing proposition, namely, that the greater the amount of contact, the greater the sales opportunity; the right side shows the impact on production efficiency as the customer exerts more influence on the operation.

The entries within the matrix list the ways in which service can be delivered. At one extreme, service contact is by mail; customers have little interaction with the system. At the other extreme, customers "have it their way" through face-to-face contact. The remaining four entries in the exhibit contain varying degrees of interaction.

As one would guess, production efficiency decreases as the customer has more contact (and therefore more influence) on the system. To offset this, the face-to-face contact provides high sales opportunity to sell additional products. Conversely, low contact, such as mail, allows the system to work more efficiently because the customer is unable to significantly affect (or disrupt) the system. However, there is relatively little opportunity for additional product sales.

There can be some shifting in the positioning of each entry. For our first example, consider the "Internet and on-site technology" entry in the matrix. The Internet clearly buffers the company from the customer, but interesting opportunities are available to provide relevant information and services to the customer. Because the Web site can be programmed to intelligently react to the inputs of the customer, significant opportunities for new sales may be possible. In addition, the system can be made to interface with real employees when the customer needs assistance that goes beyond the programming of the Web site. The Internet is truly a revolutionary technology when applied to the services that need to be provided by a company.

Another example of shifting in the positioning of an entry can be shown with the "face-to-face tight specs" entry in Exhibit 5.4. This entry refers to those situations where there is little variation in the service process—neither customer nor server has much discretion in creating the service. Fast-food restaurants and Disneyland come to mind. Face-to-face loose specs refers to situations where the service process is generally understood but there are options in how it will be performed or in the physical goods that are part of it.

A full-service restaurant and a car sales agency are examples. Face-to-face total customization refers to service encounters whose specifications must be developed through some interaction between the customer and server. Legal and medical services are of this type, and the degree to which the resources of the system are mustered for the service determines whether the system is reactive, possibly to the point of even being proactive, or merely permeable. Examples would be the mobilization of an advertising firm's resources in preparation for an office visit by a major client, or an operating team scrambling to prepare for emergency surgery.

As the degree of customer/service system contact changes, worker requirements differ. For example, if the interaction is restricted to mail contact then clerical skills might be sufficient. For Internet technology and phone contact, helping skills and verbal skills might be the primary requirements respectively. Face-to-face tight specs require procedural skills in particular, because the worker must follow the routine in conducting a generally standardized, high-volume process. Face-to-face loose specs frequently call for trade skills (bank teller, draftsperson, maître d', dental hygienist) to finalize the design for the service. Face-to-face total customization tends to call for the professional's diagnostic skills to ascertain the needs or desires of the client.

ASSEMBLY-LINE DESIGN

Though assembly lines are often associated with manufacturing layout design, they are equally applicable in service design. For example, your cafeteria, where you move along with a tray and pick up meal items (or they get served to you on your tray), is an example of a service assembly line. The most common assembly line is a moving conveyor that passes a series of workstations in a uniform time interval called the **workstation cycle time** (which is also the time between successive units coming off the end of the line). At each workstation, work is performed on a product either by adding parts or by completing assembly operations. The work performed at each station is made up of many bits of work, termed *tasks*.

The total work to be performed at a workstation is equal to the sum of the tasks assigned to that workstation. The **assembly-line balancing** problem is one of assigning all tasks to a series of workstations so that each workstation has no more work than can be done in the work-station cycle time, and the unassigned (that is, idle) time across all workstations is minimized. The problem is complicated by the relationships among tasks imposed by product design and process technologies. This is called the **precedence relationship**, which specifies the order in which tasks must be performed in the assembly process.

Operations and Supply Management in Practice

What's It Like Working on an Assembly Line?

Ben Hamper, the infamous "Rivethead" working for General Motors, describes his new job on the Chevy Suburban assembly line:

The whistle blew and the Rivet Line began to crawl. I took a seat up on the workbench and watched the guy I was re-placing tackle his duties. He'd grab one end of a long rail and, with the help of the worker up the line from him, flip it over on its back. CLAAAANNNNNNGGGG! He then raced back to the bench and grabbed a four-wheel-drive spring casting and a muffler hanger. He would rivet the pieces onto the rail. With that completed, he'd jostle the rail back into an upright position and grab a cross member off the over-hanging feeder line that curled above the bench. Reaching up with his spare arm, he'd grab a different rivet gun while fidgeting to get the cross member firmly planted so that it

aligned with the proper set of holes. He then inserted the rivets and began squashing the cross member into place. Just watching this guy go at it made my head hurt.

"How about takin' a stab at it?" the guy asked me after a while. "You're not gonna get the feel of the job sittin' up there on the bench."

I politely declined. I didn't want to learn any portion of this monster maze before it was absolutely necessary. Once the bossman thought you had a reasonable grasp of the setup, he was likely to step in and turn you loose on your own. I needed to keep delaying in order to give Art some time to reel me back up to Cab Shop.

"Well, you've got three days," the guy replied. "After that, this baby's all yours."

■ Source: Excerpt from B. Hamper's *Rivethead: Tales from the Assembly Line* (New York: Warner Books, 1992), p. 90.

Interactive Operations Management

The steps in balancing an assembly line are straightforward:

1. Specify the sequential relationships among tasks using a precedence diagram. The diagram consists of circles and arrows. Circles represent individual tasks; arrows indicate the order of task performance.
2. Determine the required workstation cycle time (C), using the formula

$$C = \frac{\text{Production time per day}}{\text{Required output per day (in units)}}$$

3. Determine the theoretical minimum number of workstations (N_t) required to satisfy the workstation cycle time constraint using the formula (note that this must be rounded up to the next highest integer)

$$N_t = \frac{\text{Sum of all task times } (T)}{\text{Cycle time } (C)}$$

4. Select a primary rule by which tasks are to be assigned to workstations, and a secondary rule to break ties.
5. Assign tasks, one at a time, to the first workstation until the sum of the task times is equal to the workstation cycle time, or no other tasks are feasible because of time or sequence restrictions. Repeat the process for Workstation 2, Workstation 3, and so on until all tasks are assigned.
6. Evaluate the efficiency of the balance derived using the formula

$$\text{Efficiency} = \frac{\text{Sum of all task times } (T)}{\text{Actual number of workstations } (N_a) \times \text{Workstation cycle time } (C)}$$

7. If efficiency is unsatisfactory, rebalance using a different decision rule.

EXAMPLE 5.2: ASSEMBLY-LINE BALANCING

The Model J Wagon is to be assembled on a conveyor belt. Five hundred wagons are required per day. Production time per day is 420 minutes, and the assembly steps and times for the wagon are given in Exhibit 5.5. Assignment: Find the balance that minimizes the number of workstations, subject to cycle time and precedence constraints.

Assembly Steps and Times for Model J Wagon   EXHIBIT 5.5

TASK	TASK TIME (IN SECONDS)	DESCRIPTION	TASKS THAT MUST PRECEDE
A	45	Position rear axle support and hand fasten four screws to nuts.	—
B	11	Insert rear axle.	A
C	9	Tighten rear axle support screws to nuts.	B
D	50	Position front axle assembly and hand fasten with four screws to nuts.	—
E	15	Tighten front axle assembly screws.	D
F	12	Position rear wheel #1 and fasten hubcap.	C
G	12	Position rear wheel #2 and fasten hubcap.	C
H	12	Position front wheel #1 and fasten hubcap.	E
I	12	Position front wheel #2 and fasten hubcap.	E
J	8	Position wagon handle shaft on front axle assembly and hand fasten bolt and nut.	F, G, H, I
K	<u>9</u> 195	Tighten bolt and nut.	J

SOLUTION

1. Draw a precedence diagram. Exhibit 5.6 illustrates the sequential relationships identified in Exhibit 5.4. (The length of the arrows has no meaning.)

Precedence Graph for Model J Wagon   EXHIBIT 5.6

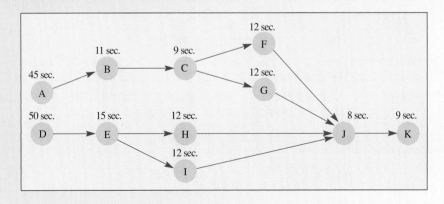

2. Determine workstation cycle time. Here we have to convert to seconds because our task times are in seconds.

$$C = \frac{\text{Production time per day}}{\text{Output per day}} = \frac{60 \text{ sec.} \times 420 \text{ min.}}{500 \text{ wagons}} = \frac{25\,200}{500} = 50.4$$

3. Determine the theoretical minimum number of workstations required (the actual number may be greater):

$$N_t = \frac{T}{C} = \frac{195 \text{ seconds}}{50.4 \text{ seconds}} = 3.87 = 4 \text{ (rounded up)}$$

EXHIBIT 5.7	Assembly Line Design for Model J Wagon

A. Balance Made According to Largest-Number-of-Following-Tasks Rule

	TASK	TASK TIME (IN SECONDS)	REMAINING UNASSIGNED TIME (IN SECONDS)	FEASIBLE REMAINING TASKS	TASK WITH MOST FOLLOWERS	TASK WITH LONGEST OPERATION TIME
Station 1	A	45	5.4 idle	None		
Station 2	D	50	0.4 idle	None		
Station 3	B	11	39.4	C, E	C, E	E
	E	15	24.4	C, H, I	C	
	C	9	15.4	F, G, H, I	F, G, H, I	F, G, H, I
	F*	12	3.4 idle	None		
Station 4	G	12	38.4	H, I	H, I	H, I
	H*	12	26.4	I		
	I	12	14.4	J		
	J	8	6.4 idle	None		
Station 5	K	9	41.4 idle	None		

*Denotes task arbitrarily selected where there is a tie between longest operation times.

B. Precedence Graph for Model J Wagon

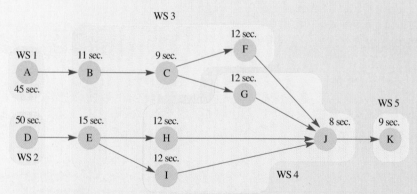

C. Efficiency Calculation

$$\text{Efficiency} = \frac{T}{N_a C} = \frac{195}{(5)(50.4)} = 0.77, \text{ or } 77\%$$

4. Select assignment rules. Research has demonstrated that some rules are better than others for certain problem structures. In general, the strategy is to use a rule assigning tasks that either have many followers or are of long duration because they effectively limit the balance achievable. In this case, we use the following as our primary rule:

   a. Prioritize tasks in order of the largest number of following tasks.

TASK	NUMBER OF FOLLOWING TASKS
A	6
B or D	5
C or E	4
F, G, H, or I	2
J	1
K	0

   Our secondary rule, to be invoked where ties exist from our primary rule, is

   b. Prioritize tasks in order of longest task time (shown in Exhibit 5.7). Note that D should be assigned before B, and E assigned before C due to this tiebreaking rule.

5. Make task assignments to form Workstation 1, Workstation 2, and so forth until all tasks are assigned. The actual assignment is given in Exhibit 5.7A and is shown graphically in Exhibit 5.7B. It is important to meet precedence and cycle time requirements as the assignments are made.

6. Calculate the efficiency. This is shown in Exhibit 5.7C.

7. Evaluate the solution. An efficiency of 77 percent indicates an imbalance or idle time of 23 percent (1.0–0.77) across the entire line. From Exhibit 5.7A we can see that there are 57 total seconds of idle time, and the "choice" job is at Workstation 5. Is a better balance possible? In this case, yes. Try balancing the line with rule *b* and breaking ties with rule *a*. (This will give you a feasible four-station balance.)

Possible Physical Layout of an Assembly Line   EXHIBIT 5.8

WS 1	WS 2	WS 3	WS 4	WS 5
Task A	Task D	Tasks B, E, C, F	Tasks G, H, I, J	Task K
45 sec	50 sec	47 sec	44 sec	9 sec

   Note that the diagram in Exhibit 5.7B is only a schematic showing the assignment of task to stations and the precedence. It is not the actual physical layout. An example of the actual physical layout is seen in Exhibit 5.8 where each station might be an area of the factory floor along a line with a conveyor belt moving the vehicle from station to station. Each workstation might have one or more employees. Assuming that there is only one employee at each station, it means that the employee at station 1 does task A when the wagon reaches the station area. The wagon then moves on to the station 2 area where another employee does task D. Then the vehicle moves to the station 3 area where another employee does tasks B, C, E and F. From station 3 it moves on to station 4 and then to station 5 where the completed vehicle leaves the line. Because of the absence of precedence relationships, the tasks at stations 1 and 2 can be interchanged. The work at stations

1 and 2 have to be completed before the tasks B and E at station 3 can start, due to precedence requirements. Also note that as soon as one vehicle moves from the station, another vehicle takes its place. So multiple vehicles are worked on simultaneously. Other possible physical layouts are shown in Exhibit 5.9

Splitting Tasks

Often the longest required task time forms the shortest workstation cycle time for the production line. This task time is the lower time bound unless it is possible to split the task into two or more workstations.

Consider the following illustration: Suppose that an assembly line contains the following task times in seconds: 40, 30, 15, 25, 20, 18, 15. The line runs for $7\frac{1}{2}$ hours per day and demand for output is 750 per day.

The workstation cycle time required to produce 750 per day is 36 seconds ($[7\frac{1}{2}$ hours $\times$ 60 minutes $\times$ 60 seconds]/750). Our problem is that we have one task that takes 40 seconds. How do we deal with this task?

There are several ways that we may be able to accommodate the 40-second task in a 36-second cycle. Possibilities are

1. **Split the task.** Can we split the task so that complete units are processed in two workstations?
2. **Share the task.** Can the task somehow be shared so an adjacent workstation does part of the work? This differs from the split task in the first option because the adjacent station acts to assist, not to do some units containing the entire task.
3. **Use parallel workstations.** It may be necessary to assign the task to two work stations that would operate in parallel.
4. **Use a more skilled worker.** Because this task exceeds the workstation cycle time by just 11 percent, a faster worker may be able to meet the 36-second time.
5. **Work overtime.** Producing at a rate of one every 40 seconds would create 675 per day, 75 short of the needed 750. The amount of overtime required to produce the additional 75 is 50 minutes (75 $\times$ 40 seconds/60 seconds).
6. **Redesign.** It may be possible to redesign the product to reduce the task time slightly.

Other possibilities to reduce the task time include an equipment upgrade, a roaming helper to support the line, a change of materials, and multiskilled workers to operate the line as a team rather than as independent workers.

Flexible and U-Shaped Line Layouts

As we saw in the preceding example, assembly-line balances frequently result in unequal workstation times. Flexible line layouts such as those shown in Exhibit 5.9 are a common way of dealing with this problem.

Mixed-Model Line Balancing

This approach is used by JIT manufacturers such as Toyota. Its objective is to meet the demand for a variety of products and to avoid building high inventories. Mixed-model line balancing involves scheduling several different models to be produced over a given day or week on the same line in a cyclical fashion. The Toyota system is discussed in more detail in "Lean Manufacturing" (Chapter 10).

Flexible Line Layouts   **EXHIBIT 5.9**

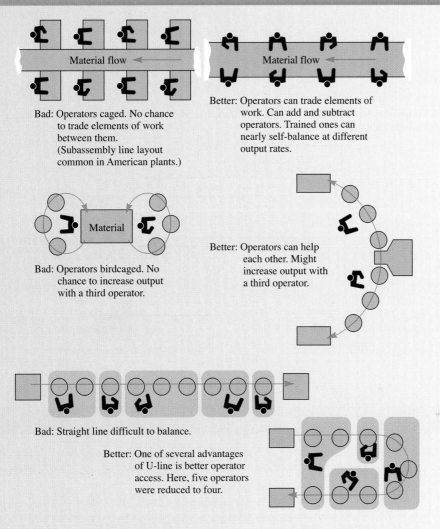

Bad: Operators caged. No chance
to trade elements of work
between them.
(Subassembly line layout
common in American plants.)

Better: Operators can trade elements of
work. Can add and subtract
operators. Trained ones can
nearly self-balance at different
output rates.

Bad: Operators birdcaged. No
chance to increase output
with a third operator.

Better: Operators can help
each other. Might
increase output with
a third operator.

Bad: Straight line difficult to balance.

Better: One of several advantages
of U-line is better operator
access. Here, five operators
were reduced to four.

Source: R. W. Hall, *Attaining Manufacturing Excellence*? (Homewood, IL: Dow Jones-Irwin, 1987), p. 125. Copyright
© 1987 McGraw-Hill Companies Inc.

EXAMPLE 5.3:   MIXED-MODEL LINE BALANCING

To illustrate how this is done, suppose our toy company has a fabrication line to bore holes in its
Model J wagon frame and its Model K wagon frame. The time required to bore the holes is different for each wagon type.

Assume that the final assembly line downstream requires equal numbers of Model J and Model K
wagon frames. Assume also that we want to develop a cycle time for the fabrication line that is
balanced for the production of equal numbers of J and K frames. Of course, we could produce Model J
frames for several days and then produce Model K frames until an equal number of frames have been
produced. However, this would build up unnecessary work-in-process inventory.

If we want to reduce the amount of in-process inventory, we could develop a cycle mix that greatly reduces inventory buildup while keeping within the restrictions of equal numbers of J and K wagon frames.

Process times: 6 minutes per J and 4 minutes per K.
The day consists of 480 minutes (8 hours × 60 minutes).

SOLUTION

6J + 4K = 480

Because equal numbers of J and K are to be produced (or J = K), produce 48J and 48K per day, or 6J and 6K per hour.

The following shows one balance of J and K frames.

Balanced Mixed-Model Sequence

Model sequence	J J	K K K	J J	J J	K K K	
Operation time	6 6	4 4 4	6 6	6 6	4 4 4	Repeats 8 times per day
Minicycle time	12	12	12	12	12	
Total cycle time			60			

This line is balanced at 6 frames of each type per hour with a minicycle time of 12 minutes.

Another balance is J K K J K J, with times of 6, 4, 4, 6, 4, 6. This balance produces 3J and 3K every 30 minutes with a minicycle time of 10 minutes (JK, KJ, KJ).

Operations and Supply Management in Practice

Improved Layouts Help any Facility— Manufacturing, Distribution, or Service

Spartan Plastics is a London, Ontario-based, medium-sized company that extrudes plastic parts primarily for the auto industry. The company realized that its inefficient warehouse layout resulted in employees walking more than 500 km every year to fill orders. Furthermore, an ABC analysis (described in Chapter 13) revealed that the top twenty items alone generated 40 percent of all sales. Previously, the warehouse shelves had been organized by item serial number, so that items could be located easily The company rearranged the warehouse by placing the most popular items closest to the packing and shipping area, at eye level and within arm's reach. Less popular items were placed farther away from the packing area. Finally, the shelf location was computerized. As a result of all these layout changes, walking time was reduced. Spartan also reorganized its manufacturing lines, which resulted in increased flexibility and vastly shorter completion times. This included removing in-process inventory, moving machines closer to each other, and making the machines easily movable by installing wheels.

When investment dealer CIBC Wood Gundy moved to its new facility in BCE Place in Toronto, the new layout design had to incorporate many considerations. In addition to the data and communication cabling, the new trading floor had to accommodate the needs of traders, support staff, offices, and meeting rooms. For example, to help communicate verbally, dealers were located near employees whose work was most closely related to theirs. Says Don Gibson, vice-president of office services at Wood Gundy, "I have done about a dozen trading floors here in Canada, and this is the first time there has been no negative feedback from *anybody*."

■ Sources: Narendar Sumukadas and Chris Piper, *Spartan Plastics* (London, Ontario: University of Western Ontario, Ivey Management Services, 1997).
Patricia Fernberg, "Focus on Facilities: Wood Gundy BCE Place," *Modern Office Technology* (March 1991), pp. 53–54.

The simplicity of mixed-model balancing (under conditions of a level production schedule) is seen in Yasuhiro Mondon's description of Toyota Motor Corporation's operations:

> Final assembly lines of Toyota are mixed product lines. The production per day is averaged by taking the number of vehicles in the monthly production schedule classified by specifications, and dividing by the number of working days.
>
> In regard to the production sequence during each day, the cycle time of each different specification vehicle is calculated. To have all specification vehicles appear at their own cycle time, different specification vehicles are ordered to follow each other.

WORKCENTRE (PROCESS) LAYOUT DESIGN

Unlike assembly lines, where the equipment is laid out according the flow of material, in workcentres the facility is laid out by placing similar equipment together. The reason is that there no standardized material flow, as in assembly lines. Consider a clinic, shown in Exhibit 5.10 with five departments, radiology, pharmacy, examination offices, and the like. The different coloured arrows represent a sample of the flow of different patients. For example, one patient (blue arrow) starts in department B (perhaps an examination) then proceeds to department D (perhaps pharmacy), and finally to department E before departing the clinic. The other patients have very different paths. Thus, it is difficult to design this facility like an assembly line because there is no "standard patient" flow. Typically, a department consists of similar equipment or personnel. So, in a hospital, one department may consist of the cardiologists all located in the same physical area, and another department may have all the neurologists. All the equipment related to radiology may be in one department.

The issue then is to decide which departments should be physically close to each other to reduce travel distances. In Exhibit 5.10, why are departments A and B next to each other while departments A and C are not? Perhaps department A is the orthopaedic department and department B is the radiology department. Since patients seen by orthopaedic surgeons often need x-ray analysis, it is logical to locate these two departments close to each other to minimize patient and service provider travel. Department C may consist of cardiologists who do not interact much with orthopaedic surgeons and so need not be close to them. A factory producing customized products is similar, except that the patient flow would be replaced by material flow and clinic personnel would be replaced by factory employees and machines (see Exhibit 5.3a). Given flow data between each pair of departments and an existing layout, the following are the steps to designing an optimal workcentre layout.

1. Determine the annual cost of flow between each pair of departments.
   Annual cost of flow between each pair of departments = Material handling cost per unit load per unit distance × Distance between department pair × Number of loads moved between department pair
2. Determine the annual cost of flow for the layout.
   Annual cost of flow for the layout = Sum of the annual costs of flow between each pair of departments
3. Find a layout with lower annual cost of flow
4. Repeat steps 1 though 3 until no cost improvements can be made

EXHIBIT 5.10   Workcentre Layout for a Clinic

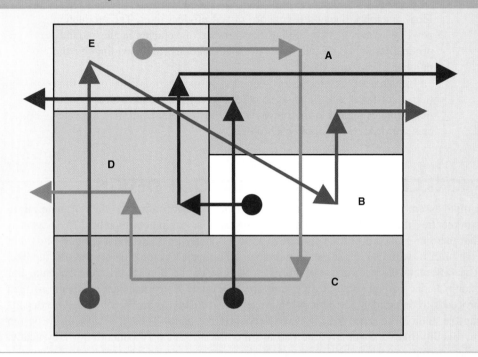

EXAMPLE 5.4:   WORKCENTRE LAYOUT DESIGN

The factory of a Fort McMurray manufacturer of customized oil field equipment has six departments. Since the products are customized, there is no "standard product." Based on historical material flow, the company has prepared a from–to (trip or flow) matrix in Exhibit 5.11. This matrix shows the annual material flow between each pair of departments.

For example, historically, in each period, 140 loads of material have moved from department 1 to 6. A "load" could be a forklift load, 100 kg, or any appropriate measure. Exhibit 5.12 shows the current layout (also called a block plan)

EXHIBIT 5.11   Flow Matrix

FROM/TO	1	2	3	4	5	6
1	—					140
2	40	—			90	
3		20	—	30		40
4	40			—	80	
5		60		60	—	
6	20		140			

EXHIBIT 5.12

2	4	3
6	5	1

4m ←5m→

This means that department 2 is located at the top left corner of the facility, department 6 is at the bottom left corner, and so on. Each department is 5 m long (horizontally) and 4 m wide (vertically). This means that the distance between the centres of each department is 5 m horizontally and 4 m vertically. We will design a better layout that reduces the interdepartmental movement cost. Assume that the cost to transport one load (unit load) a distance of 1 m (unit distance) is $1.

SOLUTION

1. Determine the annual cost of flow between each pair of departments.

Annual cost of flow between each pair of departments = Material handling cost per unit load per unit distance × Distance between department pair × Number of loads moved between department pair

The data required for this can be found in Exhibits 5.11 and 5.12. For example, the annual cost of moving material between departments 4 and 5 in both directions is given by

$$\$1 \times 4m \times (80+60) \text{ loads} = \$560$$

Note that the distances are measured rectilinearly, i.e., we cannot move diagonally across a department, only horizontally or vertically. Similarly, the annual cost of moving material between departments 6 and 3 (using the aisle via departments 2 and 4 or 5 and 1) is given by:

$$\$1 \times (5+5+4)m \times (140+40) \text{ loads} = \$2520$$

Exhibit 5.13 shows the annual cost of flow between each pair of departments

2. Determine the annual cost of flow for the layout.

Annual cost of flow for the layout = Sum of the annual costs of flow between each pair of departments

Here the flow cost of each pair of departments calculated in Step 1 is added to obtain the total cost of the layout. As seen in Exhibit 5.13, the annual cost of flow in the layout is $7300.

3. Find a layout with the lower annual cost of flow.

There are many methods to do this. But for layouts with many departments, it is difficult to determine mathematically the layout with the lowest flow cost. For example, in a six-department problem there are 6! (or 720) possible layout arrangements. A fifteen-department problem would have 15! possible arrangements—a very large number (you can determine this using your calculator). So it is not possible to find the best possible workcentre layout in many practical situations. Therefore, to solve this problem we will use a method similar to one called Computerized Relative Allocation of Facilities Technique (CRAFT),[1] which performs intelligent pairwise exchanges of departments and locations. Many other types of algorithms are also available to solve the

EXHIBIT 5.13	Initial Costs of Flow in Layout

DEPARTMENTS FROM/TO	DISTANCE (M)	FLOW	COST ($)
2-5	9	150	1350
4-5	4	140	560
4-3	5	30	150
4-1	9	40	360
2-3	10	20	200
2-1	14	40	560
6-1	10	160	1600
6-3	14	180	2520
Total Layout Cost			7300

workcentre layout problem. CRAFT attempts to find a good solution, but not necessarily the lowest cost solution. CRAFT involves switching pairs of departments intelligently to examine whether the cost can be reduced. How does this work? Consider the costs in Exhibit 5.13. Note in Step 1 that the flow cost between each department pair depends on the flow between them as well as the distance. In Exhibit 5.11 we see that interdepartmental flows between departments 6 and 3 (both ways) totals 180—quite high. Yet we see that these departments are diagonally at opposite ends of the layout. Thus, each of the 180 loads between departments 6 and 3 has to travel 14 m, resulting in a cost of $2520 in Exhibit 5.13. At the same time, the flow between department 3 and its neighbour, department 1, is 0. Thus, from a flow cost perspective it might make more sense to switch departments 6 and 1. Exhibit 5.14 shows the proposed layout with the switch and Exhibit 5.15 shows the reduction in cost.

EXHIBIT 5.14	Revised Block Plan

As seen in Exhibit 5.15, the costs of flow between department pairs 6-3, and 2-1 have been reduced by $1800 and $400, respectively, resulting in a total cost reduction of $2200.

4. Find the optimal layout by repeating steps 1 through 3.

Of course, there are many other possible department switches, and for most practical size layouts, we would need a computer to do all the calculations. Methods such as CRAFT do pairwise switches as long as the switch decreases costs. As mentioned earlier, there is no guarantee that the solution generated by CRAFT will be the lowest cost one. In the example shown here, however, since there are only 720 possibilities, each was evaluated using a computer. Exhibit 5.16 shows the lowest cost layout, with a flow cost of $3610.[2]

While we considered only the cost of material flow, qualitative considerations such as locating a painting department far away from clerical offices for health and safety can be included by using other types of workcentre design methods.

Improved Costs of Flow in Layout

EXHIBIT 5.15

DEPARTMENTS FROM/TO	DISTANCE (M)	FLOW	COST ($)
2-5	9	150	1350
4-5	4	140	560
4-3	5	30	150
4-1	9	40	360
2-3	10	20	200
2-1	4	40	160
6-1	10	160	1600
6-3	4	180	720
Total Layout Cost			5100

Optimal Layout

EXHIBIT 5.16

Summary

Designing a customer-pleasing product is an art. Building that product is a science. Moving the product from design to the customer is management. World-class manufacturers excel in the speedy and flexible integration of these processes. Effective manufacturing process design requires a clear understanding of what the factory can and cannot do relative to process structures. Many plants use a combination of the layouts identified in this chapter: workcentres for some parts, assembly operations for others. Frequently, a choice exists as to when demand seems likely to favour a switch from one to the other. Making such decisions also requires understanding the nuances of each process choice to determine whether the process really fits new product specifications.

Service businesses are in many ways very similar to manufacturing businesses. In both types of businesses, there is a need to make trade-offs in developing a focus. Just as in manufacturing, a service business cannot be all things to all people. The service-system design matrix is in many ways similar to the product–process matrix we used to categorize manufacturing operations. Services are, however, very different from manufacturing when we consider the high degree of personalization often required, the speed of delivery needed, the direct customer contact, and the inherent variability of service encounters. The buffering and scheduling mechanisms that we have available to smooth the demand placed on a manufacturing operation is often not available to a service operation. Services generally require much higher levels of capacity relative to demand. In addition, they impose a greater need for flexibility on the workers involved in providing the services.

Assembly line balancing methods and workcentre layout optimization methods are useful in designing effective layouts for both manufacturing and service processes.

Key Terms

Assembly line   A process structure designed to make discrete parts. Parts are moved through a set of specially designed workstations at a controlled rate.

Assembly-line balancing   The problem of assigning all the tasks to a series of workstations so that each workstation has no more than can be done in the workstation cycle time and so that idle time across all workstations is minimized.

Continuous process   An often automated process that converts raw materials into a finished product in one continuous process.

High and low degree of customer contact   The physical presence of the customer in the system and the percentage of time the customer must be in the system relative to the total time it takes to perform the service

Manufacturing cell   An area where items that are similar in processing requirements are produced.

Project layout   The product, because of its sheer bulk or weight, remains fixed in a location. Equipment is moved to the product rather than vice versa.

Product–process matrix   Shows the relationships between different production units and how they are used depending on product volume and the degree of product standardization.

Precedence relationship   The order in which tasks must be performed in the assembly process.

Workcentre   A process structure suited for low-volume production of a great variety of nonstandard products. Workcentres sometimes are referred to as departments and are focused on a particular type of operation

Workstation cycle time   The time between successive units coming off the end of an assembly line.

Solved Problems

Solved Problem 1

A company is considering adding a new feature that will increase unit sales by 6 percent and product cost by 10 percent. Profit is expected to increase by 16 percent of the increased sales. Initially the product cost incurred by the company was 63 percent of the sales price. Should the new feature be added?

SOLUTION

Let the sales be $100 M.

Sales increase by 6% = $100 M × 6% = $6 M.

Benefits: Profits increase by 16% of the increased sales = $6 M × 16% = $0.96 M.
Cost: Increase product cost by 10% = ($100 M × 63%) × 10% = $6.3 M.

Because costs exceed benefits, the new feature should not be added.

Solved Problem 2

An automobile manufacturer is considering a change in an assembly line that should save money due to a reduction in labour and material cost. The change involves the installation of four new robots that will automatically install windshields. The cost of the four robots, including installation and initial programming, is $400 000. Current practice is to amortize the initial cost of the robots over two years on a straight-line basis. The process engineer estimates that one full-time technician will be needed to monitor, maintain, and reprogram the robots on an ongoing basis. This person will cost approximately $60 000 per year. Currently, the company uses four full-time employees on this job and each makes about $52 000 per year. One of these employees is a material handler, and this person will still be needed with the new process. To complicate matters, the process engineer estimates that the robots will apply the windshield sealing material in a manner that will result in a savings of $0.25 per windshield installed. How many automobiles need to be produced over the next two years to make the new robots an attractive investment? Due to the relatively short horizon, do not consider the time value of money.

Cost of the current process over the next two years is just the cost of the four full-time employees.

$$\$52\,000/\text{employee} \times 4 \text{ employees} \times 2 \text{ years} = \$416\,000$$

The cost of the new process over the next two years, assuming the robot is completely costed over that time, is the following:

$$(\$52\,000/\text{material handler} + \$60\,000/\text{technician}) \times 2 + \$400\,000/\text{robots} - \$0.25 \times \text{autos}$$

Equating the two alternatives:

$$\$416\,000 = \$624\,000 - \$0.25 \times \text{autos}$$

Solving for the break-even point:

$$-\$208\,000/-\$0.25 = 832\,000 \text{ autos}$$

This indicates that to break even, 832 000 autos would need to be produced with the robots over the next two years.

Solved Problem 3

The following tasks must be performed on an assembly line in the sequence and times specified:

TASK	TASK TIME (SECONDS)	TASKS THAT MUST PRECEDE
A	50	—
B	40	—
C	20	A
D	45	C
E	20	C
F	25	D
G	10	E
H	35	B, F, G

a. Draw the schematic diagram.

b. What is the theoretical minimum number of stations required to meet a forecast demand of 400 units per eight-hour day?

c. Use the longest-task-time rule and balance the line in the minimum number of stations to produce 400 units per day.

a.

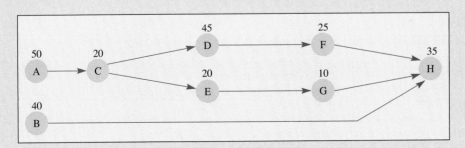

b. The theoretical minimum number of stations to meet $D = 400$ is

$$N_t = \frac{T}{C} = \frac{245 \text{ seconds}}{\left(\dfrac{60 \text{ seconds} \times 480 \text{ minutes}}{400 \text{ units}}\right)} = \frac{245}{72} = 3.4 \text{ stations}$$

c.

	TASK	TASK TIME (SECONDS)	REMAINING UNASSIGNED TIME	FEASIBLE REMAINING TASK
Station 1	A	50	22	C
	C	20	2	None
Station 2	D	45	27	E, F
	F	25	2	None
Station 3	B	40	32	E
	E	20	12	G
	G	10	2	None
Station 4	H	35	37	None

Solved Problem 4

The manufacturing engineers at Suny Manufacturing were working on a new remote controlled toy Monster Truck. They hired a production consultant to help them determine the best type of production process to meet the forecasted demand for this new product. The consultant recommended that they use an assembly line. He told the manufacturing engineers that the line must be able to produce 600 Monster Trucks per day to meet the demand forecast. The workers in the plant work eight hours per day. The task information for the new monster truck is given below:

TASK	TASK TIME (SECONDS)	TASK THAT MUST PRECEDE
A	28	—
B	13	—
C	35	B
D	11	A
E	20	C
F	6	D,E
G	23	F
H	25	F
I	37	G
J	11	G,H
K	27	I,J
Total	236	

a. Draw the schematic diagram.
b. What is the required cycle time to meet the forecasted demand of 600 trucks per day based on an eight-hour work day?
c. What is the theoretical minimum number of workstations given the answer in part b?
d. Use longest task time with alphabetical order as the tie breaker and balance the line in the minimum number of stations to produce 600 trucks per day.
e. Use the largest number of following tasks and as a tie breaker use the shortest task time, to balance the line in the minimum number of stations to produce 600 trucks per day.

SOLUTION

a.

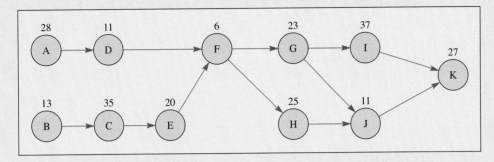

b. $C = \dfrac{\text{Production time per day}}{\text{Output per day}} = \dfrac{60 \text{ seconds} \times 480 \text{ minutes}}{600 \text{ trucks}} = \dfrac{28\,800}{600} = 48 \text{ seconds}$

c. $N_t = \dfrac{T}{C} = \dfrac{236 \text{ seconds}}{48 \text{ seconds}} = 4.92 = 5 \text{ (rounded up)}$

d.

	FEASIBLE TASKS	TASK	TASK TIME (SECONDS)	REMAINING UNASSIGNED TIME
Station 1	A, B	A	28	20
	B, D	B	13	7
Station 2	C, D	C	35	13
	D	D	11	2
Station 3	E	E	20	28
	F	F	6	22
Station 4	G, H	G	23	25
	H, I	H	25	0
Station 5	I, J	I	37	11
	J	J	11	0
Station 6	K	K	27	21

e. Solution same as above.

Solved Problem 5[3]

A university advising office has four rooms, each dedicated to specific problems: petitions (Room A), schedule advising (Room B), grade complaints (Room C), and student counselling (Room D). The office is 40 m long and 10 m wide. Each room is 10 m by 10 m. The present location of rooms is A, B, C, D; that is, a straight line. The contact summary shows the number of contacts that each advisor in a room has with other advisors in the other rooms. Assume that all advisors are equal in this value.

Contact summary: AB = 10, AC = 20, AD = 30.
BC = 15, BD = 10, CD = 20.

a. Evaluate this workcentre layout.
b. Improve the layout by exchanging functions within rooms. Show your amount of improvement using the same method as in *a*.

SOLUTION

a. Evaluate this workcentre layout.

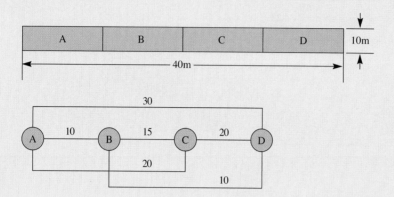

Using the material handling cost method shown in Example 5.4, we obtain the following costs, assuming $1 per contact between adjacent rooms and an additional $1 per contact for each room in between.

$$AB = 10 \times 1 = 10$$
$$AC = 20 \times 2 = 40$$
$$AD = 30 \times 3 = 90$$
$$BC = 15 \times 1 = 15$$
$$BD = 10 \times 2 = 20$$
$$CD = 20 \times 1 = 20$$
$$\text{Current cost} = 195$$

b. Improve the layout by exchanging functions within rooms. Show your amount of improvement using the same method as in *a.* A better layout would be either BCDA or ADCB.

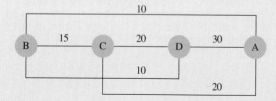

$$AB = 10 \times 3 = \$30$$
$$AC = 20 \times 2 = 40$$
$$AD = 30 \times 1 = 30$$
$$BC = 15 \times 1 = 15$$
$$BD = 10 \times 2 = 20$$
$$CD = 20 \times 1 = 20$$
$$\text{Improved cost} = \$155$$

Review and Discussion Questions

1. What kind of layout is used in a physical fitness centre?
2. What is the objective of assembly-line balancing? How would you deal with a situation in which one worker, although trying hard, is 20 percent slower than the other 10 people on a line?
3. How do you determine the idle time percentage from a specific assembly-line balance?
4. What is the essential requirement for mixed-model lines to be practical?
5. Why might it be difficult to develop a manufacturing cell?
6. How would you characterize the most important difference for the following issues when comparing a facility organized with workcentres versus a continuous process?

ISSUE	WORKCENTRES	CONTINUOUS PROCESS
Number of changeovers		
Labour content of product		
Flexibility		

7. A certain custom engraving shop has traditionally had orders for between 1 and 50 units of whatever a customer orders. A large company has contacted this shop about engraving "reward" plaques (which are essentially identical to each other). It wants the shop to place a bid for this order. The expected volume is 12 000 units per year and will most likely last four years. To successfully bid (low enough price) for such an order, what will the shop likely have to do?

8. The product–process matrix is a convenient way of characterizing the relationship between product volumes (one-of-a-kind to continuous) and the processing system employed by a firm at a particular location. In the boxes presented below, describe the nature of the intersection between the type of shop (column) and process dimension (row).

	WORKCENTRES	CONTINUOUS PROCESS
Engineering emphasis		
General workforce skill		
Statistical process control		
Facility layout		
WIP inventory level		

9. For each of the following variables, explain the differences (in general) as one moves from a workcentre process to a continuous process environment.
   a. Throughput time (time to convert raw material into product).
   b. Capital/labour intensity.
   c. Bottlenecks.

Problems

1. Kulwinder, a book publisher, has fixed costs of $300 000 and variable costs of $8.00 per book. The book sells for $23.00 per copy.
   a. How many books must be sold to break even?
   b. If the fixed cost increased, would the new break-even point be higher or lower?
   c. If the variable cost per unit decreased, would the new break-even point be higher or lower?

2. A manufacturing process has a fixed cost of $150 000 per month. Each unit of product being produced contains $25 worth of material and takes $45 of labor. How many units are needed to break even if each completed unit has a value of $90?

3. Assume a fixed cost of $900, a variable cost of $4.50, and a selling price of $5.50.
   a. What is the break-even point?
   b. How many units must be sold to make a profit of $500.00?
   c. How many units must be sold to average $0.25 profit per unit? $0.50 profit per unit? $1.50 profit per unit?

4. Pablo DeSouza drives his own car on company business. His employer reimburses him for such travel at the rate of 36 cents per km. Aldo estimates that his fixed costs per year such as taxes, insurance, and depreciation are $2052. The direct or variable costs such as gas, oil, and maintenance average about 14.4 cents per km. How many kilometres must he drive to break even?

5. A firm is selling two products, chairs and bar stools, each at $50 per unit. Chairs have a variable cost of $25 and bar stools $20. Fixed cost for the firm is $20 000.
   a. If the sales mix is 1:1 (one chair sold for every bar stool sold), what is the break-even point in dollars of sales? In units of chairs and bar stools?
   b. If the sales mix changes to 1:4 (one chair sold for every four bar stools sold), what is the break-even point in dollars of sales? In units of chairs and bar stools?

6. The desired daily output for an assembly line is 360 units. This assembly line will operate 450 minutes per day. The following table contains information on this product's task times and precedence relationships:

TASK	TASK TIME (SECONDS)	IMMEDIATE PREDECESSOR
A	30	—
B	35	A
C	30	A
D	35	B
E	15	C
F	65	C
G	40	E, F
H	25	D, G

a. Draw the precedence diagram.
b. What is the workstation cycle time?
c. Balance this line using the largest number of following tasks. Use the longest task time as a secondary criterion.
d. What is the efficiency of your line balance?

7. Some tasks and the order in which they must be performed according to their assembly requirements are shown in the following table. These are to be combined into workstations to create an assembly line. The assembly line operates $7\frac{1}{2}$ hours per day. The output requirement is 1000 units per day.

TASKS	PRECEDING TASK	TIME (SECONDS)	TASK	PRECEDING TASKS	TIME (SECONDS)
A	—	15	G	C	11
B	A	24	H	D	9
C	A	6	I	E	14
D	B	12	J	F, G	7
E	B	18	K	H, I	15
F	C	7	L	J, K	10

a. What is the workstation cycle time?
b. Balance the line using the longest task time based on the 1000-unit forecast, stating which tasks would be done in each workstation.
c. For b, what is the efficiency of your line balance?
d. After production was started, Marketing realized that they understated demand and must increase output to 1100 units. What action would you take? Be specific in quantitative terms, if appropriate.

8. An assembly line at Bouchard Inc. is to be designed to operate $7\frac{1}{2}$ hours per day and supply a steady demand of 300 units per day. Here are the tasks and their performance times:

TASK	PRECEDING TASKS	PERFORMANCE TIME (SECONDS)	TASK	PRECEDING TASKS	PERFORMANCE TIME (SECONDS)
a	—	70	g	d	60
b	—	40	h	e	50
c	—	45	i	f	15
d	a	10	j	g	25
e	b	30	k	h, i	20
f	c	20	l	j, k	25

a. Draw the precedence diagram.
b. What is the workstation cycle time?
c. What is the theoretical minimum number of workstations?
d. Assign tasks to workstations using the longest operating time.

e. What is the efficiency of your line balance?

f. Suppose demand increases by 10 percent. How would you react to this? Assume that you can operate only $7\frac{1}{2}$ hours per day.

9. The following tasks are to be performed on an assembly line:

TASK	SECONDS	TASKS THAT MUST PRECEDE
A	20	—
B	7	A
C	20	B
D	22	B
E	15	C
F	10	D
G	16	E, F
H	8	G

The workday is seven hours long. Demand for completed product is 750 per day.

a. Find the cycle time.

b. What is the theoretical number of workstations?

c. Draw the precedence diagram.

d. Balance the line using the longest-operating-time rule.

e. What is the efficiency of the line balanced as in *d*?

f. Suppose that demand rose from 750 to 800 units per day. What would you do? Show any amounts or calculations.

g. Suppose that demand rose from 750 to 1000 units per day. What would you do? Show any amounts or calculations.

10. The Larsson firm uses a serial assembly system and needs answers to the following:

a. An output of 900 units per shift (7.5 hours) is desired for a new processing system. The *system* requires product to pass through four stations where the work content at each station is 30 seconds. What is the required cycle time for such a system?

b. How efficient is your system with the cycle time you calculated?

c. Station 3 changes and now requires 45 seconds to complete. What will need to be done to meet demand (assume only 7.5 hours are available)? What is the efficiency of the new system?

11. An initial solution has been given to the following process layout problem. Given the flows described and a transportation cost of $2.00 per unit per metre (m), compute the total cost for the layout. Each location is 100 m long and 50 m wide, as shown on the figure below. Use the centres of departments for distances and compute using rectilinear distances.[4]

Department

	Department			
	A	**B**	**C**	**D**
A	0	10	25	55
B		0	10	5
C			0	15
D				0

```
        100 m  100 m  100 m
50 m  |   A  |   B  |   C  | 50 m
                    |   D  | 50 m
```

12. A Whitehorse Credit Union branch has six departments with a from–to (trip or flow) matrix shown below. Each value represents the number of trips made by office personnel between a pair of departments.

FROM/TO	1	2	3	4	5	6
1. Bank tellers	—					70
2. Bank reps	20	—	35		45	
3. Commercial tellers		10	—	40		10
4. Information desk	20			—	40	
5. Bank manager		30		30	—	90
6. Cash department	10		70			

CURRENT BLOCK PLAN

2	4	3
6	5	1

The distance between the centres of each department is 4 m horizontally and 3 m vertically. Design a better layout that reduces the interdepartmental movement cost. Assume that the trip cost per metre walked is $1.

Advanced Problems

13. Francis Johnson's plant needs to design an efficient assembly line to make a new product. The assembly line needs to produce 15 units per hour and there is room for only four workstations. The tasks and the order in which they must be performed are shown in the following table. Tasks cannot be split, and it would be too expensive to duplicate any task.

TASK	TASK TIME (MINUTES)	IMMEDIATE PREDECESSOR
A	1	—
B	2	—
C	3	—
D	1	A, B, C
E	3	C
F	2	E
G	3	E

a. Draw the precedence diagram.
b. What is the workstation cycle time?
c. Balance the line so that only four workstations are required. Use whatever method you feel is appropriate.
d. What is the efficiency of your line balance?

CASE 1	Designing Toshiba's Notebook Computer Line

Toshihiro Nakamura, manufacturing engineering section manager, examined the prototype assembly process sheet (shown in Exhibit 5.17) for the newest subnotebook computer model. With every new model introduced, management felt that the assembly line had to increase productivity and lower costs, usually resulting in changes to the assembly process.

When a new model was designed, considerable attention was directed toward reducing the number of components and simplifying parts production and assembly requirements. This new computer was a marvel of high-tech, low-cost innovation and should give Toshiba an advantage during the upcoming fall/winter selling season.

A Prototype Assembly Line for the Subnotebook Computer			EXHIBIT 5.17

STATION	OPN. #	TIME (SEC)	DESCRIPTION OF OPERATIONS
1	1	100	Lay out principal components on conveyor
110 sec	2	6	Peel adhesive backing from cover assembly
	3	4	Put screws for Opn 8 in foam tray, place on belt
2	4	50	Scan serial number bar code
114 sec	5	13	Connect LCD cable-1 to LCD-printed circuit board (PCB)
	6	16	Connect LCD cable-1 to LCD display panel
	7	13	Connect LCD cable-2 to LCD-PCB
	8	16	Screw LCD-PCB into cover assembly
	9	6	Put screws for Opns 13, 16 in foam tray on belt
3	10	26	Install LCD display panel in cover assembly
101 sec	11	10	Fold and insulate cables
	12	13	Install LCD frame in cover assembly
	13	23	Screw in frame
	14	6	Place PCB-1 in base assembly
	15	6	Install CPU bracket on PCB-1
	16	13	Screw CPU bracket into base assembly
	17	4	Put screws for Opn 23 in foam tray
4	18	15	Connect ribbon cable to hard disk drive (HDD)
107 sec	19	11	Connect ribbon cable to PCB-1
	20	8	Place insulator sheet on HDD
	21	8	Stack PCB-2 on PCB-1
	22	8	Stack PCB-3 on PCB-1
	23	13	Screw in both PCBs
	24	6	Install condenser microphone in holder
	25	13	Connect microphone cable to PCB-1
	26	8	Tape microphone cable down
	27	13	Connect backup battery to PCB-2 and install in base
	28	4	Put screws for Opn 31 in foam tray
5	29	6	Install support frame on base assembly
103 sec	30	13	Stack PCB-3 on PCB-1
	31	6	Screw in PCB-3
	32	8	Install Accupoint pointing device pressure sensor
	33	11	Connect PCB-5 to PCB-2 and PCB-4
	34	6	Set speaker holder on base
	35	11	Install speaker holder and connect cable to PCB-2
	36	10	Install clock battery on PCB-4

EXHIBIT 5.17   (Continued)

STATION	OPN. #	TIME (SEC)	DESCRIPTION OF OPERATIONS
	37	10	Tape down speaker and battery cable
	38	16	Check voltage of clock battery and backup battery
	39	6	Put screws for Opns 44, 46 in foam tray
6	40	13	Install wrist rest over Accupoint buttons
107 sec	41	6	Connect LCD cable to PCB-1
	42	6	Tape cable down
	43	5	Install keyboard support plate to base
	44	23	Screw in support plate
	45	18	Install keyboard, connect cable and set in base
	46	18	Screw in keyboard
	47	8	Install keyboard mask
	48	10	Place cushion pads on LCD mask
7	49	18	Place protective seal on LCD display
108 sec	50	10	Place brand name seal on LCD mask
	51	11	Place brand name seal on outside of cover
	52	8	Connect cable to DVD drive
	53	33	Install DVD on base
	54	22	Install cover on DVD
	55	6	Put screws for Opns 56, 57 in foam tray
8	56	58	Turn over machine and put screws in base
93 sec	57	8	Put in grounding screw
	58	8	Install connector protective flap
	59	8	Install DVD assembly
	60	6	Install battery cover on battery pack
	61	5	Install battery cover
9	62	31	Insert memory card for hardware test and start software
310 sec	63	208	Software load (does not require operator)
	64	71	Test DVD, LCD, keyboard, and pointer; remove memory
10	65	5	Place unit on shock test platform
105 sec	66	75	Perform shock test
	67	10	Scan bar codes
	68	15	Place unit on rack for burn-in

Adapted from: *Toshiba: Ome Works*, Harvard Business School (9-696-059).

Production of the subnotebook was scheduled to begin in 10 days. Initial production for the new model was to be at 150 units per day, increasing to 250 units per day the following week (management thought that eventually production would reach 300 units per day). Assembly lines at the plant were normally staffed by 10 operators who worked at a 14.4 m-long assembly line. The line could accommodate up to 12 operators if there was a need. The line normally operated for 7.5 hours a day (employees worked from 8:15 a.m. to 5:00 p.m. and regular hours included 1 hour of unpaid lunch and 15 minutes of scheduled breaks). It is possible to run one, two, or three hours of overtime, but employees need at least three days' notice for planning purposes.

The Assembly Line

At the head of the assembly line, a computer displayed the daily production schedule, consisting of a list of model types and corresponding lot sizes scheduled to be assembled on the line. The models were simple variations of hard-disk size, memory, and battery power. A typical production schedule included seven or eight model types in lot sizes varying from 10 to 100 units. The models were assembled sequentially: All the units of the first model were assembled, followed by all the units of the second, and so on. This computer screen also indicated how far along the assembly line was in completing its daily schedule, which served as a guide for the material handlers who supplied parts to the assembly lines.

The daily schedules were shared with the nearby Fujihashi Parts Collection and Distribution Centre. Parts were brought from Fujihashi to the plant within two hours of when they were needed. The material supply system was very tightly coordinated and worked well.

The assembly line consisted of a 14.4-m conveyor belt that carried the computers, separated at 1.2-m intervals by white stripes on the belt. Workers stood shoulder to shoulder on one side of the conveyor and worked on the units as they moved by. In addition to 10 assembly workers, a highly skilled worker, called a "supporter," was assigned to each line. The supporter moved along the line, assisting workers who were falling behind and replacing workers who needed to take a break. Supporters also made decisions about what to do when problems were encountered during the assembly process (such as a defective part). The line speed and the number of workers varied from day to day, depending on production demand and the workers' skills and availability. Although the assembly line was designed for 10 workers, the number of workers could vary between 8 and 12.

Exhibit 5.17 provides details of how the engineers who designed the new subnotebook computer felt that the new line should be organized. These engineers design the line assuming that one notebook is assembled every two minutes by 10 line workers. The following is a brief description of what each operator does:

1. The first operator lays out the major components of a computer between two white lines on the conveyor.
2. The second operator enters the bar codes on those components into a centralized computer system by scanning the bar codes with a hand-held scanning wand. On a shelf above the conveyor, portable computers display the operations that are performed at each station.
3. The next six steps of the assembly process involve a large number of simple operations performed by hand or with simple tools, such as electric screwdrivers. Typical operations involve snapping connectors together or attaching parts with small screws. All tools are hung by a cable above the operators, within easy reach. Although the individual operations are simple, they require manual dexterity and speed.
4. The last two operations are the hardware and shock tests. To prepare for the hardware test, an operator inserts a memory card into the USB port containing software designed to test different components of the computer circuitry. Because it takes nearly four minutes to load the testing software, the cycle time of this operation is longer than the other cycle times on the line. To achieve a lower cycle time for the line, the hardware test is performed in parallel on three different units. The units remain on the moving conveyor, and the tests are staggered so that they can be performed by a single operator. The shock test (the last operation on the assembly line) tests the ability of the computer to withstand vibrations and minor impacts.

The computers are moved to a burn-in area after the assembly line shock test. Here computers are put in racks for a 24-hour 25°C "burn-in" of the circuit components. After burn-in, the computer is tested again, software is installed, and the finished notebook computer is packaged and placed on pallets.

Tweaking the Initial Assembly Line Design

From past experience Toshihiro has found that the initial assembly line design supplied by the engineers often needs to be tweaked. Consider the following questions that Toshihiro is considering:

1. What is the daily capacity of the assembly line designed by the engineers?
2. When it is running at maximum capacity, what is the efficiency of the line?
3. How should the line be redesigned to operate at the target 300 units per day, assuming that no overtime will be used? What is the efficiency of your new design?
4. What other issues might Toshihiro consider when bringing the new assembly line up to speed?

CASE 2 | First Detect: Linking Product Strategy and Process Design

FirstDetect designs and manufactures fire safety monitoring equipment for corporate customers in the North American market. Their equipment can detect a fire less than half a second after ignition through a technology that identifies specific light waves known to be emitted by the ignition of a fire, based on the accelerant involved (natural gas, propane, ammonia, sulphur, hydrogen, etc.). Furthermore, their fire detection equipment can be integrated into a facility's fire suppression system, enabling a fire to be detected and actively suppressed within seconds of ignition. This equipment provides a company with a safer work environment, reduces the probability of fire damage and corresponding production downtime, while also reducing insurance premiums.

With growing demand for such fire detection equipment, new competitors have entered the market in recent years. A market for "standardized" models of this fire detection equipment developed in which suppliers such as FirstDetect manufacture and stock finished models that are most frequently desired by customers. More recently, a competitor from China has aggressively targeted the North American market by offering its version of the standardized models for prices below FirstDetect's production costs for their equivalent model. As a result, FirstDetect's sales have declined steadily, and management is discussing alternative strategies for the new market conditions in which they find themselves.

Currently, FirstDetect manufactures standardized fire detection models in an assembly line process. Employees work exclusively at one of the component machining or final assembly stages (each final assembly line is similar in nature to Exhibit 5.8). Production commences when a shop employee withdraws the required materials from the central stockroom. The fixtures used at the machining stages are old, and dedicated to one product model each. When they want to manufacture a different model, all fixtures must be disassembled and removed, and then the fixtures required for the next model are installed and assembled. Because of the significant set-up, or switchover times, production scheduling staff consolidate common customer orders as much as possible before providing a bulk production order to the shop. Furthermore, production scheduling often bumps up the quantity on the production order if customer demand quantity is deemed too low. Although this helps to spread out the set-up costs over a higher volume, FirstDetect then has finished goods inventory, and must trust that another customer eventually will order that model. First-Detect also has a work-in-process inventory to store batches that are machined but not scheduled immediately for final assembly. All customer orders are currently entered into the computer system by selecting information such as the finished standard model item number, quantity, and delivery date.

At a recent management meeting, sales manager Farima Hashemi commented that more customers are requesting fire detection equipment other than FirstDetect's standard offering.

In the past, FirstDetect occasionally accepted custom orders, since some customers are willing to pay a significant premium to get a product that fits their specific requirements. To avoid confusion with regular production, custom orders were machined and assembled in a separate area (similar in nature to Exhibit 5.3A) by a single shop employee who had completed a general engineering diploma at a local technical college. After the meeting, accounting manager Aidan Richards performed a cost analysis on some recent custom orders and found that although the sales price per unit was significantly higher than for standard models, excessive engineering administration costs related to preparing a complete drawing and production (machining and assembly) instructions for each custom order exceeded the increase in sales price. The result was a financial loss in the majority of the custom orders analyzed. Based on these findings, accounting recommended a significant price increase for future custom orders. However, the sales manager is concerned that the price increase proposed by accounting might deter customers from choosing FirstDetect for their custom order requirements.

With foreign competitors significantly undercutting their prices for their standard models, FirstDetect's management team began investigating the strategic option of focusing on the growing custom order market and essentially vacating the standard market. Farima and the engineering manager, Shari Vandelee, determined that their custom order requests were actually various configurations of the three purchased sub-components (housing, signal range, and accelerant type) that were machined and assembled into a finished fire detector. Further investigation revealed that over 95 percent of custom order requests could be configured by selecting one of 20 possible housings, one of 5 possible detection ranges, and one of 15 possible accelerant types (although some restrictions would apply depending on which housing was selected). Upon presenting these findings to the management team, the operations manager, Fal Levin, commented that the scenario sounds ideal for the concept of manufacturing cells in the assembly area:

a. Given the rectangular facility in Exhibit 5.18, qualitatively, where do you think the different areas should be located in relation to each other given the current situation? Assume that in addition to the three manufacturing areas (machining, assembly and custom manufacturing) described, there are raw material/purchased components, work in process, and finished goods inventory areas. Show via arrows, the general flow of material.

b. Briefly explain where the current manufacturing processes would appear on the Product-Process matrix.

c. What are some of the pros and cons of manufacturing cells for both the customer and for FirstDetect (as compared to FirstDetect's current process for handling custom orders)?

d. Considering FirstDetect's current production capabilities, what operational changes would be required so that operations could effectively support a cellular manufacturing approach for the growing custom order market? Consider equipment, employees, layout, information systems procedures, and inventory management.

Source: This case was written for classroom discussion by Brent Snider and Jaydeep Balakrishnan of the Haskayne School of Business at the University of Calgary. It is based on a real situation in a Canadian company.

First Detect Facility	EXHIBIT 5.18

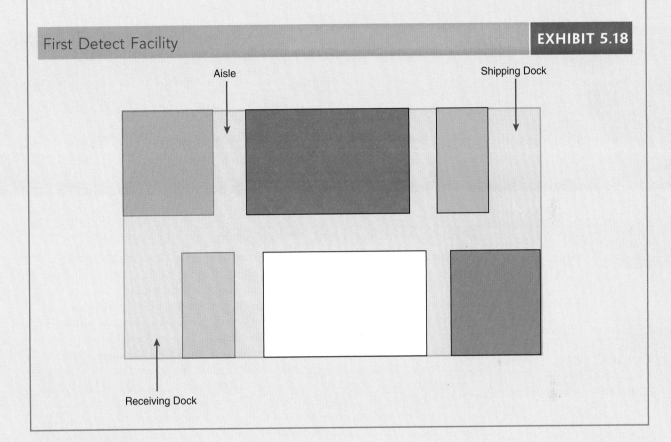

| Aisle | Shipping Dock |

Receiving Dock

Footnotes

[1] E. S. Buffa, G. C. Armour, and T. E. Vollmann, "Allocating Facilities with CRAFT," *Harvard Business Review*, 42, no. 2 (1964), pp. 136–158.

[2] The authors are thankful to Sherry Weaver of the Haskayne School of Business for her Excel VBA software, which did the computations.

[3] Adopted from F.R. Jacobs, R.B. Chase and N.J. Aquilano, *Operations & Supply Management*, New York, NY:McGraw-Hill Irwin, 2009, p241–242.

[4] Ibid, p. 247.

Selected Bibliography

Heragu, S. *Facilities Design*. Boston: PWS Publishing, 1997.

Hyer, N., and U. Wemmerlöv. *Reorganizing the Factory: Competing through Cellular Manufacturing*. Portland, OR: Productivity Press, 2002.

Tompkins, J. A., and J. A. While. *Facilities Planning*. New York: John Wiley & Sons, 2003.

Fitzsimmons, J. A., and M. J. Fitzsimmons. *Service Management,* 4th ed. New York: Irwin/McGraw-Hill, 2003.

WAITING-LINE ANALYSIS

Learning Objectives:

1. Understand what waiting-line (queuing) analysis is.
2. Be able to model some common waiting-line situations and estimate server utilization, the length of a waiting line, and average customer wait time.

THE WAITING-LINE PROBLEM

Everyone of us is involved in a waiting line on a daily basis, whether it is in a queue at a fast food restaurant, waiting for service at the bank, at a traffic light, or on the phone on hold. In modern society, we spend a considerable amount of time waiting in queues. Thus, the issue of managing queues (waiting lines), whether in a factory where customer orders wait for processing, or in services where customers wait for service, has taken on increasing importance in recent years. Managers must weigh the added cost of providing more rapid service (more traffic lanes, additional healthcare professionals, more checkout stands) against the inherent cost of waiting.

Frequently, the cost trade-off decision is straightforward. For example, if we find that the total time our employees spend in line waiting to use a copying machine would otherwise be spent in productive activities, we could compare the cost of installing one additional machine to the value of employee time saved. The decision could then be reduced to dollar terms, and the choice easily made.

On the other hand, suppose that our waiting-line problem centres on demand for beds in a hospital. We can compute the cost of additional beds by summing the costs for building construction, additional equipment required, and increased maintenance. But what is on the other side of the scale? Here we are confronted with the problem of trying to place a dollar figure on a patient's need for a hospital bed that is unavailable. Can we estimate the human cost arising from this lack of adequate hospital care?

The Practical View of Waiting Lines

Before we proceed with a technical presentation of waiting-line theory, it is useful to look at the intuitive side of the issue to see what it means. Exhibit S5.1 shows arrivals at a service facility (such as a bank) and service requirements at that facility (such as tellers and loan officers). One important variable is the number of arrivals over the hours that the service system is open. From the service delivery viewpoint, customers demand varying amounts of service, often exceeding normal capacity. We can control arrivals in a variety of ways. For example, we can have a

Arrival and Service Profiles

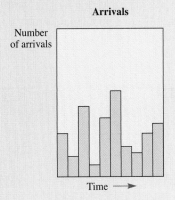

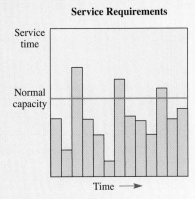

short line (such as a drive-in at a fast-food restaurant with only several spaces), we can establish specific hours for specific customers, or we can run specials. For the server, we can affect service time by using faster or slower servers, faster or slower machines, different tooling, different material, different layout, faster set-up time, and so on.

The essential point is waiting lines are *not* a fixed condition of a productive system but are, to a very large extent, within the control of the system management and design. Useful suggestions for managing queues based on research in the banking industry are given in Exhibit S5.2.

Common Methods for Managing Queues

- **Segment the customers.**
  If a group of customers needs something that can be done very quickly, give them a special line so that they do not have to wait for the slower customers.

- **Train your servers to be friendly.**
  Greeting the customer by name or providing another form of special attention can go a long way toward overcoming the negative feeling of a long wait. Psychologists suggest that servers should be told when to invoke specific friendly actions, such as smiling when greeting customers, taking orders, and giving change (for example, in a convenience store). Tests using such specific behavioural actions have shown significant increases in the perceived friendliness of the servers in the eyes of the customer.

- **Inform your customers of what to expect.**
  This is especially important when the waiting time will be longer than normal. Tell customers why the waiting time is longer than usual and what you are doing to alleviate the wait.

- **Try to divert the customer's attention when waiting.**
  Providing music, a video, or some other form of entertainment may help distract the customers from the fact that they are waiting.

- **Encourage customers to come during slack periods.**
  Inform customers of times when they usually would not have to wait; also tell them when the peak periods are—this may help smooth the load.

THE QUEUING SYSTEM

The **queuing system** consists essentially of three major components: (1) the source population and the way customers arrive at the system, (2) the servicing system, and (3) the condition of the customers exiting the system (back to source population or not?), as seen in Exhibit S5.3. The following sections discuss each of these areas.

EXHIBIT S5.3	Components of a Queuing System

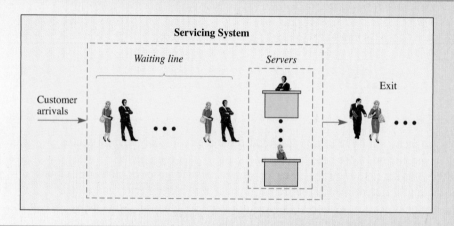

Customer Arrivals

Arrivals at a service system may be drawn from a *finite* or an *infinite* population. The distinction is important because the analyses are based on different premises and require different equations for their solution.

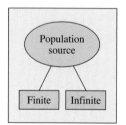

Finite Population   A *finite population* refers to the limited-size customer pool that will use the service and, at times, form a line. The reason this finite classification is important is that when a customer leaves its position as a member of the population (a machine breaking down and requiring service, for example), the size of the user group is reduced by one, which reduces the probability of the next occurrence. Conversely, when a customer is serviced and returns to the user group, the population increases and the probability of a user requiring service also increases. This finite class of problems requires a separate set of formulas from that of the infinite population case.

As an example, consider a group of six machines maintained by one repairperson. When one machine breaks down, the source population is reduced to five, and the chance of one of the remaining five breaking down and needing repair is certainly less than when six machines were operating. If two machines are down with only four operating, the probability of another breakdown is again changed. Conversely, when a machine is repaired and returned to service, the machine population increases, thus raising the probability of the next breakdown.

Infinite Population   An *infinite population* is large enough in relation to the service system so that the population size caused by subtractions or additions to the population (a customer needing service or a serviced customer returning to the population) does not significantly affect the system probabilities. If, in the preceding finite explanation, there were 100 machines instead of six, then if one or two machines broke down, the probabilities for the next breakdowns would not be very different and the assumption could be made without a great deal of error that the population (for all practical purposes) was infinite. Nor would the formulas for "infinite" queuing problems cause much error if applied to a physician with 1000 patients or a department store with 10 000 customers.

Distribution of Arrivals

When describing a waiting system, we need to define the manner in which customers or the waiting units are arranged for service.

Waiting-line formulas generally require an **arrival rate**, or the number of units per period (such as an average of one every six minutes). A *constant* arrival distribution is periodic, with exactly the same time between successive arrivals. In productive systems, the only arrivals that truly approach a constant interval period are those subject to machine control. Much more common are *variable* (random) arrival distributions.

In observing arrivals at a service facility, we can look at them from two viewpoints: First, we can analyze the time between successive arrivals to see if the times follow some statistical distribution. Usually we assume that the time between arrivals is exponentially distributed. Second, we can set some time length (T) and try to determine how many arrivals might enter the system within T. We typically assume that the number of arrivals per time unit is Poisson distributed.

Exponential Distribution In the first case, when arrivals at a service facility occur in a purely random fashion, a plot of the interarrival times yields an **exponential distribution** such as that shown in Exhibit S5.4. The probability function is

[S5.1] $$f(t) = \lambda e^{-\lambda t}$$

where λ is the mean number of arrivals per time period.

The cumulative area beneath the curve in Exhibit S5.4 is the summation of equation (S5.1) over its positive range, which is $e^{-\lambda t}$. This integral allows us to compute the probabilities of arrivals within a specified time. For example, for the case of single arrivals to a waiting line ($\lambda = 1$), the following table can be derived either by solving $e^{-\lambda t}$ or by

Exponential Distribution   EXHIBIT S5.4

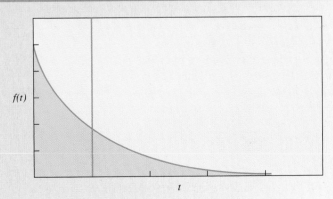

using Appendix D. Column 2 shows the probability that it will be more than t minutes until the next arrival. Column 3 shows the probability of the next arrival within t minutes (computed as 1 minus the value in column 2)

(1) t (MINUTES)	(2) PROBABILITY THAT THE NEXT ARRIVAL WILL OCCUR IN t MINUTES OR MORE (FROM APPENDIX D OR SOLVING e^{-t})	(3) PROBABILITY THAT THE NEXT ARRIVAL WILL OCCUR IN t MINUTES OR LESS [1 − COLUMN (2)]
0	1.00	0
0.5	0.61	0.39
1.0	0.37	0.63
1.5	0.22	0.78
2.0	0.14	0.86

Poisson Distribution In the second case, where one is interested in the number of arrivals during some time period T, the distribution appears as in Exhibit S5.5 and is obtained by finding the probability of exactly n arrivals during T. If the arrival process is random, the distribution is the **Poisson**, and the formula is

[S5.2]
$$P_T(n) = \frac{(\lambda T)^n e^{-\lambda T}}{n!}$$

Equation (S5.2) shows the probability of exactly n arrivals in time T. For example, if the mean arrival rate of units into a system is three per minute ($\lambda = 3$) and we want to find the probability that exactly five units will arrive within a one-minute period ($n = 5$, $T = 1$), we have

$$P_1(5) = \frac{(3 \times 1)^5 e^{-3 \times 1}}{5!} = \frac{3^5 e^{-3}}{120} = 2.025 e^{-3} = 0.101$$

EXHIBIT S5.5　Poisson Distribution for $\lambda T = 3$

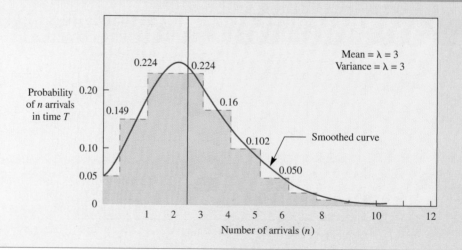

Mean $= \lambda = 3$
Variance $= \lambda = 3$

That is, there is a 10.1 percent chance that there will be five arrivals in any one-minute interval.

Although often shown as a smoothed curve, as in Exhibit S5.5, the Poisson is a discrete distribution. (The curve becomes smoother as n becomes large.) The distribution is discrete because n refers, in our example, to the number of arrivals in a system, and this must be an integer. (For example, there cannot be 1.5 arrivals.)

Also note that the exponential and Poisson distributions can be derived from one another. The mean and variance of the Poisson are equal and denoted by λ. The mean of the exponential is $1/\lambda$ and its variance is $1/\lambda^2$. (Remember that the time between arrivals is exponentially distributed and the number of arrivals per unit of time is Poisson distributed.)

Other arrival characteristics include arrival patterns, size of arrival units, and degree of patience. (See Exhibit S5.6.)

Arrival patterns.   The arrivals at a system are far more controllable than is generally recognized. Barbers may decrease their Saturday arrival rate (and supposedly shift it to other days of the week) by charging an extra $1 for adult haircuts or charging adult prices for children's haircuts. Department stores run sales during the off-season or hold one-day-only sales in part for purposes of control. Airlines offer excursion and off-season rates for similar reasons. The simplest of all arrival-control devices is the posting of business hours.

Some service demands are clearly uncontrollable, such as emergency medical demands on a city's hospital facilities. But even in these situations, arrivals at emergency rooms in specific hospitals are controllable to some extent by, say, keeping ambulance drivers in the service region informed of the status of their respective host hospitals.

Customer Arrivals in Queues   **EXHIBIT S5.6**

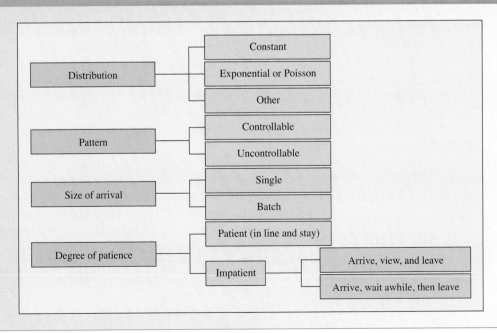

Size of arrival units.   A *single arrival* may be thought of as one unit. (A unit is the smallest number handled.) A single arrival on the floor of the New York Stock Exchange (NYSE) is 100 shares of stock; a single arrival at an egg-processing plant might be a dozen eggs or a flat of 2½ dozen; a single arrival at a restaurant is a single person.

A *batch arrival* is some multiple of the unit, such as a block of 1000 shares on the NYSE, a case of eggs at the processing plant, or a party of five at a restaurant.

Degree of patience.   A *patient* arrival is one who waits as long as necessary until the service facility is ready to serve him or her. (Even if arrivals grumble and behave impatiently, the fact that they wait is sufficient to label them as patient arrivals for purposes of waiting-line theory.)

There are two classes of *impatient* arrivals. Members of the first class arrive, survey both the service facility and the length of the line, and then decide to leave. Those in the second class arrive, view the situation, join the waiting line, and then, after some period of time, depart. The behaviour of the first type is termed *balking,* while the second is termed *reneging.*

The Queuing System: Factors

The queuing system consists primarily of the waiting line(s) and the available number of servers. Here we discuss issues pertaining to waiting-line characteristics and management, line structure, and service rate. Factors to consider with waiting lines include the line length, number of lines, and queue discipline.

Length.   In a practical sense, an infinite line is simply one that is very long in terms of the capacity of the service system. Examples of *infinite potential length* are a line of vehicles backed up for miles at a bridge crossing and customers who must form a line around the block as they wait to purchase tickets at a theater.

Gas stations, loading docks, and parking lots have *limited line capacity* caused by legal restrictions or physical space characteristics. This complicates the waiting-line problem, not only in service system utilization and waiting-line computations, but also in the shape of the actual arrival distribution. The arrival denied entry into the line because of lack of space may rejoin the population for a later try or may seek service elsewhere. Either action makes an obvious difference in the finite population case.

Number of lines.   A single line or single file is, of course, one line only. The term *multiple lines* refers to the single lines that form in front of two or more servers or to single lines that converge at some central redistribution point. The disadvantage of multiple lines in a busy facility is that arrivals often shift lines if several previous services have been of short duration or if those customers currently in other lines appear to require a short service time.

Queue discipline.   A queue discipline is a priority rule or set of rules for determining the order of service to customers in a waiting line. The rules selected can have a dramatic effect on the system's overall performance. The number of customers in line, the average waiting time, the range of variability in waiting time, and the efficiency of the service facility are just a few of the factors affected by the choice of priority rules.

Probably the most common priority rule is first come, first served (FCFS). This rule states that cus-

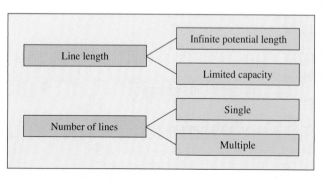

tomers in line are served on the basis of their chronological arrival; no other characteristics have any bearing on the selection process. This is popularly accepted as the fairest rule, although in practice it discriminates against the arrival requiring a short service time.

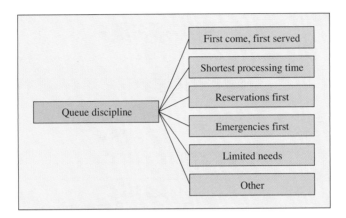

Reservations first, emergencies first, highest-profit customer first, largest orders first, best customers first, longest waiting time in line, and soonest promised date are other examples of priority rules. There are two major practical problems in using any rule: One is ensuring that customers know and follow the rule. The other is ensuring that a system exists to enable employees to manage the line (such as take-a-number systems).

Service Time Distribution Another important feature of the waiting structure is the time the customer or unit spends with the server once the service has started. Waiting-line formulas generally specify **service rate** as the capacity of the server in number of units per time period (such as 12 completions per hour) and *not* as service time, which might average five minutes each. A constant service time rule states that each service takes exactly the same time. As in constant arrivals, this characteristic is generally limited to machine-controlled operations.

When service times are random, they can be approximated by the exponential distribution. When using the exponential distribution as an approximation of the service times, we will refer to μ as the average number of units or customers that can be served per time period.

Line Structures As Exhibit S5.7 shows, the flow of items to be serviced may go through a single line, multiple lines, or some mixture of the two. The choice of format depends partly on the volume of customers served and partly on the restrictions imposed by sequential requirements governing the order in which service must be performed.

1. **Single channel, single phase.**   This is the simplest type of waiting-line structure, and straightforward formulas are available to solve the problem for standard distribution patterns of arrival and service. When the distributions are nonstandard, the problem is easily solved by computer simulation. A typical example of a single-channel, single-phase situation is the one-person barbershop.
2. **Single channel, multiphase.**   A car wash is an illustration because a series of services (vacuuming, wetting, washing, rinsing, drying, window cleaning, and parking) is performed in a fairly uniform sequence. A critical factor in the single-channel

EXHIBIT S5.7 | Line Structures

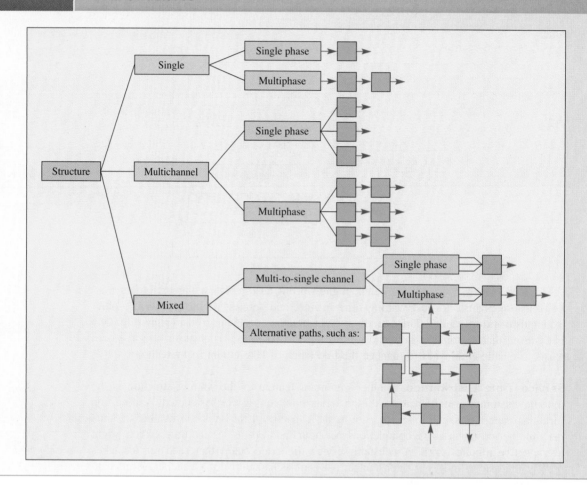

case with service in series is the amount of buildup of items allowed in front of each service, which in turn constitutes separate waiting lines.

3. **Multichannel, single phase.** Checkout counters in high-volume department stores exemplify this type of structure. The difficulty with this format is that the uneven service time given each customer results in unequal speed or flow among the lines. This results in some customers being served before others who arrived earlier, as well as in some degree of line shifting. Varying this structure to ensure the servicing of arrivals in chronological order would require forming a single line, from which, as a server becomes available, the next customer in the queue is assigned as is done in banks and airport check-ins.

The major problem of this structure is that it requires rigid control of the line to maintain order and to direct customers to available servers. In some instances, assigning numbers to customers in order of their arrival helps alleviate this problem.

4. **Multichannel, multiphase.** This case is similar to the preceding one except that two or more services are performed in sequence. The admission of patients in a

hospital follows this pattern because a specific sequence of steps is usually followed: initial contact at the admissions desk, filling out forms, making identification tags, obtaining a room assignment, escorting the patient to the room, and so forth. Because several servers are usually available for this procedure, more than one patient at a time may be processed.

5. **Mixed.**   Under this general heading, we consider two subcategories: (1) multiple-to-single channel structures and (2) alternative path structures. Under (1), we find either lines that merge into one for single-phase service, as at a bridge crossing where two lanes merge into one, or lines that merge into one for multiphase service, such as subassembly lines feeding into a main line. Under (2), we encounter two structures that differ in directional flow requirements. The first is similar to the multichannel–multiphase case, except that (a) there may be switching from one channel to the next after the first service has been rendered and (b) the number of channels and phases may vary—again—after performance of the first service.

Exiting the Queuing System

Once a customer is served, two exit fates are possible: (1) The customer may return to the source population and immediately become a competing candidate for service again or (2) there may be a low probability of reservice. The first case can be illustrated by a machine that has been routinely repaired and returned to duty but may break down again; the second can be illustrated by a machine that has been overhauled or modified and has a low probability of reservice over the near future. In a lighter vein, we might refer to the first as the "recurring-common-cold case" and to the second as the "appendectomy-only-once case."

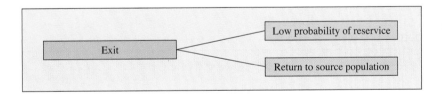

It should be apparent that when the population source is finite, any change in the service performed on customers who return to the population modifies the arrival rate at the service facility. This, of course, alters the characteristics of the waiting line under study and necessitates reanalysis of the problem.

Queue_Models

Queue

WAITING-LINE MODELS

In this section we present three sample waiting-line problems followed by their solutions. Each has a slightly different structure (see Exhibit S5.8) and solution equation (see Exhibit S5.9). There are more types of models than these three, but the formulas and solutions become quite complicated, and those problems are generally solved using computer simulation. Also, in using these formulas, keep in mind that they are steady-state formulas derived on the assumption that the process under study is ongoing. Thus, they may provide inaccurate results when applied to processes where the arrival rates and/or service rates change over time. The Excel Spreadsheet QueueModels.xls included on the OLC can be used to solve these problems.

EXHIBIT S5.8	Properties of Some Specific Waiting-line Models

MODEL	LAYOUT	SERVICE PHASE	SOURCE POPULATION	ARRIVAL PATTERN	QUEUE DISCIPLINE	SERVICE PATTERN	PERMISSIBLE QUEUE LENGTH	TYPICAL EXAMPLE
1	Single channel	Single	Infinite	Poisson	FCFS	Exponential	Unlimited	Drive-in teller at bank; one-lane toll bridge
2	Single channel	Single	Infinite	Poisson	FCFS	Constant	Unlimited	Roller coaster rides in amusement park
3	Multichannel	Single	Infinite	Poisson	FCFS	Exponential	Unlimited	Airport check-in

EXHIBIT S5.9	Notations for Equations

INFINITE QUEUING NOTATION: MODELS 1–3

λ = Average arrival rate

μ = Average service rate

$\dfrac{1}{\mu}$ = Average service time

$\dfrac{1}{\lambda}$ = Average time between arrivals

ρ = Ratio of total arrival rate to service rate for a single server $\left(\dfrac{\lambda}{\mu}\right)^{*}$

L_q = Average number waiting in line

L_s = Average number in system (including any being served)

W_q = Average time waiting in line

W_s = Average total time in system (including time to be served)

n = Number of units in the system

S = Number of identical service channels

P_n = Probability of exactly n units in system

P_w = Probability of waiting in line

EQUATIONS FOR SOLVING THREE MODEL PROBLEMS

Model 1

$$\begin{cases} L_q = \dfrac{\lambda^2}{\mu(\mu - \lambda)} \\ L_s = \dfrac{\lambda}{\mu - \lambda} \end{cases} \qquad \begin{aligned} W_q &= \dfrac{L_q}{\lambda} \\ W_s &= \dfrac{L_s}{\lambda} \end{aligned} \qquad \begin{aligned} P_n &= \left(1 - \dfrac{\lambda}{\mu}\right)\left(\dfrac{\lambda}{\mu}\right)^{n} \\ \rho &= \dfrac{\lambda}{\mu} \end{aligned} \qquad P_o = \left(1 - \dfrac{\lambda}{\mu}\right) \qquad \text{(S5.3)}$$

Model 2

$$\begin{cases} L_q = \dfrac{\lambda^2}{2\mu(\mu - \lambda)} \\ L_s = L_q + \dfrac{\lambda}{\mu} \end{cases} \qquad \begin{aligned} W_q &= \dfrac{L_q}{\lambda} \\ W_s &= \dfrac{L_s}{\lambda} \end{aligned} \qquad \text{(S5.4)}$$

Model 3

$$\begin{cases} L_s = L_q + \lambda/\mu \\ W_q = L_q/\lambda \end{cases} \qquad \begin{aligned} W_s &= L_s/\lambda \\ P_w &= L_q\left(\dfrac{S M_\mu}{\lambda} - 1\right) \end{aligned} \qquad \text{(S5.5)}$$

(Exhibit S5.10 provides the value of L_q given λ/μ and the number of servers S.)
*For single-server queues, this is equivalent to utilization.

Here is a quick preview of our three problems to illustrate each of the three waiting-line models in Exhibits S5.8 and S5.9.

Problem 1: Customers in line.   A bank wants to know how many customers are waiting for a drive-in teller, how long they have to wait, the utilization of the teller, and what the service rate would have to be so that 95 percent of the time there will not be more than three cars in the system at any time.

Problem 2: Equipment selection. A franchise for Robot Car Wash must decide which equipment to purchase out of a choice of three. Larger units cost more but wash cars faster. To make the decision, costs are related to revenue.

Problem 3: Determining the number of servers. An auto agency parts department must decide how many clerks to employ at the counter. More clerks cost more money, but there is a savings because mechanics wait less time.

EXAMPLE 5.1: CUSTOMERS IN LINE

Western Nunavut Bank is considering opening a drive-through window for customer service. Management estimates that customers will arrive at the rate of 15 per hour. The teller who will staff the window can service customers at the rate of one every three minutes or 20 per hour.

Part 1 Assuming Poisson arrivals and exponential service, find

1. Utilization of the teller.
2. Average number in the waiting line.
3. Average number in the system.
4. Average waiting time in line.
5. Average waiting time in the system, including service.

SOLUTION—PART 1

1. The average utilization of the teller is (using Model 1)

$$\rho = \frac{\lambda}{\mu} = \frac{15}{20} = 75 \text{ percent}$$

2. The average number in the waiting line is

$$L_q = \frac{\lambda^2}{\mu(\mu - \lambda)} = \frac{15^2}{20(20 - 15)} = 2.25 \text{ customers}$$

3. The average number in the system is

$$L_S = \frac{\lambda}{\mu - \lambda} = \frac{15}{20 - 15} = 3 \text{ customers}$$

4. Average waiting time in line is

$$W_q = \frac{L_q}{\lambda} = \frac{2.25}{15} = 0.15 \text{ hour, or 9 minutes}$$

5. Average waiting time in the system is

$$W_S = \frac{L_S}{\lambda} = \frac{3}{15} = 0.2 \text{ hour, or 12 minutes}$$

Queue

Part 2 Because of limited space availability and a desire to provide an acceptable level of service, the bank manager would like to ensure, with 95 percent confidence, that no more than three cars will be in the system at any time. What is the present level of service for the three-car limit? What level of teller use must be attained and what must be the service rate of the teller to ensure the 95 percent level of service?

SOLUTION—PART 2

The present level of service for three or fewer cars is the probability that there are 0, 1, 2, or 3 cars in the system. From Model 1, Exhibit S5.9,

$$P_n = \left(1 - \frac{\lambda}{\mu}\right)\left(\frac{\lambda}{\mu}\right)^n$$

at $n = 0$, $P_0 = (1 - 15/20)$ $(15/20)^0 = 0.250$
at $n = 1$, $P_1 = (1/4)$ $(15/20)^1 = 0.188$
at $n = 2$, $P_2 = (1/4)$ $(15/20)^2 = 0.141$
at $n = 3$, $P_3 = (1/4)$ $(15/20)^3 = \underline{0.105}$
                                        0.684 or   68.5 percent

The probability of having more than three cars in the system is 1.0 minus the probability of three or fewer cars ($1.0 - 0.685 = 31.5$ percent).

For a 95 percent service level of three or fewer cars, this states that $P_0 + P_1 + P_2 + P_3 = 95$ percent.

$$0.95 = \left(1 - \frac{\lambda}{\mu}\right)\left(\frac{\lambda}{\mu}\right)^0 + \left(1 - \frac{\lambda}{\mu}\right)\left(\frac{\lambda}{\mu}\right)^1 + \left(1 - \frac{\lambda}{\mu}\right)\left(\frac{\lambda}{\mu}\right)^2 + \left(1 - \frac{\lambda}{\mu}\right)\left(\frac{\lambda}{\mu}\right)^3$$

$$0.95 = \left(1 - \frac{\lambda}{\mu}\right)\left[1 + \frac{\lambda}{\mu} + \left(\frac{\lambda}{\mu}\right)^2 + \left(\frac{\lambda}{\mu}\right)^3\right]$$

We can solve this by trial and error for values of λ/μ. If $\lambda/\mu = 0.50$,

$$0.95 \overset{?}{=} 0.5(1 + 0.5 + 0.25 + 0.125)$$
$$0.95 \neq 0.9375$$

With $\lambda/\mu = 0.45$,

$$0.95 \overset{?}{=} (1 - 0.45)(1 + 0.45 + 0.203 + 0.091)$$
$$0.95 \neq 0.96$$

With $\lambda/\mu = 0.47$,

$$0.95 \overset{?}{=} (1 - 0.47)(1 + 0.47 + 0.221 + 0.104) = 0.9512$$
$$0.95 \approx 0.95135$$

Therefore, with the utilization $\rho = \lambda/\mu$ of 47 percent, the probability of three or fewer cars in the system is 95 percent.

To find the rate of service required to attain this 95 percent service level, we simply solve the equation $\lambda/\mu = 0.47$, where λ = number of arrivals per hour. This gives $\mu = 32$ per hour. That is, the teller must serve approximately 32 people per hour (a 60 percent increase over the original 20-per-hour capability) for 95 percent confidence that not more than three cars will be in the system. Perhaps service may be speeded up by modifying the method of service, adding another teller, or limiting the types of transactions available at the drive-through window. Note that with the condition of 95 percent confidence that three or fewer cars will be in the system, the teller will be idle 53 percent of the time.

EXAMPLE 5.2:   EQUIPMENT SELECTION

The Robot Company franchises combination gas and car wash stations throughout the Maritimes. Robot gives a free car wash for a gasoline fill-up or, for a wash alone, charges $0.50. Past experience shows that the number of customers that have car washes following fill-ups is about the same as for a wash alone. The average profit on a gasoline fill-up is about $0.70, and the cost of the car wash to Robot is $0.10. Robot stays open 14 hours per day.

Queue

Robot has three power units and drive assemblies, and a franchisee must select the unit preferred. Unit I can wash cars at the rate of one every five minutes and is leased for $12 per day. Unit II, a larger unit, can wash cars at the rate of one every four minutes but costs $16 per day. Unit III, the largest, costs $22 per day and can wash a car in three minutes.

The franchisee estimates that customers will not wait in line more than five minutes for a car wash. A longer time will cause Robot to lose the gasoline sales as well as the car wash sale.

If the estimate of customer arrivals resulting in washes is 10 per hour, which wash unit should be selected?

SOLUTION

Using unit I, calculate the average waiting time of customers in the wash line (μ for unit I = 12 per hour). From the Model 2 equations (Exhibit S5.9),

$$L_q = \frac{\lambda^2}{2\mu(\mu - \lambda)} = \frac{10^2}{2(12)(12 - 10)} = 2.08333$$

$$W_q = \frac{L_q}{\lambda} = \frac{2.08333}{10} = 0.208 \text{ hour, or } 12\tfrac{1}{2} \text{ minutes}$$

For unit II at 15 per hour,

$$L_q = \frac{10^2}{2(15)(15 - 10)} = 0.667$$

$$W_q = \frac{0.667}{10} = 0.0667 \text{ hour, or 4 minutes}$$

If waiting time is the only criterion, unit II should be purchased. But before we make the final decision, we must look at the profit differential between both units.

With unit I, some customers would balk and renege because of the 12½-minute wait. And, although this greatly complicates the mathematical analysis, we can gain some estimate of lost sales with unit I by increasing $W_q = 5$ minutes or $\frac{1}{12}$ hour (the average length of time customers will wait) and solving for λ. This would be the effective arrival rate of customers:

$$W_q = \frac{L_q}{\lambda} = \left(\frac{\lambda^2/2\mu(\mu - \lambda)}{\lambda} \right)$$

$$W_q = \frac{\lambda}{2\mu(\mu - \lambda)}$$

$$\lambda = \frac{2W_q\mu^2}{1 + 2W_q\mu} = \frac{2(\frac{1}{12})(12)^2}{1 + 2(\frac{1}{12})(12)} = 8 \text{ per hour}$$

Therefore, because the original estimate of λ was 10 per hour, an estimated 2 customers per hour will be lost. Lost profit of 2 customers per hour × 14 hours × $\frac{1}{2}$ ($0.70 fill-up profit + $0.40 wash profit) = $15.40 per day.

Because the additional cost of unit II over unit I is only $4 per day, the loss of $15.40 profit obviously warrants installing unit II.

The original five-minute maximum wait constraint is satisfied by unit II. Therefore, unit III is not considered unless the arrival rate is expected to increase.

Queue

EXAMPLE 5.3:   DETERMINING THE NUMBER OF SERVERS

In the service department of the Glenn-Mark Auto Agency, mechanics requiring parts for auto repair or service present their request forms at the parts department counter. The parts clerk fills a request while the mechanic waits. Mechanics arrive in a random (Poisson) fashion at the rate of 40 per hour, and a clerk can fill requests at the rate of 20 per hour (exponential). If the cost for a parts clerk is $6 per hour and the cost for a mechanic is $12 per hour, determine the optimum number of clerks to staff the counter. (Because of the high arrival rate, an infinite source may be assumed.)

SOLUTION

First, assume that three clerks will be used because having only one or two clerks would create infinitely long lines (since $\lambda = 40$ and $\mu = 20$). The equations for Model 3 from Exhibit S5.9 will be used here. But first we need to obtain the average number in line using the table of Exhibit S5.10. Using the table and values $\lambda/\mu = 2$ and $S = 3$, we obtain $L_q = 0.8888$ mechanic.

At this point, we see that we have an average of 0.8888 mechanic waiting all day. For an eight-hour day at $12 per hour, there is a loss of mechanic's time worth 0.8888 mechanic × $12 per hour × 8 hours = $85.32.

Our next step is to reobtain the waiting time if we add another parts clerk. We then compare the added cost of the additional employee with the time saved by the mechanics. Again, using the table of Exhibit S5.10 but with $S = 4$, we obtain

$$L_q = 0.1730 \text{ mechanic in line}$$

$0.1730 × \$12 × 8$ hours $= \$16.61$ cost of a mechanic waiting in line

Value of mechanics' time saved is $85.32 - \$16.61 \quad = \$68.71$

Cost of an additional parts clerk is 8 hours × $6/hour = $\underline{\quad 48.00}$

Cost of reduction by adding fourth clerk $\qquad\qquad = \$20.71$

This problem could be expanded to consider the addition of runners to deliver parts to mechanics; the problem then would be to determine the optimal number of runners. This, however, would have to include the added cost of lost time caused by errors in parts receipts. For example, a mechanic would recognize a wrong part at the counter and obtain immediate correction, whereas the parts runner might not.

COMPUTER SIMULATION OF WAITING LINES

Some waiting-line problems that seem simple at first turn out to be extremely difficult or impossible to solve. Throughout this chapter, we have been treating waiting-line situations that are independent; that is, either the entire system consists of a single phase, or else each service that is performed in a series is independent. (This could happen if the output of one service location is allowed to build up in front of the next one so that this, in essence, becomes a calling population for the next service.) When a series of services is performed in sequence, where the output rate of one becomes the input rate of the next, we can no longer use the simple formulas. This is also true for any problem where conditions do not meet the requirements of the equations, as specified in Exhibit S5.8. The technique best suited to solving this type of problem is computer simulation.

Expected Number of People Waiting in Line (L_q) for Various Values of S and λ/μ EXHIBIT S5.10

NUMBER OF SERVICE CHANNELS, S

λ/μ	1	2	3	4	5	6	7	8	9	10	11	12	13	14	15
0.10	0.0111														
0.15	0.0264	0.0006													
0.20	0.0500	0.0020													
0.25	0.0833	0.0039													
0.30	0.1285	0.0069													
0.35	0.1884	0.0110													
0.40	0.2666	0.0166													
0.45	0.3681	0.0239	0.0019												
0.50	0.5000	0.0333	0.0030												
0.55	0.6722	0.045	0.0043												
0.60	0.9090	0.0593	0.0061												
0.65	1.2071	0.0767	0.0084												
0.70	1.6333	0.0976	0.0112												
0.75	2.2500	0.1227	0.0147												
0.80	3.2000	0.1523	0.0189												
0.85	4.8165	0.1873	0.0239	0.0031											
0.90	8.1000	0.2285	0.0300	0.0041											
0.95	18.0500	0.2767	0.0371	0.0053											
1.0		0.3333	0.0454	0.0067											
1.2		0.6748	0.0940	0.0158											
1.4		1.3449	0.1778	0.0324	0.0059										
1.6		2.8441	0.3128	0.0604	0.0121										
1.8		7.6731	0.5320	0.1051	0.0227	0.0047									
2.0			0.8888	0.1730	0.0390	0.0090									
2.2			1.4907	0.2770	0.066	0.0158									
2.4			2.1261	0.4205	0.1047	0.0266	0.0065								
2.6			4.9322	0.6581	0.1609	0.0425	0.0110								
2.8			12.2724	1.0000	0.2411	0.0659	0.0180								
3.0				1.5282	0.3541	0.0991	0.0282	0.0077							
3.2				2.3855	0.5128	0.1452	0.0427	0.0122							
3.4				3.9060	0.7365	0.2085	0.0631	0.0189							
3.6				7.0893	1.0550	0.2947	0.0912	0.0283	0.0084						
3.8				16.9366	1.5181	0.4114	0.1292	0.0412	0.0127						
4.0					2.2164	0.5694	0.1801	0.0590	0.0189						
4.2					3.3269	0.7837	0.2475	0.0827	0.0273	0.0087					
4.4					5.2675	1.0777	0.3364	0.1142	0.0389	0.0128					
4.6					9.2885	1.4857	0.4532	0.1555	0.0541	0.0184					
4.8					21.6384	2.0708	0.6071	0.2092	0.0742	0.0260					
5.0						2.9375	0.8102	0.2785	0.1006	0.0361	0.0125				
5.2						4.3004	1.0804	0.3680	0.1345	0.0492	0.0175				
5.4						6.6609	1.4441	0.5871	0.1779	0.0663	0.0243	0.0085			
5.6						11.5178	1.9436	0.6313	0.2330	0.0683	0.0330	0.0119			
5.8						26.3726	2.6481	0.8225	0.3032	0.1164	0.0443	0.0164			
6.0							3.6878	1.0707	0.3918	0.1518	0.0590	0.0224			
6.2							5.2979	1.3967	0.5037	0.1964	0.0775	0.0300	0.0113		
6.4							8.0768	1.8040	0.6454	0.2524	0.1008	0.0398	0.0153		
6.6							13.7992	2.4198	0.8247	0.3222	0.1302	0.0523	0.0205		
6.8							31.1270	3.2441	1.0533	0.4090	0.1666	0.0679	0.0271	0.0105	
7.0								4.4471	1.3471	0.5172	0.2119	0.0876	0.0357	0.0141	
7.2								6.3133	1.7288	0.6521	0.2677	0.1119	0.0463	0.0187	
7.4								9.5102	2.2324	0.8202	0.3364	0.1420	0.0595	0.0245	0.0097
7.6								16.0379	2.9113	1.0310	0.4211	0.1789	0.0761	0.0318	0.0129
7.8								35.8956	3.8558	1.2972	0.5250	0.2243	0.0966	0.0410	0.0168
8.0									5.2264	1.6364	0.6530	0.2796	0.1214	0.0522	0.0220
8.2									7.3441	2.0736	0.8109	0.3469	0.1520	0.0663	0.0283
8.4									10.9592	2.6470	1.0060	0.4288	0.1891	0.0834	0.0361
8.6									18.3223	3.4160	1.2484	0.5236	0.2341	0.1043	0.0459
8.8									40.6824	4.4805	1.5524	0.6501	0.2885	0.1208	0.0577
9.0										6.0183	1.9366	0.7980	0.3543	0.1603	0.0723
9.2										8.3869	2.4293	0.9788	0.4333	0.1974	0.0899
9.4										12.4183	3.0732	1.2010	0.5267	0.2419	0.1111
9.6										20.6160	3.9318	1.4752	0.5437	0.2952	0.1367
9.8										45.4769	5.1156	1.8165	0.7827	0.3699	0.16731
10.0											6.8210	2.2465	0.9506	0.4352	0.2040

Expected Length

Summary

Waiting-line analysis is relevant to many service situations. The basic objective is to balance the cost of waiting with the cost of adding more resources. For a service system this means that the utilization of a server may be quite low to provide a short waiting time to the customer. Many queuing problems appear simple until an attempt is made to solve them. This chapter has dealt with the simpler problems. When situations become more complex, when there are multiple phases, or when services are performed only in a particular sequence, computer simulation is necessary.

Key Terms

Arrival rate   The expected number of customers that arrive each period.

Exponential distribution   A probability distribution often associated with interarrival times.

Poisson distribution   Probability distribution often used to describe the number of arrivals during a given time period.

Queuing system   Consists of three major components: (1) the source population and the way customers arrive at the system, (2) the serving systems, and (3) how customers exit the system.

Service rate   The capacity of a server measured in number of units that can be processed over a given time period.

Formula Review

Exponential distribution

[S5.1] $f(t) = \lambda e^{-\lambda t}$

Poisson distribution

[S5.2] $P_T(n) = \dfrac{(\lambda T)^n e^{-\lambda T}}{n!}$

Model 1 (See Exhibit S5.9.)

[S5.3]   Model 1

$$L_q = \frac{\lambda^2}{\mu(\mu - \lambda)} \qquad W_q = \frac{L_q}{\lambda} \qquad P_n = \left(1 - \frac{\lambda}{\mu}\right)\left(\frac{\lambda}{\mu}\right)^n \qquad P_o = \left(1 - \frac{\lambda}{\mu}\right)$$

$$L_s = \frac{\lambda}{\mu - \lambda} \qquad W_s = \frac{L_s}{\lambda} \qquad \rho = \frac{\lambda}{\mu}$$

[S5.4]   Model 2

$$L_q = \frac{\lambda^2}{2\mu(\mu - \lambda)} \qquad W_q = \frac{L_q}{\lambda}$$

$$L_s = L_q + \frac{\lambda}{\mu} \qquad W_s = \frac{L_S}{\lambda}$$

[S5.5]   Model 3

$$L_S = L_q + \lambda/\mu \qquad W_S = L_S/\lambda$$

$$W_q = L_q/\lambda$$

$$P_w = L_q\left(\frac{S\mu}{\lambda} - 1\right)$$

Exhibit S5.10 provides the value of L_q given λ/μ and the number of servers S.

Solved Problems

Solved Problem 1

Quick Lube Inc. operates a fast lube and oil change garage. On a typical day, customers arrive at the rate of three per hour, and lube jobs are performed at an average rate of one every 15 minutes. The mechanics operate as a team on one car at a time.

Assuming Poisson arrivals and exponential service, find

a. Utilization of the lube team.

b. The average number of cars in line.

c. The average time a car waits before it is lubed.

d. The total time it takes to go through the system (that is, waiting in line plus lube time).

Queue

SOLUTION

$\lambda = 3, \mu = 4$

a. Utilization $\rho = \dfrac{\lambda}{\mu} = \dfrac{3}{4} = 75\%$

b. $L_q = \dfrac{\lambda^2}{\mu(\mu - \lambda)} = \dfrac{3^2}{4(4 - 3)} = \dfrac{9}{4} = 2.25$ cars in line.

c. $W_q = \dfrac{L_q}{\lambda} = \dfrac{2.25}{3} = 0.75$ hour, or 45 minutes.

d. $W_s = \dfrac{L_s}{\lambda} = \dfrac{\lambda}{\mu - \lambda} / \lambda = \dfrac{3}{4 - 3} / 3 = 1$ hour (waiting + lube).

Solved Problem 2

Alberta Vending Inc. (AVI) supplies vended food to a large university. Because students often kick the machines out of anger and frustration, management has a constant repair problem. The machines break down on an average of three per hour, and the breakdowns are distributed in a Poisson manner. Downtime costs the company \$25/hour per machine, and each maintenance worker gets \$4 per hour. One worker can service machines at an average rate of five per hour, distributed exponentially; two workers working together can service seven per hour, distributed exponentially; and a team of three workers can do eight per hour, distributed exponentially.

What is the optimal maintenance crew size for servicing the machines?

SOLUTION

Case 1—One worker:

$\lambda = 3$/hour Poisson, $\mu = 5$/hour exponential

There is an average number of machines in the system of

$$L_s = \frac{\lambda}{\mu - \lambda} = \frac{3}{5 - 3} = \frac{3}{2} = 1\tfrac{1}{2} \text{ machines}$$

Downtime cost is \$25 × 1.5 = \$37.50 per hour; repair cost is \$4.00 per hour; and total cost per hour for 1 worker is \$37.50 + \$4.00 = \$41.50.

Downtime (1.5 × \$25) = \$37.50

Labour (1 worker × \$4) =   4.00

\$41.50

Case II—Two workers:
$$\lambda = 3, \mu = 7$$

$$L_s = \frac{\lambda}{\mu - \lambda} = \frac{3}{7 - 3} = 0.75 \text{ machine}$$

Downtime $(0.75 \times \$25)$ $= \$18.75$

Labour (2 workers $\times$ \$4.00) $=$ $\underline{8.00}$

$\overline{\$26.75}$

Case III—Three workers:
$$\lambda = 3, \mu = 8$$

$$L_s = \frac{\lambda}{\mu - \lambda} = \frac{3}{8 - 3} = \frac{3}{5} = 0.60 \text{ machine}$$

Downtime $(0.60 \times \$25)$ $= \$15.00$

Labour (3 workers $\times$ \$4) $=$ $\underline{12.00}$

$\overline{\$27.00}$

Comparing the costs for one, two, or three workers, we see that Case II with two workers is the optimal decision.

Review and Discussion Questions

1. Cultural factors affect waiting lines. For example, fast checkout lines (e.g., 10 items or less) are uncommon in Japan. Why do you think this is so?
2. How many waiting lines did you encounter during your last flight?
3. Distinguish between a *channel* and a *phase*.
4. What is the major cost trade-off that must be made in managing waiting-line situations?
5. Which assumptions are necessary to employ the formulas given for Model 1?
6. In what way might the first-come, first-served rule be unfair to the customer waiting for service in a bank or hospital?
7. Define, in a practical sense, what is meant by an *exponential service time*.
8. Would you expect the exponential distribution to be a good approximation of service times for
   a. Buying an airline ticket at the airport?
   b. Riding a merry-go-round at a carnival?
   c. Checking out of a hotel?
   d. Completing a midterm exam in your OSM class?
9. Would you expect the Poisson distribution to be a good approximation of
   a. Runners crossing the finish line in the Boston Marathon?
   b. Arrival times of the students in your OSM class?
   c. Arrival times of the bus to your stop at school?

Problems

1. Students arrive at the University of Ontario Administrative Services Office at an average of one every 15 minutes, and their requests take on average 10 minutes to be processed. The service counter is staffed by only one clerk, Judy Chan, who works eight hours per day. Assume Poisson arrivals and exponential service times.
   a. What percentage of time is Judy idle?
   b. How much time, on average, does a student spend waiting in line?
   c. How long is the (waiting) line on average?
   d. What is the probability that an arriving student (just before entering the Administrative Services Office) will find at least one other student waiting in line?

2. The managers of the Administrative Services Office estimate that the time a student spends waiting in line costs them (due to goodwill loss and so on) $10 per hour. To reduce the time a student spends waiting, they know that they need to improve Judy's processing time (see Problem 1). They are currently considering the following two options:

    a. Install a computer system, with which Judy expects to be able to complete a student request 40 percent faster (from 2 minutes per request to 1 minute and 12 seconds, for example).

    b. Hire another temporary clerk, who will work at the same rate as Judy.

       If the computer costs $99.50 to operate per day, while the temporary clerk gets paid $75 per day, is Judy right to prefer the hired help? Assume Poisson arrivals and exponential service times.

3. The Saskatoon Discounts Wholesale Club has two service desks, one at each entrance of the store. Customers arrive at each service desk at an average of one every six minutes. The service rate at each service desk is four minutes per customer.

    a. How often (what percentage of time) is each service desk idle?

    b. What is the probability that both service clerks are busy?

    c. What is the probability that both service clerks are idle?

    d. How many customers, on average, are waiting in line in front of each service desk?

    e. How much time does a customer spend at the service desk (waiting plus service time)?

4. Saskatoon Discounts Wholesale Club is considering consolidating its two service desks (see Problem 3) into one location, staffed by two clerks. The clerks will continue to work at the same individual speed of four minutes per customer.

    a. What is the probability of waiting in line?

    b. How many customers, on average, are waiting in line?

    c. How much time does a customer spend at the service desk (waiting plus service time)?

    d. Do you think the Saskatoon Discounts Wholesale Club should consolidate the service desks?

5. Burrito King (a new fast-food franchise opening up nationwide) has successfully automated burrito production for its drive-up fast-food establishments. The Burro-Master 9000 requires a constant 45 seconds to produce a batch of burritos. It has been estimated that customers will arrive at the drive-up window according to a Poisson distribution at an average of one every 50 seconds. To help determine the amount of space needed for the line at the drive-up window, Burrito King would like to know the expected average time in the system, the average line length (in cars), and the average number of cars in the system (both in line and at the window).

6. The Bijou Theater in Clarke's Beach, Newfoundland, shows vintage movies. Customers arrive at the theater line at the rate of 100 per hour. The ticket seller averages 30 seconds per customer, which includes placing validation stamps on customers' parking lot receipts and punching their frequent watcher cards. (Because of these added services, many customers don't get in until after the feature has started.)

    a. What is the average customer time in the system?

    b. What would be the effect on customer time in the system of having a second ticket taker doing nothing but validations and card punching, thereby cutting the average service time to 20 seconds?

    c. Would system waiting time be less than you found in b if a second window was opened with each server doing all three tasks?

7. To support National Heart Week, the Heart Association plans to install a free blood pressure testing booth in Deerfoot Mall for the week. Previous experience indicates that, on average, 10 persons per hour request a test. Assume arrivals are Poisson from an infinite population. Blood pressure measurements can be made at a constant time of five minutes each. Assume the queue length can be infinite with FCFS discipline.

    a. What average number in line can be expected?

    b. What average number of persons can be expected to be in the system?

    c. What is the average amount of time that a person can expect to spend in line?

    d. On average, how much time will it take to measure a person's blood pressure, including waiting time?

    e. On weekends, the arrival rate can be expected to increase to over 12 per hour. What effect will this have on the number in the waiting line?

8. A cafeteria serving line has a coffee urn from which customers serve themselves. Arrivals at the urn follow a Poisson distribution at the rate of three per minute. In serving themselves, customers take about 15 seconds, exponentially distributed.
   a. How many customers would you expect to see on the average at the coffee urn?
   b. How long would you expect it to take to get a cup of coffee?
   c. What percentage of time is the urn being used?
   d. What is the probability that three or more people are in the cafeteria?
   e. If the cafeteria installs an automatic vendor that dispenses a cup of coffee at a constant time of 15 seconds, how does this change your answers to a and b?

9. L. Winston Messier (an allergist in Winnipeg) has an excellent system for handling his regular patients who come in just for allergy injections. Patients arrive for an injection and fill out a name slip, which is then placed in an open slot that passes into another room staffed by one or two nurses. The specific injections for a patient are prepared, and the patient is called through a speaker system into the room to receive the injection. At certain times during the day, patient load drops and only one nurse is needed to administer the injections.

   Let's focus on the simpler case of the two—namely, when there is one nurse. Also assume that patients arrive in a Poisson fashion and the service rate of the nurse is exponentially distributed. During this slower period, patients arrive with an interarrival time of approximately three minutes. It takes the nurse an average of two minutes to prepare the patients' serum and administer the injection.
   a. What is the average number you would expect to see in Dr. Messier's facilities?
   b. How long would it take for a patient to arrive, get an injection, and leave?
   c. What is the probability that there will be three or more patients on the premises?
   d. What is the utilization of the nurse?
   e. Assume three nurses are available. Each takes an average of two minutes to prepare the patients' serum and administer the injection. What is the average total time of a patient in the system?

10. The Judy Gomes Income Tax Service is analyzing its customer service operations during the month prior to the April filing deadline. On the basis of past data it has been estimated that customers arrive according to a Poisson process with an average interarrival time of 12 minutes. The time to complete a return for a customer is exponentially distributed with a mean of 10 minutes. Based on this information, answer the following questions:
   a. If you went to Judy, how much time would you allow for getting your return done?
   b. On average, how much room should be allowed for the waiting area?
   c. If Judy stayed in the office 12 hours per day, how many hours on average, per day, would she be busy?
   d. What is the probability that the system is idle?
   e. If the arrival rate remained unchanged but the average time in system must be 45 minutes or less, what would need to be changed?

11. Benny the Barber owns a one-chair shop. At barber college, Benny was told that his customers would exhibit a Poisson arrival distribution and that he would provide an exponential service distribution. His market survey data indicate that customers arrive at a rate of two per hour. It will take Benny an average of 20 minutes to give a haircut. Based on these figures, find the following:
   a. The average number of customers waiting.
   b. The average time a customer waits.
   c. The average time a customer is in the shop.
   d. The average utilization of Benny's time.

12. Benny the Barber (see Problem 11) is considering adding a second chair. Customers would be selected for a haircut on a FCFS basis from those waiting. Benny has assumed that both barbers would take an average of 20 minutes to give a haircut, and that business would remain unchanged with customers arriving at a rate of two per hour. Find the following information to help Benny decide if a second chair should be added:
   a. The average number of customers waiting.
   b. The average time a customer waits.
   c. The average time a customer is in the shop.

13. Customers enter the camera department of a store at an average rate of six per hour. The department is staffed by one employee, who takes an average of six minutes to serve each arrival. Assume this is a simple Poisson arrival exponentially distributed service time situation.

    a. As a casual observer, how many people would you expect to see in the camera department (excluding the clerk)? How long would a customer expect to spend in the camera department (total time)?

    b. What is the utilization of the clerk?

    c. What is the probability that there are more than two people in the camera department (excluding the clerk)?

    d. Another clerk has been hired for the camera department who also takes an average of six minutes to serve each arrival. How long would a customer expect to spend in the department now?

14. Cathy Lee, bartender at the Fredericton Racquet Club, can serve drinks at the rate of one every 50 seconds. During a hot evening recently, the bar was particularly busy and every 55 seconds someone was at the bar asking for a drink.

    a. Assuming that everyone in the bar drank at the same rate and that Cathy served people on a first-come, first-served basis, how long would you expect to have to wait for a drink?

    b. How many people would you expect to be waiting for drinks?

    c. What is the probability that three or more people are waiting for drinks?

    d. What is the utilization of the bartender (how busy is she)?

    e. If the bartender is replaced with an automatic drink dispensing machine (with a constant service time), how would this change your answer in part a?

15. An office employs several clerks who originate documents and one operator who enters the document information in a word processor. The group originates documents at a rate of 25 per hour. The operator can enter the information with average exponentially distributed time of two minutes. Assume the population is infinite, arrivals are Poisson, and queue length is infinite with FCFS discipline.

    a. Calculate the percentage utilization of the operator.

    b. Calculate the average number of documents in the system.

    c. Calculate the average time in the system.

    d. Calculate the probability of four or more documents being in the system.

    e. If another clerk were added, the document origination rate would increase to 30 per hour. What would this do to the word processor workload? Show why.

16. A study-aid desk staffed by a graduate student has been established to answer students' questions and help in working problems in your OSM course. The desk is staffed eight hours per day. The dean wants to know how the facility is working. Statistics show that students arrive at a rate of four per hour, and the distribution is approximately Poisson. Assistance time averages 10 minutes, distributed exponentially. Assume population and line length can be infinite and queue discipline is FCFS.

    a. Calculate the percentage utilization of the graduate student.

    b. Calculate the average number of students in the system.

    c. Calculate the average time in the system.

    d. Calculate the probability of four or more students being in line or being served.

    e. Before a test, the arrival of students increases to six per hour on the average. What does this do to the average length of the line?

17. At a Quebec border inspection station, vehicles arrive at the rate of 10 per minute in a Poisson distribution. For simplicity in this problem, assume that there is only one lane and one inspector, who can inspect vehicles at the rate of 12 per minute in an exponentially distributed fashion.

    a. What is the average length of the waiting line?

    b. What is the average time that a vehicle must wait to get through the system?

    c. What is the utilization of the inspector?

    d. What is the probability that when you arrive there will be three or more vehicles ahead of you?

18. The Quebec border inspection station (see Problem 17) is considering the addition of a second inspector. The vehicles would wait in one lane and then be directed to the first available inspector. Arrival rates would remain the same (10 per minute) and the new inspector would process vehicles at the same rate as the first inspector (12 per minute).

a. What would be the average length of the waiting line?

b. What would be the average time that a vehicle must wait to get through the system?

   If a second lane was added (one lane for each inspector):

c. What would be the average length of the waiting line?

d. What would be the average time that a vehicle must wait to get through the system?

19. During the campus Spring Fling, the bumper car amusement attraction has a problem of cars becoming disabled and in need of repair. Repair personnel can be hired at the rate of $20 per hour, but they only work as one team. Thus, if one person is hired, he or she works alone; two or three people work together on the same repair.

   One repairer can fix cars in an average time of 30 minutes. Two repairers take 20 minutes, and three take 15 minutes. While these cars are down, lost income is $40 per hour. Cars tend to break down at the rate of two per hour.

   How many repairers should be hired?

20. A toll tunnel has decided to experiment with the use of a debit card for the collection of tolls. Initially, only one lane will be used. Cars are estimated to arrive at this experimental lane at the rate of 750 per hour. It will take exactly four seconds to verify the debit card.

   a. In how much time would you expect the customer to wait in line, pay with the debit card, and leave?

   b. How many cars would you expect to see in the system?

CASE | Community Hospital Evening Operating Room

National or provincial/state Colleges of Surgeons have developed criteria for determining operating room standards in different jurisdictions. In general, Level I and II trauma centres are required to have in-house operating room (OR) staff 24 hours per day. So a base level of a single OR team available 24 hours a day is mandatory. During normal business hours, a hospital will typically have additional OR teams available since surgery is scheduled during these times and these additional teams can be used in an emergency. An important decision, though, must be made concerning the availability of a backup team during the evening hours.

A backup team is needed during the evening hours if the probability of having two or more cases simultaneously is significant. "Significant" is difficult to judge, but for the purposes of this case assume that a backup OR team should be employed if the expected probability of two or more cases occurring simultaneously is greater than 1 percent.

A real application was recently studied by doctors at the Columbia University College of Physicians and Surgeons in Stamford, CT. The doctors studied emergency OR patients that arrived after 11 p.m. and before 7 a.m. during a one year period. During this time period, 62 patients required OR treatment. The average service time was 80.79 minutes.

In analyzing the problem, think about this as a single-channel, single-phase system with Poisson arrivals and Exponential service times.

1. Calculate the average customer arrival rate and service rate per hour.

2. Calculate the probability of zero patients in the system (P_0), probability of one patient (P_1), and the probability of two or more patients simultaneously arriving during the night shift.

3. Using the criterion that if the probability is greater than 1 percent, a backup OR team should be employed, make a recommendation to hospital administration.

Source: Tucker, J.B., Barone, J.E., Cecere, J., Blabey, R.G., Rha, C.K. "Using Queuing Theory to Determine Operating Room Staffing Needs," *Journal of Trauma*, Vol. 46(1), pp. 71–79.

Selected Bibliography

Fitzsimmons, J. A., and M. J. Fitzsimmons. *Service Management,* 4th ed. New York: Irwin/McGraw-Hill, 2003.

Gross, D., and C. M. Harris. *Fundamentals of Queuing Theory.* New York: Wiley, 1997.

Hillier, F. S., et al. *Queuing Tables and Graphs.* New York: Elsevier–North Holland, 1981.

Kleinrock, L., and R. Gail. *Queuing Systems: Problems and Solutions.* New York: Wiley, 1996.

Winston, W. L., and S. C. Albright. *Practical Management Science: Spreadsheet Modeling and Application.* New York: Duxbury, 2000.

PROCESS ANALYSIS

Learning Objectives:

1. Understand process analysis.
2. Know how to prepare a process flowchart.
3. Understand the different types of processes used by businesses.
4. Calculate the different measures of process performance.

FASTER SERVICE HAS BENEFITS AND COSTS

Saying "HimayItakeyourorderplease?" takes only one second for the drive-through greeter at Wendy's Old-Fashioned Hamburgers. This is two seconds faster than Wendy's guidelines and illustrates the effort fast food chains are putting into speeding up their drive-through pick-up windows. Cars spent on average 150.3 seconds at Wendy's, the leader in this category, which made it 16.7 seconds and 21 seconds faster than McDonald's and Burger King respectively. Yet, far from resting on its laurels, Wendy's is working hard to reduce this time even further.

Why this emphasis on reducing process and waiting times? The drive-through business has been growing at a faster rate than on-premise sales. Since the growth in the number of new restaurants is slowing, the big chains are focusing on this newer battleground, drive-through sales. Using product development, employee retraining, and new technology, McDonald's, Burger King, Arby's, Taco Bell, and others are battling to be the fastest in the business. It is estimated that increasing drive-through efficiency by 10 percent bolsters sales for the average fast-food restaurant by about 10 percent per year.

Wendy's and Burger King are building special drive-through kitchens, while McDonald's is experimenting with windshield transponders that can automatically bill the purchaser's account, making the cash transaction redundant. McDonald's estimates that it can shave off 15 seconds from its drive-through time and boost sales by 2 percent. Timers, kitchen choreography designed to eliminate unnecessary movement, and wireless headsets that let all workers hear customer orders, are other initiatives. Sounding alarms such as beeps, sirens, and even voices congratulating or admonishing crews are also being used. Tim Horton's recently stopped making donuts at is locations and outsourced them to Maidstone Bakeries of Brantford, Ontario. Maidstone ships frozen donuts to Tim Horton's locations in Canada and the U.S. This allows the Tim Horton's stores to make donuts quickly by reheating them.

Is there a trade-off in speeding up the service? The same survey that placed Wendy's on top in speed also ranked it eleventh in accuracy. University student Clint Toland and his girlfriend recently drove through a Taco Bell to get a late-night meal of nachos with meat but no beans, only to discover back at home that the order contained beans and no meat. Says he, "I am never coming back."

Speed can also be stressful for employees. After nine months at a drive-through, night manager Tiffany Swan Holloway vows never to work again in fast food. Her small night crew had a hard time keeping up with the 60-second service goal, and the beepers irritated her too. In the case of Tim Hortons, some may argue that freezing donuts and reheating them later could reduce their taste quality (though others might argue that making fresh donuts in the store in large batches can result in donuts becoming stale a few hours later).

This is a good illustration of some of the trade-offs in process design. Although faster processes are desirable, ultimately they may not be desirable at the cost of lower quality or higher server stress.

■ Sources: http://en.wikipedia.org/wiki/Tim_Hortons, retrieved, February 7, 2009.
http://www.brantfordbrant.com/publications/E.D.NewsletterSummer.07.pdf, retrieved, February 7, 2009.
Jennifer Ordonez, "Next! An Efficiency Drive: Fast-Food Lanes Are Getting Even Faster—Big Chains, Vying for Traffic, Use High-Tech Timers, 'Kitchen Choreography'—Mesclun in a Milkshake Cup?" *Wall Street Journal*, May 18, 2000, A1.

PROCESS ANALYSIS

What is a process? A **process** is any part of an organization that takes inputs and transforms them into outputs that, it is hoped, are of greater value to the organization than the original inputs. Consider some examples of processes. Honda Motors assembles the Civic in a plant in Alliston, Ontario. The assembly plant takes in parts and components that have been fabricated for the plant. Using labour, equipment along an assembly line, and energy, these parts and components are transformed into automobiles. McDonald's, at each of its restaurants, uses inputs such as hamburger meat, lettuce, tomatoes, and potatoes. To these inputs, trained labour is added in the form of cooks and order takers, and capital equipment is used to transform the inputs into hamburgers, french fries, and other foods.

In both of these examples, the process produces products as output. However, the outputs of many processes are services. In a hospital, for example, specialized equipment and highly trained doctors, nurses, and technicians are combined with another input, the patient. The patient is transformed through proper treatment and care into a healthy patient. An airline is another example of a service organization. The airline uses airplanes, ground equipment, flight crews, ground crews, reservation personnel, and fuel to transport customers and freight between locations all over the world.

This chapter describes how to analyze a process. Analyzing a process allows some important questions to be answered, such as these: How many customers can the process

A stage in the assembly line process of producing an automobile where inputs are transformed into outputs. The line is paced as the car moves from one stage to the next after a fixed time interval.

handle per hour? How long will it take to serve a customer? What change is needed in the process to expand capacity? How much does the process cost? A difficult, but important, first step in process analysis is to clearly define the purpose of the analysis. Is the purpose to solve a problem? Is it to better understand the impact of a change in how business will be done in the future?

Clearly understanding the purpose of the analysis is critical to setting the level of detail in modelling the process. Keep the analysis as simple as possible. The following sections of this chapter discuss the details of constructing flowcharts and measures that are appropriate for different types of processes. But first, consider a simple example.

PROCESS FLOWCHARTING

Often, the activities associated with a process affect one another, so it is important to consider the simultaneous performance of a number of activities, all operating at the same time. A good way to start analyzing a process is with a diagram showing the basic elements of a process—typically, tasks, flows, and storage areas. Tasks are shown as rectangles, flows as arrows, and the storage of goods or other items as inverted triangles. Sometimes, flows through a process can be diverted in multiple directions depending on some condition. Decision points are depicted as a diamond, with the different flows running from the points on the diamond. Exhibit 6.1 displays examples of these symbols, along with their use in an example.

EXHIBIT 6.1

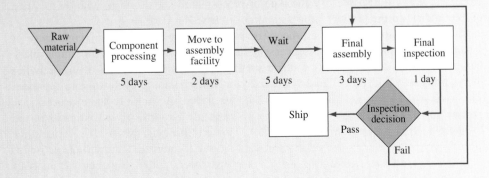

The example shown is that of a product that is made from processed components. The raw material for processing is held in inventory. When the product is ready to be manufactured, the raw material is withdrawn from the inventory in appropriate quantities and the components are made. Then these components are shipped to the second facility where they wait for some time before being assembled into the final product. The product then goes through a final inspection. If it passes inspection it is shipped. Otherwise, it is returned to the final assembly area for rework. The flowchart could be more or less detailed, as required. For example, Exhibit 6.1 does not include the option for inspection after component processing. This could be added if appropriate. Further, the component processing and final assembly process nodes could be expanded to show more detail. One important advantage of process flowcharting is that it allows decision makers to identify opportunities for improving the process. For example, one may question why components need to be moved to a second facility for assembly, thus encountering delays. This might lead to reorganization of the process so that all the processing is done in one facility, resulting in a faster process. Thus, process flowcharting is related to a concept called Value Stream Mapping (VSM) which analyzses processes for improvement.

An easy way to draw flowcharts is to use the Shapes gallery available in the Microsoft Office programs (i.e., Word, Excel, and PowerPoint). For more sophisticated flow charting, other, more dedicated, flowcharting software is also available.

Cycle Time and Utilization

The cycle time (discussed in Chapter 5) of a repetitive process is the average time between completions of successive units. Suppose we have an automatic car wash that can wash one car in 3 minutes. Assuming that there are many cars waiting to be washed all the time, the cycle time for the wash is then 3 minutes, i.e., a car comes out of the wash every 3 minutes. However, if, on average, only 10 cars come in an hour, then the actual cycle time is 6 minutes (one car coming out every 6 minutes on average), even though the fastest cycle time for the car wash is 3 minutes. To be consistent, in this text the term "cycle time" refers to the fastest cycle time

Note that this car wash can handle 20 cars an hour (3 minutes per car). If, in reality, only 10 cars on average arrive in an hour, the utilization of this facility is only 50 percent (10 cars per hour/20 cars per hour). Utilization is the ratio of the time that a resource is actually activated relative to the time that it is available for use (also see Chapter 4).

TYPES OF PROCESSES

It is useful to categorize processes to describe how a process is designed. By being able to quickly categorize a process, we can show the similarities and differences between processes. We will also see that the type of process used should tie in with the position of the product on the product–process matrix discussed in Chapter 5.

The first way to categorize a process is to determine whether it is a *single-stage* or a *multiple-stage* process. If the process in Exhibit 6.1 were viewed as a simple black box, it would be categorized as a single-stage process. In this case, all of the activities in the process would be collapsed and analyzed using a single cycle time to represent its speed. A multiple-stage process has multiple groups of activities that are linked through flows. The term *stage* is used to indicate that multiple activities have been pulled together for analysis purposes.

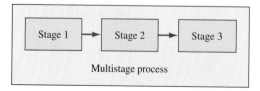

Multistage process

Buffering, Blocking, and Starving

A multiple-stage process may be buffered internally. **Buffering** refers to a storage area between stages where the output of a stage is placed prior to being used in a downstream stage. Buffering allows the stages to operate independently. If one stage feeds a second stage with no intermediate buffer, then the assumption is that the two stages are directly linked. When a process is designed this way, the most common problems that can happen are blocking and starving. **Blocking** occurs when the activities in the stage must stop because there is no place to deposit the item just completed. **Starving** occurs when the activities in a stage must stop because there is no work.

Consider a two-stage process where the first stage has a cycle time of 30 seconds and the second a cycle time of 45 seconds. If this process needs to produce 100 units, then the first stage would be blocked for 15 seconds for each unit produced.

What would happen if an inventory buffer were placed between the two stages? In this case, the first stage would complete the 100 units in 3000 seconds (30 seconds/unit × 100 units). During these 3000 seconds, the second stage would complete only 66 units ((3000 − 30) seconds/45 seconds/unit). The 30 seconds are subtracted from the 3000 seconds because the second stage is starved for the first 30 seconds. This would mean that the inventory would build up to 34 units (100 units − 66 units) over that first 3000 seconds. All of the units would be produced in 4530 seconds. The second stage in this case is called a **bottleneck** because it limits the capacity of the process.

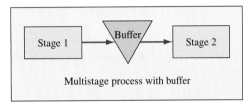

Multistage process with buffer

What would happen if the first stage required 45 seconds and the second stage had the 30-second cycle time? In this case, the first stage would be the bottleneck, and each unit would go directly from the first stage to the second. The second stage would be starved for 15 seconds waiting for each unit to arrive; however, it would still take 4530 seconds to complete all 100 units. Note that the cycle time is 45 seconds (one unit comes out every 45 seconds) which is the time required to process each unit at the bottleneck stage. So the cycle time is related to the processing time at the bottleneck. All of this assumes that there is no variability in the cycle time. With the relatively low 67 percent utilization on the second stage, variability would have little impact on the performance of this system, but if the cycle times were closer, some inventory might collect in the buffer.

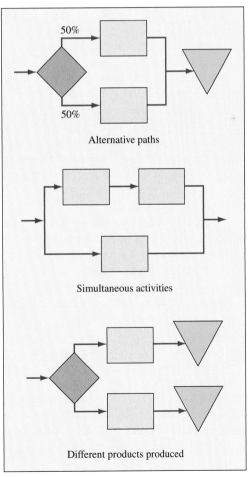

Alternative paths

Simultaneous activities

Different products produced

Often, activities, stages, and even entire processes are operated in parallel. For example, operating two identical activities in parallel would theoretically double capacity. Or perhaps two different sets of activities can be done at the same time on the unit being produced. In analyzing a system with parallel activities or stages, it is important to understand the context. In the case where parallel processes represent alternatives, for example, a diamond should show that flows divert and what percentage of the flow moves in each direction. Sometimes, two or more processes terminate in a common inventory buffer. Normally, this indicates that the two processes make identical items that are going into this inventory. Separate inventories should be used in the diagram if the outputs of the parallel processes are different.

Make-to-Stock versus Make-to-Order

Another useful way to characterize a process is whether the process *makes to stock* or *makes to order*. To illustrate these concepts, consider the processes used to make hamburgers at the three major fast-food restaurant chains in North America: McDonald's, Burger King, and Wendy's. In the case of McDonald's, in 1999 the company converted to a new make-to-order process, but the company has now revised that into a "hybrid" system. We begin our tour of the approaches used by the top fast-food restaurants by first reviewing the traditional approach.

Consider a traditional restaurant making hamburgers. Before the era of fast food, hamburgers were always made to order. In the traditional process, the customer places an order specifying the degree of cooking (medium or well done) and requests specific condiments (pickles, cheese, mustard, onions, ketchup). Using this specification, the cook takes raw hamburger meat from inventory (typically, this inventory is refrigerated and the patties have already been made), cooks the hamburger, and warms the bun. The hamburger is then assembled and delivered to the customer. The quality of the hamburger is highly dependent on the skill of the cook.

This **make-to-order** process is activated only in response to an actual order. Inventory (both work-in-process and finished goods) is kept to a minimum. Theoretically, one would expect that response time would be slow because all the activities need to be completed before the product is delivered to the customer. Services by their very nature often use make-to-order processes. A make-to-order process is used for products in the project and job shop part of the diagonal in the product process matrix, i.e., for customized products produced in low volumes.

McDonald's revolutionized the hamburger-making process by developing a high-volume approach. A diagram of McDonald's traditional process is shown in Exhibit 6.2A. Until recently, hamburgers were grilled in batches. Standard hamburgers (for example, the "Big Mac" consists of two beef patties, sauce, lettuce, cheese, pickles, and onion on a sesame seed bun) were then prepared and stored in a holding bin for immediate delivery to the customer. A person who judged current demand and placed orders to keep inventory in the bin at an appropriate level controlled the whole process. This is a highly efficient **make-to-stock** process that produces standard products that can be delivered quickly to the customer. This quick process appeals to families with small children, for whom speed of delivery is important.

In general, a make-to-stock process ends with finished goods inventory; customer orders are then served from this inventory. A make-to-stock process can be controlled based on the actual or anticipated amount of finished goods inventory. A target stocking level, for example, might be set, and the process would be periodically activated to maintain that target stocking level. Make-to-stock processes are also used when demand is seasonal. In this case, inventory can be built during the slow season and used during

Making Hamburgers at McDonald's, Burger King, and Wendy's

EXHIBIT 6.2

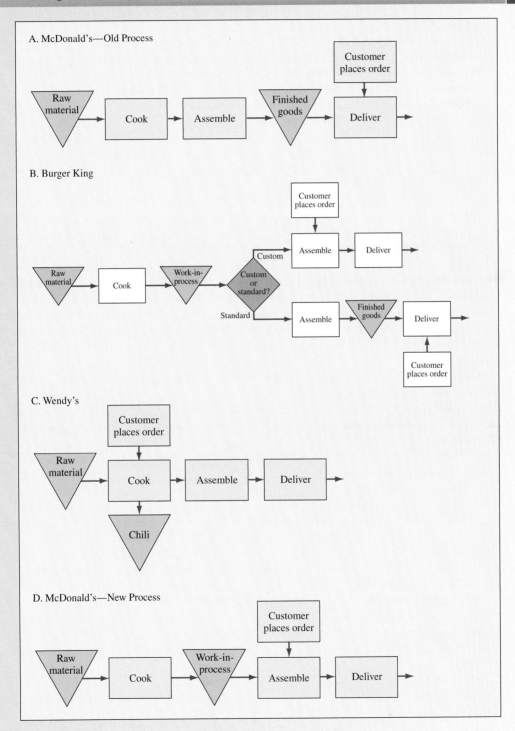

A. McDonald's—Old Process

B. Burger King

C. Wendy's

D. McDonald's—New Process

the peak season, thus allowing the process to run at a constant rate throughout the year. Make-to-stock processes are used for products in the assembly line and continuous process part of the product process matrix, i.e., those products with high volume but little customization.

The unique feature of the Burger King process, shown in Exhibit 6.2B, is a highly specialized conveyor–broiler. Raw hamburger patties are placed on a moving conveyor that runs through a flaming broiler. In exactly 90 seconds, the patties are cooked on both sides with a unique broiler taste. Due to the fixed time for a patty to move through the conveyor–broiler, the thickness of the patties must be the same for all the hamburger products. The buns are also warmed on a conveyor. This system results in a unique, highly consistent product. The cooked patties are stored in a warmed storage container. During periods of high demand, some standard hamburgers are prepared and inventoried for immediate delivery. Custom hamburgers with unique combinations of condiments are prepared to order. This *hybrid* process provides flexibility to respond to customer preferences through the assemble-to-order backend process—thus, the Burger King "have it your way" slogan. In general, **hybrid** processes combine the features of both make-to-order and make-to-stock. Here, two types of process are parallel alternatives at the end of the Burger King process.

Modularized products are made using a hybrid process. In modularized products, generic components (sub-assemblies or modules) are first made-to-stock. The components are then assembled in different combinations, when actual customer demand occurs. As shown in the OSMP, a company like Silent Witness is able to offer more than 1000 different end products, with fewer than 40 standard modules. Modularization thus uses the characteristics of both make-to-order and make-to-stock processes.

Modularization is also related to **mass customization**. Mass customization implies that mass production methods (high volume process for the modules with the advantages discussed in Chapter 5) are employed, while at the same time offering customization (assembling the standard modules into many different end products). Mass customization is discussed in more detail in Chapter 8.

A key trade-off in modularization is the speed of design, quality, and reliability versus uniqueness. For example, while Mercedes realized that while having every model as unique as possible (differentiating between the various models) was important to a luxury car brand, having too many unique parts in each model can bring its own problems. Designing unique parts requires increasing the time needed to design a new model. This could be a disadvantage if a competitor like Lexus or BMW introduces a state-of-the art model more quickly. Also, new and untested parts have a higher risk of unanticipated failure in the field, resulting in product recalls, whereas using common parts that have already been field tested would be more reliable. At the same time, though, Mercedes wants to keep its reputation for innovation in each model. Thus, it does not want too many common components either. So Mercedes is using limited modularization.[1]

Continuing with our tour, Wendy's uses a make-to-order process (as shown in Exhibit 6.2C) that is in full view of the customer. Hamburger patties are cooked on a grill. During high-volume times, the cook tries to get a little ahead and anticipates the arrival of customers. Patties that are on the grill too long are used in the chili soup. When a customer order arrives, a patty is taken from the grill and the hamburger is assembled to the exact specifications of the customer. Because the process starts with the cooking of the patty, it is a little slower. The customer can see what is going on, and the perception is of a high-quality custom product.

Design Your Own Surveillance Camera on the Web

Founded in 1986 and based in Surrey, British Columbia, Silent Witness (now a unit of Honeywell Video Systems), is a company that designs and manufactures a full range of video monitoring technology for the global marketplace, including high-performance closed circuit television (CCTV) cameras, digital and analog storage solutions, digital processing technologies, and network-based remote video surveillance. You can design your preferred surveillance camera by going to the Silent Witness Web site. With about 19 types of housings, 12 types of cameras, and 6 types of lenses (each for two different types of television systems), and some other options, you can have more than 1000 camera configurations, yet the company needs to produce and carry only a little more than 40 stock keeping units (SKUs). So they don't have to forecast demand and manage the supply chain for 1000 items, only for 40. This is a good example of how modular design gives the customer more choices while making operations management easier for the provider.

■ Source: www.honeywellvideo.com/support/configurations/modular

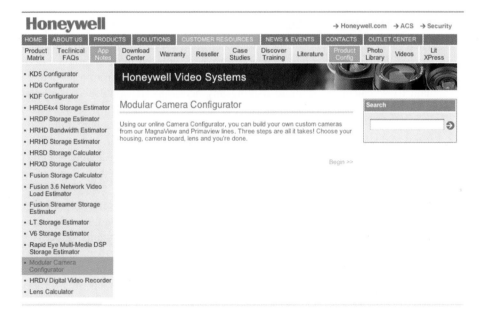

Finally, the new McDonald's process introduced in 1999 (Exhibit 6.2D) is a hybrid process. Cooked hamburger patties are inventoried in a special storage device that maintains the moistness of the cooked patties for up to 30 minutes. The process makes extensive use of the latest cooking technologies. Hamburger patties are cooked in less than 45 seconds. Buns are toasted in only 11 seconds. Individual items on each customer order are transmitted immediately to the area where the hamburgers are assembled, using a specially designed computer system. The assembly process that includes toasting the buns is designed to respond to a customer order in only 15 seconds. By combining the latest technology and clever process engineering, McDonald's has developed a very quick response process. The product is fresh, delivered quickly, and made to the exact specifications of the customer.

Each of the processes used by these companies has its strengths and weaknesses. McDonald's is the high-volume leader, catering to families with young children. Burger

King has its unique taste. Wendy's appeals to those who want their hamburgers prepared the old-fashioned way. Each company focuses advertising and promotional efforts toward attracting the segment of the market its process characteristics best support.

One final method for categorizing a process is by whether it is paced or nonpaced. Recall that Burger King uses the conveyor–broiler to cook hamburgers in exactly 90 seconds. **Pacing** refers to the fixed timing of the movement of items through the process. In a serial process, the movement of items through each activity (or stage) is often paced in some mechanical way to coordinate the line. An assembly line may, for example, move every 45 seconds. Another mechanism used is a clock that counts down the amount of time left in each cycle. When the clock reaches zero, the parts are manually moved to the next activity. Dividing the time available to produce a certain product by customer demand for the product calculates the required cycle time for a process. For example, if an automobile manufacturer needs to produce 1000 automobiles during a shift where the assembly line operates 420 minutes, the cycle time is 25.2 seconds (420 minutes/1000 automobiles × 60 seconds/minute = 25.2 seconds/automobile).

MEASURING PROCESS PERFORMANCE

There is much variation in the way performance metrics are calculated in practice. This section defines metrics in a manner consistent with the most common use in practice. It is vital, though, to understand exactly how a metric coming from a particular company or industry is calculated prior to making any decisions. It would be easier if metrics were calculated more consistently, but this is just not the case. So, if a manager says that his utilization is 90 percent or her efficiency is 115 percent, a standard follow-up question is "How did you calculate that?" Metrics are often calculated in the context of a particular process. Metrics used in cases that you are studying may be defined slightly differently from what is given here. It is important to understand, within the context of the case, how a term is being used.

Comparing the metrics of one company to another, often referred to as *benchmarking,* is an important activity. Metrics tell a firm if progress is being made toward improvement. Similar to the value of financial measures to accountants, process performance metrics give the operations manager a gauge on how productively a process is currently operating and how productivity is changing over time. Often, operations managers need to improve the performance of a process or project the impact of a proposed change. The metrics described in this section are important for answering these questions. To help in understanding these calculations, Exhibit 6.3 shows how these metrics relate to one another.

Possibly the most common process metric is utilization. As discussed earlier in the chapter, utilization is the ratio of the time that a resource is actually being used relative to the time that it is available for use. Utilization is always measured in reference to some resource—for example, the utilization of direct labour or the utilization of a machine resource. The distinction between productivity and utilization is important.

Productivity is the ratio of output to input. Total factor productivity is usually measured in monetary units, dollars, for example, by taking the dollar value of the output (such as goods and services sold) and dividing by the cost of all the inputs (that is, material, labour, and capital investment). Alternatively, *partial factor productivity* is measured based on an individual input, labour being the most common. Partial factor productivity answers the question of how much output we can get from a given level of input; for example, how many computers are made per employee working in the computer manufacturing plant. (See Chapter 2 for additional information about productivity.) Utilization measures the

Process Performance Metrics

EXHIBIT 6.3

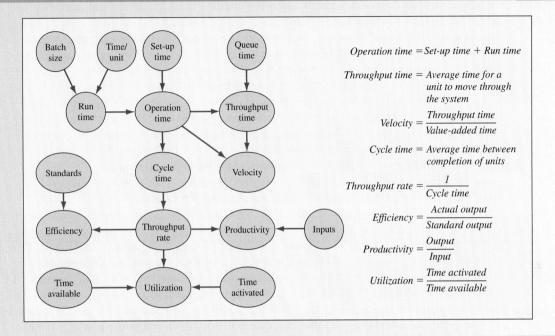

$Operation\ time = Set\text{-}up\ time + Run\ time$

$Throughput\ time = Average\ time\ for\ a\ unit\ to\ move\ through\ the\ system$

$Velocity = \dfrac{Throughput\ time}{Value\text{-}added\ time}$

$Cycle\ time = Average\ time\ between\ completion\ of\ units$

$Throughput\ rate = \dfrac{1}{Cycle\ time}$

$Efficiency = \dfrac{Actual\ output}{Standard\ output}$

$Productivity = \dfrac{Output}{Input}$

$Utilization = \dfrac{Time\ activated}{Time\ available}$

actual activation of the resource. For example, what is the percentage of time that an expensive machine is actually operating?

Efficiency is a ratio of the actual output of a process relative to some standard. For example, consider a machine designed to package cereal at a rate of 30 boxes per minute. If, during a shift, the operators actually produce at a rate of 36 boxes per minute, then the efficiency of the machine is 120 percent (36/30). An alternative way to use the term *efficiency* is to measure the loss or gain in a process. For example, if 1000 units of energy are put into a process designed to convert that energy to some alternative form, and the process produces only 800 units of energy in the new form, then the process is 80 percent efficient.

Run time is the time required to produce a batch of parts. This is calculated by multiplying the time required to produce each unit by the batch size. The **set-up time** is the time required to prepare a machine to make a particular item. Machines that have significant set-up time will typically run parts in batches. The **operation (process) time** is the sum of the set-up time and run time for a batch of parts that are run on a machine. Consider the cereal-boxing machine that is designed to produce at a rate of 30 boxes per minute. The run time for each box is 2 seconds. To switch the machine from 500 g boxes to 250 g boxes requires a set-up time of 30 minutes. The operation time to make a batch of 10 000 250 g boxes is 21 800 seconds (30 minutes' set-up × 60 seconds/minute + 2 seconds/box × 10 000 boxes), or 363.33 minutes.

In practice, set-up time is often not included in the utilization of the process. In essence, set-up time is categorized like the downtime caused by repair or some other disruption to the process. This assumption can vary from company to company, so it is important when comparing the utilization of a machine or other resource to understand exactly how the company categorizes set-up time.

Another related term is **throughput time**. Throughput time includes the time that the unit spends actually being worked on together with the time spent waiting in a queue. As a simple example, consider a paced assembly line that has six stations and runs with a cycle time of 30 seconds. If the stations are located one right after another and every 30 seconds parts move from one station to the next, then the throughput time is three minutes (30 seconds × 6 stations/60 seconds per minute). The **throughput rate** is the output rate that the process is expected to produce over a period of time. The throughput rate of the assembly line is 120 units per hour (60 minutes/hour × 60 seconds/minute ÷ 30 seconds/unit). In this case, the throughput rate is the mathematical inverse of the cycle time. Sometimes throughput time and cycle time are used interchangeably (recall that cycle time is related to the operation time at the bottleneck). So in practice it is important to determine how the term is being used in the context of the process being studied. In this text, cycle time and throughput time are considered to be different.

It has been long recognized that cycle time depends on the bottleneck and that managing the bottleneck is important in ensuring the effectiveness of a process. In fact, in Chapter 3, the "critical path" in a project schedule is the bottleneck in the process since it determines when the project can be completed. Thus, the chapter emphasized the importance of managing the critical path. Lean Manufacturing (Chapter 10) and more recently the Theory of Contraints[2] have also reiterated the importance of bottlenecks in process management.

Often, units are not worked on 100 percent of the time as they move through a process. Because the cycle time of the individual parts of a process often varies, buffers are incorporated in the process to allow individual activities to operate independently, at least to some extent. In the six-station assembly line just described, consider the impact of having 10 additional buffer positions along the line. Assume that two of these positions are between the first and second workstations, two are between stations 2 and 3, and so forth. If these positions are always occupied, then the average throughput time would be eight minutes (assuming a total of 16 positions along the assembly line and an average cycle time of 30 seconds).

A cereal production line running a particular package size. Changing the package size would entail a set-up during which the production line would be idle. To minimize this idle time, each package size is produced in large batches, often called a lot size.

Process velocity (also known as **throughput ratio**) is the ratio of the total throughput time to the value-added time. **Value-added time** is the time in which useful work is actually being done on the unit. Assuming that all of the activities that are included in the process are value-added activities, value-added time should be the sum of the activity operation times in the process. The process velocity (or throughput ratio) for our assembly line with the 10 additional buffer positions, assuming the positions are used 100 percent of the time, is 2.66 (8 minutes/3 minutes).

Summary

Process analysis is a basic skill you need to understand how a business operates. You can obtain great insight by drawing a simple flowchart showing the flow of materials or information through an enterprise. The diagram should include all the operating elements and show how they fit together. Be sure to indicate where material is stored or where orders are queued. Often, 90 percent or more of the time required for a customer to be served is spent just waiting. Hence, merely eliminating the waiting time can dramatically improve the performance of the process.

Remember this fundamental concept when analyzing a process: What goes into the process must come out of the process. A process taken as a whole is like the funnel shown in Exhibit 6.4. The outlet of the funnel restricts the amount that can flow through. In a real business process, certain resources limit output. If liquid is poured into the funnel at a rate greater than it can exit, the level in the funnel will continue to grow. As the level of liquid in the funnel grows, the time it takes the liquid to flow through the funnel increases. If too much liquid is poured into the funnel, it just spills over the top and never flows through.

The same is true of a real process. If too many jobs are pumped into the process, the time that it takes to complete a job will increase because the waiting time will increase. At some point, customers will go somewhere else and the business will be lost. When a process is operating at capacity, the only way to take on more work without increasing the waiting time is to add more capacity. This requires finding what activity is limiting the output of the process and increasing the capacity of that activity. In essence, the tube leading out of the funnel needs to be made larger.

What Goes into a Process Must Come Out of the Process. Input Rate Must Be Less Than or Equal to the Output Rate; Otherwise, the System Will Overflow.

EXHIBIT 6.4

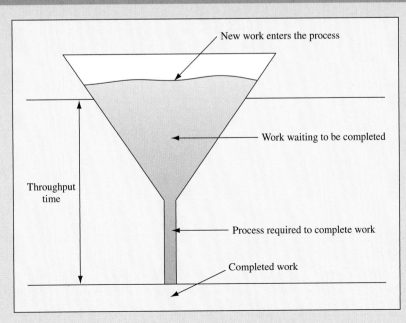

Key Terms

Blocking   The activities in the stage must stop because there is no place to deposit the item just completed.

Bottleneck   A stage or activity (or resource) that limits the capacity or maximum output of the process.

Buffering   A storage area between stages where the output of a stage is placed prior to being used in a downstream stage. Buffering allows the stages to operate independently.

Cycle time   The average time between completions of successive units in a process (this is the definition used in this book). The term is sometimes used to mean the elapsed time between starting and completing a job (throughput time).

Efficiency   A ratio of the actual output of a process relative to some standard.

Hybrid   Combines the features of both make-to-order and make-to-stock. Typically, generic components are made and stocked at some point in the process. These generic components are customized in a final process to meet actual orders.

Make-to-order   A process that is activated only in response to an actual order.

Make-to-stock   A process that produces standard products that are stored in finished goods inventory. The product is delivered quickly to the customer from the finished goods inventory.

Mass customization   Providing customized end products while at the same time using the efficiencies of a high volume manufacturing process.

Modular products   Products that are assembled into different end products from standard modules (components).

Operation time   The sum of the set-up time and run time for a batch of parts that are run on a machine.

Pacing   Movement of items through a process is coordinated through a timing mechanism. Most processes are not paced, but assembly lines are usually paced.

Process   Any set of activities performed by an organization that takes inputs and transforms them into outputs, ideally of greater value to the organization than the original inputs.

Process velocity or throughput ratio   The ratio of the total throughput time to the value-added time.

Productivity   The ratio of output to input. Taking the dollar value of the output and dividing by the dollar value of the inputs usually measures total factor productivity. Alternatively, *partial factor productivity* is measured based on an individual input and often is not calculated using dollar values (an example would be units/person).

Run time   The time required to produce a batch of parts.

Set-up time   The time required to prepare a machine to make a particular item.

Starving   The activities in a stage must stop because there is no work.

Throughput rate   The output rate that the process is expected to produce over a period of time.

Throughput time   The average time that it takes a unit to move through an entire process. Usually, the term *lead time* is used to refer to the total time that it takes a customer to receive an order (includes time to process the order, throughput time, and delivery time).

Utilization   The ratio of the time that a resource is actually activated relative to the time that it is available for use.

Value-added time   The time in which useful work is actually being done on the unit.

Value stream mapping   Visually describing a process and analyzing it for improvement.

Solved Problems

Daffy Dave's Sub Shop makes custom submarine sandwiches to order. Dave is analyzing the processes at the shop. The general flow of the process is shown below. A separate person works at each of the steps in the process.

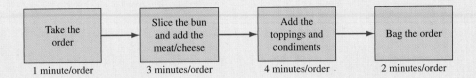

Take the order		Slice the bun and add the meat/cheese		Add the toppings and condiments		Bag the order
1 minute/order		3 minutes/order		4 minutes/order		2 minutes/order

Daffy Dave wants to figure out the following for a typical 8-hour work day.

a. What is the current maximum output of the process?

b. If we add another person, where would we add him or her and what is the benefit?

c. Is there a benefit if we can shift 1 minute from Bun and Meat to Order Taking? Assume we do not make the change in part b above.

d. Is there a benefit if we shift 1 minute of work from Condiments to Bagging? Assume we do not make the changes in parts b and c above.

SOLUTION

a. Maximum output is 120 subs per day.

OPERATION	OUTPUT
Take Orders	(60 min. per hour/1 min. per order) * 8 hours = 480 subs per day
Bun and Meat	(60 min. per hour/3 min. per order) * 8 hours = 160 subs per day
Toppings/Condiments	(60 min. per hour/4 min. per order) * 8 hours = 120 subs per day
Bag the Order	(60 min. per hour/2 min. per order) * 8 hours = 240 subs per day

Output per day is determined by the slowest station; therefore, we can only produce 120 per day because that is the limit of the Toppings/Condiments station.

b. Dave should add the person to the slowest station (Condiments/Toppings) since it is the bottleneck.

OPERATION	OUTPUT
Take Orders	480 subs per day
Bun and Meat	160 subs per day
Toppings/Condiments	120 * 2 = 240 subs per day
Bag the Order	240 subs per day

The impact is not a very big one. Even though the Toppings/Condiments station now can do 240 subs per day, the Bun and Meat station can only do 160, so that is the maximum output.

c. Order Taking station will go from 1 minute to 2 minutes, and Bun and Meat goes from 3 minutes to 2 minutes.

OPERATION	OUTPUT
Take Orders	(60 min. per hour/2 min. per order) * 8 hours = 240 subs per day
Bun and Meat	(60 min. per hour/2 min. per order) * 8 hours = 240 subs per day
Toppings/Condiments	(60 min. per hour/4 min. per order) * 8 hours = 120 subs per day
Bag the Order	(60 min. per hour/2 min. per order) * 8 hours = 240 subs per day

There is no benefit to this change. Dave can still only make 120 subs per day since we can only produce 120 per day because that is the limit of the Toppings/Condiments station.

d. Toppings/Condiments station will go from 4 minutes to 3 minutes, and Bagging goes from 2 minutes to 3 minutes.

OPERATION	OUTPUT
Take Orders	(60 min. per hour/1 min. per order) * 8 hours = 480 subs per day
Bun and Meat	(60 min. per hour/3 min. per order) * 8 hours = 160 subs per day
Toppings/Condiments	(60 min. per hour/3 min. per order) * 8 hours = 160 subs per day
Bag the Order	(60 min. per hour/3 min. per order) * 8 hours = 160 subs per day

There is a benefit to this change. Dave can now make 160 subs per day. This will provide the same benefit as hiring another worker. However, if Dave wants to increase output further, he will have to hire some additional staff.

Review and Discussion Questions

1. Compare McDonald's old and new processes for making hamburgers. How valid is McDonald's claim that the new process will produce fresher hamburgers for the customer? Comparing McDonald's new process to the processes used by Burger King and Wendy's, which process appears to produce the freshest hamburgers?
2. Explain how having more work-in-process inventory can improve the efficiency of a process. How can this be bad?
3. Recently, some operations management experts have begun insisting that simply minimizing process velocity, which actually means minimizing the time that it takes to process something through the system, is the single most important measure for improving a process. Can you think of a situation in which this might not be true?
4. What is a bottleneck and how does it help manage a process?
5. What are the advantages and disadvantages of a modularized process compared to make-to-stock and make-to-order processes?
6. For what type of products or services would it not be appropriate to use a hybrid process?
7. Give an example of a process where you have observed a reduction in set-up time through the use of better technology or better techniques. How has this set-up time reduction helped?

Problems[3]

1. Osakwe, an enterprising student, has set up an internship clearinghouse for business students. Each student who uses the service fills out a form and lists up to 10 companies that he or she would like to have contacted. The clearinghouse has a choice of two methods to use for processing the forms. The traditional method requires about 20 minutes to review the form and arrange the information in the proper order for processing. Once this set-up is done, it takes only two minutes per company requested to complete the processing. The other alternative uses an optical scan/retrieve system, which takes only a minute to prepare but requires five minutes per company for completing the processing. If it costs about the same amount per minute for processing with either of the two methods, when should each be used?
2. Rockness Recycling refurbishes rundown business students. The process uses a moving belt, which carries each student through the five steps of the process in sequence. The five steps are as follows:

STEP	DESCRIPTION	TIME REQUIRED PER STUDENT
1	Unpack and place on belt	1.0 minute
2	Strip off bad habits	1.5 minutes
3	Scrub and clean mind	0.8 minute
4	Insert modern methods	1.0 minute
5	Polish and pack	1.2 minutes

One faculty member is assigned to each of these steps. Faculty members work a 40-hour week and rotate jobs each week. Mr. Rockness has been working on a contract from General Eclectic, which requires delivery of 2000 refurbished students per week. A representative of the human resources department has just called, complaining that the company hasn't been receiving the agreed-upon number of students. A check of finished goods inventory by Mr. Rockness reveals that there is no stock left. What is going on?

3. A local market research firm has just won a contract for several thousand small projects involving data gathering and statistical analysis. In the past, the firm has assigned each project to a single member of its highly trained professional staff. This person would both gather and analyze the data. Using this approach, an experienced person can complete an average of 10 such projects in an eight-hour day.

The firm's management is thinking of assigning two people to each project in order to allow them to specialize and become more efficient. The process would require the data gatherer to fill out a matrix on the computer, check it, and transmit it to the statistical analysis program for the analyst to complete. Data can be gathered on one project while the analysis is being completed on another, but the analysis must be complete before the statistical analysis program can accept the new data. After some practice, the new process can be completed with a standard time of 20 minutes for the data gathering and 30 minutes for the analysis.

   a. What is the production (output per hour) for each alternative? What is the productivity (output per labour hour)?

   b. How long would it take to complete 1000 projects with each alternative? What would the labour content (total number of labour hours) for 1000 projects be for each alternative?

4. The following represents a process used to assemble a chair with an upholstered seat. Stations A, B, and C make the seat; stations J, K, and L assemble the chair frame; station X is where the two subassemblies are brought together; and some final tasks are completed in stations Y and Z. One worker is assigned to each of the stations. Generally, no inventory is kept anywhere in the system, although there is room for one unit between each of the stations that might be used for a brief amount of time.

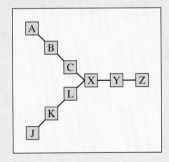

Given the following amount of work in seconds required at each station:

A	38	J	32	X	22
B	34	K	30	Y	18
C	35	L	34	Z	20

   a. What is the possible daily output of this "process" if 8 hours of processing time is available each day?

   b. Given your output rate in part a, what is the efficiency of the process?

   c. What is the throughput time of the process?

5. Wally's Widget Warehouse takes orders from 7 a.m. to 7 p.m. The manager wants to analyze the process. There are three steps required to ship a customer order. The first step is to take the order from a customer (capacity: 100 customers/hr). The second step is to pick the order for the customer (capacity: 80 customers/hr), and then the warehouse has to pack the order ready for shipping (capacity: 60 customers/hr). Wally promises that every order placed today gets shipped tomorrow. That means that the picking and packing operations must finish all orders before they go home.

Wally wants to figure out the following.

a. Draw the flowchart of the process from customer order placement to shipping

b. What is the current maximum output of the process assuming that no one works overtime?

c. How long will the picking and packing operations have to work if we have a day where the order taker works at his maximum capacity?

d. Given c, what is the maximum number of orders waiting to be picked?

e. Given c, what is the maximum number of orders waiting to be packed?

f. If we double the packing capacity (from 60 to 120 orders per hour), what impact does this have on your answers in parts c, d, and e?

6. Anvi, the manager of a bakery, is interested in analyzing her bread-making process. The raw materials required for making bread are carried in inventory. Two steps are required in preparing the bread. The first is preparing the dough and baking the loaves, here referred to as bread making. The second is packaging the loaves. Due to the size of the mixers in the bakery, bread is made in batches of 100 loaves. A batch of 100 loaves is baked every hour. The loaves are then put into an intermediate stocking area ready for packing. Packaging needs only 0.75 hour to place the 100 loaves in bags. The loaves are then stored, waiting for shipment

Anvi is considering buying an additional bread-making machine (though not an additional packaging machine). The time for each individual bread-making operation is still one hour per 100 loaves. Assume that the bakery can sell all it can bake.[4]

a. Draw flowcharts for the situations with both one and two bread-making machines.

b. When there is only one bread-making machine what is the capacity of the bakery per hour? What are the utilizations of the bread-making and packing operations?

c. When there are two bread-making machines what is the capacity of the bakery per hour? What are the utilizations of the bread-making and packing operations?

CASE 1	Kristen's Cookie Company (A)

You and your roommate are preparing to start Kristen's Cookie Company in your on-campus apartment. The company will provide fresh cookies to starving students late at night. You need to evaluate the preliminary design for the company's production process to figure out many variables there are, including what prices to charge, whether you will be able to make a profit, and how many orders to accept.

Business Concept

Your idea is to bake fresh cookies to order, using any combination of ingredients that the buyer wants. The cookies will be ready for pickup at your apartment within an hour.

Several factors will set you apart from competing products such as store-bought cookies. First, your cookies will be completely fresh. You will not bake any cookies before receiving the order; therefore, the buyer will be getting cookies that are literally hot out of the oven.

Second, like Steve's Ice Cream,[5] you will have a variety of ingredients available to add to the basic dough, including chocolate chips, M&M's, Crispy Crunch bars, coconut, walnuts, and raisins. Buyers will telephone in their orders and specify which of these ingredients they want in their cookies. You guarantee completely fresh cookies. In short, you will have the freshest, most exotic cookies anywhere, available right on campus.

The Production Process

Baking cookies is simple: mix all the ingredients in a food processor; spoon out the cookie dough onto a tray; put the cookies into the oven; bake them; take the tray of cookies out of the oven; let the cookies cool; and, finally, take the cookies off the tray and carefully pack them in a box. You and your roommate already own all the necessary capital equipment: one food processor, cookie sheets, and spoons. Your apartment has a small oven that will hold one tray at a time. Your land-lord pays for all the electricity. The variable costs, therefore, are merely the cost of the ingredients (estimated to be $0.60/dozen), the cost of the box in which the cookies are packed ($0.10 per box; each box holds a dozen cookies), and your time (what value do you place on your time?).

A detailed examination of the production process, which specifies how long each of the steps will take, follows. The first step is to take an order, which your roommate has figured out how to do quickly and with 100 percent accuracy. (Actually, you and your roommate devised a method using the Internet to accept orders and to inform customers when their orders will be ready for pickup. Because this runs automatically on your personal computer, it does not take any of your time.) There-fore, this step will be ignored in further analysis.

You and your roommate have timed the necessary physical operations. The first physical production step is to wash out the mixing bowl from the previous batch, add all of the ingredients, and mix them in your food processor. The mixing bowls hold ingredients for up to three dozen cookies. You then dish up the cookies, one dozen at a time, onto a cookie tray. These activities take six minutes for the washing and mixing steps, regardless of how many cookies are being made in the batch. That is, to mix enough dough and ingredients for two dozen cookies takes the same six minutes as one dozen cookies. However, dishing up the cookies onto the sheet takes two minutes per sheet.

The next step, performed by your roommate, is to put the cookies in the oven and set the thermostat and timer, which takes about one minute. The cookies bake for the next nine minutes. So total baking time is 10 minutes, during the first minute of which your roommate is busy setting the oven. Be-cause the oven holds only one cookie sheet, a second dozen take an additional 10 minutes to bake.

Your roommate also performs the last steps of the process by first removing the cookies from the oven and putting them aside to cool for five minutes, then carefully packing them in a box and accepting payment. Removing the cookies from the oven takes only a negligible amount of time, but it must be done promptly. It takes two minutes to pack each dozen and about one minute to accept payment for the order.

That is the process for producing cookies by the dozen in Kristen's Cookie Company. As experienced bakers know, a few simplifications were made in the actual cookie production process. For example, the first batch of cookies for the night requires preheating the oven. However, such complexities will be put aside for now. Begin your analysis by developing a process flow diagram of the cookie-making process.

Key Questions to Answer Before You Launch the Business

To launch the business, you need to set prices and rules for accepting orders. Some issues will be resolved only after you get started and try out different ways of producing the cookies.

Before you start, however, you at least want a preliminary plan, with as much as possible specified, so that you can do a careful calculation of how much time you will have to devote to this business each night, and how much money you can expect to make. For example, when you conduct a market survey to determine the likely demand, you will want to specify exactly what your order policies will be. Therefore, answering the following operational questions should help you:

1. How long will it take you to fill an order?
2. How many orders can you fill in a night, assuming you are open four hours each night?
3. How much of your own and your roommate's valuable time will it take to fill each order?
4. Because your cookie sheets can hold exactly one dozen cookies, you will produce and sell cookies by the dozen. Should you give any discount for people who order two dozen cookies, three dozen cookies, or more? If so, how much? Will it take you any longer to fill a two-dozen cookie order than a one-dozen cookie order?
5. How many food processors and cookie sheets will you need?
6. Are there any changes you can make in your production plans that will allow you to make better cookies, or more cookies in less time or at lower cost? For example, is there a bottleneck operation in your production process that you can expand cheaply? What is the effect of adding another oven? How much would you be willing to pay to rent an additional oven?

Questions

1. What happens if you are trying to do this by yourself with-out a roommate?
2. Should you offer special rates for rush orders? Suppose you have just put a sheet of cookies into the oven and someone calls up with a "crash priority" order for a dozen cookies of a different flavour. Can you fill the priority order while still fulfilling the order for the cookies that are already in the oven? If not, how much of a premium should you charge for filling the rush order?
3. When should you promise delivery? How can you look quickly at your order board (list of pending orders) and tell a caller when his or her order will be ready? How much of a safety margin for timing should you allow?
4. What other factors should you consider at this stage of planning your business?
5. Your product must be made to order because each order is potentially unique. If you decide to sell standard cookies instead, how should you change the production system? The order-taking process?

Source: Kristen's Cookie Company (A), Case 9-686-093, Written by Roger Bohn. Copyright © 1986 by The Harvard Business School Publishing Corpora-tion. All Rights Reserved.

CASE 2 | Canadian Blood Services (CBS)[1]

Canadian Blood Services is a not-for-profit organization created in 1998 that manages the blood supply for Canadians on behalf of the government.[2] It often organizes blood drives in local communities, setting up a temporary blood collection centre in places like gymnasiums. The process of blood collection at such places is as follows: When a potential donor arrives, his or her name and address are recorded manually and he or she is assigned a number in order of arrival. Donors are also given a card with their name on it. Donors then wait in a queue till their number is called. At that time, a nurse records and verifies details about the donor. The nurse also pricks the donor's finger, using a special needle to draw blood into a mini-test tube. Both needle and test tube are disposable. This blood sample is tested immediately for sufficient iron. If donors pass this test, they are given a questionnaire to fill out. This questionnaire elicits information on any current illnesses and recent travel. After completing the questionnaire, donors drop the card obtained upon arrival into a box, which ensures first-drop-first-called sequence. Donors then wait with the questionnaire until their card is taken out of the box and their name is called.

A nurse goes through the questionnaire with the donor to ensure eligibility. For example, if a person has travelled to a region with malaria in the last year, they are ineligible to donate blood (even if they did not contract malaria). On a busy day, potential donors can spend more than an hour in the system before being sent back because they are ineligible. This has caused a lot of annoyance to potential donors. Some have commented that they would not return even when eligible.

1. Draw a flow chart of the process. Times are not necessary.
2. How might you improve the process to avoid wasting the time of ineligible donors? Would there be any material cost savings?
3. If you could do some market intelligence on the community, such as income or ethnicity or any other relevant information, what might you do at the collection centre or other point to expeditiously weed out ineligible donors?

[1]This case is adopted from a real situation observed at a CBS blood collection drive.
[2]*Source:* www.bloodservices.ca

Footnotes

[1]Stephen Power, "Betting on the S; Mercedes Looks to New Model Of Flagship S-Class to Reverse An Image of Sagging Quality," *Wall Street Journal*, July 11, 2005. p. B.1.

[2]Eliyahu Goldratt, *Theory of Constraints* (Great Barrington MA: North River Press, 1990).

[3]The authors are indebted to D. Clay Whybark of the University of North Carolina for contributing Problems 1–3.

[4]This example is similar to one given by A. E. Gray in "Capacity Analysis: Sample Problems," *Harvard Business School* 9-696-058.

[5]Steve's Ice Cream was started in the Boston area by a young entrepreneur to provide make-to-order ice cream, using mix-ins.

Selected Bibliography

Anupindi, R.; S. Chopra; S.D. Deshmukh; J.A. van Mieghem; and E. Zemel. *Managing Business Process Flows.* 2nd ed. Upper Saddle River, NJ: Prentice Hall, 2005.

Gray, A.E., and J. Leonard. "Process Fundamentals." *Harvard Business School* 9-696-023.

Jeston, J., and J. Nelis. *Business Process Management: Practical Guidelines to Successful Implementation.* Burlington, MA: Butterworth-Heinemann, 2006.

MANAGING QUALITY

Learning Objectives:

1. Understand total quality management.
2. Know how quality is measured and be aware of the different dimensions of quality.
3. Understand quality management certification.
4. Know how good quality is recognized through awards.
5. Understand the Define, Measure, Analyze, Improve, and Control (DMAIC) phases of the quality improvement process.
6. Know how to calculate the capability of a process.
7. Understand how processes are monitored with control charts.
8. Be familiar with acceptance sampling concepts.

GE SIX-SIGMA SUPPLY CHAIN PROCESSES

General Electric (GE) has been a major advocate of Six Sigma for over 10 years. Jack Welch, the legendary, now retired, CEO, declared that "the big myth is that Six Sigma is about quality control and statistics. It is that—but it's much more. Ultimately, it drives leadership to be better by providing tools to think through tough issues. At Six Sigma's core is an idea that can turn a company inside out, focusing the organization outward on the customer." GE's commitment to quality centres on Six Sigma. Six Sigma is defined on the GE Web site as follows:

First, What is Six Sigma? First, what it is not. It is not a secret society, a slogan or a cliché. Six Sigma is a highly disciplined process that helps us focus on developing and delivering near-perfect products and services. Why "Sigma"? The word is a statistical term that measures how far a given process deviates from perfection. The central idea behind Six Sigma is that if you can measure how many "defects" you have in a process, you can systematically figure out how to eliminate them and get as close to "zero defects" as possible. To achieve Six Sigma Quality, a process must produce no more than 3.4 defects per million opportunities. An "opportunity" is defined as a chance for nonconformance, or not meeting the required specifications. This means we need to be nearly flawless in executing our key processes.

At its core, Six Sigma revolves around a few key concepts.

Critical to Quality:	Attributes most important to the customer
Defect:	Failing to deliver what the customer wants
Process Capability:	What your process can deliver
Variation:	What the customer sees and feels
Stable Operations:	Ensuring consistent, predictable processes to improve what the customer sees and feels
Design for Six Sigma:	Designing to meet customer needs and process capability

TOTAL QUALITY MANAGEMENT

Total quality management (TQM) may be defined as "managing the entire organization so that it excels on all dimensions of products and services that are important to the customer." It has two fundamental operational goals, namely

1. Careful design of the product or service.
2. Ensuring that the organization's systems can consistently produce the design.

These two goals can only be achieved if the entire organization is oriented toward them—hence the term *total* quality management. TQM became a national concern in North America in the 1980s, primarily as a response to Japanese quality superiority in manufacturing automobiles and other durable goods such as room air conditioners. A widely cited study of Japanese and U.S. air-conditioning manufacturers showed that the best-quality North American products had *higher* average defect rates than those of the poorest Japanese manufacturers.[1] One response to this quality challenge was the institution of **The Canada Awards for Excellence** (CAE) in 1984. These are quality awards given annually to Canadian organizations by the National Quality Institute (NQI) on behalf of the Canadian government.[2] In the U.S., the Department of Commerce established the **Malcolm Baldrige National Quality Award** in 1987 to help companies review and structure their quality programs. Also gaining major attention at this time was the requirement that suppliers demonstrate that they are measuring and documenting their quality practices according to specified criteria, called ISO standards, if they wished to compete for international contracts. We will have more to say about this later.

The philosophical leaders of the quality movement, the so-called Quality Gurus—had slightly different definitions of what quality is and how to achieve it but they all had the same general message: To achieve outstanding quality requires quality leadership from senior management, a customer focus, total involvement of the workforce, and continuous improvement based upon rigorous analysis of processes. Later in the chapter, we will discuss how these precepts are applied in the latest approach to TQM—Six Sigma.

To put the quality movement in perspective we will now discuss the contributions by the Quality Gurus. Of course there are many others who have contributed to the quality movement but we focus here on the more important contributors.

Walter A Shewhart: Shewhart, a statistician at Bell Laboratories, developed the principles of statistical quality control (SQC) in the 1920s. He also created the Plan-Do-Check-Act (PDCA) principle of continuous improvement: we Plan for the improvement, then we Do the improvement, after which we Check the results against the plan. Finally, we Act to improve again which leads us back to the beginning of the next

Operations and Supply Management in Practice

TQM and Leadership at High Liner Foods

High Liner Foods (formerly National Sea Products) is a 100-year-old food processing company based in Lunenburg, Nova Scotia. It has weathered the decline in fish stocks on the East Coast by launching new products, eliminating unprofitable lines, acquiring non-seafood based businesses, and focusing on total quality management (TQM). Today its profits are increasing and the company is successfully penetrating U.S. markets, where it lists major grocery chains, club stores, and Wal-Mart among its customers. In fact, Fisher Boy, the company's U.S. and Mexican seafood brand, was the bestselling fish stick in the United States in 2002. In 1995, the Canadian grocery trade gave a "Best New Product Award" to the company's Gourmet Fillets. Since then, High Liner has won the Grand Prix Awards (grocery industry Junos or Grammys) from the Canadian Council of Grocery Distributors for different products.

A few years earlier, the company had launched a TQM campaign. Top management recognized that leadership would be a key in the success of the campaign. Said President and CEO Henry Demone, "When you launch something like this (TQM) in a company, you have to assume that the people in middle management and front lines are going to be skeptical. Okay (they say), the guys went to a seminar or they read a book and this is the flavour of the month. They test your commitment and you have to prove your commitment by your actions day to day."

Demone also introduced a broad and regular consultation process for planning to improve communication and decision making in an era where tough decisions had to be made, such as getting out of some seafood businesses, laying off employees, and reorganizing.

For example, at the company's Arnold's Cove plant in Newfoundland, employees organized themselves into work teams along with management "coaches" to learn new processing skills and interact with technology.

Today, Demone considers quality and innovation to be key parts of the company's competitive strengths.

■ Sources: Quality Imperative, VHS (Ottawa, Ontario: Stonehaven Productions, 1991).

Casey Mahood, "National Sea Stock Hits 52-Week High, CEO Suggest Investors Eyeing Its New Product and Strategic Success," *The Globe and Mail*, April 29, 1997, B17.

Kevin Cox, "High Liner Charts a Sea Change," *The Globe and Mail*, February 5, 1999, B25.

Henry Demone, Address to Shareholders, May 1, 2003, www.highlinerfoods.com.

PDCA cycle. Shewhart's work greatly influenced W. Edwards Deming, probably the best known of the quality gurus.

W. Edwards Deming: In addition to SQC, Deming emphasized the importance of organization-wide quality management. He placed great importance on the change in attitude of senior management since, according to him, 94 percent of quality problems were not attributable to workers but rather to the failings of senior management. Deming would do a "red bead" experiment in workshops to effectively demonstrate this. His well-known 14-point plan for quality improvement helps achieve long-term competitiveness. The plan focuses on the following major themes in quality improvement; a) defect prevention rather than inspection, b) doing business with suppliers based on quality rather than price, c) leadership from top management that provides an atmosphere in which employees can focus on continuous improvement and can take pride in their work though producing quality goods and services, and d) the importance of continuous training and education. It was also his view that by focusing on quality, cost would be automatically reduced in the long run. In Japan, where he first visited just after World War II, his work influenced the rise in quality of Japanese products in the latter half of the twentieth century. The Japanese honoured him by naming their highest quality award the Deming Prize, in 1951, decades before such awards were created in North America.

Joseph M. Juran: Juran, who also influenced the Japanese during his visits there after World War II, developed the concept of quality as "fitness for use," i.e., the product must satisfy the customer's need. He also promoted the Pareto analysis in quality control and costs of quality.[2] His methods of preventing quality problems included *quality improvement* (finding ways of doing better than standard) and *quality planning* (launching new products and processes in ways that result in minimal need for future quality improvement).[3]

Genichi Taguchi: Beginning in the 1950s in Japan, Taguchi began to apply the concept of design of experiments (changing various parameters of the process), also referred to as DOE, in optimizing process quality. His work on the relationship of reduced variability to improved process quality is discussed later in this chapter. Taguchi's work has influenced major companies, such as Toyota.[4]

Philip Crosby: Crosby developed the notion that "quality is free." This philosophy maintains that the cost and effort spent preventing defects will be more than offset by the benefits, such as reduced repair costs (less warranty work, for example), better reputation, and more market share. Crosby (like another Japanese pioneer in quality, Shigeo Shingo) focused on defect prevention or "zero defects."

We will now turn to some fundamental concepts, which underlie any quality effort: quality specifications and quality costs.

QUALITY SPECIFICATION AND QUALITY COSTS

Determining quality specifications and the costs of achieving (or *not* achieving) those specifications are fundamental to any quality program.

Developing Quality Specifications

The quality specifications of a product or service derive from decisions and actions made because of the quality of its design and the quality of its conformance to that design. **Design quality** refers to the inherent value of the product in the marketplace and is thus a strategic decision for the firm. The dimensions of quality are listed in Exhibit 7.1. These dimensions refer to features of the product or service that relate directly to design issues.

A firm designs a product or service with certain performance characteristics and features based on what the intended market expects. Materials and manufacturing process attributes can greatly impact the reliability and durability of a product. Here the company attempts to design a product or service that can be produced or delivered at reasonable cost. The serviceability of the product may have a great impact on the cost of the product or service to the customer after the initial purchase is made. It may also affect the warranty and repair cost to the firm. Aesthetics may greatly impact the desirability of the product or service, in particular consumer products. The design often represents the next generation of an ongoing stream of products or services, especially when a brand name

EXHIBIT 7.1	The Dimensions of Design Quality

DIMENSION	MEANING
Performance	Primary product or service characteristics
Features	Added touches, bells and whistles, secondary characteristics
Reliability/durability	Consistency of performance over time, probability of failing, useful life
Serviceability	Ease of repair
Aesthetics	Sensory characteristics (sound, feel, look, and so on)
Perceived quality	Past performance and reputation

is involved. Consistency in the relative performance of the product compared to the state of the art, for example, may have a great impact on how the quality of the product is perceived. This may be very important to the long-run success of the product or service.

Quality function deployment (QFD) is an important tool in improving design quality. OFD uses multifunctional teams from different departments, such as marketing, design engineering, and manufacturing, to ensure that the designed product is fit for use. The QFD process begins with understanding the customer to determine the characteristics of the required product. The customers' product needs and preferences are then defined and broken down into categories called *customer attributes*. For example, an appliance manufacturer might like to improve the design of a refrigerator door (see Exhibit 7.2). Through

Completed House of Quality Matrix for Refrigerator Door   EXHIBIT 7.2

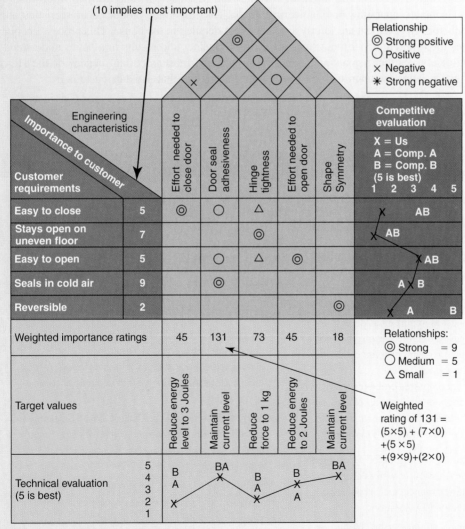

Source: Adapted from F.R Jacobs, R.B Chase, and N. J. Aquilano. *Operations and Supply Management.* New York: Irwin McGraw-Hill, 2009, p. 104.

customer surveys and interviews, the manufacturer might determine that the most important customer attribute desired in a refrigerator door is that it "seal in the cold air." As well, a weighted importance rating for each engineering characteristic that relates to customer attributes is developed. The consumer is also asked to compare and rate the company's products with those of its competitors. Thus, the QFD process helps the company to determine those product characteristics that are important to the consumer and to evaluate its product in relation to others. The end result is a better understanding of and focus on the product characteristics that require improvement.

Customer attribute information forms the basis for the QFD matrix in Exhibit 7.2, also called the house of quality (HOQ). The matrix depicts (a) customer attributes, (b) design characteristics required to satisfy customer requirements, (c) weighted importance ratings for the design characteristics, (d) interrelationships between design characteristics (that could lead to trade-offs), and (e) competitor comparisons. By building a HOQ matrix, the cross-functional QFD team can use customer feedback to make engineering, marketing, and design decisions. The matrix helps the team translate customer attribute information into concrete operating or engineering goals. The important product characteristics and goals for improvement are jointly agreed on and detailed in the house. This process encourages the different departments to work closely together and results in a better understanding of one another's goals and issues. However, the most important benefit of the HOQ is that it helps the team to focus on building a product that satisfies customers.

Operations and Supply Management in Practice

J. D. Power and Associates Redefines Quality

J..D. Power and Associates, the watchdog organization that aims to provide consumers with product quality and customer satisfaction data recently redefined its "Initial Quality Study" in a manner similar to what is discussed in this section. This study, oriented toward new car purchases, recognizes that technology integrated into the overall design of a new vehicle is just as important as defects and malfunctions when it comes to determining quality. The study is designed to capture problems experienced by new owners in two distinct categories:

Quality of Production encompasses problems that have caused a complete breakdown or malfunction of any component, feature or item, including those that stop working or trim pieces that break or come loose. This includes:

- Mechanical Manufacturing Quality: based on problems with the engine or transmission, as well as problems that affect the driving experience, such as pulling on the brakes, abnormal noises, or vibrations.

- Body and Interior Manufacturing Quality: based on problems with wind noise, water leaks, poor interior fit and finish, paint imperfection, and squeaks and rattles.

- Feature and Accessory Manufacturing Quality: based on problems with the seats, windshield wipers, navigation system, rear-seat entertainment system, heater, air conditioner, stereo system, sunroof, and trip computer.

Quality of Design addresses scenarios in which controls or features work as designed, but are difficult to use or understand. This includes:

- Mechanical Design Quality: based on problems with the engine or transmission, and those that affect the driving experience, such as ride smoothness, responsiveness of the steering system and brakes, handling, and stability.

- Body and Interior Design Quality: based on problems with the front- and rear-end styling, the appearance of the interior and exterior, and the sound of the doors when closing.

- Feature and Accessory Design Quality: based on problems with the seats, stereo or navigation system, heater, air conditioner, and sunroof.

Adapted from *J. D. Power and Associates' Study Redefines Quality,* The McGraw-Hill Companies Employee Newsletter, Vol. 19, No. 6 (June, 2006).

| | MEASURES | |
DIMENSION	PRODUCT EXAMPLE: LASER PRINTER	SERVICE EXAMPLE: CHEQUING ACCOUNT AT A BANK
Performance	Pages per minute Print density	Time to process customer requests Online security
Features	Multiple paper trays Colour capability	Automatic bill paying Online inter-account transfers
Reliability/durability	Mean time between failures Estimated time to obsolescence Expected life of major components	Variability of time to process requests Keeping pace with industry trends Online 24/7 availability
Serviceability	Availability of authorized repair centres Number of copies per print cartridge Modular design	Online reports Ease of getting updated information
Aesthetics	Control button layout Case style Courtesy of dealer	Appearance of bank lobby Courtesy of teller Appearance of printed material and Web site
Perceived quality	Brand name recognition Rating in *Consumer Reports*	Endorsed by community leaders Business newspaper reviews

Examples of Dimensions of Quality — EXHIBIT 7.3

Conformance quality refers to the degree to which the product or service design specifications are met. The activities involved in achieving conformance are of a tactical, day-to-day nature. It should be evident that a product or service can have high design quality but low conformance quality, and vice versa.

Quality at the source is frequently discussed in the context of conformance quality. This means that the person who does the work takes responsibility for making sure that his or her output meets specifications. Where a product is involved, achieving the quality specifications is typically the responsibility of manufacturing management; in a service firm, it is usually the responsibility of the branch operations management. Exhibit 7.3 shows two examples of the **dimensions of quality.** One is a laser printer that meets the pages-per-minute and print density standards; the second is a chequing account transaction in a bank (Internet as well as branches).

Both quality of design and quality of conformance should provide products that meet the customer's objectives for those products. This is often termed the product's *fitness for use,* developed, as mentioned earlier, by Joseph Juran. It entails identifying the dimensions of the product (or service) that the customer wants (that is, the voice of the customer) and developing a quality control program to ensure that these dimensions are met.

Cost of Quality

Although few can quarrel with the notion of prevention, management often needs hard numbers to determine how much prevention activities will cost. This issue was recognized by Juran, who wrote about it in 1951 in his *Quality Control Handbook.* Today, cost of quality (COQ) analyses are common in industry and constitute one of the primary functions of QC departments.

There are a number of definitions and interpretations of the term *cost of quality*. From the purist's point of view, it means all of the costs attributable to the production of quality that is not 100 percent perfect. A less stringent definition considers only those costs that are the difference between what can be expected from excellent performance and the current costs that exist.

How significant is the cost of quality? It has been estimated at between 15 and 20 percent of every sales dollar—the cost of reworking, scrapping, repeated service, inspections, tests, warranties, and other quality-related items. Philip Crosby states that the correct cost for a well-run quality management program should be under 2.5 percent.[5]

Three basic assumptions justify an analysis of the costs of quality: (1) failures are caused, (2) prevention is cheaper, and (3) performance can be measured.

The costs of quality are generally classified into four types:

1. **Appraisal costs.**   Costs of the inspection, testing, and other tasks to ensure that the product or process is acceptable.
2. **Prevention costs.**   The sum of all the costs to prevent defects, such as the costs to identify the cause of the defect, to implement corrective action to eliminate the cause, to train personnel, to redesign the product or system, and to purchase new equipment or make modifications. Fail-safing measures to prevent defects are sometimes referred to by the Japanese term poke-yoke (see OSMP on costs of poor quality).
3. **Internal failure costs.**   Costs for defects incurred within the system: scrap, rework, repair.
4. **External failure costs.**   Costs for defects that pass through the system: customer warranty replacements, loss of customers or goodwill, handling complaints, and product repair.

Exhibit 7.4 illustrates the type of report that might be submitted to show the various costs by categories. Prevention is the most important influence. A rule of thumb says that for every dollar you spend in prevention, you can save $10 in failure and appraisal costs.

Often, increases in productivity occur as a by-product of efforts to reduce the cost of quality. A bank, for example, set out to improve quality and reduce the cost of quality and found that it had also boosted productivity. The bank developed this productivity measure for the loan processing area: the number of tickets processed divided by the resources required (labour cost, computer time, ticket forms). Before the quality improvement program, the productivity index was 0.2660 [2080/($11.23 × 640 hours + $0.05 × 2600 forms + $500 for systems costs)]. After the quality improvement project was completed, labour time fell to 546 hours and the number of forms rose to 2100, for a change in the index to 0.3088, an increase in productivity of 16 percent.

INTERNATIONAL QUALITY MANAGEMENT SYSTEMS STANDARDS

ISO 9000

ISO 9000 is a series of international quality standards that have been developed by the International Organization for Standardization. The idea behind the standards is that defects can be prevented through the planning and application of *best practices* at every stage of business—from design through manufacturing, installation, and servicing. These standards focus on

| Quality Cost Report | | EXHIBIT 7.4 |

	CURRENT MONTH'S COST	PERCENTAGE OF TOTAL
Prevention costs		
Quality training	$ 2000	1.3%
Reliability consulting	10 000	6.5
Pilot production runs	5000	3.3
Systems development	8000	5.2
Total prevention	25 000	16.3
Appraisal costs		
Materials inspection	6000	3.9
Supplies inspection	3000	2.0
Reliability testing	5000	3.3
Laboratory testing	25 000	16.3
Total appraisal	39 000	25.5
Internal failure costs		
Scrap	15 000	9.8
Repair	18 000	11.8
Rework	12 000	7.8
Downtime	6000	3.9
Total internal failure	51 000	33.3
External failure costs		
Warranty costs	14 000	9.2
Out-of-warranty repairs and replacement	6000	3.9
Customer complaints	3000	2.0
Product liability	10 000	6.5
Transportation losses	5000	3.3
Total external failure	38 000	24.9
Total quality costs	$153 000	100.0

identifying criteria by which any organization, regardless of whether it is manufacturing- or service-oriented, can ensure that product leaving its facility meets the requirements of its customers. These standards ask a company to first document and implement its systems for quality management and then to verify, by means of an audit conducted by an independent accredited third party, the compliance of those systems to the requirements of the standards.

ISO 9000 currently includes three quality standards: ISO 9000:2000, ISO 9001:2000, and ISO 9004:2000. ISO 9001:2000 presents requirements, while ISO 9000:2000 and ISO 9004:2000 present *guidelines*. All these are process standards (not product standards), meaning that they indicate how processes should be measured and documented from a quality view, but do not prescribe specific tolerances for individual products (which may be covered by industry-specific or jurisdiction-specific standards).

ISO first published its quality standards in 1987, revised them in 1994, and then republished an updated version in 2000. These new standards are referred to as the "ISO 9000 2000 Standards." The purpose of ISO is to facilitate international trade by providing a

Global

Operations and Supply Management in Practice

Cost of Poor Quality

The following examples highlight the need for defect prevention (fail-safing or poke-yoke, concepts promoted by Shigeo Shingo and Philip Crosby) in different organizations.

A misaligned row of information in an electronic spreadsheet used to bid for electricity transmission contracts in New York state cost Calgary-based TransAlta Corp US$24 million. This was expected to wipe out 10 percent of the company's profit for that year. The error meant that TransAlta overpaid for certain transmission contracts as well as buying more capacity than it intended in certain cases. Since New York state rules do not allow bids to be changed even in the event of human blunder, TransAlta had to honour the contracts that it did not need.

A misrouted order at high-tech brokerage house ITG Canada Corp to buy and sell $30 million worth of stocks at the Toronto Stock Exchange (TSX) meant thousands of dollars in losses to the company. Trades are done through an electronic network. Said a Bay Street veteran, "what is interesting is that ITG did not have a fail-safe system that worked."

The cost of quality can be described in human terms, too. In Canadian health care, it is estimated that 70 000 health care workers (mostly nurses) are injured annually by needles and other sharp objects. As many as 300 of these result in the transmission of serious diseases such as HIV-AIDS and hepatitis C. At the same time, research in the United States shows that the use of safety-engineered devices such as retractable needles and self-sheathing scalpels can reduce injuries by more than 50 percent. In 2004, Saskatchewan became the first province to introduce regulations making it mandatory for health-care facilities to use retractable needles and other safety-engineered medical devices. It is expected this will result in savings of $1.4-million annually in treating the aftermath of needle injuries. Similarly, after some children in the U.S. were given adult doses of the drug Heparin (for treating blood clots), resulting in a number of deaths, the manufacturer of the drug redesigned its packaging so that the adult and child packages were dissimilar (poke-yoke). This should prevent people from mistaking one package for another.

■ Sources: Patrick Brethour, "Human Error Costs TransAlta $24-Million on Contract Bids," *The Globe and Mail,* June 4, 2003, B11.
Andrew Willis, "High-Tech Broker Hurt by Misrouted Order," *The Globe and Mail,* June 5, 2003, B1.
André Picard, "A Tiny Pinprick, a Deadly Outcome," *The Globe and Mail,* December 1, 2003, A1.
André Picard, "Saskatchewan to be First Province to Insist on Safer Needles," *The Globe and Mail,* November 2, 2004, A15
Crystal Phend, "MedPage Today," November 27, 2007, http://www.medpagetoday.com/Pediatrics/GeneralPediatrics/7469, retrieved, February 8, 2009.

single set of standards that people everywhere will recognize and respect. The ISO 9000 2000 Standards apply to all kinds of organizations in many industries. Some of these are manufacturing, processing, servicing, printing, forestry, electronics, steel, computing, legal services, financial services, accounting, trucking, banking, retailing, drilling, recycling, aerospace, construction, exploration, textiles, pharmaceuticals, oil and gas, pulp and paper, petrochemicals, publishing, shipping, energy, telecommunications, plastics, metals, research, health care, hospitality, utilities, pest control, aviation, machine tools, food processing, agriculture, government, education, recreation, fabrication, sanitation, software development, consumer products, transportation, design, instrumentation, tourism, communications, biotechnology, chemicals, engineering, farming, entertainment, horticulture, consulting, and insurance. The list continues to grow.

ISO 9000 Certification

Registration procedures to become certified differ depending on the country.[7] In Canada, although it is possible for organizations to self-declare conformity, most companies are assessed by third-party quality system registrars for ISO 9000 certification, since most customers prefer their supplier to be independently assessed. The Standards Council of Canada (SCC) is the accreditation body for registrars.

Although SCC's accreditation of a company does not mean that the certification is recognized worldwide, mutual agreements signed between the SCC and its counterparts in other countries mean participating accreditation bodies (which include those of most of Canada's major trading partners) will recognize the SCC's accreditation program as equivalent to their own.

Companies will typically take 12 to 18 months to prepare for and undergo the registration process to become certified. Some companies undertake the registration process on their own; others engage outside consultants. The usual certification period is three years, after which the company has to seek recertification, although this can vary by registrar. During the certification period, surveillance audits are conducted once a year.

ISO 14000 Series

The ISO 14000 series is a set of international standards and guidance documents for environmental management. Environmental management refers to the practice of managing the impact of an organization's activities on the environment. The ISO 14000 series provides a set of tools for determining the environmental aspects of an organization's activities, establishing goals and targets for those aspects, evaluating how well those goals and targets are being achieved, and for auditing, labelling, and continuously improving performance. Since the standards apply to all industries, the ISO 14000 series does not provide specific environmental targets or describe ways of achieving them. Instead, the documents provide generic frameworks and general principles. The series covers aspects such as consumption of natural resources and energy, and measuring and managing emissions, effluents, and other waste streams.

Having ISO 14000 does not necessarily indicate that a company's environmental performance is better than that of its competitors. However, since establishing and maintaining an environmental management system (EMS) requires a significant investment of time and resources, the registration indicates a company's commitment to monitoring, managing, and improving its environmental performance on an ongoing basis. To maintain its registration, the company must show not only consistency, but also improvement in its performance over time. In Canada, EPCOR in the electricity generating industry, and Canfor and Domtar in the forestry industry, have already become partially or fully certified. In 1999, Suncor's Sarnia Refinery became the first refinery in Canada to receive ISO 14001 certification, and every one of the company's operating businesses is expected to implement the ISO 14001 requirements.[8] In 2002, Dofasco's Hamilton steel plant became ISO 14001 certified.[9] In both cases, these steps form a part of the company's goal to become more environmentally friendly.

The ISO standards are constantly evolving. To see the latest developments, check out the official ISO Web site at www.iso.org. For example, ISO 22000 relates to food safety management.

RECOGNITION FOR GOOD ORGANIZATION-WIDE QUALITY

To foster better quality in products and services, many countries have instituted annual awards for companies that achieve organization-wide quality. In Canada, we have the Canada Awards for Excellence (CAE). The U.S. has the Malcolm Baldrige National Quality Award (MBNQA), the European Union has the European Quality Award, and Japan has the Deming Award (which is open to companies outside Japan also).

EXHIBIT 7.5   The Integrated Framework for the Canada Award for Excellence

Canada Awards for Excellence

The Canada Awards for Excellence (CAE) are quality awards given annually to Canadian organizations by the National Quality Institute (NQI) on behalf of the Canadian government to recognize outstanding achievement across major functions of the organization.[6] Although some awards are unidimensional, the CAE criteria are broad based and look at many factors to ensure that excellence is evident throughout an organization. The seven main criteria are shown in Exhibit 7.5. The criteria are leadership and governance, planning and environmental sustainability, customer/citizen/client focus, people focus and healthy workplace, process management, supplier/partner focus, and overall organizational performance. Each of the seven main criteria have sub-criteria. Since its inception in 1984, hundreds of organizations have been honoured for their impressive accomplishments (see the OSMP box on the NQI, on the next page).

CAE Criteria Criteria for assessing overall quality of an organization and determining the winner(s) of the CAE awards.

Categories   There are eight categories of Canada Awards for Excellence, adjudicated according to various NQI criteria. For example, the Quality Award is for both private and public sector businesses in general. The Customer Service Award for Small Business recognizes excellence in organizations with fewer than 50 employees. The Healthy Workplace Award for Small Organizations evaluates employee well-being (see the opening vignette of Chapter 2 for the Dofasco example). The Education Award is for institutions involved in kindergarten to K12 education

Forms of Recognition for the Awards   The Canada Awards for Excellence Gold trophy is awarded to organizations that have fully met the intent of the NQI criteria, with documented overall achievements and results. The Canada Awards for Excellence Silver and Bronze are awarded to organizations that have completed some good work toward meeting the intent of the NQI criteria, but need some more time to get desired documented results, and are usually one or two years away from Gold Trophy recognition. There is also an Order of Excellence award given to those who sustain past excellence. Recent winners (see www.nqi.com) include manufacturing and service organizations, both for-profit and not-for-profit, from different parts of the country.

The U.S. equivalent of the CAE is the Malcolm Baldrige National Quality Award (MBNQA), given to organizations that have demonstrated outstanding quality in their products and processes. Four awards may be given annually in each of these categories: manufacturing, service, small business, education and health care, and not-for-profit.

Candidates for the award must submit an application of up to 75 pages that details the approach, deployment, and results of their quality activities under seven major categories: Leadership, Strategic Planning, Customer and Market Focus, Information and Analysis, Human Resource Focus, Process Management, and Business Results. These applications are scored on total points out of 1000 by examiners and judges. Those who score above roughly 650 are selected for site visits. Winners selected from this group are then honoured at an annual meeting in Washington, DC. A major benefit to all applicants is feedback from the examiners, which is essentially an audit of their practices. Many states have used the Baldrige Criteria as the basis of their own quality award programs. A report, *Building on Baldrige: American Quality for the 21st Century,* by the private U.S. Council on Competitiveness, said, "More than any other program, the Baldrige Quality Award is responsible for making quality a national priority and disseminating best practices across the United States." More details on this award can be found at the Baldrige Web site (www.quality.nist.gov).

SIX-SIGMA QUALITY

Six Sigma refers to the philosophy and methods developed by Motorola and made popular by companies such as General Electric to eliminate defects in their products and processes. A defect is simply any component that does not fall within the customer's specification limits. Each step or activity in a company represents an opportunity

Operations and Supply Management in Practice

Canada's National Quality Institute (NQI)

Created in 1992, the National Quality Institute (NQI) is a not-for-profit organization that provides strategic focus and direction for Canadian organizations to achieve excellence in quality and healthy workplace practices. Funds are generated through memberships and the sales of products and services. The services are all focused on assisting Canadian organizations, both public and private, to increase productivity, heighten the level of organizational excellence, and develop healthy workplaces.

The NQI also offers the multiple-level Progressive Excellence Program (PEP) certification, giving companies a roadmap to implement NQI criteria into their organization in stages. Unlike the Canadian Awards for Excellence (CAE), which are one-time awards, the PEPs are certifications that have to be maintained through periodic assessments. In that respect, they are similar to the ISO standards. The organizations are assessed at each level periodically, at which time they can

also move up a level. Other certifications include Leadership Excellence Program, Certified Excellence Professional, Certified Excellence Leader, and Improvement Champion.

In addition to for-profit organizations, governmental organizations, such as the municipalities of St. John, New Brunswick (Canada's oldest incorporated city), and Markham, Parry Sound, Sault. Ste. Marie, and Peel, all in Ontario, have achieved various levels of PEP certification. St. Luke Elementary School in Mississauga, Ontario recently became the first school in Canada to be certified. Details on these and other certified organizations can be found on the Web site of the NQI (www.nqi.com).

■ Sources: David Helwig, "City of Sault Ste. Marie on PEP Journey," SooToday.com, April 9, 2003.
John Stewart, "Quality Marks Life at St. Luke," *Mississauga News,* March 3, 2003.
Dan Corbett, "PEP in the City," *Excellence Magazine,* National Quality Institute, November 29, 2002.
National Quality Institute, www.nqi.com.

for defects to occur, and Six-Sigma programs seek to reduce the variation in the processes that lead to these defects. Indeed, Six-Sigma advocates see variation as the enemy of quality, and much of the theory underlying Six Sigma is devoted to dealing with this problem. Motorola's definition of a Six-Sigma process is one that will produce no more than about 4 (actually 3.4) defects out of every million defect opportunities. Today, many companies use **Lean Six Sigma**, a philosophy that combines traditional Six Sigma methods with Lean Manufacturing techniques(discussed in Chapter 10).

Six Sigma implementations can be found among a cross-section of Canadian business, including Bombardier, and Pratt and Whitney Canada (aerospace), RIM (high technology), Noranda (mining), Maple Leaf Foods (meat processing), Air Canada (transportation), Imperial Oil (petroleum), Celestica (electronics), Ford Canada, (automobiles), TD Canada Trust (financial services), and Starwood (hospitality).

One of the benefits of Six-Sigma thinking is that it allows managers to readily describe the performance of a process in terms of its variability and to compare different processes using a common metric. This metric is **defects per million opportunities (DPMO)**. This calculation requires three pieces of data:

1. **Unit.** The item produced or being serviced.
2. **Defect.** Any item or event that does not meet the customer's requirements.
3. **Opportunity.** A chance for a defect to occur.

A straightforward calculation is made using the following formula:

$$\text{DPMO} = \frac{\text{Number of Defects}}{\text{Number of opportunities for error per unit} \times \text{Number of units}} \times 1\,000\,000$$

EXAMPLE 7.1:

The customers of a mortgage bank expect to have their mortgage applications processed within 10 days of filing. This would be called a *critical customer requirement,* or CCR, in Six-Sigma terms. Suppose all defects are counted (loans in a monthly sample taking more than 10 days to process), and it is determined that there are 150 loans in the 1000 applications processed last month that don't meet this customer requirement. Thus, the DPMO = 150/1000 × 1 000 000, or 150 000 loans out of every million processed that fail to meet a CCR. Put differently, it means that only 850 000 loans out of a million are approved within time expectations. Statistically, 15 percent of the loans are defective and 85 percent are correct. This is a case where all the loans processed in less than 10 days meet our criteria. Often, there are upper and lower customer requirements, rather than just a single upper requirement, as we have here.

There are two aspects to Six-Sigma programs: the methodology side and the people side. We will take these up in order.

Six-Sigma Methodology

While Six Sigma's methods include many of the statistical tools that were employed in other quality movements, here they are employed in a systematic project-oriented fashion through the Define, Measure, Analyze, Improve, and Control (**DMAIC**) cycle. The overarching focus of the methodology is understanding and achieving what the customer wants, since that is seen as the key to profitability of a production process. In fact, to get across this point, some use the DMAIC as an acronym for "Dumb Managers Always Ignore Customers."

The standard approach to Six-Sigma projects is the DMAIC methodology developed by General Electric, described below:[10]

1. Define (D)
   • Identify customers and their priorities.
   • Identify a project suitable for Six-Sigma efforts based on business objectives as well as customer needs and feedback.
   • Identify CTQs (critical-to-quality characteristics) that the customer considers to have the most impact on quality.
2. Measure (M)
   • Determine how to measure the process and how it is performing.
   • Identify the key internal processes that influence CTQs and measure the defects currently generated relative to those processes.
3. Analyze (A)
   • Determine the most likely causes of defects.
   • Understand why defects are generated by identifying the key variables that are most likely to create process variation.
4. Improve (I)
   • Identify means to remove the causes of defects.
   • Confirm the key variables and quantify their effects on the CTQs.
   • Identify the maximum acceptance ranges of the key variables and a system for measuring deviations of the variables.
   • Modify the process to stay within an acceptable range.
5. Control (C)
   • Determine how to maintain the improvements.
   • Put tools in place to ensure that the key variables remain within the maximum acceptance ranges under the modified process.

Analytical Tools for Six Sigma

The analytical tools of Six Sigma have been used for many years in traditional quality improvement programs. What makes their application to Six Sigma unique is the integration of these tools in a corporatewide management system. The tools common to all quality efforts are flowcharts, run charts, Pareto charts, histograms, checksheets, cause-and-effect diagrams, and control charts. Examples of these, along with an opportunity flow diagram, are shown in Exhibit 7.6, arranged according to DMAIC categories where they commonly appear.

Flowcharts. There are many types of flowcharts. The one shown in Exhibit 7.6 depicts the process steps as part of a SIPOC (supplier, input, process, output, customer) analysis. In essence, SIPOC is a formalized input-output model, used in the define stage of a project.

Run charts. They depict trends in data over time, and thereby help to understand the magnitude of a problem at the define stage. Typically, they plot the median of a process.

EXHIBIT 7.6 Analytical Tools for Six Sigma and Continuous Improvement

Define

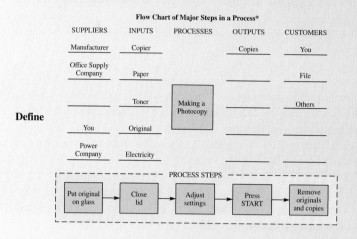

Flow Chart of Major Steps in a Process*

Measure

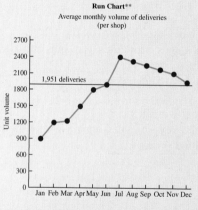

Run Chart**
Average monthly volume of deliveries
(per shop)

1,951 deliveries

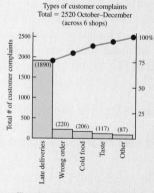

Pareto Chart**
Types of customer complaints
Total = 2520 October–December
(across 6 shops)

Illustration note: Delivery time was defined
by the total time from when the order was
placed to when the customer received it.

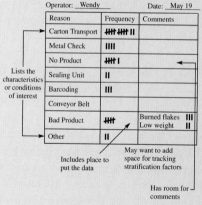

DATA COLLECTION FORMS*
Checksheets are basic forms that help standardize data collection
by providing specific spaces where people should record data.

*Source: Rath & Strong, *Rath & Strong's Six Sigma Pocket Guide*, 2001.

**Source: From *The Memory Jogger*™II, 2001. Used with permission of GOAL/QPC.

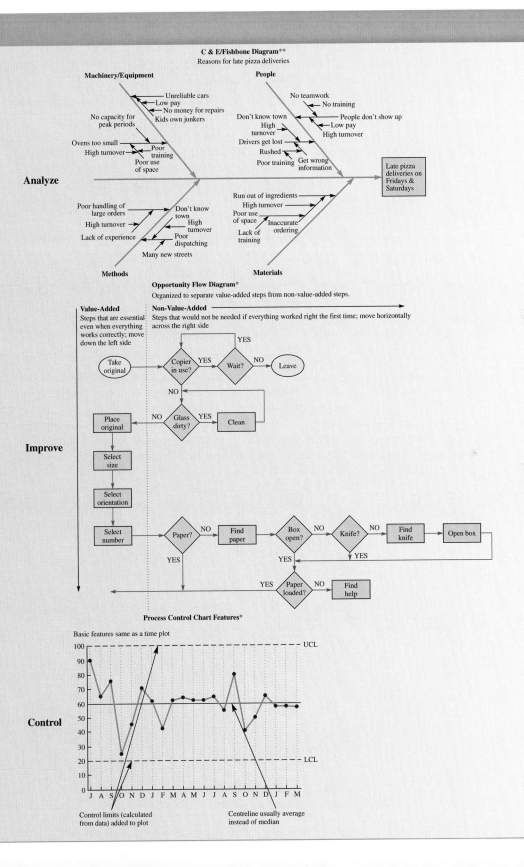

C & E/Fishbone Diagram**
Reasons for late pizza deliveries

Machinery/Equipment

- Unreliable cars
- Low pay
- No money for repairs
- Kids own junkers

No capacity for peak periods

Ovens too small
High turnover
Poor training
Poor use of space

People

No teamwork
No training
Don't know town
People don't show up
High turnover
Low pay
High turnover
Drivers get lost
Rushed
Poor training
Get wrong information

Analyze

Late pizza deliveries on Fridays & Saturdays

Poor handling of large orders
High turnover
Lack of experience
Don't know town
High turnover
Poor dispatching
Many new streets

Run out of ingredients
High turnover
Poor use of space
Inaccurate ordering
Lack of training

Methods

Materials

Opportunity Flow Diagram*
Organized to separate value-added steps from non-value-added steps.

Value-Added
Steps that are essential even when everything works correctly; move down the left side

Non-Value-Added
Steps that would not be needed if everything worked right the first time; move horizontally across the right side

Improve

Take original → Copier in use? — YES → Wait? — YES (up) ; Wait? — NO → Leave

Copier in use? — NO → Place original

Place original ← NO — Glass dirty? — YES → Clean

Select size
Select orientation
Select number → Paper? — NO → Find paper → Box open? — NO → Knife? — NO → Find knife → Open box
Paper? — YES
Box open? — YES
Knife? — YES

Paper loaded? — YES ; Paper loaded? — NO → Find help

Process Control Chart Features*

Basic features same as a time plot

UCL

LCL

Control

J A S O N D J F M A M J J A S O N D J F M

Control limits (calculated from data) added to plot

Centreline usually average instead of median

Pareto charts. These charts help to break down a problem into the relative contributions of its components. They are based on the common empirical finding that a large percentage of problems are due to a small percentage of causes. In the example, 75 percent (1890 out of 2520) of customer complaints are due to late deliveries, which are 20 percent (one out of five) of the causes listed.

Checksheets. These are basic forms that help standardize data collection. They are used to create histograms such as shown on the Pareto chart.

Cause-and-effect diagrams. Also called *fishbone diagrams* or *Ishikawa diagrams* (after its creator Kaoru Ishikawa, a Japanese quality guru who also pioneered *quality circles*, i.e., employee groups who work on quality improvement), C&E diagrams show hypothesized relationships between potential causes and the problem under study. Once the C&E diagram is constructed, the analysis would proceed to find out which of the potential causes were contributing to the problem.

Opportunity flow diagram. This is used to separate value-added from non-value-added steps in a process.

Process control charts. These are time-sequenced charts showing plotted values of a statistic including a centreline average and one or more control limits. They are used to assure that processes are in statistical control.

Other tools that have seen extensive use in Six-Sigma projects are failure mode and effect analysis (FMEA) and design of experiments (DOE).

Failure mode and effect analysis. This is a structured approach to identify, estimate, prioritize, and evaluate risk of possible failures at each stage of a process. It begins with identifying each element, assembly, or part of the process and listing the potential failure modes, potential causes, and effects of each failure. A risk priority number (RPN) is calculated for each failure mode. It is an index used to measure the rank importance of the items listed in the FMEA chart. See Exhibit 7.7. These conditions

EXHIBIT 7.7   FMEA Form

FMEA Analysis

Project: _____   Date: _____ (original)

Team: _____   _____ (revised)

Item or Process Step	Potential Failure Mode	Potential Effects of Failure	Severity	Potential Cause(s)	Occurrence	Current Controls	Detection	RPN	Recommended Action	Responsibility and Target Date	"After" → Action Taken	Severity	Occurrence	Detection	RPN
			Total Risk Priority Number:								"After" Risk Priority Number:				

Source: Rath & Strong, *Rath & Strong's Six Sigma Pocket Guide*: 2001, p. 31.

include the probability that the failure takes place (occurrence), the damage resulting from the failure (severity), and the probability of detecting the failure in-house (detection). High RPN items should be targeted for improvement first. The FMEA suggests a recommended action to eliminate the failure condition by assigning a responsible person or department to resolve the failure by redesigning the system, design, or process and recalculating the RPN.

Design of experiments (DOE).   DOE, sometimes referred to as *multivariate testing,* is a statistical methodology used for determining the cause-and-effect relationship between process variables (X's) and the output variable (Y). In contrast to standard statistical tests, which require changing each individual variable to determine the most influential one, DOE permits experimentation with many variables simultaneously by carefully selecting a subset of them. As mentioned, Genichi Taguchi pioneered the use of DOE in quality management.

STATISTICAL QUALITY CONTROL

This section on statistical quality control (SQC) covers the quantitative aspects of quality management. In general, SQC is a number of different techniques designed to evaluate quality from a conformance view. That is, how well are we doing at meeting the specifications that have been set during the design of the parts or services that we are providing? Managing quality performance using SQC techniques usually involves periodic sampling of a process and analysis of these data using statistically derived performance criteria.

As you will see, SQC can be applied to logistics, manufacturing, and service processes. Here are some examples of situations where SQC can be applied:

- How many paint defects are there in the finish of a car? Have we improved our painting process by installing a new sprayer?
- How long does it take to execute market orders in our Web-based trading system? Has the installation of a new server improved the service? Does the performance of the system vary over the trading day?
- How well are we able to maintain the dimensional tolerance on our 3 cm ball-bearing assembly? Given the variability of our process for making this ball bearing, how many defects would we expect to produce per million bearings that we make?
- How long does it take for customers to be served from our drive-through window during the busy lunch period?

Processes that provide goods and services usually exhibit some variation in their output. This variation can be caused by many factors, some of which we can control, others that are inherent in the process. Variation that is caused by factors that can be clearly identified and possibly even managed is called **assignable variation.** For example, variation caused by workers not being equally trained or by improper machine adjustment is assignable variation. Variation that is inherent in the process itself is called **common variation.** Common variation is often referred to as *random variation* and may, for example, be the result of the type of equipment used to complete a process.

As the title of this section implies, this material requires an understanding of very basic statistics. Recall from your study of statistics the definition of the population mean and standard deviation. The mean (μ) is just the average value of a set of numbers. Mathematically, this is

[7.1]
$$\mu = \sum_{i=1}^{N} x_i / N$$

where:

x_i = Observed value

N = Total number of observed values

The standard deviation is

[7.2]
$$\sigma = \sqrt{\dfrac{\sum\limits_{i=1}^{N}(x_i - \overline{X})^2}{N}}$$

In monitoring a process using SQC, samples of the process output would be taken and sample statistics calculated. Using samples allows for the quick detection of changes in the actual distribution of the process. The purpose of sampling is to find when the process has changed in some nonrandom way, so that the reason for the change can be quickly determined.

As you will see in the examples, sample standard deviation is calculated in a few different ways, depending on the underlying theoretical distribution (i.e., a normal distribution or a Poisson distribution).

Variation Around Us

It is generally accepted that as variation is reduced, quality is improved. Sometimes that knowledge is intuitive. If a train is always on time, schedules can be planned more precisely. If clothing sizes are consistent, time can be saved by ordering from a catalogue. But rarely are such things thought about in terms of the value of low variability. With engineers, the knowledge is better defined. Pistons must fit cylinders, doors must fit openings, electrical components must be compatible, and boxes of cereal must have the right amount of raisins—otherwise, quality will be unacceptable and customers will be dissatisfied.

However, engineers also know that it is impossible to have zero variability. For this reason, designers establish specifications that define not only the target value of something but also acceptable limits about the target. For example, if the aim value of a dimension is 10 cm, the design specifications might then be 10.00 cm ±0.02 cm. This would tell the manufacturing department that, while it should aim for exactly 10 cm, anything between 9.98 and 10.02 cm is OK. These design limits are often referred to as the **upper and lower specification limits**.

A traditional way of interpreting such a specification is that any part that falls within the allowed range is equally good, whereas any part falling outside the range is totally bad. This is illustrated in Exhibit 7.8. (Note that the cost is zero over the entire specification range, and then there is a quantum leap in cost once the limit is violated.)

Genichi Taguchi has pointed out that the traditional view illustrated in Exhibit 7.8 is nonsense for two reasons:

1. From the customer's view, there is often practically no difference between a product just inside specifications and a product just outside. Conversely, there is a far

A Traditional View of the Cost of Variability

EXHIBIT 7.8

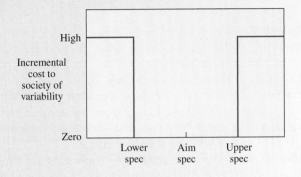

Taguchi's View of the Cost of Variability

EXHIBIT 7.9

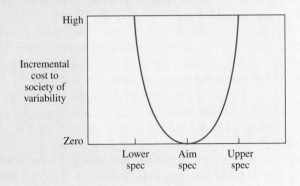

greater difference in the quality of a product that is the target and the quality of one that is near a limit.

2. As customers get more demanding, there is pressure to reduce variability. However, Exhibit 7.8 does not reflect this logic.

Taguchi suggests that a more correct picture of the loss is shown in Exhibit 7.9. Notice that in this graph the cost is represented by a smooth curve. There are dozens of illustrations of this notion: the meshing of gears in a transmission, the amount of sugar in a dessert, the temperature in a workplace or department store. In nearly anything that can be measured, the customer sees, not a sharp line, but a gradation of acceptability away from the "Aim" specification. Customers see the loss function as Exhibit 7.9 rather than Exhibit 7.8.

Of course, if products are consistently scrapped when they are outside specifications, the loss curve flattens out in most cases at a value equivalent to scrap cost in the ranges outside specifications. This is because such products, theoretically at least, will never be sold, so there is no external cost to society. However, in many practical situations, either the process is capable of producing a very high percentage of product within specifications and 100 percent checking is not done, or, if the process is not capable of producing within specifications,

100 percent checking is done and out-of-spec products can be reworked to bring them within specs. In any of these situations, the parabolic loss function is usually a reasonable assumption.

Process Capability

Taguchi argues that being within specification is not a yes/no decision, but rather a continuous function. The Motorola quality experts, on the other hand, argue that the process used to produce a good or deliver a service should be so good that the probability of generating a defect should be very, very low. Motorola made process capability and product design famous by adopting Six-Sigma limits. When we design a part, we specify that certain dimensions should be within the upper and lower specification limits. Otherwise, the bearing will be too loose or will not fit on the axle.

As a simple example, assume that we are designing a bearing for a rotating shaft—say an axle for the wheel of a bicycle. There are many variables involved for both the bearing and the axle—for example, the width of the bearing, the size of the rollers, the size of the axle, the length of the axle, how it is supported, and so on. The designer specifies limits for each of these variables to ensure that the parts will fit properly. Suppose that initially a design is selected and the diameter of the bearing is set at 1.250 cm $\pm$0.005 cm. This means that acceptable parts may have a diameter that varies between 1.245 and 1.255 cm (which are the lower and upper specification limits).

Next, consider the process by which the bearing will be made. Consider that we can select many different processes for making the bearing. Usually, there are trade-offs that need to be considered when designing a process for making a part. The process, for example, might be very fast but not very consistent, or, alternatively, it might be very slow but very consistent. The consistency of a process for making our bearing can be measured by the standard deviation of the diameter measurement. We can run a test by, say, measuring the diameter of each bearing produced over a long run, assuming that the process is under control.

Let's say that after running our test we find that the average or mean diameter is 1.250 cm. Another way of saying this is that the process is "centred" right in the middle of the upper and lower specification limits. In reality, it may be very difficult to have a perfectly centred process like our example. Let's say that the individual diameter values have a standard deviation or sigma equal to 0.002 cm. What this means is that our process does not make each bearing exactly the same size.

As we will see later in this chapter, normally we monitor a process using control charts such that if the process starts making bearings that have a diameter more than three standard deviations ($\pm$0.006 cm) above or below 1.250 cm, we stop the process. This means that we will produce parts that vary between 1.244 (this is $1.250 - 3 \times 0.002$) and 1.256 (this is $1.250 + 3 \times 0.002$) cm. The 1.244 and 1.256 are referred to as the upper and lower process limits. Be careful not to get confused with the terminology here. The "process" limits relate to how consistent our process is for making the bearing. The "specification" limits are related to the design of the part. Recall that, from a design view, acceptable parts have a diameter between 1.245 and 1.255 cm (which are the lower and upper specification limits). This was set by the designers based on fitness for use and had nothing to do with the sigma of 0.002.

Also note that in calculating the process limits, we used 0.002 cm as the sigma since we assume that we are examining individual bearings. Normally in control charts, as we will see later in this chapter, we will be examining samples of bearings (or any other products or services) as a group. Thus, we will have to use the standard deviation of the sample mean rather than the standard deviation of individual units (0.002). So the formulas to calculate process limits when using samples will differ somewhat. But since the principles of variation are the same whether we are looking at individual units or samples (we mentioned this earlier also in relation to equations 7.1 and 7.2), we won't worry about it now—what is important here is the difference between process limits and specification limits.

As we can see, our process limits are slightly greater than the specification limits given to us by the designer. This is not good because we will produce some parts that do not meet specifications. Companies with Six-Sigma processes insist that a process making a part be capable of operating so that the design specification limits are six standard deviations away from the process mean. For our bearing process, how small would the process standard deviation need to be for it to be Six-Sigma capable? Recall that our design specification was 1.250 cm plus or minus 0.005 cm. When you think about it, that 0.005 cm must relate to the variation in the process. By dividing 0.005 cm by 6, which equals 0.00083, we can determine our process standard deviation for a Six-Sigma process. So for our process to be Six-Sigma capable, the mean diameter produced by the process would need to be exactly 1.250 cm and the process standard deviation would need to be less than or equal to 0.00083 cm. The concept of Six Sigma developed by Motorola is somewhat different from what we have explained here. This difference will be explained later, but, in any case, the notion of Six Sigma is one of an extremely capable process.

We can imagine that some of you are really confused at this point with the whole idea of Six Sigma. Why doesn't our company, for example, just check the diameter of each bearing and throw out the ones with a diameter less than 1.245 or greater than 1.255? This could certainly be done and for many, many parts, 100 percent testing is done. The problem is that for a company that is making thousands of parts each hour, testing each critical dimension of each part made can be very expensive. For our bearing, there could easily be 10 or more additional critical dimensions in addition to the diameter. These would all need to be checked. Using a 100 percent testing approach, the company would spend more time testing than it takes to actually make the part! This is why a company uses small samples to periodically check that the process is in statistical control. We discuss exactly how this statistical sampling works later in the chapter.

We say that a process is *capable* when the mean and standard deviation of the process are operating such that the upper and lower control limits are acceptable relative to the upper and lower specification limits. Consider diagram A in Exhibit 7.10. This represents the distribution of the bearing diameter dimension in our original process (assumed to be normally distributed). The average or mean value is 1.250 and the lower and upper design specifications are 1.245 and 1.255, respectively. Process control limits are plus and minus three standard deviations (1.244 and 1.256). Notice that there is a probability (the yellow areas) of producing defective parts.

If we can improve our process by reducing the standard deviation associated with the bearing diameter, the probability can be reduced. Diagram B in Exhibit 7.10 shows a new process where the standard deviation has been reduced to 0.00083 (the yellow area). Even though we cannot see it in the diagram, there is some probability that a defect could be produced by this new process, but that probability is very, very small.

Suppose that the central value or mean of the process shifts away from the mean. Exhibit 7.11 shows that the mean shifted approximately one standard deviation closer to the upper specification limit. This, of course, causes a slightly higher number of expected defects (since the right edge of the yellow area is now closer to the USL), but we can see that this is still very, very good. We use the *capability index* to measure how well our process is capable of producing relative to the design specifications. We describe how to calculate this index in the next section.

EXHIBIT 7.10   Process Capability

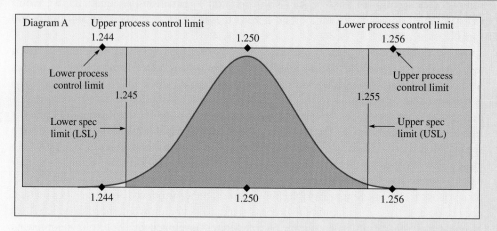

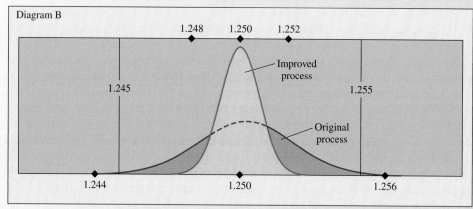

EXHIBIT 7.11   Process Capability with a Shift in the Process Mean

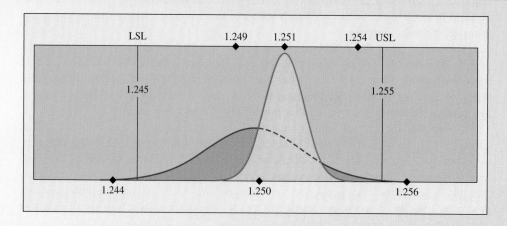

SPC

Capability Index (C_{pk}) The **capability index (C_{pk})** shows how well the parts being produced fit into the range specified by the design specification limits. If the specification limits are larger than the three sigma allowed in the process, then the mean of the process can be allowed to drift off-centre before readjustment, and a high percentage of good parts will still be produced.

Referring to Exhibits 7.10 and 7.11, the capability index (C_{pk}) is the position of the mean and tails of the process relative to design specifications. The more off-centre, the greater the chance to produce defective parts.

Because the process mean can shift in either direction, the direction of shift and its distance from the design specification set the limit on the process capability. The direction of shift is toward the smaller number.

Formally stated, the capability index (C_{pk}) is calculated as the smaller number as follows:

[7.3]
$$C_{pk} = \min\left[\frac{\overline{\overline{X}} - \text{LSL}}{3\sigma} \quad \text{or} \quad \frac{\text{USL} - \overline{\overline{X}}}{3\sigma}\right]$$

where

$\overline{\overline{X}}$ = Average of sample means or a target value set for the process

Working with our example in Exhibit 7.11, let's assume our process is centred at 1.251 and σ = 0.00083 (σ is the symbol for standard deviation).

$$C_{pk} = \min\left[\frac{1.251 - 1.245}{3(0.00083)} \quad \text{or} \quad \frac{1.255 - 1.251}{3(0.00083)}\right]$$

$$= \min\left[\frac{0.006}{0.00249} \quad \text{or} \quad \frac{0.004}{0.00249}\right]$$

$$C_{pk} = \min[2.4 \quad \text{or} \quad 1.6]$$

C_{pk} = 1.6, which is the smaller number. This is a pretty good capability index. Note that based on our previous discussion, C_{pk} has to be at least 1 for a process to be capable.

This tells us that the process mean has shifted to the right, similar to Exhibit 7.11, but parts are generally still well within design specification limits.

At times, it is useful to calculate the actual probability of producing a defect. Assuming that the process is producing with a consistent standard deviation, this is a fairly straightforward calculation, particularly when we have access to a spreadsheet. The approach to use is to calculate the probability of producing a part outside the lower and upper design specification limits, given the mean and standard deviation of the process.

Working with our example, where the process is not centred, with a mean of 1.251 cm, σ = 0.00083 cm, LSL = 1.245, and USL = 1.255, we first need to calculate the Z score associated with the upper and lower specification limits. Recall from your study of statistics that the Z score is the number of standard deviations either to the right or to the left of zero in a standard normal distribution.

$$Z_{\text{LSL}} = \frac{\text{LSL} - \overline{\overline{X}}}{\sigma} \qquad Z_{\text{USL}} = \frac{\text{USL} - \overline{\overline{X}}}{\sigma}$$

For our example,

$$Z_{\text{LSL}} = \frac{1.245 - 1.251}{0.00083} = -7.2289 \qquad Z_{\text{USL}} = \frac{1.255 - 1.251}{0.00083} = 4.8193$$

An easy way to get the probabilities associated with these Z values is to use the NORMSDIST function built into Excel (you can also use the table in Appendix E). The format for this function is NORMSDIST(Z), where Z is the Z value calculated above. Excel returns the following values. (We have found that you might get slightly different results from those given here, depending on the version of Excel you are using.)

$$\text{NORMSDIST}(-7.2289) = 2.43461\text{E-}13 \quad \text{and} \quad \text{NORMSDIST}(4.8193) = 0.99999928$$

Interpreting this information requires understanding exactly what the NORMSDIST function is providing. NORMSDIST is giving the cumulative probability to the left of the given Z value. Since $Z = -7.2289$ is the number of standard deviations associated with the lower specification limit, the fraction of parts that will be produced lower than this is 2.43461E-13. This number is in scientific notation and E-13 at the end means we need to move the decimal over 13 places to get the real fraction defective. So the fraction defective is 0.00000000000024361, which is a very small number! Similarly, we see that approximately 0.99999928 of our parts will be below our upper specification limit. What we are really interested in is the fraction that will be above this limit since these are the defective parts. This fraction defective above the upper spec is $1 - 0.99999928 = 0.00000082$ of our parts.

Adding these two fraction defective numbers together, we get 0.00000082000024361. We can interpret this to mean that we only expect about 0.82 parts per million to be defective. Clearly, this is a great process. You will discover as you work the problems at the end of the chapter that this is not always the case.

EXAMPLE 7.2:

The quality assurance manager is assessing the capability of a process that puts pressurized grease in an aerosol can for industrial purposes. The design specifications call for an average of 60 kg per cm^2 of pressure in each can, with an upper specification limit of 65 kg per cm^2 and a lower specification limit of 55 kg per cm.^{2} A long-run sample is taken from production and it is found that the cans average 61 kg per cm^2 with a standard deviation of 2 kg per cm.^{2} What is the capability of the process? What is the probability of producing a defect?

SOLUTION

Step 1—Interpret the data from the problem

$$\text{LSL} = 55 \quad \text{USL} = 65 \quad \overline{\overline{X}} = 61 \quad \sigma = 2$$

Step 2—Calculate the C_{pk}

$$C_{pk} = \min\left[\frac{\overline{\overline{X}} - \text{LSL}}{3\sigma}, \frac{\text{USL} - \overline{\overline{X}}}{3\sigma}\right]$$

$$C_{pk} = \min\left[\frac{61 - 55}{3(2)}, \frac{65 - 61}{3(2)}\right]$$

$$C_{pk} = \min[1, 0.6667] = 0.6667$$

This is not a very good capability index.

Step 3—Calculate the probability of producing a defect
Probability of a can with less than 55 kg per cm^2

$$Z = \frac{X - \overline{\overline{X}}}{\sigma} = \frac{55 - 61}{2} = -3$$

$$\text{NORMSDIST}(-3) = 0.001349898$$

Probability of a can with more than 65 kg per cm^2

$$Z = \frac{X - \overline{\overline{X}}}{\sigma} = \frac{65 - 61}{2} = 2$$

$$1 - NORMSDIST(2) = 1 - 0.977249868 = 0.022750132$$

Probability of a can less than 55 kg per cm^2 or more than 65 kg per cm^2

Probability $= 0.001349898 + 0.022750132 = 0.024100030$

Or approximately 2.4% of the cans will be defective.

The following table is a quick reference for the fraction of defective units for various design specification limits (expressed in standard deviations). This table assumes that the standard deviation is constant and that the process is centred exactly between the design specification limits.

DESIGN LIMITS	DEFECTIVE PARTS	FRACTION DEFECTIVE
$\pm 1\sigma$	317 per thousand	0.3173
$\pm 2\sigma$	45 per thousand	0.0455
$\pm 3\sigma$	2.7 per thousand	0.0027
$\pm 4\sigma$	63 per million	0.000063
$\pm 5\sigma$	574 per billion	0.000000574
$\pm 6\sigma$	2 per billion	0.000000002

If $\pm 6\sigma$ has a defect level of 2 per billion, why does Motorola's Six-Sigma definition refer to 3.4 per million? The reason is that Motorola's definition allows for a shift in the process mean itself by 1.5σ ($C_{pk} = 1.5$). From the previous C_{pk} calculation examples, we know that a shift in the mean implies reduced process capability and increased probability of defects. In our previous explanation of process capability and in the table above, we assume that that mean does not shift (which is not generally true in practice, hence Motorola's allowance for a mean shift). If the mean is exactly in the centre ($C_{pk} = 2$), then 2 defects per *billion* are expected, as the table above shows. So it is important to understand that Motorola's Six-Sigma process definition is closely related to $\pm 6\sigma$ but is not identical.

PROCESS CONTROL PROCEDURES

Process control is concerned with monitoring quality *while the product or service is being produced*. Typical objectives of process control plans are to provide timely information on whether currently produced items are meeting design specifications and to detect shifts in the process that signal that future items (units) may not meet specifications. **Statistical process control (SPC)** involves testing a random sample of output from a process to determine whether the process is producing items within a preselected range.

The examples given so far have all been based on quality characteristics (or *variables*) that are measurable, such as the diameter or weight of a part. **Attributes** are quality characteristics that are classified as either conforming or not conforming to specification. Goods or services may be observed to be either good or bad, or functioning or malfunctioning. For example, a lawnmower either runs or it doesn't; it attains a certain level of torque and horsepower or it doesn't. This type of measurement is known as sampling by attributes. Alternatively, a lawnmower's torque and horsepower can be measured as an amount of deviation from a set standard. This type of measurement is known as sampling by variables. The following section describes some standard approaches to controlling processes: first, an approach useful for attribute measures and then an approach for variable measures. Both of these techniques result in the construction of control charts. Exhibit 7.12 shows some examples for how control charts can be analyzed to understand how a process is operating.

EXHIBIT 7.12	Process Control Chart Evidence for Investigation

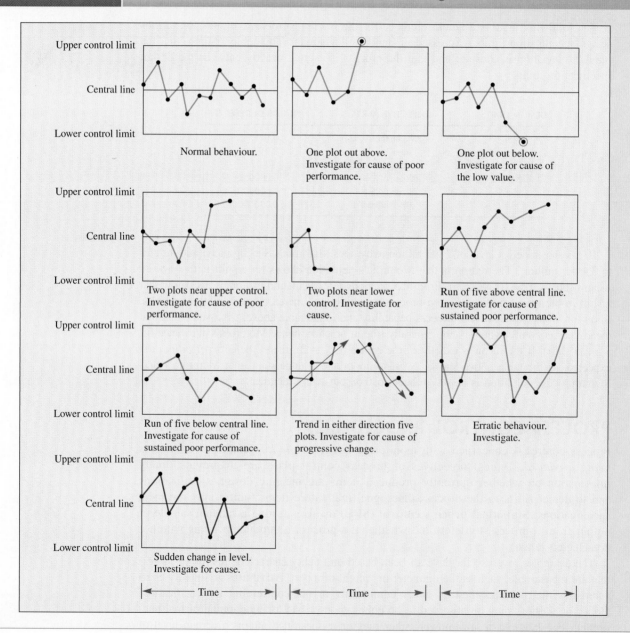

Process Control with Attribute Measurements: Using *p* Charts

Measurement by attributes means taking samples and using a single decision—the item is good or it is bad. Because it is a yes or no decision, we can use simple statistics to create a *p* chart with an upper process control limit (UCL) and a lower process control limit (LCL). We can draw these control limits on a graph and then plot the fraction defective of each individual sample tested. The process is assumed to be working correctly when the samples, which are taken periodically during the day, continue to stay between the control limits.

[7.4]
$$\bar{p} = \frac{\text{Total number of defects from all samples}}{\text{Number of samples} \times \text{Sample Size}}$$

[7.5]
$$s_p = \sqrt{\frac{\bar{p}(1 - \bar{p})}{n}}$$

[7.6]
$$\text{UCL} = \bar{p} + zs_p$$

[7.7]
$$\text{LCL} = \bar{p} - zs_p$$

SPC

where $\bar{p}$ is the fraction defective, s_p is the standard deviation, n is the sample size, and z is the number of standard deviations for a specific confidence. Typically, $z = 3$ (99.7 percent confidence) or $z = 2.58$ (99 percent confidence) is used.

Size of the Sample The size of the sample must be large enough to allow counting of the attribute. For example, if we know that a machine produces 1 percent defects, then a sample size of five would seldom capture a defect. A rule of thumb when setting up a *p* chart is to make the sample large enough to expect to count the attribute twice in each sample. So an appropriate sample size if the defect rate were approximately 1 percent would be 200 units. One final note: In the calculations shown in equations 7.4 through 7.7, the assumption is that the sample size is fixed. The calculation of the standard deviation depends on this assumption. If the sample size varies, the standard deviation and upper and lower process control limits should be recalculated for each sample.

EXAMPLE 7.3:   PROCESS CONTROL CHART DESIGN

An insurance company wants to design a control chart to monitor whether insurance claim forms are being completed correctly. The company intends to use the chart to see if improvements in the design of the form are effective. To start the process, the company collected data on the number of incorrectly completed claim forms over the past 10 days. The insurance company processes thousands of these forms each day. Due to the high cost of inspecting each form, only a small representative sample was collected each day. The data and analysis are shown in Exhibit 7.13.

SOLUTION

To construct the control chart, first calculate the overall fraction defective from all samples. This sets the centreline for the control chart.

$$\bar{p} = \frac{\text{Total number of defects from all samples}}{\text{Number of samples} \times \text{Sample size}} = \frac{91}{3000} = 0.03033$$

Next, calculate the sample standard deviation:

$$s_p = \sqrt{\frac{\bar{p}(1 - \bar{p})}{n}} = \sqrt{\frac{0.03033(1 - 0.03033)}{300}} = 0.00990$$

Finally, calculate the upper and lower process control limits. A z-value of 3 gives 99.7 percent confidence that the process is within these limits.

$$UCL = \bar{p} + 3s_p = 0.03033 + 3(0.00990) = 0.06003$$

$$LCL = \bar{p} - 3s_p = 0.03033 - 3(0.00990) = 0.00063$$

The calculations in Exhibit 7.13, including the control chart, are included in the spreadsheet SPC.xls.

SPC

EXHIBIT 7.13	Insurance Company Claim Form

SAMPLE	NUMBER INSPECTED	NUMBER OF FORMS COMPLETED INCORRECTLY	FRACTION DEFECTIVE
1	300	10	0.03333
2	300	8	0.02667
3	300	9	0.03000
4	300	13	0.04333
5	300	7	0.02333
6	300	7	0.02333
7	300	6	0.02000
8	300	11	0.03667
9	300	12	0.04000
10	300	8	0.02667
Totals	3000	91	0.03033
Sample standard deviation			0.00990

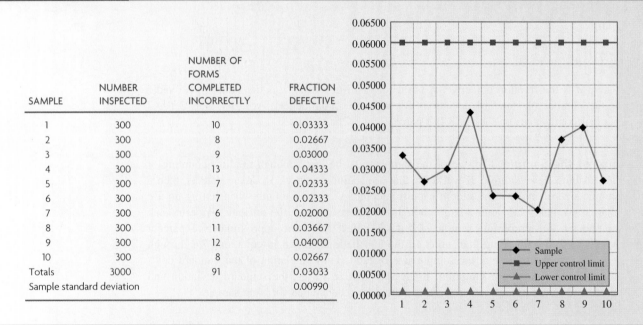

Process Control with Variable Measurements: Using $\bar{X}$ and R Charts

$\bar{X}$ and R (range) charts are widely used in statistical process control.

In attribute sampling, we determine whether something is good or bad, fits or doesn't fit—it is a go/no-go situation. In **variables** sampling, however, we measure the actual weight, volume, length, or other variable measurements, and we develop control charts to determine the acceptability or rejection of the process based on those measurements. For example, in attribute sampling, we might decide that if something is over 10 kg we will reject it and under 10 kg we will accept it. In variable sampling, we measure a sample and may record weights of 9.8 kg or 10.2 kg. These values are used to create or modify control charts and to see whether they fall within the acceptable limits.

Four main issues need to be addressed in creating a control chart: the size of the samples, number of samples, frequency of samples, and control limits.

A foreman and team coach examine process control charts at the Ford Fiesta assembly line in Cologne-Niehl, Germany.

Size of Samples As mentioned when we compared process limits and specification limits, the normal method in process control is to use sample sizes greater than one (though sample sizes of one are also used in some cases). For industrial applications in process control involving the measurement of variables, it is preferable to keep the sample size small. There are two main reasons. First, the sample needs to be taken within a reasonable length of time; otherwise, the process might change while the samples are taken. Second, the larger the sample, the more it costs to take.

Sample sizes of four or five units seem to be the preferred numbers. The *means* of samples of this size have an approximately normal distribution, no matter what the distribution of the parent population looks like. Sample sizes greater than five give narrower process control limits and thus more sensitivity. For detecting finer variations of a process, it may be necessary, in fact, to use larger sample sizes. However, when sample sizes exceed 15 or so, it would be better to use $\overline{X}$ charts with standard deviation σ rather than $\overline{X}$ charts with the range R as we use in Example 7.4.

Number of Samples Once the chart has been set up, each sample taken can be compared to the chart and a decision can be made about whether the process is acceptable. To set up the charts, however, prudence and statistics suggest that 25 or so samples be taken.

Frequency of Samples How often to take a sample is a trade-off between the cost of sampling (along with the cost of the unit if it is destroyed as part of the test) and the benefit of adjusting the system. Usually, it is best to start off with frequent sampling of a process and taper off as confidence in the process builds. For example, one might start with a sample of five units every half hour and end up feeling that one sample per day is adequate.

Control Limits Standard practice in statistical process control for variables is to set control limits three standard deviations above the mean and three standard deviations below. This means that 99.7 percent of the sample means are expected to fall within these process control limits (that is, within a 99.7 percent confidence interval). Thus, if one sample mean falls outside this obviously wide band, we have strong evidence that the process is out of control.

How to Construct $\bar{X}$ and R Charts

If the standard deviation of the process distribution is known, the $\bar{X}$ chart may be defined:

[7.8]
$$\text{UCL}_{\bar{X}} = \bar{\bar{X}} + zS_{\bar{X}} \text{ and } \text{LCL}_{\bar{X}} = \bar{\bar{X}} - zS_{\bar{X}}$$

where

$S_{\bar{X}} = s/\sqrt{n} = $ Standard deviation of sample means

$s = $ Estimated standard deviation of the process distribution (based on multiple samples)

$n = $ Sample size

$\bar{\bar{X}} = $ Average of sample means or a target value set for the process

$z = $ Number of standard deviations for a specific confidence level (typically, $z = 3$)

An $\bar{X}$ chart is simply a plot of the means of the samples that were taken from a process. $\bar{\bar{X}}$ is the average of the means.

In practice, the standard deviation of the process is not known. For this reason, an approach that uses actual sample data is commonly used. This practical approach is described in the next section.

An R chart is a plot of the range within each sample. The range is the difference between the highest and the lowest numbers in that sample. R values provide an easily calculated measure of variation used like a standard deviation. An $\bar{R}$ chart is the average of the range of each sample. More specifically defined, these are

[Same as 7.1]
$$\bar{X} = \frac{\sum\limits_{i=1}^{n} X_i}{n}$$

where

$\bar{X} = $ Mean of the sample

$i = $ Item number

$n = $ Total number of items in the sample

[7.9]
$$\bar{\bar{X}} = \frac{\sum\limits_{j=1}^{m} \bar{X}_j}{m}$$

where

$\bar{\bar{X}} = $ The average of the means of the samples

$j = $ Sample number

$m = $ Total number of samples

[7.10]
$$\bar{R} = \frac{\sum\limits_{j=1}^{m} R_j}{m}$$

where

R_j = Difference between the highest and lowest measurement in the sample

$\overline{R}$ = Average of the measurement differences R for all samples

E. L. Grant and R. Leavenworth computed a table (Exhibit 7.14) that allows us to easily compute the upper and lower control limits for both the $\overline{X}$ chart and the R chart.[11] These are defined as

[7.11] Upper control limit for $\overline{X} = \overline{\overline{X}} + A_2\overline{R}$

[7.12] Lower control limit for $\overline{X} = \overline{\overline{X}} - A_2\overline{R}$

[7.13] Upper control limit for $R = D_4\overline{R}$

[7.14] Lower control limit for $R = D_3\overline{R}$

Factor for Determining from $\overline{R}$ the Three-Sigma Control Limits for $\overline{X}$ and R Charts

EXHIBIT 7.14

NUMBER OF OBSERVATIONS IN SUBGROUP	FACTOR FOR $\overline{X}$ CHART	FACTORS FOR R CHART	
		LOWER CONTROL LIMIT	UPPER CONTROL LIMIT
n	A_2	D_3	D_4
2	1.88	0	3.27
3	1.02	0	2.57
4	0.73	0	2.28
5	0.58	0	2.11
6	0.48	0	2.00
7	0.42	0.08	1.92
8	0.37	0.14	1.86
9	0.34	0.18	1.82
10	0.31	0.22	1.78
11	0.29	0.26	1.74
12	0.27	0.28	1.72
13	0.25	0.31	1.69
14	0.24	0.33	1.67
15	0.22	0.35	1.65
16	0.21	0.36	1.64
17	0.20	0.38	1.62
18	0.19	0.39	1.61
19	0.19	0.40	1.60
20	0.18	0.41	1.59

Upper control limit for $\overline{X} = UCL_{\overline{X}} = \overline{\overline{X}} + A_2\overline{R}$
Lower control limit for $\overline{X} = LCL_{\overline{X}} = \overline{\overline{X}} + A_2\overline{R}$
Upper control limit for $R = UCL_R = D_4\overline{R}$
Lower control limit for $R = LCL_R = D_3\overline{R}$

Note: All factors are based on the normal distribution.

SPC

EXHIBIT 7.15   Measurements in Samples of Five from a Process

SAMPLE NUMBER	EACH UNIT IN SAMPLE					AVERAGE $\overline{X}$	RANGE $\overline{R}$
1	10.60	10.40	10.30	9.90	10.20	10.28	0.70
2	9.98	10.25	10.05	10.23	10.33	10.17	0.35
3	9.85	9.90	10.20	10.25	10.15	10.07	0.40
4	10.20	10.10	10.30	9.90	9.95	10.09	0.40
5	10.30	10.20	10.24	10.50	10.30	10.31	0.30
6	10.10	10.30	10.20	10.30	9.90	10.16	0.40
7	9.98	9.90	10.20	10.40	10.10	10.12	0.50
8	10.10	10.30	10.40	10.24	10.30	10.27	0.30
9	10.30	10.20	10.60	10.50	10.10	10.34	0.50
10	10.30	10.40	10.50	10.10	10.20	10.30	0.40
11	9.90	9.50	10.20	10.30	10.35	10.05	0.85
12	10.10	10.36	10.50	9.80	9.95	10.14	0.70
13	10.20	10.50	10.70	10.10	9.90	10.28	0.80
14	10.20	10.60	10.50	10.30	10.40	10.40	0.40
15	10.54	10.30	10.40	10.55	10.00	10.36	0.55
16	10.20	10.60	10.15	10.00	10.50	10.29	0.60
17	10.20	10.40	10.60	10.80	10.10	10.42	0.70
18	9.90	9.50	9.90	10.50	10.00	9.96	1.00
19	10.60	10.30	10.50	9.90	9.80	10.22	0.80
20	10.60	10.40	10.30	10.40	10.20	10.38	0.40
21	9.90	9.60	10.50	10.10	10.60	10.14	1.00
22	9.95	10.20	10.50	10.30	10.20	10.23	0.55
23	10.20	9.50	9.60	9.80	10.30	9.88	0.80
24	10.30	10.60	10.30	9.90	9.80	10.18	0.80
25	9.90	10.30	10.60	9.90	10.10	10.16	0.70

$$\overline{\overline{X}} = 10.21$$

$$\overline{\overline{R}} = .60$$

SPC

EXAMPLE 7.4: $\overline{X}$ AND R CHARTS

We would like to create $\overline{X}$ and R charts for a process. Exhibit 7.15 shows measurements for all 25 samples. The last two columns show the average of the sample $\overline{X}$ and the range R.

Values for A_2, D_3, and D_4 were obtained from Exhibit 7.14.

Upper control limit for $\overline{X} = \overline{\overline{X}} + A_2\overline{R} = 10.21 + .58(.60) = 10.56$

Lower control limit for $\overline{X} = \overline{\overline{X}} - A_2\overline{R} = 10.21 - .58(.60) = 9.86$

Upper control limit for $R = D_4\overline{R} = 2.11(.60) = 1.27$

Lower control limit for $R = D_3\overline{R} = 0(.60) = 0$

SOLUTION

Exhibit 7.16 shows the $\overline{X}$ chart and R chart with a plot of all the sample means and ranges of the samples. All the points are well within the control limits, although sample 23 is close to the $\overline{X}$ lower control limit.

$\overline{X}$ Chart and R Chart

EXHIBIT 7.16

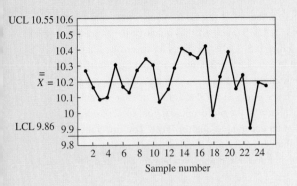

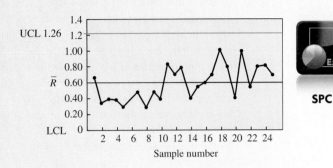

SPC

ACCEPTANCE SAMPLING

Design of a Single Sampling Plan for Attributes

Acceptance sampling is performed on goods that already exist to determine what percentage of products conforms to specifications. These products may be items received from another company and evaluated by the receiving department, or they may be components that have passed through a processing step and are evaluated by company personnel either in production or later in the warehousing function. Whether inspection should be done at all is addressed in the following example.

Acceptance sampling is executed through a sampling plan. The purpose of a sampling plan is to test the lot to either (1) find its quality or (2) ensure that the quality is what it is supposed to be. In this section, we illustrate the planning procedures for a single sampling plan—that is, a plan in which the quality is determined from the evaluation of one sample. (Other plans may be developed using two or more samples. See J. M. Juran and F. M. Gryna's *Quality Planning and Analysis* for a discussion of these plans.)

EXAMPLE 7.5:   COSTS TO JUSTIFY INSPECTION

Total (100 percent) inspection is justified when the cost of a loss incurred by not inspecting is greater than the cost of inspection. For example, suppose a faulty item results in a $10 loss and the average percentage defective of items in the lot is 3 percent.

SOLUTION

If the average percentage of defective items in a lot is 3 percent, the expected cost of faulty items is $0.03 \times \$10$, or $0.30 each. Therefore, if the cost of inspecting each item is less than $0.30, the economic decision is to perform 100 percent inspection. In other words, in the long term for each batch of 100 units inspected, we would find 3 defectives on average costing us $3 \times \$10$, or $30. At the same time, if each item costs less than $0.30 to inspect, for example, say, $0.25, then inspecting 100 units will cost only $100 \times \$0.25$, or $25 thus making 100 percent inspection feasible. Not all defective items will be removed, however, because inspectors will pass some bad items and reject some good ones.

A single sampling plan is defined by n and c, where n is the number of units in the sample and c is the acceptance number. The size of n may vary from one up to all the items in the lot (usually denoted as N) from which it is drawn. The acceptance number c denotes the maximum number of defective items that can be found in the sample before the lot is rejected. Values for n and c are determined by the interaction of four factors (AQL, α, LTPD, and β) that quantify the objectives of the product's producer and its consumer. The objective of the producer is to ensure that the sampling plan has a low probability of rejecting good lots. Lots are defined as high quality if they contain no more than a specified level of defectives, termed the *acceptable quality level (AQL)*.

There is some controversy surrounding AQLs. This is based on the argument that specifying some acceptable percentage of defectives is inconsistent with the philosophical goal of zero defects. In practice, even in the best QC companies, there is an acceptable quality level. The difference is that it may be stated in parts per million rather than in parts per hundred. This is the case in Motorola's Six-Sigma quality standard, which holds that no more than 3.4 defects per million defect opportunities are acceptable.

The objective of the consumer is to ensure that the sampling plan has a low probability of accepting bad lots. Lots are defined as low quality if the percentage of defectives is greater than a specified amount, termed *lot tolerance percent defective (LTPD)*. The probability associated with rejecting a high-quality lot is denoted by the Greek letter alpha (α) and is termed the *producer's risk*. The probability associated with accepting a low-quality lot is denoted by the letter beta (β) and is termed the *consumer's risk*. The selection of particular values for AQL, α, LTPD, and β is an economic decision based on a cost trade-off or, more typically, on company policy or contractual requirements.

There is a humorous story, supposedly about Hewlett-Packard during its first dealings with Japanese vendors, who place great emphasis on high-quality production. HP had insisted on 2 percent AQL in a purchase of 100 cables. During the purchase agreement, some heated discussion took place wherein the Japanese vendor did not want this AQL specification; HP insisted that they would not budge from the 2 percent AQL. The Japanese vendor finally agreed. Later, when the box arrived, there were two packages inside. One contained 100 good cables. The other package had 2 cables with a note stating: "We have sent you 100 good cables. Since you insisted on 2 percent AQL, we have enclosed 2 defective cables in this package, though we do not understand why you want them."

The following example, using an excerpt from a standard acceptance sampling table, illustrates how the four parameters—AQL, α, LTPD, and β—are used in developing a sampling plan.

EXAMPLE 7.6:   VALUES OF n AND C

Hi-Tech Industries manufactures Z-Band radar scanners used to detect speed traps. The printed circuit boards in the scanners are purchased from an outside vendor. The vendor produces the boards to an AQL of 2 percent defectives and is willing to run a 5 percent risk (α) of having lots of this level or fewer defectives rejected. Hi-Tech considers lots of 8 percent or more defectives (LTPD) unacceptable and wants to ensure that it will accept such poor-quality lots no more than 10 percent of the time (β). A large shipment has just been delivered. What values of n and c should be selected to determine the quality of this lot?

SOLUTION

The parameters of the problem are AQL = 0.02, α = 0.05, LTPD = 0.08, and β = 0.10. We can use Exhibit 7.17 to find c and n.

First, divide LTPD by AQL ($0.08 \div 0.02 = 4$). Then, find the ratio in column 2 that is equal to or just greater than that amount (4). This value is 4.057, which is associated with $c = 4$.

			EXHIBIT 7.17
Excerpt from a Sampling Plan Table for $\alpha = 0.05$, $\beta = 0.10$			

c	LTPD ÷ AQL	$n \times$ AQL	c	LTPD ÷ AQL	$n \times$ AQL
0	44.890	0.052	5	3.549	2.613
1	10.946	0.355	6	3.206	3.286
2	6.509	0.818	7	2.957	3.981
3	4.890	1.366	8	2.768	4.695
4	4.057	1.970	9	2.618	5.426

Finally, find the value in column 3 that is in the same row as $c = 4$, and divide that quantity by AQL to obtain n ($1.970 \div 0.02 = 98.5$).

The appropriate sampling plan is $c = 4$, $n = 99$.

Operating Characteristic Curves

While a sampling plan such as the one just described meets our requirements for the extreme values of good and bad quality, we cannot readily determine how well the plan discriminates between good and bad lots at intermediate values. For this reason, sampling plans are generally displayed graphically through the use of operating characteristic (OC) curves. These curves, which are unique for each combination of n and c, simply illustrate the probability of accepting lots with varying percentages of defectives. The procedure we have followed in developing the plan, in fact, specifies two points on an OC curve: one point defined by AQL and $1 - \alpha$ and the other point defined by LTPD and β. Curves for common values of n and c can be computed or obtained from available tables.[12]

Shaping the OC Curve A sampling plan discriminating perfectly between good and bad lots has an infinite slope (vertical) at the selected value of AQL. In Exhibit 7.18, any percentage defective to the left of 2 percent would always be accepted, and those to the right always rejected. However, such a curve is possible only with complete inspection of all units and thus is not a possibility with a true sampling plan.

An OC curve should be steep in the region of most interest (between the AQL and the LTPD), which is accomplished by varying n and c. If c remains constant, increasing the sample size n causes the OC curve to be more vertical. While holding n constant, decreasing c (the maximum number of defective units) also makes the slope more vertical, moving closer to the origin.

The Effects of Lot Size The size of the lot that the sample is taken from has relatively little effect on the quality of protection. Consider, for example, that samples—all of the same size of 20 units—are taken from different lots, ranging from a lot size of 200 units to a lot size of infinity. If each lot is known to have 5 percent defectives, the probability of accepting the lot based on the sample of 20 units ranges from about 0.34 to about 0.36. This means that as long as the lot size is several times the sample size, it makes little difference how large the lot is. This seems a bit difficult to accept, but statistically (on the average in the long run) whether we have a carload or box full, we'll get about the same answer. It just seems that a carload should have a larger sample size. Of course, this assumes that the lot is randomly chosen and that defects are randomly spread through the lot.

EXHIBIT 7.18   Operating Characteristic Curve for AQL = 0.02, α = 0.05, LTPD = 0.08, β = 0.10

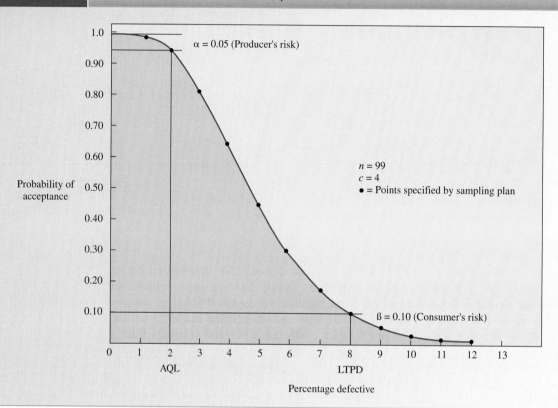

Summary

In the last decades of the last century and into this one, quality has become increasingly important in products and services. The definition of quality has also been expanded to include organization-wide quality issues such as the quality of the work environment for employees. Companies now expect employees to understand the Six-Sigma improvement methodology. DMAIC, the acronym for Define, Measure, Analyze, Improve, and Control, is a process fundamental to the approach companies use to guide improvement projects. The "capability" of a process is a measure of how often that process is expected to produce a defect, given that the process is in control. Six-Sigma processes are designed to produce very few defects. Statistical process control techniques include control charts and acceptance sampling, which ensure that processes are operating as they are designed to operate. World-class companies have implemented extensive training programs (often referred to as "green and black belt training") to ensure these concepts are understood.

Key Terms

Assignable variation Deviation in the output of a process that can be clearly identified and managed.

Attributes Quality characteristics that are classified as either conforming or not conforming to specification.

Canada Award for Excellence An award established on behalf of the Canadian government given annually to companies that excel in organization wide quality.

Capability index (C_{pk}) The ratio of the range of values produced by a process divided by the range of values allowed by the design specification.

Common variation Deviation in the output of a process that is random and inherent in the process itself.

Conformance quality The degree to which the product or service design specifications are met.

Cost of quality Expenditures related to achieving product or service quality, such as the costs of prevention, appraisal, internal failure, and external failure.

Design quality The inherent value of the product in the marketplace.

Dimensions of quality Criteria by which quality is measured.

DMAIC An acronym for the **D**efine, **M**easure, **A**nalyze, **I**mprove, and **C**ontrol improvement methodology followed by companies engaging in Six-Sigma programs.

DPMO (defects per million opportunities) A metric used to describe the variability of a process.

House of quality A matrix that helps a product design team translate consumer requirements into operating and engineering goals.

Malcolm Baldrige National Quality Award An award established by the U.S. Department of Commerce given annually to companies that excel in quality.

Poke-yoke Japanese term for fail safing or any measure to prevent defects.

Quality at the source The person who does the work is responsible for ensuring that specifications are met.

Quality function deployment A process that helps a company determine the product characteristics important to the consumer and to evaluate its own product in relation to others.

Six Sigma A statistical term to describe the quality goal of no more than four defects out of every million units. Also refers to a quality improvement philosophy and program.

Statistical process control (SPC) Techniques for testing a random sample of output from a process to determine whether the process is producing items within a prescribed range.

Total quality management (TQM) Managing the entire organization so that it excels on all dimensions of products and services that are important to the customer.

Upper and lower specification limits The range of values in a measure associated with a process that are allowable given the intended use of the product or service.

Variables Quality characteristics that are measured in actual weight, volume, length, or other measure.

Formula Review

Mean or average

[7.1]
$$\mu = \sum_{i=1}^{N} x_i / N$$

Standard deviation

[7.2]
$$\sigma = \sqrt{\frac{\sum_{i=1}^{N} (x_i - \overline{X})^2}{N}}$$

Capability index

[7.3]
$$C_{pk} = \min\left[\frac{\overline{\overline{X}} - \text{LSL}}{3\sigma}, \frac{\text{USL} - \overline{\overline{X}}}{3\sigma}\right]$$

Process control charts using attribute measurements

[7.4]
$$\bar{p} = \frac{\text{Total number of defects from all samples}}{\text{Number of samples} \times \text{Sample size}}$$

[7.5]
$$s_p = \sqrt{\frac{\bar{p}(1 - \bar{p})}{n}}$$

[7.6]
$$\text{UCL} = \bar{p} + zs_p$$

[7.7]
$$\text{LCL} = \bar{p} - zs_p$$

[7.8]
$$\text{UCL}_{\bar{X}} = \bar{\bar{X}} + zS_{\bar{X}} \quad \text{and} \quad \text{LCL}_{\bar{X}} = \bar{\bar{X}} - zS_{\bar{X}}$$

Process control $\bar{X}$ and R charts

[7.9]
$$\bar{\bar{X}} = \frac{\sum_{j=1}^{m} \bar{X}_j}{m}$$

[7.10]
$$\bar{R} = \frac{\sum_{j=1}^{m} R_j}{m}$$

[7.11]
$$\text{Upper control limit for } \bar{X} = \bar{\bar{X}} + A_2\bar{R}$$

[7.12]
$$\text{Lower control limit for } \bar{X} = \bar{\bar{X}} - A_2\bar{R}$$

[7.13]
$$\text{Upper control limit for } R = D_4\bar{R}$$

[7.14]
$$\text{Lower control limit for } R = D_3\bar{R}$$

Solved Problems

Solved Problem 1

Completed forms from a particular department of an insurance company were sampled daily to check the performance quality of that department. To establish a tentative norm for the department, one sample of 100 units was collected each day for 15 days, with these results:

SAMPLE	SAMPLE SIZE	NUMBER OF FORMS WITH ERRORS	SAMPLE	SAMPLE SIZE	NUMBER OF FORMS WITH ERRORS
1	100	4	9	100	4
2	100	3	10	100	2
3	100	5	11	100	7
4	100	0	12	100	2
5	100	2	13	100	1
6	100	8	14	100	3
7	100	1	15	100	1
8	100	3			

a. Develop a p chart using a 95 percent confidence interval ($1.96s_p$).
b. Plot the 15 samples collected.
c. What comments can you make about the process?

a. $\bar{p} = \dfrac{46}{15(100)} = 0.0307$

$s_p = \sqrt{\dfrac{\bar{p}(1 - \bar{p})}{n}} = \sqrt{\dfrac{0.0307(1 - 0.0307)}{100}} = \sqrt{0.0003} = 0.17$

$\text{UCL} = \bar{p} + 1.96s_p = 0.031 + 1.96(0.17) = 0.064$

$\text{LCL} = \bar{p} - 1.96s_p = 0.031 - 1.96(0.017) = -0.00232$ or zero

b. The defectives are plotted below.

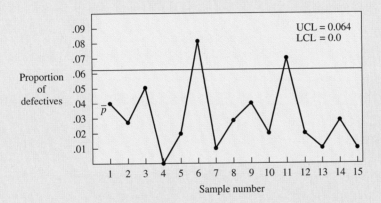

c. Of the 15 samples, 2 were out of the control limits. Because the control limits were established as 95 percent, or 1 out of 20, we would say that the process is out of control. It needs to be examined to find the cause of such widespread variation.

Solved Problem 2

Management is trying to decide whether Part A, which is produced with a consistent 3 percent defective rate, should be inspected. If it is not inspected, the 3 percent defectives will go through a product assembly phase and have to be replaced later. If all Part A's are inspected, one-third of the defectives will be found, thus raising the quality to 2 percent defectives.

a. Should the inspection be done if the cost of inspecting is $0.01 per unit and the cost of replacing a defective in the final assembly is $4.00?

b. Suppose the cost of inspecting is $0.05 per unit rather than $0.01. Would this change your answer in a?

Should Part A be inspected?

0.03 defective with no inspection.

0.02 defective with inspection.

a. This problem can be solved simply by looking at the opportunity for 1 percent improvement.

Benefit = 0.01($4.00) = $0.04

Cost of inspection = $0.01

Therefore, inspect and save $0.03 per unit.

b. A cost of $0.05 per unit to inspect would be $0.01 greater than the savings, so inspection should not be performed.

Review and Discussion Questions

1. After researching, using your library or the Internet, briefly describe Deming's red bead experiment and the lessons Deming intended to convey through it.
2. After research using your library or the Internet, expand on Juran's "fitness for use concept."
3. Explain the differences between the ISO 9000 certifications and the CAE awards.
4. Visit www.nqi.com and examine the list of recent CAE award winners. Would it be accurate to describe the winners as representing a large section of the Canadian organizational landscape?
5. "To achieve Six Sigma Quality, a process must produce no more than 3.4 defects per million opportunities." Does this mean that Six Sigma cannot be applied to projects or job shoptype businesses, since the volumes will be very low (much lower than a million)? Explain.
6. The capability index allows for some drifting of the process mean. Discuss what this means in terms of product quality output.
7. Discuss the purposes of and differences between p charts and $\overline{X}$ and R charts.
8. In an agreement between a supplier and a customer, the supplier must ensure that all parts are within specification before shipment to the customer. What is the effect on the cost of quality to the customer?
9. In the situation described in Question 8, what would be the effect on the cost of quality to the supplier?
10. Discuss the trade-off between achieving a zero AQL (acceptable quality level) and a positive AQL (such as an AQL of 2 percent).

Problems

1. A manager states that his process is really working well. Out of 1500 parts, 1477 were produced free of a particular defect and passed inspection. Based on Six-Sigma theory, how would you rate this performance, other things being equal?
2. The Ramos company currently using an inspection process in its material receiving department is trying to install an overall cost reduction program. One possible reduction is the elimination of one inspection position. This position tests material that has a defective content on the average of 0.04. By inspecting all items, the inspector is able to remove all defects. The inspector can inspect 50 units per hour. The hourly rate including fringe benefits for this position is $9. If the inspection position is eliminated, defects will go into product assembly and will have to be replaced later at a cost of $10 each when they are detected in final product testing.
   a. Should this inspection position be eliminated?
   b. What is the cost to inspect each unit?
   c. Is there benefit (or loss) from the current inspection process? How much?
3. A metal fabricator produces connecting rods with an outer diameter that has a 1 ±0.01 cm specification. A machine operator takes several sample measurements over time and determines the sample mean outer diameter to be 1.002 cm with a standard deviation of 0.003 cm.
   a. Calculate the process capability index for this example.
   b. What does this figure tell you about the process?
4. Ten samples of 15 parts each were taken from an ongoing process to establish a p chart for control. The samples and the number of defectives in each are shown in the following table:

SAMPLE	n	NUMBER OF DEFECTS IN SAMPLE	SAMPLE	n	NUMBER OF DEFECTS IN SAMPLE
1	15	3	6	15	2
2	15	1	7	15	0
3	15	0	8	15	3
4	15	0	9	15	1
5	15	0	10	15	0

 a. Develop a *p* chart for 95 percent confidence (1.96 standard deviations).

 b. Based on the plotted data points, what comments can you make?

5. Output from a process contains 0.02 defective units. Defective units that go undetected into final assemblies cost $25 each to replace. An inspection process, which would detect and remove all defectives, can be established to test these units. However, the inspector, who can test 20 units per hour, is paid $8 per hour, including fringe benefits. Should an inspection station be established to test all units?

 a. What is the cost to inspect each unit?

 b. What is the benefit (or loss) from the inspection process?

6. There is a 3 percent error rate at a specific point in a production process. If an inspector is placed at this point, all the errors can be detected and eliminated. However, the inspector is paid $8 per hour and can inspect units in the process at the rate of 30 per hour.

 If no inspector is used and defects are allowed to pass this point, there is a cost of $10 per unit to correct the defect later on.

 Should an inspector be hired?

7. Resistors for electronic circuits are manufactured on a high-speed automated machine. The machine is set up to produce a large run of resistors of 1000 ohms each.

 To set up the machine and to create a control chart to be used throughout the run, 15 samples were taken with four resistors in each sample. The complete list of samples and their measured values are as follows:

SAMPLE NUMBER	READINGS (IN OHMS)			
1	1010	991	985	986
2	995	996	1009	994
3	990	1003	1015	1008
4	1015	1020	1009	998
5	1013	1019	1005	993
6	994	1001	994	1005
7	989	992	982	1020
8	1001	986	996	996
9	1006	989	1005	1007
10	992	1007	1006	979
11	996	1006	997	989
12	1019	996	991	1011
13	981	991	989	1003
14	999	993	988	984
15	1013	1002	1005	992

 Create an X chart and an *R* chart and plot the values. From the charts, what comments can you make about the process? (Use three-sigma control limits, as in Exhibit 7.14.)

8. In the past, Menon Corporation has not performed incoming quality control inspections but has taken the word of its vendors. However, recently Menon has been having some unsatisfactory experiences with the quality of purchased items and wants to set up sampling plans for the receiving department to use.

 For a particular component, X, Menon has a lot tolerance percentage defective of 10 percent. TPJ Corporation, from which Menon purchases this component, has an acceptable quality level in its production facility of 3 percent for component X. Menon has a consumer's risk of 10 percent and TPJ has a producer's risk of 5 percent.

 a. When a shipment of Product X is received from TPJ Corporation, what sample size should the receiving department test?

 b. What is the allowable number of defects in order to accept the shipment?

9. You are the newly appointed assistant administrator at a local hospital, and your first project is to investigate the quality of the patient meals put out by the food-service department. You conducted a 10-day survey by submitting a simple questionnaire to the 400 patients with each meal, asking that they simply check off that the meal was either satisfactory or unsatisfactory. For simplicity, assume that the response was 1000 returned questionnaires from the 1200 meals each day. The results are as follows:

	NUMBER OF UNSATISFACTORY MEALS	SAMPLE SIZE
December 1	74	1000
December 2	42	1000
December 3	64	1000
December 4	80	1000
December 5	40	1000
December 6	50	1000
December 7	65	1000
December 8	70	1000
December 9	40	1000
December 10	75	1000
	600	10 000

a. Construct a *p* chart based on the questionnaire results, using a confidence interval of 95.5 percent, which is two standard deviations.

b. What comments can you make about the results of the survey?

10. Large-scale integrated (LSI) circuit chips are made in one department of Lopez Electronics. These chips are incorporated into analog devices that are then encased in epoxy. The yield is not particularly good for LSI manufacture, so the AQL specified by that department is 0.15, while the LTPD acceptable by the assembly department is 0.40.

a. Develop a sampling plan.

b. Explain what the sampling plan means; that is, how would you tell someone to do the test?

11. The RCMP and local police departments are trying to analyze crime rates so they can shift their patrols from decreasing-rate areas to areas where rates are increasing. The city and county have been geographically segmented into areas containing 5000 residences. The police recognize that not all crimes and offences are reported: people do not want to become involved, consider the offences too small to report, are too embarrassed to make a police report, or do not take the time, among other reasons. Because of this, every month, the police contact by phone a random sample of 1000 of the 5000 residences for data on crime. (Respondents are guaranteed anonymity.) Here are the data collected for the past 12 months for one area:

MONTH	CRIME INCIDENCE	SAMPLE SIZE	CRIME RATE
January	7	1000	0.007
February	9	1000	0.009
March	7	1000	0.007
April	7	1000	0.007
May	7	1000	0.007
June	9	1000	0.009
July	7	1000	0.007
August	10	1000	0.010
September	8	1000	0.008
October	11	1000	0.011
November	10	1000	0.010
December	8	1000	0.008

Construct a *p* chart for 95 percent confidence (1.96) and plot each of the months. If the next three months show crime incidences in this area as

January = 10 (out of 1000 sampled)

February = 12 (out of 1000 sampled)

March = 11 (out of 1000 sampled)

what comments can you make regarding the crime rate?

12. Some citizens complained to city council members that there should be equal protection under the law against the occurrence of crimes. The citizens argued that this equal protection should be

interpreted as indicating that high-crime areas should have more police protection than low-crime areas. Therefore, police patrols and other methods for preventing crime (such as street lighting or cleaning up abandoned areas and buildings) should be used proportionately to crime occurrence.

In a fashion similar to Problem 11, the city has been broken down into 20 geographic areas, each containing 5000 residences. The 1000 sampled from each area showed the following incidence of crime during the past month:

AREA	NUMBER OF CRIMES	SAMPLE SIZE	CRIME RATE
1	14	1000	0.014
2	3	1000	0.003
3	19	1000	0.019
4	18	1000	0.018
5	14	1000	0.014
6	28	1000	0.028
7	10	1000	0.010
8	18	1000	0.018
9	12	1000	0.012
10	3	1000	0.003
11	20	1000	0.020
12	15	1000	0.015
13	12	1000	0.012
14	14	1000	0.014
15	10	1000	0.010
16	30	1000	0.030
17	4	1000	0.004
18	20	1000	0.020
19	6	1000	0.006
20	30	1000	0.030
	300		

Suggest a reallocation of crime protection effort, if indicated, based on a p chart analysis. To be reasonably certain in your recommendation, select a 95 percent confidence level (that is, $Z = 1.96$).

13. The following table contains the measurements of the key length dimension from a fuel injector. These samples of size five were taken at one-hour intervals.
Construct a three-sigma $\overline{X}$ chart and R chart (use Exhibit 7.14) for the length of the fuel injector. What can you say about this process?

| SAMPLE NUMBER | OBSERVATIONS | | | | |
	1	2	3	4	5
1	0.486	0.499	0.493	0.511	0.481
2	0.499	0.506	0.516	0.494	0.529
3	0.496	0.500	0.515	0.488	0.521
4	0.495	0.506	0.483	0.487	0.489
5	0.472	0.502	0.526	0.469	0.481
6	0.473	0.495	0.507	0.493	0.506
7	0.495	0.512	0.490	0.471	0.504
8	0.525	0.501	0.498	0.474	0.485
9	0.497	0.501	0.517	0.506	0.516
10	0.495	0.505	0.516	0.511	0.497
11	0.495	0.482	0.468	0.492	0.492
12	0.483	0.459	0.526	0.506	0.522
13	0.521	0.512	0.493	0.525	0.510
14	0.487	0.521	0.507	0.501	0.500
15	0.493	0.516	0.499	0.511	0.513
16	0.473	0.506	0.479	0.480	0.523
17	0.477	0.485	0.513	0.484	0.496
18	0.515	0.493	0.493	0.485	0.475
19	0.511	0.536	0.486	0.497	0.491
20	0.509	0.490	0.470	0.504	0.512

14. Vladimir, Inc. is attempting to determine whether an existing machine is capable of milling an engine part that has a key specification of 4 ± 0.003 cm. After a trial run on this machine, Vladimir has determined that the machine has a sample mean of 4.001 cm with a standard deviation of 0.002 cm.

    a. Calculate the C_{pk} for this machine.

    b. Should Vladimir use this machine to produce this part? Why?

Advanced Problem

15. Design specifications require that a key dimension on a product measure 100 ± 10 units. A process being considered for producing this product has a standard deviation of four units.

    a. What can you say (quantitatively) regarding the process capability?

    b. Suppose the process average shifts to 92. Calculate the new process capability.

    c. What can you say about the process after the shift? Approximately what percentage of the items produced will be defective?

CASE 1 | Hank Kolb, Director of Quality Assurance

Hank Kolb was whistling as he walked toward his office, still feeling a bit like a stranger since being hired four weeks before as director of quality assurance. The past week he had been away from the plant at a seminar given for quality managers of manufacturing plants by the corporate training department. He was now looking forward to digging into the quality problems at this industrial products plant employing 1200 people.

Kolb poked his head into Mark Hamler's office, his immediate subordinate as the quality control manager, and asked him how things had gone during the past week. Hamler's muted smile and an "Oh, fine," stopped Kolb in his tracks. He didn't know Hamler very well and was unsure about pursuing this reply any further. Kolb was still uncertain of how to start building a relationship with him since Hamler had been passed over for the promotion to Kolb's job; Hamler's evaluation form had stated "superb technical knowledge; managerial skills lacking." Kolb decided to inquire a little further and asked Hamler what had happened. Hamlere replied, "Oh, just another typical quality snafu. We had a little problem on the Greasex line last week [a specialized degreasing solvent packed in a spray can for the high-technology sector]. A little high pressure was found in some cans on the second shift, but a supervisor vented them so that we could ship them out. We met our delivery schedule!" Because Kolb was still relatively unfamiliar with the plant and its products, he asked Hamler to elaborate. Hamler continued, painfully:

> We've been having some trouble with the new filling equipment and some of the cans were pressurized beyond the upper specification limit.
>
> The production rate is still 50 percent of standard, about 14 cases per shift, and we caught it halfway into the shift. Mac Evans [the inspector for that line] picked it up, tagged the cases "hold," and went on about his duties. When he returned at the end of the shift to write up the rejects, Wayne Simmons, first-line supervisor, was by a pallet of finished goods

finishing sealing up a carton of the rejected Greasex. The reject "hold" tags had been removed. He told Mac that he had heard about the high pressure from another inspector at coffee break, had come back, taken off the tags, individually turned the cans upside down and vented every one of them in the eight rejected cartons. He told Mac that production planning was really pushing for the stuff and they couldn't delay by having it sent through the rework area. He told Mac that he would get on the operator to run the equipment right next time. Mac didn't write it up but came in about three days ago to tell me about it. Oh, it happens every once in a while and I told him to make sure to check with maintenance to make sure the filling machine was adjusted; and I saw Wayne in the hall and told him that he ought to send the stuff through rework next time.

Kolb was a bit dumbfounded at this and didn't say much—he didn't know if this was a big deal or not. When he got to his office he thought again about what Morganthal, the general manager, had said when he had hired him. He warned Kolb about the "lack of quality attitude" in the plant, and said that Kolb "should try and do something about this." Morganthal further emphasized the quality problems in the plant: "We have to improve our quality; it's costing us a lot of money, I'm sure of it, but I can't prove it! Hank, you have my full support in this matter; you're in charge of these quality problems. This downward quality-productivity–turnover spiral has to end!"

The incident had happened a week before; the goods were probably out in the customers' hands by now, and everyone had forgotten about it (or wanted to). There seemed to be more pressing problems than this for Kolb to spend his time on, but it continued to nag him. He felt that the quality department was being treated as a joke, and he also felt that this was a personal slap from manufacturing. He didn't want to start a war with the production people, but what could he do? Kolb was troubled enough to cancel his appointments and spend the morning talking to a few people. After a long and very tactful morning, he learned the following information:

1. **From personnel.** The operator for the filling equipment had just been transferred from shipping two weeks ago. He had no formal training in this job but was being trained by Wayne, on the job, to run the equipment. When Mac had tested the high-pressure cans, the operator was nowhere to be found and had only learned of the rejected material from Wayne after the shift was over.

2. **From plant maintenance.** This particular piece of automated filling equipment had been purchased two years ago for use on another product. It had been switched to the Greasex line six months ago and maintenance completed 12 work orders during the last month for repairs or adjustments on it. The equipment had been adapted by plant maintenance for handling the lower viscosity of Greasex, which it had not originally been designed for. This included designing a special filling head. There was no scheduled preventive maintenance for this equipment, and the parts for the sensitive filling head, replaced three times in the last six months, had to be made at a nearby machine shop. Nonstandard downtime was 15 percent of actual running time.

3. **From purchasing.** The plastic nozzle heads for the Greasex can, designed by a vendor for this new product on a rush order, were often found to have slight burrs on the inside rim, and this caused some trouble in fitting the top to the can. An increase in application pressure at the filling head by maintenance adjustment had solved the burr application problem or had at least forced the nozzle heads on despite burrs. Purchasing agents said that they were going to talk to the sales representative of the nozzle head supplier about this the next time he came in.

4. **From product design and packaging.** The can, designed especially for Greasex, had been contoured to allow better gripping by the user. This change, instigated by marketing research, set Greasex apart from the appearance of its competitors and was seen as significant by the designers. There had been no test of the effects of the contoured can on filling speed or filling hydrodynamics from a high-pressured filling head. Kolb had a hunch that the new design was acting as a venturi (carrier creating suction) when being filled, but the packaging designer thought that was unlikely.

5. **From the manufacturing manager.** He had heard about the problem; in fact, Simmons had made a joke about it, bragging about how he beat his production quota to the other foremen and shift supervisors. The manufacturing manager thought Simmons was one of the "best foremen we have . . . he always got his production out." His promotion papers were actually on the manufacturing manager's desk when Kolb dropped by. Simmons was being strongly considered for promotion to shift supervisor. The manufacturing manager, under pressure from Morganthal for cost improvements and reduced delivery times, sympathized with Kolb but said that the rework area would have vented with their pressure gauges what Wayne had done by hand. "But I'll speak with Wayne about the incident," he said.

6. **From marketing.** The introduction of Greasex had been rushed to market to beat competitors, and a major promotional advertising campaign was under way to increase consumer awareness. A deluge of orders was swamping the order-taking department and putting Greasex high on the back-order list. Production had to turn the stuff out. Even being a little off spec was tolerable because "it would be better to have it on the shelf than not there at all. Who cares if the label is a little crooked or the stuff comes out with a little too much pressure? We need market share now in that high-tech segment."

What bothered Kolb most was the safety issue of the high pressure in the cans. He had no way of knowing how much of a hazard the high pressure was or if Simmons had vented them enough to effectively reduce the hazard. The data from the can manufacturer, which Hamler had showed him, indicated that the high pressure found by the inspector was not in the danger area. But, again, the inspector had used only a sample testing procedure to reject the eight cases. Even if he could morally accept that there was no product safety hazard, could Kolb make sure that this would never happen again?

Skipping lunch, Kolb sat in his office and thought about the morning's events. The past week's seminar had talked about the role of quality, productivity and quality, creating a new attitude, and the quality challenge; but where had they told him what to do when this happened? He had left a very good job to come here because he thought the company was serious about the importance of quality, and he wanted a challenge. Kolb had demanded and received a salary equal to the manufacturing, marketing, and R&D directors, and he was one of the direct reports to the general manager. Yet he still didn't know exactly what he should or shouldn't do, or even what he could or couldn't do under these circumstances.

Questions

1. What are the causes of the quality problems on the Greasex line? Display your answer on a fishbone diagram (under Equipment, Material, Personnel, and Procedure categories).

2. What general steps should Hank follow in setting up a continuous improvement program for the company? What problems will he have to overcome to make it work?

Source: Copyright 1981 by President and Fellows of Harvard College, Harvard Business School. Case 681.083. This case was prepared by Frank S. Leonard as the basis for class discussion rather than to illustrate either effective or ineffective handling of an administrative situation. Reprinted by permission of the Harvard Business School.

CASE 2 | Shortening Customers' Telephone Waiting Time

This case illustrates how a bank applied some of the basic quality tools discussed in this chapter to improve customer service. It is the story of a Quality Circle (QC) program implemented in the main office of a large bank. An average of 500 customers call this office every day. Surveys indicated that the callers tended to become irritated if it took too long for the call to be answered and for the caller to be transferred to the appropriate person. By contrast, prompt service reassured the customers and made them feel more comfortable doing business by phone. The bank feared that dissatisfied customers might move their business to another bank.

Selection of a Theme

A QC team was formed to address the telephone reception issue. Telephone reception was chosen as a QC theme for the following reasons: (*a*) Telephone reception is the first impression a customer receives from the company; (*b*) this theme coincided with the company's telephone reception slogan, "Don't make customers wait, and avoid needless switching from extension to extension;" and (*c*) it also coincided with a companywide campaign being promoted at that time that advocated being friendly to everyone one met.

First, the team discussed why the present method of answering calls made callers wait. Exhibit 7.19 illustrates a frequent situation, where a call from customer B comes in while the operator is talking with customer A. Let's see why the customer has to wait.

At (1), the operator receives a call from the customer but, due to lack of experience, does not know where to connect the call. At (2), the receiving party cannot answer the phone quickly, perhaps because he or she is unavailable, and no one else can take the call. The result is that the operator must transfer the call to another extension while apologizing for the delay.

Situation Analysis

To fully understand the situation, the QC members decided to brainstorm regarding the reasons for poor service. Some of the reasons identified for customers having to wait too long before they were connected to the appropriate person were:

1. The receiving party is out of the office for the day on other business, or is absent that day, or is not at the desk at present (these are considered three reasons). In these cases the operator would have to try somebody else who could help the caller.
2. Sometimes the customer engages the operator in lengthy conversation or spends a long time complaining to the operator.
3. Often customers are not aware whom they should contact within the bank.
4. Sometimes the delay is system related. As is common in queues, sometimes there is a high call volume, and other times it is light. If people call at lunchtime there is usually only one operator since the only other operator would be at lunch.
5. Sometimes the operator cannot find an alternate person to receive calls since everybody in the section is unavailable.
6. One or the other of the operators is sometimes absent due to illness or vacation.
7. In some cases operators may lack knowledge about the job responsibilities within the company and thus may not transfer the caller to the appropriate person at the first try. The caller would then have to be transferred again. In other cases, operators have difficulty understanding customer requests.

Operators were then asked to keep checksheets on several points to tally the reasons for poor service spanning 12 days from June 4 to 16. (See Exhibit 7.20A.) The data recorded on the checksheets unexpectedly revealed that "only one operator (partner out of the office)" topped the list by a big margin, occurring a total of 172 times. In this case, the operator on duty had to deal with large numbers of calls when the phones

EXHIBIT 7.19 | Why Customers Had to Wait

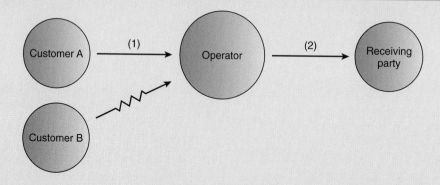

EXHIBIT 7.20

Causes of Callers' Waits

A. Checksheet—Designed to Identify the Problems

Reason / Date	No one present in the section receiving the call	Receiving party not present	Only one operator (partner out of the office)	Total
June 4	\\\\	₩ \	₩ ₩ \	24
June 5	₩	₩ \\\	₩ ₩ \\\\	32
June 6	₩ \	\\\\	₩ ₩ \\	28
June 15	₩	₩	₩ \\\	25

B. Reasons Why Callers Had to Wait

Cause type	Description	Number of occurrences
A	Customer does not know whom to contact regarding concern	19
B	Receiving party not present in office	73
C	No one present in section	61
D	One operator (partner out of office)	172
E	Lengthy conversation	16
F	Other reasons	10
	Total	351

were busy. A total of 351 customers had to wait a long time (experienced poor service), which accounted for about 6 percent of the calls received. (See Exhibit 7.20B).

System Improvement

The bank implemented a number of suggestions made by the QC. As a result, the customer waiting time improved considerably. Exhibit 7.21 shows data from a recent 12-day period comparable to the June 4 to 16 analysis, where the details on all calls considered to be poorly served (defective calls) are shown. As seen, although the poorly serviced calls could not be reduced to zero, all items presented showed a marked improvement. The total number of defective calls dropped from 351 to 59. The major cause of delays—"one operator"—plummeted from 172 incidents to 15 in the follow-up survey.

Questions

1. Create a fishbone diagram using the reasons given in the situation analysis. Use four main categories: Receiving party, Customer, System, and Operator.
2. Using the data in Exhibit 7.20B, prepare a Pareto diagram for the six reasons. Explain how it can help you improve the system.
3. How would you have solved these problems?

4. With the improved system and the data in Exhibit 7.21, prepare the following:
   a. checksheet for poorly serviced calls, similar to 7.20A, in the format shown below.

DAY	REASONS						TOTAL
	A	B	C	D	E	F	
1							
2							
.							
.							
12							

   b. Pareto diagram of the improved system using the six reasons.
5. Using the data given, comment on the overall and specific improvements in the system.
6. What would be the next step in improving the system even further?

Source: From "The Quest for Higher Quality—the Deming Prize and Quality Control," Ricoh Company, Ltd., in Masaaki Imai, *Kaizen: The Key to Japan's Competitive Success* (New York: The McGraw-Hill Companies, 1986), pp. 54–58.

EXHIBIT 7.21   Analysis of Defective Calls

DEFECTIVE CALL #	DAY	REASON	DEFECTIVE CALL #	DAY	REASON
1	1	One operator	31	7	Receiving party not present
2	1	One operator	32	7	One operator
3	1	Receiving party not present	33	7	No one in section
4	1	No one in section	34	7	No one in section
5	1	Lengthy conversation	35	8	Receiving party not present
6	1	Customer does not know whom to contact	36	8	One operator
7	1	No one in section	37	8	Customer does not know whom to contact
8	2	Other reasons	38	8	Receiving party not present
9	2	Lengthy conversation	39	8	No one in section
10	2	One operator	40	8	One operator
11	3	Receiving party not present	41	8	Receiving party not present
12	3	No one in section	42	9	One operator
13	3	Receiving party not present	43	9	No one in section
14	3	No one in section	44	10	Receiving party not present
15	3	Receiving party not present	45	10	One operator
16	3	One operator	46	10	No one in section
17	4	No one in section	47	10	One operator
18	4	Receiving party not present	48	10	No one in section
19	4	No one in section	49	10	Receiving party not present
20	4	Receiving party not present	50	10	No one in section
21	4	No one in section	51	10	No one in section
22	4	One operator	52	11	One operator
23	5	Receiving party not present	53	11	Receiving party not present
24	5	No one in section	54	11	No one in section
25	5	Receiving party not present	55	11	Customer does not know whom to contact
26	5	No one in section	56	12	No one in section
27	6	One operator	57	12	No one in section
28	6	One operator	58	12	Receiving party not present
29	6	Receiving party not present	59	12	Customer does not know whom to contact
30	6	One operator			

Footnotes

[1] D. A. Garvin, *Managing Quality* (New York: Free Press, 1988).

[2] J. Banks, *Principles of Quality Control* New York, NY: Wiley, 1989. p. 25.

[3] J. M Juran and F. M Gryna, Jr., *Quality Planning and Analysis*. New York, NY: McGraw Hill, 1980, pp. 3–4.

[4] www.wikipedia.org

[5] P. B. Crosby, *Quality Is Free* (New York: New American Library, 1979), p. 15.

[6] Canadian Framework for Business Excellence, Toronto, Ontario, National Quality Institute, 2000.

[7] Standards Council of Canada (www.scc.ca and personal conversation)

[8] www.suncor.com

[9] www.dofasco.com

[10] S. Walleck, D. O'Halloran, and C. Leader, "Benchmarking World-Class Performance," *McKinsey Quarterly*, no. 1 (1991), p. 7.

[11]E. L. Grant and R. S. Leavenworth, *Statistical Quality Control* (New York: McGraw-Hill, 1996).

[12]See, for example, H. F. Dodge and H. G. Romig, *Sampling Inspection Tables—Single and Double Sampling* (New York: John Wiley & Sons, 1959); and *Military Standard Sampling Procedures and Tables for Inspection by Attributes* (MIL-STD-105D) (Washington, DC: U.S. Government Printing Office, 1983).

Selected Bibliography

Evans, James R., and William M. Lindsay. *The Management and Control of Quality,* 6th ed. Cincinnati: South-Western College Publications, 2004.

Rath & Strong. *Rath & Strong's Six Sigma Pocket Guide.* Rath & Strong, Inc., 2000.

Small, B. B. (with committee). *Statistical Quality Control Handbook.* Western Electric Co., Inc., 1956.

Zimmerman, S. M., and M. L. Icenogel. *Statistical Quality Control; Using Excel.* 2nd ed. Milwaukee, WI: ASQ Quality Press, 2002.

SUPPLY CHAINS

Why Having an Effective Supply Chain Matters

A recent study by Accenture, INSEAD, and Stanford University has documented a strong direct relationship between supply chain operations and corporate financial performance. The bottom line is that supply chain leaders are rewarded by the stock market with substantially higher growth in stock values than companies with lesser performance in supply chain management.

The study used data from more than 600 "Global 3000" companies across 24 industries, from 1995 to 2000. Companies were classified as supply chain "leaders" or "laggards," based on their performance compared with the others on inventory turns, cost of goods sold as a percentage of revenue, and return on assets. The study then calculated the financial performance for each company based on its change in stock market capitalization during the study period, compared with other companies in its industry. It's difficult to argue with the stock market as the ultimate arbiter of company value for this purpose.

The impact was dramatic: The compound average annual growth in market capitalization of the leaders was 10 to 30 percentage points higher than the laggards. The results applied across the board—for 21 of the 24 industries the supply chain leaders had higher stock value growth over the six-year period. Companies all try to beat the Dow or the S&P 500 averages and are happy if they are ahead by a couple of percentage points on a consistent basis. The supply chain leaders beat the market by an annual average of 26 points during the period 1995–1997 and 7 points during 1998–2000.

Is it possible for a company's financial value to grow without being a supply chain leader? Sure. Fifteen percent of the "laggards" had top-tier market cap growth. But the reality is that most supply chain laggards were also under-performers in the stock market.

Armed with these results, is it easy to become a supply chain leader? Of course not. It takes processes, people, technology, leadership, discipline, and maybe a little luck. It requires knowing what to do and how to do it. It stands to reason that if you can build your product to order rather than carry inventory, closely match store requirements to actual customer sales trends, restock the shelves quickly, minimize the amount of end-of-season markdown merchandise, or reduce the property, plant, and equipment assets needed to generate a dollar's worth of profit, then you will earn an outsized return from the market.

Source: Accenture research report, available at http://www.accenture.com.

CHAPTER

8

SUPPLY CHAIN STRATEGY

Learning Objectives:

1. Recognize the important issues in managing supply chains.
2. Understand the "bullwhip effect" and know why it is important to synchronize the flow of material between supply chain partners.
3. Understand how characteristics of supply and demand have an impact on structuring supply chain
4. Know the reason for outsourcing capabilities.
5. Know how to measure supply chain performance.
6. Know the basic building blocks for an effective mass customization program.
7. Understand what a reverse supply chain is.

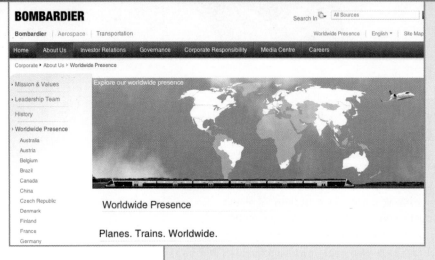

THE WORLD IS FLAT
Flattener 5: Outsourcing
Flattener 6: Offshoring

The owner of a fuel pump factory in Beijing posted the following African proverb, translated into Mandarin, on his factory floor:

Every morning in Africa, a gazelle wakes up.

It knows it must run faster than the fastest lion or it will be killed.

Every morning a lion wakes up.

It knows it must outrun the slowest gazelle or it will starve to death.

It doesn't matter whether you are a lion or a gazelle.

When the sun comes up, you better start running.

Global

The opening of China to the rest of the world started on December 11, 2001, when that country formally joined the World Trade Organization (WTO). Ever since China joined the WTO, both it and the rest of the world have had to run faster and faster. This is because China's membership in the WTO gave a huge boost to another form of collaboration: offshoring. Offshoring, which has been around for decades, is different from outsourcing. Outsourcing means taking some specific but limited function that your company was doing in-house—such as research, call centres, or accounts receivable—and having another company perform the exact same function for you, then reintegrating its work back into your overall operation. Offshoring, by contrast, is when a company takes one of its factories that is operating in Fredericton, New Brunswick, and moves the whole factory offshore to Fuzhou, China. There, it produces the very same product in the very same way, only with cheaper labour, lower taxes, subsidized energy, and lower health-care costs. Just as Y2K took India and the world to a whole new level of outsourcing, China's joining the WTO took Beijing and the world to a whole new level of offshoring, with more companies shifting production offshore and then integrating it into the global supply chain.

Offshoring is also becoming a hot trade issue in developed countries. Even the satirical television sitcom "The Simpsons" got into the act in one episode, with Mr. Burns moving the nuclear power plant to Bangalore (now called Bengaluru), India and putting Homer in charge there. But unknown to Mr. Burns, and to his horror, Homer provides benefits like vacation and healthcare to the Indian employees—very real issues for global Canadian organizations such as Bombardier, Magna, Celestica, CAE, big banks, and insurance companies and others in offshoring and outsourcing, which we will be discussing in this chapter.

■ Adapted from: Thomas L. Friedman, *The World Is Flat* [Updated and Expanded], New York: Farrar, Straus and Giroux, 2006, p. 136.

WHAT IS SUPPLY CHAIN MANAGEMENT?

Supply chain management (SCM) is a hot topic in business today. Traditionally, companies gave much of their attention to internal operations but did not consider the external supply chain. For example, the notion that providing your supplier with your production plans so that they could better manage the production and inventory of the parts supplied to you was not on most operations managers' minds. Similarly, designing your product to make it easier to ship to a customer was not on most designers' minds. This company-centric approach, while possibly optimizing operations, could result in sub-optimality in the supply chain as a whole, thus making your product more expensive and resulting in poorer customer service.

Supply chain management today, on the other hand, involves optimizing the entire supply chain operations for the product by taking a systems approach to managing the flow of information, materials, and services from raw materials suppliers through factories and warehouses to the end customer. Well-managed organizations consider supply chain management issues right from when a product or service is conceived to the very end of its life cycle, when the product or service is replaced by a newer one. The term supply chain comes from a picture of how organizations are linked together, as viewed from a particular company. Exhibit 8.1 depicts a global supply chain for both manufacturing and service companies. Note the linkage between suppliers that provide inputs, manufacturing and service support operations that transform the inputs into products and services, and the distribution and local service providers that localize the product. Localization can involve just the delivery of the product or some more involved process that tailors the product or service to the needs of the local market. As we will see later in this chapter, the structure of the supply chain is dependent on the competitive priorities of your company. So why is supply chain management such a popular topic these days? The answer is that many companies are achieving significant competitive advantage by the way they configure and manage their supply chain operations. Figure 8.7 shows a specific example of the supply chain for the BlackBerry Storm smartphone (This example is discussed in more detail later).

EXHIBIT 8.1 | The Supply Chain Network

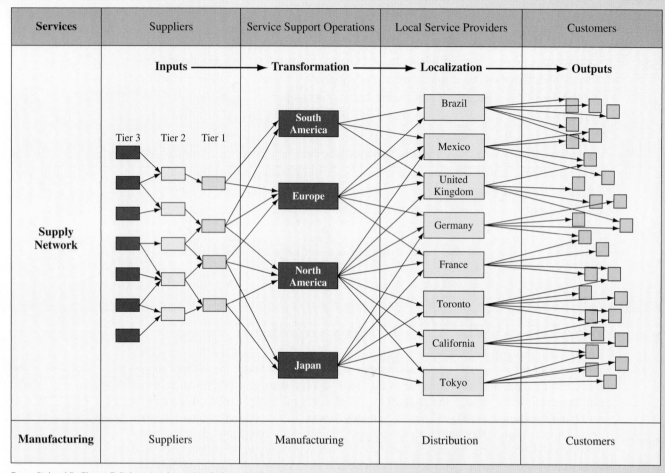

From: Richard B. Chase, F. Robert Jacobs, and Nicholas J. Aquilano, *Operations Management for Competitive Advantage* 10th ed. (New York, NY: Irwin McGraw-Hill, 2004): 365.

Operations and Supply Management in Practice

Could Better Supply Chain Management have Saved More *Titanic* Lives?

The sinking of the *Titanic* on April 14, 1912 was one of the biggest transportation tragedies in history. Naturally, researchers have been intrigued by why such a behemoth failed to survive the iceberg collision. Part of the reason many have been supply chain issues.

The *Titanic* required about three million rivets which acted like glue to hold the ship together. Clues from rivets recovered from the wreck, modern tests, computer simulations, comparisons with century-old metals, as well as care-

ful documentation of what engineers and shipbuilders of that era considered state of the art, reveal that the rivets may have been sub-standard, causing the ship to break up on impact (however, the ship builder, Harland & Wolff, still in existence, denies this).

Since there was much shipbuilding going on at the same time as the *Titanic* was being built, it was difficult to get rivets. In fact, Harland and Wolff itself was building two sister ships, the *Olympic* and the *Britannic*. Thus, it appears that, based on company and British government documents, Harland and Wolff had to search beyond its usual suppliers of rivet iron and include smaller forges.

Continued

Since forging iron rivets was done manually, it required skill and experience that these small forges may not have had. Poorly forged rivets, of course, meant they weren't as strong. Further, it appeared that the iron for the rivets, while good quality, did not match the competitive standard in shipbuilding for the day. Also, while other shipbuilders had moved to better-suited steel rivets, that could be machine made (leading to more consistent quality), Harland and Wolff was just in the process of doing so. So it appears that the state-of-the-art *Titanic* may have been fitted with less than state-of-the-art rivets.

Would any of this have saved the *Titanic*? Probably not. The iceberg was just too gigantic for any ship to survive. But scientists think that the ship might have stayed afloat longer, allowing more rescuers to arrive and save more lives.

What lesson does this have for the twenty-first century? At the beginning of this century, Canada was undergoing a boom. Supplies were hard to find. For example, a home that would have taken six months to complete in the 1990s was taking more than a year in some cities. This naturally puts a lot of pressure on manufacturers to reduce delays. However, manufacturers have to be careful in a boom time not to sacrifice quality, and to avoid other short cuts to maintain schedule, as the manufacturer of the *Titanic* may have done.

■ Source: William J. Broad, "A Riveting Take on the Sinking of the Titanic" *The Globe and Mail*, April 15, 2008. pg. A.3
William J. Broad, *The New York Times,* April 15, 2008, www.nytimes.com/2008/04/15/science/15titanic.html. Retrieved May 01, 2009.
CBS/AP. "Did Weak Rivets Help Do in the Titanic?" April 19, 2008. www.cbsnews.com. Retrieved May 01, 2009.

DESIGNING THE SUPPLY CHAIN

As seen in Exhibit 8.1, the supply chain includes suppliers, the transformation process, distributors, and customers. Thus, a number of issues need to be addressed in designing a company's supply chain. These include:

Sourcing

Logistics and inventory management

Vertical integration and outsourcing

Measuring supply chain performance

Product design to facilitate supply chain management

Information systems in supply chain management

SOURCING

Strategic sourcing is the development and management of supplier relationships to acquire goods and services in a way that aids in achieving the needs of the business. In the past the term *sourcing* was just another term for purchasing, a corporate function that financially was important but strategically was not the centre of attention. Today, as a result of globalization and inexpensive communications technology, the basis for competition is changing. A firm is no longer constrained by the capabilities it owns; what matters is its ability to make the most of available capabilities, whether they are owned by the firm or not. Outsourcing is so sophisticated that even core functions such as engineering, research and development, manufacturing, information technology, and marketing can be moved outside the firm.

The Dell Company is unique and interesting. Through a combination of innovative product design, an Internet order-taking process, an innovative assembly system, and extensive cooperation from its suppliers, Dell Computer has been able to create a supply chain that is extremely efficient. Dell Computer has now become the benchmark company for the computer industry.

A key to the success of Dell is the fact that customers now order over the Internet and are willing to wait at least a week for the delivery of their computer systems. This strategy of selling directly is called **disintermediation** because it gets rid of the intermediaries such as computer retailers.[1] Airlines do the same thing when they sell tickets directly through their Web site, because they are eliminating the intermediary, the travel agent. In appropriate

Supply Chain

situations, disintermediation can reduce costs and can also increase the contact between the vendor and buyer, thus increasing the vendor's understanding of the customer.

Dell is also an example of how supply chain strategies have to change over time. While Dell has been very successful with its strategy, it has realized that, today, personal computers have almost become a commodity. So, many consumers are satisfied with going to retail stores such as Future Shop and purchasing a computer from the available stock in the store. Often, the computer is bundled with other services that offer rebates, enticing the customer to buy the package, thus reducing the overall cost of the computer and the service. To avoid losing customers, recently Dell has also started selling personal computers through different retail stores.

Marshall Fisher[2] argues that in many cases supply chain partners are adversaries. Dysfunctional industry practices, for example, such as a reliance on price promotions, are common. Consider the common food industry practice of offering price promotions every January on a product. Retailers respond to the price cut by stocking up, in some cases buying a year's supply—a practice the industry calls *forward buying*. Nobody wins in the deal. Retailers have to pay to carry the year's supply, and the shipment bulge adds cost throughout the supplier's system. For example, the supplier plants must go on overtime starting in October to meet the bulge. Even the vendors who supply the manufacturing plants are affected because they must quickly react to the large surge in raw material requirements.

The impact of these types of practices has been studied at companies such as Procter & Gamble. Exhibit 8.2 shows typical order patterns faced by each node in a supply chain

EXHIBIT 8.2   Increasing Variability of Orders up the Supply Chain

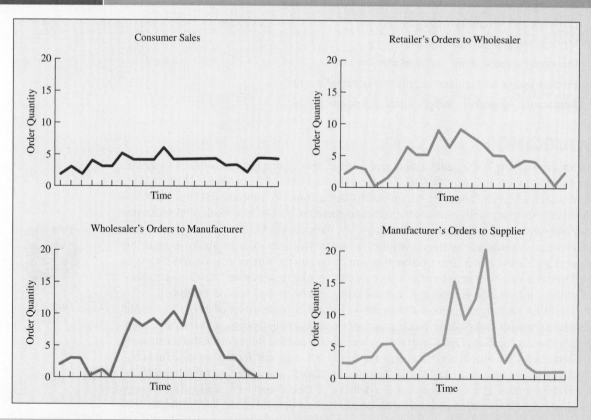

that consists of a manufacturer, a distributor, a wholesaler, and a retailer. In this case, the demand is for disposable baby diapers. The retailer's orders to the wholesaler display greater variability than the end-consumer sales; the wholesaler's orders to the manufacturer show even more oscillations; and, finally, the manufacturer's orders to its suppliers are the most volatile. This phenomenon of variability magnification as we move from the customer to the producer in the supply chain is often referred to as the **bullwhip effect**. The effect indicates a lack of synchronization among supply chain members. Even a slight change in consumer sales ripples backward in the form of magnified oscillations upstream, resembling the result of a flick of a bullwhip handle. Because the supply patterns do not match the demand patterns, inventory accumulates at various stages, and shortages and delays occur at others. This bullwhip effect has been observed by many firms in numerous industries, including Campbell Soup and Procter & Gamble in consumer products; Hewlett-Packard, IBM, and Motorola in electronics; General Motors in automobiles; and Eli Lilly in pharmaceuticals.

In addition to forward buying, the lack of information sharing, and rationing and gaming (in case of shortages, customers tend to exaggerate orders to ensure that they get at least some amount), can cause the bullwhip effect. Lee et al.[3] recommend a) information sharing, b) reducing the lead time (time from order placement to receipt), c) vendor-managed inventories (discussed later in this chapter), and d) instituting an everyday price policy (i.e., getting rid of promotional pricing) to prevent the bullwhip effect.

Campbell Soup has a program called *continuous replenishment* that typifies what many manufacturers are doing to smooth the flow of materials through their supply chain. Here is how the program works: Campbell establishes electronic data interchange (EDI) links with retailers and offers an "everyday low price" that eliminates discounts. Every morning, retailers electronically inform the company of their demand for all Campbell products and of the level of inventories in their distribution centres. Campbell uses that information to forecast future demand and to determine which products require replenishment based on upper and lower inventory limits previously established with each supplier. Trucks leave the Campbell shipping plant that afternoon and arrive at the retailers' distribution centres with the required replenishments the same day. Using this system, Campbell can cut the retailers' inventories, which under the old system averaged four weeks of supply, to about two weeks of supply.

This solves some problems for Campbell Soup, but what are the advantages for the retailer? Most retailers figure that the cost to carry the inventory of a given product for a year equals at least 25 percent of what they paid for the product. A two-week inventory reduction represents a cost savings equal to nearly 1 percent of sales. The average retailer's profits equal about 2 percent of sales, so this saving is enough to increase profits by 50 percent. Because the retailer makes more money on Campbell products delivered through continuous replenishment, it has an incentive to carry a broader line of products and to give them more shelf space. Campbell Soup found that after it introduced the program, sales of its products grew twice as fast through participating retailers as sales through other retailers.

Fisher has developed a framework to help managers understand the nature of the demand for their products and then devise the supply chain that can best satisfy that demand. Many aspects of a product's demand are important—for example, product life cycle, demand predictability, product variety, and market standards for lead times and service. Fisher has found that products can be categorized as either primarily functional or primarily innovative. Because each category requires a distinctly different kind of supply chain, the root cause of supply chain problems is a mismatch between the type of product and the type of supply chain.

Functional products include the staples that people buy in a wide range of retail outlets, such as grocery stores and gas stations. Because such products satisfy basic needs, which do not change much over time, they have stable, predictable demand, and long life cycles. But their stability invites competition, which often leads to low profit margins. Specific criteria suggested by Fisher for identifying functional products include the following: product life cycle of more than two years, contribution margin of 5 to 20 percent, only 10 to 20 product variations, an average forecast error at time of production of only 10 percent, and a lead time for make-to-order products of from six months to one year.

To avoid low margins, many companies introduce innovations in fashion or technology to give customers an additional reason to buy their products. Fashionable clothes and personal computers are good examples. Although innovation can enable a company to achieve higher profit margins, the very newness of the innovative products makes demand for them unpredictable. These **innovative products** typically have a life cycle of just a few months. Imitators quickly erode the competitive advantage that innovative products enjoy, and companies are forced to introduce a steady stream of newer innovations. The short life cycles and the great variety typical of these products further increase unpredictability.

Exhibit 8.3 summarizes the differences between functional and innovative products.

Hau Lee[4] expands on Fisher's ideas by focusing on the "supply" side of the supply chain. While Fisher has captured important demand characteristics, Lee points out that there are uncertainties revolving around the supply side that are equally important drivers for the right supply chain strategy.

Lee defines a *stable supply process* as one where the manufacturing process and the underlying technology are mature and the supply base is well established. In contrast, an *evolving supply process* is one in which the manufacturing process and the underlying technology are still under early development and are rapidly changing. As a result, the supply base may be limited in both size and experience. In a stable supply process, manufacturing

EXHIBIT 8.3	Demand and Supply Uncertainty Characteristics

DEMAND CHARACTERISTICS		SUPPLY CHARACTERISTICS	
FUNCTIONAL	INNOVATIVE	STABLE	EVOLVING
Low demand uncertainty	High demand uncertainty	Fewer breakdowns	Vulnerable to breakdowns
More predictable demand	Difficult to forecast	Stable and higher yields	Variable and lower yields
Stable demand	Variable demand	Less quality problems	Potential quality problems
Long product life	Short selling season	More supply sources	Limited supply sources
Low inventory cost	High inventory cost	Reliable suppliers	Unreliable suppliers
Low profit margin	High profit margin	Fewer process changes	More process changes
Low product variety	High product variety	Fewer capacity constraints	Potential capacity constrained
Higher volume	Low volume	Easier to change over	Difficult to change over
Low stockout cost	High stockout cost	Flexible	Inflexible
Low obsolescence	High obsolescence	Dependable lead times	Variable lead time

	EXHIBIT 8.4
Hau Lee's Uncertainty Framework—Examples and Types of Supply Chain Needed	

		DEMAND UNCERTAINTY	
		LOW (FUNCTIONAL PRODUCTS)	HIGH (INNOVATIVE PRODUCTS)
SUPPLY UNCERTAINTY	LOW (STABLE PROCESS)	Grocery, basic apparel, food, oil and gas **Efficient Supply Chain**	Fashion apparel, computers, popular music **Responsive Supply Chain**
	HIGH (EVOLVING PROCESS)	Hydroelectric power, some food produce **Risk-Hedging Supply Chain**	Telecom, high-end computers, semiconductor **Agile Supply Chain**

complexity tends to be low or manageable. Stable manufacturing processes tend to be highly automated, and long-term supply contracts are prevalent. In an evolving supply process, the manufacturing process requires a lot of fine-tuning and is often subject to breakdowns and uncertain yields. The supply base may not be reliable, as the suppliers themselves are going through process innovations. Exhibit 8.3 summarizes some of the differences between stable and evolving supply processes.

Lee argues that while functional products tend to have a more mature and stable supply process, that is not always the case. For example, the annual demand for electricity and other utility products in a locality tends to be stable and predictable, but the supply of hydroelectric power, which relies on rainfall in a region, can be erratic year by year. Some food products also have a very stable demand, but the supply (both quantity and quality) of the products depends on yearly weather conditions. Similarly, there are also innovative products with a stable supply process. Fashion apparel products have a short selling season and their demand is highly unpredictable. However, the supply process is very stable, with a reliable supply base and a mature manufacturing process technology. Exhibit 8.4 gives some examples of products that have different demand and supply uncertainties.

According to Lee, it is more challenging to operate a supply chain that is in the right column of Exhibit 8.4 than in the left column, and, similarly, it is more challenging to operate a supply chain that is in the lower row of Exhibit 8.4 than in the upper row. Before setting up a supply chain strategy, it is necessary to understand the sources of the underlying uncertainties and explore ways to reduce these uncertainties. If it is possible to move the uncertainty characteristics of the product from the right column to the left or from the lower row to the upper; then the supply chain performance will improve. Information technologies play an important role in shaping such strategies.

- **Efficient supply chains.**   These are supply chains that use strategies aimed at creating the highest cost efficiency. For such efficiencies to be achieved, non-value-added activities should be eliminated, scale economies should be pursued, optimization techniques should be deployed to get the best capacity utilization in production and distribution, and information linkages should be established to ensure the most efficient, accurate, and cost-effective transmission of information across the supply chain.
- **Risk-hedging supply chains.**   These are supply chains that use strategies aimed at pooling and sharing resources in a supply chain so that the risks in supply disruption

can be shared. A single entity in a supply chain can be vulnerable to supply disruptions, but if there is more than one supply source or if alternative supply resources are available, then the risk of disruption is reduced. A company may, for example, increase the safety stock of its key component to hedge against the risk of supply disruption, and by sharing the safety stock with other companies who also need this key component, the cost of maintaining this safety stock can be shared. This type of strategy is common in retailing, where different retail stores or dealerships share inventory. Information technology is important for the success of these strategies since real-time information on inventory and demand allows the most cost-effective management and transshipment of goods between partners sharing the inventory.

- **Responsive supply chains.**   These are supply chains that use strategies aimed at being responsive and flexible to the changing and diverse needs of the customers. To be responsive, companies use build-to-order and mass customization processes as a means to meet the specific requirements of customers.

- **Agile supply chains.**   These are supply chains that use strategies aimed at being responsive and flexible to customer needs, while the risks of supply shortages or disruptions are hedged by pooling inventory and other capacity resources. Essentially, these supply chains have strategies in place that combine the strengths of "hedged" and "responsive" supply chains. They are agile because they have the ability to be responsive to the changing, diverse, and unpredictable demands of customers on the front end, while minimizing the back-end risks of supply disruptions. See the OSMP on the no-one-size-fits-all supply chain for an example of different types of supply chains.

Demand and supply uncertainty is a good framework for understanding supply chain strategy. Innovative products with unpredictable demand and an evolving supply process face a major challenge. Because of shorter and shorter product life cycles, the pressure for dynamically adjusting and adopting a company's supply chain strategy is great. In the following, we explore the concepts of outsourcing, global sourcing, mass customization, and postponement: important tools for coping with demand and supply uncertainty.

Operations and Supply Management in Practice

The One-Size-Fits-All Supply Chain Does Not Exist

Exhibits 8.3 and 8.4 clearly show that different supply chain structures are required for different types of products. For example, compare the supply chain for a can or soup with that of the BlackBerry Storm smartphone. With groceries, the profit margin is very low and thus the supply chain must be cost effective (the product is functional based on Exhibit 8.4). You probably would not want to airfreight cans of soup, because that would probably eat up all of the profit margin. Since soup demand is quite predictable, managing the required inventory is not too difficult. On the other hand, in Exhibit 8.7 we see that the BlackBerry Storm costs a little more than $250 to manufacture. As of February 2009, it was being sold for $700

(without a contract) at one Canadian retailer. Clearly, even after adding the logistics and service costs, the Storm provides a high margin (the product is innovative based on Exhibit 8.4). For RIM, BlackBerry's manufacturer, it is not the cost of shipping that matters but the opportunity cost of not having the product in stock. If this happens, the customer may go for competing products from Apple or Samsung, and RIM loses a huge profit margin. So for RIM it would make perfect sense, if necessary, to airfreight chips from supplier Qualcomm to RIM's assembly facility and to airfreight assembled Storms to the distributors. Further, given that the life cycle of a smartphone model is short, predicting demand is difficult. So optimizing the inventory of components and assembled products in the supply chain is more challenging. In summary, the supply chain management objectives for the two products are very different.

There has also been a move in recent years toward dealing with fewer high quality and reliable suppliers. This allows the company to establish long-term and collaborative relationships with fewer suppliers rather than having many suppliers compete primarily on price. Recall from Chapter 7 that this was one of the Deming's 14 points. For example, in a space of five years, IBM reduced its number of suppliers from 1156 to 321, and Sony is planning to reduce the number of its suppliers from 4700 to 1000 within a few years. Other companies have also achieved reductions of this order. We will talk more about collaborative relationships with vendors in Chapter 10.

When selecting a supplier it is important to consider all of the costs involved, in other words, the **total cost of ownership**. For example, the purchase price may only be the tip of the iceberg. One or more of the following costs may be added to the purchase price depending on the product or service that is being procured: transportation and installation, inventory management, administration and order processing, training employees to use the product, data acquisition and evaluation, operating and maintenance, and disposal.

There are a number of qualitative factors that have to be considered when selecting suppliers. These factors include the potential supplier's engineering capability, manufacturing strength, financial situation, information systems strength, management capabilities, research facilities, proximity, knowledge of sales personnel, labour relations, technical assistance capability, and so on. Other factors to examine may include the ability of the potential vendor to deliver consistently on time (reliability), to maintain consistent quality, and to react to unexpected increases in demand or a different product mix from the customer. For example, Toronto-based Nortel uses a Supplier Business Engagement Model (SBEM) defined on its Web site as "a collaborative approach to supplier selection, designed to strengthen supplier relationships and drive greater spending with few suppliers—those with the products, capabilities, innovation and talent that best complement Nortel's own strengths."

One issue that is becoming increasingly important is that of **fair trade practices**. Companies are recognizing the importance of corporate responsibility within their supply chains. Thus, it is important to ensure that supplier companies are environmentally conscious, provide acceptable working conditions, and respect human rights in issues such as the use of child labour. For example, at some universities students have ensured that products sold on the campus through the university, such as clothing with the university logo, are purchased only from companies that follow fair trade practices. Companies like Lululemon have made purchasing from companies that follow fair trade practices a priority.

Another emerging issue is that of fakes, or counterfeits and, related to this, intellectual property theft. Some of you may have seen counterfeits of luxury goods such as watches, golf clubs, and handbags, but many other products are counterfeited as well. With the availability of better manufacturing and computer technology it is becoming easier to produce counterfeit products. Furthermore, with globalization there are now many more suppliers and they are widely dispersed geographically. Some deal with counterfeit products, which are often difficult to detect. Thus, it is important to ensure the integrity, not only of your suppliers but also of the suppliers upstream in the supply chain, to ensure that counterfeit products do not enter your supply chain.

In addition to violating intellectual property rights, suppliers of counterfeit products may not follow fair trade or environmental practices. In some cases, suppliers contracted to produce authorized goods produce excess amounts not authorized by the customer and sell them illegally or give designs and equipment illegally to other suppliers to make counterfeits. The counterfeiting industry has even targeted automobile brakes, aircraft parts, and pharmaceuticals, where the results can be disastrous. Counterfeits may often contain toxic ingredients. The recent examples of contaminated pet food in Canada and milk in China are good examples of the product safety-oriented risks that have to be managed in supply chains. Counterfeiting is thus getting increasing global attention because of the dangers it poses.

We are in the middle of a major change in the global economy. Great opportunities in global sourcing are available because of the collapse of communism in the Eastern Bloc, the issuance of the euro currency, and new markets in Turkey, India, South Africa, and so on. We have seen the results of agreements such as the North American Free Trade Agreement and the General Agreement on Tariffs and Trade. China is a huge market and is now a powerful trading partner.

Global

Managers face an interesting predicament in global procurement management. Let's take the example of Nike, the maker of high-quality tennis shoes. For Nike, a key raw material is leather, which is available from many sources around the world. The lowest-cost leather, though, might be available in South America, while the least expensive labour is in China, locations that are on opposite sides of the globe. These locations are far removed from the major markets for the shoes in North America, Europe, and Japan. To make matters worse, those customers in North America, Europe, and Japan do not even agree on what they want.

Companies that face such diverse sourcing, production, and distribution decisions need to weigh the costs associated with materials, transportation, production, warehousing, and distribution to develop a comprehensive network designed to minimize costs. Of course, this network must be designed while considering outsourcing alternatives, as described later in this chapter. Chapter 9 describes techniques useful for minimizing these costs.

LOGISTICS AND INVENTORY MANAGEMENT

Logistics is a term that refers to the management functions that support the complete cycle of material flow: from the purchase and internal control of production materials; to the planning and control of work-in-process; to the purchasing, shipping, and distribution of the finished product. Logistics is discussed in more detail in Chapter 9.

Supply chains convert raw material to finished products, which involves the storage and movement of different types of inventory. Therefore, organizations have to make decisions about how the inventory is controlled, such as how much to stock and when to order replenishments. Furthermore, organizations have to make decisions about how to co-ordinate these decisions among the supply chain partners. Inventory management is discussed in detail in Chapters 13 and 14. Lean manufacturing (just-in-time) systems, the subject of Chapter 10, also relates to the management of inventory within supply chains. Managing inventory across the supply chain is sometimes called multi-echelon inventory management.

Inventory positioning involves deciding where and in what form to stock inventory in the supply chain. For example, if a company had only one warehouse in Canada, located in southwestern Ontario, the advantage would be that the operating costs of the warehouse would be lower because of economies of scale. However, customer service might suffer. For example, if a retailer in Moose Jaw, Saskatchewan, ran out of stock, it would take longer to replenish stock than if the company had a western warehouse in Calgary and thus positioned the inventory closer to the customer. However, if the item, such as electronic components, is easy to airfreight, it might be better to have only one consolidated warehouse. Another aspect of positioning is the form in which inventory is stored in various locations. For example, Dell stocks only standardized computer parts, not the whole computer itself. Thus, it postpones the assembly of the final product, assembling it only when it gets an actual order. These concepts are discussed more later in this chapter.

Many firms use a concept known as **vendor-managed inventories (VMI)**. Under this concept, vendors manage the customer's inventory of the products they supply. For example, home improvement retailer RONA allows its suppliers to access its computer system to determine when they should replenish RONA's stock.[5] The supplier has oversight of the demand for its products, which helps its supply chain management, while RONA gets the advantage of decreased purchasing and record-keeping costs.

VERTICAL INTEGRATION AND OUTSOURCING

Vertical integration refers to the proportion of the supply chain that the company owns. For example, in 1896 the Nova Scotia Steel and Forge Company merged with the New Glasgow Iron, Coal and Railway Company (a company that owned iron ore deposits and railways), to obtain a secure supply of ore. The new company was called the Nova Scotia Steel Company. Because coal is required to run steel-producing furnaces, a few years later the merged company acquired the metallurgical coalfields owned by the General Mining Association of Sydney Mines, Cape Breton. In 1912, this new company formed the Eastern Car Company to build railway cars to use some of the steel that it produced.

Nova Scotia Steel's operation could therefore be described as being more vertically integrated in comparison to other steel manufacturers of the time, who focused solely on making steel from purchased ore. The Irving Group of New Brunswick is a current example of a vertically integrated company owning oil-and-gas refining facilities, petroleum trucking, and service stations.

The current trend in many industries is to become less vertically integrated. For example, telecommunications companies such as Nortel and Cisco have outsourced their manufacturing to electronic manufacturing service (EMS) companies such as Solectron and Toronto-based Celestica. Proctor and Gamble (P&G) recently subcontracted all of its North American soap manufacturing to Newmarket, Ontario-based Trillium Health Care Products Inc. Similarly, Toronto-based Cott Corp. is one of the world's largest producers of soft drinks, which are sold by supermarkets under their own brand name.

On the other hand, clothing retailer Zara owns its own factories, which gives it more control over the supply chain and allows it to manufacture and deliver clothing quickly. Similarly, some of the EMS companies have become more vertically integrated by doing some product design, producing more of their inputs, and providing after-sales product service for the ultimate customer. In 2001, UPS acquired Mailboxes Etc., Inc. (now called UPS Store) to provide value-added services such as photocopying.

Outsourcing is the act of moving some of a firm's internal activities and decision responsibility to outside providers, i.e., becoming less vertically integrated. The terms of the agreement are established in a contract. Outsourcing goes beyond the more common purchasing and consulting contracts because not only are the activities transferred, but also resources that make the activities occur, including people, facilities, equipment, technology, and other assets, are transferred. The responsibilities for making decisions over certain elements of the activities are transferred as well. Taking complete responsibility for this is a specialty of contract manufacturers such as Flextronics, Celestica, and Solectron.[6]

The reasons why a company decides to outsource (sometimes referred to as the *make-or-buy* decision) can vary greatly. Exhibit 8.5 lists examples of reasons to outsource and the accompanying benefits. Outsourcing allows a firm to focus on activities that represent its core competencies. Thus, the company can create a competitive advantage while reducing cost. An entire function may be outsourced, or some elements of an activity may be outsourced, with the rest kept in-house. For example, some of the elements of information technology may be strategic, some may be critical, and some may be performed less expensively by a third party. Identifying a function as a potential outsourcing target, and then breaking that function into its components, allows decision makers

EXHIBIT 8.5   Reasons to Outsource and the Resulting Benefits

FINANCIALLY DRIVEN REASONS

Improve return on assets by reducing inventory and selling unnecessary assets.

Generate cash by selling low-return entities.

Gain access to new markets, particularly in developing countries.

Reduce costs through a lower cost structure.

Turn fixed costs into variable costs.

IMPROVEMENT-DRIVEN REASONS

Improve quality and productivity.

Shorten cycle time.

Obtain expertise, skills, and technologies that are not otherwise available.

Improve risk management.

Improve credibility and image by associating with superior providers.

ORGANIZATIONALLY DRIVEN REASONS

Improve effectiveness by focusing on what the firm does best.

Increase flexibility to meet changing demand for products and services.

Increase product and service value by improving response to customer needs.

to determine which activities are strategic or critical and should remain in-house and which can be outsourced like commodities. This outsourcing trend has provided opportunities for new companies to prosper. For example, Toronto-based conglomerate, the Onex Corporation, was created in 1984. Among the many businesses that it currently owns is Spirit AeroSystems (aircraft components) acquired from Boeing, Allison Transmission (serving the truck and bus market) acquired from General Motors, and Celestica (electronics manufacturing) from IBM.

There has been dramatic growth in outsourcing in the logistics area. The emphasis on lean inventory means there is less room for error in deliveries. Trucking companies such as UPS have started adding the logistics aspect to their businesses—changing from merely moving goods from point A to point B, to managing all or part of all shipments over a longer period, typically three years, and replacing the shipper's employees with their own. Logistics companies now have complex computer tracking technology that reduces the risk in transportation and allows the logistics company to add more value to the firm than it could if the function were performed in-house. Third-party logistics providers track freight using electronic data interchange technology and a satellite system to tell customers exactly where its drivers are and when deliveries will be made. Such technology is critical in some environments where the delivery window may be only 30 minutes long.

Federal Express has one of the most advanced systems available for tracking items being sent through its services. The system is available to all customers over the Internet. It tells the exact status of each item currently being carried by the company. Information on the exact time a package is picked up, when it is transferred between hubs in the company's network, and when it is delivered is available on the system. You can access this system at the FedEx Web site (www.fedex.com). Select your country on the initial screen and then select "Track Shipments" in the Track box in the lower part of the page. Of course, you will need the actual tracking number for an item currently in the system to get information. Federal Express has integrated its tracking system with many of its customers' in-house information systems.

Another example of innovative outsourcing in logistics involves Hewlett-Packard. Hewlett-Packard turned over its inbound raw materials warehousing in Vancouver, Washington, to Roadway Logistics. Roadway's 140 employees operate the warehouse 24 hours a day, seven days a week, coordinating the delivery of parts to the warehouse and managing storage. Hewlett-Packard's 250 employees were transferred to other company activities. Hewlett-Packard reports savings of 10 percent in warehousing operating costs.

One of the drawbacks to outsourcing is the layoffs that often result. Even in cases where the outsourcing partner hires former employees, they are often hired back at lower wages with fewer benefits. Outsourcing is perceived by many unions as an effort to circumvent union contracts.

In theory, outsourcing is a no-brainer. Companies can unload noncore activities, shed balance sheet assets, and boost their return on capital by using third-party service providers. But in reality, things are more complicated. "It's really hard to figure out what's core and what's noncore today," says Jane Linder, senior research fellow and associate director of Accenture's Institute for Strategic Change in Cambridge, Massachusetts. "When you take another look tomorrow, things may have changed. On September 9, 2001, airport security workers were noncore; on September 12, 2001, they were core to the federal government's ability to provide security to the nation. It happens every day in companies as well."[7]

Exhibit 8.6 is a useful framework to help managers make appropriate choices for the structure of supplier relationships. The decision goes beyond the notion that "core competencies" should be maintained under the direct control of management of the firm and that other activities should be outsourced. In this framework, a continuum that ranges from vertical integration to arm's-length relationships forms the basis for the decision.

A Framework for Structuring Supplier Relationships — EXHIBIT 8.6

	VERTICAL INTEGRATION (DO NOT OUTSOURCE)	ARM'S-LENGTH RELATIONSHIPS (OUTSOURCE)
Coordination	"Messy" interfaces; adjacent tasks involve a high degree of mutual adaptation, exchange of implicit knowledge, and learning-by-doing. Requisite information is highly particular to the task.	Standardized interfaces between adjacent tasks; requisite information is highly codified and standardized (prices, quantities, delivery schedules, etc.).
Strategic control	Very high: significant investments in highly durable relationship-specific assets needed for optimal execution of tasks. Investments cannot be recovered if relationship terminates: • Collocation of specialized facilities • Investment in brand equity • Large proprietary learning curves • Long-term investments in specialized R&D programs	Very low: assets applicable to businesses with a large number of other potential customers or suppliers.
Intellectual property	Unclear or weak intellectual property protection Easy-to-imitate technology "Messy" interfaces between different technological components	Strong intellectual property protection Difficult-to-imitate technology "Clean" boundaries between different technological components

Source: Robert Hayes, Gary Pisano, David Upton, and Steven Wheelwright, *Operations Strategy and Technology: Pursuing the Competitive Edge* (New York: John Wiley & Sons, 2005), p. 137. Copyright © 2005 John Wiley & Sons. Reprinted by permission.

An activity can be evaluated using the following characteristics: required coordination, strategic control, and intellectual property. Required coordination refers to how difficult it is to ensure that the activity will integrate well with the overall process. Uncertain activities that require much back-and-forth exchange of information should not be outsourced, whereas activities that are well understood and highly standardized can easily move to business partners who specialize in the activity. Strategic control refers to the degree of loss that would be incurred if the relationship with the partner were severed. Many types of losses would be important to consider, including specialized facilities, knowledge of major customer relationships, and investment in research and development. A final consideration is the potential loss of intellectual property though the partnership.

Intel is an excellent example of a company that recognized the importance of this type of decision framework in the mid-1980s. During the early 1980s, Intel found itself being squeezed out of the market for the memory chips that it had invented by Japanese competitors such as Hitachi, Fujitsu, and NEC. These companies had developed stronger capabilities to develop and rapidly scale up complex semiconductor manufacturing processes. It was clear by 1985 that a major Intel competency was in its ability to design complex integrated circuits, not in manufacturing or developing processes for more standardized chips. As a result, faced with growing financial losses, Intel was forced to exit the memory chip market.

Global

Learning a lesson from the memory market, Intel shifted its focus to the microprocessor market, a device that it had invented in the late 1960s. To keep from repeating the mistake with memory chips, Intel felt it was essential to develop strong capabilities in process development and manufacturing. A pure "core competency" strategy would have suggested that Intel focus on the design of microprocessors and use outside partners to manufacture them. Given the close connection between semiconductor product development and process development, however, relying on outside parties for manufacturing would likely have created costs in terms of longer development lead times. Over the late 1980s, Intel invested heavily in building world-class capabilities in process development and manufacturing. These capabilities are one of the chief reasons it has been able to maintain approximately 90 percent of the personal computer microprocessor market, despite the ability of competitors like AMD to "clone" Intel designs relatively quickly. Expanding its capabilities beyond its original core capability of product design has been a critical ingredient in Intel's sustained success.

In some cases, companies leave themselves vulnerable to market coups by former partners when they outsource. Such was the case with the German consumer electronics company Blaupunkt, notes Ed Frey, a vice president at Booz Allen Hamilton. To beef up the product line it offered to its dealers, Blaupunkt decided to add VCRs and contracted the work out to Panasonic (once a lowly circuit-board stuffer). Later, with the Blaupunkt reputation attached to its products, Panasonic approached the dealers directly and, presto, it had a ready-made distribution network for its own product line. "In effect, all Blaupunkt did was give access to its dealer network to Panasonic," says Frey.

Good advice is to keep control of—or acquire—activities that are true competitive differentiators, or leave the potential to yield a competitive advantage, and to outsource the rest. It is important to make a distinction between "core" and "strategic" activities. Core activities are key to the business, but do not confer a competitive advantage, such as a bank's information technology operations. Strategic activities are a key source of competitive advantage. Because the competitive environment can change rapidly, companies need to monitor the situation constantly, and adjust accordingly. As an example, Coca-Cola, which decided to stay out of the bottling business in the early 1900s, partnered instead with independent bottlers and quickly built market share. The company reversed itself in the 1980s when bottling became a key competitive element in the industry.

MEASURING SUPPLY CHAIN PERFORMANCE

Companies evaluate the performance of their supply chain with such measures as inventory turns, number of stockouts, lead times for order delivery, and overall costs. This allows the company to benchmark its performance against competitors and its own objectives. Each group at any company has its own measures of performance. Marketing, for example, is evaluated on revenue growth, research and development on a product's functionality and the cost of its components, and manufacturing and distribution on the cost of assembling and delivering a product to the customer. The different measures focus the groups on different objectives. Marketing wants to offer as many product options as possible to attract more customers; research and development wants to offer the product with the greatest possible functionality at the lowest possible cost; and manufacturing and distribution want to make one product at a stable volume. If the groups are not properly coordinated, their attempts to optimize their own performance may hurt the company's ability to create the most efficient supply network that can deliver a customized product at the lowest cost. Negotiations among these groups are critical, with the goal being to decide to do what is best for the company as a whole. Thus, Kaplan and Norton suggest that a "balanced scorecard" approach, including financial, customer, business process, and learning and growth measures be used at all levels of the supply chain.[8]

One measurement of sourcing performance is centred on the inventories that are positioned in the system. Exhibit 8.7 shows how components are stored in various locations

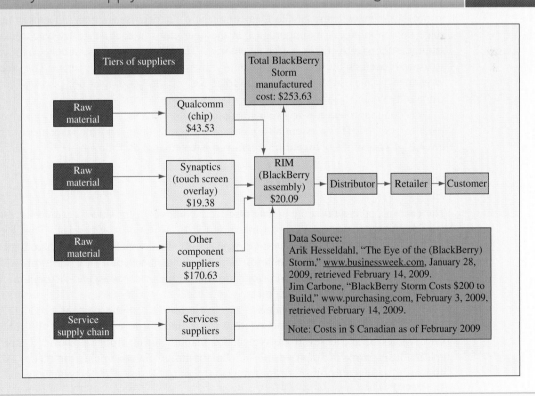

Inventory in the Supply Chain—Cell Phone Manufacturing   **EXHIBIT 8.7**

in a typical cell phone manufacturing chain. The specifics in the example are from the BlackBerry Storm smart cell phone, manufactured by Waterloo, Ontario-based RIM. Here we see the steps that raw materials move through on their way through the component- and final-assembly stages, then through distribution centres for the assembled product, to the local retail store, and, finally, to the customer. At each stage, value is added to the product, through the addition of material, processing of the material, and labour. For example, a combination of tin and silver is sometimes used for soldering on electronic circuit boards. For this, the silver has to be mined, extracted, purified, and combined with tin, adding value all along this process and is reflected in the cost of the product that is purchased by RIM. When this tin-silver combination is soldered on to a circuit board, the material cost of the tin-silver as well as the labour involved in soldering has to be added to the circuit board.

There are many suppliers as well as tiers in the chain that convert the raw material into components. For example, two components of the Storm are the chip from Qualcomm and the touch screen overlay from Synaptics, in addition to various other purchased components. iSuppli, a market intelligence firm estimates that components cost RIM $233.54. iSuppli also estimates that it costs RIM $20.09 to assemble these components into the final Storm phone. Thus, the total estimated value added manufactured cost of the Storm is $253.63. An important aspect to note in the supply chain is that there are services going into the phone, such as software, cell network services and other intellectual property services (these are not included in the $253.63 estimated by iSuppli).

At each step, inventory is carried (not shown separately), and this inventory has a particular cost to the company. Inventory serves as a buffer, thus allowing each stage to operate independently of the others. For example, the distribution centre inventory allows the system that supplies the retail stores to operate independently of the assembly operations. Similarly, inventory of Qualcomm chips at the Storm assembly facility allows it to operate independently of the Qualcomm chip factory. Because the inventory at each stage ties up money, it is important that the operations at each stage be synchronized to minimize the size of these buffer inventories. The efficiency of the supply chain can be measured based on the size of the inventory investment in the supply chain. The inventory investment is measured relative to the total cost of the goods that are provided through the supply chain.

Two common measures to evaluate supply chain efficiency are *inventory turnover* and *weeks-of-supply*. These essentially measure the same thing and mathematically are the inverse of one another. **Inventory turnover** is calculated as follows:

[8.1] $$\text{Inventory turnover} = \frac{\text{Cost of goods sold}}{\text{Average aggregate inventory value}}$$

The **cost of goods sold** is the annual cost for a company to produce the goods or services provided to customers; it is sometimes referred to as the *cost of revenue*. This does not include the selling and administrative expenses of the company. The **average aggregate inventory value** is the total value of all items held in inventory for the firm valued at cost. It includes the raw material, work-in-process, finished goods, and distribution inventory considered owned by the company.

Good inventory turnover values vary by industry and the type of products being handled. At one extreme, a grocery store chain may turn inventory over 100 times per year. Values of six to seven are typical for manufacturing firms. However, many firms continuously work to improve the number of turns. For example, car maker Porsche improved its inventory turns from 6 turns a year to close to 20 per year between 1990 and 2006.[9]

In many situations, particularly when distribution inventory is dominant, **weeks of supply** is the preferred measure. This is a measure of how many weeks' worth of inventory is in the system at a particular point in time. The calculation is as follows:

$$[8.2] \qquad \text{Week of supply} = \left(\frac{\text{Average aggregate inventory value}}{\text{Cost of goods sold}} \right) \times 52 \text{ weeks}$$

When company financial reports cite inventory turnover and weeks of supply, we can assume that the measures are being calculated firm-wide. We show an example of this type of calculation in the example that follows, using Dell Computer data. These calculations, though, can be done on individual entities within the organization. For example, we might be interested in the production raw materials inventory turnover or the weeks of supply associated with the warehousing operation of a firm. In these cases, the cost would be that associated with the total amount of inventory that runs through the specific inventory. In some very-low-inventory operations, days or even hours are a better unit of time for measuring supply.

A firm considers inventory an investment because the intent is for it to be used in the future. Inventory ties up funds that could be used for other purposes, and a firm may have to borrow money to finance the inventory investment. The objective is to have the proper amount of inventory and to have it in the correct locations in the supply chain. Determining the correct amount of inventory to have in each position requires a thorough analysis of the supply chain coupled with the competitive priorities that define the market for the company's products.

EXAMPLE 8.1: INVENTORY TURNOVER CALCULATION

Dell Computer reported the following information in its 2005 annual report (all amounts are expressed in millions of USD):

Net revenue (fiscal year 2005)	$49 205
Cost of revenue (fiscal year 2005)	40 190
Production materials on hand (28 January 2005)	228
Work-in-process and finished goods on hand (28 January 2005)	231
Days of supply in inventory	4 days

The cost of revenue corresponds to what we call cost of goods sold. One might think that U.S. companies, at least, would use a common accounting terminology, but this is not true. The inventory turnover calculation is

$$\text{Inventory turnover} = \frac{40\ 190}{228 + 231} = 87.56 \text{ turns per year}$$

This is amazing performance for a high-tech company, but it explains much of why the company is such a financial success.

The corresponding weeks of supply calculation is

$$\text{Week of supply} = \left(\frac{228 + 231}{40\ 190} \right) \times 52 = 0.59 \text{ week}$$

PRODUCT DESIGN TO FACILITATE SUPPLY CHAIN MANAGEMENT

Companies have come to realize that product design can help or hinder supply chain management. Earlier, we talked about the advantages of stocking standardized components and postponing assembly of the final product until receipt of a customer order. Clearly, in order to do this the product must be modularly designed. Also, the product has to be designed in such a way as to ensure that the recycling or disposal can be done in a cost-effective manner.

A company that wishes to sell to global retailers such as French company Carrefour or Wal-Mart may have to design product to fit the shelf sizes or transportation equipment used by these customers. In Europe, many retailers have to take back packaging. Thus, there is an incentive to design better packaging that is easier to handle from a supply chain perspective. These examples show that it is important to keep the supply chain in mind when designing products. This idea is explored further under reverse supply chain management, discussed later in this chapter.

The term **mass customization** has been used to describe the ability of a company to deliver highly customized products and services to different customers around the world.[10] The key to mass-customizing effectively is by postponing the task of differentiating a product for a specific customer until the latest possible point in the supply network. In order to do this, companies must rethink and integrate the designs of their products, the processes used to make and deliver those products, and the configuration of the entire supply network. By adopting such a comprehensive approach, companies can operate at maximum efficiency and quickly meet customers' orders with a minimum amount of inventory.

Three organization design principles together form the basic building blocks of an effective mass customization program.

Global

Principle 1: *A product should be designed so it consists of independent modules that can be assembled into different forms of the product easily and inexpensively.* Hewlett-Packard decided to use a modular product design to allow its DeskJet printers to be easily customized for the European and Asian markets. The company decided to customize the printers at its local distribution centres rather than at its factories. For example, instead of customizing the DeskJets at its factory in Singapore before shipping them to Europe, Hewlett-Packard has its European distribution centre near Stuttgart, Germany, perform this job. The company designed the new printer with a country-specific external power supply that the customer plugs in when setting up the printer. The distribution centre not only customizes the product but also purchases the materials that differentiate it (the power supplies, packaging, and manuals). As a result of this redesign, manufacturing costs are slightly higher than when the factories customized the printers, but the total manufacturing, shipping, and inventory costs dropped by 25 percent.

Principle 2: *Manufacturing and service processes should be designed so that they consist of independent modules that can be moved or rearranged easily to support different distribution network designs.* The way neighborhood hardware and paint stores match paint colours on their premises is a good example. Instead of making a broad range of different paints to meet customers' specific requirements, factories make generic paint and a variety of colour pigments, which hardware and paint stores stock. The stores use a chromatograph to analyze a customer's paint sample and to determine the paint-and-pigment mixture that will match it. This process provides

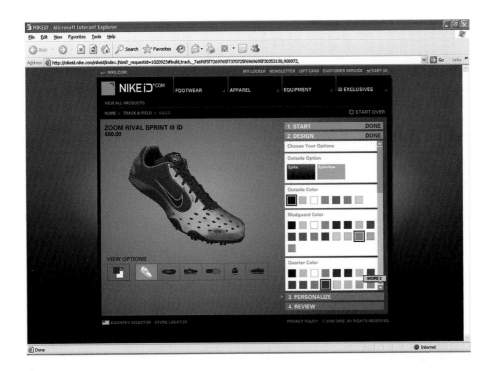

Nike's Web site and stores through NikeID allow customers to create and customize their own shoe, choosing elements from available designs. Nike has an exclusive contract with UPS, so customized products go from creation to doorstep in three to four weeks. Once customers place an order, they begin receiving regular e-mail updates as the product goes from initial production to final shipping. Customers can track the status of their order anytime throughout the shipping process.

customers with a virtually unlimited number of consistent choices and, at the same time, significantly reduces the inventory of paint that the stores need to stock in order to match every customer's desired colour on demand. **Process postponement** is the term used to describe delay of the process step that differentiates the product to as late in the supply chain as possible. The key to postponement, in this case, was separating the production of the paint and the mixing of the pigment and paint and creating a low-cost chromatograph.

Principle 3: *The supply network—the positioning of inventory and the location, number, and structure of service, manufacturing, and distribution facilities—should be designed to provide two capabilities. First, it must be able to supply the basic product to the facilities performing the customization in a cost-effective manner. Second, it must have the flexibility and the responsiveness to take individual customers' orders and deliver the finished, customized good quickly.* To support mass customization, an agile supply network is needed. A company with many product options benefits little from having many distribution centres around the world if those centres perform only the tasks of warehousing and distribution. The investments in inventory that are required to support all the options would be enormous. The example of the paint production process just described is ideal because the paint manufacturing company now has a ready source of capacity to handle the final mixing step: the local paint stores. The generic paint can be shipped in bulk and the final product produced while the customer is in the store. The manufacturing economics change radically when a company redesigns its products and processes into modules, so that the final customization steps take place on receipt of a customer's order. It becomes cost-effective to have more distribution centres or stores as in the case of the paint example, each of which stocks basic products and performs the final steps in the customization process.

Having distribution centres perform light manufacturing or assembly can help a company both comply with the local-content rules that are prevalent in emerging markets and respond to customers who are unwilling to wait for a customized product to be shipped from a factory in another region. In this way, a company enjoys the best of both worlds: on the one hand, it can concentrate its manufacturing of critical parts in a few sites around the world so that it can achieve economies of scale, and on the other hand, it can maintain a local presence.

Making decisions like these is not easy. It involves people from at least five areas of the company: marketing, research and development, manufacturing, distribution, and finance. These five groups must play the following roles to support an effective mass customization program:

Cross Functional

- Marketing must determine the extent to which mass customization is needed to fulfill customers' requirements.
- Research and development must redesign the product so that it can be customized at the most efficient point in the supply network.
- Manufacturing and distribution must coordinate both the supply and redesign of materials and situate manufacturing or assembly processes in the most efficient locations.
- Finance must provide activity-based cost information and financial analyses of the alternatives.

Supply Chain

INFORMATION SYSTEMS IN SUPPLY CHAIN MANAGEMENT

A supply chain links all of the stages together from raw materials through production to the consumer. The supply chain is coordinated with an electronic information system. Many options define the logic of these systems; in all cases, the frequency and speed of communicating information through the chain have a great effect on inventory levels, efficiencies, and costs. For large manufacturing companies, the new enterprise resource planning systems (ERP), discussed in Chapter 14, are now being used extensively. Companies like *i*2 and Manugistics are providers of SCM-specific software, while others, like Emptoris, provide software for Internet-based procurement management.

Managing the supply chain is being shifted, to a large extent, to the vendor. Purchasing contracts are now tied to delivery schedules; we look at the coordination needed to do this when we study lean production systems in Chapter 10. Electronic information flow has shifted routine activities to the vendor by allowing direct access to point-of-sales data and giving responsibility for forecasting and delivery of product directly to the vendor. Today, such relationships tend to be long-term, but one can speculate whether the relationships will be long-term in the future.

Collaborative Planning, Forecasting, and Replenishment (CPFR)

Proposed in 1995, **Collaborative Planning, Forecasting, and Replenishment (CPFR)**[11] has evolved into a Web-based tool used to coordinate demand forecasting, production and purchase planning, and inventory replenishment between supply chain trading partners.

CPFR is being used as a means of integrating all members of an *n*-tier supply chain, including manufacturers, distributors, and retailers. As depicted in Exhibit 8.8, the ideal point of collaboration utilizing CPFR is the retail-level demand forecast (forecasting is discussed in Chapter 11), which is successively used to synchronize forecasts, production, and replenishment plans upstream through the supply chain.

Although the methodology can be applied to any industry, CPFR applications to date have largely focused on the food, apparel, and general merchandise industries. The potential benefits of sharing information for enhanced planning visibility in any supply chain are enormous. Various estimates for cost savings attributable to improved supply chain coordination have been proposed, including $30 billion annually in the food industry alone.[2]

CPFR's objective is to exchange selected internal information on a shared Web server to provide for reliable, longer-term future views of demand in the supply chain. CPFR uses a cyclic and iterative approach to derive consensus supply chain forecasts. It consists of the following five steps.

Step 1. Creation of a front-end partnership agreement. This agreement specifies (1) objectives (e.g., inventory reductions, lost sale elimination, lower product obsolescence) to be gained through collaboration, (2) resource requirements (e.g., hardware, software, performance metrics) necessary for the collaboration, and (3) expectations of confidentiality concerning the prerequisite trust necessary to share sensitive company information, which represents a major implementation obstacle.

Step 2. Joint business planning. Typically, partners create partnership strategies, design a joint calendar identifying the sequence and frequency of planning activities to follow that affect product flows, and specify exception criteria for handling planning variances between the trading partners' demand forecasts.

Step 3. Development of demand forecasts. Forecast development may follow preexisting company procedures. Retailers should play a critical role as shared *point-of-sale* (POS) data permit the development of more accurate and timely expectations (compared with extrapolated warehouse withdrawals or aggregate store orders) for both retailers and vendors. Given the frequency of forecast generation and the potential for vast numbers of items requiring forecast preparation, a simple forecast procedure such as a moving average is commonly used within CPFR. Simple techniques are easily used in conjunction with expert knowledge of promotional or pricing events to modify forecast values accordingly.

Supply Chain

n-Tier Supply Chain with Retail Activities

EXHIBIT 8.8

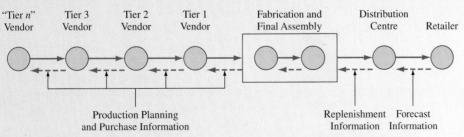

Note: Solid arrows represent material flows; dashed arrows represent information flows.

Step 4. Sharing forecasts.   Retailer (order forecasts) and vendor (sales forecasts) then electronically post their latest forecasts for a list of products on a shared, dedicated server. The server examines pairs of corresponding forecasts and issues an exception notice for any forecast pair where the difference exceeds a pre-established safety margin (e.g., 5 percent). If the safety margin is exceeded, planners from both firms may collaborate electronically to derive a consensus forecast.

Step 5. Inventory replenishment.   Once the corresponding forecasts are in agreement, the order forecast becomes an actual order, which commences the replenishment process. Each of these steps is then repeated iteratively in a continuous cycle, at varying times, by individual products and the calendar of events established between trading partners. For example, partners may review the front-end partnership agreement annually, evaluate the joint business plans quarterly, develop forecasts weekly to monthly, and replenish daily.

The early exchange of information between trading partners provides for reliable, longer-term future views of demand in the supply chain. The forward visibility based on information sharing leads to a variety of benefits within supply chain partnerships (See OSMP on CPFR). ERP systems and SCM software are useful in facilitating the intercompany collaboration required for CPFR.

As with most new corporate initiatives, there is skepticism and resistance to change. One of the largest hurdles hindering collaboration is the lack of trust over complete information sharing between supply chain partners. The conflicting objective between the profit-maximizing vendor and cost-minimizing customer gives rise to adversarial supply chain relationships. Sharing sensitive operating data may enable one trading partner to take advantage of the other. Similarly, there is the potential loss of control as a barrier to implementation. Some companies are rightfully concerned about the idea of placing strategic data such as financial reports, manufacturing schedules, and inventory values online. Companies open themselves to security breaches. The front-end partnership agreements, nondisclosure agreements, and limited information access may help overcome these fears.

Operations and Supply Management in Practice

Collaborative Forecasting and Planning for Smooth Sailing

Ensuring that the right merchandise is in stock is a challenge for retailers selling seasonal products, as West Marine Inc. has found. The California-based company, the world's largest for boating supplies, has over US$500 million in annual sales. In Canada, it has retail locations in Nanaimo, Sidney, Vancouver, and Victoria, all in British Columbia.

Recently, it was unable to stock the right products at its stores due to poor supply chain management. The company realized that the key to improvement was to improve the front end of the supply chain—forecasting. They felt this would drive supply chain savings. The improvement process started with better forecasting and by linking store sales to warehouse replenishment. It also involved increased collaboration with its 200 top vendors, who accounted for over 90 percent of stocked items.

The process is called collaborative planning, forecasting, and replenishment (CPFR). CPFR involves collaboration between supply chain partners in forecasting, distribution, and production. For example, West Marine installed software that allowed it to track and analyze sales and shifts in consumer trends and then to make the necessary changes

Continued

rapidly throughout the entire supply chain. As a result, the forecast accuracy increased to 85 percent. Other software improved supply chain visibility among its partners, linked point-of-sale forecasting to the order forecasts sent to suppliers, and provided electronic data interchange (EDI) capabilities with more than two-thirds of its suppliers.

Within the company, point-of-sale data are processed and forecasts are updated nightly. Merchandise and assortment planning as well as promotion decisions are based on these forecasts. Suppliers participate in building forecasts, and performance metrics are routinely reviewed with vendors, who keep West Marine informed of shortages. As a result of their changes, West Marine increased its peak season in-stock rate to 96 percent while reducing costs at its distribution centres by US$3 million.

■ Sources: "Accurate Forecasts Mean Smooth Sailing for West Marine," *Frontline Solutions* (October 2003), p. 39.

Walter McKaige, "Collaborating on the Supply Chain," *IIE Solutions* (March 2001), pp. 34–36.

West Marine Inc., www.westmarine.com.

THE REVERSE SUPPLY CHAIN

Guide and Van Wassenhove define the reverse supply chain as the series of activities required to retrieve a used product or return from a customer and either dispose of it or reuse it.[12] Product returns are becoming an increasingly important issue for many reasons, including the existence of catalogue and Internet purchasing. In addition, regulatory authorities are increasingly mandating companies to pay more attention to reverse supply chains, and both consumers and regulations are encouraging companies to pay attention to the environment. For example, many European countries require vendors to take back transportation packaging.[13] Toxic materials such as mercury have to be recovered or disposed of properly.

Even where there are no regulations, companies are finding there are competitive advantages to being more proactive about reverse logistics. For example, Kodak has reduced its operating costs by remanufacturing its single use cameras after the film has been developed. Similarly, Noranda's new recycling facility in Brampton, Ontario, will process obsolete goods from electronics manufacturers and consumers, and expects to make a profit after extracting metals and sending them to its refineries, such as its copper smelter in Rouyn, Quebec. Other companies such as Bosch have created a new market by selling remanufactured power hand tools.

Guide and Van Wassenhove divide the reverse supply chain into five components, one or more of which might be done by a third party.

1. Product acquisition, which involves planning the quality, quantity, and timing of product returns. This is important, because reverse supply chain aspects such as product returns or used product repairs and recycling are unpredictable in nature with respect to timing and quantity.
2. Reverse logistics, which involves the transportation of the collected products to facilities that inspect, sort, and dispose of them.
3. Inspection and disposition involves determining what to do with the returned products. The returns might go to resellers, scrap merchants, or charities, for example.
4. Reconditioning involves capturing value from returned products by remanufacturing products for resale.
5. Distribution and sales involves distributing the returned, repaired, or recycled products through existing markets and creating new markets.

Companies successful in their reverse supply chains have often closely coordinated them with their forward supply chains, creating a closed-loop system. This implies that they design and manufacture products with eventual recycling in mind. Bosch, for example, places sensors in its power tool parts that indicate whether the parts are worth reconditioning. Other companies take steps to avoid unnecessary reverse supply chain occurrences by educating customers on product usage. For example, electronics giant Philips found that customers often returned items such as DVD players because they couldn't understand the instruction manual. These returns dropped significantly when Philips revised the product manual so that customers could understand it more easily.

INTEGRATING IT ALL: THE SUCCESSFUL SUPPLY CHAIN

This chapter discussed many aspects of supply chain management. At the end, it is important to discuss how these aspects translate into effective supply chain management strategic themes. The discussions in this chapter can be related to the following important themes:

Supply chains should be customized.   As discussed earlier in the chapter, there is no one-size-fits-all supply chain. A supply chain has to be designed to fit the product and process characteristics. You may manage the supply chain very well but if it is the wrong type of supply chain, success will be elusive. It would be like an automaker designing a car that customers don't want, under budget and on time, in other words managing the project effectively but doing the wrong project, resulting in failure.

Partnerships are important.   It is important to realize that in order for your organization to be successful, your partners in the supply chain have to be successful. Thus, your actions should be geared toward the improved management of the entire supply chain rather than being focused on your company's improvement, to the detriment of others. Evidence from practice shows that this latter strategy has not worked in the long run. Thus, it important to build long-term trust-based relationships with suppliers and customers.

Information should be shared.   If you build effective partnerships, it will be easier to share information, which is another key ingredient of successful supply chains. Information sharing allows for smoothing of the supply chain and also helps avoid the negative consequences of the bullwhip effect. For example, Procter & Gamble found that when they started sharing information with their customers, they were able to greatly reduce the demand variations in their factories. In fact, they were able to close down factories because they did not need that extra capacity to respond to the variation caused by the lack of information sharing.[14]

Holistic and evolving supply chain management.   It is important to remember that supply chain issues affect management aspects from product concept inception all the way to the end of its life cycle and disposal, i.e., it is more than just inventory management (discussed in Chapter 13) or logistics (which is discussed in Chapter 9). Further, what is done during the design stage can affect how well the supply chain can be managed during the product life cycle. The ease of production, vertical integration, logistics, and the ability to reduce the environmental footprint of the product and process are examples of product life cycle supply chain issues that have to considered up front. One should not wait for a product to be in the manufacturing stage before thinking of supply chain issues and one should stop thinking about supply chain issues because the product is now in production. As the product or service enters the different stages in its life cycle, the supply chain must evolve accordingly.

Summary

Managing your supply chain effectively is a prerequisite for business success today. Decision makers have to think strategically about supply chain design. These include the sourcing, inventory management, logistics, level of vertical integration, performance measurement, information system, product design, and the design of the reverse supply chain. Strategic sourcing is important in business today. Outsourcing is an important way to reduce cost while improving the strategic focus of a firm. Many companies have enjoyed significant success as a result of the unique ways in which they work with their suppliers.

Measures of sourcing efficiency are inventory turnover and weeks of supply. Efficient processes should be used for functional products, and responsive processes for innovative products. This alignment of sourcing strategy and product demand characteristics is extremely important to the operational success of a company.

Companies that face diverse sourcing, production, and distribution decisions need to weigh the costs associated with materials, transportation, production, warehousing, and distribution to develop a comprehensive network designed to minimize costs. In addition, managers will have to collaborate with supply chain partners and consider reverse supply chain issues.

Key Terms

Average aggregate inventory value   The total value of all items held in inventory for the firm, valued at cost.

Balanced scorecard   Including multi-dimensional measures in performance assessment.

Bullwhip effect   The variability in demand is magnified as we move from the customer to the producer in the supply chain.

Collaborative Planning, Forecasting, and Replenishment (CPFR)   An Internet tool to coordinate forecasting, production, and purchasing in a firm's supply chain.

Cost of goods sold   The annual cost for a company to produce the goods or services provided to customers.

Fair trade practices   Following ethical and socially responsible practices.

Functional products   Staples that people buy in a wide range of retail outlets, such as grocery stores and gas stations.

Innovative products   Products such as fashionable clothes and personal computers that typically have a life cycle of just a few months.

Inventory positioning   Deciding where and in what form to stock inventory in the supply chain.

Inventory turnover and weeks of supply   Measures of supply chain efficiency that are mathematically the inverse of one another.

Logistics   Management functions that support the complete cycle of material flow: from the purchase and internal control of production materials; to the planning and control of work-in-process; to the purchasing, shipping, and distribution of the finished product.

Mass customization   The ability of a company to deliver highly customized products and services to different customers around the world.

Outsourcing   Moving some of a firm's internal activities and decision responsibility to outside providers.

Process postponement   Delay of the process step that differentiates a product to as late in the supply chain as possible.

Reverse supply chain   Series of activities required to retrieve a used product or return from a customer and either dispose of it or reuse it.

Strategic sourcing   The development and management of supplier relationships to acquire goods and services in a way that aids in achieving the immediate needs of a business.

Supply chain management   Optimizing the entire supply chain operations for the product by taking a systems approach to managing the flow of information, materials, and services from raw materials suppliers through factories and warehouses to the end customer.

Total cost of ownership   Incorporating all relevant costs in the purchasing decision, not only the purchase price.

Vendor managed inventory (VMI)   Vendor manages customer's inventory of the products they supply.

Vertical integration   Level of ownership of partners in the supply chain.

Weeks of supply   A measure of how many weeks' worth of inventory is in the system at a particular point in time.

Formula Review

[8.1] $\text{Inventory turnover} = \dfrac{\text{Cost of goods sold}}{\text{Average aggregate inventory value}}$

[8.2] $\text{Week of supply} = \left(\dfrac{\text{Average aggregate inventory value}}{\text{Cost of goods sold}} \right) \times 52 \text{ weeks}$

Review and Discussion Questions

1. What recent changes have caused supply chain management to gain importance?
2. With so much productive capacity and room for expansion in Canada, why would a company based in Canada choose to purchase items from a foreign firm? Discuss the pros and cons.
3. Describe the differences between functional and innovative products.
4. What are characteristics of efficient, responsive, risk-hedging, and agile supply chains? Can a supply chain be both efficient and responsive? Risk-hedging and agile? Why or why not?
5. As a supplier, which factors about a buyer (your potential customer) would you consider to be important in setting up a long-term relationship?
6. What are the advantages of using the postponement strategy?
7. Describe how outsourcing works. Why would a firm want to outsource?
8. What are the basic building blocks of an effective mass customization program? What kind of company-wide cooperation is required for a successful mass customization program?

Problems

1. The McGann fast-food restaurant on an American university campus sells an average of 4000 quarter-pound hamburgers each week. Hamburger patties are resupplied twice a week, and on average the store has 350 lbs of hamburger in stock. Assume that the hamburger costs $1.00 a lb. What is the inventory turnover for the hamburger patties? On average, how many days of supply are on hand?
2. The Laval Airfilter company has hired you as a supply chain consultant. The company makes air filters for residential heating and air-conditioning systems. These filters are made in a single plant located in Laval, Quebec. They are distributed to retailers through wholesale centres in 100 locations in the United States, Canada, and Europe. You have collected the following data (on the next page) relating to the value of inventory in its supply chain:
   a. What is the average inventory turnover for the firm?
   b. If you were given the assignment to increase inventory turnover, what would you focus on? Why?
   c. The company reported that it used $500M worth of raw material during the year. On average, how many weeks of supply of raw material are on hand at the factory?

	QUARTER 1 (JANUARY THROUGH MARCH)	QUARTER 2 (APRIL THROUGH JUNE)	QUARTER 3 (JULY THROUGH SEPTEMBER)	QUARTER 4 (OCTOBER THROUGH DECEMBER)
Sales (total quarter):				
United States	300	350	405	375
Canada	75	60	75	70
Europe	30	33	20	15
Cost of goods sold (total quarter)	280	295	340	350
Raw materials at the Laval plant (end-of-quarter)	50	40	55	60
Work-in-process and finished goods at the Laval plant (end-of-quarter)	100	105	120	150
Distribution centre inventory (end-of-quarter):				
United States	25	27	23	30
Canada	10	11	15	16
Europe	5	4	5	5

All amounts in millions of U.S. dollars

I. S. Airfilter

CASE | Pepe Jeans

Pepe began to produce and sell denim jeans in the early 1970s in the United Kingdom and has achieved enormous growth. Pepe's success was the result of a unique approach in a product market dominated by strong brands and limited variety. Pepe presented a range of jeans styles that offered a better fit than traditional five-pocket Western jeans (such as those made by Levi Strauss in the United States)—particularly for female customers. The Pepe range of basic styles is modified each season, but each style keeps its identity, with a slightly whimsical name featured prominently on the jeans and on the point-of-sale material. Variations such as modified washes, leather trim, and even designer wear marks are applied to respond to changing fashion trends. To learn more about Pepe and its products, visit its Web site at http://www.pepejeans.com.

Pepe's brand strength is such that the company can demand a retail price that averages about £45 for its standard products. A high percentage of Pepe sales are through about 1500 independent outlets throughout the United Kingdom. The company maintains contact with its independent retailers via a group of approximately 10 agents, who are self-employed and work exclusively for Pepe. Each agent is responsible for retailers in a particular area of the country.

Pepe is convinced that a good relationship with the independent retailers is vital to its success. The agent meets with each independent retailer three to four times each year to present the new collections and to take sales orders. Because the number of accounts for each agent is so large, contact is often achieved by holding a presentation in a hotel for several retailers. Agents take orders from retailers for six-month delivery. After Pepe receives an order, the retailer has only one week in which to cancel because of the need to place immediate firm orders in Hong Kong to meet the delivery date. The company has had a longstanding policy of not holding any inventory of jeans in the United Kingdom.

After an order is taken and confirmed, the rest of the process up to delivery is administered from the Pepe office in Willesden. The status of orders can be checked from a Web site maintained by Pepe. The actual orders are sent to a sourcing agent in Hong Kong who arranges for manufacturing the jeans. The sourcing agent handles all the details associated with materials, fabrication, and shipping the completed jeans to the retailer. Pepe has an outstanding team of young in-house designers who are responsible for developing new styles and the accompanying point-of-sale material. Jeans are made to specifications provided by this team. The team works closely with the

Hong Kong sourcing agent to ensure that the jeans are made properly and that the material used is of the highest quality.

A recent survey of the independent retailers indicated some growing problems. The independents praised the fit, quality, and variety of Pepe's jeans, although many thought that they had become much less of a trendsetter than in their early days. It was felt that Pepe's variety of styles and quality were the company's key advantage over the competition. However, the independents were unhappy with Pepe's requirements to place firm orders six months in advance with no possibility of amendment, cancellation, or repeat ordering. Some claimed that the inflexible order system forced them to order less, resulting in stockouts of particular sizes and styles. The retailers estimated that Pepe's sales would increase by about 10 percent with a more flexible ordering system.

The retailers expected to have some slow-moving inventory, but the six-month order lead time made it difficult to accurately order and worsened the problem. Because the fashion market is so impulsive, the current favourites were often not in vogue six months later. On the other hand, when demand exceeded expectations, it took a long time to fill the gap. What the retailers wanted was some method of limited returns, exchange, or reordering to overcome the worst of these problems. Pepe was feeling some pressure to respond to these complaints because some of Pepe's smaller competitors offered delivery in only a few days.

Pepe has enjoyed considerable financial success with its current business model. Sales last year were approximately £200M. Cost of sales was approximately 40 percent, operating expenses 28 percent, and profit before taxes nearly 32 percent of sales. The company has no long-term debt and has a very healthy cash position.

Pepe was feeling considerable pressure and felt that a change was going to be needed soon. In evaluating alternatives, the company found that the easiest thing to do would be to work with the Hong Kong sourcing agent to reduce the lead time associated with orders. The agent agreed that the lead time could be shortened, possibly to as little as six weeks, but costs would increase significantly. Currently, the agent collects orders over a period of time and about every two weeks puts these orders out on bid to about 1000 potential suppliers. The sourcing agent estimated that costs might go up 30 percent if the lead time were shortened to six weeks.

Even with the significant increase in cost, consistent delivery schedules would be difficult to keep.

The sourcing agent suggested that Pepe consider building a finishing operation in the United Kingdom. The agent indicated that a major retail chain in the United States had moved to this type of structure with considerable success. All the finishing operation did for the U.S. retail chain was apply different washes to the jeans to give them different "worn" looks. The U.S. operation also took orders for the retail stores and shipped the orders. The U.S. firm found that it could give a two-day response time to the retail stores.

The sourcing agent indicated that costs for the basic jeans (jeans where the wash has not been applied) could probably be reduced by 10 percent because the volumes would be higher. In addition, lead time for the basic jeans could be reduced to approximately three months because the finishing step would be eliminated and the orders would be larger.

The Pepe designers found this an interesting idea, so they visited the U.S. operation to see how the system worked. They found that they would have to keep about six weeks' supply of basic jeans on hand in the United Kingdom and that they would have to invest in about £1 000 000 worth of equipment. They estimated that it would cost about £500 000 to operate the facility each year. They could locate the facility in the basement of the current Willesden office building, and the renovations would cost about £300 000.

Questions

1. Acting as an outside consultant, what would you recommend that Pepe do? Given the data in the case, perform a financial analysis to evaluate the alternatives that you have identified. (Assume that the new inventory could be valued at six weeks' worth of the yearly cost of sales. Use a 30 percent inventory carrying cost rate.) Calculate a payback period for each alternative.
2. Are there other alternatives that Pepe should consider?

The idea for this case came from a case titled "Pepe Jeans" written by D. Bramley and C. John of the London Business School. Pepe Jeans is a real company, but the data given in the case do not represent actual company data.

Footnotes

[1] Stanley Davis, *Future Perfect* (Reading, MA: Addison-Wesley, 1987).

[2] M. L. Fisher, "What Is the Right Supply Chain for Your Product?" *Harvard Business Review,* March–April 1997, pp. 105–16.

[3] H. Lee, V. Padmanabhan, and S. Whang, "The Bullwhip Effect in Supply Chains," *Sloan Management Review* (Spring 1997), pp. 93–102.

[4]Hau L. Lee, "Aligning Supply Chain Strategies with Product Uncertainties," *California Management Review* 44, no. 3 (Spring 2002), pp. 105–19. Copyright © 2002 by the Regents of the University of California. By permission of the Regents.

[5]"Retailer to Suppliers: Track Inventory, Restock Shelves," *Information Week*, July 2, 2001, p. 24.

[6]"Have Factory Will Travel," *The Economist,* February 12–18, 2000, pp. 61–62.

[7]Adapted from Martha Craumer, "How to Think Strategically about Outsourcing," *Harvard Management Update*, May 2002, p. 4.

[8]R. S. Kaplan and D. P. Norton, *The Balanced Scorecard: Translating Strategy into Action* (Cambridge: Harvard Business School Press, 1996).

[9]R. Schonberger, "Tracking Toyota's Position," *APICS Magazine*, 18, 6, 2008, pp. 34–37

[10]This section is adapted from E. Feitzinger and H. Lee, "Mass Customization at Hewlett-Packard: The Power of Postponement," *Harvard Business Review*, January–February 1997, pp. 116–21.

[11]Special thanks to Gene Fliedner for help with this section. Gene Fliedner, "Hierarchical Forecasting: Issues and Use Guidelines," *Industrial Management & Data Systems* 101, no. 1 (2001), pp. 5–12.

[12]V. D. R. Guide Jr. and L.N. Van Wassenhove, "The Reverse Supply Chain," *Harvard Business Review* (February 2002), p. 25.

[13]R. S. Tibben-Lembke, "Life After Death: Reverse Logistics and the Product Life Cycle," *International Journal of Physical Distribution and Logistics Management,* 32, no. 3 (2002), pp. 223–244.

[14]T.H. Clarke and J.L. McKenney, "Proctor & Gamble: Improving Customer Value Through Process Redesign," Harvard Business School Publishing, Case 9-195-126, 1995.

Selected Bibliography

Bowersox, D. J.; D. J. Closs; and M. B. Cooper. *Supply Chain and Logistics Management.* New York: Irwin/McGraw-Hill, 2002.

Burt, D. N.; D. W. Dobler; and S. L. Starling. *World Class Supply Management[SM]: The Key to Supply Chain Management.* 7th ed. New York: McGraw-Hill/Irwin, 2003.

Chopra, S., and P. Meindl. *Supply Chain Management: Strategy, Planning, and Operations.* 2nd ed. Upper Saddle River, NJ: Prentice Hall, 2003.

da Silveira, G.; D. Borenstein; and F.S. Fogliatto. "Mass Customization: Literature Review and Research Directions," *International Journal of Production Economics,* 72, 1, 1–13, 2001.

Greaver II, M. F. *Strategic Outsourcing: A Structured Approach to Outsourcing Decisions and Initiatives.* New York: American Management Association, 1999.

Hayes, R.; G. Pisano; D. Upton; and S. Wheelwright. *Operations Strategy and Technology: Pursuing the Competitive Edge.* New York: John Wiley & Sons, 2005.

Simchi-Levi, D.; P. Kaminski; and E. Simchi-Levi. *Supply Chain Management.* 2nd ed. New York: McGraw-Hill, 2003.

Vollmann, T.; W. L. Berry; D. C. Whybark; and F. R. Jacobs. *Manufacturing Planning and Control Systems for Supply Chain Management: The Definitive Guide for Professionals.* New York: McGraw-Hill/Irwin, 2004.

LOGISTICS

1. Know what a third-party logistics provider is.
2. Understand the major issues that need to be considered in locating a plant or warehouse facility.
3. Know how a factor-rating system can be used to narrow potential location sites.
4. Be able to use the "transportation" method of linear programming to analyze location problems.
5. Understand the "centroid" method for locating entities such as cell phone communication towers.

LOGISTICS PROVIDERS ARE PROVIDING MORE VALUE-ADDED SERVICES...

Not long ago, all companies such as DHL, Federal Express (FedEx), UPS, and Canada Post's Purolator did was pick up an item from you and deliver it to the addressee. Now they do a lot more than that. They provide supply chain solutions. Purolator offers consulting services that help the customer comply with increased security regulations in this post-9/11 world. In 2004, FedEx bought Kinko's, a chain of copy stores, as a value-added service. Now, from your computer you can electronically deliver a document to Kinko's. Kinko's will then do the production of the documents, and FedEx will deliver the documents to your customer. For the same reason, UPS bought Mail Boxes Etc. (now being rebranded as the UPS Store) in 2001. UPS also offers services in order fulfillment (picking, packing, and making required kits), repair and refurbishment, reverse logistics, and service parts logistics. DHL offers to take over management of customers' in-house logistics including distribution, transport, back-office, supply chain, and after sales. These value-added services are not unique. Most logistics service providers are moving in the same direction. They see this as a way to survive in the future.

LOGISTICS

A major issue in designing a great supply chain for manufactured goods is determining the way those items are moved from the manufacturing plant to the customer. For consumer products, this often involves moving product from the manufacturing plant to a warehouse and then to a retail store. You probably do not think about this often, but consider all those items with "Made in China" on the label. That sweatshirt has probably made a longer trip than you may ever make. If you live in Winnipeg and the sweatshirt is made in the Fujian region of China, that sweatshirt travelled over 10 000 kilometres, nearly halfway around the world, to get to the retail store where you bought it. To keep the price of the sweatshirt down, that trip must be made as efficiently as possible. There is no telling how that sweatshirt made the trip. It might have been flown in an airplane or might have travelled in a combination of vehicles, possibly going by truck part of the way and by boat or plane the rest. Logistics is about this movement of goods through the supply chain.

Supply Chain

APICS, The Association for Operations Management defines **logistics** as "the art and science of obtaining, producing, and distributing material and product in the proper place and in proper quantities." This is a fairly broad definition, and this chapter will focus on how to analyze where we locate warehouses and plants and how to evaluate the movement of materials to and from those locations. The term **international logistics** refers to managing these functions when the movement is on a global scale.

Supply Chain

There are companies that specialize in logistics, such as United Parcel Service (UPS), Federal Express (FedEx), and DHL. These global companies are in the business of moving everything from flowers to industrial equipment. Today, a manufacturing company will most often contract with one of those companies to handle many of its logistics functions. In this case, those transportation companies are often called a **third-party logistics (3PL) company**. The most basic function would be simply moving the goods from one place to another.

As discussed in the opening vignette, the logistics company may also provide additional services such as warehouse management, inventory control, and other customer service functions.

Logistics is big business, accounting for about 12 percent of Canada's gross domestic product, and growing.[1] Today's modern efficient warehouse and distribution centres are the heart of logistics. These centres are carefully managed and efficiently operated to ensure the secure storage and quick flow of goods, services, and related information from the point of origin to the point of consumption.

DECISIONS RELATED TO LOGISTICS

The problem of deciding how best to transport goods from plants to customers is a complex one that affects the cost of a product. Major trade-offs related to the cost of transporting the product, speed of delivery, and flexibility to react to changes are involved. Information systems play a major role in coordinating activities and include activities such as allocating resources, managing inventory levels, scheduling, and order tracking. A full discussion of these systems is beyond the scope of this book, but we cover basic inventory control and scheduling in later chapters.

A key decision area is deciding how material will be transported. There are five widely recognized modes of transportation: highway (trucks), water (ships), air (aircraft), rail (trains), and pipelines. Each mode is uniquely suited to handle certain types of products, as described next:

Highway (truck)—Actually, few products are moved without some highway transportation. The highway offers great flexibility for moving goods to virtually any location not separated by water. The size of the product, weight, and liquid or bulk can all be accommodated with this mode.

Water (ship)—Very high capacity and very low cost, but transit times are long, and large areas of the world are not directly accessible to water carriers. This mode is especially useful for bulk items such as oil, coal, and chemical products.

Air—Fast but expensive. Small, light, expensive items are most appropriate for this mode of transportation.

Rail (trains)—This is a fairly low-cost alternative, but transit times can be long and may be subject to variability. The suitability of rail can vary depending on the rail infrastructure in a particular region of the world. The European infrastructure is highly developed, making this an attractive alternative compared to trucks. In parts of North America, the rail infrastructure has declined significantly over the last 50 years, making this less attractive.

Pipelines—This is highly specialized and limited to liquids, gases, and solids in slurry forms. No packaging is needed, and the costs per km are low. The initial cost to build a pipeline is very high.

Few companies use a single mode of transportation. Multimodal solutions are the norm, and finding the correct multimode strategies can be a significant problem. The problem of coordination and scheduling the carriers requires comprehensive information systems capable of tracking goods through the system. Standardized containers often are used so that a product can be transferred efficiently from a truck to an airplane or ship. It is important to include all the costs of delivery in making the transportation mode decision. Thus, a cost-benefit analysis should be undertaken before choosing the mode. Consider the example in Exhibit 9.1 The Good Earth

EXHIBIT 9.1	Air vs Rail for Good Earth

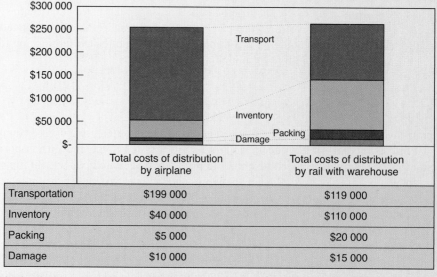

	Total costs of distribution by airplane	Total costs of distribution by rail with warehouse
Transportation	$199 000	$119 000
Inventory	$40 000	$110 000
Packing	$5 000	$20 000
Damage	$10 000	$15 000

Stanley Shapiro; Kenneth Wong; William Perreault, Jr.; E. Jerome McCarthy; *Basic Marketing* (Toronto, Ontario: McGraw-Hill Ryerson, 2002), p. 353.

Vegetable Company was shipping produce to distant markets by train. The cost of shipping a tonne of vegetables by train averaged less than half the cost of airfreight, so the company assumed that rail was the best method. But then Good Earth managers did a more complete analysis. To their surprise, they found that the airfreight system was faster and cheaper.

Cross-Docking Special consolidation warehouses are used when shipments from various sources are pulled together and combined into larger shipments with a common destination. This improves the efficiency of the entire system. **Cross-docking** is an approach used in these consolidation warehouses, where, rather than making larger shipments, large shipments are broken down into small shipments for local delivery in an area.

Retailers receive shipments from many suppliers in their regional warehouses and immediately sort those shipments for delivery to individual stores by using cross-docking systems coordinated by computerized control systems. This results in a minimal amount of inventory being carried in the warehouses. This is the case at Canadian Tire and Walmart warehouses.

Hub-and-spoke systems combine the idea of consolidation and that of cross-docking. Here the warehouse is referred to as a "hub," and its sole purpose is sorting goods. Incoming goods are sorted immediately to consolidation areas where each area is designated for shipment to a specific location. Hubs are located in strategic locations near the geographic centre of the region they are to serve to minimize the distance a good must travel.

Designing these systems is an interesting and complex task. The following section focuses on the plant and warehouse location problem as representative of the types of logistics decisions that need to be made. Logistics is a broad topic, and its elements evolve as the value-added services provided by major logistics vendors expand. Having the proper network design is fundamental to efficiency in the industry.

ISSUES IN FACILITY LOCATION

The problem of facility location is faced by both new and existing businesses, and its solution is critical to a company's eventual success. An important element in designing a company's supply chain is the location of its facilities. For instance, U.S. oilfield services giant Haliburton recently moved its corporate headquarters to Dubai in the United Arab Emirates (while maintaining a corporate office in the current headquarters in Houston, Texas), since the Persian Gulf region is a major energy source and Asia is emerging as a high demand region. Toys "Я" Us has opened a location in Japan as a part of its global strategy. Disney chose Paris, France, for its European theme park, and Honda assembles cars in Ontario. Manufacturing and service companies' location decisions are guided by a variety of criteria defined by competitive imperatives. Criteria that influence manufacturing plant and warehouse location planning (sometimes called *critical success factors* or CSFs) are discussed next (see OSMPs on Toyota and Palliser for examples).

Global

> **Proximity to customers.**   For example, Aurora, Ontario-based Magna has many manufacturing plants in Europe to be closer to European auto makers whose buyers want their goods delivered "yesterday." Such proximity also helps ensure that customer needs are incorporated into products being developed and built.

Business climate.   A favourable business climate can include the presence of similar-sized businesses, the presence of companies in the same industry, and, in the case of international locations, the presence of other foreign companies. Pro-business government legislation and local government intervention to facilitate businesses locating in an area via subsidies, tax abatements, and other support are also factors.

Total costs.   The objective is to select a site with the lowest total cost. This includes regional costs, inbound distribution costs, and outbound distribution costs. Land, construction, labour, taxes, and energy costs make up the regional costs. In addition, there are hidden costs that are difficult to measure. These involve (1) excessive moving of preproduction material between locations before final delivery to the customers and (2) loss of customer responsiveness arising from locating away from the main customer base.

Infrastructure.   Adequate road, rail, air, and sea transportation is vital. Energy and telecommunications requirements also must be met. In addition, the local government's willingness to invest in upgrading infrastructure to the levels required may be an incentive to select a specific location.

Quality of labour.   The educational and skill levels of the labour pool must match the company's needs. Even more important are the willingness and ability to learn.

Suppliers.   A high-quality and competitive supplier base makes a given location suitable. The proximity of important suppliers' plants also supports the lean production methods discussed in Chapter 10.

Other facilities.   The location of other plants or distribution centres of the same company may influence a new facility's location in the network. Issues of product mix and capacity are strongly interconnected to the location decision in this context.

Alcoa's Portland, Victoria plant in Australia is one of over two dozen smelters producing primary aluminum for Alcoa. The creation of Parklands around the plant site has earned the title "smelter in the park," and the only one granted certification as a viable habitat, by the Wildlife Habitat Enhancement Council of the United States, outside the country.

Operations and Supply Management in Practice

Toyota Chooses Woodstock, Ontario, for its New Assembly Plant

October 11, 2005: Toyota president, Katsuaki Watanabe and Prime Minister Paul Martin attend the sod-turning ceremony for Toyota's latest planned North American plant in Woodstock, a small town between Toronto and London. The completed plant will employ 2000 workers and churn out 200 000 automobiles per year (production started in November 2008, though initially output is expected to be less than planned, because of the global economic crisis).

What made Woodstock attractive to Toyota? Location and aggregate capacity are major decisions and thus are made on the basis of multiple factors, not cost alone. In the case of Toyota, now the world's largest automobile manufacturer, one factor would have been that in 2004 Ontario became the number one jurisdiction for assembling automobiles in North America (a distinction it wrested from Michigan), with a very strong auto parts industry as well. Besides, southwestern Ontario, along with the nearby U.S. midwest, forms the traditional heart of the North American auto industry. Thus, developing suppliers close by that can deliver parts frequently and in small batches, something crucial to its Just-In-Time (JIT) system (discussed in Chapter 10) is feasible at Woodstock.

Another important factor is the existence of another Toyota plant nearby in Cambridge, Ontario. Due to significant capacity expansion in recent years, Toyota will have to rely on its existing plants to train employees in the new plants in its JIT system, which focuses on waste elimination. So having Cambridge nearby was a plus.

Also, rural locations close to big cities are ideal. The cost of land is lower than in the city, yet highways make it easy to get parts in and vehicles out to cities such as Toronto, a road, rail, air, and sea transportation hub. In addition, the major North American markets of central Canada and the midwestern, eastern, and south-eastern U.S. are nearby.

It helped that the Ontario government contributed $70 million in incentives to help land the deal and that the federal government chipped in another $55 million. Lobbying by top ministers in Ontario and the federal government (including the prime minister) probably also helped.

Another advantage of Woodstock is the many universities and technical institutions nearby from which Toyota can recruit skilled employees. Canada's socialized health system is also a plus since Toyota won't be burdened as much by employee health care costs as it would be in the United States. Furthermore, general liberalization of trade rules means that Toyota can take advantage of a good location in Canada and yet not be limited by Canada's small market. It can export Woodstock-built vehicles to the United States and beyond.

■ Sources: Greg Keenan, "Toyota May Double Output, Boost Hiring at New Plant," *The Globe and Mail*, October 12, 2005, B1.
Norihiko Shirouzu, "Mean but Lean, Toyota Seeks Outside Help; With In-House Quality Gurus in Short Supply, Auto Maker Turns to Its Assembler Affiliates," *Wall Street Journal*, July 14, 2005, B4.
The Canadian Press, "Toyota Celebrates Opening of Ontario Plant," December 4, 2008, retrieved from www.theglobeandmail.com. February, 25, 2009.

Free trade zones.   A foreign trade zone or a **free trade zone** is typically a closed facility (under the supervision of the customs department) into which foreign goods can be brought without being subject to the normal customs requirements. Such specialized locations exist in many countries. Manufacturers in free trade zones can use imported components duty free in the final product if exported and delay payment of customs duties if the product is shipped into the host country.

Global

Political risk.   The fast-changing geopolitical scenes in numerous nations present exciting, challenging opportunities. But the extended phase of transformation that many countries are undergoing makes the decision to locate in those areas extremely difficult. Political risks in both the country of location and the host country influence location decisions.

Government barriers.   Barriers to enter and locate in many countries are being removed today through legislation. Yet many nonlegislative and cultural barriers should be considered in location planning.

Operations and Supply Management in Practice

Evolution of a Global Location Strategy at a Winnipeg Furniture Maker

Palliser Furniture, which originated as a woodworking shop in 1944 in a Winnipeg basement, is Canada's largest furniture manufacturer, employing about 5000 people worldwide. With suppliers on four continents, and factories in Canada, the United States, Mexico, and Indonesia, it stands among the industry leaders in global presence. As this example describes, the company chose these global locations after careful consideration and for various strategic reasons.

It was only in 1981 that Palliser opened its first international plant in Fargo, North Dakota, allowing it to secure a beachhead in the United States, the world's largest furniture market. The U.S. expansion also allowed it to hedge against currency fluctuations. In 1991, another plant in North Carolina was established and the Fargo plant closed in 1994. The arrival of the Free Trade Agreement (FTA) in 1984 and the North American Free Trade Agreement (NAFTA) in 1994 and the resulting lowering of tariffs had a profound effect on Palliser. These agreements brought tremendous opportunities since the U.S. and Mexican markets were now more accessible. At the same time the Canadian market was no longer protected. Thus, Palliser had to become more competitive. As a result, the company redefined its markets, rationalized its distribution locations, and shifted its manufacturing locations. Mexico was seen as an attractive location because of its cheap labour. By the late 1990s, Palliser had established a factory in Saltillo, a city close to Monterey, as its Mexican location. Saltillo has a stable economic base, including manufacturing operations of Chrysler, GM, Lear Seating, Fruit of the Loom, etc. Thus the city also had experience in tanning, cutting, and sewing operations, skills valuable to Palliser.

In 2000, it opened its first Asian factory in Indonesia because of the country's highly skilled labour force and its wood processing tradition, among other reasons. The plant

produces wood components for furniture to be assembled in Winnipeg. With the ability to design, produce, and source in different parts of the globe (it also has a partnership with a Lithuanian company), Palliser can come to market with both inexpensive offerings and pricier goods. Just as important, with multiple plants in North America it has the ability to juggle production between plants for the important North American market. It can provide two- to four-week deliveries on even custom orders, which its Asian competition cannot match. Palliser has not abandoned its Canadian base, however. Currently, four (three in Winnipeg and one in Alberta) of its seven locations are in Canada.

■   Sources: Michael Chazin, "The New Global Reality," *Upholstery Design and Management* (December 2002), pp. 12–16.

Anthony Goerzen, *Palliser Furniture* (London, Ontario: University of Western Ontario, Ivey Management Services, 1998).

Geoff Kirbyson, "Winnipeg Furniture Maker Sets Up Shops in Asia, Europe," *Winnipeg Free Press*, August 11, 2000, B5.

"Palliser Looks for 400-M in Canadian Sales," *Winnipeg Free Press*, March 5, 1999, B12. Palliser Furniture, www.palliser.com.

Trading blocs.   The Central America Free Trade Agreement (CAFTA) is one of the new **trading blocs** in our hemisphere. Such agreements influence location decisions, both within and outside trading bloc countries. Firms typically locate or relocate within a bloc to take advantage of new market opportunities or lower total costs afforded by the trading agreement. Other companies (those outside the trading bloc countries) decide on locations within the bloc so as not to be disqualified from competing in the new market. Examples include the location of various Japanese auto manufacturing plants in Europe before 1992 as well as recent moves by many communications and financial services companies into Mexico in a post-NAFTA environment.

Environmental issues and regulations.   The environmental issues and regulations that affect a certain industry in a given location should be included in the location decision. Besides measurable cost implications, these influence the relationship with the local community.

Host community.   The host community's interest in having the plant in its midst is a necessary part of the evaluation process. Local educational facilities and the broader issue of quality of life are also important.

Competitive advantage.   An important decision for multinational companies is which nation they decide to locate the home base in for each distinct business. Porter suggests that a company can have different home bases for distinct businesses or segments. Competitive advantage is created at a home base where strategy is set, the core product and process technology are created, and a critical mass of production takes place. So a company should move its home base to a country that stimulates innovation and provides the best environment for global competitiveness.[2] This concept can also be applied to domestic companies seeking to gain sustainable competitive advantage. It partly explains the southeastern states' recent emergence as the preferred corporate destination within the United States (that is, their business climate fosters innovation and low-cost production).

Corporate social responsibility.   As discussed in Chapter 8, companies also have to be concerned about corporate social responsibility issues. For example, in some cases, locations with lower business costs may also be ones that do not place an emphasis on working conditions, product safety, or on human rights. While companies may benefit in the short term by locating in such areas, the reputation of the company in the long run may be damaged.

Global

PLANT LOCATION METHODS

As we will see, there are many techniques available for identifying potential sites for plants or other types of facilities. The process required to narrow the decision down to a particular area can vary significantly depending on the type of business we are in and the competitive pressures that must be considered. As we have discussed, there are often many different criteria that need to be considered when selecting from the set of feasible sites.

In this section, we sample three different types of techniques that have proven to be very useful to many companies. The first is the *factor-rating system* that allows us to consider many different types of criteria using simple point-rating scales. Next, we consider the *transportation method* of linear programming, a powerful technique for estimating the cost of using a network of plants and warehouses. Following this, we consider the *centroid method,* a technique often used by communications companies (cell phone providers) to locate their transmission towers. Finally, later in the chapter we consider how service firms such as McDonald's and State Farm Insurance use statistical techniques to find desirable locations for their facilities.

Factor-Rating Systems

Factor-rating systems are perhaps the most widely used of the general location techniques because they provide a mechanism to combine diverse factors in an easy-to-understand format.

By way of example, a refinery assigned the following range of point values to major factors affecting a set of possible sites:

	RANGE
Fuels in region	0 to 330
Power availability and reliability	0 to 200
Labour climate	0 to 100
Living conditions	0 to 100
Transportation	0 to 50
Water supply	0 to 10
Climate	0 to 50
Supplies	0 to 60
Tax policies and laws	0 to 20

Each site was then rated against each factor, and a point value was selected from its assigned range (the higher the point value assigned to a site, the more desirable it was with respect to that factor). The sums of assigned points for each site were then compared. The site with the most points was selected.

A major problem with simple point-rating schemes is that they do not account for the wide range of costs that may occur within each factor. For example, there may be only a few hundred dollars' difference between the best and worst locations on one factor and several thousands of dollars' difference between the best and the worst on another. The first factor may have the most points available to it but provide little help in making the location decision; the second may have few points available but potentially show a real difference in the value of locations. To deal with this problem, it has been suggested that points possible for each factor be derived using a weighting scale based on standard deviations of costs rather than simply total cost amounts. In this way, relative costs can be considered.

Transportation Method of Linear Programming

The **transportation method** is a special linear programming method. (Note that linear programming is developed in detail in Web Appendix F (online).) It gets its name from its application to problems involving transporting products from several sources to several destinations. The two common objectives of such problems are either (1) minimize the cost of shipping n units to m destinations or (2) maximize the profit of shipping n units to m destinations.

Interactive Operations Management

EXAMPLE 9.1:   BRUNSWICK PHARMACEUTICAL COMPANY

Suppose the Brunswick Pharmaceutical Company has four factories supplying the warehouses of four major customers and its management wants to determine the minimum-cost shipping schedule for its monthly output to these customers. Factory supply, warehouse demands, and shipping costs per case for these drugs are shown in Exhibit 9.2.

EXHIBIT 9.2   Data for Brunswick Pharmaceutical Transportation Problem

					SHIPPING COSTS PER CASE (IN DOLLARS)			
FACTORY	SUPPLY	WAREHOUSE	DEMAND	FROM	TO REGINA	TO LONDON	TO QUEBEC CITY	TO HALIFAX
Calgary	16	Regina	10	Calgary	$25	$35	$36	$60
Sudbury	6	London	12	Sudbury	55	30	25	25
Vancouver	14	Quebec City	15	Vancouver	40	50	80	90
Edmonton	11	Halifax	9	Edmonton	30	40	66	75

Graphical Representation of the Brunswick Pharmaceutical Problem   **EXHIBIT 9.3**

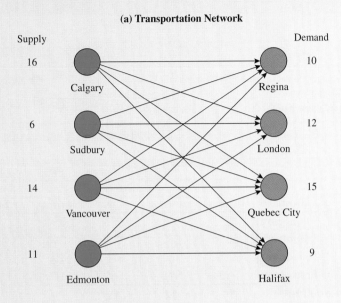

(a) Transportation Network

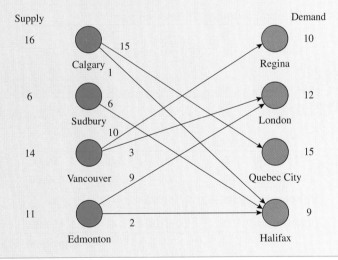

(b) Optimal Transportation Solution

The network for this example appears in Exhibit 9.3a, where supply availability at each factory is shown beside each supply node and the warehouse demands are shown beside each demand node.

SOLUTION

This problem can be solved by using Microsoft® Excel's® Solver function. Exhibit 9.4 shows how the problem can be set up in the spreadsheet. Cells B6 through E6 contain the requirement for each customer warehouse. Cells F2 through F5 contain the amount that can be supplied from each plant. Cells B2 through E5 are the cost of shipping one unit for each potential plant and warehouse combination.

Cells for the solution of the problem are B9 through E12. These cells can initially be left blank when setting up the spreadsheet. Column cells F9 through F12 are the sum of each row, indicating how much is actually being shipped from each factory in the candidate solution (this is also the optimal

EXHIBIT 9.4   Excel® Screen Showing the Brunswick Pharmaceutical Problem

Brunswick Pharmaceutical

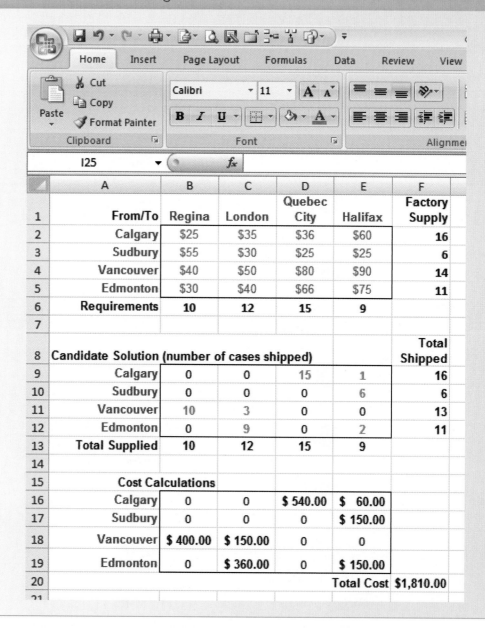

From/To	Regina	London	Quebec City	Halifax	Factory Supply
Calgary	$25	$35	$36	$60	16
Sudbury	$55	$30	$25	$25	6
Vancouver	$40	$50	$80	$90	14
Edmonton	$30	$40	$66	$75	11
Requirements	10	12	15	9	

Candidate Solution (number of cases shipped)					Total Shipped
Calgary	0	0	15	1	16
Sudbury	0	0	0	6	6
Vancouver	10	3	0	0	13
Edmonton	0	9	0	2	11
Total Supplied	10	12	15	9	

Cost Calculations					
Calgary	0	0	$ 540.00	$ 60.00	
Sudbury	0	0	0	$ 150.00	
Vancouver	$ 400.00	$ 150.00	0	0	
Edmonton	0	$ 360.00	0	$ 150.00	
				Total Cost	$1,810.00

solution). Similarly, row cells B13 through E13 are sums of the amount being shipped to each customer in the candidate solution. The Excel® Sum function can be used to calculate these values.

The cost of the candidate solution is calculated in cells B16 through E19. Multiplying the amount shipped in the candidate solution by the cost per unit of shipping over that particular route makes this calculation. For example, multiplying B4 by B11 in cell B18 gives the cost of shipping between Vancouver and Regina for the candidate solution ($400). The total cost shown in cell F20 is the sum of all these individual costs.

To solve the problem, the Excel® Solver application needs to be accessed. In Office 2007, Solver is found by selecting Data and then Solver from the Excel® menu (in Office 2003, instead of Data you have to select Tools). A screen similar to what is shown below should appear. If you cannot find Solver at that location, the required add-in might not have been added when Excel® was initially installed on your computer. Solver can easily be added if you have your original Excel® installation disk.

Solver parameters now need to be set. First set the target cell. This is the cell where the total cost associated with the solution is calculated. In our sample problem, this is cell F20. Next we need to indicate that we are minimizing this cell. Selecting the "Min" button does this. The location of our solution is indicated in the "Changing Cells." These cells are B9 through E12 in our example.

Next we need to indicate the constraints for our problem. For our transportation problem we need to be sure that customer demand is met and that we do not exceed the capacity of our manufacturing plants. To ensure that demand is met, click on "Add" and highlight the range of cells where we have calculated the total amount being shipped to each customer. This range is B13 to E13 in our example. Next select "=" indicating that we want the amount shipped to equal demand. Finally, on the right side enter the range of cells where the actual customer demand is stated in our spreadsheet. This range is B6 to E6 in our example.

The second set of constraints that ensures that the capacity of our manufacturing plants is not exceeded is entered similarly. The range of cells that indicated how much is being shipped from each factory is F9 to F12. These values need to be less than or equal to (<=) the capacity of each factory, which is in cells F2 to F5. To set up the Solver, a few options need to be set as well. Click on the "Options" button and the following screen should appear:

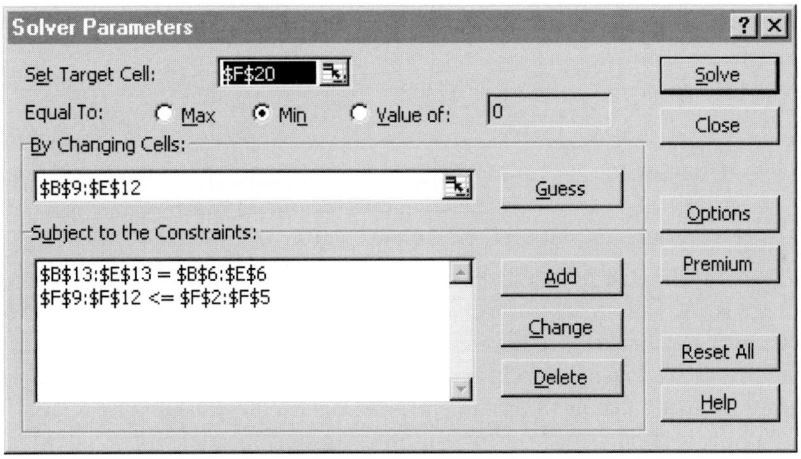

Excel® Screen shots from Microsoft® Excel © 2001 Microsoft Corporation.

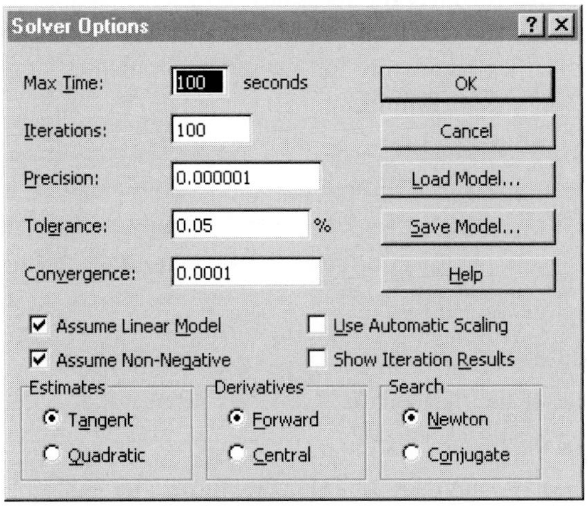

Two options need to be set for solving transportation problems. First we need "Assume Linear Model." This tells the Solver that there are no nonlinear calculations in our spreadsheet. This is important because the Solver can use a very efficient algorithm to calculate the optimal solution to this problem if this condition exists. Next, the "Assume Non-Negative" box needs to be checked. This tells Solver that the values in our solution need to be greater than or equal to zero. In transportation problems, shipping negative quantities does not make any sense. Click "OK" to return to the main Solver box, and then click "Solve" to actually solve the problem. Solver will notify you that it found a solution. Indicate that you want that solution saved. Finally, click "OK" to go back to the main spreadsheet. The solution should be in cells B9 to E12. It is also shown graphically in Exhibit 9.3b, with the amounts shipped shown on the arrows. Note that since there is one more case of supply than is needed, the Vancouver factory needs to ship only thirteen out of the fourteen cases that it has.

The transportation method can be used to solve many different types of problems if it is applied innovatively. For example, it can be used to test the cost impact of different candidate locations on the entire production–distribution network. To do this, we might add a new row that contains the unit shipping cost from a factory in a new location, say, Winnipeg, to the existing set of customer warehouses, along with the total amount it could supply. We could then solve this particular matrix for minimum total cost. Next, we would replace the factory located in Winnipeg in the same row of the matrix with a factory at a different location, Hamilton, and again solve for minimum total cost. Assuming the factories in Winnipeg and Hamilton would be identical in other important ways, the location resulting in the lowest total cost for the network would be selected.

For additional information about using the Solver, see the Web Appendix F, "Linear Programming Using the Excel Solver," online.

Centroid Method

The **centroid method (also called the centre-of-gravity method)** is a technique for locating single facilities that considers the existing facilities, the distances between them, and the volumes of goods to be shipped. The technique is often used to locate intermediate or distribution warehouses. In its simplest form, this method assumes that inbound and outbound transportation costs are equal, and it does not include special shipping costs for less than full loads.

Another major application of the centroid method today is the location of communication towers in urban areas. Examples include radio, TV, and cell phone towers. In this application, the goal is to find sites that are near clusters of customers, thus ensuring clear radio signals.

The centroid method begins by placing the existing locations on a coordinate grid system. Coordinates are usually based on longitude and latitude measures due to the rapid adoption of GPS systems for mapping locations. To keep it simple for our examples, we use arbitrary X, Y coordinates. Exhibit 9.5 shows an example of a grid layout.

The centroid is found by calculating the X and Y coordinates that result in the minimal transportation cost. We use the formulas

$$C_x = \frac{\sum d_{ix}V_i}{\sum V_i} \qquad C_y = \frac{\sum d_{iy}V_i}{\sum d_{iy}V_i}$$

where

Interactive Operations Management

$C_x = X$ coordinate of the centroid

$C_y = Y$ coordinate of the centroid

$d_{ix} = X$ coordinate of the ith location

$d_{iy} = Y$ coordinate of the ith location

$V_i = $ Volume of goods moved to or from the ith location

Grid Map for Centroid Example

EXHIBIT 9.5

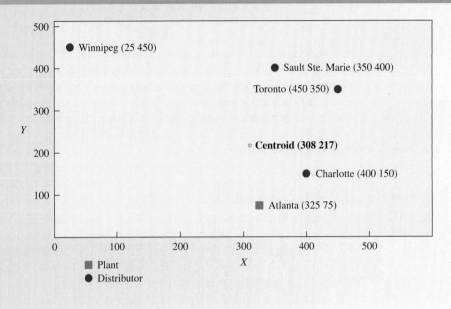

Centroid_Method

Shipping Volumes, Centroid Example

EXHIBIT 9.6

LOCATIONS	GALLONS OF GASOLINE PER MONTH (000 000)
Atlanta, GA	1500
Charlotte, NC	250
Toronto	450
Sault Ste. Marie	350
Winnipeg	450

Centroid_Method

EXAMPLE 9.2: HIOCTANE REFINING COMPANY

The HiOctane Refining Company needs to locate an intermediate holding facility between its refining plant in Atlanta and its major distributors. Exhibit 9.5 shows the coordinate map. The amount of gasoline shipped to or from the plant and distributors appears in Exhibit 9.6.

In this example, for the Atlanta location (the first location), $d_{1x} = 325$, $d_{1y} = 75$, and $V_1 = 1,500$.

SOLUTION

Using the information in Exhibits 9.5 and 9.6, we can calculate the coordinates of the centroid:

$$C_x = \frac{(325 \times 1500) + (400 \times 250) + (450 \times 450) + (350 \times 350) + (25 \times 450)}{1500 + 250 + 450 + 350 + 450}$$

$$= \frac{923,750}{3000} = 307.9$$

$$C_x = \frac{(75 \times 1500) + (150 \times 250) + (350 \times 450) + (400 \times 350) + (450 \times 450)}{1500 + 250 + 450 + 350 + 450}$$

$$= \frac{650\,000}{3000} = 216.7$$

This gives management the X and Y coordinates of approximately 308 and 217, respectively, and provides an initial starting point to search for a new site. By examining the location of the calculated centroid on the grid map, we can see that it might be more cost-efficient to ship directly between the Atlanta plant and the Charlotte distributor than to ship via a warehouse near the centroid. Before a location decision is made, management would probably recalculate the centroid, changing the data to reflect this (that is, decrease the gallons shipped from Atlanta by the amount Charlotte needs and remove Charlotte from the formula).

LOCATING SERVICE FACILITIES

Because of the variety of service firms and the relatively low cost of establishing a service facility compared to one for manufacturing, new service facilities are far more common than new factories and warehouses. Indeed, there are few communities in which rapid population growth has not been paralleled by concurrent rapid growth in retail outlets, restaurants, municipal services, and entertainment facilities.

Services typically have multiple sites to maintain close contact with customers. The location decision is closely tied to the market selection decision. If the target market is college-age groups, locations in retirement communities—despite desirability in terms of cost, resource availability, and so forth—are not viable alternatives. Market needs also affect the number of sites to be built and the size and characteristics of the sites. Whereas manufacturing location decisions are often made by minimizing costs, many service location decision techniques maximize the profit potential of various sites. Next, we present a multiple regression model that can be used to help select good sites.

A map showing the location of fire and rescue locations in Victoria, BC. For emergency services such as fire, police and ambulance, since we are dealing with life and death situations, there have to be enough locations (though not too many as these are expensive) so that everybody is accessible within a safe time limit.

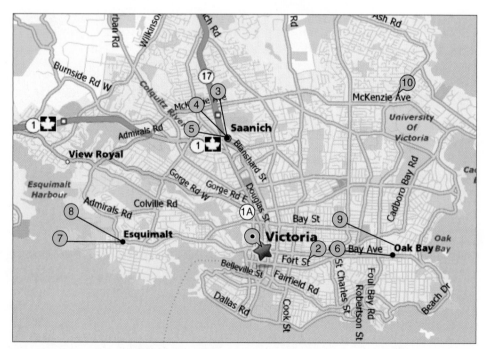

Source: MapQuest and the MapQuest logo are registered trademarks of MapQuest, Inc. Map content © 2009 by MapQuest, Inc. and its respective copyright holders. Used with permission.

| | Independent Variables Collected for the Initial Model-Building Stage | EXHIBIT 9.7 |

CATEGORY	NAME	DESCRIPTION
Competitive	INNRATE	Inn price
	PRICE	Room rate for the inn
	RATE	Average competitive room rate
	RMS 1	Hotel rooms within 1 km
	RMSTOTAL	Hotel rooms within 3 km
	ROOMSINN	Inn rooms
Demand generators	CIVILIAN	Civilian personnel on base
	COLLEGE	College enrollment
	HOSP1	Hospital beds within 1 km
	HOSPTOTL	Hospital beds within 4 km
	HVYIND	Heavy industrial employment
	LGTIND	Light industrial acreage
	MALLS	Shopping mall square footage
	CFBBLKD	Canadian Forces base blocked
	CFP	Canadian Forces personnel
	CFTOT	CFP + CIVILIAN
	OFC1	Office space within 1 km
	OFCTOTAL	Office space within 4 km
	OFCCBD	Office space in Central Business District
	PASSENGR	Airport passengers enplaned
	RETAIL	Scale ranking of retail activity
	TOURISTS	Annual tourists
	TRAFFIC	Traffic count
	VAN	Airport van
Demographic	EMPLYPCT	Unemployment percentage
	INCOME	Average family income
	POPULACE	Residential population
Market awareness	AGE	Years inn has been open
	NEAREST	Distance to nearest inn
	PROV	Provincial population per inn
	URBAN	Urban population per inn
Physical	ACCESS	Accessibility
	ARTERY	Major traffic artery
	DISTCBD	Distance to downtown
	SIGNVIS	Sign visibility

EXAMPLE 9.3:   SCREENING HOTEL LOCATION SITES

Selecting good sites is crucial to a hotel chain's success. Of the four major marketing considerations (price, product, promotion, and location), location and product have been shown to be most important for multisite firms. As a result, hotel chain owners who can pick good sites quickly have a distinct competitive advantage.

Exhibit 9.7 shows the initial list of variables included in a study to help a hotel chain screen potential locations for its new hotels. Data were collected on 57 existing sites. Analysis of the data identified the variables that correlated with operating profit in two years. (See Exhibit 9.8.)

EXHIBIT 9.8	A Summary of the Variables That Correlated with Operating Margin

VARIABLE	YEAR 1	YEAR 2
ACCESS	.20	
AGE	.29	0.49
COLLEGE		0.25
DISTCBD		−0.22
EMPLYPCT	−.22	−0.22
INCOME		−0.23
CFTOT		0.22
NEAREST	−.51	
OFCCBD	.30	
POPULACE	.30	0.35
PRICE	.38	0.58
RATE		0.27
PROV	−.32	−0.33
SIGNVIS	.25	
TRAFFIC	.32	
URBAN	−.22	−0.26

SOLUTION

A *regression model* (see Chapter 11) was constructed. Its final form was

$$\text{Profitability} = 39.05 - 5.41 \times \text{Provincial population per inn (1000)}$$
$$+5.86 \times \text{Price of the inn}$$
$$-3.91 \times \text{Square root of the median income of the area (1000)}$$
$$+1.75 \times \text{College students within four km}$$

The model shows that profitability is negatively affected by market penetration, positively affected by price, negatively affected by higher incomes (the inns do better in lower-median-income areas), and positively affected by colleges nearby.

The hotel chain implemented the model on a spreadsheet and routinely uses the spreadsheet to screen potential real estate acquisitions. The founder and president of the hotel chain has accepted the model's validity and no longer feels obligated to personally select the sites.

This example shows that a specific model can be obtained from the requirements of service organizations and used to identify the most important features in site selection.

Summary

In this chapter, the focus was on locating the manufacturing and distribution sites in the supply chain. Certainly the term *logistics* is more comprehensive in scope and includes not only the design issues addressed in this chapter, but also the more comprehensive problem involved with moving goods through the supply chain.

In the chapter, we covered common techniques for designing the supply chain. Linear programming and in particular the transportation method is a useful way to structure these logistics design problems. The problems can be easily solved using the Excel Solver and how to do this is covered in the chapter. Dramatic changes in the global business environment have placed a premium on making decisions relating to how products will be sourced and delivered. These decisions need to be made quickly and must be based on the actual costs involved. Cost modeling using spreadsheets when combined with optimization is a powerful tool for analysis of these problems.

The chapter also briefly looked at locating service facilities such as restaurants and retail stores by using regression analysis. These problems are challenging and spreadsheet modelling is again an important analysis tool.

Key Terms

Centroid method   A technique for locating single facilities that considers the existing facilities, the distances between them, and the volumes of goods to be shipped.

Cross-docking   An approach used in consolidation warehouses where rather than making larger shipments, large shipments are broken down into small shipments for local delivery in an area.

Factor-rating system   An approach for selecting a facility location by combining a diverse set of factors. Point scales are developed for each criterion. Each potential site is then evaluated on each criterion and the points are combined to calculate a rating for the site.

Free trade zone   A closed facility (under the supervision of government customs officials) into which foreign goods can be brought without being subject to the payment of normal import duties.

Hub-and-spoke systems   Systems that combine the idea of consolidation and that of cross-docking.

International logistics   All functions concerned with the movement of materials and finished goods on a global scale.

Logistics   (1) In an industrial context, the art and science of obtaining, producing, and distributing material and product in the proper place and in the proper quantities. (2) In a military sense (where it has greater usage), its meaning also can include the movement of personnel.

Third-party logistics company   A company that manages all or part of another company's product delivery operations.

Trading bloc   A group of countries that agree on a set of special arrangements governing the trading of goods between member countries. Companies may locate in places affected by the agreement to take advantage of new market opportunities.

Transportation method   A special linear programming method that is useful for solving problems involving transporting products from several sources to several destinations.

Formula Review

Centroid

$$C_x = \frac{\sum d_{ix} V_i}{\sum V_i} \quad C_y = \frac{\sum d_{iy} V_i}{\sum d_{iy} V_i}$$

Solved Problem

Cool Air, a manufacturer of automotive air conditioners, currently produces its XB-300 line at three different locations: Plant A, Plant B, and Plant C. Recently management decided to build all compressors, a major product component, in a separate dedicated facility, Plant D.

Using the centroid method and the information displayed in Exhibits 9.9 and 9.10, determine the best location for Plant D. Assume a linear relationship between volumes shipped and shipping costs (no premium charges).

| EXHIBIT 9.9 | Plant Location Matrix |

Centroid_Method

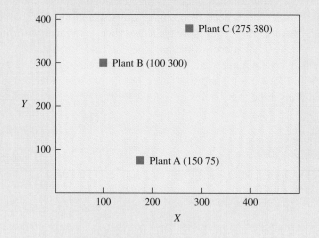

| EXHIBIT 9.10 | Quantity of Compressors Required by Each Plant |

PLANT	COMPRESSORS REQUIRED PER YEAR
A	6000
B	8200
C	7000

SOLUTION

$$d_{1x} = 150 \quad d_{1y} = 75 \quad V_1 = 6000$$
$$d_{2x} = 100 \quad d_{2y} = 300 \quad V_2 = 8200$$
$$d_{3x} = 275 \quad d_{3y} = 380 \quad V_3 = 7000$$

$$C_x = \frac{\sum d_{ix} V_i}{\sum V_i} = \frac{(150 \times 6000) + (100 \times 8200) + (275 \times 7000)}{6000 + 8200 + 7000} = 172$$

$$C_y = \frac{\sum d_{iy} V_i}{\sum d_{iy} V_i} = \frac{(75 \times 6000) + (300 \times 8200) + (380 \times 7000)}{6000 + 8200 + 7000} = 262.7$$

Plant $D[C_x, C_y] = D[172, 263]$

Review and Discussion Questions

1. What motivations typically cause firms to initiate a facilities location or relocation project?
2. List five major reasons why a new electronic components manufacturing firm should move into your city or town.

3. How do facility location decisions differ for service facilities and manufacturing plants?
4. What are the pros and cons of relocating a small or midsized manufacturing firm (that makes mature products) from Canada to Mexico in the post-NAFTA environment?
5. If you could locate your new software development company anywhere in the world, which place would you choose, and why?

Problems

1. Refer to the information given in the solved problem. Suppose management decides to shift 2000 units of production from Plant B to Plant A. Does this change the proposed location of Plant D, the compressor production facility? If so, where should Plant D be located?
2. A small manufacturing facility is being planned that will feed parts to three heavy manufacturing facilities. The locations of the current plants with their coordinates and volume requirements are given in the following table:

PLANT LOCATION	COORDINATES (X, Y)	VOLUME (PARTS PER YEAR)
Windsor	300 320	4000
Detroit	375 470	6000
Kitchener	470 180	3000

Use the centroid method to detsermine the best location for this new facility.
3. Bindley Corporation has a one-year contract to supply motors for all washing machines produced by Rinso Ltd. Rinso manufactures the washers at four locations around the country: Toronto, Fort Worth, San Diego, and Winnipeg. Plans call for the following numbers of washing machines to be produced at each location:

Toronto	50 000
Fort Worth	70 000
San Diego	60 000
Winnipeg	80 000

Bindley has three plants that can produce the motors. The plants and production capacities are

Lethbridge	100 000
Fredericton	100 000
Bloomington	150 000

Due to varying production and transportation costs, the profit Bindley earns on each 1000 units depends on where they were produced and where they were shipped. The following table gives the accounting department estimates of the dollar profit per unit. (Shipment will be made in lots of 1000.)

PRODUCED AT	SHIPPED TO			
	TORONTO	FORT WORTH	SAN DIEGO	WINNIPEG
Lethbridge	7	11	8	13
Fredericton	20	17	12	10
Bloomington	8	18	13	16

Given profit maximization as a criterion, Bindley would like to determine how many motors should be produced at each plant and how many motors should be shipped from each plant to each destination.

a. Develop a transportation grid for this problem.

b. Find the optimal solution using Microsoft® Excel Solver.

4. Rent'R Cars is a multisite car rental company in the city. It is trying out a new "return the car to the location most convenient for you" policy to improve customer service. But this means that the company has to constantly move cars around the city to maintain required levels of vehicle availability. The supply and demand for economy cars, and the total cost of moving these vehicles between sites, are shown below.

From/To	D	E	F	G	Supply
A	$9	$8	$6	$5	50
B	$9	$8	$8	$0	40
C	$5	$3	$3	$10	75
Demand	50	60	25	30	

a. Find the solution that minimizes moving costs using Microsoft® Excel Solver.

b. What would you have to do to the costs to assure that A always sends a car to D as part of the optimal solution?

CASE   Applichem—The Transportation Problem

Applichem management is faced with the difficult problem of allocating to its customers the capacity of manufacturing plants that are located around the world. Management has long recognized that the manufacturing plants differ greatly in efficiency but has had little success in improving the operations of the inefficient plants. At this time, management has decided to focus on how best to use the capacity of its plants given the differences in manufacturing costs that currently exist. They recognize that this study may result in the significant reduction of output or possibly the shutting down of one or more of the existing plants.

Applichem makes a product called Release-ease. Plastics molding manufacturers use this chemical product. Plastic parts are made by injecting hot plastic into a mold made in the shape of the part. After the plastic has sufficiently cooled, the fresh part is removed from the mold and the mold is then reused to make subsequent parts. Release-ease is a dry powder, applied as part of the manufacturing process, which makes it easy to remove the part from the mold.

Applichem has made the product since the early 1950s, and demand has been consistent over time. A recent study by Applichem's market research team has indicated that demand for Release-ease should be fairly steady for the next five years. Although Applichem does have some competition, particularly in the European markets, management feels that as long as they can provide a quality product at a competitive cost, customers should stick with Applichem. Release-ease sells at an average price of $1.00 per kg.

The company owns plants capable of making Release-ease in the following cities: Gary, Indiana, U.S.A.; Windsor, Ontario, Canada; Frankfurt, Germany; Mexico City, Mexico; Caracas, Venezuela; and Osaka, Japan. Although the plants are focused on meeting demand for the immediate surrounding regions, there is considerable exporting and importing of product for various reasons. The following table contains data on how demand has been met during the past year:

PRODUCT MADE AND SHIPPED DURING PAST YEAR (× 100 000 KG)

From/to	Mexico	Canada	Venezuela	European Union	United States	Japan
Mexico City	3.0		6.3			7.9
Windsor		2.6				
Caracas			4.1			
Frankfurt			5.6	20.0	12.4	
Gary					14.0	
Osaka						4.0

Differences in the technologies used in the plants and in local raw material and labour costs created significant differences in the cost to produce Release-ease in the various locations. These costs may change dramatically due to currency valuation and labour law changes in some of the countries. This is especially true in Mexico and Venezuela. The capacity of each plant also differs at each location, and management has no interest in increasing capacity anywhere at this time. The following table gives details on the costs to produce and capacity of each plant:

PLANT PRODUCTION COSTS AND CAPACITY

Plant	Production Cost Plant (per 1000 kg)	Plant Capacity (× 100 000 kg)
Mexico City	95.01	22.0
Windsor, Ontario	97.35	3.7
Caracas	116.34	4.5
Frankfurt	76.69	47.0
Gary	102.93	18.5
Osaka	153.80	5.0

In considering how best to use the capacity of its plants, Applichem management needs to consider the cost of shipping product from one customer region to another. Applichem now commonly ships product in bulk around the world, but it is expensive. The costs involved are not only the transportation costs but also import duties that are assessed by customs in some countries. Applichem is committed to meeting demand, though, and sometimes this is done even though profit might not be made on all orders.

The following table details the demand in each country, the cost to transport product from each plant to each country, and the current import duty rate levied by each country. (These percentages do not reflect current duties.) Import duty is calculated on the approximate production plus transportation cost of product brought into the country. (For example, if the production and shipping cost for 1000 kg of Release-ease shipped into Venezuela were $100, the import duty would be $100 (×0.5 = $50.)

TRANSPORTATION COST (PER 1000 KG), IMPORT DUTIES, AND DEMANDS FOR RELEASE-EASE

Plant/Country	Mexico	Canada	Venezuela	Europe	United States	Japan
Mexico City	0	11.40	7.00	11.00	11.00	14.00
Windsor	11.00	0	9.00	11.50	6.00	13.00
Caracas	7.00	10.00	0	13.00	10.40	14.30
Frankfurt	10.00	11.50	12.50	0	11.20	13.30
Gary	10.00	6.00	11.00	10.00	0	12.50
Osaka	14.00	13.00	12.50	14.20	13.00	0
Total demand (× 100 000 kg)	3.0	2.6	16.0	20.0	26.4	11.9
Import duty	0.0%	0.0%	50.0%	9.5%	4.5%	6.0%

Questions

Given all these data, set up a spreadsheet (Applichem.xls is a start) and answer the following questions for management:

Applichem

1. Evaluate the cost associated with the way Applichem's plant capacity is currently being used.
2. Determine the optimal use of Applichem's plant capacity using the Solver in Excel.
3. What would you recommend that Applichem management do? Why?

Source: This case is roughly based on data contained in "Applichem (A)," Harvard Business School, 9-685-051.

Footnotes

[1]A. M. Rodrigues, D. J. Bowersox and R. J. Calantone. "Estimation of Global and National Logistics Expenditures: 2002 Data Update," *Journal of Business Logistics,* 26, 2, 2005, pp. 1–16.

[2]M. E. Porter, "The Competitive Advantage of Nation," *Harvard Business Review,* March–April 1990.

Selected Bibliography

Ballou, R. H. *Business Logistics Management.* 4th ed. Upper Saddle River, NJ: Prentice Hall, 1998.

Drezner, Z., and H. Hamacher. *Facility Location: Applications and Theory.* Berlin: Springer Verlag, 2002.

Klamroth, K. *Single Facility Location Problems with Barriers.* Berlin: Springer-Verlag Telos, 2002.

CHAPTER 100

LEAN (JIT) OPERATIONS

1. Learn how a pull operations system works.
2. Understand Toyota Production System concepts.
3. Know how value stream mapping can be used to identify wasteful activities.
4. Know how kanban cards can be used to control a pull system.
5. Understand about lean facility design.
6. Understand lean implementation issues.
7. Be familiar with examples of lean concepts applied to service systems.

LEAN SIX SIGMA AT SOLECTRON

Solectron is a leading provider of electronics manufacturing and integrated supply chain services. Solectron was acquired by Singapore based competitor Flextronics in 2008. In Canada, Flextronics has seven locations with over 65 000 square metres (over 700 000 square feet) of manufacturing and logistics space.

At Solectron, Lean Six Sigma focuses on eliminating waste and variability throughout the supply chain, and mandates that every company activity add value for customers.

Lean, which is based on the Toyota production system, is driven by five key principles at Solectron:

Value: Understanding the value of the work performed by defining it as something that customers want to pay for.

Value Chain: Mapping the process steps throughout the supply chain by identifying the steps that add value and striving to eliminate those that add waste.

Pull: Eliminating the primary sources of waste—overproduction—by only producing what customers want, when they want it. This means starting production only when the customer "pulls."

Flow: Removing other major sources of waste—bloated inventory and waiting—by ensuring that goods flow continuously through the supply chain and never stop.

Kaizen/Continuous Improvement: Striving for the total elimination of waste through a succession of small, action-oriented (kaizen) events within the production process.

To complement Lean, Six Sigma is the well-known, data-driven set of standards that drives exceptional quality in Solectron operations. It requires in-depth statistical metrics to analyze quality at all levels of the supply chain, eliminating defects. Six Sigma—when combined with Lean—allows for easier identification and quicker resolution of quality issues or problems, and reaps quick results while opening people's eyes to new and better possibilities on plant floors.

Lean Six Sigma is a differentiator in the electronic manfacturing services (EMS) industry and fundamental to Solectron's overall strategy and future success. It significantly improves Solectron's quality and reduces waste. It reinvents the way they serve customers. It empowers every employee to help make drastic improvements in the company's performance. It enhances partnerships with key suppliers across the supply chain. And it drives new ways of thinking about business.

■ Source: www.solectron.com.
www.flextronics.com

The most significant production management approach of the past 50 years is *lean*[1] or just in time (JIT) production. In the context of supply chains, *lean* production refers to a focus on eliminating as much waste as possible. Moves that are not needed, unnecessary processing steps, and excess inventory in the supply chain are targets for improvement during the *leaning* process. Some consultants in industry have coined the phrase *value* chain to refer to an emphasis that each step in the supply chain processes that delivers products and services to customers should create value. If a step does not create value, it should be removed from the process.

The term "lean production" has evolved from the JIT production concepts pioneered in Japan at Toyota (see OSMP on Toyota later in this chapter). JIT gained worldwide prominence in the 1970s, but some of its philosophy can be traced to the early 1900s in the United States. Henry Ford used JIT concepts as he streamlined his moving assembly lines to make automobiles. For example, to eliminate waste, he used the bottom of the packing crates for car seats as the floor board of the car. In 1914, as an incentive to motivate employees to work better, he reduced the work hours per day from 9 hours to 8 hours. He also set the minimum wage in his factory to $5 per day when the prevailing minimum wage in the U.S. was $2 per day. As he said of his floor sweepers, "if his heart is in his job, he can save us five dollars a day by picking up small tools instead of sweeping them out." He also believed that these higher wages would increase the purchasing power which was good for the economy.[2]

Global

Although elements of JIT were being used by Toyota from its very inception in the 1930s (in fact, some of the home-grown principles themselves predate the establishment of Toyota and originated from the textile factory that Toyota's founding family used to own), it was not fully refined until the 1970s, when Tai-ichi Ohno of Toyota Motors used JIT to take Toyota's cars to the forefront of delivery time and quality.

In the 1990s, *lean* became a more global term for the evolution of the JIT philosophy of systematically eliminating waste throughout the supply chain. This chapter relates the logic of lean production; its evolution in Japan at Toyota; how it is implemented; and its current applications in manufacturing and service companies such as Solectron described in the opening vignette. The number of Canadian companies that use aspects of lean are too numerous to mention, though some examples are discussed in the chapter to provide an illustration of lean applications as well as its popularity in Canada.

LEAN LOGIC

Lean production is an integrated set of activities designed to achieve production using minimal inventories of raw materials, work-in-process, and finished goods. Parts arrive at the next workstation "just in time" and are completed and move through the process quickly.

EXHIBIT 10.1 | Lean Production Pull System

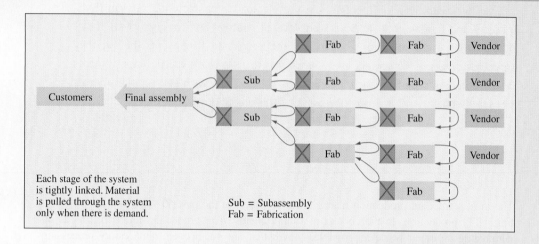

Each stage of the system is tightly linked. Material is pulled through the system only when there is demand.

Sub = Subassembly
Fab = Fabrication

Lean is also based on the logic that nothing will be produced until it is needed. Exhibit 10.1 illustrates the process. Production need is created by actual demand for the product. In theory, when an item is sold, the market pulls a replacement from the last position in the system—final assembly in this case. This triggers an order to the factory production line, where a worker then pulls another unit from an upstream station in the flow to replace the unit taken. This upstream station then pulls from the next station further upstream and so on back to the release of raw materials. To enable this pull process to work smoothly, lean production demands high levels of quality at each stage of the process, strong vendor (supplier) relations, and a fairly predictable demand for the end product.

THE TOYOTA PRODUCTION SYSTEM

In this section, we develop the philosophy and elements of lean production developed in Japan and embodied in the Toyota Production System—the benchmark for lean manufacturing. The Toyota Production System was developed to improve quality and productivity and is predicated upon two philosophies that are central to the Japanese culture: elimination of waste and respect for people.[3]

Elimination of Waste

Waste (called *muda* in Japanese), as defined by Toyota's past president Fujio Cho, is "anything other than the minimum amount of equipment, materials, parts, and workers (working time) which are absolutely essential to production." An expanded lean definition advanced by Cho identifies seven prominent types of waste to be eliminated from the supply chain: (1) waste from overproduction, (2) waste of waiting time, (3) transportation waste, (4) inventory waste, (5) processing waste, (6) waste of motion, and (7) waste from product defects.[4]

An approach that has been adopted to analyze a process to identify steps that can be improved is called **value chain mapping, also called value stream mapping**. The idea is to develop a detailed diagram of a process that clearly shows those activities that add value, activities that do not add value, and steps that involve just waiting. See the example provided by the Superfactory Learning Centre in the box on the next page. By drawing a

Global

Value Chain Mapping

Value chain mapping is widely used as a means of eliminating waste in a supply chain process. The value chain is a network of steps from beginning to end that provides the result for the customer.

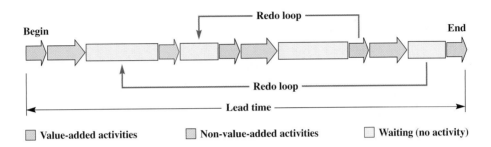

Some activities add value to the result, some do not add value, and sometimes the process stops with no activity at all.

Value Chain Principles

1. Keep the value chain moving at maximum velocity.
2. Eliminate waste that stops, slows down, or diverts the value chain.
3. Concentrate on removing waste rather than speeding up value-adding operations.
4. Look for waste in the factory, office, physical, procedural, and technical operations.

■ Source: Superfactory Learning Center, http://www.superfactory.com/.

diagram that identifies the non-value-adding activities, we can understand what changes might have the biggest impact on leaning the process. For a more complete discussion of the value stream mapping methodology, see Jared Lovelle.[5]

Value chain mapping is a great way to analyze existing processes. The following design principles guide the design of lean supply chains:

1. Just-in-time production.
2. Focus on quality.
3. Lean process and product design.
4. Workforce involvement.
5. Close supplier relationships.
6. Problem solving and continuous improvement.

JIT Production

JIT means producing what is needed when needed and no more. Anything over the minimum amount necessary is viewed as waste, because effort and material expended for something not needed now cannot be utilized now. This is in contrast to relying on extra material just in case something goes wrong. Some of the key requirements of JIT production are discussed below.

Production in Small Lots JIT is typically applied to repetitive manufacturing, which is when the same or similar items are made one after another. JIT does not require large volumes and can be applied to any repetitive segments of a business regardless of where they appear. Under JIT, the ideal lot size or production batch is one. Although workstations may be geographically dispersed, the Japanese minimize transit time and keep transfer quantities small—typically one-tenth of a day's production. Vendors even ship several times a day to their customers to keep lot sizes small and inventory low. The goal is to drive all inventory to as close to zero as possible, thus minimizing inventory investment and shortening lead times. Small lot sizes also result in less waste if a defective batch is produced. As the OSMP on lot sizes shows, small lot sizes are applicable in services too.

Small lot sizes also result in lower inventory levels. This has advantages. For example, when inventory levels are low, quality problems become very visible. Exhibit 10.2 illustrates this idea. If the water in a lake represents inventory, then rocks represent problems that could occur in a firm. In Exhibit 10.2A, the high level of water (inventory) hides the problems (rocks). Management assumes everything is fine, but the reason why production is moving smoothly (the ship is able to sail without hitting rocks) is because of the high level of inventory. In practice, this high level of inventory results in excessive costs (inventory is discussed in more detail in Chapter 13) and the firm will become uncompetitive. The lean philosophy is to reduce this inventory level (the water level drops) as in Exhibit 10.2B. The ship now hits the rocks. This means that production is no longer proceeding smoothly and customers experience shortages because the level of inventory is no longer sufficient to cover sales when the process is stopped due to the problems. To improve the situation, the company will be forced to address one or more of these problems, for example, excessive machine downtime, as shown. Once this problem is successfully addressed (the rock is removed) as in Exhibit 10.2C, the ship can sail again, i.e., production proceeds smoothly again. An important aspect of JIT is continuous improvement (to be discussed later). Lean firms follow the PDCA cycle (Plan-Do-Check-Act from Chapter 7). So, any time production is proceeding smoothly, lean firms reduce to inventory level to expose more problems (perhaps the scrap and vendor delinquency rocks in Exhibit 10.2) and they will be forced to solve these problems. So there is a focus on continuous problem identification and improvement.

Inventory Hides Problems

EXHIBIT 10.2

A.

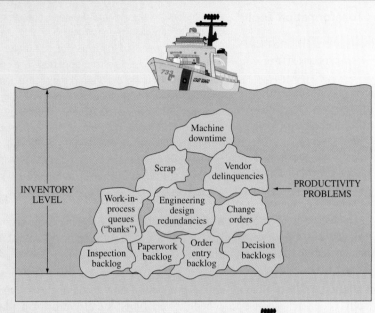

B.

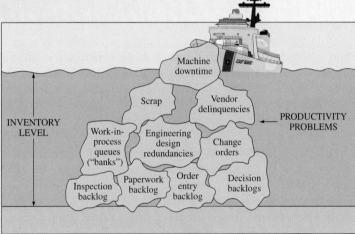

C.

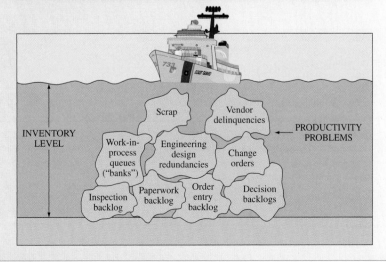

Operations and Supply Management in Practice

Small-Lot Principle Applies To Information Too!

Large-lot information processing problems are similar to those faced by manufacturing managers when producing in large batches (overtime, additional costs, transcription, identification, and calculation errors, as well as interruptions to production and costly rework of defects). Thus it is important that managers of information flow also recognize the advantages that small-lot information processing can provide.

For example, a large childcare agency was responsible for thousands of children daily. The integrity of its database of parent telephone numbers, children's known allergies, and other information was vital. However, the database never seemed to be current, making it unreliable.

Upon analysis, a consultant realized that the employees entering the data had other responsibilities. As a result,

they tended to accumulate database changes over long periods of time and then update the database in a large batch, which resulted in errors due to fatigue. When the method was changed so that updates were completed in small daily lots, the problem disappeared. Since the employees were at their computers anyway, set-up was minimal, and entering a few records each day was easier than large-lot entry. The cost of the change was virtually nothing and it was very successful. Note that small lots can be completed much quicker than large lots. This leads to lower customer wait times, a competitive advantage in any business.

■ Source: Frank Gue, "Small Lot Principle Applies to Information," *APICS—The Performance Advantage* (August 1999), p. 56.

Uniform Plant Loading Smoothing the production flow to dampen the reaction waves that normally occur in response to schedule variations is called **uniform plant loading** (or, in Japanese, **heijunka**). When a change is made in a final assembly, the changes are magnified throughout the line and the supply chain (recall the bullwhip effect from Chapter 8). The only way to eliminate the problem is to make adjustments as small as possible by setting a firm monthly production plan for which the output rate is frozen.

Interactive Operations Management

Toyota found it could do this by building the same mix of products every day in small quantities. Thus, Toyota always has a total mix available to respond to variations in demand. A Toyota example is shown in Exhibit 10.3. Monthly car style quantities are reduced to daily quantities (assuming a 20-day month) in order to compute a model *cycle time* (defined here as the time between two identical units being completed on the line). The cycle-time figure is used to adjust resources to produce the precise quantity needed. The speed of equipment or of the production line is adjusted so only the needed quantity is produced each day. JIT strives to produce on schedule, on cost, and on quality.

So lean production desires a stable schedule over a lengthy time horizon. This is accomplished by level scheduling, freeze windows, and underutilization of capacity. A **level schedule** is one that requires material to be pulled into final assembly in a pattern uniform

---

EXHIBIT 10.3   Toyota Example of Mixed-Model Production Cycle in a Japanese Assembly Plant

MODEL	MONTHLY QUANTITY	DAILY QUANTITY	MODEL CYCLE TIME (MINUTES)
Sedan	5000	250	2
Hardtop	2500	125	4
Wagon	2500	125	4

Sequence: Sedan, hardtop, sedan, wagon, sedan, hardtop, sedan, wagon, and so on (one minute apart).

enough to allow the various elements of production to respond to pull signals. It does not necessarily mean that the usage of every part on an assembly line is identified hour by hour for days on end; it does mean that a given production system equipped with flexible set-ups and a fixed amount of material in the pipelines can respond.[6]

The term **freeze window** refers to that period of time during which the schedule is fixed and no further changes are possible. An added benefit of the stable schedule is seen in how parts and components are accounted for in a pull system. Here, the concept of **backflush** is used where the parts that go into each unit of the product are periodically removed from inventory and accounted for based on the number of units produced. This eliminates much of the shop-floor data collection activity, which is required if each part must be tracked and accounted for during production.

Underutilization and overutilization of capacity are features of lean production. Conventional approaches use safety stocks and early deliveries as a hedge against production problems like poor quality, machine failures, and unanticipated bottlenecks in traditional manufacturing. Under lean production, excess labour, machines, and overtime provide the hedge. The excess capacity in labour and equipment that results is much cheaper than carrying excess inventory. When demand is greater than expected, overtime must be used. Often, part-time labour is used when additional capacity is needed. During idle periods, personnel can be put to work on other activities such as special projects, work group activities, and work station housekeeping.

Kanban Production Control Systems A kanban control system uses a signalling device to regulate JIT flows. **Kanban** means "sign" or "instruction card" in Japanese. In a paperless control system, containers can be used instead of cards. The cards or containers make up the **kanban pull system**. The authority to produce or supply additional parts comes from downstream operations. Consider Exhibit 10.4, where we show an assembly line that is supplied with parts by a machine centre. The machine centre makes two parts, A and B. These two parts are stored in containers that are located next to the assembly line and next to the machine centre. Each container next to the assembly line has a withdrawal kanban, and each container next to the machine centre has a production kanban. This is often referred to as a two-card kanban system.

When the assembly line takes the first part A from a full container, a worker takes the withdrawal kanban from the container, and takes the card to the machine centre storage area. In the machine centre area, the worker finds a container of part A, removes the production kanban, and replaces it with the withdrawal kanban. Placement of this card on the container authorizes the movement of the container to the assembly line. The freed production kanban

---

Flow of Two Kanbans   **EXHIBIT 10.4**

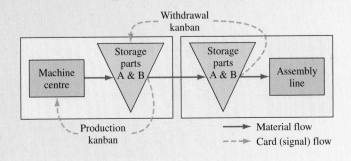

is placed on a rack by the machine centre, which authorizes the production of another lot of material. A similar process is followed for part B. The cards on the rack become the dispatch list for the machine centre. Cards are not the only way to signal the need for production of a part; other visual methods are possible, as shown in Exhibit 10.5.

The following are some other possible approaches:

Kanban squares.   Some companies use marked spaces on the floor or on a table to identify where material should be stored. When the square is empty, the supplying operations are authorized to produce; when the square is full, no parts are needed.

Container system.   Sometimes the container itself can be used as a signal device. In this case, an empty container on the factory floor visually signals the need to fill it. The amount of inventory is adjusted by simply adding or removing containers.

Coloured golf balls.   At a Kawasaki engine plant, when a part used in a subassembly is down to its reorder point, the assembler rolls a coloured golf ball down a pipe to the replenishment machine centre. This tells the operator which part to make next. Many variations on this approach have been developed.

The kanban pull approach can be used not only within a manufacturing facility but also between manufacturing facilities (pulling engines and transmissions into an automobile assembly operation, for example) and between manufacturers and external suppliers.

Determining the Number of Kanbans Needed Setting up a kanban control system requires determining the number of kanban cards (or containers) needed. In a two-card system, we are finding the number of sets of withdrawal and production cards. The kanban cards represent the number of containers of material that flow back and forth between the supplier and the user areas. Each container represents the minimum production lot size to

---

EXHIBIT 10.5   Diagram of Outbound Stockpoint with Warning Signal Marker

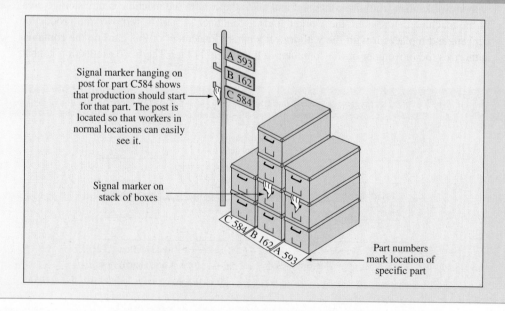

Signal marker hanging on post for part C584 shows that production should start for that part. The post is located so that workers in normal locations can easily see it.

Signal marker on stack of boxes

Part numbers mark location of specific part

be supplied. The number of containers, therefore, directly controls the amount of work-in-process inventory in the system.

Accurately estimating the lead time needed to produce a container of parts is the key to determining the number of containers. This lead time is a function of the processing time for the container, any waiting time during the production process, and the time required to transport the material to the user. Enough kanbans are needed to cover the expected demand during this lead time plus some additional amount for safety stock.

The kanban system does not produce zero inventory; rather, it controls the amount of material that can be in process at a time—the number of containers of each item. The kanban system can be easily adjusted to fit the current way the system is operating, because card sets can be easily added or removed from the system. If the workers find that they are not able to consistently replenish the item on time, an additional container of material, with the accompanying kanban cards, can be added. If it is found that excess containers of material accumulate, card sets can be easily removed, thus reducing the amount of inventory. Reducing kanbans can also be used to improve the process, as shown in Exhibit 10-2.

Minimized Set-up Times Because small lot sizes are the norm, machines must be quickly set up to produce the mixed models on the line. Would you make only one tray of cookies at a time if preheating (setting up) your oven took eight hours? You would probably make many trays to justify the set-up time. In a widely cited example from the late 1970s, Toyota teams of press operators producing car hoods and fenders were able to change an 800-ton press in 10 minutes, compared with the average of six hours for U.S. workers and four hours for German workers. (Now, however, such speed is common in most U.S. auto plants.) This set-up reduction philosophy is also called Single-Minute-Exchange-of-Die (SMED).

Set-ups consist of the **internal** part, activities that can be done only when the machine or resource is stopped (idle), and the **external** part, activities that can be done while the machine is running. For example, at the University of British Columbia Hospital in Vancouver, the complete surgery was being performed in one operating theatre. That meant the surgeon (a valuable resource) was idle while pre- and post-surgery procedures were being done (all internal set-up). Then another theatre was added and the pre- and post-procedures were separated from the critical parts of the operation. The surgeon now switches between the critical parts in the two theatres (where pre-surgery procedures have already been done), and is never idle, because pre- and post-procedures are now external set-up. Many more patients are now being operated on per day because of this improvement.[7] Thus, lean attempts to convert as much of the internal set-up as possible to external set-up in addition to reducing the internal set-up time itself.

Focus on Quality

Lean places high emphasis on quality. You may recall in Chapter 7 that quality gurus such as Deming were influential in Japan. Thus, it is not surprising that lean focuses on defect prevention or quality at the source. This means "do it right the first time" and, when something goes wrong, stop the process or assembly line immediately. Factory workers become their own inspectors, personally responsible for the quality of their output. Workers concentrate on one part of the job at a time so quality problems are uncovered. If the pace is too fast, if the worker finds a quality problem, or if a safety issue is discovered, the worker is obligated to push a button to stop the line and turn on a visual signal (this principle is called **jidoka** in Japanese; see the photo on the andon system at Kawasaki.). People from other areas respond to the alarm and the problem. Workers are empowered to do their own maintenance and housekeeping until the problem is fixed. The lean process uses as many poke-yoke (Japanese for failsafe mechanisms) as possible to prevent defects and promote safety in much the same way an electrical plug uses different size pins to ensure that the plug can be inserted in the socket only in the correct way.

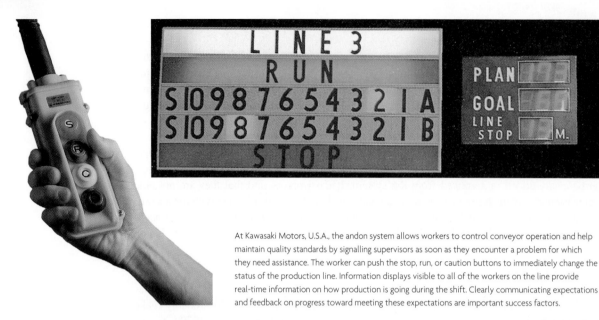

At Kawasaki Motors, U.S.A., the andon system allows workers to control conveyor operation and help maintain quality standards by signalling supervisors as soon as they encounter a problem for which they need assistance. The worker can push the stop, run, or caution buttons to immediately change the status of the production line. Information displays visible to all of the workers on the line provide real-time information on how production is going during the shift. Clearly communicating expectations and feedback on progress toward meeting these expectations are important success factors.

As will be discussed, lean often uses manufacturing cells (see photograph in the Manufacturing Cell section in Chapter 5, which shows cells at Standard Aero in Winnipeg). Inside each cell as shown there is a board where the status of the line is shown. An electronic version of this type of board, called an **andon** board, is shown in the photograph below from Kawasaki Motors. This board can be used to identify problems and bottlenecks in the line. Thus, in lean operations, there is an emphasis on visual control. The notion is that if problems are clearly visible, it will be easier to address them.

Lean and Six-Sigma quality have merged in theory and practice. Six-Sigma quality (Chapter 7) is the practice of building quality into the process rather than relying on inspection. It also refers to the theory of employees assuming responsibility for the quality of their own work. When employees are responsible for quality, lean works at its best because only good-quality products are pulled through the system. When all products are good, no "just-in-case" extra inventory is needed. Thus organizations can achieve high quality and high productivity. By using statistical quality control and other quality improvement tools (discussed in Chapter 7) and training workers to maintain quality, inspections can be reduced to the first and last units produced. If they are perfect, we can assume the other units between these points are perfect as well.

A foundation of quality is improved product design. Standard product configurations, fewer parts, and standardized parts are important elements in lean production. These design modifications reduce variability in the end item or in the materials that go into the product. Besides improving the producibility of a product, product design activities can facilitate the processing of engineering changes.

Lean Process and Product Design

Lean requires the plant layout to be designed to ensure balanced work flow with a minimum of work-in-process inventory. Each workstation is part of a production line, whether or not a physical line actually exists. Capacity is balanced using the same logic for an assembly line, and operations are linked through a pull system. In addition, the system designer must visualize how all aspects of the internal and external logistics system tie to the layout.

Preventive maintenance is emphasized to ensure that flows are not interrupted by down time or malfunctioning equipment. Preventive maintenance involves periodic inspection and repair designed to keep a machine reliable. Operators perform much of the maintenance because they are most familiar with their machines and because machines are easier to repair, as lean operations favour several simple machines rather than one large complex one.

Another factor in lean layout is how the machinery is configured. Sometimes it is set up to allow easy rearrangement as is the case at Spartan Plastics Canada Ltd. in London, Ontario, where equipment was placed on wheels to facilitate easy mixing and matching of equipment to product configurations.[8]

The **5S** philosophy is based on five Japanese words starting with S that imply a clean and safe workplace. 5S starts with sorting and discarding items that are not needed. For example, the Cutler Hammer factory in Calgary, which manufactures power supply equipment, has a designated area within the facility where all employees are expected to discard items, whether from the factory floor or offices, that have not been used for some time. This helps keep the workplace neat. FiveS implies arranging the workplace and keeping it clean. Each tool used should have its place (there may be an outline of each tool drawn on the tool board so it's easy to locate and retrieve), and the equipment and workplace should be cleaned frequently. In addition, 5S requires a proper personal and work environment, which means wearing the right clothing and safety equipment. Furthermore, the physical layout should be designed to minimize stress and the equipment must be operated in a safe manner. Finally, like the PDCA model of Shewhart, 5S requires that process improvements be made permanent by including them in standard operating procedures. ICICI Bank Canada is an example of a pure service organization that has implemented 5S.

Lean Applications for Line Flows Exhibit 10.6 illustrates a pull system in a simple line flow (assembly line, discussed in Chapter 5). In a pure lean environment, no employee does any work until the product has been pulled from the end of the line by the market. The product could be a final product or a component used in later production. When a product is pulled, a replenishment unit is pulled from upstream operations. In the exhibit, an item of finished goods is pulled from F, the finished goods inventory. The inventory clerk then goes to processing station E and takes replacement product to fill the void. This pattern continues up the line to worker A, who pulls material from the raw material inventory. The rules of the flow layout require employees to keep completed units at their work station, and if someone takes the completed work away, the employee must move upstream in the flow to get additional work to complete.

Lean Applications for Workcentre Shops Although workcentres are characterized by low volume and high variety (see Chapter 5), lean can be used if demand can be stabilized to permit repetitive manufacturing. Stabilizing demand is usually easier to accomplish when the demand is from a downstream production stage rather than an end customer. (The logic is that internal customers can smooth their input requirements far more easily than a distributor or individual purchaser.)

Lean in a Line Flow Layout   EXHIBIT 10.6

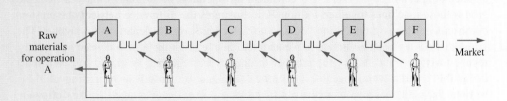

| EXHIBIT 10.7 | A Lean Job Shop Layout Showing the Materials Handling Vehicle Route Connecting Workcentres and Line Operations |

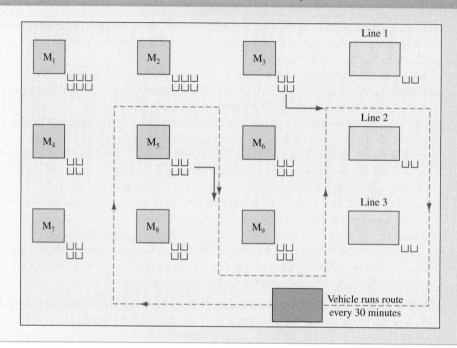

Factory machining centres, paint shops, and shirt making are examples of workcentre operations that process parts and components before they reach final production stages. By way of example, consider the production system in Exhibit 10.7. If a workcentre produces nine different parts used by several product varieties that are produced just in time, the workcentre keeps containers of completed output of all nine parts at the centre to be picked up by users. Operators could make periodic rounds throughout the facility (hourly or more frequently) to pick up empty containers and drop them off at the corresponding upstream workcentre and to pick up full containers. In Exhibit 10.7, automatic guided vehicles pick up and deliver part numbers M_5 and M_3 to lines 2 and 3 for processing. These handling procedures can be manual or automated, but either way, these periodic pickups and drop-offs allow the system to operate in a just-in-time mode.

Group Technology (GT) GT is a philosophy in which similar parts are grouped into families, and the processes required to make the parts are arranged in a specialized manufacturing cell (see discussion in the Manufacturing Cell section in Chapter 5 which shows cells at Standard Aero in Winnipeg). Instead of transferring jobs from one department to another to specialized workers, GT considers all operations required to make a part and groups those machines together. Exhibit 10.8 illustrates the difference between the clusters of various machines grouped into work centres for parts versus departmental layouts. The group technology cells eliminate movement and queue (waiting) time between operations, reduce inventory, and reduce the number of employees required. Workers, however, must be flexible to run several machines and processes. Due to their advanced skill level, these workers have increased job security. GT provides several advantages as the following example on Canon shows.

EXHIBIT 10.8

Group Technology versus Departmental Specialty

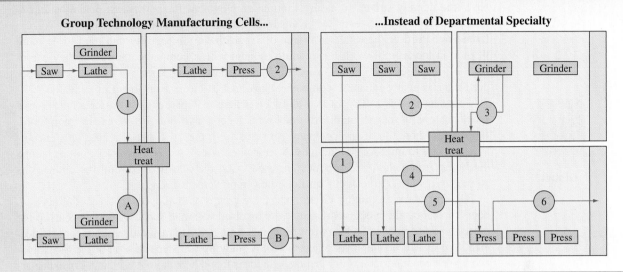

Group Technology Manufacturing Cells...   ...Instead of Departmental Specialty

Canon, a major electronic equipment maker, with 54 plants in 23 countries manufacturing cameras, printers, and copiers, recently implemented group technology in all of its assembly lines. As a result, work-in-process (WIP) inventory in its factories has been reduced from three days to six hours. Factory operating costs have been reduced by US$1.5 billion. Canon has decreased its real estate costs by $279 million because cells require less room, and because the reduced inventory level has resulted in fewer required warehouses (down from thirty-seven to eight).[9]

Focused Factory Networks The Japanese build small specialized plants rather than large vertically integrated manufacturing facilities. (Toyota has 12 plants located in and around Toyota City and other areas of Aichi Prefecture.) They find large operations and their bureaucracies difficult to manage and not in line with their management styles. Plants designed for one purpose can be constructed and operated more economically. The bulk of Japanese plants, some 60 000, have between 30 and 1000 workers. Even tire manufacturers, who normally produce in large batches, are building smaller plants with newer technology, close to the automobile factories, which will allow them to reduce inventories and transportation time, and produce just-in-time.

Concurrent Engineering In terms of product design, lean firms use **concurrent engineering**. Traditionally in product design, the design of the product was sequential. For example, the marketing department would come up with the concept, the designers would design it and manufacturing would produce it. This is ineffective from a time and quality perspective. For example, manufacturing may find that the designed product is very expensive to produce and may send it back for redesign, leading to additional time and cost. In concurrent engineering, personnel from the different functions such as marketing, design, manufacturing, costing and even customers and suppliers, are involved in product design so that issues are exposed early in the process. This avoids the problems discussed in sequential design. The result is that products are launched quicker and at a lower cost.

Workforce Involvement

Respect for people and their capabilities is a key to the Toyota production system. They have traditionally striven to assure lifetime employment for permanent positions and to maintain level payrolls even when business conditions deteriorate. Permanent workers (about one-third of the total workforce of Japan) have job security and tend to be more flexible in the type of work they can do, remain with a company, and do all they can to help a firm achieve its goals. (In recent years, because of competitive pressures and poor performance, many Japanese companies have had to move away from this ideal.)

Global

Company unions at Toyota as well as elsewhere in Japan exist to foster a cooperative relationship with management. All employees receive two bonuses a year in good times. Employees know that if the company performs well, they will get a bonus. This encourages workers to improve productivity. Management views workers as assets, not as human machines. Automation and robotics are used extensively to perform dull or routine jobs so employees are free to focus on important improvement tasks.

JIT firms often use **quality circles**, which are groups of employees that meet during work hours to analyze the processes that they are involved with and suggest improvements to the process and the product. So lean firms encourage employees to make suggestions for improvement (see OSMP on employee suggestions). A study by Christer Karlsson of the Stockholm School of Economics points out that the lean ideas found here are not used in all manufacturing companies in Japan. Rather, they are applied situationally and where appropriate. However, the fundamental ideas of elimination of waste and respect for workers are still foundations of the exceptional productivity of most Japanese manufacturing companies.[10]

Close Supplier Relationships

Lean firms like Toyota rely heavily on subcontractor networks. Indeed, more than 90 percent of all Japanese companies are part of the supplier network of small firms. Some suppliers are specialists in a narrow field, usually serving multiple customers. Firms have long-term partnerships with their suppliers and customers. Suppliers consider themselves part of a customer's family. The company and suppliers may be part of a close network of companies, not all of which may be suppliers, called a **keiretsu**. For example, a keiretsu may have a bank as one of the organizations in the network, which makes it easier for the companies in the network to obtain financing.

In Chapter 8, we discussed the recent change in procurement philosophy from one of trying to make many vendors compete with each other to get the best price to one that fosters long-term collaborative relationships with fewer suppliers. Lean was one of the influential factors in this phenomenon. This is called *single sourcing*, though in practice

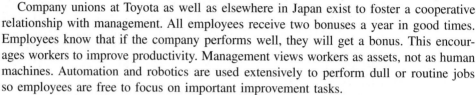

Operations and Supply Management in Practice

Employee Suggestions Pay Off at Canada Post

Canada Post employee Craig Johnson earned a company reward of $10 000 (as well as the respect of his bosses and the admiration of his peers) for an innovation developed late one night in October 2004 on a Canada Post assembly line. He modified the sorting line machinery to generate mail barcodes on the fly. Previously, packages without barcodes had to be sorted manually by clerks like Mr. Johnston and clogged up the machines. The time-saving idea, now being rolled out nationwide, has reduced the number of unmarked wayward parcels employees have to sort by 20 percent. The savings to Canada Post is expected to be significant.

The $10 000 came through the Canada Post employee involvement award program, an initiative designed to encourage and reward innovation on the job. This is an example of a culture of innovation at work, in which employees are encouraged to generate new ideas that benefit both themselves and their organization.

■ Source: Rob Shaw, "Reward Employee Ideas—Literally," *The Globe and Mail*, August 19, 2005, C1.

each component will have more than one vendor as most customers do not want to put all their eggs in one basket.

Another aspect of lean sourcing is that vendors are often located close to the customer. This allows for frequent deliveries in small lots and face to face meetings to improve the product and the supply chain. The philosophy of close relationships with geographically proximal suppliers has many benefits, as the OSMP on Toyota shows.

Lean firms share their projected usage requirements with its vendors, so the vendors have a long-run picture of the demands that will be placed on their production and distribution systems. This avoids the bullwhip effect. Some vendors are linked online with a customer to share production scheduling and input needs data. This permits vendors to develop level production systems thus perpetuating the lean system all along the supply chain. Confidence in the supplier or vendor's delivery commitment allows reductions of buffer inventories. Maintaining stock at a lean level requires frequent deliveries during the day. Some suppliers even deliver to a location on the production line and not at a receiving dock. When vendors adopt quality practices, incoming receiving inspections of their products can be bypassed.

North American manufacturers have moved in the direction of closer co-operation with suppliers. For example, Intier Automotive Inc. of Newmarket, Ontario, got not only a contract to supply interiors for the next generation of small cars for General Motors, but also to manage the design and development of the interiors.[11] Intier's parent company, Aurora, Ontario-based Magna International, is a leading global supplier of technologically-advanced automotive systems, components, and complete modules to the major automobile manufacturers. Not only does Magna have 238 manufacturing divisions, it also has 50 product development and engineering centres throughout North America, Europe, Asia, Africa and South America.[12] This allows them to move from being just a supplier to being a partner to the automobile companies. In fact, Magna has even moved one step further. It designs and assembles entire vehicles for BMW. Despite these examples, it still appears that, compared to their North American competitors, Japanese automakers collaborate more with their suppliers, and help improve their cost and quality, rather than just demanding lower prices.[13, 14]

Operations and Supply Management in Practice

JIT at Toyota's North American Plants

No discussion about JIT is complete without mentioning Toyota, the creator of the JIT manufacturing system and still one of its leading practitioners. However, Toyota will still tell you it has not mastered the art and views JIT as a process that can be continually improved upon. Different Toyota plants, such as the ones in Cambridge, Ontario, and Georgetown, Kentucky, employ JIT principles in a slightly different fashion depending on the plant attributes and supply base. Here are some of the features and results at those plants:

Eighty percent of materials used in Georgetown come from North America. The closer suppliers deliver more often than the farther ones. At Georgetown, most suppliers are within 300 km of the plant. At any given time at the Kentucky (or Cambridge) plant there is only three to four hours' worth of inventory; however, parts sourced from overseas may have up to five days worth of inventory. Between 1996

and 1997, Toyota was able to reduce the time it takes to produce an engine at Georgetown from 1.6 hours to 1.26 hours (21 percent). This was achieved through a kaizen (problem solving and continuous improvement) program.

In Cambridge, by working with TMM Canada, its logistics provider, Toyota has been able to cut in-house inventories by 28 percent, transportation lead time by 31 percent, and parts storage space by 37 percent. Only once has a parts shortage apparently hampered production. The Cambridge facility has about 200 suppliers. On average, TMM Canada picks up material 7.8 times per day from each supplier. At the plant, the parts bins are kept close to the line, eliminating five steps between workers and parts bins and gaining the equivalent of 6.25 workers in efficiency.

Toyota's production control process uses simple (though not simplistic) techniques such as the kanban system and co-operating with suppliers to ensure timely delivery and good quality. Toyota does not inspect incoming inventory.

Continued

As an example of simplicity and supplier co-operation, consider the following: With a US$12 dryer, a Toyota executive proved to engineers from Michigan's Summit Polymers Inc., a supplier, that their US$280 000 investment in robots and a paint oven to bake the dashboard vents they produce was actually causing quality problems and increasing costs. The equipment took up to 90 minutes to dry the paint and also caused quality flaws because parts gathered dust as they crept along a conveyor. The hair dryer did the job in less than three minutes. Summit's engineers replaced their paint system with some US$150 spray guns and a few light bulbs for drying and integrated the painting into the final assembly process. Along with some other changes using Toyota's help, Summit cut its defect rate to less than 60 per million parts from 3000 per million. As another example, Automotive Sunroof-Customcraft (ASC) Inc., of Kitchener, Ontario, which converts Solara coupe bodies to convertibles, developed many error-proofing techniques and process improvements with Toyota's help.

As part of its continuous improvement philosophy, Toyota is now moving beyond production management to improvement in the marketing area. It plans to improve customer choice and satisfaction by allowing customers to pick the colour and options on some vehicle models and have the vehicle delivered in two weeks.

Toyota's plants are among the most flexible in the auto industry, with the ability to build multiple models on the same line and to redesign the lines faster than its competitors. Toyota also avoids laying off workers as part of its commitment to the well-being of its employees. As of February 2009, despite the severe global economic downturn, while competitors are laying off workers, Toyota has no plans to do so. All employees, including executives, will be taking pay cuts as shared sacrifice. The slowdown in production is also seen as an opportunity because there will be time to identify ares in which to improve.

Ironically for Toyota as a whole, inventory turns dropped from the close-to-23 per year in 1994 (very impressive in manufacturing) to 10 per year by 2007. This is due in part to Toyota's rapid global expansion in recent years. This means that its supply chain has also become global, thus resulting in it having to carry more inventory. In contrast, competitor General Motor's inventory turns were about 12 per year in 2007. This reinforces the notion that continuous improvement is necessary to remain competitive in the rapidly changing global market place. Competitive advantages are never static, since the environment is dynamic. Companies have to be eternally vigilant to maintain their edge.

■ Sources: Dave Zoia, "Toyota's Production System Comes to Logistics," *Ward's Auto World* (September 1999), pp. 77–78.

Tim Minahan, "JIT, A Process with Many Faces," *Purchasing* (September 4, 1997), pp. 42–43.

Norihiko Shirouzu, "Toyota Finds Success in Details," *The Globe and Mail*, March 15, 2001, B11.

Jeff Sabatini, "The Chop House," *Automotive Manufacturing and Production* (September 2000), pp. 68–71.

"Toyota Trumpets Quick Custom Delivery," *Calgary Herald*, August 8, 2003.

Greg Keenan, "Nimble Toyota Retools Amid Slump," *The Globe and Mail*, July 11, 2008, B1.

R. Schonberger, "Tracking Toyota's Position," *APICS Magazine*, 18, 6, 2008, pp. 34-37.

G. Keenan, "In Crisis, Toyota's New Way Turns to Self-Sacrifice," *The Globe and Mail*, February 13, 2009, B1.

As we discussed in Chapter 8, a supply chain is the sum total of organizations involved—from raw materials firms through tiers of suppliers to original equipment manufacturers, onward to the ultimate distribution and delivery of the finished product to the customer. Womack and Jones, in their seminal work *Lean Thinking*, provide the following guidelines for implementing a lean supply chain:[15]

- Value must be defined jointly for each product family along with a target cost based on the customer's perception of value.
- All firms along the value stream must make an adequate return on their investments related to the value stream.
- The firms must work together to identify and eliminate *muda* (waste) to the point where the overall target cost and return-on-investment targets of each firm are met.
- When cost targets are met, the firms along the stream will immediately conduct new analyses to identify remaining muda and set new targets.
- Every participating firm has the right to examine every activity in every firm relevant to the value stream as part of the joint search for waste.

To summarize: To be lean, everyone's got to be on the same page!

Problem Solving and Continuous Process Improvement

Exhibit 10.9 discusses ways to accomplish lean production, which integrates the concepts that we have discussed so far. These suggestions are geared to repetitive production systems—those that make the same products again and again. Also, bear in mind that these elements are linked: Any changes in part of the production system affect other features of the system. It is also important to note that lean is not a one-time improvement and it involves everybody in the workforce, management and non-management employees.

In fact, lean firms are big believers in the PDCA cycle (called **kaizen** in Japan). As discussed in many of the previous topics, the focus is on always looking from ways to improve the product and process. These include providing regular training to employees, giving them time on the job to think about improvement, using inventory reduction as a tool to identify problems, implementing pull production and a focus on quality. Lean firms also recognize that the lean journey does not happen overnight. It takes a long time. In fact, it is never ending. Thus, it requires patience and commitment. In fact, as with any improvement process, initially results may be negative. Firms must not lose heart and give up.

How to Accomplish Lean Production	EXHIBIT 10.9

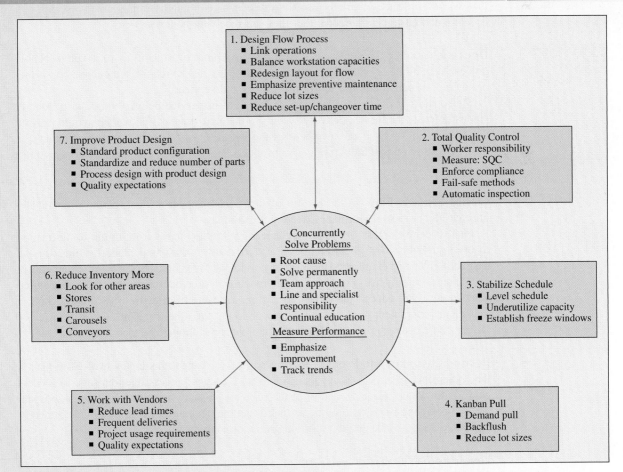

This diagram is modelled after the one used by Hewlett-Packard's Boise plant to accomplish its Lean Production program.

LEAN SERVICES

Many lean techniques have been successfully applied by service firms (as seen in some of the examples in this chapter). Just as in manufacturing, the suitability of each technique and the corresponding work steps depend on the characteristics of the firm's markets, production and equipment technology, skill sets, and corporate culture. Service firms are not different in this respect. Here are ten of the more successful applications.

Organize Problem-Solving Groups Honeywell is extending its quality circles from manufacturing into its service operations. Other corporations as diverse as banks and breweries are using similar approaches to improve service. British Airways used quality circles as a fundamental part of its strategy to implement new service practices.

Upgrade Housekeeping Good housekeeping means more than winning the clean broom award (see discussion in 5S). It means that only the necessary items are kept in a work area, that there is a place for everything, and that everything is clean and in a constant state of readiness. Employees clean their own areas.

Service organizations such as McDonald's, Disneyland, and ICICI Bank Canada have recognized the critical nature of housekeeping. Their dedication to housekeeping has meant that service processes work better, the attitude of continuous improvement is easier to develop, and customers perceive that they are receiving better service.

Upgrade Quality The only cost-effective way to improve quality is to develop reliable process capabilities. Process quality is quality at the source—it guarantees first-time production of consistent and uniform products and services.

McDonald's is famous for building quality into its service delivery process. It literally "industrialized" the service delivery system so that part-time, casual workers could provide the same eating experience anywhere in the world. Quality doesn't mean producing the best; it means consistently producing products and services that give customers their money's worth.

Clarify Process Flows Clarification of flows, based on lean themes, can dramatically improve the process performance. Here are examples.

First, Federal Express Corporation changed air flight patterns from origin-to-destination to origin-to-hub, where the freight is transferred to an outbound plane heading for the destination. This revolutionized the air transport industry. Second, the order-entry department of a manufacturing firm converted from functional subdepartments to customer-centred work groups and reduced the order processing lead time from eight to two days. Third, a municipal government used the lean approach to cut the time to record a deed transfer by 50 percent. Changes in process flows can literally revolutionize service industries.

Revise Equipment and Process Technologies Revising technologies involves evaluating the equipment and processes for their ability to meet the process requirements, to process consistently within tolerance, and to fit the scale and capacity of the work group. A hospital reduced operating room set-up time so that it had the flexibility to perform a wider range of operations without reducing the operating room availability.

Level the Facility Load Service firms synchronize production with demand. They have developed unique approaches to levelling demand so they can avoid making customers wait for service. McDonald's offers a special breakfast menu in the morning. Retail stores use take-a-number systems. The post office charges more for next-day delivery. These are all examples of the service approach for creating uniform facility loads.

Eliminate Unnecessary Activities A step that does not add value is a candidate for elimination. A step that does add value may be a candidate for reengineering, to improve the process consistency or to reduce the time to perform the tasks.

A hospital discovered that significant time was spent during an operation waiting for an instrument that was not available when the operation began. It developed a checklist of instruments required for each category of operation.

Reorganize Physical Configuration Work area configurations frequently require reorganization during a lean implementation. Often manufacturers accomplish this by setting up manufacturing cells to produce items in small lots, synchronous to demand. These cells amount to microfactories inside the plant.

Most service firms are far behind manufacturers in this area. However, a few interesting examples do come out of the service sector. Some hospitals—instead of routing patients all over the building for tests, exams, X-rays, and injections—are reorganizing their services into work groups based on the type of problem. Teams that treat only trauma are common, but other work groups have been formed to treat less immediate conditions like hernias. These teams amount to microclinics within the hospital facility.

Introduce Demand-Pull Scheduling Due to the nature of service production and consumption, demand-pull (customer-driven) scheduling is necessary for operating a service business. Moreover, many service firms are separating their operations into "back room" and "customer contact" facilities. This approach creates new problems in coordinating schedules between the facilities. The original Wendy's restaurants were set up so cooks could see cars enter the parking lot. They put a pre-established number of hamburger patties onto the grill for each car. This pull system was designed to have a fresh patty on the grill before the customer even placed an order.

Develop Supplier Networks The term *supplier networks* in the lean context refers to the cooperative association of suppliers and customers working over the long term for mutual benefit. Service firms have not emphasized supplier networks for materials because the service costs are often predominantly labour. Notable exceptions must include service organizations like McDonald's, one of the biggest food products purchasers in the world, which has been developing lean practices. Manpower and other employment agencies have established lean-type relationships with a temporary employment service and a trade school to develop a reliable source of trained assemblers.

Summary

Lean production has proven its value to thousands of companies throughout the world. The idea behind *lean* is achieving high volume with minimal inventory. Toyota pioneered the ideas associated with *lean* production with the Toyota Production System. There are six elements to the concept: just-in-time production, focus on quality, lean product and process design, workforce involvement, close supplier relationships and, problem solving and continuous improvement. Lean concepts are best applied in environments where the same products are produced over and over at relatively high volume, though many of the principles can be applied to any environment, even services.

Key Terms

5S Philosophy based on five Japanese words starting with S that imply a clean and safe workplace.

Andon board A board showing performance measures of the production line.

Backflush Calculating how many of each part were used in production and using these calculations to adjust actual on-hand inventory balances. This eliminates the need to actually track each part used in production.

Concurrent engineering Product design using multifunctional teams.

External set-up Set-up activities that can be done while the machine is running.

Freeze window The period of time during which the schedule is fixed and no further changes are possible.

Group technology A philosophy in which similar parts are grouped into families, and the processes required to make the parts are arranged in a specialized work cell.

Internal set-up Set-up activities that can be done only when the machine is stopped.

Jidoka Ability to stop a production line if there are problems.

Kaizen Japanese term for continuous improvement or the PDCA cycle.

Kanban and the kanban pull system An inventory or production control system that uses a signaling device to regulate flows.

Keiretsu A close network of companies related to each other in the supply chain.

Lean production Integrated activities designed to achieve high-volume, high-quality production using minimal inventories of raw materials, work-in-process, and finished goods.

Level schedule A schedule that pulls material into final assembly at a constant rate.

Muda Waste of any kind in a production system.

Preventive maintenance Periodic inspection and repair designed to keep equipment reliable.

Quality at the source Philosophy of making factory workers personally responsible for the quality of their output. Workers are expected to make the part correctly the first time and to stop the process immediately if there is a problem.

Quality circles Groups of employees that meet during work hours for process and product improvement.

Uniform plant loading (heijunka) Smoothing the production flow to dampen schedule variation.

Value chain mapping A graphical way to analyze where value is or isn't being added as material flows though a process.

Review and Discussion Questions

1. Is it possible to achieve zero inventories? Why or why not?
2. Stopping waste is a vital part of lean. Using value stream mapping, identify some sources of waste in your home or dorm and discuss how they may be eliminated.
3. Why must lean have a stable schedule?
4. Will lean work in service environments? Why or why not?
5. Discuss ways to use lean to improve one of the following where you might have noticed some inefficiencies: a pizza restaurant, a hospital, or an auto dealership.
6. What objections might a marketing manager have to uniform plant loading?
7. What are the implications for cost accounting of lean production?
8. What are the roles of suppliers and customers in a lean system?
9. Explain how cards are used in a kanban system.
10. In which ways, if any, are the following systems analogous to kanban: returning empty bottles to the supermarket and picking up filled ones; running a hot dog stand at lunchtime; withdrawing money from a chequing account; raking leaves into bags?
11. Why is lean hard to implement in practice?
12. Explain the relationship between quality and productivity under the lean philosophy.

CASE | Cheng Parts Company

Cheng Parts Company supplies gizmos for a computer manufacturer located a few miles away. The company produces two different models of gizmos in production runs ranging from 100 to 300 units.

The production flow of models X and Y is shown in Exhibit 10.10. Model Z requires milling as its first step, but otherwise follows the same flow pattern as X and Y. Skids can hold up to 20 gizmos at a time. Approximate times per unit by operation number and equipment set-up times are shown in Exhibit 10.11.

Demand for gizmos from the computer company ranges between 125 and 175 per month, equally divided among X, Y, and Z. Subassembly builds up inventory early in the month to make certain that a buffer stock is always available. Raw materials and purchased parts for subassemblies each constitute 40 percent of the manufacturing cost of a gizmo. Both categories of parts are multiple-sourced from about 80 vendors and are delivered at random times. (Gizmos have 40 different part numbers.)

Gizmo Production Flow
EXHIBIT 10.10

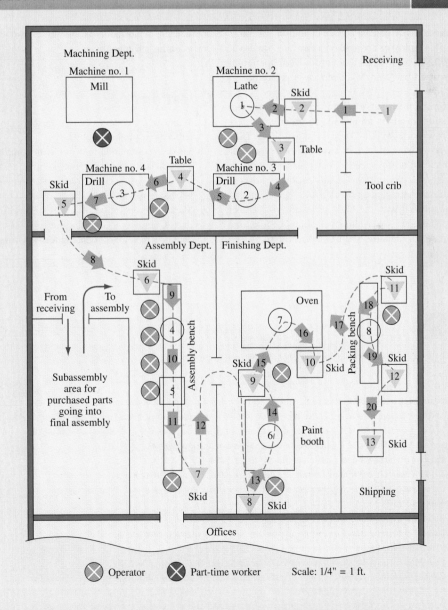

EXHIBIT 10.11	Operations and Set-up Time

OPERATION NUMBER AND NAME	OPERATION TIME (MINUTES)	SET-UP TIME (MINUTES)
Milling for Model Z	20	60
1. Lathe	50	30
2. Mod. 14 drill	15	5
3. Mod. 14 drill	40	5
4. Assembly step 1	50	
Assembly step 2	45	
Assembly step 3	50	
5. Inspection	30	
6. Paint	30	20
7. Oven	50	
8. Packing	5	

Scrap rates are about 10 percent at each operation, inventory turns twice yearly, employees are paid on a day rate, employee turnover is 25 percent per year, and net profit from operations is steady at 5 percent per year. Maintenance is performed as needed.

Cindy Cheng, the manager of Cheng Parts Company has been contemplating installing an automated ordering system to help control inventories and to "keep the skids filled." (She feels that two days of work in front of a workstation motivates the worker to produce at top speed.) She is also planning to add three inspectors to clean up the quality problem. Further, she is thinking about setting up a rework line to speed repairs. Although she is pleased with the high utilization of most of her equipment and labour, she is concerned about the idle time of the milling machine. Finally, she has asked the industrial

engineering department to look into high-rise shelving to store parts coming off machine 4.

Questions

1. Which of the changes being considered by Cindy are counter to the lean philosophy?
2. Make recommendations for lean improvements in such areas as scheduling, layout, kanban, task groupings, and inventory. Use quantitative data as much as possible; state necessary assumptions.
3. Sketch the operation of a pull system for running Cheng Parts Company's current system.
4. Outline a plan for introducing lean at Cheng Parts Company.

Footnotes

[1]J. P. Womack, D. T. Jones, and D. Roos, *The Machine That Changed the World* (New York: R. A. Rawston Associates, 1990).

[2]G. Garrett, *The Wild Wheel,* New York, NY: Pantheon, 1952, pp. 9–11.

[3]K. A. Wantuck, *The Japanese Approach to Productivity* (Southfield, MI: Bendix Corporation, 1983).

[4]K. Suzaki, *The New Manufacturing Challenge: Techniques for Continuous Improvement* (New York: Free Press, 1987), pp. 7–25.

[5]J. Lovelle, "Mapping the Value Stream," *IIE Solutions* 33, no. 2 (February 2001), pp. 26–33.

[6]R. H. Hall, *Zero Inventories* (Homewood, IL: Dow Jones-Irwin, 1983), p. 64.

[7]*The Current*, CBC Radio, May 11, 2009 (http://www.cbc.ca/thecurrent/2009/200905/20090511.html)

[8]Navendar Sumukadas and Chris Piper, *Spartan Plastics* (London, Ontario: University of Western Ontario, Ivey Management Services, 1997).

[9]Dreyfuss, J., "Profit Machine," *Bloomberg Markets*, October 2003, pp. 29–38.

[10]C. Karlsson, *Japanese Production Management in Sunrise or Sunset* (Stockholm, Sweden: Stockholm School of Economics, EFI/The Economic Research Institute. 1999).

[11]Greg Keenan, "Intier Wins 'Huge' GM Small-Car Contract," *The Globe and Mail*, May 8, 2002, B7.

[12]Magna International Inc., www.magna.com.

[13]Greg Keenan, "Ford Yanks Contract from Decoma," *The Globe and Mail*, December 20, 2003, B1.

[14]Greg Keenan, "Big 3's Ties to Suppliers Are Eroding," *The Globe and Mail*, August 2, 2004, B1.

[15]J. P. Womack and D. T. Jones, *Lean Thinking* (New York: Simon & Shuster, 1996), p. 277.

Selected Bibliography

Allen, M. "Picture-Perfect Manufacturing [Using Value Stream Mapping]," *Modern Machine Shop Magazine Online*, August 2004.

George, M. L. *Lean Six Sigma.* New York: McGraw-Hill, 2002.

Gross, J. M., and K. R. McInnis. *Kanban Made Simple: Demystifying and Applying Toyota's Legendary Manufacturing Process.* New York: AMACOM, 2003.

Monden, Y. *Toyota Production System: An Integrated Approach to Just-in-Time.* Atlanta, GA:Institute of Industrial Engineers, 1998.

Phelps, T.; M. Smith; and T. Hoenes. "Building a Lean Supply Chain," *Manufacturing Engineering* 132, no. 5 (May 2004), pp. 107–13.

Womack, J. P., and D. T. Jones. *Lean Thinking: Banish Waste and Create Wealth in Your Corporation.* New York: Simon & Schuster, 1996.

Womack, J. P.; D. T. Jones and D. Roos. *The Machine That Changed the World.* New York: R. A. Rawston Associates, 1990.

MEDIUM- AND SHORT-RANGE OPERATIONS PLANNING

In Running a Business, Computers Can Do More than Just Word Processing and E-Mail

Running a business requires a great planning system. What do we expect to sell in the future? How many people should we hire to handle the Christmas rush? How much inventory do we need? What should we make today? This section discusses various approaches used to answer these questions. The use of comprehensive software packages is common practice but it is important to understand the basic planning concepts that underlie them so that the right software can be purchased and configured correctly. Moreover, given this basic understanding, a spreadsheet can be created for simple production planning situations.

DEMAND MANAGEMENT AND FORECASTING

Learning Objectives:

1. Understand the role of forecasting as a basis for supply chain planning.
2. Know how independent demand and dependent demand differ.
3. Know the basic components of independent demand: average, trend, seasonal, and random variation.
4. Become familiar with common qualitative forecasting techniques such as the Delphi method.
5. Know how to make time series forecasts using moving averages, exponential smoothing, and regression.

WALMART'S DATA WAREHOUSE

Walmart's size and power in the retail industry is having a huge influence in the database industry. Walmart manages one of the world's largest data warehouses with more than 35 terabytes of data. A terabyte is equal to 1024 gigabytes or a trillion bytes. Your computer hard drive probably has less than 500 gigabytes. Walmart's formula for success— getting the right product on the appropriate shelf at the lowest price—owes much to the company's multimillion-dollar investment in data warehousing. WalMart has more detail than most of its competitors on what's going on by product, by store, and by day.

The systems track point-of-sale (POS) data at each store, inventory levels by store, products in transit, market statistics, customer demographics, finance, product returns, and supplier performance. The data are used for three broad areas of decision support: analyzing trends, managing inventory, and understanding customers. What emerges are "personality traits" for each of Walmart's 3000 or so outlets, which Walmart managers use to determine product mix and presentation for each store.

Data mining is next. Walmart has developed a demand-forecasting application that looks at individual items for individual stores to decide the seasonal sales profile of each item. The system keeps a year's worth of data on the sales of 100 000 products and predicts which items will be needed in each store.

Walmart is now doing market-basket analysis. Data are collected on items that make up a shopper's total purchase so that the company can analyze relationships and patterns in customer purchases. The data warehouse is made available over the Web to its store managers and suppliers.

**Cross
Functional**

Forecasts are vital to every business organization and for every significant management decision. Forecasting is the basis of corporate long-run planning. In the functional areas of finance and accounting, forecasts provide the basis for budgetary planning and cost control. Marketing relies on sales forecasting to plan new products, compensate sales personnel, and make other key decisions. Production and operations personnel use forecasts to make periodic decisions involving supplier selection, process selection, capacity planning, and facility layout, as well as for continual decisions about purchasing, production planning, scheduling, and inventory (see the OSMP on Kellogg in Chapter 12).

Bear in mind that a perfect forecast is virtually impossible. In fact, a recent study by the Economic Intelligence Unit for KPMG revealed that only 22 percent of financial projections by companies were accurate to within 5 percent.[1] Too many factors in the business environment cannot be predicted with certainty. Therefore, rather than search for the perfect forecast, it is far more important to establish the practice of continual review of forecasts and to learn to live with inaccurate forecasts. This is not to say that we should not try to improve the forecasting model or methodology, but that we should try to find and use the best forecasting method available, *within reason*.

When forecasting, a good strategy is to use two or three methods and look at them for the commonsense view. Will expected changes in the general economy affect the forecast? Are there changes in industrial and private consumer behaviours? Will there be a shortage of essential complementary items? Continual review and updating in light of new data are basic to successful forecasting. In this chapter we look at *qualitative* and *quantitative* forecasting and concentrate primarily on several quantitative time series techniques. We cover in some depth moving averages, linear regression and trends. We also discuss sources and measurement of errors.

DEMAND MANAGEMENT

The purpose of demand management is to coordinate and control all sources of demand so the supply chain can be run efficiently and the product delivered on time.

Where does demand for a firm's product or service come from, and what can a firm do to manage it? There are two basic sources of demand: dependent demand and independent demand. **Dependent demand** is the demand for a product or service caused by the demand for other products or services. For example, if a firm sells 1000 tricycles, then 1000 front wheels and 2000 rear wheels are needed. This type of internal demand does not need a forecast, just a tabulation. As to how many tricycles the firm might sell, this is called **independent demand** because its demand cannot be derived directly from that of other products.[2] We discuss dependence and independence more fully in Chapters 13 and 14.

There is not much a firm can do about dependent demand. It must be met (although the product or service can be purchased rather than produced internally). But there is a lot a firm can do about independent demand—if it wants to. The firm can

An RFID tag compared to the size of a Canadian loonie. It is paper-thin and lightweight, so it can be easily used in tracking any type of package. The tag responds to an RFID scanner, which in turn can be used to access and enter information about the package. RFID tags offer opportunities for better forecasts, by providing suppliers with better information on real-time demand for products, thus improving the speed of distribution. Tag courtesy of Omron Electronics Pte Ltd, Singapore.

1. **Take an active role to influence demand.**   The firm can apply pressure on its sales force, it can offer incentives both to customers and to its own personnel, it can wage campaigns to sell products, and it can cut prices. These actions can increase demand. Conversely, demand can be decreased through price increases or reduced sales efforts.
2. **Take a passive role and simply respond to demand.**   There are several reasons a firm may not try to change demand but simply accept what happens. If a firm is running at full capacity, it may not want to do anything about demand. Other reasons are a firm may be powerless to change demand because of the expense to advertise; the market may be fixed in size and static; or demand is beyond its control (such as in the case of sole supplier). There are other competitive, legal, environmental, ethical, and moral reasons that market demand is passively accepted.

A great deal of coordination is required to manage these dependent, independent, active, and passive demands. These demands originate both internally and externally in the form of new product sales from marketing, repair parts for previously sold products from product service, restocking from the factory warehouses, and supply items for manufacturing. In this chapter, our primary interest is in forecasting for independent items.

TYPES OF FORECASTING

Forecasting can be classified into four basic types: *qualitative, time series analysis, causal relationships,* and *simulation.*

Qualitative techniques are subjective or judgmental and are based on estimates and opinions. **Time series analysis**, the primary focus of this chapter, is based on the idea that data relating to past demand can be used to predict future demand. Past data may include several components, such as trend, seasonal, or cyclical influences, and are described in the following section. Causal forecasting, which we discuss using the linear regression technique, assumes that demand is related to some underlying factor or factors in the environment. Simulation models allow the forecaster to run through a range of assumptions about the condition of the forecast. In this chapter we focus on qualitative and time series techniques since these are most often used in supply chain planning and control.

COMPONENTS OF DEMAND

In most cases, demand for products or services can be broken down into six components: average demand for the period, a trend, seasonal element, cyclical elements, random variation, and autocorrelation. Exhibit 11.1 illustrates a demand over a four-year period, showing the average, trend, and seasonal components and randomness around the smoothed demand curve.

EXHIBIT 11.1   Historical Product Demand Consisting of a Growth Trend and Seasonal Demand

Components of Demand

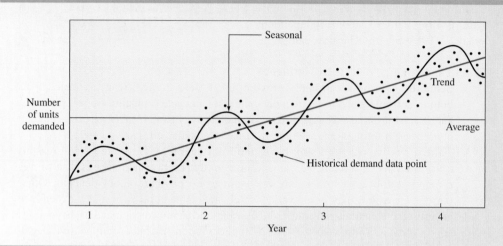

Cyclical factors are more difficult to determine because the time span may be unknown or the cause of the cycle may not be considered. Cyclical influence on demand may come from such occurrences as political elections, war, economic conditions, or sociological pressures.

Random variations are caused by chance events. Statistically, when all the known causes for demand (average, trend, seasonal, cyclical, and autocorrelative) are subtracted from total demand, what remains is the unexplained portion of demand. If we cannot identify the cause of this remainder, it is assumed to be purely random chance.

Autocorrelation denotes the persistence of occurrence. More specifically, the value expected at any point is highly correlated with its own past values. In waiting-line theory, the length of a waiting line is highly autocorrelated. That is, if a line is relatively long at one time, then shortly after that time, we would still expect the line to be long.

When demand is random, it may vary widely from one week to another. Where high autocorrelation exists, demand is not expected to change very much from one week to the next.

Trend lines are the usual starting point in developing a forecast. These trend lines are then adjusted for seasonal effects, cyclical elements, and any other expected events that may influence the final forecast. Exhibit 11.2 shows four of the most common types of trends. A linear trend is obviously a straight continuous relationship. An S-curve is typical of a product growth and maturity cycle. The most important point in the S-curve is where the trend changes from slow growth to fast growth, or from fast to slow. An asymptotic trend starts with the highest demand growth at the beginning but then tapers off. Such a curve could happen when a firm enters an existing market with the objective of saturating and capturing a large share of the market. An exponential curve is common in products with explosive growth. The exponential trend suggests that sales will continue to increase—an assumption that may not be safe to make.

A widely used forecasting method plots data and then searches for the curve pattern (such as linear, S-curve, asymptotic, or exponential) that fits best. This is an attractive method because the mathematics for the curve are then known, and solving for values for future time periods is easy.

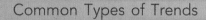

Common Types of Trends

EXHIBIT 11.2

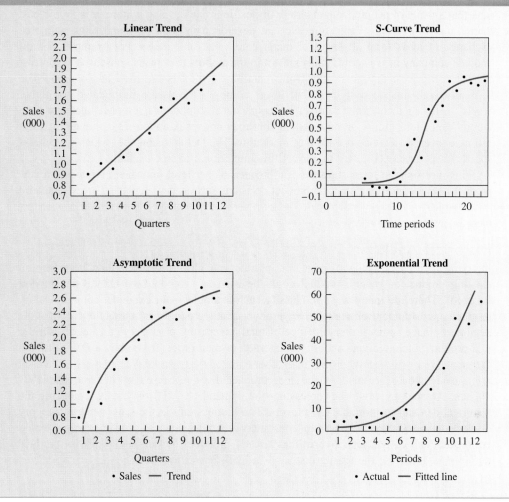

Sometimes our data do not seem to fit any standard curve. This may be due to several causes essentially beating the data from several directions at the same time. For these cases, a simplistic but often effective forecast can be obtained by simply plotting data.

QUALITATIVE TECHNIQUES IN FORECASTING

Market Research

Firms often hire outside companies that specialize in **market research** to conduct this type of forecasting. You may have been involved in market surveys through a marketing class. Certainly you have not escaped telephone calls asking you about product preferences, your income, habits, and so on.

Market research is used mostly for product research in the sense of looking for new product ideas, likes and dislikes about existing products, which competitive products within a particular class are preferred, and so on. Again, the data collection methods are primarily surveys and interviews.

Panel Consensus

In a *panel consensus*, the idea that two heads are better than one is extrapolated to the idea that a panel of people from a variety of positions can develop a more reliable forecast than a narrower group. Panel forecasts are developed through open meetings with free exchange of ideas from all levels of management and individuals. For example, one oil and gas company in Western Canada known to the authors uses panel consensus to forecast natural gas prices, though results from quantitative models are used as an input. The difficulty with this open style is that lower employee levels are intimidated by higher levels of management. For example, a salesperson in a particular product line may have a good estimate of future product demand but may not speak up to refute a much different estimate given by the vice president of marketing. The Delphi technique (which we discuss shortly) was developed to try to correct this impairment to free exchange.

When decisions in forecasting are at a broader, higher level (as when introducing a new product line or concerning strategic product decisions such as new marketing areas), the term *executive judgment* is generally used. The term is self-explanatory: a higher level of management is involved.

Historical Analogy

In trying to forecast demand for a new product, an ideal situation would be where an existing product or generic product could be used as a model (see OSMP on Hewlett Packard). There are many ways to classify such analogies—for example, complementary products, substitutable or competitive products, and products as a function of income. Again, you have surely gotten a deluge of mail advertising products in a category similar to a product purchased via catalog, the Internet, or mail order. If you buy a DVD through the mail, you will receive more mail about new DVDs and DVD players. A causal relationship would be that demand for compact discs is caused by demand for DVD players. An analogy would be forecasting the demand for MP3 players by analyzing the historical demand for portable CD players. The products are in the same general category of electronics and may be bought by consumers at similar rates. A simpler example would be toasters and coffee pots. A firm that already produces toasters and wants to produce coffee pots could use the toaster history as a likely growth model.

Operations and Supply Management in Practice

Forecasting for Short-Lived Products at Hewlett Packard

Traditional forecasting methods assume that product life cycles are long, at least a few years. For Hewlett Packard (HP) in North America, this long-life assumption is no longer valid. Many HP products have life cycles of between 9 to 18 months, a short life cycle. To complicate matters further, these products have high uncertainty in demand and a steep obsolescence curve. HP found that traditional forecasting methods were ill-suited to these products. So the company's Strategic Planning and Modelling Group (SPaM) developed a Product Life Cycle (PLC) forecasting method specifically for these types of products.

SPaM recognized that the usual short life cycle product demonstrated the following characteristics: well-defined life cycle phases from introduction to maturity and then to end of life, a high demand spike during the introduction phase followed by a gradual downward levelling off during maturity, and finally, a steep end-of-life drop-off often caused by planned product rollovers. These characteristics formed the basis of the forecasting method (historical data from similar products served as a good starting point). To these were added templates for seasonality, price drops, and special promotions. The method was developed with the involvement of forecasters and included development of a good user interface, ensuring that it was actually used. It is estimated that the increased forecast accuracy saves HP US$15 million or so annually.

■ Source: Jim Burruss and Dorothea Kuettner, "Forecasting for Short Lived Products: Hewlett Packard's Journey," *Journal of Business Forecasting* (Winter 2002–2003), pp. 9–14.

Delphi Method

As we mentioned, under panel consensus a statement or opinion of a higher-level person will likely be weighted more than that of a lower-level person. The worst case is one in which lower-level people feel threatened and do not contribute their true beliefs. To prevent this problem, the *Delphi method* conceals the identity of the individuals participating in the study. Everyone has the same weight. Procedurally, a moderator creates a questionnaire and distributes it to participants. Their responses are summed and given back to the entire group along with a new set of questions.

The Delphi method was developed by the Rand Corporation in the 1950s. The step-by-step procedure is

1. Choose the experts to participate. There should be a variety of knowledgeable people in different areas.
2. Through a questionnaire (or e-mail), obtain forecasts (and any premises or qualifications for the forecasts) from all participants.
3. Summarize the results and redistribute them to the participants along with appropriate new questions.
4. Summarize again, refining forecasts and conditions, and again develop new questions.
5. Repeat Step 4 if necessary. Distribute the final results to all participants.

The Delphi technique can usually achieve satisfactory results in three rounds. The time required is a function of the number of participants, how much work is involved for them to develop their forecasts, and their speed in responding.

TIME SERIES ANALYSIS

Time series forecasting models try to predict the future based on past data. For example, sales figures collected for the past six weeks can be used to forecast sales for the seventh week. Quarterly sales figures collected for the past several years can be used to forecast future quarters. Even though both examples contain sales, different forecasting time series models would likely be used, as explained below.

Exhibit 11.3 shows the time series models discussed in the chapter and some of their characteristics. Terms such as *short, medium*, and *long* are relative to the context in which they are used. However, in business forecasting, *short-term* usually refers to under three months; *medium-term*, three months to two years; and *long-term*, greater than two years. In general, the short-term models compensate for random variation and adjust for short-term changes (such as consumers' responses to a new product). Medium-term forecasts are useful for seasonal effects, and long-term models detect general trends and are especially useful in identifying major turning points.

Which forecasting model a firm should choose depends on

1. Time horizon to forecast.
2. Data availability.
3. Accuracy required.
4. Size of forecasting budget.
5. Availability of qualified personnel.

In selecting a forecasting model, there are other issues such as the firm's degree of flexibility. (The greater the ability to react quickly to changes, the less accurate the forecast needs to be.) Another item is the consequence of a bad forecast. If a large capital investment decision is to be based on a forecast, it should be a good forecast.

Interactive Operations Management

EXHIBIT 11.3 | A Guide to Selecting an Appropriate Forecasting Method

FORECASTING METHOD	AMOUNT OF HISTORICAL DATA	DATA PATTERN	FORECAST HORIZON
Simple moving average	6 to 12 months, weekly data are often used	Data should be stationary (i.e., no trend or seasonality)	Short
Weighted moving average and simple exponential smoothing	5 to 10 observations needed to start	Data should be stationary	Short
Exponential smoothing with trend	5 to 10 observations needed to start	Stationary and trend	Short
Linear regression	10 to 20 observations; for seasonality, at least 5 observations per season	Stationary, trend, and seasonality	Short to medium

Simple Moving Average

When demand for a product is neither growing nor declining rapidly, and if it does not have seasonal characteristics, a moving average can be useful in removing the random fluctuations for forecasting. Although *moving averages* are frequently centred, it is more convenient to use past data to predict the following period directly. To illustrate, a centred five-month average of January, February, March, April, and May gives an average centred on March. However, all five months of data must already exist. If our objective is to forecast for June, we must project our moving average—by some means—from March to June. If the average is not centred but is at the forward end, we can forecast more easily, though we may lose some accuracy. Thus, if we want to forecast June with a five-month moving average, we can take the average of January, February, March, April, and May. When June passes, the forecast for July would be the average of February, March, April, May, and June. This is how Exhibits 11.4 and 11.5 were computed.

Although it is important to select the best period for the moving average, there are several conflicting effects of different period lengths. The longer the moving average period, the more the random elements are smoothed (which may be desirable in many cases). But if there is a trend in the data—either increasing or decreasing—the moving average has the adverse characteristic of lagging the trend. Therefore, while a shorter time span produces more oscillation, there is a closer following of the trend. Conversely, a longer time span gives a smoother response but lags the trend.

The formula for a simple moving average is

[11.1]
$$F_t = \frac{A_{t-1} + A_{t-2} + A_{t-3} + \cdots + A_{t-n}}{n}$$

where

$$F_t = \text{Forecast for the coming period}$$
$$n = \text{Number of periods to be averaged}$$
$$A_{t-1} = \text{Actual occurrence in the past period}$$
$$A_{t-2}, A_{t-3}, \text{ and } A_{t-n} = \text{Actual occurrences two periods ago, three periods ago, and so on up to } n \text{ periods}$$

				EXHIBIT 11.4

Forecast Demand Based on a Three- and a Nine-Week Simple Moving Average

WEEK	DEMAND	3 WEEK	9 WEEK	WEEK	DEMAND	3 WEEK	9 WEEK
1	800			16	1700	2200	1811
2	1400			17	1800	2000	1800
3	1000			18	2200	1833	1811
4	1500	1067		19	1900	1900	1911
5	1500	1300		20	2400	1967	1933
6	1300	1333		21	2400	2167	2011
7	1800	1433		22	2600	2233	2111
8	1700	1533		23	2000	2467	2144
9	1300	1600		24	2500	2333	2111
10	1700	1600	1367	25	2600	2367	2167
11	1700	1567	1467	26	2200	2367	2267
12	1500	1567	1500	27	2200	2433	2311
13	2300	1633	1556	28	2500	2333	2311
14	2300	1833	1644	29	2400	2300	2378
15	2000	2033	1733	30	2100	2367	2378

Forecasting

	EXHIBIT 11.5

Moving Average Forecast of Three- and Nine-Week Periods versus Actual Demand

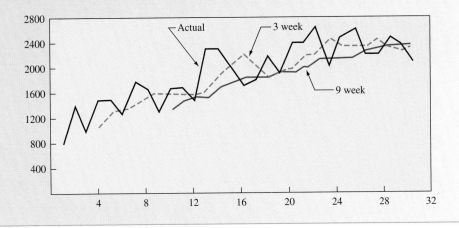

Forecasting

Exhibit 11.5, a plot of the data in Exhibit 11.4, shows the effects of various lengths of the period of a moving average. We see that the growth trend levels off at about the 23rd week. The three-week moving average responds better in following this change than the nine-week average, although overall the nine-week average is smoother.

The main disadvantage in calculating a moving average is that all individual elements must be carried as data because a new forecast period involves adding new data and dropping the earliest data. For a three- or six-period moving average, this is not too severe.

But plotting a 60-day moving average for the usage of each of 20 000 items in inventory would involve a significant amount of data.

Weighted Moving Average

Whereas the simple moving average gives equal weight to each component of the moving average database, a weighted moving average allows any weights to be placed on each element, providing, of course, that the sum of all weights equals 1. For example, a department store may find that in a four-month period, the best forecast is derived by using 40 percent of the actual sales for the most recent month, 30 percent of two months ago, 20 percent of three months ago, and 10 percent of four months ago. If actual sales experience was

MONTH 1	MONTH 2	MONTH 3	MONTH 4	MONTH 5
100	90	105	95	?

the forecast for month 5 would be

$$F_5 = 0.40(95) + 0.30(105) + 0.20(90) + 0.10(100)$$
$$= 38 + 31.5 + 18 + 10$$
$$= 97.5$$

The formula for a weighted moving average is

[11.2]
$$F_t = w_1 A_{t-1} + w_2 A_{t-2} + \cdots + w_n A_{t-n}$$

where

w_1 = Weight to be given to the actual occurrence for the period $t - 1$

w_2 = Weight to be given to the actual occurrence for the period $t - 2$

w_n = Weight to be given to the actual occurrence for the period $t - n$

n = Total number of periods in the forecast

Although many periods may be ignored (that is, their weights are zero) and the weighting scheme may be in any order (for example, more distant data may have greater weights than more recent data), the sum of all the weights must equal 1.

$$\sum_{i=1}^{n} w_i = 1$$

Suppose sales for month 5 actually turned out to be 110. Then the forecast for month 6 would be

$$F_6 = 0.40(110) + 0.30(95) + 0.20(105) + 0.10(90)$$
$$= 44 + 28.5 + 21 + 9$$
$$= 102.5$$

Choosing Weights Experience and trial and error are the simplest ways to choose weights. As a general rule, the most recent past is the most important indicator of what to expect in the future, and, therefore, it should get higher weighting. The past month's revenue or plant capacity, for example, would be a better estimate for the coming month than the revenue or plant capacity of several months ago.

However, if the data are seasonal, for example, weights should be established accordingly. Bathing suit sales in July of last year should be weighted more heavily than bathing suit sales in December (in the Northern Hemisphere).

The weighted moving average has a definite advantage over the simple moving average in being able to vary the effects of past data. However, it is more inconvenient and costly to use than the exponential smoothing method, which we examine next.

Exponential Smoothing

In the previous methods of forecasting (simple and weighted moving averages), the major drawback is the need to continually carry a large amount of historical data. (This is also true for regression analysis techniques, which we soon will cover.) As each new piece of data is added in these methods, the oldest observation is dropped, and the new forecast is calculated. In many applications (perhaps in most), the most recent occurrences are more indicative of the future than those in the more distant past. If this premise is valid—that the importance of data diminishes as the past becomes more distant—then **exponential smoothing** may be the most logical and easiest method to use.

The reason this is called exponential smoothing is that each increment in the past is decreased by $(1 - \alpha)$. If α is 0.05, for example, weights for various periods would be as follows (α is defined below):

	WEIGHTING AT $\alpha = 0.05$
Most recent weighting $= \alpha(1 - \alpha)^0$	0.0500
Data one time period older $= \alpha(1 - \alpha)^1$	0.0475
Data two time periods older $= \alpha(1 - \alpha)^2$	0.0451
Data three time periods older $= \alpha(1 - \alpha)^3$	0.0429

Therefore, the exponents 0, 1, 2, 3, . . . , and so on, give it its name.

Exponential smoothing is the most used of all forecasting techniques. It is an integral part of virtually all computerized forecasting programs, and it is widely used in ordering inventory in retail firms, wholesale companies, and service agencies.

Exponential smoothing techniques have become well accepted for six major reasons:

1. Exponential models are surprisingly accurate.
2. Formulating an exponential model is relatively easy.
3. The user can understand how the model works.
4. Little computation is required to use the model.
5. Computer storage requirements are small because of the limited use of historical data.
6. Tests for accuracy as to how well the *model* is performing are easy to compute.

In the exponential smoothing method, only three pieces of data are needed to forecast the future: the most recent forecast, the actual demand that occurred for that forecast period, and a **smoothing constant alpha (α)**. This smoothing constant determines the level of smoothing and the speed of reaction to differences between forecasts and actual occurrences. The value for the constant is determined both by the nature of the product and by the manager's sense of what constitutes a good response rate. For example, if a firm produced a standard item with relatively stable demand, the reaction rate to differences between actual and forecast demand would tend to be small, perhaps just 5 or 10 percentage points. However, if the firm were experiencing growth, it would be desirable to have a higher reaction rate, perhaps 15 to 30 percentage points, to give greater importance to recent growth experience. The more rapid the growth, the higher the reaction rate should be. Sometimes, users of the simple moving average switch to exponential smoothing but like to keep the forecasts about the same as the simple moving average. In this case, α is approximated by $2 \div (n + 1)$, where n is the number of time periods.

The equation for a single exponential smoothing forecast is simply

[11.3]
$$F_t = F_{t-1} + \alpha(A_{t-1} - F_{t-1})$$

where

F_t = The exponentially smoothed forecast for period t

F_{t-1} = The exponentially smoothed forecast made for the prior period

A_{t-1} = The actual demand in the prior period

α = The desired response rate, or smoothing constant

This equation states that the new forecast is equal to the old forecast plus a portion of the error (the difference between the previous forecast and what actually occurred).[3]

To demonstrate the method, assume that the long-run demand for the product under study is relatively stable and a smoothing constant (α) of 0.05 is considered appropriate. If the exponential method were used as a continuing policy, a forecast would have been made for last month.[4] Assume that last month's forecast (F_{t-1}) was 1050 units. If 1000 actually were demanded, rather than 1050, the forecast for this month would be

$$F_t = F_{t-1} + \alpha(A_{t-1} - F_{t-1})$$
$$= 1050 + 0.05(1000 - 1050)$$
$$= 1050 + 0.05(-50)$$
$$= 1047.5 \text{ units}$$

Because the smoothing coefficient is small, the reaction of the new forecast to an error of 50 units is to decrease the next month's forecast by only $2\frac{1}{2}$ units.

Single exponential smoothing has the shortcoming of lagging changes in demand. Exhibit 11.6 presents actual data plotted as a smooth curve to show the lagging effects of the exponential forecasts. The forecast lags during an increase or decrease but overshoots when a change in direction occurs. Note that the higher the value of alpha, the more closely the forecast follows the actual. To more closely track actual demand, a trend factor may be added. Adjusting the value of alpha also helps. This is termed *adaptive forecasting*. Both trend effects and adaptive forecasting are briefly explained in following sections.

Trend Effects in Exponential Smoothing Remember that an upward or downward trend in data collected over a sequence of time periods causes the exponential forecast to always lag behind (be above or below) the actual occurrence. Exponentially smoothed forecasts can be corrected somewhat by adding in a trend adjustment. To correct the trend, we need two smoothing constants. Besides the smoothing constant α, the trend equation also uses a **smoothing constant delta (δ)**. The delta reduces the impact of the error that occurs between the actual and the forecast. If both alpha and delta are not included, the trend overreacts to errors.

Exponential Forecasts versus Actual Demand for Units
of a Product over Time Showing the Forecast Lag

EXHIBIT 11.6

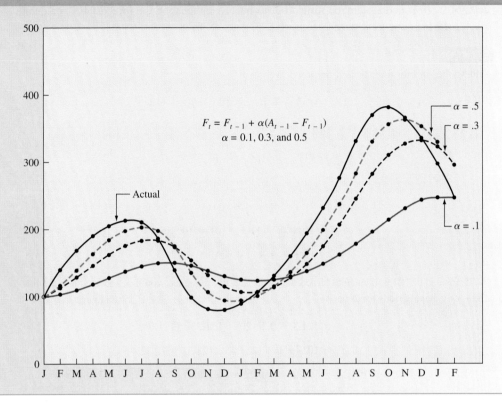

To get the trend equation going, the first time it is used the trend value must be entered manually. This initial trend value can be an educated guess or a computation based on observed past data.

The equation to compute the forecast including trend (FIT) is

[11.4]
$$\text{FIT}_t = F_t + T_t$$

[11.5]
$$F_t = \text{FIT}_{t-1} + \alpha(A_{t-1} - \text{FIT}_{t-1})$$

[11.6]
$$T_t = T_{t-1} + \delta(F_t - \text{FIT}_{t-1})$$

where

F_t = The exponentially smoothed forecast for period t

T_t = The exponentially smoothed trend for period t

FIT_t = The forecast including trend for period t

FIT_{t-1} = The forecast including trend made for the prior period

A_{t-1} = The actual demand for the prior period

α = Smoothing constant

δ = Smoothing constant

EXAMPLE 11.1:   FORECAST INCLUDING TREND

Assume an initial starting F_t of 100 units, a trend of 10 units, an alpha of 0.20, and a delta of 0.30. If actual demand turned out to be 115 rather than the forecast 100, calculate the forecast for the next period.

SOLUTION

Adding the starting forecast and the trend, we have

$$\text{FIT}_{t-1} = F_{t-1} + T_{t-1} = 100 + 10 = 110$$

The actual A_{t-1} is given as 115. Therefore,

$$F_t = \text{FIT}_{t-1} + \alpha(A_{t-1} - \text{FIT}_{t-1})$$
$$= 110 + 0.2(115 - 110) = 111.0$$
$$T_t = T_{t-1} + \delta(F_t - \text{FIT}_{t-1})$$
$$= 10 + 0.3(111 - 110) = 10.3$$
$$\text{FIT}_t = F_t + T_t = 111.0 + 10.3 = 121.3$$

If, instead of 121.3, the actual turned out to be 120, the sequence would be repeated and the forecast for the next period would be

$$F_{t+1} = 121.3 + 0.2(120 - 121.3) = 121.04$$
$$T_{t+1} = 10.3 + 0.3(121.04 - 121.3) = 10.22$$
$$\text{FIT}_{t+1} = 121.04 + 10.22 = 131.26$$

Choosing the Appropriate Value for Alpha Exponential smoothing requires that the smoothing constant alpha (a) be given a value between 0 and 1. If the real demand is stable (such as demand for electricity or food), we would like a small alpha to lessen the effects of short-term or random changes. If the real demand is rapidly increasing or decreasing (such as in fashion items or new small appliances), we would like a large alpha to try to keep up with the change. It would be ideal if we could predict which alpha we should use. Unfortunately, two things work against us. First, it would take some time to determine the alpha that would best fit our actual data. This would be tedious to follow and revise. Second, because demands do change, the alpha we pick this week may need to be revised soon. Therefore, we need some automatic method to track and change our alpha values.

There are two approaches to controlling the value of alpha. One uses various values of alpha. The other uses a tracking signal.

1. **Two or more predetermined values of alpha.**   The amount of error between the forecast and the actual demand is measured. Depending on the degree of error, different values of alpha are used. If the error is large, alpha is 0.8; if the error is small, alpha is 0.2.
2. **Computed values for alpha.**   A tracking alpha computes whether the forecast is keeping pace with genuine upward or downward changes in demand (as opposed to random changes). In this application, the tracking alpha is defined as the exponentially smoothed actual error divided by the exponentially smoothed absolute error. Alpha changes from period to period within the possible range of 0 to 1.

Forecast Errors

In using the word *error*, we are referring to the difference between the forecast value and what actually occurred. In statistics, these errors are called *residuals*. As long as the forecast value is within the confidence limits, as we discuss later in "Measurement of Error," this is not really an error. But common usage refers to the difference as an error.

Demand for a product is generated through the interaction of a number of factors too complex to describe accurately in a model. Therefore, all forecasts certainly contain some error. In discussing forecast errors, it is convenient to distinguish between *sources of error* and the *measurement of error*.

Sources of Error

Errors can come from a variety of sources. One common source that many forecasters are unaware of is projecting past trends into the future. For example, when we talk about statistical errors in regression analysis, we are referring to the deviations of observations from our regression line. It is common to attach a confidence band (that is, statistical control limits) to the regression line to reduce the unexplained error. But when we then use this regression line as a forecasting device by projecting it into the future, the error may not be correctly defined by the projected confidence band. This is because the confidence interval is based on past data; it may not hold for projected data points and therefore cannot be used with the same confidence. In fact, experience has shown that the actual errors tend to be greater than those predicted from forecast models.

Errors can be classified as bias or random. *Bias errors* occur when a consistent mistake is made. Sources of bias include the failure to include the right variables; the use of the wrong relationships among variables; employing of the wrong trend line; a mistaken shift in the seasonal demand from where it normally occurs; and the existence of some undetected secular trend. *Random errors* can be defined as those that cannot be explained by the forecast model being used.

Measurement of Error

Several common terms used to describe the degree of error are *standard error, mean squared error* (or *variance*), and *mean absolute deviation*. In addition, tracking signals may be used to indicate any positive or negative bias in the forecast.

Standard error is discussed in the section on linear regression in this chapter. Because the standard error is the square root of a function, it is often more convenient to use the function itself. This is called the mean square error or variance.

The **mean absolute deviation (MAD)** was in vogue in the past but subsequently was ignored in favour of standard deviation and standard error measures. In recent years, MAD has made a comeback because of its simplicity and usefulness in obtaining tracking signals. MAD is the average error in the forecasts, using absolute values. It is valuable because MAD, like the standard deviation, measures the dispersion of some observed value from some expected value.

MAD is computed using the differences between the actual demand and the forecast demand without regard to sign. It equals the sum of the absolute deviations divided by the number of data points, or, stated in equation form,

[11.7]

$$\text{MAD} = \frac{\sum_{t=1}^{n} |A_t - F_t|}{n}$$

where

t = Period number

A = Actual demand for the period

F = Forecast demand for the period

n = Total number of periods

$|\,|$ = A symbol used to indicate the absolute value disregarding positive and negative signs

When the errors that occur in the forecast are normally distributed (the usual case), the mean absolute deviation relates to the standard deviation as

$$1 \text{ standard deviation} = \sqrt{\frac{\pi}{2}} \times \text{MAD, or approximately } 1.25 \text{ MAD}$$

Conversely,

$$1 \text{ MAD} = 0.8 \text{ standard deviation}$$

The standard deviation is the larger measure. If the MAD of a set of points was found to be 60 units, then the standard deviation would be 75 units. In the usual statistical manner, if control limits were set at plus or minus 3 standard deviations (or ± 3.75 MADs), then 99.7 percent of the points would fall within these limits.

A **tracking signal** is a measurement that indicates whether the forecast average is keeping pace with any genuine upward or downward changes in demand. As used in forecasting, the tracking signal is the *number* of mean absolute deviations that the forecast value is above or below the actual occurrence. Exhibit 11.7 shows a normal distribution with a mean of 0 and a MAD equal to 1. Thus, if we compute the tracking signal and

EXHIBIT 11.7   A Normal Distribution with Mean = 0 and MAD = 1

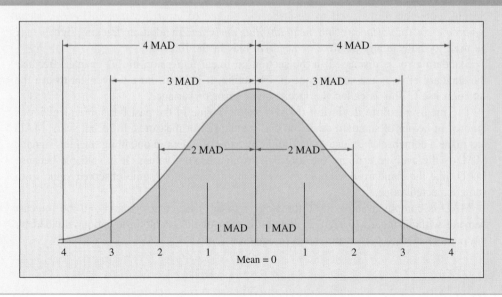

EXHIBIT 11.8

Computing the Mean Absolute Deviation (MAD), the Running Sum of Forecast Errors (RSFE), and the Tracking Signal (TS) from Forecast and Actual Data

MONTH	DEMAND FORECAST	ACTUAL	DEVIATION	RSFE	ABS. DEV.	SUM OF ABS. DEV.	MAD*	$TS = \dfrac{RSFE^\dagger}{MAD}$
1	1000	950	−50	−50	50	50	50	−1
2	1000	1070	+70	+20	70	120	60	0.33
3	1000	1100	+100	+120	100	220	73.3	1.64
4	1000	960	−40	+80	40	260	65	1.2
5	1000	1090	+90	+170	90	350	70	2.4
6	1000	1050	+50	+220	50	400	66.7	3.3

*For month 6, MAD = 400 ÷ 6 = 66.7.

†For month 6, $TS = \dfrac{RSFE}{MAD} = \dfrac{220}{66.7} = 3.3$ MADs.

Forecasting

find it equal to minus 2, we can see that the forecast model is providing forecasts that are quite a bit above the mean of the actual occurrences.

A tracking signal (TS) can be calculated using the arithmetic sum of forecast deviations divided by the mean absolute deviation:

[11.8]
$$TS = \frac{RSFE}{MAD}$$

where

RSFE = The running sum of forecast errors, considering the nature of the error. (For example, negative errors cancel positive errors and vice versa.)

MAD = The average of all the forecast errors (disregarding whether the deviations are positive or negative). It is the average of the absolute deviations.

Exhibit 11.8 illustrates the procedure for computing MAD and the tracking signal for a six-month period where the forecast had been set at a constant 1000 and the actual demands that occurred are as shown. In this example, the forecast, on the average, was off by 66.7 units and the tracking signal was equal to 3.3 mean absolute deviations.

We can get a better feel for what the MAD and tracking signal mean by plotting the points on a graph. Though this is not completely legitimate from a sample-size standpoint, we plotted each month in Exhibit 11.9 to show the drift of the tracking signal. Note that it drifted from minus 1 MAD to plus 3.3 MADs. This happened because actual demand was greater than the forecast in four of the six periods. If the actual demand does not fall below the forecast to offset the continual positive RSFE, the tracking signal would continue to rise and we would conclude that assuming a demand of 1000 is a bad forecast.

Linear Regression Analysis

Regression can be defined as a functional relationship between two or more correlated variables. It is used to predict one variable, given the other. The relationship is usually developed from observed data. The data should be plotted first to see if they appear linear or at least if parts of the data are linear. *Linear regression* refers to the special class of regression where the relationship between variables forms a straight line.

EXHIBIT 11.9   A Plot of the Tracking Signals Calculated in Exhibit 11.8

Forecasting

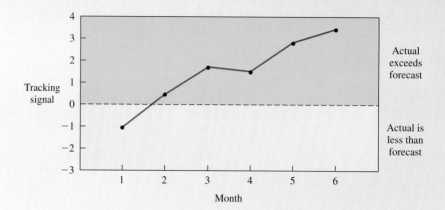

Operations and Supply Management in Practice

Forecasting in Services

With the Canadian economy becoming more services oriented, forecasting demand in services is becoming more important. Inaccurate forecasts can mean either a lack of personnel to service customers (leading to queues and poor customer service) or a surfeit of employees, leading to unnecessary costs. Remember, in services one cannot inventory capacity, therefore accurate forecasts are even more critical than in manufacturing.

Forecasting demand in services uses many of the techniques discussed in this chapter, both quantitative and qualitative. Naturally, one of the popular uses is in call centres all over the world. But there are other, more innovative, uses. A joint project between the Worker's Compensation Board (WCB) of British Columbia, Marsh Canada (an insurance company), and The Sauder School of Business at the University of British Columbia developed a method, based partly on regression, that helps predict high-risk claims from work-related injuries and diseases. This helps the WCB intervene earlier, which can result in lower costs and the employee returning to work earlier. Others have developed forecasting models of the calls to Emergency Medical System (EMS) services in Calgary, and the revenues of the British Columbia government. Thus, you can see the universal applicability of forecasting. The American Automobile Association in Michigan used time series and regression models to improve forecasting at their different divisions (emergency road service, member services, claims, and travel).

Carlos Leitao, chief economist for Montreal-based Laurentian Bank Securities and Tim Harford, economist and columnist for the London, U.K.-based *Financial Times* pointed out in a recent interview on CBC Radio that forecasting should also involve looking at a range of scenarios. Point forecasts are generally wrong (we discussed error measurements earlier) and therefore it is important for the company to have different views of the future to determine how they might respond to actual scenarios that might occur, i.e., proactive planning. This will help the company avoid facing unpredicted situations and having to develop reactive strategies and tactics to respond. It may also be useful to work with simple models that the decision maker can understand and interpret, rather than use more sophisticated "black box" models where the results are implemented without intuitive understanding. While their message was specific to financial forecasting, this principle is applicable to forecasting in general.

■ Sources: E. Urbanovich, E. E Young, M. L Puterman, and S. O. Fattedad, "Early Detection of High-Risk Claims at the Workers' Compensation Board of British Columbia," *Interfaces*, 33, 4, Jul/Aug 2003, pp. 15–26,

N. Channouf, P. L'Ecuyer, A. Ingolfsson, and A. N. Avramidis, "The Application of Forecasting Techniques to Modeling Emergency Medical System Calls in Calgary," *Alberta Health Care Management Science*, 10, 1, Feb 2007, pp. 25–45.

R. Klungle and J. Maluchnik, "Call Center Forecasting at AAA Michigan," *The Journal of Business Forecasting Methods and Systems*; 16, 4, Winter 1997/1998, pp 8–13.

The Current, CBC Radio 1, March 9, 2009.

The linear regression line is of the form $Y = a + bX$, where Y is the value of the dependent variable that we are solving for, a is the Y intercept, b is the slope, and X is the independent variable (actually, there can be many of these). In time series analysis, X is units of time.

Linear regression is useful for long-term forecasting of major occurrences and aggregate planning. For example, linear regression would be very useful to forecast demands for product families. Even though demand for individual products within a family may vary widely during a time period, demand for the total product family is surprisingly smooth.

The major restriction in using **linear regression forecasting** is, as the name implies, that past data and future projections are assumed to fall about a straight line. Although this does limit its application, sometimes, if we use a shorter period of time, linear regression analysis can still be used. For example, there may be short segments of the longer period that are approximately linear.

Linear regression is used both for time series forecasting and for causal relationship forecasting. When the dependent variable (usually the vertical axis on a graph) changes as a result of time (plotted as the horizontal axis), it is time series analysis. If one variable changes because of the change in another variable, this is a causal relationship (such as the number of deaths from lung cancer increasing with the number of people who smoke).

We use the following example to demonstrate linear least squares regression analysis.

EXAMPLE 11.2:   LEAST SQUARES METHOD

A firm's sales for a product line during the 12 quarters of the past three years were as follows:

QUARTER	SALES	QUARTER	SALES
1	600	7	2600
2	1550	8	2900
3	1500	9	3800
4	1500	10	4500
5	2400	11	4000
6	3100	12	4900

The firm wants to forecast each quarter of the fourth year—that is, quarters 13, 14, 15, and 16.

SOLUTION

The least squares equation for linear regression is

[11.9] $$Y = a + bx$$

where

Y = Dependent variable computed by the equation

y = The actual dependent variable data point (used below)

a = Y intercept

b = Slope of the line

x = Time period

The least squares method tries to fit the line to the data *that minimizes the sum of the squares of the vertical distance* between each data point and its corresponding point on the line. If a straight line is drawn through the general area of the points, the difference between the point and the line

EXHIBIT 11.10 Least Squares Regression Line

Forecasting

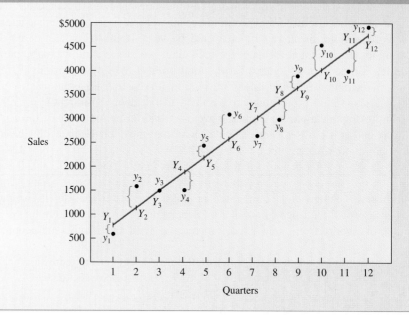

is $y - Y$. Exhibit 11.10 shows these differences. The sum of the squares of the differences between the plotted data points and the line points is

$$(y_1 - Y_1)^2 + (y_2 - Y_2)^2 + \cdots + (y_{12} - Y_{12})^2$$

The best line to use is the one that minimizes this total.

As before, the straight line equation is

$$Y = a + bx$$

Previously we determined a and b from the graph. In the least squares method, the equations for a and b are

[11.10]
$$a = \bar{y} - b\bar{x}$$

[11.11]
$$b = \frac{\sum xy - n\bar{x} \cdot \bar{y}}{\sum x^2 - n\bar{x}^2}$$

where

$a = Y$ intercept

$b = $ Slope of the line

$\bar{y} = $ Average of all ys

$\bar{x} = $ Average of all xs

$x = x$ value at each data point

$y = y$ value at each data point

$n = $ Number of data points

$Y = $ Value of the dependent variable computed with the regression equation

Least Squares Regression Analysis						**EXHIBIT 11.11**

(1)x	(2)y	(3)xy	(4)x^2	(5)y^2	(6)Y
1	600	600	1	360 000	801.3
2	1550	3100	4	2 402 500	11 60.9
3	1500	4500	9	2 250 000	15 20.5
4	1500	6000	16	2 250 000	18 80.1
5	2400	12 000	25	5 760 000	22 39.7
6	3100	18 600	36	9 610 000	25 99.4
7	2600	18 200	49	6 760 000	29 59.0
8	2900	23 200	64	8 410 000	33 18.6
9	3800	34 200	81	14 440 000	36 78.2
10	4500	45 000	100	20 250 000	40 37.8
11	4000	44 000	121	16 000 000	43 97.4
12	4900	58 800	144	24 010 000	47 57.1
78	33 350	268 200	650	112 502 500	

$\bar{x} = 6.5$ $b = 359.6153$

$\bar{y} = 2,779.17$ $a = 441.6666$

Therefore $Y = 441.66 + 359.6x$

$S_{yx} = 363.9$

Forecasting

Exhibit 11.11 shows these computations carried out for the 12 data points in the problem. Note that the final equation for Y shows an intercept of 441.6 and a slope of 359.6. The slope shows that for every unit change in X, Y changes by 359.6.

Strictly based on the equation, forecasts for periods 13 through 16 would be

$$Y_{13} = 441.6 + 359.6(13) = 5,116.4$$
$$Y_{14} = 441.6 + 359.6(14) = 5,476.0$$
$$Y_{15} = 441.6 + 359.6(15) = 5,835.6$$
$$Y_{16} = 441.6 + 359.6(16) = 6,195.2$$

The standard error of estimate, or how well the line fits the data, is[5]

[11.12]
$$S_{yx} = \sqrt{\frac{\sum_{i=1}^{n}(y_i - Y_i)^2}{n - 2}}$$

The standard error of estimate is computed from the second and last columns of Exhibit 11.11:

$$S_{yx} = \sqrt{\frac{(600 - 801.3)^2 + (1550 - 1160.9)^2 + (1500 - 1520.5)^2 + \cdots + (4900 - 4757.1)^2}{10}}$$

$$= 363.9$$

Microsoft® Excel has a very powerful regression tool designed to perform these calculations. To use the tool, a table is needed that contains data relevant to the problem (see Exhibit 11.12). The tool is part of the Data Analysis ToolPak that is accessed from the Data tab in Excel 2007 (you may need to add this by using the Add-In options).

EXHIBIT 11.12   Excel Regression Tool

	A	B	C	D	E	F	G	H	I
1		Qtr	Demand						
2		1	600						
3		2	1550						
4		3	1500						
5		4	1500						
6		5	2400						
7		6	3100						
8		7	2600						
9		8	2900						
10		9	3800						
11		10	4500						
12		11	4000						
13		12	4900						
14									
15									
16	SUMMARY OUTPUT								
17									
18		Regression Statistics							
19	Multiple R	0.96601558							
20	R Square	0.933186102							
21	Adjusted R Square	0.926504712							
22	Standard Error	363.8777972							
23	Observations	12							
24									
25	ANOVA								
26		df	SS	MS	F	Significance F			
27	Regression	1	18493221.15	18493221	139.6695	3.37202E-07			
28	Residual	10	1324070.513	132407.1					
29	Total	11	19817291.67						
30									
31		Coefficients	Standard Error	t Stat	P-value	Lower 95%	Upper 95%	Lower 95.0%	Upper 95.0%
32	Intercept	441.6666667	223.9513029	1.972155	0.076869	-57.3279302	940.661264	-57.3279302	940.6612636
33	X Variable 1	359.6153846	30.42899005	11.81818	3.37E-07	291.8153699	427.415399	291.81537	427.4153993
34									

Regression dialog box:

Input
Input Y Range: $B$2:$B$13
Input X Range: $A$2:$A$13
☐ Labels   ☐ Constant is Zero
☐ Confidence Level: 95 %

Output options
◉ Output Range: $A$16
◯ New Worksheet Ply:
◯ New Workbook

Residuals
☐ Residuals   ☐ Residual Plots
☐ Standardized Residuals   ☐ Line Fit Plots

Normal Probability
☐ Normal Probability Plots

[OK] [Cancel] [Help]

Forecasting

To use the tool, first input the data in two columns in your spreadsheet, then access the Regression option from the Data → Data Analysis menu. Next, specify the Y Range, which is B2:B13, and the X Range, which is A2:A13 in our example. Finally, an Output Range is specified. This is where you would like the results of the regression analysis placed in your spreadsheet. In the example A16 is entered. There is some information provided that goes beyond what we have covered, but what you are looking for is the Intercept and X Variable coefficients that correspond to the intercept and slope values in the linear equation. These are in rows 32 and 33 in Exhibit 11.12.

Summary

Developing a forecasting system is not easy. However, it must be done because forecasting is fundamental to any planning effort. In the short run, a forecast is needed to predict the requirements for materials, products, services, or other resources to respond to changes in demand. Forecasts permit adjusting schedules and varying labour and materials. In the long run, forecasting is required as a basis for strategic changes, such as developing new markets, developing new products or services, and expanding or creating new facilities.

Short- and intermediate-term forecasting (such as required for inventory control as well as staffing and material scheduling) may be satisfied with simpler models, such as exponential smoothing with perhaps an adaptive feature or a trend index. In these applications, thousands of items are usually being forecast. The forecasting routine should therefore be simple and run quickly on a computer. The routines should also detect and respond rapidly to definite short-term changes in demand while at the same time ignoring the occasional spurious demands. Exponential smoothing, when monitored by management to control the value of alpha, is an effective technique.

In summary, forecasting is tough. A perfect forecast is like a hole in one in golf: great to get but we should be satisfied just to get close to the cup—or, to push the analogy, just to land on the green. The ideal philosophy is to create the best forecast that you reasonably can and then hedge by maintaining flexibility in the system to account for the inevitable forecast error.

Key Terms

Dependent demand Requirements for a product or service caused by the demand for other products or services. This type of internal demand does not need a forecast, but can be calculated based on the demand for the other products or services.

Exponential smoothing A time series forecasting technique in which each increment of past demand data is decreased by $(1 - \alpha)$.

Independent demand Demand that cannot be directly derived from the demand for other products.

Linear regression forecasting A forecasting technique that assumes that past data and future projections fall around a straight line.

Mean absolute deviation (MAD) The average forecast error using absolute values of the error of each past forecast.

Smoothing constant alpha (α) The parameter in the exponential smoothing equation that controls the speed of reaction to differences between forecasts and actual demand.

Smoothing constant delta (δ) An additional parameter used in an exponential smoothing equation that includes an adjustment for trend.

Time series analysis A type of forecast in which data relating to past demand are used to predict future demand.

Tracking signal A measure that indicates whether the forecast average is keeping pace with any genuine upward or downward changes in demand.

Formula Review

Simple moving average

[11.1]
$$F_t = \frac{A_{t-1} + A_{t-2} + A_{t-3} + \cdots + A_{t-n}}{n}$$

Weighted moving average

[11.2]
$$F_t = w_1 A_{t-1} + w_2 A_{t-2} + \cdots + w_n A_{t-n}$$

Single exponential smoothing

[11.3]
$$F_t = F_{t-1} + \alpha(A_{t-1} - F_{t-1})$$

Exponential smoothing with trend

[11.4]
$$\text{FIT}_t = F_t + T_t$$

[11.5]
$$F_t = \text{FIT}_{t-1} + \alpha(A_{t-1} - \text{FIT}_{t-1})$$

[11.6]
$$T_t = T_{t-1} + \delta(F_t - \text{FIT}_{t-1})$$

Mean absolute deviation

[11.7]
$$\text{MAD} = \frac{\sum_{t=1}^{n} |A_t - F_t|}{n}$$

Tracking signal

[11.8]
$$\text{TS} = \frac{\text{RSFE}}{\text{MAD}}$$

Least squares regression

[11.9]
$$Y = a + bx$$

[11.10]
$$a = \bar{y} - b\bar{x}$$

[11.11]
$$b = \frac{\sum xy - n\bar{x} \cdot \bar{y}}{\sum x^2 - n\bar{x}^2}$$

Standard error of estimate

[11.12]
$$S_{yx} = \sqrt{\frac{\sum_{i=1}^{n}(y_i - Y_i)^2}{n - 2}}$$

Solved Problems

Solved Problem 1

Sunrise Baking Company markets donuts through a chain of food stores. It has been experiencing over- and underproduction because of forecasting errors. The following data are its demand in dozens of donuts for the past four weeks. Donuts are made for the following day; for example, Sunday's donut production is for Monday's sales, Monday's production is for Tuesday's sales, and so forth. The bakery is closed Saturday, so Friday's production must satisfy demand for both Saturday and Sunday.

Forecasting

	4 WEEKS AGO	3 WEEKS AGO	2 WEEKS AGO	LAST WEEK
Monday	2200	2400	2300	2400
Tuesday	2000	2100	2200	2200
Wednesday	2300	2400	2300	2500
Thursday	1800	1900	1800	2000
Friday	1900	1800	2100	2000
Saturday				
Sunday	2800	2700	3000	2900

Make a forecast for this week on the following basis:
a. Daily, using a simple four-week moving average.
b. Daily, using a weighted average of 0.40, 0.30, 0.20, and 0.10 for the past four weeks.
c. Sunrise is also planning its purchases of ingredients for bread production. If bread demand had been forecast for last week at 22 000 loaves and only 21 000 loaves were actually demanded, what would Sunrise's forecast be for this week using exponential smoothing with $\alpha = 0.10$?
d. Suppose, with the forecast made in c, this week's demand actually turns out to be 22 500. What would the new forecast be for the next week?

SOLUTION

a. Simple moving average, four-week.

$$\text{Monday} \quad \frac{2400 + 2300 + 2400 + 2200}{4} = \frac{9300}{4} = 2325 \text{ doz.}$$

$$\text{Tuesday} \quad \frac{2200 + 2200 + 2100 + 2000}{4} = \frac{8500}{4} = 2125 \text{ doz.}$$

$$\text{Wednesday} \quad \frac{2500 + 2300 + 2400 + 2300}{4} = \frac{9500}{4} = 2375 \text{ doz.}$$

$$\text{Thursday} \quad \frac{2200 + 1800 + 1900 + 1800}{4} = \frac{7500}{4} = 1875 \text{ doz.}$$

$$\text{Friday} \quad = \frac{7800}{4} = 1950 \text{ doz.}$$

$$\text{Saturday and Sunday} \quad = \frac{11\,400}{4} = 2850 \text{ doz.}$$

b. Weighted average with weights of .40, .30, .20, and .10.

	(.10)		(.20)		(.30)		(.40)		
Monday	220	+	480	+	690	+	960	=	2350
Tuesday	200	+	420	+	660	+	880	=	2160
Wednesday	230	+	480	+	690	+	1000	=	2400
Thursday	180	+	380	+	540	+	800	=	1900
Friday	190	+	360	+	630	+	800	=	1980
Saturday and Sunday	280	+	540	+	900	+	1160	=	2880
	1300	+	2660	+	4110	+	5600	=	13 670

c. Exponentially smoothed forecast for bread demand

$$F_t = F_{t-1} + \alpha(A_{t-1} - F_{t-1})$$
$$= 22\,000 + 0.10(21\,000 - 22\,000)$$
$$= 22\,000 - 100 = 21\,900 \text{ loaves}$$

d. Exponentially smoothed forecast

$$F_{t+1} = 21\,900 + 0.10(22\,500 - 21\,900)$$
$$= 21\,900 + 0.10(600) = 21\,960 \text{ loaves}$$

Solved Problem 2

A specific forecasting model was used to forecast demand for a product. The forecasts and the corresponding demand that subsequently occurred are shown below. Use the MAD and tracking signal technique to evaluate the accuracy of the forecasting model.

	ACTUAL	FORECAST
October	700	660
November	760	840
December	780	750
January	790	835
February	850	910
March	950	890

Forecasting

SOLUTION

Evaluate the forecasting model using MAD and tracking signal.

	ACTUAL DEMAND	FORECAST DEMAND	ACTUAL DEVIATION	CUMULATIVE DEVIATION (RSFE)	ABSOLUTE DEVIATION
October	700	660	40	−40	40
November	760	840	−80	−40	80
December	780	750	30	−10	30
January	790	835	−45	−55	45
February	850	910	−60	−115	60
March	950	890	60	−55	60
				Total dev. =	315

$$\text{MAD} = \frac{315}{6} = 52.5$$

$$\text{Tracking singal} = \frac{-55}{52.5} = -1.05$$

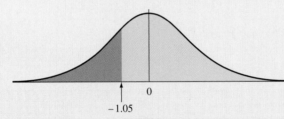

There is not enough evidence to reject the forecasting model, so we accept its recommendations.

Review and Discussion Questions

1. What is the difference between dependent and independent demand?
2. Examine Exhibit 11.3 and suggest which model you might use for (*a*) bathing suit demand, (*b*) demand for new houses, (*c*) electrical power usage, (*d*) new plant expansion plans.
3. Give some very simple rules you might use to manage demand for a firm's product. (An example is "limited to stock on hand.")
4. What strategies are used by supermarkets, airlines, hospitals, banks, and cereal manufacturers to influence demand?
5. All forecasting methods using exponential smoothing, adaptive smoothing, and exponential smoothing including trend require starting values to get the equations going. How would you select the starting value for, say, F_{t-1}?
6. From the choice of simple moving average, weighted moving average, exponential smoothing, and linear regression analysis, which forecasting technique would you consider the most accurate? Why?
7. What are the main problems with using adaptive exponential smoothing in forecasting?
8. Discuss the basic differences between the mean absolute deviation and the standard deviation.
9. What implications do forecast errors have for the search for ultrasophisticated statistical forecasting models?

Problems

1. Demand for stereo headphones and CD players for joggers has caused Nina Industries to grow almost 50 percent over the past year. The number of joggers continues to expand, so Nina expects demand for headsets to also expand, because, as yet, no safety laws have been passed to prevent joggers from wearing them. Demand for the stereo units for last year was as follows:

MONTH	DEMAND (UNITS)	MONTH	DEMAND (UNITS)
January	4200	July	5300
February	4300	August	4900
March	4000	September	5400
April	4400	October	5700
May	5000	November	6300
June	4700	December	6000

a. Using least squares regression analysis, what would you estimate demand to be for each month next year? Using a spreadsheet, follow the general format in Exhibit 11.11. Compare your results to those obtained by using the forecast spreadsheet function.

b. To be reasonably confident of meeting demand, Nina decides to use three standard errors of estimate for safety. How many additional units should be held to meet this level of confidence?

2. Historical demand for a product is

	DEMAND
January	12
February	11
March	15
April	12
May	16
June	15

a. Using a weighted moving average with weights of 0.60, 0.30, and 0.10, find the July forecast.

b. Using a simple three-month moving average, find the July forecast.

c. Using single exponential smoothing with $\alpha = 0.2$ and a June forecast $= 13$, find the July forecast. Make whatever assumptions you wish.

d. Using simple linear regression analysis, calculate the regression equation for the preceding demand data.

e. Using the regression equation in d, calculate the forecast for July.

3. The following tabulations are actual sales of units for six months and a starting forecast in January.

a. Calculate forecasts for the remaining five months using simple exponential smoothing with $\alpha = 0.2$.

b. Calculate MAD for the forecasts.

	ACTUAL	FORECAST
January	100	80
February	94	
March	106	
April	80	
May	68	
June	94	

4. Sales data for two years are as follows. Data are aggregated with two months of sales in each "period."

MONTHS	SALES	MONTHS	SALES
January–February	109	January–February	115
March–April	104	March–April	112
May–June	150	May–June	159
July–August	170	July–August	182
September–October	120	September–October	126
November–December	100	November–December	106

a. Plot the data.

b. Fit a simple linear regression model to the sales data.

5. The tracking signals computed using past demand history for three different products are as follows. Each product used the same forecasting technique.

	TS 1	TS 2	TS 3
1	−2.70	1.54	0.10
2	−2.32	−0.64	0.43
3	−1.70	2.05	1.08
4	−1.1	2.58	1.74
5	−0.87	−0.95	1.94
6	−0.05	−1.23	2.24
7	0.10	0.75	2.96
8	0.40	−1.59	3.02
9	1.50	0.47	3.54
10	2.20	2.74	3.75

Discuss the tracking signals for each and what the implications are.

6. Not all the items in your office supply store are evenly distributed as far as demand is concerned, so you decide to forecast demand to help plan your stock. Past data for legal-sized yellow tablets for the month of August are

Week 1	300	Week 3	600
Week 2	400	Week 4	700

   a. Using a three-week moving average, what would you forecast the next week to be?
   b. Using exponential smoothing with $\alpha = 0.20$, if the exponential forecast for week 3 was estimated as the average of the first two weeks [(300 + 400)\2 = 350], what would you forecast week 5 to be?

7. Here are the actual tabulated demands for an item for a nine-month period (January through September). Your supervisor wants to test two forecasting methods to see which method was better over this period.

MONTH	ACTUAL	MONTH	ACTUAL
January	110	June	180
February	130	July	140
March	150	August	130
April	170	September	140
May	160		

   a. Forecast April through September using a three-month moving average.
   b. Use simple exponential smoothing with an alpha of 0.3 to estimate April through September. Start the forecast with the average of January, February, and March demands.
   c. Use MAD to decide which method produced the better forecast over the six-month period.

8. A particular forecasting model was used to forecast a six-month period. Here are the forecasts and actual demands that resulted:

	FORECAST	ACTUAL
April	250	200
May	325	250
June	400	325
July	350	300
August	375	325
September	450	400

Find the tracking signal and state whether you think the model being used is giving acceptable answers.

9. Harlen Industries has a simple forecasting model: Take the actual demand for the same month last year and divide that by the number of fractional weeks in that month. This gives the average weekly demand for that month. This weekly average is used as the weekly forecast for the same month this year. This technique was used to forecast eight weeks for this year, which are shown below along with the actual demand that occurred.

The following eight weeks show the forecast (based on last year) and the demand that actually occurred:

WEEK	FORECAST DEMAND	ACTUAL DEMAND	WEEK	FORECAST DEMAND	ACTUAL DEMAND
1	140	137	5	140	180
2	140	133	6	150	170
3	140	150	7	150	185
4	140	160	8	150	205

   a. Compute the MAD of forecast errors.
   b. Using the RSFE, compute the tracking signal.
   c. Based on your answers to a and b, comment on Harlen's method of forecasting.

10. The following table contains the demand from the last 10 months:

MONTH	ACTUAL DEMAND	MONTH	ACTUAL DEMAND
1	31	6	36
2	34	7	38
3	33	8	40
4	35	9	40
5	37	10	41

   a. Calculate the single exponential smoothing forecast for these data using an α of .30 and an initial forecast (F_1) of 31.
   b. Calculate the exponential smoothing with trend forecast for these data using an α of .30, a δ of .30, an initial trend forecast (T_1) of 1, and an initial exponentially smoothed forecast (F_1) of 30.
   c. Calculate the mean absolute deviation (MAD) for each forecast. Which is best?

11. In this problem, you are to test the validity of your forecasting model. Here are the forecasts for a model you have been using and the actual demands that occurred:

WEEK	FORECAST	ACTUAL
1	800	900
2	850	1000
3	950	1050
4	950	900
5	1000	900
6	975	1100

Use the method stated in the text to compute the MAD and tracking signal. Then decide whether the forecasting model you have been using is giving reasonable results.

12. Assume that your stock of sales merchandise is maintained based on the forecast demand. If the distributor's sales personnel call on the first day of each month, compute your forecast sales by each of the three methods requested here.

	ACTUAL
June	140
July	180
August	170

a. Using a simple three-month moving average, what is the forecast for September?
b. Using a weighted moving average, what is the forecast for September, with weights of 0.20, 0.30, and 0.50 for June, July, and August, respectively?
c. Using single exponential smoothing and assuming that the forecast for June had been 130, forecast sales for September with a smoothing constant alpha of 0.30.

13. Historical demand for a product is as follows:

	DEMAND
April	60
May	55
June	75
July	60
August	80
September	75

a. Using a simple four-month moving average, calculate a forecast for October.
b. Using single exponential smoothing with $\alpha = 0.2$ and a September forecast = 65, calculate a forecast for October.
c. Using simple linear regression, calculate the trend line for the historical data. Say the X axis is April = 1, May = 2, and so on, while the Y axis is demand.
d. Calculate a forecast for October.

14. The following table shows predicted product demand using your particular forecasting method along with the actual demand that occurred:

FORECAST	ACTUAL
1500	1550
1400	1500
1700	1600
1750	1650
1800	1700

a. Compute the tracking signal using the mean absolute deviation and running sum of forecast errors.
b. Discuss whether your forecasting method is giving good predictions.

15. Your manager is trying to determine what forecasting method to use. Based upon the following historical data, calculate the following forecast and specify what procedure you would utilize.

MONTH	ACTUAL DEMAND	MONTH	ACTUAL DEMAND
1	62	7	76
2	65	8	78
3	67	9	78
4	68	10	80
5	71	11	84
6	73	12	85

a. Calculate the simple three-month moving average forecast for periods 4–12.
b. Calculate the weighted three-month moving average using weights of 0.50, 0.30, and 0.20 for periods 4–12.
c. Calculate the single exponential smoothing forecast for periods 2–12 using an initial forecast (F_1) of 61 and an α of 0.30.
d. Calculate the exponential smoothing with trend component forecast for periods 2–12 using an initial trend forecast (T_1) of 1.8, an initial exponential smoothing forecast (F_1) of 60, an α of 0.30, and a δ of 0.30.
e. Calculate the mean absolute deviation (MAD) for the forecasts made by each technique in periods 4–12. Which forecasting method do you prefer?

16. Actual demand for a product for the past three months was

Three months ago	400 units
Two months ago	350 units
Last month	325 units

a. Using a simple three-month moving average, make a forecast for this month.

b. If 300 units were actually demanded this month, what would your forecast be for next month?

c. Using simple exponential smoothing, what would your forecast be for this month if the exponentially smoothed forecast for three months ago was 450 units and the smoothing constant was 0.20?

17. After using your forecasting model for six months, you decide to test it using MAD and a tracking signal. Here are the forecast and actual demands for the six-month period:

PERIOD	FORECAST	ACTUAL
May	450	500
June	500	550
July	550	400
August	600	500
September	650	675
October	700	600

a. Find the tracking signal.

b. Decide whether your forecasting routine is acceptable.

18. Assume an initial starting F_t of 300 units, a trend of 8 units, an alpha of .30, and a delta of .40. If actual demand turned out to be 288, calculate the forecast for the next period.

CASE | Altavox Electronics

Altavox is a manufacturer and distributor of many different electronic instruments and devices, including digital/analog multimeters, function generators, oscilloscopes, frequency counters, and other test and measuring equipment. Altavox sells a line of test meters that are popular with professional electricians. The model VC202 is sold through six distributors to retail stores in Canada. These distributors are located in St. John's, Laval, Kitchener, Regina, and Kelowna, and have been selected to serve different regions in the country.

The model VC202 has been a steady seller over the years due to its reliability and rugged construction. Altavox does not consider this a seasonal product, but there is some variability in demand. Demand for the product over the past 13 weeks is shown in the following table.

These data are contained in an Excel Spreadsheet *Altavox Data* included on the OLC with the book. The demand in the regions varies between a high of 40 units on average per week in St. John's and 48 units in Regina. This quarter's data are pretty close to the demand last quarter.

WEEK	1	2	3	4	5	6	7	8	9	10	11	12	13	AVERAGE
St. John's	33	45	37	38	55	30	18	58	47	37	23	55	40	40
Laval	26	35	41	40	46	48	55	18	62	44	30	45	50	42
Kitchener	44	34	22	55	48	72	62	28	27	95	35	45	47	47
Regina	27	42	35	40	51	64	70	65	55	43	38	47	42	48
Kelowna	32	43	54	40	46	74	40	35	45	38	48	56	50	46
Total	162	199	189	213	246	288	245	204	236	257	174	248	229	222

Management would like you to experiment with some forecasting models to determine what should be used in a new system being implemented. The new system is programmed to use one of two models: simple moving average or exponential smoothing.

Altavox Data

Questions

1. Consider using a simple moving average model. Experiment with models using five weeks' and three weeks' past data. The past data in each region is given below. Evaluate the forecasts that would have been made over the past 13 weeks using the mean absolute deviation and tracking signal as criteria.

WEEK	−5	−4	−3	−2	−1
St. John's	45	38	30	58	37
Laval	62	18	48	40	35
Kitchener	62	22	72	44	48
Regina	42	35	40	64	43
Kelowna	43	40	54	46	35
Total	254	153	244	252	198

2. Next consider using a simple exponential smoothing model. In your analysis, test two alpha values, .2 and .4. Use the same criteria for evaluating the model as in part 1. Assume that the initial previous forecast for the model using an alpha value of .2 is the past three-week average. For the model using an alpha of .4, assume that the previous forecast is the past five-week average.

3. Altavox is considering a new option for distributing the model VC202 where, instead of using five vendors, only a single vendor would be used. Evaluate this option by analyzing how accurate the forecast would be, based on the demand aggregated across all regions. Use the model that you think is best, from your analysis of parts 1 and 2. Use a new criterion that is calculated by taking the MAD and dividing by the average demand. This criterion is called the mean absolute percent error (MAPE) and gauges the error of a forecast as a percent of the average demand. What are the advantages and disadvantages of aggregating demand from a forecasting view? Are there other things that should be considered when going from multiple distributors to a single distributor?

Footnotes

[1] S. Spooner, *CA Magazine*, 141, 3, April 2008, p10.

[2] In addition to dependent and independent demands, other relationships include complementary products and causal relationships where demand for one causes the demand for another.

[3] Some writers prefer to call F_t a smoothed average.

[4] When exponential smoothing is first introduced, the initial forecast or starting point may be obtained by using a simple estimate or an average of preceding periods such as the average of the first two or three periods.

[5] An equation for the standard error that is often easier to compute is $S_{yx} = \sqrt{\dfrac{\sum y^2 - a \sum y - b \sum xy}{n - 2}}$

Selected Bibliography

De Lurgio, S. *Forecasting Principles and Applications.* New York: Irwin/McGraw-Hill, 1998.

Diebold, F. X. *Elements of Forecasting.* 2nd ed. Cincinnati, OH: South-Western College Publishing, 2000.

Hanke, J. E.; A. G. Reitsch; and D. W. Wichem. *Business Forecasting.* 7th ed. Upper Saddle River, NJ: Prentice Hall, 2001.

Makridakis, S.; S. C. Wheelwright; and R. J. Hyndman. *Forecasting: Methods for Management.* New York: John Wiley & Sons, 1998.

AGGREGATE SALES AND OPERATIONS PLANNING

1. Understand what sales and operations planning is and how it coordinates manufacturing, logistics, service, and marketing plans.
2. Know how to construct aggregate plans that employ different strategies for meeting demand.
3. Understand aggregate plan implementation issues.
4. Understand what yield management is and why it is an important strategy for levelling demand.

AGGREGATE PLANNING

Let's eavesdrop on an executive staff meeting at the Acme Widget Company. The participants are not happy campers.

President: This shortage situation is terrible. When will we ever get our act together? Whenever business gets good, we run out of product and our customer service is lousy.

VP Operations: I'll tell you when. When we start to get some decent forecasts from the Sales Department . . .

VP Sales
(interrupting): Wait a minute. We forecast this upturn.

VP Operations: . . . . in time to do something about it. Yeah, we got the revised forecast—four days after the start of the month. By then it was too late.

VP Sales: I could have told you months ago. All you had to do was ask.

VP Finance: I'd like to be in on those conversations. We've been burned more than once by building inventories for a business upturn that doesn't happen. Then we get stuck with tons of inventory and run out of cash.

And the beat goes on. Back orders, dissatisfied customers, high inventories, late shipments, finger-pointing, cash-flow problems, demand and supply out of balance, missing the business plan. This is the norm in many companies.

It does not, however, have to be that way. Today many companies are using a business process called sales and operations planning (S&OP) to help avoid such problems. To learn what it is, and how to make it work, read on.

■ Source: Adapted from Thomas F. Wallace, *Sales and Operations Planning: The How-To Handbook* (Cincinnati, OH: T. F. Wallace & Co., 2000), p. 3. Copyright © 2000 Thomas Wallace. Used with permission.

In this chapter, we focus on the aggregate operations plan, which translates annual and quarterly business plans into broad labour and output plans for the intermediate term (3 to 18 months). The objective of the aggregate operations plan is to minimize the cost of resources required to meet demand over that period.

WHAT IS SALES AND OPERATIONS PLANNING?

Sales and operations planning is a process that helps firms provide better customer service, lower inventory, shorten customer lead times, stabilize production rates, and give top management a handle on the business. The process is designed to coordinate activities in the field with the manufacturing and service functions that are required to meet demand over time. Depending on the situation, activities in the field may include the supply of warehouse distribution centres, retail sales outlets, or direct sales channels. The process is designed to help a company get demand and supply in balance and keep them in balance over time. This process requires teamwork among sales, distribution and logistics, operations, finance, and product development.

The sales and operations planning process consists of a series of meetings, finishing with a high-level meeting where key intermediate-term decisions are made. The end goal is an agreement between various departments on the best course of action to achieve the optimal balance between supply and demand. The idea is to put the operational plan in line with the business plan.

This balance must occur at an aggregate level and also at the detailed individual product level. By *aggregate* we mean at the level of major groups of products. Over time, we need to ensure that we have enough total capacity. Since demand is often quite dynamic, it is important that we monitor our expected needs 3 to 18 months or further in the future. When planning this far into the future, it is difficult to know exactly how much of a particular product we will need, but we should be able to know how a larger group of similar products should sell. The term *aggregate* refers to this group of products. Given that we have enough aggregate capacity, our individual product schedulers, working within aggregate capacity constraints, can handle the daily and weekly launching of individual product orders to meet short-term demand.

OVERVIEW OF SALES AND OPERATIONS PLANNING ACTIVITIES

Exhibit 12.1 positions sales and operations planning relative to other major operations planning activities. The term sales and operations planning was coined by companies to refer to the process that helps firms keep demand and supply in balance. In operations management, this process was traditionally called *aggregate planning*. The new terminology is meant to

Overview of Major Operations and Supply Planning Activities   EXHIBIT 12.1

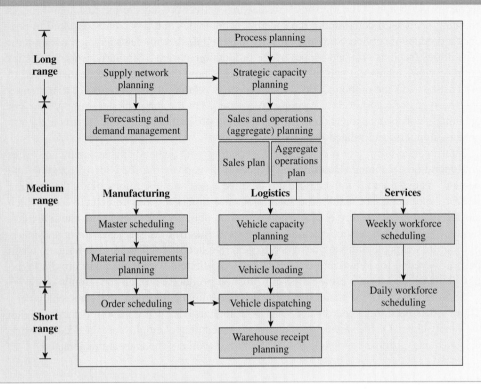

capture the importance of cross-functional work. Typically, this activity requires an integrated effort with cooperation from sales, distribution and logistics, operations, finance, and product development.

Within sales and operations planning, marketing develops a sales plan that extends through the next 3 to 18 months. This sales plan is typically stated in units of aggregate product groups and is often tied into sales incentive programs and other marketing activities. The operations side develops an operations plan as an output of the process, which is discussed in depth in this chapter. By focusing on aggregate product and sales volumes, the marketing and operations functions are able to develop plans for the way demand will be met. This is a particularly difficult task when there are significant changes in demand over time as a result of market trends or other factors.

Aggregation on the supply side is done by product families, and on the demand side by groups of customers. Individual product production schedules and matching customer orders can be handled more readily as a result of the sales and operations planning process. Typically, sales and operations planning occurs on a monthly cycle. Sales and operations planning links a company's strategic plans and business plan to its detailed operations and supply processes. These detailed processes include manufacturing, logistics, and service activities, as shown in Exhibit 12.1.

In Exhibit 12.1, the time dimension is shown as long, intermediate, and short range. Generally, **long-range planning** is done annually, focusing on a horizon greater than one year. **Intermediate-range planning** usually covers a period from 3 to 18 months, with weekly, monthly, or sometimes quarterly time increments. **Short-range planning** covers a period from one day to six months, with daily or weekly time increments.

Cross Functional

Long-range planning activities are done in two major areas. The first is the design of the manufacturing and service processes that produce the products of the firm, and the second is the design of the logistics activities that deliver products to the customer. Process planning deals with determining the specific technologies and procedures required to produce a product or service. Strategic capacity planning deals with determining the long-term capabilities (such as size and scope) of the production systems. Similarly, from a logistics point of view, supply network planning determines how the product will be distributed to the customer on the outbound side, with decisions relating to the location of warehouses and the types of transportation systems to be used. On the inbound side, supply network planning involves decisions relating to outsourcing production, selection of parts and component suppliers, and related decisions.

Intermediate-term activities include forecasting and demand management and sales and operations planning. Determining expected demand is the focus of forecasting and demand management. From these data, detailed sales and operations plans for meeting these requirements are made. The sales plans are inputs to sales force activities, which are the focus of marketing books. The operations plan provides input into the manufacturing, logistics, and service planning activities of the firm. Master scheduling and material requirements planning are designed to generate detailed schedules that indicate when parts are needed for manufacturing activities. Coordinated with these plans are the logistics plans needed to move the parts and finished products through the supply chain.

Short-term details are focused mostly on scheduling production and shipment orders. These orders need to be coordinated with the actual vehicles that transport material through the supply chain. On the service side, short-term scheduling of employees is needed to ensure that adequate customer service is provided and fair worker schedules are maintained.

THE AGGREGATE OPERATIONS PLAN

The aggregate operations plan is concerned with setting production rates by product group or other broad categories for the intermediate term (3 to 18 months). Note again from Exhibit 12.1 that the aggregate plan precedes the master schedule. *The main purpose of the aggregate plan is to specify the optimal combination of production rate, workforce level, and inventory on hand.* **Production rate** refers to the number of units completed per unit of time (such as per hour or per day). **Workforce level** is the number of workers needed for production (production = production rate × workforce level). **Inventory on hand** is unused inventory carried over from the previous period.

Here is a formal statement of the aggregate planning problem: Given the demand forecast F_t for each period t in the planning horizon that extends over T periods, determine the production level P_t, inventory level I_t, and workforce level W_t for periods $t = 1, 2, \ldots, T$ that minimize the relevant costs over the planning horizon.

The form of the aggregate plan varies from company to company. In some firms, it is a formalized report containing planning objectives and the planning premises on which it is based. In other companies, particularly smaller ones, the owner may make simple calculations of workforce needs that reflect a general staffing strategy.

The process by which the plan itself is derived also varies. One common approach is to derive it from the corporate annual plan, as shown in Exhibit 12.1. A typical corporate plan contains a section on manufacturing that specifies how many units in each major product line need to be produced over the next 12 months to meet the sales forecast. The planner takes this information and attempts to determine how best to meet these requirements with available resources. Alternatively, some organizations combine output requirements into equivalent units and use this as the basis for the aggregate plan. For example, a division of

Bombardier Aerospace of Montreal makes different types of aircraft such as regional jets, business jets, and amphibious aircraft.

The corporate plan specifies how many units to produce of each type of aircraft based on forecasts; the aggregate plan determines how to meet this requirement with available resources and how to acquire more resources if needed.

General Motors may be asked to produce a certain number of cars of all types at a particular facility. The production planner would then take the average labour hours required for all models as a basis for the overall aggregate plan. Refinements to this plan, specifically model types to be produced, would be reflected in shorter-term production plans.

Another approach is to develop the aggregate plan by simulating various master production schedules and calculating corresponding capacity requirements to see if adequate labour and equipment exist at each work centre. If capacity is inadequate, additional requirements for overtime, subcontracting, extra workers, and so forth are specified for each product line and combined into a rough-cut plan. This plan is then modified by cut-and-try or mathematical methods to derive a final and (one hopes) lower-cost plan.

Production Planning Environment

Exhibit 12.2 illustrates the internal and external factors that constitute the production planning environment. In general, the external environment is outside the production planner's direct control, but in some firms, demand for the product can be managed. Through close cooperation between marketing and operations, promotional activities and price cutting can be used to build demand during slow periods. Conversely, when demand is strong, promotional activities can be curtailed and prices raised to maximize the revenues from those products or services that the firm has the capacity to provide. The current practices in managing demand will be discussed later in the section titled "Yield Management."

Complementary products may work for firms facing cyclical demand fluctuations. Demands on the production system can be smoothed out by producing a complementary product with high demand during fall and winter, and low demand during spring and summer. For example, Bombardier Recreational Products makes snowmobiles for winter recreation and motorized watercraft and all-terrain vehicles for summer recreation. Similarly, since air travel in Canada drops off during the winter, WestJet uses its aircraft (which would otherwise have been idle) to charter passengers to the Caribbean for Air Transat. The complementary offerings help level demand, allowing for a level strategy without disadvantages, such as reduced prices for national destinations during winter or fluctuations in the size of the workforce.

With services, cycles are more often measured in hours than months. Restaurants with strong demand during lunch and dinner will often add a breakfast menu to increase demand during the morning hours.

Cross Functional

EXHIBIT 12.2 | Required Inputs to the Production Planning System

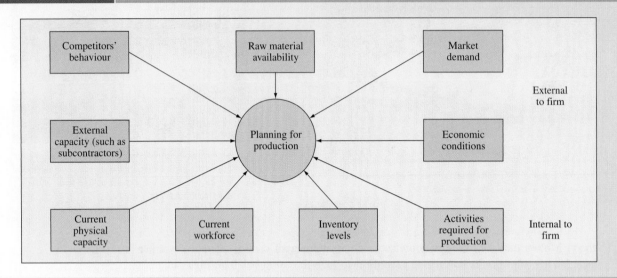

But even so, there are limits to how much demand can be controlled. Ultimately, the production planner must live with the sales projections and orders promised by the marketing function, leaving the internal factors as variables that can be manipulated in deriving a production plan. A new approach to facilitate managing these internal factors is termed *accurate response*. This entails refined measurement of historical demand patterns blended with expert judgment to determine when to begin production of particular items. The key element of the approach is clearly identifying those products for which demand is relatively predictable from those for which demand is relatively unpredictable.[1]

The internal factors themselves differ in their controllability. Current physical capacity (plant and equipment) is usually nearly fixed in the short run; union agreements often constrain what can be done in changing the workforce; physical capacity cannot always be increased; and top management may limit the amount of money that can be tied up in inventories. Still, there is always some flexibility in managing these factors, and production planners can implement one or a combination of the **production planning strategies** discussed here.

Production Planning Strategies There are three production planning strategies. These strategies involve trade-offs among the workforce size, work hours, inventory, and backlogs.

1. **Chase strategy.** Match the production rate to the order rate by hiring and laying off employees as the order rate varies. The success of this strategy depends on having a pool of easily trained applicants to draw on as order volumes increase. Some of the quantifiable costs of the layoff/hiring strategy are: (*a*) hiring/training costs, (*b*) reduced productivity and capacity, due to the learning employees have to acquire after being hired, (*c*) quality problems during ramp up, due to untrained employees, and (*d*) reduced productivity, due to employees slowing down out of fear of being laid off. Qualitative costs of the layoff/hiring strategy include: (*a*) loss of morale, (*b*) loss of knowledge through layoffs, and (*c*) poor customer service due to untrained employees.

2. **Stable workforce—variable work hours.** Vary the output by varying the number of hours worked through flexible work schedules or overtime. By varying the

number of work hours, you can match production quantities to orders. This strategy provides workforce continuity and avoids many of the emotional and tangible costs of hiring and firing associated with the chase strategy.

3. **Level strategy.**   Maintain a stable workforce working at a constant output rate. Shortages and surpluses are absorbed by fluctuating inventory levels, order backlogs, and lost sales. Employees benefit from stable work hours at the cost of potentially decreased customer service levels and increased inventory costs. Another concern is the possibility of inventoried products becoming obsolete.

When just one of these variables is used to absorb demand fluctuations, it is termed a **pure strategy**; two or more used in combination constitute a **mixed strategy**. As you might suspect, mixed strategies are more widely applied in industry (see the section on Aggregate Planning in Practice).

Subcontracting In addition to these strategies, managers also may choose to subcontract some portion of production. This strategy is similar to the chase strategy, but hiring and laying off are translated into subcontracting and not subcontracting. Some level of subcontracting can be desirable to accommodate demand fluctuations. However, unless the relationship with the supplier is particularly strong, a manufacturer can lose some control over schedule and quality. Subcontracting is different from outsourcing in that outsourcing implies permanent transfer of production to another company whereas subcontracting is considered temporary.

Relevant Costs

Four costs are relevant to the aggregate production plan. These relate to the production cost itself as well as the cost to hold inventory and to have unfilled orders. More specifically, these are

1. **Basic production costs.**   These are the fixed and variable costs incurred in producing a given product type in a given time period. Included are direct and indirect labour costs and regular as well as overtime compensation.
2. **Costs associated with changes in the production rate.**   Typical costs in this category are those involved in hiring, training, and laying off personnel. Hiring temporary help is a way of avoiding these costs.
3. **Inventory holding costs.**   A major component is the cost of capital tied up in inventory. Other components are storing, insurance, taxes, spoilage, and obsolescence.
4. **Backordering costs.**   Usually these are very hard to measure and include costs of expediting, loss of customer goodwill, and loss of sales revenues resulting from backordering.

Budgets To receive funding, operations managers are generally required to submit annual, and sometimes quarterly, budget requests. The aggregate plan is key to the success of the budgeting process. Recall that the goal of the aggregate plan is to minimize the total production-related costs over the planning horizon by determining the optimal combination of workforce levels and inventory levels. Thus, the aggregate plan provides justification for the requested budget amount. Accurate medium-range planning increases the likelihood of (1) receiving the requested budget and (2) operating within the limits of the budget.

In the next section we provide an example of medium-range planning in a manufacturing setting. This example illustrates the trade-offs associated with different production planning strategies.[2]

Operations and Supply Management in Practice

It's All in the Planning

You're sitting anxiously in the suddenly assembled general manager's staff meeting. Voices are nervous, subdued. The rumour mill is in high gear about another initiative-of-the-month about to be loosed among the leery survivors of the last purge. The meeting begins. Amid the tricolour visuals and 3D spreadsheets, the same old message is skeptically received by managers scrambling for politically correct responses in an endless game of shoot the messenger.

This is a familiar scene in corporations around the world. But interestingly, firms such as Advanced Optical Components, a division of Finisar, formerly VCSEL, have learned how to manage the process of successfully matching supply and demand. Advanced Optical Components has developed a new semiconductor laser used in computing, networking, and sensing applications. Forecasting and managing production capacity is a unique challenge for companies with a stream of new and innovative products coming to market. Using a monthly sales and operations planning process, Advanced Optical Components has been able to improve its short- and long-term forecasting accuracy from 60 percent to consistently hitting 95 percent or better. The specific steps within its plan focus the executive team on (1) the demand opportunities for current and new products and (2) the constraints on the organization's ability to produce product to meet this demand. The plan, developed in a monthly sales and operations planning executive meeting, ensures that demand is synchronized with supply, so customers get the product they want, when they want it, while inventory and costs are kept to a minimum.

Advanced Optical Components managers said that a critical step was getting the general manager to champion the process. The second step was achieving a complete understanding of required behaviour from the team, including committing to a balanced and synchronized demand/supply plan, being accountable for meeting the performance standards, having open and honest communication, not promising what cannot be delivered, and making the decisions needed to address the identified opportunities and constraints.

AGGREGATE PLANNING TECHNIQUES

Companies commonly use simple cut-and-try charting and graphic methods to develop aggregate plans. A cut-and-try approach involves costing out various production planning alternatives and selecting the one that is best. Elaborate spreadsheets are developed to facilitate the decision process. Sophisticated approaches involving linear programming and simulation are often incorporated into these spreadsheets (see OSMP on Kellogg's and Appendix F online). In the following, we demonstrate a spreadsheet approach to evaluate four strategies for meeting demand for the JCB Company.

Operations and Supply Management in Practice

Medium-Term Production and Inventory Planning at Kellogg's

The Kellogg Company is the world's largest producer of cereal and is also a leading producer of convenience foods. It operates four plants in the United States and one in London, Ontario. It has seven main distribution centres (DCs) and fifteen co-packers that contract to produce or pack some of Kellogg's products; that is, a total of 27 locations. In the cereal business alone, the firm coordinates the production of about 80 products and the packaging, inventorying, and distribution of over 600 stock keeping units at the 27 locations. It has 90 production lines and 180 packaging lines. How do Kellogg's managers stay abreast of all these operations? They use a computerized planning system called the Kellogg Planning System (KPS) to manage the five plants in North America.

In the tactical version of the KPS, the company uses a mathematical technique called linear programming along with some rules of thumb (heuristics) to find the best

(Continued)

medium-term, cost-minimizing and integrated production, inventory, and distribution plan—keeping capacity constraints in mind. Time periods are four weeks long and the planning horizon is 18 months. Prior to the start of each fiscal year, planners estimate the plant costs and demands for the next 18 months. KPS then determines the best production allocation to the plants. This plan is then used to allocate the financial budgets within the plants, the inventory space requirements with the DC networks, and the equipment projection for transportation. The plan also ensures that items are never stocked more than five months to ensure freshness.

The system allows the company to do what-ifs with these allocations. For example, if the plan calls for an item to be produced at multiple locations (if no one plant is large enough to produce the forecasted demand), but some of the locations are poorly utilized, it can evaluate increasing the capacity at the lower-cost locations and fully or partially shutting down the higher-cost, poorly utilized lines. It can also answer questions such as how much inventory should be carried in general and how much extra inventory may

be needed while shifting capacity from one plant to another. The KPS also helps determine the buffer inventory at various locations for different SKUs to protect against forecast errors. Presumably, the production allocation plans can then also be used to determine the employment plan at the different locations.

The KPS also has a detailed planning model (in the operational version) that determines the weekly production and packaging schedule for each quarter, subject to constraints of the 18-month plan determined by the KPS. This allows planners to adjust capacity to meet short-term demand through additional shifts, reallocation of production to a different facility, and so on. The KPS therefore is a hierarchical planning system (doing both medium-term and short-term planning) similar to that seen in Exhibit 12.1.

The operational KPS reduced production, inventory, and distribution costs by $4.5 million in 1995. Tactical KPS was expected to yield savings between $35 and $40 million per year.

■ Source: Gerald Brown, Joseph Keegan, Brian Vigus, and Kevin Wood, "The Kellogg Company Optimizes Production, Inventory, and Distribution," *Interfaces*, 31, no. 6 (2001), pp. 1–14.

A Cut-and-Try Example: The JCB Company

A firm with pronounced seasonal variation normally plans production for a full year to capture the extremes in demand during the busiest and slowest months. But we can illustrate the general principles involved with a shorter horizon. Suppose we wish to set up a production plan for the JCB Company for the next six months. We are given the following information:

DEMAND AND WORKING DAYS

	JANUARY	FEBRUARY	MARCH	APRIL	MAY	JUNE	TOTALS
Demand forecast	1800	1500	1100	900	1100	1600	8000
Number of working days	22	19	21	21	22	20	125

COSTS

Materials	$100.00/unit
Inventory holding cost	$1.50/unit/month
Marginal cost of stockout	$5.00/unit/month
Marginal cost of subcontracting	$20.00/unit ($120 subcontracting cost less $100 material savings)
Hiring and training cost	$200.00/worker
Layoff cost	$250.00/worker
Labour hours required	5/unit
Straight-time cost (first eight hours each day)	$4.00/hour
Overtime cost (time and a half)	$6.00/hour

INVENTORY

Beginning inventory	400 units
Safety stock	25% of month demand

EXHIBIT 12.3 Aggregate Production Planning Requirements

	JANUARY	FEBRUARY	MARCH	APRIL	MAY	JUNE
Beginning inventory	400	450	375	275	225	275
Demand forecast	1800	1500	1100	900	1100	1600
Safety stock (0.25 × Demand forecast)	450	375	275	225	275	400
Production requirement (Demand forecast + Safety stock − Beginning inventory)	1850	1425	1000	850	1150	1725
Ending inventory (Beginning inventory + Production requirement − Demand forecast)	450	375	275	225	275	400

Aggregate Planning

Cross Functional

In solving this problem, we can exclude the material costs. We could have included this $100 cost in all our calculations, but if we assume that a $100 cost is common to each demanded unit, then we need only concern ourselves with the marginal costs. Because the subcontracting cost is $120, our true cost for subcontracting is just $20 because we save the materials.

Note that many costs are expressed in a different form than what is typically found in the accounting records of a firm. Therefore, do not expect to obtain all these costs directly from such records, but obtain them indirectly from management personnel, who can help interpret the data.

Inventory at the beginning of the first period is 400 units. Because the demand forecast is imperfect, the JCB Company has determined that a *safety stock* (buffer inventory) should be established to reduce the likelihood of stockouts. For this example, assume the safety stock at one-quarter of the demand forecast. (Chapter 13 covers this topic in depth.)

Before investigating alternative production plans, it is often useful to convert demand forecasts into *production requirements,* which take into account the safety stock estimates. In Exhibit 12.3, note that these requirements assume that the safety stock is never actually used, so that the ending inventory each month equals the safety stock for that month. For example, the January safety stock of 450 (25 percent of January demand of 1800) becomes the inventory at the end of January. The production requirement for January is demand plus safety stock minus beginning inventory (1800 + 450 − 400 = 1850).

Now we must formulate alternative production plans for the JCB Company. Using a spreadsheet (Exhibit 12.4), we investigate four different plans with the objective of finding the one with the lowest total cost.

Plan 1. Produce to exact monthly production requirements using a regular eight-hour day by varying workforce size.

Plan 2. Produce to meet expected average demand over the next six months by maintaining a constant workforce. This constant number of workers is calculated by finding the average number of workers required each day over the horizon. Take the total production requirements and multiply by the time required for each unit. Then divide by the total time that one person works over the horizon [(8000 units × 5 hours per unit) ÷ (125 days × 8 hours per day) = 40 workers]. Inventory is allowed to accumulate, with shortages filled from next month's production by backordering. Negative beginning inventory balances indicate that demand is backordered. In some cases, sales may be lost if demand is not met. The lost sales can be shown with a negative ending inventory balance followed by a zero beginning inventory balance in the next period. Notice that in this plan we use our safety stock in January, February, March, and June to meet expected demand.

Plan 3. Produce to meet the minimum expected demand (April) using a constant workforce on regular time. Subcontract to meet additional output requirements. The number of workers is calculated by locating the minimum monthly production requirement and determining how many workers would be needed for that month [(850 units × 5 hours per unit) ÷ (21 days × 8 hours per day) = 25 workers] and subcontracting any monthly difference between requirements and production.

Plan 4. Produce to meet expected demand for all but the first two months using a constant workforce on regular time. Use overtime to meet additional output requirements. The number of workers is more difficult to compute for this plan, but the goal is to finish June with an ending inventory as close as possible to the June safety stock. By trial and error it can be shown that a constant workforce of 38 workers is the closest approximation.

The next step is to calculate the cost of each plan. This requires the series of simple calculations shown in Exhibit 12.4. Note that the headings in each row are different for each plan because each is a different problem requiring its own data and calculations.

The final step is to tabulate and graph each plan and compare their costs. From Exhibit 12.5 we can see that using subcontractors resulted in the lowest cost (Plan 3). Exhibit 12.6 shows the effects of the four plans. This is a cumulative graph illustrating the expected results on the total production requirement. Exhibit 12.7 shows the projected monthly employment for the four plans. This will help managers plan their employment strategy.

Note that we have made one other assumption in this example: The plan can start with any number of workers with no hiring or layoff cost. This is usually the case because an aggregate plan draws on existing personnel, and we can start the plan that way. However, in an actual application, the availability of existing personnel transferable from other areas of the firm may change the assumptions.

Each of these four plans focused on one particular cost, and the first three were simple pure strategies. Obviously, there are many other feasible plans, some of which would use a combination of workforce changes, overtime, and subcontracting. The problems at the end of this chapter include examples of such mixed strategies. In practice, the final plan chosen would come from searching a variety of alternatives and future projections beyond the six-month planning horizon we have used.

Keep in mind that the cut-and-try approach does not guarantee finding the minimum-cost solution. However, spreadsheet programs, such as Microsoft Excel, can perform cut-and-try cost estimates in seconds and have elevated this kind of what-if analysis to a fine art. More sophisticated programs can generate much better solutions without the user having to intercede, as in the cut-and-try method. In fact, in the problems at the end of this chapter, a slightly modified version of the JCB problem, using linear programming, has been assigned for you to solve. In the linear programming model, neither the requirement for level production nor chase production is imposed, since we want you to find the best solution. As you can imagine, there are many possible plans if these restrictions are removed.

EXHIBIT 12.4   Costs of Four Production Plans

Aggregate Planning

PRODUCTION PLAN 1: EXACT PRODUCTION; VARY WORKFORCE

	JANUARY	FEBRUARY	MARCH	APRIL	MAY	JUNE	TOTAL
Production requirement (from Exhibit 12.3)	1850	1425	1000	850	1150	1725	
Production hours required (Production requirement × 5 hr./unit)	9250	7125	5000	4250	5750	8625	
Working days per month	22	19	21	21	22	20	
Hours per month per worker (Working days × 8 hrs./day)	176	152	168	168	176	160	
Workers required (Production hours required/Hours per month per worker)	53	47	30	25	33	54	
New workers hired (assuming opening workforce equal to first month's requirement of 53 workers)	0	0	0	0	8	21	
Hiring cost (New workers hired × $200)	$0	$0	$0	$0	$1600	$4200	$5800
Workers laid off	0	6	17	5	0	0	
Layoff cost (Workers laid off × $250)	$0	$1500	$4250	$1250	$0	$0	$7000
Straight-time cost (Production hours required × $4)	$37 000	$28 500	$20 000	$17 000	$23 000	$34 500	$160 000
						Total cost	$172 800

PRODUCTION PLAN 2: CONSTANT WORKFORCE; VARY INVENTORY AND STOCKOUT

	JANUARY	FEBRUARY	MARCH	APRIL	MAY	JUNE	TOTAL
Beginning inventory	400	8	−276	−32	412	720	
Working days per month	22	19	21	21	22	20	
Production hours available (Working days per month × 8 hr./day × 40 workers)*	7040	6080	6720	6720	7040	6400	
Actual production (Production hours available/5 hr./unit)	1408	1216	1344	1344	1408	1280	
Demand forecast (from Exhibit 12.3)	1800	1500	1100	900	1100	1600	
Ending inventory (Beginning inventory + Actual production − Demand forecast)	8	−276	−32	412	720	400	
Shortage cost (Units short × $5)	$0	$1380	$160	$0	$0	$0	$1540
Safety stock (from Exhibit 12.3)	450	375	275	225	275	400	
Units excess (Ending inventory − Safety stock) only if positive amount	0	0	0	187	445	0	
Inventory cost (Units excess × $1.50)	$0	$0	$0	$281	$668	$0	$948
Straight-time cost (Production hours available × $4)	$28 160	$24 320	$26 880	$26 880	$28 160	$25 600	$160 000
						Total cost	$162 488

*(Sum of production requirement in Exhibit 12.3 × 5 hr./unit)/(Sum of production hours available × 8 hr./day) = (8000 × 5)/(125 × 8) = 40.

(Continued)

PRODUCTION PLAN 3: CONSTANT LOW WORKFORCE; SUBCONTRACT

	JANUARY	FEBRUARY	MARCH	APRIL	MAY	JUNE	TOTAL
Production requirement (from Exhibit 12.3)	1850	1425	1000	850	1150	1725	
Working days per month	22	19	21	21	22	20	
Production hours available (Working days × 8 hrs./day × 25 workers)*	4400	3800	4200	4200	4400	4000	
Actual production (Production hours available/5 hr. per unit)	880	760	840	840	880	800	
Units subcontracted (Production requirement − Actual production)	970	665	160	10	270	925	
Subcontracting cost (Units subcontracted × $20)	$19 400	$13 300	$3200	$200	$5400	$18 500	$60 000
Straight-time cost (Production hours available × $4)	$17 600	$15 200	$16 800	$16 800	$17 600	$16 000	$100 000
						Total cost	$160 000

*Minimum production requirement. In this example, April is minimum of 850 units. Number of workers required for April is (850 × 5)/(21 × 8) = 25.

PRODUCTION PLAN 4: CONSTANT WORKFORCE; OVERTIME

	JANUARY	FEBRUARY	MARCH	APRIL	MAY	JUNE	TOTAL
Beginning inventory	400	0	0	177	554	792	
Working days per months	22	19	21	21	22	20	
Production hours available (Working days × 8 hr./day × 38 workers)*	6688	5776	6384	6384	6688	6080	
Regular shift production (Production hours available/5 hrs. per unit)	1338	1155	1277	1277	1338	1216	
Demand forecast (from Exhibit 12.3)	1800	1500	1100	900	1100	1600	
Units available before overtime (Beginning inventory + Regular shift production − Demand forecast). This number has been rounded to the nearest integer.	62	345	177	554	792	408	
Units overtime	62	375	0	0	0	0	
Overtime cost (Units overtime × 5 hr./unit + $6/hr.)	$1860	$10 350	$0	$0	$0	$0	$12 210
Safety stock (from Exhibit 12.3)	450	375	275	225	275	400	
Units excess (Units available before overtime − Safety stock) only if positive amount	0	0	0	329	517	8	
Inventory cost (Units excessive × $1.50)	$0	$0	$0	$494	$776	$12	$1281
Straight-time cost (Production hours available × $4)	$26 752	$23 104	$25 536	$25 536	$26 752	$24 320	$152 000
						Total cost	$165 491

*Workers determined by trial and error. See text for explanation.

EXHIBIT 12.5   Comparison of Four Plans

**Aggregate
Planning**

COST	PLAN 1: EXACT PRODUCTION; VARY WORKFORCE	PLAN 2: CONSTANT WORKFORCE; VARY INVENTORY AND STOCKOUT	PLAN 3: CONSTANT LOW WORKFORCE; SUBCONTRACT	PLAN 4: CONSTANT WORKFORCE; OVERTIME
Hiring	$ 5800	$ 0	$ 0	$ 0
Layoff	7000	0	0	0
Excess inventory	0	948	0	1281
Shortage	0	1540	0	0
Subcontract	0	0	60 000	0
Overtime	0	0	0	12 210
Straight time	160 000	160 000	100 000	152 000
	$172 800	$162 488	$160 000	$165 491

EXHIBIT 12.6   Four Plans for Satisfying a Production Requirement over the Number of Production Days Available

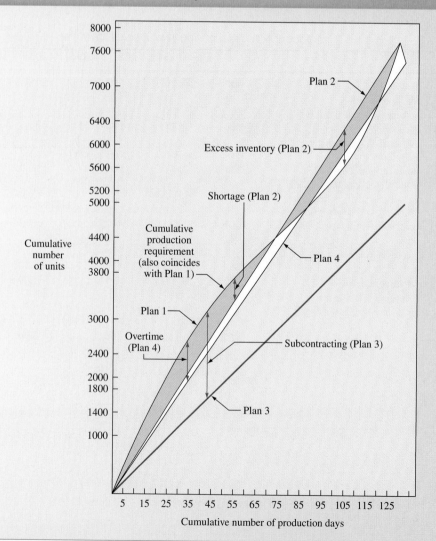

Monthly Employment under the Four Different Plans   EXHIBIT 12.7

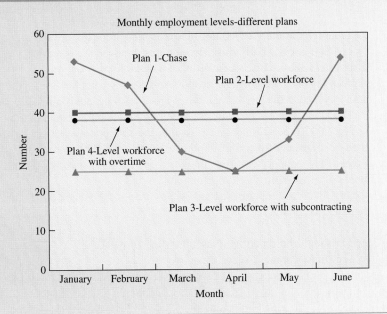

Evaluating this myriad of possibilities manually to determine the optimal plan would be nearly impossible. Linear programming is thus an effective alternative in determining the best plan. When solved (not shown), the workforce remains level in this plan during contiguous periods, though over the six periods, the workforce level is adjusted through hiring and layoffs. In addition, inventory is carried in some periods. So the best plan, given the assumptions in the modified problem, is not pure chase or pure level, but mixed. As we mentioned earlier and as we will discuss later, in practice mixed plans are more popular than pure plans because they offer many different solutions. The case at the end of this chapter also discusses the use of Excel Solver to solve aggregate sales and operations planning problems.

Level Scheduling

In this chapter, we looked at four primary strategies for production planning: vary workforce size to meet demand, work overtime and part-time, vary inventory through excesses and shortages, and subcontract.

A level schedule holds production constant over a period of time. It is a combination of the strategies we have mentioned here. For each period, it keeps the workforce constant and inventory low, and depends on demand to pull products through. Level production has a number of advantages, which makes it the backbone of JIT production:

1. The entire system can be planned to minimize inventory and work-in-process.
2. Product modifications are up-to-date because of the low amount of work-in-process.
3. There is a smooth (more stable) flow throughout the production system.
4. Purchased items from vendors can be delivered when needed, and, in fact, often directly to the production line.

Toyota Motor Corporation, for example, creates a yearly production plan that shows the total number of cars to be made and sold. The aggregate production plan creates the system requirements to produce this total number with a level schedule. The secret to success in the Japanese level schedule is *production smoothing*. The aggregate plan is translated into monthly and daily schedules that *sequence* products through the production system. The procedure is essentially this: Two months in advance, the car types and quantities needed are established. This is converted to a detailed plan one month ahead. These quantities are given to subcontractors and vendors so that they can plan on meeting Toyota's needs. The monthly needs of various car types are then translated into daily schedules. For example, if 8000 units of car type A are needed in one month, along with 6000 type B, 4000 type C, and 2000 type D, and if we assume the line operates 20 days per month, this would then be translated to a daily output of 400, 300, 200, and 100, respectively. Further, this would be sequenced as four units of A, three of B, two of C, and one of D each 9.6 minutes of a two-shift day (960 minutes).

Each worker operates a number of machines, producing a sequence of products. To use this level scheduling technique,

1. Production should be repetitive (assembly-line format).
2. The system must contain excess capacity.
3. Output of the system must be fixed for a period of time (preferably a month).
4. There must be a smooth relationship among purchasing, marketing, and production.
5. The cost of carrying inventory must be high.
6. Equipment costs must be low.
7. The workforce must be multiskilled.

For more about level scheduling, see uniform plant loading in Chapter 10 on lean manufacturing systems. Also see the discussion on mixed-model line balancing in Chapter 5.

AGGREGATE PLANNING IN PRACTICE

Buxey[3] surveyed 42 Australian manufacturers in different industries to examine the type of aggregate plans they used. He found that almost three-quarters of the companies used chase or modified chase strategy (similar to a mixed strategy, but very close to chase). These were primarily companies with high product variety and/or high seasonality in demand. They did not want to carry excess inventory because they could not be sure it would be sold. Also, if the product is perishable or bulky, carrying inventory is expensive. Thus, the chase strategy reduced the financial exposure. Furthermore, many of the companies operated on a JIT basis that discouraged inventory buildup.

Recall, however, that the chase strategy has disadvantages, in loss of worker morale and excessive training costs if workers are laid off frequently. Most companies following a chase or modified chase strategy did not lay off permanent employees. Another reason why companies avoided layoffs is that in some industries, it is difficult to find and train skilled employees, so it was important to retain them. Companies were even willing to let employees be idle for part of the time rather than lay them off. Companies also developed complementary products (such as cooling fans and heaters) so that employees could be switched from one product to another when the seasons changed. The study also indicated that overtime is usually not planned, but is left for emergency situations, such as an unexpected sales order or machine breakdown. Some of the strategies used by companies following a chase or modified chase strategy are shown in Exhibit 12.8.

Chase and Modified-Chase Strategies Used in Practice to Avoid Layoffs of Full-Time Employees	EXHIBIT 12.8

WHEN DEMAND IS LOW	WHEN DEMAND IS HIGH
• Idle time • Employees are assigned to complementary products • Employees are assigned to activities such as quality and productivity improvement or retooling the line • Vacations • Subcontract work from other firms (even in other, related industries) • Employee attrition	• Additional shifts • Part-time employees (especially for simpler work) • Overtime • Subcontracting out work • Producing some customer orders earlier (acceptable to carry inventory that is guaranteed to be sold)

The study also indicated that a level strategy was followed by companies manufacturing a small variety of stable products with little seasonality. Thus, sales forecasts were quite reliable and, because of the stability in demand, not much buildup of inventory was needed. In some cases, items were made to order (backorders), but were usually delivered within 24 hours. So backordering did not seem to be a common strategy. Some companies used modularization in their product line to ensure a fairly stable demand for components. Customer orders are then assembled from standard components.

Yet other companies used mixed strategies because they did not have enough flexibility to follow a chase strategy. At the same time, issues such as perishability or limited warehouse capacity did not allow them to build the amount of inventory a level strategy might require. Others employed "demand management" by changing prices to reduce or increase demand.

The companies in the survey did not use mathematical algorithms to develop aggregate plans; they tended to use trial-and-error-type (cut-and-try) methods. The production plans for periods in the immediate future were considered "firm" or "frozen" (changes were discouraged); periods further in the future were considered more flexible or "open."

YIELD MANAGEMENT

Why is it that the guy sitting next to you on the plane paid half the price you paid for your ticket? Why was a hotel room you booked more expensive when you booked it six months in advance than when you checked in without a reservation (or vice versa)? The answers lie in the practice known as yield management. Yield management can be defined as the process of allocating the right type of capacity to the right type of customer at the right price and time to maximize revenue or yield. **Yield management** can be a powerful approach to making demand more predictable, which is important to aggregate planning.

Yield management has existed as long as there has been limited capacity for serving customers. However, its widespread scientific application began with American Airlines' computerized reservation system (SABRE), introduced in the mid-1980s. The system allowed the airline to change ticket prices on any routes instantaneously as a function of

Air carriers such as Singapore Airlines utilize yield management strategies to maximize revenue for the capacity they have.

forecast demand. Peoples' Express, a no-frills, low-cost competitor airline, was one of the most famous victims of American's yield management system. The system enabled hour-by-hour updating on competing routes so that American could match or better prices wherever Peoples' Express was flying. The president of Peoples' Express realized that the game was lost when his mother flew on American to Peoples' hub for a lower price than Peoples' could offer!

From an operational perspective, yield management is most effective when

1. Demand can be segmented by customer.
2. Fixed costs are high and variable costs are low.
3. Inventory is perishable.
4. Product can be sold in advance.
5. Demand is highly variable.

Hotels illustrate these five characteristics well. They offer one set of rates during the week for the business traveller and another set during the weekend for the vacationer. The variable costs associated with a room (such as cleaning) are low compared with the cost of adding rooms to the property. Available rooms cannot be transferred from night to night, and blocks of rooms can be sold to conventions or tours. Finally, potential guests may cut short their stay or not show up at all.

Most organizations (such as airlines, rental car agencies, cruise lines, and hotels) manage yield by establishing decision rules for opening or closing rate classes as a function of expected demand and available supply. The methodologies for doing this can be quite sophisticated. A common approach is to forecast demand over the planning horizon and then use marginal analysis to determine the rates that will be charged if demand is forecast as being above or below set control limits around the forecast mean.

Summary

Sales and operations planning and the aggregate plan translate corporate strategic and capacity plans into broad categories of workforce size, inventory quantity, and production levels.

Demand variations are a fact of life, so the planning system must include sufficient flexibility to cope with such variations. Flexibility can be achieved by developing alternative sources of supply, cross-training workers to handle a wide variety of orders, and engaging in more frequent replanning during high-demand periods.

Decision rules for production planning should be adhered to once they have been selected. However, they should be carefully analyzed prior to implementation by checks such as simulation of historical data to see what really would have happened if the decision rules had operated in the past.

Yield management is an important tool that can be used to shape demand patterns so a firm can operate more efficiently.

Key Terms

Aggregate operations plan Translating annual and quarterly business plans into labour and production output plans for the intermediate term. The objective is to minimize the cost of resources required to meet demand.

Intermediate-range planning Activity that usually covers a period from 3 to 18 months with weekly, monthly, or quarterly time increments.

Inventory on hand Unused inventory carried from a previous period.

Long-range planning Activity typically done annually and focusing on a horizon of a year or more.

Mixed strategy A plan that combines options available for meeting demand.

Production planning strategies Plans that involve trade-offs among workforce size, work hours, inventory, and backlogs.

Production rate The number of units completed per unit of time.

Pure strategy A plan that uses just one of the options available for meeting demand. Typical options include chasing demand, using a stable workforce with overtime or part-time work, and constant production with shortages and overages absorbed by inventory.

Sales and operations planning A term that refers to the process that helps companies keep demand and supply in balance. The terminology is meant to capture the importance of cross-functional work.

Short-range planning Planning that covers a period less than six months with either daily or weekly increments of time.

Workforce level The number of production workers needed each period.

Yield management Allocating the right type of capacity to the right type of customer at the right price and time to maximize revenue or yield.

Solved Problem

Jason Enterprises (JE) produces video telephones for the home market. Quality is not quite as good as it could be at this point, but the selling price is low and Jason can study market response while spending more time on R&D.

Aggregate Planning Solved Problem

At this stage, however, JE needs to develop an aggregate production plan for the six months from January through June. You have been commissioned to create the plan. The following information should help:

DEMAND AND WORKING DAYS

	JANUARY	FEBRUARY	MARCH	APRIL	MAY	JUNE	TOTALS
Demand forecast	500	600	650	800	900	800	4250
Number of working days	22	19	21	21	22	20	125

COSTS

Materials	$100.00/unit
Inventory holding cost	$10.00/unit/month
Marginal cost of stockout	$20.00/unit/month
Marginal cost of subcontracting	$100.00/unit ($200 subcontracting cost less $100 material savings)
Hiring and training cost	$50.00/worker
Layoff cost	$100.00/worker
Labour hours required	4/unit
Straight-time cost (first eight hours each day)	$12.50/hour
Overtime cost (time and a half)	$18.75/hour

INVENTORY

Beginning inventory	200 units
Safety stock required	0% of month demand

What is the cost of each of the following production strategies?

a. Produce exactly to meet demand; vary workforce (assuming opening workforce equal to first month's requirements).
b. Constant workforce; vary inventory and allow shortages only (assuming a starting workforce of 10).
c. Constant workforce of 10; use subcontracting.

SOLUTION

AGGREGATE PRODUCTION PLANNING REQUIREMENTS

	JANUARY	FEBRUARY	MARCH	APRIL	MAY	JUNE	TOTAL
Beginning inventory	200	0	0	0	0	0	
Demand forecast	500	600	650	800	900	800	
Safety stock (0.0 × Demand forecast)	0	0	0	0	0	0	
Production requirement (Demand forecast + Safety stock − Beginning inventory)	300	600	650	800	900	800	
Ending inventory (Beginning inventory + Production requirement − Demand forecast)	0	0	0	0	0	0	

PRODUCTION PLAN 1: EXACT PRODUCTION; VARY WORKFORCE

	JANUARY	FEBRUARY	MARCH	APRIL	MAY	JUNE	TOTAL
Production requirement	300	600	650	800	900	800	
Production hours required (Production requirement × 4 hr./unit)	1200	2400	2600	3200	3600	3200	

(Continued)

PRODUCTION PLAN 1: EXACT PRODUCTION; VARY WORKFORCE

	JANUARY	FEBRUARY	MARCH	APRIL	MAY	JUNE	TOTAL
Working days per month	22	19	21	21	22	20	
Hours per month per worker (Working days × 8 hrs./day)	176	152	168	168	176	160	
Workers required (Production hours required/Hours per month per worker)	7	16	15	19	20	20	
New workers hired (assuming opening workforce equal to first month's requirement of 7 workers)	0	9	0	4	1	0	
Hiring cost (New workers hired × $50)	$0	$450	$0	$200	$50	$0	$700
Workers laid off	0	0	1	0	0	0	
Layoff cost (Workers laid off × $100)	$0	$0	$100	$0	$0	$0	$100
Straight-time cost (Production hours required × $12.50)	$15 000	$30 000	$32 500	$40 000	$45 000	$40 000	$202 500
						Total cost	$203 300

*Assume a constant workforce of 10.

PRODUCTION PLAN 2: CONSTANT WORKFORCE; VARY INVENTORY AND STOCKOUT

	JANUARY	FEBRUARY	MARCH	APRIL	MAY	JUNE	TOTAL
Beginning inventory	200	140	−80	−310	−690	−1150	
Working days per month	22	19	21	21	22	20	
Production hours available (Working days per month × 8 hr./day × 10 workers)*	1760	1520	1680	1680	1760	1600	

*Assume a constant workforce of 10.

	JANUARY	FEBRUARY	MARCH	APRIL	MAY	JUNE	TOTAL
Actual production (Production hours available/4 hr./unit)	440	380	420	420	440	400	
Demand forecast	500	600	650	800	900	800	
Ending inventory (Beginning inventory + Actual production − Demand forecast)	140	−80	−310	−690	−1150	−1550	
Shortage cost (Units short × $20)	$0	$1600	$6200	$13 800	$23 000	$31 000	$75 600
Safety stock	0	0	0	0	0	0	
Units excess (Ending inventory − Safety stock; only if positive amount)	140	0	0	0	0	0	
Inventory cost (Units excess × $10)	$1400	$0	$0	$0	$0	$0	$1400
Straight-time cost (Production hours available × $12.50)	$22,000	$19 000	$21 000	$21 000	$22 000	$20 000	$125 000
						Total cost	$202 000

PRODUCTION PLAN 3: CONSTANT WORKFORCE; SUBCONTRACT

	JANUARY	FEBRUARY	MARCH	APRIL	MAY	JUNE	TOTAL
Production requirement	300	460[†]	650	800	900	800	
Working days per month	22	19	21	21	22	20	
Production hours available (Working days × 8 hrs./day × 10 workers)*	1760	1520	1680	1680	1760	1600	
Actual production (Production hours available/4 hr. per unit)	440	380	420	420	440	400	

(Continued)

PRODUCTION PLAN 3: CONSTANT WORKFORCE; SUBCONTRACT

	JANUARY	FEBRUARY	MARCH	APRIL	MAY	JUNE	TOTAL
Units subcontracted (Production requirements − Actual production)	0	80	230	380	460	400	
Subcontracting cost (Units subcontracted × $100)	$0	$8000	$23 000	$38 000	$46 000	$40 000	$155 000
Straight-time cost (Production hours available × $12.50)	$22 000	$19 000	$21 000	$21 000	$22 000	$20 000	$125 000
						Total cost	$280 000

*Assume a constant workforce of 10.

†600 − 140 units of beginning inventory in February.

SUMMARY

PLAN DESCRIPTION	HIRING	LAYOFF	SUBCONTRACT	STRAIGHT TIME	SHORTAGE	EXCESS INVENTORY	TOTAL COST
1. Exact production; vary workforce	$700	$100		$202 500			$203 300
2. Constant workforce; vary inventory and shortages				$125 000	$75 600	$1400	$202 000
3. Constant workforce; subcontract			$155 000	$125 000			$280 000

Review and Discussion Questions

1. What are the major differences between aggregate planning in manufacturing and aggregate planning in services?
2. What are the basic controllable variables of a production planning problem? What are the four major costs?
3. Distinguish between pure and mixed strategies in production planning.
4. Define level scheduling. How does it differ from the pure strategies in production planning?
5. How does forecast accuracy relate, in general, to the practical application of the aggregate planning models discussed in the chapter?
6. In which way does the time horizon chosen for an aggregate plan determine whether it is the best plan for the firm?
7. Review the opening vignette. How does sales and operations planning help resolve product shortage problems?
8. How would you apply yield management concepts to a barbershop? A soft-drink-vending machine?

Problems

1. For the solved problem, devise the least costly plan you can. You may choose your starting workforce level.
2. Develop a production plan and calculate the annual cost for a firm whose demand forecast is: fall, 10 000; winter, 8000; spring, 7000; summer, 12 000. Inventory at the beginning of fall is 500 units. At the beginning of fall you currently have 30 workers, but you plan to hire temporary workers at the beginning of summer and lay them off at the end of the summer. In addition, you have negotiated with the union an option to use the regular workforce on overtime during

winter or spring if overtime is necessary to prevent stockouts at the end of those quarters. Overtime is *not* available during the fall. Relevant costs are: hiring, $100 for each temp; layoff, $200 for each worker laid off; inventory holding, $5 per unit-quarter; backorder, $10 per unit; straight time, $5 per hour; overtime, $8 per hour. Assume that the productivity is 0.5 unit per worker hour, with eight hours per day and 60 days per season.

3. Plan production for a four-month period: February through May. For February and March, you should produce to exact demand forecast. For April and May, you should use overtime and inventory with a stable workforce; *stable* means that the number of workers needed for March will be held constant through May. However, government constraints put a maximum of 5000 hours of overtime labour per month in April and May (zero overtime in February and March). If demand exceeds supply, then backorders occur. There are 100 workers on January 31. You are given the following demand forecast: February, 80 000; March, 64 000; April, 100 000; May, 40 000. Productivity is four units per worker hour, eight hours per day, 20 days per month. Assume zero inventory on February 1. Costs are hiring, $50 per new worker; layoff, $70 per worker laid off; inventory holding, $10 per unit-month; straight-time labour, $10 per hour; overtime, $15 per hour; backorder, $20 per unit. Find the total cost of this plan.

4. Plan production for the next year. The demand forecast is spring, 20 000; summer, 10 000; fall, 15 000; winter, 18 000. At the beginning of spring you have 70 workers and 1000 units in inventory. The union contract specifies that you may lay off workers only once a year, at the beginning of summer. Also, you may hire new workers only at the end of summer to begin regular work in the fall. The number of workers laid off at the beginning of summer and the number hired at the end of summer should result in planned production levels for summer and fall that equal the demand forecasts for summer and fall, respectively. If demand exceeds supply, use overtime in spring only, which means that backorders could occur in winter. You are given these costs: hiring, $100 per new worker; layoff, $200 per worker laid off; holding, $20 per unit-quarter; backorder cost, $8 per unit; straight-time labour, $10 per hour; overtime, $15 per hour. Productivity is 0.5 unit per worker hour, eight hours per day, 50 days per quarter. Find the total cost.

5. DAT, Inc., needs to develop an aggregate plan for its product line. Relevant data are

Production time	1 hour per unit	Beginning inventory	500 units
Average labour cost	$10 per hour	Safety stock	One-half month
Workweek	5 days, 8 hours each day	Shortage cost	$20 per unit per month
Days per month	Assume 20 work days per month	Carrying cost	$5 per unit per month

The forecast for next year is

JAN.	FEB.	MAR.	APR.	MAY	JUNE	JULY	AUG.	SEPT.	OCT.	NOV.	DEC.
2500	3000	4000	3500	3500	3000	3000	4000	4000	4000	3000	3000

Management prefers to keep a constant workforce and production level, absorbing variations in demand through inventory excesses and shortages. Demand not met is carried over to the following month.

Develop an aggregate plan that will meet the demand and other conditions of the problem. Do not try to find the optimum; just find a good solution and state the procedure you might use to test for a better solution. Make any necessary assumptions.

6. Old Pueblo Engineering Contractors creates six-month "rolling" schedules, which are recomputed monthly. For competitive reasons (it would need to divulge proprietary design criteria, methods, and so on), Old Pueblo does not subcontract. Therefore, its only options to meet customer requirements are (1) work on regular time; (2) work on overtime, which is limited to 30 percent of regular time; (3) do customers' work early, which would cost an additional $5 per hour per month; and (4) perform customers' work late, which would cost an additional $10 per hour per month penalty, as provided by their contract.

Old Pueblo has 25 engineers on its staff at an hourly rate of $30. The overtime rate is $45. Customers' hourly requirements for the six months from January to June are

JANUARY	FEBRUARY	MARCH	APRIL	MAY	JUNE
5000	4000	6000	6000	5000	4000

Develop an aggregate plan using a spreadsheet. Assume 20 working days in each month.

7. Alan Industries is expanding its product line to include new models: Model A, Model B, and Model C. These are to be produced on the same production equipment, and the objective is to meet the demands for the three products using overtime where necessary. The demand forecast for the next four months, in required hours, is

PRODUCT	APRIL	MAY	JUNE	JULY
Model A	800	600	800	1200
Model B	600	700	900	1100
Model C	700	500	700	850

Because the products deteriorate rapidly, there is a high loss in quality and, consequently, a high carryover cost into subsequent periods. Each hour's production carried into future months costs $3 per productive hour of Model A, $4 for Model B, and $5 for Model C.

Production can take place during either regular working hours or overtime. Regular time is paid at $4 when working on Model A, $5 for Model B, and $6 for Model C. Overtime premium is 50 percent.

The available production capacity for regular time and overtime is

	APRIL	MAY	JUNE	JULY
Regular time	1500	1300	1800	1700
Overtime	$700	650	900	850

a. Set up the problem in matrix form and show appropriate costs.
b. Show a feasible solution.

8. Al-Jazayer Video Concepts produces a line of videodisc players to be linked to personal computers for video games. Videodiscs have much faster access time than tape. With such a computer/video link, the game becomes a very realistic experience. In a simple driving game where the joystick steers the vehicle, for example, rather than seeing computer graphics on the screen, the player is actually viewing a segment of a videodisk shot from a real moving vehicle. Depending on the action of the player (hitting a guard rail, for example), the disk moves virtually instantaneously to that segment and the player becomes part of an actual accident of real vehicles (staged, of course).

Al-Jazayer is trying to determine a production plan for the next 12 months. The main criterion for this plan is that the employment level is to be held constant over the period. Al-Jazayer is continuing in its R&D efforts to develop new applications and prefers not to cause any adverse feeling with the local workforce. For the same reason, all employees should put in full workweeks, even if this is not the lowest-cost alternative. The forecast for the next 12 months is

MONTH	FORECAST DEMAND	MONTH	FORECAST DEMAND
January	600	July	200
February	800	August	200
March	900	September	300
April	600	October	700
May	400	November	800
June	300	December	900

Manufacturing cost is $200 per set, equally divided between materials and labour. Inventory storage cost is $5 per month. A shortage of sets results in lost sales and is estimated to cost an overall $20 per unit short.

The inventory on hand at the beginning of the planning period is 200 units. Ten labour hours are required per videodisk player. The workday is eight hours.

Develop an aggregate production schedule for the year using a constant workforce. For simplicity, assume 22 working days each month except July, when the plant closes down for three weeks' vacation (leaving seven working days). Assume that total production capacity is greater than or equal to total demand.

9. Develop a production schedule to produce the exact production requirements by varying the workforce size for the following problem. Use the example in the chapter as a guide (Plan 1).

The monthly forecasts for Product X for January, February, and March are 1000, 1500, and 1200, respectively. Safety stock policy recommends that half of the forecast for that month be defined as safety stock. There are 22 working days in January, 19 in February, and 21 in March. Beginning inventory is 500 units.

Manufacturing cost is $200 per unit, storage cost is $3 per unit per month, standard pay rate is $6 per hour, overtime rate is $9 per hour, cost of stockout is $10 per unit per month, marginal cost of subcontracting is $10 per unit, hiring and training cost is $200 per worker, layoff cost is $300 per worker, and worker productivity is 0.1 unit per hour. Assume that you start off with 50 workers and that they work 8 hours per day.

10. Bebehani Industries, a company that produces a line of women's bathing suits, hires temporaries to help produce its summer product demand. For the current four-month rolling schedule, there are three temps on staff and 12 full-time employees. The temps can be hired when needed and can be used as needed, whereas the full-time employees must be paid whether they are needed or not. Each full-time employee can produce 205 suits, while each part-time employee can produce 165 suits per month.

Demand for bathing suits for the next four months is as follows:

MAY	JUNE	JULY	AUGUST
3200	2800	3100	3000

Beginning inventory in May is 403 complete (a complete two-piece includes both top and bottom) bathing suits. Bathing suits cost $40 to produce and carrying cost is 24 percent per year.

Develop an aggregate plan using a spreadsheet.

11. Let us revisit the JCB aggregate sales and operations planning example problem. You have just presented the four plans that you prepared to the VP Operations, Pearl Okalik. While she is grateful to you for your work, she is wondering whether a mixed plan would be more cost effective. The company's next sales and operations planning meeting is coming up soon. This meeting will be attended by the president and other top executives and she would like to present these plans and get approval for one of them to be implemented. However since developing an effective mixed plan would be very time consuming using the cut-and-try approach, she has asked you try a linear programming approach. She also knows that using linear programming would be more complex that the regular cut-and-try approach. So Pearl has allowed you to make some simplifying assumptions as follows. All other data are identical to the JCB problem.

1. Inventory costs are calculated as $1.5 per month for each unit of ending inventory as well as safety stock.
2. Overtime production in units is limited to 25 percent of regular-time production.
3. Shortages are not allowed, i.e., monthly ending inventory has to be greater or equal to zero.
4. It appears that there will be 40 employees at the beginning of the planning horizon.

She would like you to build a spreadsheet for the linear programming model and solve it using Excel Solver. She has asked you to ensure that the solution has integer values for the number of employees hired or fired. However, the number of units produced can be non-integer, as this just implies that the final unit is only partially completed in that month.

a. What is the optimal sales and operations plan in terms of production, inventory and work force levels? What is the projected cost of the plan?

b. What are the advantages and disadvantages of this plan when compared to pure level and pure chase plans? You will not be able to compare this plan with the ones in the chapter directly as the assumptions are somewhat different. You only have to answer it conceptually.

JCB LP Template

CASE | Bradford Manufacturing—Planning Plant Production

The Situation

You are the operations manager for a manufacturing plant that produces pudding food products. One of your important responsibilities is to prepare an aggregate plan for the plant. This plan is an important input into the annual budget process. The plan provides information on production rates, manufacturing labour requirements, and projected finished goods inventory levels for the next year.

You make those little boxes of pudding mix on packaging lines in your plant. A packaging line has a number of machines that are linked by conveyors. At the start of the line the pudding is mixed; it is then placed in small packets. These packets are inserted into the small pudding boxes, which are collected and placed in cases that hold 48 boxes of pudding. Finally, 160 cases are collected and put on a pallet. The pallets are staged in a shipping area from which they are sent to four distribution centres. Over the years, the technology of the packaging lines has improved so that all the different flavours can be made in relatively small batches with no set-up time to switch between flavors. The plant has 15 of these lines, but currently only 10 are being used. Six employees are required to run each line.

The demand for this product fluctuates from month to month. In addition, there is a seasonal component, with peak sales before Thanksgiving, Christmas, and Easter each year. To complicate matters, at the end of the first quarter of each year the marketing group runs a promotion in which special deals are made for large purchases. Business is going well, and the company has been experiencing a general increase in sales.

The plant sends product to four large distribution warehouses strategically located in the United States. Trucks move product daily. The amounts shipped are based on maintaining target inventory levels at the warehouses. These targets are calculated based on anticipated weeks of supply at each warehouse. Current targets are set at two weeks of supply.

In the past, the company has had a policy of producing very close to what it expects sales to be because of limited capacity for storing finished goods. Production capacity has been adequate to support this policy.

Bradford Manufacturing

A sales forecast for next year has been prepared by the marketing department. The forecast is based on quarterly sales quotas, which are used to set up an incentive program for the salespeople. Sales are mainly to the large U.S. retail grocers. The pudding is shipped to the grocers from the distribution warehouses based on orders taken by the salespeople.

Your immediate task is to prepare an aggregate plan for the coming year. The technical and economic factors that must be considered in this plan are shown next.

Technical and Economic Information

1. Currently, the plant is running 10 lines with no overtime. Each line requires six people to run it. For planning purposes, the lines are run for 7.5 hours each normal shift. Employees, though, are paid for eight hours' work. It is possible to run up to two hours of overtime each day, but it must be scheduled for a week at a time, and all the lines must run overtime when it is scheduled. Workers are paid $20.00/hour during a regular shift and $30.00/hour on overtime. The standard production rate for each line is 450 cases/hour.
2. The marketing forecast for demand is as follows: Q1—2000; Q2—2200; Q3—2500; Q4—2650; and Q1 (next year)—2200. These numbers are in 1000-case units. Each number represents a 13-week forecast.
3. Management has instructed manufacturing to maintain a two-week supply of pudding inventory in the warehouses. The two-week supply should be based on future expected sales. The following are ending inventory target levels for each quarter: Q1—338; Q2—385; Q3—408; Q4—338.
4. Inventory carrying cost is estimated by accounting to be $1.00 per case per year. This means that if a case of pudding is held in inventory for an entire year, the cost to just carry that case in inventory is $1.00. If a case is carried for only one week, the cost is $1.00/52, or $.01923. The cost is proportional to the time carried in inventory. There are 200 000 cases in inventory at the beginning of Q1 (this is 200 cases in the 1000-case units that the forecast is given in).
5. If a stockout occurs, the item is backordered and shipped at a later date. The cost when a backorder occurs is $2.40 per case due to the loss of goodwill and the high cost of emergency shipping.
6. The human resource group estimates that it costs $5000 to hire and train a new production employee. It costs $3000 to lay off a production worker.

Questions

1. Prepare an aggregate plan for the coming year, assuming that the sales forecast is perfect. Use the spreadsheet "Bradford Manufacturing" included on the OLC. In the

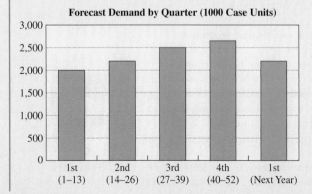

Forecast Demand by Quarter (1000 Case Units)

spreadsheet an area has been designated for your aggregate plan solution. Supply the number of packaging lines to run and the number of overtime hours for each quarter. You will need to set up the cost calculations in the spreadsheet.

You may want to try using the Excel (2007) Solver to find a solution. You will need to "unprotect" the spreadsheet to run the Solver (Review > Unprotect sheet). You will also need to set the "not-negativity" box in the

"options" area. Remember that your final solution needs an integer number of lines and an integer number of overtime hours for each quarter. (Solutions that require 8.9134 lines and 1.256 hours of overtime are not feasible.)

2. Review your solution carefully and be prepared to defend it. Bring a printout of your solution to class. If you have a notebook computer, bring it to class with a copy of your completed spreadsheet. Your instructor may run a simulation in class using your solution.

Footnotes

[1] M. L. Fisher, J. H. Hammond, W. R. Obermeyer, and A. Raman, "Making Supply Meet Demand in an Uncertain World," *Harvard Business Review* 72, no. 3 (May–June 1994), p. 84.

[2] For an interesting application of aggregate planning in nonprofit humanitarian organizations, see C. Sheu and J. G. Wacker, "A Planning and Control Framework for Nonprofit Humanitarian Organizations," *International Journal of Operations and Production Management* 14, no. 4 (1994), pp. 64–77.

[3] Geoff Buxey, "Strategy Not Tactics Drives Aggregate Planning," *International Journal of Production Economics*, 85, 2003, pp 331–346.

Selected Bibliography

Brandimarte, P., and A. Villa (eds.). *Modeling Manufacturing Systems: From Aggregate Planning to Real-Time Control.* New York: Springer, 1999.

Fisher, M., L.; J. H. Hammond; W. R. Obermeyer; and A. Raman. "Making Supply Meet Demand in an Uncertain World," *Harvard Business Review* 72, no. 3 (May–June 1994), pp. 83–93.

Narasimhan, S.; D.W. McLeavey; and P. J. Billington. *Production Planning and Inventory Control.* Englewood Cliffs, NJ: Prentice Hall, 1995.

Silver, E. A.; D. F. Pyke; and R. Peterson. *Inventory Management and Production Planning and Scheduling.* New York: Wiley, 1998.

Vollmann, T. E.; W. L. Berry; D. C. Whybark; and F. R. Jacobs. *Manufacturing Planning and Control for Supply Chain Management.* 5th ed. New York: Irwin/McGraw-Hill, 2004.

Wallace, T. F. *Sales and Operations Planning: The How-To Handbook.* Cincinnati, OH: T. F. Wallace & Company, 2000.

13

INVENTORY CONTROL

Learning Objectives:

1. Understand the different purposes for keeping inventory.
2. Understand that the type of inventory system logic that is appropriate for an item depends on the type of demand for that item.
3. Know how to calculate the appropriate order size when a one-time purchase must be made.
4. Understand what the economic order quantity is and know how to calculate it.
5. Understand fixed-order quantity and fixed-time period models, including ways to determine safety stock when there is variability in demand.
6. Know why inventory turn is directly related to order quantity and safety stock.

HOSPITALS HOPE TO SAVE BY EFFECTIVE INVENTORY MANAGEMENT

Lahey Clinic is hoping to save up to $17 million over five years by acting more like a big-box retailer and automaker when it comes to managing a mundane aspect of the health-care business: medical supplies. The Burlington, Massachusetts teaching hospital's managers decided more than two years ago that they needed to eliminate the hospital's ponderous ordering and stocking bureaucracy and wring savings out of its supply chain. They studied systems deployed by Walmart and Toyota.

Now Lahey is rolling out a system that features secure supply cabinets, bar codes, and computers that keep track of each bottle of antibiotics, every syringe and intravenous bag, and all surgical masks, gowns, and latex gloves. Using thumbprint security technology, nurses open the cabinets, which resemble vending machines, and sit in every ward. Computers keep count of stock and automatically reorder from a vendor's off-site warehouse. Moreover, the system links the use of supplies to individual patients, so now the hospital knows exactly what it is spending on every type of illness and surgical procedure. In an emergency, nurses and doctors can override the system, open the entire supply cabinet, and grab anything they need quickly. However, the day-to-day goal is to squeeze waste and excess out of the supply chain, said Dr. Sanford R. Kurtz, chief operating officer at Lahey.

"The hospital represents a very chaotic environment for supply," Kurtz said. "Now, when the supplies are taken out, all the charges and supply information go into the purchasing system, and we're able to generate reports." Among the big challenges has been training doctors and nurses to change the way they operate. "There is a learning curve here," Kurtz said. "This is a major, major change."

But, he said, the savings to Lahey will be worth it. Beyond eliminating wasted and idle inventory, the system gives administrators a way to analyze how the hospital's staff actually uses expensive materials to treat patients, from operating rooms to outpatient clinics. "It's important to see how different physicians use different supplies to treat the same diagnosis," he said. "This gives us an opportunity to standardize."

The system is provided under a five-year contract with Cardinal Health of Dublin, Ohio, one of the nation's three largest pharmaceutical wholesale companies (Its Canadian division is located in Vaughn, Ontario.). Cardinal Health says its sophisticated supply systems can save Lahey Clinic $29 million in gross pharmaceutical and supply costs and $17 million in net reductions during the five years of the contract.

■ Source: Adapted from Christopher Rowland, "Hospitals Hope to Save by Supply Management," *Boston Globe*, April 10, 2006.

You should visualize inventory as stacks of money sitting on forklifts, on shelves, and in trucks and planes while in transit. That's what inventory is—money. For many businesses, inventory is the largest asset on the balance sheet at any given time, even though it is often not very liquid. It is a good idea to try to get your inventory down as far as possible.

A few years ago, Heineken, the Netherlands beer company, figured it could save a whole bunch of money on inventory-in-transit if it could just shorten the forecasting lead time. It expected two things to happen. First, it expected to reduce the need for inventory in the pipeline, thereby cutting down the amount of money devoted to inventory itself. Second, it figured that with a shorter forecasting time, forecasts would be more accurate, reducing emergencies and waste. The Heineken system, called HOPS, cut overall inventory in the system from 16 to 18 weeks to 4 to 6 weeks—a huge drop in time, and a big gain in cash. Forecasts were more accurate, and there was another benefit, too.

Heineken found that its salespeople were suddenly more productive. That's because they were not dealing with all those calls to check on inventory, or solve bad forecasting problems, or change orders that were already in process. Instead, they could concentrate on good customer service and helping distributors do better. It was a "win" all the way around.

The key here involves doing things that decrease your inventory order cycle time and increase the accuracy of your forecast. Look for ways to use automated systems and electronic communication to substitute the rapid movement of electrons for the cumbersome movement of masses of atoms.

The economic benefit from inventory reduction is evident from the following statistics: A commonly accepted annual average cost of inventory in Canada is 20 percent of its value.[1]

For example, if a firm carries an average inventory of $20 million, it costs the firm more than $4 million per year. These costs are due mainly to obsolescence, insurance, and opportunity costs. If the amount of inventory could be reduced to $10 million, for instance, the firm would save over $2 million, which goes directly to the bottom line. That is, the savings from reduced inventory results in increased profit. This cost of inventory can be much higher in the case of perishables such as food, or short-life-cycle products such as fashion or electronic goods.

This chapter and Chapter 14 present techniques designed to manage inventory in different supply chain settings. In this chapter the focus is on settings where the desire is to maintain a stock of inventory that can be delivered to the customer on demand. Good examples of where the models described in this chapter are used include retail stores, grocery stores, wholesale distributors, hospital supplies, and repair parts needed to fix or maintain equipment quickly. Situations where it is necessary to have the item "in-stock" are ideal candidates for the models described in this chapter.

Exhibit 13.1 depicts different types of supply chain inventories, such as raw materials, manufacturing plant, and warehouse inventories. In the upper echelons of the supply chain, which are supply points closer to the customer, stock is usually kept so that an item can be delivered quickly when the customer need occurs. Of course, there are many exceptions, but in general this is the case. The techniques most appropriate for these inventories assume that demand is random and cannot be predicted with great precision. In the cases of the models we describe in this chapter, we characterize demand by using a probability distribution and maintain stock so that the risk associated with stocking out is managed. For these applications, the following three models are discussed in the chapter:

1. **The single-period model.** This is used when we are making a one-time purchase of an item. An example might be purchasing T-shirts to sell at a one-time sporting event.

EXHIBIT 13.1 | Supply Chain Inventories

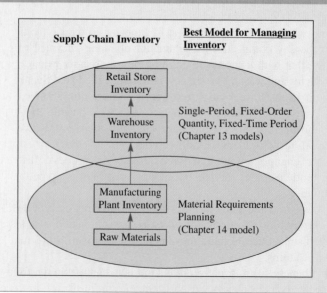

2. **The fixed-order-quantity model.**   This is used when we want to maintain an item "in-stock," and when we resupply the item, a certain number of units must be ordered each time. Inventory for the item is monitored until it gets down to a level where the risk of stocking out is great enough that we are compelled to order.

3. **The fixed-time period model.**   This is similar to the fixed-order-quantity model; it is used when the item should be in-stock and ready to use. In this case, rather than monitoring the inventory level and ordering when the level gets down to a critical quantity, the item is ordered at certain intervals of time, for example, every Friday morning. This is often convenient when a group of items are ordered together. An example is the delivery of different types of bread to a grocery store. The bakery supplier may have 10 or more products stocked in a store. Rather than delivering each product individually at different times, it is much more efficient to deliver all 10 together at the same time and on the same schedule.

In this chapter, we want to show not only the mathematics associated with effective inventory control but also the "art" of managing inventory. Ensuring accuracy in inventory records is essential to running an efficient inventory control process. Techniques such as ABC analysis and cycle counting are essential to the actual management of the system since they focus attention on the high-value items and ensure the quality of the transactions that affect the tracking of inventory levels.

DEFINITION OF INVENTORY

Inventory is the stock of any item or resource used in an organization. An *inventory system* is the set of policies and controls that monitor levels of inventory and determine what levels should be maintained, when stock should be replenished, and how large orders should be.

By convention, *manufacturing inventory* generally refers to items that contribute to or become part of a firm's product output. Manufacturing inventory is typically classified into *raw materials, finished products, component parts, supplies,* and *work-in-process.* In services, *inventory* generally refers to the tangible goods to be sold and the supplies necessary to administer the service.

The basic purpose of inventory analysis in manufacturing and stockkeeping services is to specify (1) when items should be ordered and (2) how large the order should be. Many firms are tending to enter into longer-term relationships with vendors to supply their needs for perhaps the entire year. This changes the "when" and "how many to order" to "when" and "how many to deliver."

PURPOSES OF INVENTORY

All firms (including JIT operations) keep a supply of inventory for the following reasons:

1. **To maintain independence of operations.**   A supply of materials at a work centre allows that centre flexibility in operations. For example, because there are costs for making each new production set-up, this inventory allows management to reduce the number of set-ups.

   Independence of workstations is desirable on assembly lines as well. The time that it takes to do identical operations will naturally vary from one unit to the next.

Therefore, it is desirable to have a cushion of several parts within the workstation so that shorter performance times can compensate for longer performance times. This way, the average output can be fairly stable.

2. **To meet variation in product demand.** If the demand for the product is known precisely, it may be possible (though not necessarily economical) to produce the product to exactly meet the demand. Usually, however, demand is not completely known, and a safety or buffer stock must be maintained to absorb variation.

3. **To allow flexibility in production scheduling.** A stock of inventory relieves the pressure on the production system to get the goods out. This allows for longer lead times, which permit production planning for smoother flow and lower-cost operation through larger lot-size production. High set-up costs, for example, favour producing a larger number of units once the set-up has been made.

4. **To provide a safeguard for variation in raw material delivery time.** When material is ordered from a vendor, delays can occur for a variety of reasons: a normal variation in shipping time, a shortage of material at the vendor's plant causing backlogs, an unexpected strike at the vendor's plant or at one of the shipping companies, a lost order, or a shipment of incorrect or defective material. This applies to within-the-facility production and delivery as well.

5. **To take advantage of economic purchase order size.** There are costs to place an order: labour, phone calls, typing, postage, and so on. Therefore, the larger each order is, the fewer the orders that need be written. Also, shipping costs favour larger orders—the larger the shipment, the lower the per-unit cost.

For each of the preceding reasons (especially for items 3, 4, and 5), be aware that inventory is costly and large amounts are generally undesirable. Long cycle times are caused by large amounts of inventory and are undesirable as well.

INVENTORY COSTS

In making any decision that affects inventory size, the following costs must be considered.

1. **Holding (or carrying) costs.** This broad category includes the costs for storage facilities, handling, insurance, pilferage, breakage, obsolescence, depreciation, taxes, and the opportunity cost of capital. Obviously, high holding costs tend to favour low inventory levels and frequent replenishment.

2. **Set-up (or production change) costs.** Making each different product involves obtaining the necessary materials, arranging specific equipment set-ups, filling out the required papers, appropriately charging time and materials, and moving out the previous stock of material.

   If there were no costs or loss of time in changing from one product to another, many small lots would be produced. This would reduce inventory levels, with a resulting savings in cost. One challenge today is to try to reduce these set-up costs to permit smaller lot sizes. (This is one objective of a JIT system.)

3. **Ordering (order preparation) costs.** These costs refer to the managerial and clerical costs to place the purchase order. Ordering costs include all the details, such as counting items and calculating order quantities. The costs associated with maintaining the system needed to track orders are also included in ordering costs. So this cost is similar to set-up cost except that it is related to a purchase order rather than a production order. Sometimes set-up cost and ordering cost are used interchangeably.

Toyota Priuses and other vehicles clad in protective covering await shipment to dealers at a port. In 2006, the value of the company's inventory totalled about ¥1.62 trillion and the cost of goods sold was ¥15.73 trillion. So Toyota's inventory turned over about 9.7 times per year, or roughly 38 days of inventory on hand.

4. **Shortage costs.**   When the stock of an item is depleted, an order for that item must either wait until the stock is replenished or be cancelled. There is a trade-off between carrying stock to satisfy demand and the costs resulting from stockout. This balance is sometimes difficult to obtain, because it may not be possible to estimate lost profits, the effects of lost customers, or lateness penalties. Frequently, the assumed shortage cost is little more than a guess, although it is usually possible to specify a range of such costs.

Establishing the correct quantity to order from vendors or the size of lots submitted to the firm's productive facilities involves a search for the minimum total cost resulting from the combined effects of the individual costs: holding costs, set-up costs, ordering costs, and shortage costs. Of course, the timing of these orders is a critical factor that may affect inventory cost.

INDEPENDENT VERSUS DEPENDENT DEMAND

In inventory management, it is important to understand the difference between dependent and independent demand. The reason is that entire inventory systems are predicated on whether demand is derived from an end item or is related to the item itself.

Briefly, the distinction between **independent and dependent demand** is this: In independent demand, the demands for various items are unrelated to each other. For example, a workstation may produce many parts that are unrelated but meet some external demand requirement. In dependent demand, the need for any one item is a direct result of the need for some other item, usually a higher-level item of which it is a part.

In concept, dependent demand is a relatively straightforward computational problem. Needed quantities of a dependent-demand item are simply computed, based on the number needed in each higher-level item in which it is used. For example, if an automobile company plans on producing 500 cars per day, then obviously it will need 2000 wheels and tires (plus spares). The number of wheels and tires needed is *dependent* on the production levels and is not derived separately. The demand for cars, on the other hand, is *independent*— it comes from many sources external to the automobile firm and is not a part of other products; it is unrelated to the demand for other products.

To determine the quantities of independent items that must be produced, firms usually turn to their sales and market research departments. They use a variety of techniques, including customer surveys, forecasting techniques, and economic and sociological trends, as we discussed in Chapter 11 on forecasting. Because independent demand is uncertain, extra units (safety stock) must be carried in inventory. This chapter presents models to determine how many units need to be ordered, and how many extra units should be carried to reduce the risk of stocking out.

Cross Functional

INVENTORY SYSTEMS

An inventory system provides the organizational structure and the operating policies for maintaining and controlling goods to be stocked. The system is responsible for ordering and receipt of goods: timing the order placement and keeping track of what has been ordered, how much, and from whom. The system must also follow up to answer such questions as, has the supplier received the order? Has it been shipped? Are the dates correct? Are the procedures established for reordering or returning undesirable merchandise?

This section divides systems into single-period systems and multiple-period systems. The classification is based on whether the decision is just a one-time purchasing decision where the purchase is designed to cover a fixed period of time and the item will not be reordered, or if the decision involves an item that will be purchased periodically and inventory should be kept in stock to be used on demand. We begin with a look at the one-time purchasing decision and the single-period inventory model.

A Single-Period Inventory Model

Certainly, an easy example to think about is the classic single-period "newsperson" problem. For example, consider the problem that the newsperson has in deciding how many newspapers to put in the sales stand outside a hotel lobby each morning. If the newsperson does not put enough papers in the stand, some customers will not be able to purchase a paper and the newsperson will lose the profit from these sales. On the other hand, if too many papers are placed in the stand, the newsperson will have paid for papers that were not sold during the day, lowering profit for the day.

Actually, this is a very common type of problem. Consider the person selling T-shirts promoting a championship hockey or soccer game. This is especially difficult, since the person must wait to learn what teams will be playing. The shirts can then be printed with the proper team logos. Of course, the person must estimate how many people will actually want the shirts. The shirts sold prior to the game can probably be sold at a premium price, whereas those sold after the game will need to be steeply discounted.

A simple way to think about this is to consider how much risk we are willing to take for running out of inventory. Let's consider that the newsperson selling papers in the sales stand had collected data over a few months and had found that on average each Monday 90 papers were sold, with a standard deviation of 10 papers (assume that during this time the papers were purposefully overstocked in order not to run out, so the newsperson would know what "real" demand was). With these data, our newsperson could simply state a service rate he or she felt to be acceptable. For example, the newsperson might want to be 80 percent sure of not running out of papers each Monday.

Recall from your study of statistics that, assuming that the probability distribution associated with the sales of the paper is normal, then if we stocked exactly 90 papers each Monday morning, the risk of stocking out would be 50 percent, since 50 percent of the time we expect demand to be less than 90 papers and 50 percent of the time we expect demand to be greater than 90. To be 80 percent sure of not stocking out, we need to carry a few more papers. From the "cumulative standard normal distribution" table given in Appendix E, we see that we need approximately .85 standard deviation of extra papers to be 80 percent sure of not stocking out. A quick way to find the exact number of standard deviations needed for a given probability of stocking out is with the NORMSINV(probability) function in Microsoft Excel (NORMSINV(.8) = .84162). Given our result from Excel, which is more accurate than what we can get from the tables, the number of extra papers would be .84162 $\times$ 10 = 8.416, or 9 papers (there is no way to sell .4 paper!).

To make this more useful, it would be good to actually consider the potential profit and loss associated with stocking either too many or too few papers on the stand. Let's say that our newspaper person pays $.20 for each paper and sells the papers for $.50. In this case, the marginal cost associated with underestimating demand is $.30, the lost profit. Similarly, the marginal cost of overestimating demand is $.20, the cost of buying too many papers. The optimal stocking level, using marginal analysis, occurs at the point where the expected benefits derived from carrying the next unit are less than the expected costs for that unit. Keep in mind that the specific benefits and costs depend on the problem.

In symbolic terms, define

$$C_o = \text{Cost per unit of demand overestimated}$$
$$C_u = \text{Cost per unit of demand underestimated}$$

By introducing probabilities, the expected marginal cost equation becomes

$$P(C_o) \leq (1 - P)\, C_u$$

where P is the probability that the unit will not be sold and $1 - P$ is the probability of it being sold, because one or the other must occur. (The unit is sold or is not sold.)[2]

Then, solving for P, we obtain a distribution independent equation

[13.1]
$$P \leq \frac{C_u}{C_o + C_u}$$

This equation states that we should continue to increase the size of the order as long as the probability of selling what we order is equal to or less than the ratio $C_u/(C_o + C_u)$.

Returning to our newspaper problem, our cost of overestimating demand (C_o) is $.20 per paper and the cost of underestimating demand (C_u) is $.30. The probability therefore is .3/(.2 + .3) = .6. Now, we need to find the point on our demand distribution that corresponds to the cumulative probability of .6. Using the NORMSINV function to get the number of standard deviations (commonly referred to as the Z-score) of extra newspapers to carry, we get .253, which means that we should stock .253(10) = 2.53 or 3 extra papers. The total number of papers for the stand each Monday morning, therefore, should be 93 papers.

This model is very useful and, as we will see in our solved sample problem, can even be used for many service sector problems, such as the number of seats to book on a full airline flight or the number of reservations to book on a full night at a hotel.

EXAMPLE 13.1: HOTEL RESERVATIONS

A hotel near a CFL stadium always fills up on the evening before football games. History has shown that when the hotel is fully booked, the number of last-minute cancellations has a mean of 5 and a standard deviation of 3. The average room rate is $80. When the hotel is overbooked, its policy is to find a room in a nearby hotel and pay for the room for the customer. This usually costs the hotel approximately $200 since rooms booked on such late notice are expensive. How many rooms should the hotel overbook?

SOLUTION

The cost of underestimating the number of cancellations is $80 and the cost of overestimating cancellations is $200.

$$P \leq \frac{C_u}{C_o + C_u} = \frac{\$80}{\$200 + \$80} = .2857$$

Using NORMSINV(.2857) from Excel® gives a Z-score of −.56599. The negative value indicates that we should overbook by a value less than the average of 5. The actual value should be −.56599(3) = −1.69797, or 2 reservations less than 5. The hotel should overbook three reservations on the evening prior to a football game.

Another common method for analyzing this type of problem is with a discrete probability distribution found using actual data and marginal analysis. For our hotel, consider that we have collected data and our distribution of no-shows is as follows:

NUMBER OF NO-SHOWS	PROBABILITY	CUMULATIVE PROBABILITY
0	0.05	0.05
1	0.08	0.13
2	0.10	0.23
3	0.15	0.38
4	0.20	0.58
5	0.15	0.73
6	0.11	0.84
7	0.06	0.90
8	0.05	0.95
9	0.04	0.99
10	0.01	1.00

Using these data, a table showing the impact of overbooking is created. Total expected cost of each overbooking option is then calculated by multiplying each possible outcome by its probability and summing the weighted costs. The best overbooking strategy is the one with minimum cost.

NUMBER OF RESERVATIONS OVERBOOKED

NO-SHOWS	PROBABILITY	0	1	2	3	4	5	6	7	8	9	10
0	0.05	0	200	400	600	800	1000	1200	1400	1600	1800	2000
1	0.08	80	0	200	400	600	800	1000	1200	1400	1600	1800
2	0.1	160	80	0	200	400	600	800	1000	1200	1400	1600
3	0.15	240	160	80	0	200	400	600	800	1,000	1,200	1,400
4	0.2	320	240	160	80	0	200	400	600	800	1,000	1,200
5	0.15	400	320	240	160	80	0	200	400	600	800	1,000
6	0.11	480	400	320	240	160	80	0	200	400	600	800
7	0.06	560	480	400	320	240	160	80	0	200	400	600
8	0.05	640	560	480	400	320	240	160	80	0	200	400
9	0.04	720	640	560	480	400	320	240	160	80	0	200
10	0.01	800	720	640	560	480	400	320	240	160	80	0
Total cost		337.6	271.6	228	212.4	238.8	321.2	445.6	600.8	772.8	958.8	1,156

Inventory Control

From the table, the minimum total cost is when three extra reservations are taken. This approach using discrete probability is useful when valid historic data are available.

Single-period inventory models are useful for a wide variety of service and manufacturing applications. Consider the following:

1. **Overbooking of airline flights.**   It is common for customers to cancel flight reservations for a variety of reasons. Here the cost of underestimating the number of cancellations is the revenue lost due to an empty seat on a flight. The cost of overestimating cancellations is the awards, such as free flights or cash payments, that are given to customers unable to board the flight.
2. **Ordering of fashion items.**   A problem for a retailer selling fashion items is that often only a single order can be placed for the entire season. This is often caused by long lead times and the limited life of the merchandise. The cost of underestimating demand is the lost profit due to sales not made. The cost of overestimating demand is the cost that results when it is discounted.
3. **Any type of one-time order.**   For example, ordering T-shirts for a sporting event, spare parts, or printing maps that become obsolete after a certain period of time.

Multiperiod Inventory Systems

There are two general types of multiperiod inventory systems: **fixed-order-quantity models** (also called the *economic order quantity,* EOQ, and ***Q*-model**) and **fixed-time-period models** (also referred to variously as the *periodic* system, *periodic review* system, *fixed-order interval* system, and ***P*-model**). Multiperiod inventory systems are designed to ensure that an item will be available on an ongoing basis throughout the year. Usually the item will be ordered multiple times throughout the year where the logic in the system dictates the actual quantity ordered and the timing of the order.

The basic distinction is that fixed-order-quantity models are "event triggered" and fixed-time-period models are "time triggered." That is, a fixed-order-quantity model initiates an order when the event of reaching a specified reorder level occurs. This event may take place at any time, depending on the demand for the items considered. In contrast, the fixed-time-period model is limited to placing orders at the end of a predetermined time period; only the passage of time triggers the model.

EXHIBIT 13.2   Fixed-Order-Quantity and Fixed-Time-Period Differences

FEATURE	Q-MODEL FIXED–ORDER QUANTITY MODEL	P-MODEL FIXED–TIME PERIOD MODEL
Order quantity	Q—constant (the same amount ordered each time)	q—variable (varies each time order is placed)
When to place order	R—when inventory position drops to the reorder level	T—when the review period arrives
Recordkeeping	Each time a withdrawal or addition is made	Counted only at review period
Size of inventory	Less than fixed–time period model	Larger than fixed–order quantity model
Time to maintain	Higher due to perpetual recordkeeping	
Type of items	Higher-priced, critical, or important items	

To use the fixed-order quantity model (which places an order when the remaining inventory drops to a predetermined order point, R), the inventory remaining must be continually monitored. Thus, the fixed-order-quantity model is a *perpetual* system, which requires that every time a withdrawal from inventory or an addition to inventory is made, records must be updated to reflect whether the reorder point has been reached. In a fixed-time-period model, counting takes place only at the review period. (We will discuss some variations of systems that combine features of both.)

Some additional differences tend to influence the choice of systems (also see Exhibit 13.2):

- The fixed-time-period model has a larger average inventory because it must also protect against stockout during the review period, T; the fixed-order quantity model has no review period.
- The fixed-order-quantity model favours more expensive items because average inventory is lower.
- The fixed-order-quantity model is more appropriate for important items such as critical repair parts because there is closer monitoring and therefore quicker response to potential stockout.
- The fixed-order-quantity model requires more time to maintain because every addition or withdrawal is logged.

Exhibit 13.3 shows what occurs when each of the two models is put into use and becomes an operating system. As we can see, the fixed-order-quantity system focuses on order quantities and reorder points. Procedurally, each time a unit is taken out of stock, the withdrawal is logged and the amount remaining in inventory is immediately compared to the reorder point. If it has dropped to this point, an order for Q items is placed. If it has not, the system remains in an idle state until the next withdrawal.

In the fixed-time-period system, a decision to place an order is made after the stock has been counted or reviewed. Whether an order is actually placed depends on the inventory position at that time.

EXHIBIT 13.3

Comparison for Fixed-Order-Quantity and Fixed-Time-Period Reordering Inventory Systems

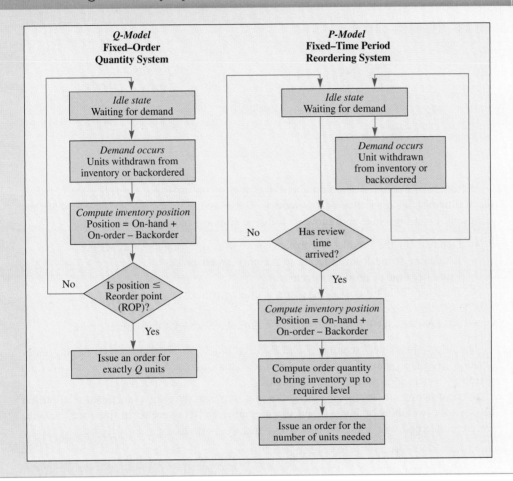

FIXED-ORDER-QUANTITY MODELS

Determining Optimal Order Quantities

Fixed-order-quantity models attempt to determine the specific point, R, at which an order will be placed and the size of that order, Q. The order point, R, is always a specified number of units. An order of size Q is placed when the inventory available (currently in stock and on order) reaches the point R. **Inventory position** is defined as the on-hand plus on-order minus backordered quantities. The solution to a fixed-order-quantity model may stipulate something like this: When the inventory position drops to 36, place an order for 57 more units.

The simplest models in this category occur when all aspects of the situation are known with certainty. If the annual demand for a product is 1000 units, it is precisely 1000—not 1000 plus or minus 10 percent. The same is true for set-up costs and holding costs. Although the assumption of complete certainty is rarely valid, it provides a good basis for our coverage of inventory models.

EXHIBIT 13.4	Basic Fixed-Order-Quantity Model

Inventory Control

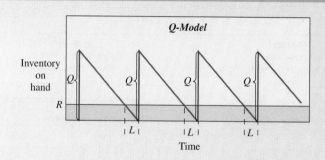

Exhibit 13.4 and the discussion about deriving the optimal order quantity are based on the following characteristics of the model. These assumptions are unrealistic, but they represent a starting point and allow us to use a simple example.

- Demand for the product is constant and uniform throughout the period.
- Lead time (time from ordering to receipt) is constant.
- Price per unit of product is constant.
- Inventory holding cost is based on average inventory.
- Ordering or set-up costs are constant.
- All demands for the product will be satisfied. (No backorders are allowed.)

The "sawtooth effect" relating Q and R in Exhibit 13.4 shows that when the inventory position drops to point R, a reorder is placed. This order is received at the end of time period L, which does not vary in this model.

In constructing any inventory model, the first step is to develop a functional relationship between the variables of interest and the measure of effectiveness. In this case, because we are concerned with cost, the following equation pertains:

$$\begin{array}{ccccc} \text{Total} & = & \text{Annual} & + & \text{Annual} & + & \text{Annual} \\ \text{annual cost} & & \text{purchase cost} & & \text{ordering cost} & & \text{holding cost} \end{array}$$

or

[13.2]
$$TC = DC + \frac{D}{Q}S + \frac{Q}{2}H$$

where

TC = Total annual cost

D = Demand (annual)

C = Cost per unit

Q = Quantity to be ordered (the optimal amount is termed the *economic order quantity*—EOQ—or Q_{opt})

S = Set-up cost or cost of placing an order

R = Reorder point (ROP)

L = Lead time

H = Annual holding and storage cost per unit of average inventory (often holding cost is taken as a percentage of the cost of the item, such as $H = iC$, where i is the percent carrying cost)

Annual Product Costs, Based on Size of the Order	EXHIBIT 13.5

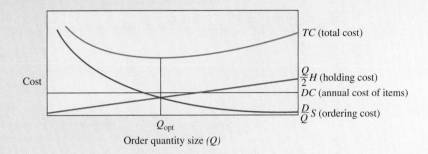

On the right side of the equation, DC is the annual purchase cost for the units, $(D/Q)S$ is the annual ordering cost (the actual number of orders placed, D/Q, times the cost of each order, S), and $(Q/2)H$ is the annual holding cost (the average inventory, $Q/2$, times the cost per unit for holding and storage, H). These cost relationships are graphed in Exhibit 13.5.

The second step in model development is to find that order quantity Q_{opt} at which total cost is a minimum. In Exhibit 13.5, the total cost is minimal at the point where the slope of the curve is zero. Using calculus, we take the derivative of total cost with respect to Q and set this equal to zero. For the basic model considered here, the calculations are

$$TC = DC + \frac{D}{Q}S + \frac{Q}{2}H$$

$$\frac{dTC}{dQ} = 0 + \left(\frac{-DS}{Q^2}\right) + \frac{H}{2} = 0$$

Interactive Operations Management

[13.3]
$$Q_{opt} = \sqrt{\frac{2DS}{H}}$$

Because this simple model assumes constant demand and lead time, neither safety stock nor stockout cost are necessary, and the reorder point, R, is simply

[13.4]
$$R = \bar{d}L$$

where

$\bar{d}$ = Average daily demand (stationary)

L = Lead time in days (constant)

EXAMPLE 13.2: ECONOMIC ORDER QUANTITY AND REORDER POINT

Find the economic order quantity and the reorder point, given

$$
\begin{aligned}
\text{Annual demand } (D) &= 1,000 \text{ units} \\
\text{Average daily demand } (\bar{d}) &= 1,000/365 \\
\text{Ordering cost } (S) &= \$5 \text{ per order} \\
\text{Holding cost } (H) &= \$1.25 \text{ per unit per year} \\
\text{Lead time } (L) &= 5 \text{ days} \\
\text{Cost per unit } (C) &= \$12.50
\end{aligned}
$$

What quantity should be ordered?

Inventory Control

SOLUTION

The optimal order quantity is

$$Q_{opt} = \sqrt{\frac{2DS}{H}} = \sqrt{\frac{2(1,000)5}{1.25}} = \sqrt{8,000} = 89.4 \text{ units}$$

The reorder point is

$$R = \bar{d}L = \frac{1,000}{365}(5) = 13.7 \text{ units}$$

Rounding to the nearest unit, the inventory policy is as follows: When the inventory position drops to 14, place an order for 89 more.

The total annual cost will be

$$TC = DC + \frac{D}{Q}S + \frac{Q}{2}H$$

$$= 1,000(12.50) + \frac{1,000}{89}(5) + \frac{89}{2}(1.25)$$

$$= \$12,611.81$$

Note that in this example, the purchase cost of the units was not required to determine the order quantity and the reorder point because the cost was constant and unrelated to order size.

Operations and Supply Management in Practice

Determining Optimal Lot Sizes in Practice

In this chapter, we discuss inventory models based primarily on the EOQ model. Historically, EOQ-based models have been popular because of their simplicity and because they give good approximations even when the assumptions are violated to some extent. However, most practitioners would caution against using the EOQ or any other model blindly (which is what companies have often done, to the detriment of their costs and customer service).

There are many inventory models for managers to choose from. It is important to choose the inventory model that fits the situation of the item or items under consideration. Sometimes a simple modification to the EOQ can produce good results, as was the case with a Big 3 automaker and its service parts supply chain in the U.S. Furthermore, with improvements in computing power

in recent years, many supply chain management and ERP software programs incorporate sophisticated methods for determining optimal order quantities in today's complex and fast-changing operational environment. These methods may be very different from EOQ-type models. Computer simulation is another method used for determining order quantities. 3M is a company that has started institutionalizing the use of sophisticated inventory modelling and computer simulation to improve its inventory management across its diverse product lines. So far, it has saved millions of dollars without compromising customer service levels.

■ Sources: Dan Strike, "Reducing Inventory through Safety Stock and Lot-Size Optimization," 2003 APICS International Conference Proceedings, F10, pp. 1–9.
Alan R. Cannon and Richard E. Crandall, "The Way Things Never Were," *APICS—The Performance Advantage*, January 2004, pp. 32–36.
Chuck LaMacchia, "A New Take," *APICS—The Performance Advantage*, January 2003, pp. 20–23.

| Relationship Between Lot Size and Set-up Cost | EXHIBIT 13.6 |

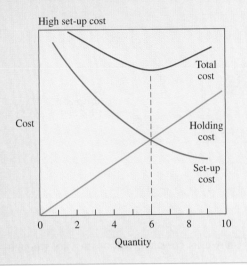
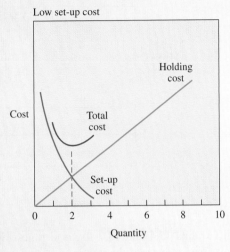

Role of Ordering Cost in Optimal Order Quantity Determination In the EOQ model (Equation 13.3), one can see that the optimal order quantity (or lot size) is related to the ordering cost (set-up cost in manufacturing). The lower this cost, the lower the optimal order quantity. Lean manufacturers were influential in showing the importance of this relationship (you may recall the Toyota example in Chapter 10 where Toyota was taking 10 minutes to change a die compared to six hours for its North American competitors). Exhibit 13.6 shows the benefits of reducing ordering cost. Not only does your optimal order quantity decrease, which leads to carrying less inventory and its associated benefits, but the total cost decreases too. In Example 13.2, if the ordering cost decreased by 50 percent to $2.50 per order, the optimal order quantity would decrease to 63 units and the sum of the holding and ordering cost would decrease by nearly 30 percent. Further, since items are being produced in smaller batches, customers have to wait less (imagine that you are waiting in line to make photocopies; if everybody in front of you had only 10 copies to make, you would wait a lot less than if everybody had 100 copies to make). Given all these benefits of smaller lot sizes, it is no wonder that in recent years firms have been putting in great efforts to reduce ordering costs.

Fixed-Order-Quantity Model with Safety Stock

Recall that in the fixed-order-quantity model discussed thus far, the inventory is adjusted every time a sale or withdrawal is made, and when the ROP, R, is reached, an order for a fixed quantity, Q, is placed. However, in practice, the demand may not be known with certainty (hence our use of the general term $\bar{d}$ for average daily demand). As a result, the inventory depletion line will not be straight, as in Exhibit 13.4, but will be crooked, as in Exhibit 13.7. Thus, exactly when (on the time axis in Exhibit 13.7) a new order will be placed is not known. For example, because sales were slower in the second time interval (t_2), the reorder point was reached later than during t_1; i.e., $t_2 > t_1$. Note that, regardless of the inventory level, when an order is placed it will be for a fixed quantity, Q. Although

EXHIBIT 13.7   Fixed-Order-Quantity Model under Uncertainty

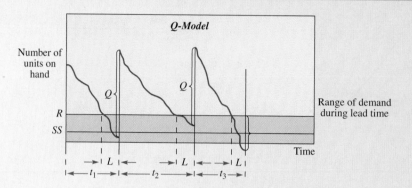

in Exhibits 13.4 and 13.7 the lead time L is shown as constant, it too can vary (though this issue is beyond this text).

A fixed-order-quantity system perpetually monitors the inventory level and places a new order when stock reaches some level, R. The danger of stockout in this model occurs only during the lead time, between the time an order is placed and the time it is received. As shown in Exhibit 13.7, during this lead time L, a range of demands is possible. Because of this range, sometimes when the new order arrives, we have some inventory on hand, and at other times we are actually stocked out by the time the new order arrives. This range, as shown in the exhibit, is determined either from an analysis of past demand data or from an estimate (if past data are not available).

Safety stock must therefore be maintained to provide some level of protection against stockouts. **Safety stock** can be defined as the amount of inventory carried in addition to the expected demand (so it can be applied to any inventory model, including the single period inventory model discussed earlier). For example, note that in time interval t_1, the sales level was higher than normal. As a result, some of the safety stock had to be used to satisfy demand. In fact, had there been no safety stock, a shortage would have occurred. As seen in Exhibit 13.7, R is higher than in the case in which there is no uncertainty (Exhibit 13.4) because it has to incorporate not only the expected or average demand during lead time ($\overline{d}L$), but also the safety stock.

Safety stock can be determined based on many different criteria. A common approach is for a company to simply state that a certain number of weeks of supply be kept in safety stock. It is better, though, to use an approach that captures the variability in demand.

For example, an objective may be something like "set the safety stock level so that there will only be a 5 percent chance of stocking out if demand exceeds 300 units." We call this approach to setting safety stock the probability approach.

The Probability Approach   Using the probability criterion to determine safety stock is pretty simple. With the models described in this chapter, we assume that the demand over a period of time is normally distributed with a mean and a standard deviation. *Again, remember that this approach considers only the probability of running out of stock, not how many units we are short.* To determine the probability of stocking out over the time period, we can simply plot a normal distribution for the expected demand and note where the amount we have on hand lies on the curve.

Let's take a few simple examples to illustrate this. Say we expect demand to be 25 units per week and our lead time is 4 weeks. Our $\bar{dL}$ is then 25 × 4, or 100 units. Suppose we know that the standard deviation of $\bar{dL}$ is 20 units. Assume we have just placed an order for 1000 units (Q) at the beginning of the month, when we had 100 units on hand (i.e., $R = \bar{dL} = 100$ units). Since we know that that the order will be delivered at the end of the month (since $L = 4$ weeks or 1 month), this 100 units on hand should cover us for a month of sales. Ideally, in the absence of any uncertainty, this policy should work well, because, just as we deplete our inventory at the end of the month, the new order for 1000 units should be delivered.

As mentioned, in practice we may sell more or less than the $\bar{dL}$ of 100 units during the month. $\bar{dL}$ Distribution A in Exhibit 13.8 depicts the probability distribution. If our R was 100 units, i.e., we go into the month with just 100 units (no safety stock), we know that our probability of stocking out is 50 percent (the area of the curve to the left of $\bar{dL}$). In half of the lead times, we would expect demand to be greater than 100 units; in the other half, we would expect it to be less than 100 units.

If running out this often was not acceptable, we would want to carry extra inventory to reduce this risk of stocking out. One idea might be to carry an extra 20 units of inventory for the item. In this case, we would still order 1000 units of inventory at a time, but we would schedule the delivery to arrive when we still have 20 units remaining in inventory. Thus, we would have 100 + 20, or 120 units when placing the order. This would give us that little cushion of safety stock to reduce the probability of stocking out. Let R_1 in Exhibit 13.8 represent the reorder point of 120 units in stock. Since the standard deviation associated with our demand is 20 units, we would then be carrying one standard deviation worth of safety stock. Looking at the Cumulative Standard Normal Distribution (Appendix E), online, and moving one standard deviation to the right of the mean, gives a probability of 0.84134. So we would expect approximately 84 percent of the lead times not to stock out, and 16 percent of the lead times to stock out (the area to the left of R_1 in Exhibit 13.8 represents 84 percent of the total area of $\bar{dL}$ Distribution A and the area to the right of R_1 represents 16 percent).

It is common for companies using this approach to set the probability of not stocking out at 95 percent. This means we would carry about 1.64 standard deviations of safety stock, or 33 units (1.64 × 20 = 32.8) for our example. This means that our ROP would have to be 133 units ($\bar{dL}$ of 100 units plus a safety stock of 33 units). Let R_2 in $\bar{dL}$ Distribution A in Exhibit 13.8 represent this ROP (implying that 95 percent of the area under the curve is to the left of R_2, i.e., 95 percent of the lead times would not stock out). Once again, keep in mind that every time we place an order we would still be ordering 1000 units. But we would schedule the receipt so that we could expect to have 33 units in inventory when the order arrives, by placing the order when there are 133 units on hand. So the higher the level of service desired, the higher the amount of safety stock that has to be carried.

$\bar{dL}$ Distribution B in Exhibit 13.8 represents a situation where the $\bar{dL}$ has not changed from 100 units per month, but the variability of demand has increased. For example, assume that the standard deviation of this $\bar{dL}$ has increased to 30 units. Based on $\bar{dL}$ Distribution B, which has more variability than $\bar{dL}$ Distribution A, it is clear that reorder point level R_2 will not provide a 95 percent service level (if the area to the left of R_2 under $\bar{dL}$ Distribution A is 95 percent, then the area to the left of R_2 under $\bar{dL}$ Distribution B is clearly less than 95 percent). To restore the service level to 95 percent, the reorder point will have to increase to an appropriate level R_3.

Thus, the safety stock level that one should have for any given item depends on: (1) demand variation (2) the desired service level, and (3) the variability in order delivery lead time, L (though lead time variability was not discussed here, it behaves in a similar manner to demand variability). Also, as seen in Exhibit 13.7, where in time period t_3 a shortage

EXHIBIT 13.8 | Safety Stock Determination

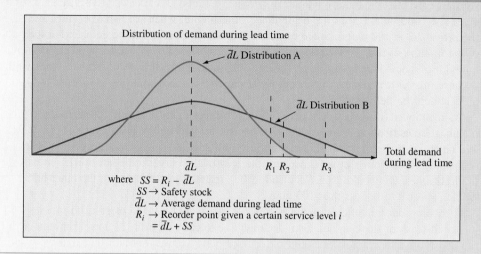

Distribution of demand during lead time

where $SS = R_i - \overline{d}L$
$SS \rightarrow$ Safety stock
$\overline{d}L \rightarrow$ Average demand during lead time
$R_i \rightarrow$ Reorder point given a certain service level i
$= \overline{d}L + SS$

occurred even with safety stock, in practice it is difficult to achieve a 100 percent service level. The amount of safety stock required would cost too much to justify that level.

The quantity to be ordered, Q, is calculated in the usual way, considering the demand, shortage cost, ordering cost, holding cost, and so forth. The reorder point is then set to cover the expected demand during the lead time plus a safety stock determined by the desired service level. Thus, *the key difference between a fixed-order-quantity model where demand is known and one where demand is uncertain is in computing the reorder point. The order quantity is the same in both cases.* The uncertainty element is taken into account in the safety stock.

The reorder point is

[13.5] $$R = \overline{d}L + z\sigma_L$$

where

R = Reorder point in units
$\overline{d}$ = Average daily demand
L = Lead time in days (assumed to be constant)
z = Number of standard deviations for a specified service probability
σ_L = Standard deviation of usage (demand) during lead time

The term $z\sigma_L$ is the amount of safety stock. Note that if safety stock is positive, the effect is to place a reorder sooner. That is, R without safety stock is simply the average demand during the lead time. If lead time usage was expected to be 20, for example, and safety stock was computed to be 5 units, then the order would be placed sooner, when 25 units remained. The greater the safety stock, the sooner the order is placed.

Computing $\overline{d}$, σ_L, and z Demand during the replenishment lead time is really an estimate or forecast of expected use of inventory from the time an order is placed to when it is received. It may be a single number (for example, if the lead time is a month, the demand may be taken as the previous year's demand divided by 12), or it may be a summation of expected demands over the lead time (such as the sum of daily demands over a 30-day lead time). For the daily demand situation, d can be a forecast demand using any of the models in Chapter 11 on forecasting. For example, if a 30-day period was used to calculate d, then a simple average would be

[13.6]
$$\bar{d} = \frac{\sum_{i=1}^{n} d_i}{n}$$
$$= \frac{\sum_{i=1}^{30} d_i}{30}$$

where n is the number of days.

The standard deviation of the daily demand is

[13.7]
$$\sigma_d = \sqrt{\frac{\sum_{i=1}^{n} (d_i - \bar{d})^2}{n}}$$
$$= \sqrt{\frac{\sum_{i=1}^{30} (d_i - \bar{d})^2}{30}}$$

Because σ_d refers to one day, if lead time extends over k (several) days, we can use the statistical premise that the standard deviation of a series of independent occurrences is equal to the square root of the sum of the variances. That is, in general,

[13.8]
$$\sigma_L = \sqrt{\sigma_1^2 + \sigma_2^2 + \cdots + \sigma_k^2}$$

For example, suppose we computed the standard deviation of demand to be 10 units per day. If our lead time to get an order is five days, the standard deviation of total demand for the five-day period, assuming each day can be considered independent, is

$$\sigma_5 = \sqrt{(10)^2 + (10)^2 + (10)^2 + (10)^2 + (10)^2} = 22.36$$

Next we need to find z, the number of standard deviations of safety stock.

Suppose we wanted our probability of not stocking out during the lead time to be 0.95. The z value associated with a 95 percent probability of not stocking out is 1.64 (see Appendix E online or use the Excel NORMSINV function). Given this, safety stock is calculated as follows:

[13.9]
$$SS = z\sigma_L$$
$$= 1.64 \times 22.36$$
$$= 36.67$$

We now compare two examples. The difference between them is that in the first, the variation in demand is stated in terms of standard deviation over the entire lead time, while in the second, it is stated in terms of standard deviation per day.

EXAMPLE 13.3:   ECONOMIC ORDER QUANTITY

Consider an economic order quantity case where annual demand $D = 1000$ units, economic order quantity $Q = 200$ units, the desired probability of not stocking out $P = 0.95$, the standard deviation of demand during lead time units, and lead time $\sigma_L = 15$ days. Determine the reorder point. Assume that demand is over a 250-workday year.

SOLUTION

In our example, $\bar{d} = \frac{1000}{250} = 4$, and lead time is 15 days. We use the equation

$$R = \bar{d}L + z\sigma_L$$
$$= 4(15) + z(25)$$

In this case z is 1.64.

Completing the solution for R, we have

$$R = 4(15) + 1.64(25) = 60 + 41 = 101 \text{ units}$$

This says that when the stock on hand gets down to 101 units, order 200 more.

EXAMPLE 13.4:   ORDER QUANTITY AND REORDER POINT

Inventory Control

Daily demand for a certain product is normally distributed with a mean of 60 and standard deviation of 7. The source of supply is reliable and maintains a constant lead time of six days. The cost of placing the order is $10 and annual holding costs are $0.50 per unit. There are no stockout costs, and unfilled orders are filled as soon as the order arrives. Assume sales occur over the entire 365 days of the year. Find the order quantity and reorder point to satisfy a 95 percent probability of not stocking out during the lead time.

SOLUTION

In this problem we need to calculate the order quantity Q as well as the reorder point R.

$$\bar{d} = 60 \qquad\qquad S = \$10$$
$$\sigma_d = 7 \qquad\qquad H = \$0.50$$
$$D = 60(365) \qquad L = 6$$

The optimal order quantity is

$$Q_{opt} = \sqrt{\frac{2DS}{H}} = \sqrt{\frac{2(60)365(10)}{0.50}} = \sqrt{876\ 000} = 936 \text{ units}$$

To compute the reorder point, we need to calculate the amount of product used during the lead time and add this to the safety stock.

The standard deviation of demand during the lead time of six days is calculated from the variance of the individual days. Because each day's demand is independent.[3]

$$\sigma_L = \sqrt{\sum_{i=1}^{L} \sigma_d^2} = \sqrt{6(7)^2} = 17.15$$

Once again, z is 1.64.

$$R = \bar{d}L + z\sigma_L = 60(6) + 1.64(17.15) = 388 \text{ units}$$

To summarize the policy derived in this example, an order for 936 units is placed whenever the number of units remaining in inventory drops to 388.

FIXED-TIME-PERIOD MODELS

In a fixed-time-period system, inventory is counted only at particular times, such as every week or every month. Counting inventory and placing orders periodically is desirable in certain situations, such as when vendors make routine visits to customers and take orders for their complete line of products, or when buyers want to combine orders to save transportation costs. Other firms operate on a fixed time period to facilitate planning their inventory count; for example, Distributor X calls every two weeks and employees know that all Distributor X's product must be counted.

Fixed-time-period models generate order quantities that vary from period to period, depending on the usage rates. These generally require a higher level of safety stock than a fixed-order-quantity system. The fixed-order-quantity system assumes continual tracking of inventory on hand, with an order immediately placed when the reorder point is reached. In contrast, the standard fixed-time-period models assume that inventory is counted only at the time specified for review. It is possible that some large demand will draw the stock down to zero right after an order is placed. This condition could go unnoticed until the next review period. Then the new order, when placed, still takes time to arrive. Thus, it is possible to be out of stock throughout the entire review period, T, and order lead time, L. Safety stock, therefore, must protect against stockouts during the review period itself as well as during the lead time from order placement to order receipt.

Thumbs Up Foods of Calgary, a manufacturer of packaged Indian food, follows a fixed-time-period production model, in general, in which an item such as a samosa might be made only once a week. Orders have to be placed by the day before the samosas are made (although extra quantities are made to cater to drop-in customers). One reason Thumbs Up follows the fixed-time-period model is that it doesn't have the physical space to set up a separate line for each product it manufactures (where it is easy to start production if the reorder point is reached). It therefore uses the same line with different fixtures. Changing fixtures entails a significant set-up activity, which makes it difficult to respond when a reorder point is reached randomly (as is usually the case in practice with a fixed-order-quantity model).

From the planning perspective of both its customers and itself, it is better for Thumbs Up to use the fixed-time-period model. Customers know that orders have to be placed on a fixed day of the week; Thumbs Up can plan ahead knowing that it makes certain items only on certain days. As mentioned, the disadvantage of the fixed-time-period model is that, because the inventory is replenished only after a fixed time interval, there is a greater chance of running out of stock than with a fixed-order-quantity model. For example, if Thumbs Up runs out of samosas midweek, customers might have to wait for the next run of samosas to be done at the end of the week. If Thumbs Up had used the fixed-order-quantity model, it could have started a new batch of samosas as soon as the reorder point was reached before midweek, thus preventing a stockout.

Fixed-Time-Period Model with Safety Stock

In a fixed-time period system, reorders are placed at the time of review (T), and the safety stock that must be reordered is

[13.10] $$\text{Safety stock} = z\sigma_{T+L}$$

Exhibit 13.9 shows a fixed-time-period system with a review cycle of T and a constant lead time of L. In this case, demand is randomly distributed about a mean $\bar{d}$. The quantity to order, q, is

| EXHIBIT 13.9 | Fixed-Time-Period Inventory Model |

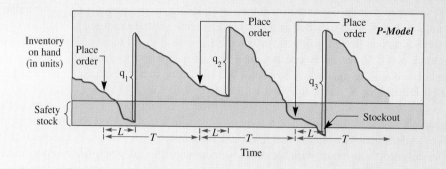

$$[13.11] \quad \underset{q}{\overset{\text{Order}}{\text{quantity}}} = \underset{\bar{d}(T+L)}{\overset{\text{Average demand over the vulnerable period}}{}} + \underset{z\sigma_{T+L}}{\overset{\text{Safety stock}}{}} - \underset{I}{\overset{\text{Inventory currently on hand (plus on order, if any)}}{}}$$

where

q = Quantity to be ordered

T = The number of days between reviews

L = Lead time in days (time between placing an order and receiving it)

$\bar{d}$ = Forecast average daily demand

z = Number of standard deviations for a specified service probability

σ_{T+L} = Standard deviation of demand over the review and lead time

I = Current inventory level (includes items on order)

Note: The demand, lead time, review period, and so forth can be any time units such as days, weeks, or years so long as they are consistent throughout the equation.

In this model, demand $\bar{d}$ can be forecast and revised each review period if desired or the yearly average may be used if appropriate. We assume that demand is normally distributed.

The value of z is dependent on the probability of stocking out and can be found using Appendix E or by using the Excel® NORMSINV function.

Thus, with regard to safety stock levels, in a fixed-time-period model, in addition to the three factors (demand variability, variability in lead time, and service level), the length of the interval is also a factor. So, if a firm such as Thumbs Up made samosas only once weekly, it would have to carry more safety stock than if it made samosas daily.

As discussed in Exhibit 13.2 and from Exhibits 13.7 and 13.9, it can be seen that the fixed-order-quantity period and fixed-time-period models respond differently to demand level changes over time. In the fixed-order-quantity model (Exhibit 13.7), when demand changes, the amount ordered (Q) remains the same, but the frequency at which this amount is ordered changes (t_1, t_2 etc). In the fixed-time-period model (Exhibit 13.9), when demand changes, the frequency of ordering does not change (the time between orders is always T), but the amount of each order changes (q_1, q_2 etc).

EXAMPLE 13.5: QUANTITY TO ORDER

Daily demand for a product is 10 units with a standard deviation of 3 units. The review period is 30 days, and lead time is 14 days. Management has set a policy of satisfying 98 percent of demand from items in stock. At the beginning of this review period, there are 150 units in inventory.

How many units should be ordered?

SOLUTION

The quantity to order is

$$q = \overline{d}\,(T + L) + z\sigma_{T+L} - I$$
$$= 10(30 + 14) + z\sigma_{T+L} - 150$$

Before we can complete the solution, we need to find σ_{T+L} and z. To find σ_{T+L}, we use the notion, as before, that the standard deviation of a sequence of independent random variables equals the square root of the sum of the variances. Therefore, the standard deviation during the period $T + L$ is the square root of the sum of the variances for each day:

[13.12]
$$\sigma_{T+L} = \sqrt{\sum_{d=1}^{T+L} \sigma_d^2}$$

Because each day is independent and is constant,

$$\sigma_{T+L} = \sqrt{(T + L)\sigma_d^2} = \sqrt{(30 + 14)(3)^2} = 19.90$$

The z value for $P = 0.98$ is 2.05.

The quantity to order, then, is

$$q = \overline{d}\,(T + L) + z\sigma_{T+L} - I = 10(30 + 14) + 2.05(19.90) - 150 = 331 \text{ units}$$

To ensure a 98 percent probability of not stocking out, order 331 units at this review period.

INVENTORY CONTROL AND SUPPLY CHAIN MANAGEMENT

It is important for managers to realize that how they run items using inventory control logic relates directly to the financial performance of the firm. A key measure that relates to company performance is inventory turn. Recall that inventory turn is calculated as follows:

$$\text{Inventory turn} = \frac{\text{Cost of goods sold}}{\text{Average inventory value}}$$

So what is the relationship between how we manage an item and the inventory turn for that item? Let us simplify things and consider just the inventory turn for an individual item or a group of items. First, if we look at the numerator, the cost of goods sold for an individual item relates directly to the expected yearly demand (D) for the item. Given a cost per unit (C) for the item, the cost of goods sold is just D times C. Recall that this is the same as what was used in our EOQ equation. Next, consider average inventory value. Recall from EOQ that the average inventory is $Q/2$, which is true if we assume that demand is constant. When we bring uncertainty into the equation, safety stock is needed to manage the risk created by demand variability. The fixed-order-quantity model and fixed-time-period model both have equations for calculating the safety stock required for a given probability of stocking out. In both models, we assume that when going through an order cycle, half the time we need to use the safety stock and half the time we do not. So, on average, we expect the safety stock (SS) to be on hand. Given this, the average inventory is equal to the following:

[13.13]
$$\text{Average inventory value} = (Q/2 + SS)C$$

The inventory turn for an individual item then is

[13.14]
$$\text{Inventory turn} = \frac{DC}{(Q/2 + SS)C} = \frac{D}{Q/2 + SS}$$

EXAMPLE 13.6: AVERAGE INVENTORY CALCULATION—FIXED-ORDER-QUANTITY MODEL

Suppose the following item is being managed using a fixed-order-quantity model with safety stock.

Annual demand (D) = 1000 units

Order quantity (Q) = 300 units

Safety stock (SS) = 40 units

What are the average inventory level and inventory turn for the item?

SOLUTION

$$\text{Average inventory} = Q/2 + SS = 300/2 + 40 = 190 \text{ units}$$

$$\text{Inventory turn} = \frac{D}{Q/2 + SS} = \frac{1000}{190} = 5.263 \text{ turns per year}$$

EXAMPLE 13.7: AVERAGE INVENTORY CALCULATION—FIXED-TIME-PERIOD MODEL

Consider the following item that is being managed using a fixed-time-period model with safety stock.

Weekly demand (d) = 50 units

Review cycle (T) = 3 weeks

Safety stock (SS) = 30 units

What are the average inventory level and inventory turn for the item?

SOLUTION

Here we need to determine how many units we expect to order each cycle. If we assume that demand is fairly steady, then we would expect to order the number of units that we expect demand to be during the review cycle. This expected demand is equal to dT if we assume that there is no trend or seasonality in the demand pattern.

$$\text{Average inventory} = dT/2 + SS = 50(3)/2 + 30 = 105 \text{ units}$$

$$\text{Inventory turn} = \frac{52d}{dT/2 + SS} = \frac{50(52)}{105} = 24.8 \text{ turns per year}$$

assuming there are 52 weeks in the year.

ABC INVENTORY PLANNING

Maintaining inventory through counting, placing orders, receiving stock, and so on, takes personnel time and costs money. When there are limits on these resources, the logical move is to try to use the available resources to control inventory in the best way. In other words, focus on the most important items in inventory.

In the nineteenth century, Vilfredo Pareto, in a study of the distribution of wealth in Milan, found that 20 percent of the people controlled 80 percent of the wealth. This logic of the few having the greatest importance and the many having little importance has been broadened to include many situations and is termed the *Pareto principle*.[4] This is true in our everyday lives (most of our decisions are relatively unimportant, but a few shape our future) and is certainly true in inventory systems (where a few items account for the bulk of our investment).

Any inventory system must specify when an order is to be placed for an item and how many units to order. Most inventory control situations involve so many items that it is not practical to model and give thorough treatment to each item. To get around this problem, the ABC classification scheme divides inventory items into three groupings: high dollar volume (A), moderate dollar volume (B), and low dollar volume (C). Dollar volume is a measure of importance; an item low in cost but high in volume can be more important than a high-cost item with low volume.

ABC Classification If the annual usage of items in inventory is generally listed according to dollar volume, the list shows that a small number of items account for a large dollar volume and that a large number of items account for a small dollar volume. Exhibit 13.10 illustrates the relationship.

Annual Usage of Inventory by Value		EXHIBIT 13.10

ITEM NUMBER	ANNUAL DOLLAR USAGE	PERCENTAGE OF TOTAL VALUE
22	$ 95 000	40.69%
68	75 000	32.13
27	25 000	10.71
03	15 000	6.43
82	13 000	5.57
54	7500	3.21
36	1500	0.64
19	800	0.34
23	425	0.18
41	225	0.10
	$233 450	100.0%

The ABC approach divides this list into three groupings by value: A items constitute roughly the top 15 percent of the items, B items the next 35 percent, and C items the last 50 percent. From observation, it appears that the list in Exhibit 13.10 may be meaningfully grouped with A including 20 percent (2 of the 10), B including 30 percent, and C including 50 percent. These points show clear delineations between sections. The result of this segmentation is shown in Exhibit 13.11 and plotted in Exhibit 13.12.

EXHIBIT 13.11	ABC Grouping of Inventory Items

CLASSIFICATION	ITEM NUMBER	ANNUAL DOLLAR USAGE	PERCENTAGE OF TOTAL
A	22, 68	$170 000	72.9%
B	27, 03, 82	53 000	22.7
C	54, 36, 19, 23, 41	10 450	4.4
		$233 450	100.0%

EXHIBIT 13.12	ABC Inventory Classification (inventory value for each group versus the group's portion of the total list)

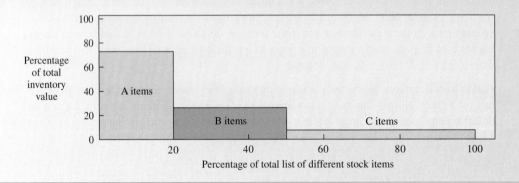

Segmentation may not always occur so neatly. The objective, though, is to try to separate the important from the unimportant. Where the lines actually break depends on the particular inventory under question and on how much personnel time is available. (With more resources available to manage their inventory, a firm could define larger A or B categories.)

The purpose of classifying items into groups is to establish the appropriate degree of control over each item. On a periodic basis, for example, class A items may be more clearly controlled with weekly ordering (with higher safety stock control), B items may be ordered biweekly, and C items may be ordered monthly or bimonthly. Note that the unit cost of items is not related to their classification. An A item may have a high dollar volume through a combination of either low cost and high usage or high cost and low usage. Similarly, C items may have a low dollar volume because of either low demand or low cost. In an automobile service station, gasoline would be an A item with daily or weekly replenishment; tires, batteries, oil, grease, and transmission fluid may be B items and ordered every two to four weeks; and C items would consist of valve stems, windshield wiper blades, radiator caps, hoses, fan belts, oil and gas additives, car wax, and so forth. C items may be ordered every two or three months and may even have higher safety stock levels for better service since the cost of carrying excess inventory is low. Some C items could even be managed manually without the complexity of computer records.

Sometimes an item may be critical to a system if its absence creates a sizable loss. In this case, regardless of the item's classification, sufficiently large stocks should be kept on hand to prevent runout. ABC classification may also be done based on multiple criteria rather than on dollar volume alone.

INVENTORY ACCURACY AND CYCLE COUNTING

Inventory records usually differ from the actual physical count; inventory accuracy refers to how well the two agree. Companies such as Walmart understand the importance of inventory accuracy and expend considerable effort ensuring it. The question is, how much error is acceptable? If the record shows a balance of 683 of part X and an actual count shows 652, is this within reason? Suppose the actual count shows 750, an excess of 67 over the record; is this any better?

Every production system must have agreement, within some specified range, between what the record says is in inventory and what actually is in inventory. There are many reasons why records and inventory may not agree. For example, an open stockroom area allows items to be removed for both legitimate and unauthorized purposes. The legitimate removal may have been done in a hurry and simply not recorded. Sometimes parts are misplaced, turning up months later. Parts are often stored in several locations, but records may be lost or the location recorded incorrectly. Sometimes stock replenishment orders are recorded as received, when in fact they never were. Occasionally, a group of parts is recorded as removed from inventory, but the customer order is cancelled and the parts are replaced in inventory without cancelling the record. To keep the production system flowing smoothly without parts shortages and efficiently without excess balances, records must be accurate.

How can a firm keep accurate, up-to-date records? Using bar codes and RFID tags is important for minimizing errors caused by inputting wrong numbers into the system. It is also important to keep the storeroom locked. If only storeroom personnel have access, and one of their measures of performance for personnel evaluation and merit increases is record accuracy, there is a strong motivation to comply. Every location of inventory storage, whether in a locked storeroom or on the production floor, should have a recordkeeping mechanism. A second way is to convey the importance of accurate records to all personnel and depend on them to assist in this effort. (It all boils down to this: Nobody can pull parts without having the transaction authorized and recorded.)

Another way to ensure accuracy is to count inventory frequently and match this against records. A widely used method is called *cycle counting*.

Cycle counting is a physical inventory-taking technique in which inventory is counted frequently rather than once or twice a year. The key to effective cycle counting and, therefore, to accurate records, lies in deciding which items are to be counted, when, and by whom.

Virtually all inventory systems these days are computerized. Computers can be programmed to produce a cycle count notice in the following cases:

1. When the record shows a low or zero balance on hand. (It is easier to count fewer items.)
2. When the record shows a positive balance but a backorder was written (indicating a discrepancy).
3. After some specified level of activity.
4. To signal a review based on the importance of the item (as in the ABC system) such as in the following table:

ANNUAL DOLLAR USAGE	REVIEW PERIOD
$10 000 or more	30 days or less
$3000–$10 000	45 days or less
$250–3000	90 days or less
Less than $250	180 days or less

The easiest time for stock to be counted is when there is no activity in the stockroom or on the production floor. This means on the weekends or during the second or third shift, when the facility is less busy. If this is not possible, more careful logging and separation of items are required to count inventory while production is going on and transactions are occurring.

The counting cycle depends on the available personnel. Some firms schedule regular stockroom personnel to do the counting during lulls in the regular working day. Other companies hire private firms that come in and count inventory. Still other firms use full-time cycle counters who do nothing but count inventory and resolve differences with the records. Although this last method sounds expensive, many firms believe that it is actually less costly than the usual hectic annual inventory count generally performed during the two- or three-week annual vacation shutdown.

The question of how much error is tolerable between physical inventory and records has been much debated. Some firms strive for 100 percent accuracy, whereas others accept 1, 2, or 3 percent error. The accuracy level often recommended by experts is ± 0.2 percent for A items, ± 1 percent for B items, and ± 5 percent for C items. Regardless of the specific accuracy decided on, the important point is that the level be dependable so that safety stocks may be provided as a cushion. Accuracy is important for a smooth production process so that customer orders can be processed as scheduled and not held up because of unavailable parts.

Summary

This chapter introduced the two main classes of demand: (1) independent demand, referring to the external demand for a firm's end product, and (2) dependent demand, usually referring—within the firm—to the demand for items created because of the demand for more complex items of which they are a part. Most industries have items in both classes. In manufacturing, for example, independent demand is common for finished products, service and repair parts, and operating supplies; and dependent demand is common for those parts and materials needed to produce the end product. In wholesale and retail sales of consumer goods, most demand is independent—each item is an end item, with the wholesaler or retailer doing no further assembly or fabrication.

Independent demand, the focus of this chapter, is based on statistics. In the fixed-order-quantity and fixed-time-period models, the influence of service level was shown on safety stock and reorder point determinations. One special-purpose model—the single-period model—was also presented.

To distinguish among item categories for analysis and control, the ABC method was offered. The importance of inventory accuracy was also noted, and cycle counting was described.

In this chapter, we also pointed out that inventory reduction requires a knowledge of the operating system. It is not simply a case of selecting an inventory model off the shelf and plugging in some numbers. In the first place, a model might not even be appropriate. In the second case, the numbers might be full of errors or even based on erroneous data. Determining order quantities is often referred to as a trade-off problem; that is, trading off holding costs for set-up costs. Note that companies really want to reduce both.

The simple fact is that firms have very large investments in inventory, and the cost to carry this inventory can be more than 20 percent of the inventory's annual worth. Therefore, a major goal of most firms today is to reduce inventory.

A caution is in order, though. The formulas in this chapter try to minimize cost. Bear in mind that a firm's objective should be something like "making money"—so be sure that reducing inventory cost does, in fact, support this. Usually, correctly reducing inventory lowers cost, improves quality and performance, and enhances profit.

Key Terms

Cycle counting   A physical inventory-taking technique in which inventory is counted on a frequent basis rather than once or twice a year.

Dependent demand   The need for any one item is a direct result of the need for some other item, usually an item of which it is a part.

Fixed-order-quantity model (or Q-model)   An inventory control model where the amount requisitioned is fixed and the actual ordering is triggered by inventory dropping to a specified level of inventory.

Fixed-time-period model (or P-model)   An inventory control model that specifies inventory is ordered at the end of a predetermined time period. The interval of time between orders is fixed and the order quantity varies.

Independent demand   The demands for various items are unrelated to each other.

Inventory   The stock of any item or resource used in an organization.

Inventory position   The amount on-hand plus on-order minus backordered quantities. In the case where inventory has been allocated for special purposes, the inventory position is reduced by these allocated amounts.

Safety stock   The amount of inventory carried in addition to the expected demand.

Formula Review

Single-period model. Cumulative probability of not selling the last unit. Ratio of marginal cost of underestimating demand and marginal cost of overestimating demand.

[13.1]
$$P \leq \frac{C_u}{C_o + C_u}$$

Q-model. Total annual cost for an order Q, a per-unit cost C, set-up cost S, and per-unit holding cost H.

[13.2]
$$TC = DC + \frac{D}{Q}S + \frac{Q}{2}H$$

Q-model. Optimal (or economic) order quantity.

[13.3]
$$Q_{opt} = \sqrt{\frac{2DS}{H}}$$

Q-model. Reorder point R based on average daily demand $\bar{d}$ and lead time L in days.

[13.4]
$$R = \bar{d}L$$

Q-model. Reorder point providing a safety stock of $z\sigma_L$.

[13.5]
$$R = \bar{d}L + z\sigma_L$$

Average daily demand over a period of n days.

**Inventory
Control**

[13.6]
$$\bar{d} = \frac{\sum_{i=1}^{n} d_i}{n}$$

Standard deviation of demand over a period of n days.

[13.7]
$$\sigma_d = \sqrt{\frac{\sum_{i=1}^{n} (d_i - \bar{d})^2}{n}}$$

Standard deviation of total lead time demand for a series of k independent demands.

[13.8]
$$\sigma_L = \sqrt{\sigma_1^2 + \sigma_2^2 + \cdots + \sigma_k^2}$$

Q-model. Safety stock calculation.

[13.9]
$$SS = z\sigma_L$$

P-model. Safety stock calculation.

[13.10]
$$SS = z\sigma_{T+L}$$

P-model. Optimal order quantity in a fixed-period system with a review period of T days and lead time of L days.

[13.11]
$$q = \bar{d}(T + L) + z\sigma_{T+L} - I$$

P-model. Standard deviation of a series of independent demands over the review period T and lead time L.

[13.12]
$$\sigma_{T+L} = \sqrt{\sum_{d=1}^{T+L} \sigma_d^2}$$

[13.13]
$$\text{Average inventory value} = (Q/2 + SS)C$$

[13.14]
$$\text{Inventory turn} = \frac{DC}{(Q/2 + SS)C} = \frac{D}{Q/2 + SS}$$

Solved Problems

Solved Problem 1

A product is priced to sell at $100 per unit, and its cost is constant at $70 per unit. Each unsold unit has a salvage value of $20. Demand is expected to range between 35 and 40 units for the period; 35 can definitely be sold and no units over 40 will be sold. The demand probabilities and the associated cumulative probability distribution (P) for this situation are shown below.

NUMBER OF UNITS DEMANDED	PROBABILITY OF THIS DEMAND	CUMULATIVE PROBABILITY
35	.10	0.10
36	.15	0.25
37	.25	0.50
38	.25	0.75
39	.15	0.90
40	.10	1.00

Inventory Control

How many units should be ordered?

SOLUTION

The cost of underestimating demand is the loss of profit, or $C_u = \$100 - \$70 = \$30$ per unit. The cost of overestimating demand is the loss incurred when the unit must be sold at salvage value, $C_o = \$70 - \$20 = \$50$.

The optimal probability of not being sold is

$$P \leq \frac{C_u}{C_o + C_u} = \frac{30}{50 + 30} = 0.375$$

From the distribution data above, this corresponds to the 37th unit.

The following is a full marginal analysis for the problem. Note that the minimum cost is when 37 units are purchased.

		NUMBER OF UNITS PURCHASED					
UNITS DEMANDED	PROBABILITY	35	36	37	38	39	40
35	0.1	0	50	100	150	200	250
36	0.15	30	0	50	100	150	200
37	0.25	60	30	0	50	100	150
38	0.25	90	60	30	0	50	100
39	0.15	120	90	60	30	0	50
40	0.1	150	120	90	60	30	0
Total cost		75	53	43	53	83	125

Solved Problem 2

Items purchased from a vendor cost $20 each, and the forecast for next year's demand is 1000 units. If it costs $5 every time an order is placed for more units and the storage cost is $4 per unit per year, what quantity should be ordered each time?
a. What is the total ordering cost for a year?
b. What is the total storage cost for a year?

SOLUTION

The quantity to be ordered each time is

$$Q = \sqrt{\frac{2DS}{H}} = \sqrt{\frac{2(1000)5}{4}} = 50 \text{ units}$$

a. The total ordering cost for a year is

$$\frac{D}{Q}S = \frac{1000}{50}(\$5) = \$100$$

b. The storage cost for a year is

$$\frac{Q}{2}H = \frac{50}{2}(\$4) = \$100$$

Solved Problem 3

Daily demand for a product is 120 units, with a standard deviation of 30 units. The review period is 14 days and the lead time is 7 days. At the time of review, 130 units are in stock. If only a 1 percent risk of stocking out is acceptable, how many units should be ordered?

SOLUTION

$$\sigma_{T+L} = \sqrt{(14 + 7)(30)^2} = \sqrt{18\ 900} = 137.5$$

$$z = 2.33$$

$$q = \bar{d}(T + L) + z\sigma_{T+L} - I$$

$$= 120(14 + 7) + 2.33(137.5) - 130$$

$$= 2710 \text{ units}$$

**Inventory
Control**

Solved Problem 4

A company currently has 200 units of a product on hand that it orders every two weeks when the salesperson visits the premises. Demand for the product averages 20 units per day with a standard deviation of 5 units. Lead time for the product to arrive is seven days. Management has a goal of a 95 percent probability of not stocking out for this product.

The salesperson is due to come in late this afternoon when 180 units are left in stock (assuming that 20 are sold today). How many units should be ordered?

**Inventory
Control**

SOLUTION

Given $I = 180, T = 14, L = 7, \bar{d} = 20$

$$\sigma_{T+L} = \sqrt{21(5)^2} = 23$$

$$z = 1.64$$

$$q = \bar{d}(T + L) + z\sigma_{T+L} - I$$

$$= 20(14 + 7) + 1.64(23) - 180$$

$$q = 278 \text{ units}$$

Review and Discussion Questions

1. Distinguish between dependent and independent demand in a McDonald's restaurant, in an integrated manufacturer of personal copiers, and in a pharmaceutical supply house.
2. Distinguish between in-process inventory, safety stock inventory, and seasonal inventory.
3. Discuss the nature of the costs that affect inventory size.
4. Under which conditions would a plant manager elect to use a fixed-order-quantity model as opposed to a fixed-time-period model? What are the disadvantages of using a fixed-time-period ordering system?
5. What two basic questions must be answered by an inventory-control decision rule?
6. Discuss the assumptions that are inherent in production set-up cost, ordering cost, and carrying costs. How valid are they?
7. "The nice thing about inventory models is that you can pull one off the shelf and apply it as long as your cost estimates are accurate." Comment.
8. Which type of inventory system would you use in the following situations?
   a. Supplying your kitchen with fresh food.
   b. Obtaining a daily newspaper.
   c. Buying gas for your car.
   To which of these items do you impute the highest stockout cost?
9. Why is it desirable to classify items into groups, as the ABC classification does?

Problems

1. The local supermarket buys lettuce each day to ensure really fresh produce. Each morning any lettuce that is left from the previous day is sold to a dealer that resells it to farmers who use it to feed their animals. This week the supermarket can buy fresh lettuce for $4.00 a box. The lettuce is sold for $10.00 a box and the dealer that sells old lettuce is willing to pay $1.50 a box. Past history says that tomorrow's demand for lettuce averages 250 boxes with a standard deviation of 34 boxes. How many boxes of lettuce should the supermarket purchase tomorrow?

2. Next week, Ntini Airlines has a flight from Montreal to Windsor that will be booked to capacity. The airline knows from past history that an average of 25 customers (with a standard deviation of 15) cancel their reservation or do not show up for the flight. Revenue from a ticket on the flight is $125. If the flight is overbooked, the airline has a policy of getting the customer on the next available flight and giving the person a free round-trip ticket on a future flight. The cost of this free round-trip ticket averages $250. Ntini considers the cost of flying the plane from Montreal to Windsor a sunk cost. By how many seats should Ntini overbook the flight?

3. Sukhi Kaur's Satellite Emporium wishes to determine the best order size for its best-selling satellite dish (model TS111). Sukhi has estimated the annual demand for this model at 1000 units. His cost to carry one unit is $100 per year per unit, and he has estimated that each order costs $25 to place. Using the EOQ model, how many should Sukhi order each time?

4. Dunstreet's Department Store would like to develop an inventory ordering policy of a 95 percent probability of not stocking out. To illustrate your recommended procedure, use as an example the ordering policy for white percale sheets.

   Demand for white percale sheets is 5000 per year. The store is open 365 days per year. Every two weeks (14 days) inventory is counted and a new order is placed. It takes 10 days for the sheets to be delivered. Standard deviation of demand for the sheets is five per day. There are currently 150 sheets on hand.

   How many sheets should you order?

5. Charlie's Pizza orders all of its pepperoni, olives, anchovies, and mozzarella cheese to be shipped directly from Italy. An American distributor stops by every four weeks to take orders. Because the orders are shipped directly from Italy, they take three weeks to arrive.

   Charlie's Pizza uses an average of 68 kilograms of pepperoni each week, with a standard deviation of 14 kilograms. Charlie's prides itself on offering only the best-quality ingredients and a high level of service, so it wants to ensure a 98 percent probability of not stocking out on pepperoni.

   Assume that the sales representative just walked in the door and there are currently 227 kg of pepperoni in the walk-in cooler. How many kilograms of pepperoni would you order?

6. Given the following information, formulate an inventory management system. The item is demanded 50 weeks a year.

Item cost	$10.00	Standard deviation of weekly demand	25 per week
Order cost	$250.00		
Annual holding cost (%)	33% of item cost	Lead time	1 week
Annual demand	25 750	Service probability	95%
Average demand	515 per week		

   a. State the order quantity and reorder point.
   b. Determine the annual holding and order costs.
   c. If a price break of $50 per order was offered for purchase quantities of over 2000, would you take advantage of it? How much would you save annually?

7. Lieutenant Commander Choudhary is planning to make his monthly (every 30 days) trek to Gamma Hydra City to pick up a supply of isolinear chips. The trip will take Choudhary about two days. Before he leaves, he calls in the order to the GHC Supply Store. He uses chips at an average rate of five per day (seven days per week) with a standard deviation of demand of one per day. He needs a 98 percent service probability. If he currently has 35 chips in inventory, how many should he order? What is the most he will ever have to order?

8. Jill's Job Shop buys two parts (Tegdiws and Widgets) for use in its production system from two different suppliers. The parts are needed throughout the entire 52-week year. Tegdiws are used at a relatively constant rate and are ordered whenever the remaining quantity drops to the reorder level. Widgets are ordered from a supplier who stops by every three weeks. Data for both products are as follows:

ITEM	TEGDIW	WIDGET
Annual demand	10 000	5000
Holding cost (% of item cost)	20%	20%
Set-up or order cost	$150.00	$25.00
Lead time	4 weeks	1 week
Safety stock	55 units	5 units
Item cost	$10.00	$2.00

   a. What is the inventory control system for Tegdiws? That is, what is the reorder quantity and what is the reorder point?
   b. What is the inventory control system for Widgets?

9. Demand for an item is 1000 units per year. Each order placed costs $10; the annual cost to carry items in inventory is $2 each. In what quantities should the item be ordered?

10. The annual demand for a product is 15 600 units. The weekly demand is 300 units with a standard deviation of 90 units. The cost to place an order is $31.20, and the time from ordering to receipt is four weeks. The annual inventory carrying cost is $0.10 per unit. Find the reorder point necessary to provide a 98 percent service probability.

   Suppose the production manager is asked to reduce the safety stock of this item by 50 percent. If she does so, what will the new service probability be?

11. Daily demand for a product is 100 units, with a standard deviation of 25 units. The review period is 10 days and the lead time is 6 days. At the time of review there are 50 units in stock. If 98 percent service probability is desired, how many units should be ordered?

12. Item X is a standard item stocked in a company's inventory of component parts. Each year the firm, on a random basis, uses about 2000 of item X, which costs $25 each. Storage costs, which include insurance and cost of capital, amount to $5 per unit of average inventory. Every time an order is placed for more item X, it costs $10.
   a. Whenever item X is ordered, what should the order size be?
   b. What is the annual cost for ordering item X?
   c. What is the annual cost for storing item X?

13. Annual demand for a product is 13 000 units; weekly demand is 250 units, with a standard deviation of 40 units. The cost of placing an order is $100, and the time from ordering to receipt is four weeks. The annual inventory carrying cost is $0.65 per unit. To provide a 98 percent service probability, what must the reorder point be?

   Suppose the production manager is told to reduce the safety stock of this item by 100 units. If this is done, what will the new service probability be?

14. In the past, Taylor Industries has used a fixed-time period inventory system that involved taking a complete inventory count of all items each month. However, increasing labour costs are forcing Taylor Industries to examine alternative ways to reduce the amount of labour involved in inventory stockrooms, yet without increasing other costs, such as shortage costs. Here is a random sample of 20 of Taylor's items.

ITEM NUMBER	ANNUAL USAGE	ITEM NUMBER	ANNUAL USAGE
1	$ 1500	11	$13 000
2	12 000	12	600
3	2200	13	42 000
4	50 000	14	9900
5	9600	15	1200
6	750	16	10 200
7	2000	17	4000
8	11 000	18	61 000
9	800	19	3500
10	15 000	20	2900

a. What would you recommend Taylor do to cut back its labour cost? (Illustrate using an ABC plan.)

b. Item 15 is critical to continued operations. How would you recommend that it be classified?

15. Gentle Ben's Bar and Restaurant uses 5000 quart bottles of an imported wine each year. The effervescent wine costs $3 per bottle and is served only in whole bottles because it loses its bubbles quickly. Ben figures that it costs $10 each time an order is placed, and holding costs are 20 percent of the purchase price. It takes three weeks for an order to arrive. Weekly demand is 100 bottles (closed two weeks per year) with a standard deviation of 30 bottles.

Ben would like to use an inventory system that minimizes inventory cost and will provide a 95 percent service probability.

a. What is the economic quantity for Ben to order?

b. At what inventory level should he place an order?

16. Retailers Warehouse (RW) is an independent supplier of household items to department stores. RW attempts to stock enough items for a 98 percent service probability.

A stainless steel knife set is one item it stocks. Demand (2400 sets per year) is relatively stable over the entire year. Whenever new stock is ordered, a buyer must assure that numbers are correct for stock on hand and then phone in a new order. The total cost involved to place an order is about $5. RW figures that holding inventory in stock and paying for interest on borrowed capital, insurance, and so on, adds up to about $4 holding cost per unit per year.

Analysis of the past data shows that the standard deviation of demand from retailers is about four units per day for a 365-day year. Lead time to get the order is seven days.

a. What is the economic order quantity?

b. What is the reorder point?

17. Daily demand for a product is 60 units with a standard deviation of 10 units. The review period is 10 days, and lead time is 2 days. At the time of review there are 100 units in stock. If 98 percent service probability is desired, how many units should be ordered?

18. Pham Drug Pharmaceuticals orders its antibiotics every two weeks (14 days) when a salesperson visits from one of the pharmaceutical companies. Tetracycline is one of its most prescribed antibiotics, with average daily demand of 2000 capsules. The standard deviation of daily demand was derived from examining prescriptions filled over the past three months and was found to be 800 capsules. It takes five days for the order to arrive. Pham Drug would like to satisfy 99 percent of the prescriptions. The salesperson just arrived, and there are currently 25 000 capsules in stock.

How many capsules should be ordered?

19. Angkor's Silk Screening produces specialty T-shirts that are primarily sold at special events. They are trying to decide how many to produce for an upcoming event. During the event itself, which lasts one day, Angkor can sell T-shirts for $20 apiece. However, when the event ends, any unsold T-shirts are sold for $4 apiece. It costs Angkor $8 to make a specialty T-shirt. Using Angkor's estimate of demand that follows, how many T-shirts should they produce for the upcoming event?

DEMAND	PROBABILITY
300	0.05
400	0.10
500	0.40
600	0.30
700	0.10
800	0.05

20. Famous Albert prides himself on being the Cookie King of the West. Small, freshly baked cookies are the specialty of his shop. Famous Albert has asked for help to determine the number of cookies he should make each day. From an analysis of past demand he estimates demand for cookies as

DEMAND	PROBABILITY OF DEMAND
1800 dozen	0.05
2000	0.10
2200	0.20
2400	0.30
2600	0.20
2800	0.10
3000	0.05

Each dozen sells for $0.69 and costs $0.49, which includes handling and transportation. Cookies that are not sold at the end of the day are reduced to $0.29 and sold the following day as day-old merchandise.

a. Construct a table showing the profits or losses for each possible quantity.

b. What is the optimal number of cookies to make?

c. Solve this problem by using marginal analysis.

21. Sarah's Muffler Shop has one standard muffler that fits a large variety of cars. Sarah wishes to establish a reorder point system to manage inventory of this standard muffler. Use the following information to determine the best order size and the reorder point:

Annual demand	3500 mufflers	Ordering cost	$50 per order
Standard deviation of daily demand	6 mufflers per working day	Service probability	90%
Item cost	$30 per muffler	Lead time	2 working days
Annual holding cost	25% of item value	Working days	300 per year

22. Volkov Products, Inc., is having a problem trying to control inventory. There is insufficient time to devote to all its items equally. Here is a sample of some items stocked, along with the annual usage of each item expressed in dollar volume.

ITEM	ANNUAL DOLLAR USAGE	ITEM	ANNUAL DOLLAR USAGE
a	$ 7000	k	$80 000
b	1000	l	400
c	14 000	m	1100
d	2000	n	30 000
e	24 000	o	1900
f	68 000	p	800
g	17 000	q	90 000
h	900	r	12 000
i	1700	s	3000
j	2300	t	32 000

a. Can you suggest a system for allocating control time?

b. Specify where each item from the list would be placed.

23. A distributor of large appliances needs to determine the order quantities and reorder points for the various products it carries. The following data refer to a specific refrigerator in its product line:

Cost to place an order	$100
Holding cost	20 percent of product cost per year
Cost of refrigerator	$500 each
Annual demand	500 refrigerators
Standard deviation during lead time	10 refrigerators
Lead time	7 days

Consider an even daily demand and a 365-day year.

a. What is the economic order quantity?

b. If the distributor wants a 97 percent service probability, what reorder point, R, should be used?

24. It is your responsibility, as the new head of the automotive section of Nichols Department Store, to ensure that reorder quantities for the various items have been correctly established. You decide to test one item and choose Michelin tires, XW size 185 × 14 BSW. A perpetual inventory system has been used, so you examine this as well as other records and come up with the following data:

Cost per tire	$35 each
Holding cost	20 percent of tire cost per year
Demand	1000 per year
Ordering cost	$20 per order
Standard deviation of daily demand	3 tires
Delivery lead time	4 days

Because customers generally do not wait for tires but go elsewhere, you decide on a service probability of 98 percent. Assume the demand occurs 365 days per year.

a. Determine the order quantity.

b. Determine the reorder point.

25. UA Hamburger Hamlet (UAHH) places a daily order for its high-volume items (hamburger patties, buns, milk, and so on). UAHH counts its current inventory on hand once per day and phones in its order for delivery 24 hours later. Determine the number of hamburgers UAHH should order for the following conditions:

Average daily demand	600
Standard deviation of demand	100
Desired service probability	99%
Hamburger inventory	800

26. Cho, Inc., produces digital audiotapes to be used in the consumer audio division. Cho lacks sufficient personnel in its inventory supply section to closely control each item stocked, so it has asked you to determine an ABC classification. Here is a sample from the inventory records

ITEM	AVERAGE MONTHLY DEMAND	PRICE PER UNIT	ITEM	AVERAGE MONTHLY DEMAND	PRICE PER UNIT
1	700	$6.00	6	100	10.00
2	200	4.00	7	3000	2.00
3	2000	12.00	8	2500	1.00
4	1100	20.00	9	500	10.00
5	4000	21.00	10	1000	2.00

Develop an ABC classification for these 10 items.

27. A local service station is open 7 days per week, 365 days per year. Sales of 10W40 grade premium oil average 20 cans per day. Inventory holding costs are $0.50 per can per year. Ordering costs are $10 per order. Lead time is two weeks. Backorders are not practical—the motorist drives away.

   a. Based on these data, choose the appropriate inventory model and calculate the economic order quantity and reorder point. Describe in a sentence how the plan would work. Hint: Assume demand is deterministic.

   b. The boss is concerned about this model because demand really varies. The standard deviation of demand was determined from a data sample to be 6.15 cans per day. The manager wants a 99.5 percent service probability. Determine a new inventory plan based on this information and the data in a. Use Q_{opt} from a.

28. Dave Danielevich's Auto Supply custom mixes paint for its customers. The shop performs a weekly inventory count of the main colors that are used for mixing paint. Determine the amount of white paint that should be ordered, using the following information:

Average weekly demand	91 L
Standard deviation of demand	23 L/week
Desired service probability	98%
Current inventory	114 L
Lead time	1 week

CASE 1   Batching Patients for MRI Exams Because of Set-up Time[1]

Consider the following example, adapted from the process used at the Pan Am Clinic in Winnipeg for MRI exams, which demonstrates the effect of set-up times on batching. In the original process used by the clinic, patients were seen on a first-come-first-served (FCFS) basis. Assume that knee and shoulder patients (using only two types, for simplicity) alternate. The first patient needs a knee MRI, the second a shoulder MRI, the third a knee MRI, and so on. Though the same MRI machine is used for knee and shoulder MRIs, the radio frequency coils need to be reconfigured when changing from a knee MRI to a shoulder MRI, and vice versa, as they are specific to different parts of the body. This set-up takes 30 minutes. An MRI exam, regardless of whether it is for a knee or shoulder, also takes 30 minutes. At the beginning of the day, 8 a.m., the machine is ready for a knee exam. The facility closes at 5:30 p.m., without any breaks or other delays.

The Pan Am Clinic recently changed its process, scheduling patients in alternating batches instead of FCFS. For example, assume that five knee patients are seen (FCFS within the batch), followed by five shoulder patients and so on.

Questions

1. Explain how the new process improves capacity for the MRI machine.
2. Despite this increased capacity, do some patients get scheduled later in the new process?
3. How might you alleviate the situation in 2 (Hint: consider the JIT set up philosophy)?
4. In terms of batch size, explain the parallel between this situation and the EOQ model.

[1]Times and batch sizes are hypothetical.
Source: Based on outline information from The Current, CBC Radio, May 11, 2009 (http://www.cbc.ca/thecurrent/2009/200905/20090511.html).

CASE 2 | Merdeka Gas Grills: Inventory and Supply Chain Management

Merdeka manufactures premium gas grills for the North American market. Its gas grills require over 30 separate components, ranging from the relatively expensive bowl, lid, and burner (unit costs greater than $50), down to the many low-unit-cost (less than $1) items such as grill clips and screws. All Merdeka models use common low-unit-cost components which can be purchased from any industrial supply company.

Merdeka uses an enterprise resource planning (ERP) software package to manage its purchasing, sales, inventory and production management, and accounting functions. Excited by the information and control the software can provide, Merdeka entered into the computer system as an item every single component required for its gas grills. Furthermore, by having shop floor staff enter into the system the quantity consumed of every component used during the assembly process, the computer system keeps constant track of on-hand inventory of every component. Purchasing staff then print inventory reordering reports each morning and compare on-hand inventory to previously calculated reorder points to determine if a purchase order needs to be prepared.

In an effort to keep material costs down, Merdeka's purchasing department has identified multiple suppliers for each component. When an order for a component is required, a buyer contacts potential suppliers requesting a quote, then orders from the supplier that quoted the lowest unit cost. By using various suppliers for each component, with each supplier having various delivery lead times, Merdeka maintains a significant safety stock on each component to buffer this delivery variability.

Once a year, production shuts down for a two-day inventory count of all components. After the year-end count is entered, discrepancies between the actual physical inventory and the on-hand quantity in the computer system are corrected (they typically range from a 10 percent to 15 percent quantity loss for each individual component). Recognizing this pattern over the years, Merdeka's purchasing staff "mentally adjust down" the on-hand quantities that appear on their daily inventory reordering reports. This uncertainty regarding on-hand inventory quantities also causes purchasing staff to bump up their required order quantities throughout the year, typically by at least 20 percent.

Recently, increased competition has forced Merdeka to review its operations for potential efficiency improvements. One manager suggested starting with an ABC analysis of the inventory. A study was initiated to do this. Exhibit 13.13 shows a representative sample from this study.

Questions

1. Classify the 10 items shown into A, B, and C categories. Do the sample data indicate that Merdeka's inventory could be classified into more than three categories?

2. How might your inventory management policies differ for the A versus the C categories? For example, how would the frequency of ordering, using fixed-order-quantity versus fixed time-period models, computerization, vendor development, inventory counting, and other management aspects differ conceptually?

3. Are there other potential improvements for Merdeka that you can think of?

Source: This case was written by Brent Snider and Jaydeep Balakrishnan of the Haskayne School of Business at the University of Calgary. It is based on a real situation.

EXHIBIT 13.13

ITEM NO.	UNIT VALUE ($)	ANNUAL USAGE (UNITS)
1013	68.13	105
2691	0.54	4368
2862	11.67	298
3846	0.77	3067
4456	23.43	564
5066	2.43	1264
6392	6.12	1994
6547	0.8	2476
7675	1.65	656
8725	99.84	297

CASE 3　Hewlett-Packard—Supplying the DeskJet Printer in Europe

The DeskJet printer was introduced in 1988 and has become one of Hewlett-Packard's (HP's) most successful products. Sales have grown steadily, now reaching a level of over 600 000. Unfortunately, inventory growth has closely tracked sales growth. HP's distribution centres are filled with pallets of the DeskJet printer. Worse yet, the organization in Europe claims that inventory levels there need to be raised even further to maintain satisfactory product availability.

The DeskJet Supply Chain

The network of suppliers, manufacturing sites, distribution centres (DCs), dealers, and customers for the DeskJet product make up the DeskJet supply chain (see Exhibit 13.14). HP in Vancouver manufactures the product. There are two key stages in the manufacturing process: (1) printed circuit assembly and test (PCAT) and (2) final assembly and test (FAT). PCAT involves the assembly and testing of electronic components (like integrated circuits, read-only memories, and raw printed circuit boards) to make logic boards used in the printer. FAT involves the assembly of other subassemblies (like motors, cables, keypads, plastic chassis, gears, and the printed circuit assemblies from PCAT) to produce a working printer, as well as the final testing of the printer. The components needed for PCAT and FAT are sourced from other HP divisions as well as from external suppliers worldwide.

Selling the DeskJet in Europe requires customizing the printer to meet the language and power supply requirements of the local countries, a process known as "localization." Specifically, the localization of the DeskJet of different countries involves assembling the appropriate power supply module, which reflects the correct voltage requirements (110 or 220) and power cord plug, and packaging it with the working printer and a manual written in the appropriate language. Currently, the final test is done with the actual power supply module included with the printer. The finished products of the factory are thus "localized" versions of the printer destined for all the different countries. For the European Market, six different versions are currently produced. These are designated A, AA, AB, AQ, AU, and AY, as indicated in the Bills of Materials shown in Exhibit 13.15.

The total factory throughput time through the PCAT and FAT stages is about one week. The transportation time from Vancouver to the European DC is five weeks. The long shipment time to Europe is due to ocean transit and the time to clear customs and duties at port of entry. The plant sends a weekly shipment of printers to the DC in Europe.

The printer industry is highly competitive. Resellers want to carry as little inventory as possible. Consequently there has been increasing pressure for HP as a manufacturer to provide high levels of availability at the DC. In response, management has decided to stock the DCs so that a high level of availability is maintained.

The Inventory Service Crisis

To limit the amount of inventory throughout the DeskJet supply chain and at the same time provide the high level of service needed has been quite a challenge to Vancouver's management. The manufacturing group has been very successful in

---

EXHIBIT 13.14　HP DeskJet Supply Chain

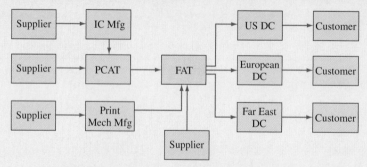

Key: IC Mfg—Integrated Circuit Manufacturing
PCAT—Printed Circuit Assembly and Test
FAT—Final Assembly and Test
Print Mech Mfg—Print Mechanism Manufacturing

EXHIBIT 13.15   HP DeskJet Bill of Materials

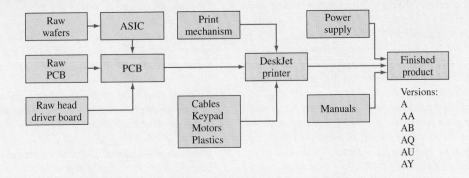

reducing the uncertainties caused by delivery to the European DC. Forecasting demand in Europe, though, is a significant problem. It has become common to have product shortages for model demands from some countries, while inventory of other models keeps piling up. In the past, the target inventory levels at the DCs were based on safety stocks that were a result of some judgmental rule of thumb. Specifically, target inventory levels, equal to one-month average sales, were set for each model carried in the DC. Now, however, it seems that the increasing difficulty of getting accurate forecasts means the safety stock rules should be revisited.

HP has put together a team of employees to help implement a scientifically-based safety stock system that will be responsive to forecast errors and replenishment lead times. They are to recommend a method for calculating appropriate safety stock levels for the various DeskJet models carried in the European DC. The team has a good sample of demand data that can be used for developing the safety stock methodology (see Exhibit 13.16). HP hopes this new methodology will solve the inventory and service problem.

One issue that continually comes up is the choice of inventory carrying cost to be used in safety stock analyses. Estimates within

the company range from 12 percent (HP's cost of debt plus some warehousing expenses) to 60 percent (based on the ROI expected of new product development projects). Management has decided to use 25 percent for this study. Assume that all printers cost an average of approximately $250 each to produce and ship to Europe. Another issue is the choice of safety stock probability for the model. The company has decided to use a probability of 98 percent, a number that marketing feels is appropriate.

The Distribution Process

The DCs have traditionally envisioned their process as a simple, straight-line, standardized process. There are four process stops:

1. Receive (complete) products from various suppliers and stock them.
2. Pick the various products needed to fill a customer order.
3. Shrink-wrap the complete order and label it.
4. Ship the order via the appropriate carrier.

The DeskJet printer fits well into the standard process. In contrast, other products, such as personal computers and

EXHIBIT 13.16   DeskJet Demand Data from Europe

EUROPE OPTIONS	NOV.	DEC.	JAN.	FEB.	MAR.	APR.	MAY	JUN.	JUL.	AUG.	SEP.	OCT.
A	80	—	60	90	21	48	—	9	20	54	84	42
AB	20 572	20 895	19 252	11 052	19 864	20 316	13 336	10 578	6 095	14 496	23 712	9792
AU	4564	3207	7485	4908	5295	90	—	5004	4385	5103	4302	6153
AA	400	255	408	645	210	87	432	816	430	630	456	273
AQ	4008	2196	4761	1953	1008	2358	1676	540	2310	2046	1797	2961
AY	248	450	378	306	219	204	248	484	164	363	384	234
Total	29 872	27 003	32 344	18 954	26 617	23 103	15 692	17 431	13 405	22 692	30 735	19 455

monitors, require special processing called "integration," which includes addition of an appropriate keyboard and manual for the destination country. Although this extra processing does not require much extra labour, it is difficult to accommodate in the standard process and disrupts the material flow. There is considerable frustration within DC management regarding the support of assembly processes. In general, DC management stresses the DCs' role as warehouses and the need to continue to do what they are best at—distribution.

Top management, though, feels that integration of the product at the warehouse is extremely valuable because it allows generic products to be sent to the DC with final configuration of the product done just prior to shipment to the customer. Rather than the factory making products specific to a country, generic products could be produced and shipped to Europe. Management is very interested in studying the value of this approach, as it could be applied to the DeskJet printers.

Questions

1. Develop an inventory model for managing the DeskJet printers in Europe assuming that the Vancouver plant continues to produce the six models sold in Europe. Using the data in Exhibit 13.16, apply your model and calculate the expected yearly investment in DeskJet printer inventory in the Europe DC.
2. Compare your results from question 1 to the current policy of carrying one month's average inventory at the DC.
3. Evaluate the idea of supplying generic printers to the Europe DC and integrating the product by packaging the power supply and the instruction manual at the DC just prior to delivery to the European resellers. Focus on the impact on DC inventory investment in this analysis.
4. What is your recommendation to HP?

Footnotes

[1] Industry Canada, http://www.strategis.gc.ca/epic/site/dsib-logi.nsf/en/pj00356e.html, retrieved July 2, 2008.

[2] P is actually a cumulative probability because the sale of the nth unit depends not only on exactly n being demanded but also on the demand for any number greater than n.

[3] As previously discussed, the standard deviation of a sum of independent variables equals the square root of the sum of the variances.

[4] The Pareto principle is also widely applied in quality problems through the use of Pareto chart. (See Chapter 7).

Selected Bibliography

Brooks, R. B., and L. W. Wilson. *Inventory Record Accuracy: Unleashing the Power of Cycle Counting.* Essex Junction, VT: Oliver Wight, 1993.

Silver, E.; D. Pyke; and R. Peterson. *Decision Systems for Inventory Management and Production Planning and Control.* 3rd ed. New York: Wiley, 1998.

Sipper, D., and R. L. Bulfin Jr. *Production Planning, Control, and Integration.* New York: McGraw-Hill, 1997.

Tersine, R. J. *Principles of Inventory and Materials Management.* 4th ed. New York: North-Holland, 1994.

Vollmann, T. E.; W. L. Berry; D. C. Whybark; and F. R. Jacobs. *Manufacturing Planning and Control Systems for Supply Chain Management.* 5th ed. New York: McGraw-Hill, 2004.

Wild, T. *Best Practices in Inventory Management.* New York: Wiley, 1998.

Zipkin, P. H. *Foundations of Inventory Management.* New York: Irwin/McGraw-Hill, 2000.

MATERIAL REQUIREMENTS PLANNING

Learning Objectives:

1. Understand what MRP is and where it is best applied.
2. Understand the source of the information used by the system.
3. Know how to do an MRP "explosion."
4. Know how order quantities are calculated in MRP systems.
5. Understand the extensions of MRP.

FROM PUSH TO PULL

In the 1980s, manufacturing was a leader in the move from batch-oriented data processing systems to online transaction processing systems. The focus was MRP (initially material requirements planning, evolving to manufacturing resource planning), which later evolved into enterprise resource planning (ERP). It has been a long ride, and anyone who has been there for the duration deserves a rest.

However, the winds of change are blowing again as yet another new paradigm comes roaring through manufacturing. Specifically, we are speaking of the change in our economy from a build-to-stock to a build-to-order model of doing business.

The weak link in the build-to-stock model is inventory management, and this can be traced to an even weaker link, reliance on sales forecasts. A build-to-order model begins with the order, not the forecast. The old problem of coordinating the procurement of parts, production of the product, and shipping the product still exists.

Today, the term *flow management* is used to describe new hybrid production planning systems that combine the information integration and planning capability of MRP with the response of a JIT kanban system. Major ERP and SCM software vendors such as Oracle, SAP, and i2 Technologies are selling these new systems.

Essentially, the idea with flow management is to produce a constantly changing mix of products, a mix that is based on current orders, using a stream of parts that are supplied just-in-time. It's important not to be tricked into thinking that all these new words really represent something new. Actually, flow manufacturing just combines things that have been used for years. In this case the combination is JIT kanban logic, MRP logic for planning material requirements, and client–server ERP.

In Chapter 13, we discussed the inventory management of items that are considered to have independent demand, generally end items such as appliances or automobiles. In this chapter we discuss the inventory management of components that go into the manufacturing of these end items. Although some of the models used in Chapter 13 can be used for managing certain components, others cannot. This chapter introduces new methods for managing the inventory and production schedule of components and subassemblies. Furthermore, because each end item may have thousands of components, the use of a computerized system is necessary. Thus, not only do we have inventory management issues, we also have data processing and system implementation and management issues.

Material requirements planning (MRP) has come a long way. From humble beginnings computing the schedules and amounts of materials required, MRP has grown to become fully integrated, interactive, real-time systems capable of multisite global applications. In this chapter we go back to the beginning and introduce the basic MRP system and take you through the logic and calculations of scheduling and materials ordering.

Material requirements planning (MRP) systems have been installed almost universally in manufacturing firms, even those considered small. The reason is that MRP is a logical, easily understandable approach to the problem of determining the number of parts, components, and materials needed to produce each end item. MRP also provides the schedule specifying when each of these materials, parts, and components should be ordered or produced.

MRP is based on dependent demand. Dependent demand is caused by the demand for a higher-level item. Tires, wheels, and engines are dependent demand items based on the demand for automobiles.

Cross Functional

Determining the number of dependent demand items needed is essentially a straightforward multiplication process. If one Part A takes five parts of B to make, then five parts of A require 25 parts of B. The basic difference in independent demand covered in the previous chapter and dependent demand covered in this chapter is as follows: If Part A is sold outside the firm, the amount of Part A that we sell is uncertain. We need to create a forecast using past data or do something like a market analysis. Part A is an independent item. However, Part B is a dependent part and its use depends on Part A. The number of B needed is simply the number of A times five. As a result of this type of multiplication, the requirements of other dependent demand items tend to become more and more lumpy as we go farther down into the product creation sequence. Lumpiness means that the requirements tend to bunch or lump rather than having an even dispersal. It is also caused by the way manufacturing is done. When manufacturing occurs in lots, items needed to produce the lot are withdrawn from inventory in quantities (perhaps all at once) rather than one at a time.

WHERE MRP CAN BE USED

MRP is most valuable in industries where a number of products are made in batches using the same productive equipment. The list in Exhibit 14.1 includes examples of different industry types and the expected benefit from MRP. As you can see in the exhibit, MRP is most valuable to companies involved in assembly operations and least valuable to those in fabrication. Numerous Canadian companies in these industries use MRP. One more point to note: MRP does not work well in companies that produce a low number of units annually. Especially for companies producing complex, expensive products requiring advanced research and design, experience has shown that lead times tend to be too long and too uncertain, and the product configuration too complex. Such companies need the control features that network scheduling techniques offer. These project management methods are covered in Chapter 3. While many companies purchase MRP software packages, as the OSMP on MRP shows, smaller companies can create their own MRP software packages.

Industry Applications and Expected Benefits of MRP

EXHIBIT 14.1

INDUSTRY TYPE	EXAMPLES	EXPECTED BENEFITS
Assemble-to-stock	Combines multiple component parts into a finished product, which is then stocked in inventory to satisfy customer demand. Examples: watches, tools, appliances.	High
Fabricate-to-stock	Items are manufactured by machine rather than assembled from parts. These are standard stock items carried in anticipation of customer demand. Examples: piston rings, electrical switches.	Low
Assemble-to-order	A final assembly is made from standard options that the customer chooses. Examples: trucks, generators, motors.	High
Fabricate-to-order	Items are manufactured by machine to customer order. These are generally industrial orders. Examples: bearings, gears, fasteners.	Low
Manufacture-to-order	Items are fabricated or assembled completely to customer specification. Examples: turbine generators, heavy machine tools.	High
Process	Includes industries such as foundries, rubber and plastics, specialty paper, chemicals, paint, drug, food processors.	Medium

Operations and Supply Management in Practice

Manufacturing Your Own MRP System to Help Manufacturing

Canada Sportswear Corp. (CSW) is a Toronto-based apparel producer and retailer of products such as outerwear, knit shirts, woven shirts, tracksuits, fleece, and even scarves and blankets. A few years ago, it was struggling to keep up with customer demand, with fill rates lower than 50 percent. Not surprisingly, it had some unhappy clients.

Part of the problem was determining quantities. CSW had a manual method of figuring out just how much product it needed, but it was a slow process. It took two months to complete a forecast for the company's entire product line. Thus, it needed a faster way to do this. Though, typically, most firms would purchase MRP software, CSW decided to build its own unique MRP system. On the surface, CSW's MRP system is little more than an Excel spreadsheet that shows product stock keeping units (SKUs) and presents a number indicating how many of each item is required. But behind this is a computer program

that does a series of MRP logic-based calculations, comparing orders made, order history, and other parameters to decide how much product CSW needs from its suppliers. But not everything was unique. CSW purchased Forecast Pro software from Business Forecast Systems Inc. to help with forecasts. CSW's MRP system also interfaces with an inventory control system it purchased from Momentis Systems Inc. in Montreal.

Because the system was custom built, features such as a "day's planned inventory" measure, not normally available in MRP systems, could be calculated by combining the forecast and the current day's orders to tell planners how many days of inventory the company had in stock. In six months, CSW had its Forecast Pro–Momentis-linking MRP system up and running and started enjoying the benefits of better planning and operation.

■ Source: S. Dubowski, "Clothing Maker Zips Up Bespoke MRP Platform," ITWorldCanada.com, January 1, 2005.

MATERIAL REQUIREMENTS PLANNING SYSTEM STRUCTURE

The material requirements planning portion of manufacturing activities most closely interacts with the master schedule, bill of materials file, inventory records file, and the output reports, as shown in Exhibit 14.2.

Each facet of Exhibit 14.2 is detailed in the following sections, but, essentially, the MRP system works as follows: Orders for products are used to create a **master production schedule**, which states the number of items to be produced during specific time periods. A *bill of materials* file identifies the specific materials used to make each item and the correct quantities of each. The inventory records file contains data such as the number of units on hand and on order. These three sources—master production schedule, bill of materials file, and inventory records file—become the data sources for the material requirements program, which expands the production schedule into a detailed order scheduling plan for the entire production sequence.

Demand for Products

Product demand for end items comes primarily from two main sources. The first is known customers who have placed specific orders, such as those generated by sales personnel, or from interdepartment transactions. These orders usually carry promised delivery dates. There is no forecasting involved in these orders—simply add them up. The second source

EXHIBIT 14.2

Overall View of the Inputs to a Standard Material Requirements Planning Program and the Reports Generated by the Program

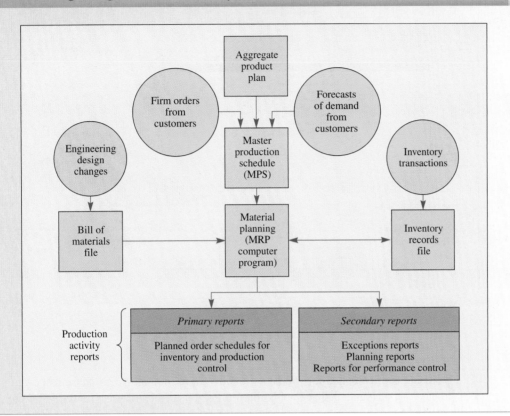

is forecast demand. These are the usual independent-demand orders; the forecasting models presented in Chapter 11 can be used to predict the quantities. The demand from the known customers and the forecast demand are combined and become the input for the master production schedule.

In addition to the demand for end products, customers also order specific parts and components either as spares or for service and repair. These demands are not usually part of the master production schedule; instead, they are fed directly into the material requirements planning program at the appropriate levels. That is, they are added in as a gross requirement for that part or component.

Bill of Materials

The **bill of materials (BOM)** file contains the complete product description, listing not only the materials, parts, and components but also the sequence in which the product is created. This BOM file is one of the three main inputs to the MRP program. (The other two are the master schedule and the inventory records file.)

BlueCielo's System's Enterprise software, Solidworks, interacts with various systems to link CAD designs to the bill of materials for engineering projects. The ERP systems allow companies to share information across the organization to prevent errors and omit redundancy, thus improving efficiency.

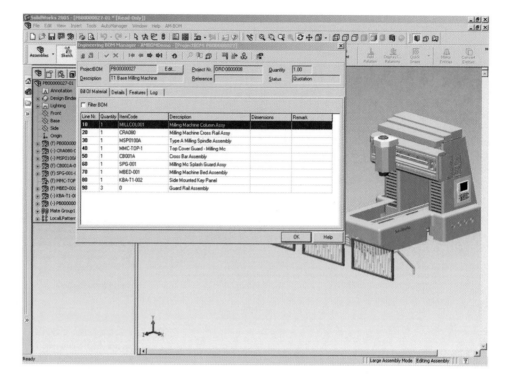

The BOM file is often called the *product structure file* or *product tree* because it shows how a product is put together. It contains the information to identify each item and the quantity used per unit of the item of which it is a part.

To illustrate this, consider the manufacture of a saucepan (end item), which is shown in an exploded view in Exhibit 14.3. The saucepan consists of a top and a base. The top is assembled using a lid and top handle. The top handle consists of the knob, screw, and washer. Similarly, the base can be broken down into its constituent components, as shown in the exhibit. Some of the components may be manufactured, others purchased.

The product structure tree for the product is shown in Exhibit 14.4 with the part (component) names and part numbers. The number in brackets beside the part name shows the number of units required for each parent. For example, two base handles and brackets are required for each saucepan. Each part has a unique part number to identify it throughout the supply chain. You have probably experienced this when you called in to order a replacement part for a product such as a household appliance or electronic equipment, and the customer service agent asked you for the item part number (or had you describe it so that the part number could be identified). Note that both the top and base use the same type of screw and washer (same part number). By using common parts, the company has less stockkeeping units to manage, and this will help better control the inventory as well as reduce the database resources required. In addition, the company may get a price discount from its supplier for larger volumes.

Bills of materials often list parts using an indented structure. This clearly identifies each item and the manner in which it is assembled because each indentation signifies the components of the item. A comparison of the indented parts in Exhibit 14.5 with the item

Exploded View of End Item

EXHIBIT 14.3

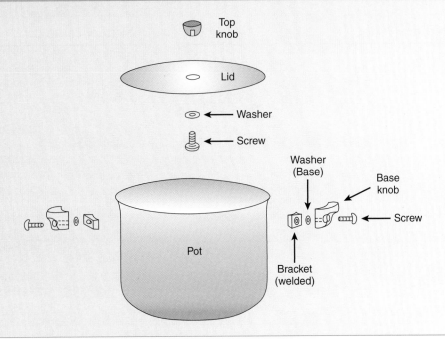

structure in Exhibit 14.4 shows the ease of relating the two displays. From a computer standpoint, however, storing items in indented parts lists is very inefficient. To compute the amount of each item needed at the lower levels, each item would need to be expanded ("exploded") and summed. A more efficient procedure is to store parts data in simple

Bill of Materials (Product Structure Tree) for Saucepan

EXHIBIT 14.4

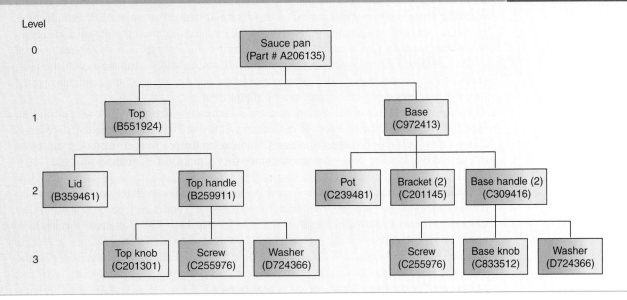

EXHIBIT 14.5   Parts List for Saucepan in an Indented Format and in a Single Level List

INDENTED PARTS LIST				SINGLE-LEVEL PARTS LIST		
A206135				A206135		
	B551924(1)					B551924(1)
		B359461				C972413(1)
		B259911		B551924		
			C201301(1)			B359461(1)
			C255976(1)			B259911(1)
			D724366(1)	B259911		
	C972413(1)					C201301(1)
		C239481(1)				C255976(1)
		C201145(2)				D724366(1)
		C309416(2)		C972413		
			C255976(1)			C239481(1)
			C833512(1)			C201145(2)
			D724366(1)			C309416(2)
				C309416		
						C255976(1)
						C833512(1)
						D724366(1)

single-level lists. That is, each item and component is listed showing only its parent and the number of units needed per unit of its parent. This avoids duplication because it includes each assembly only once. Exhibit 14.5 shows both the indented parts list and the single-level parts list for the saucepan.

A *modular* bill of materials is the term for a buildable item that can be produced and stocked as a subassembly. It is also a standard item with no options within the module. Many end items that are large and expensive are better scheduled and controlled as modules (or subassemblies). It is particularly advantageous to schedule subassembly modules when the same subassemblies appear in different end items. For example, a manufacturer of cranes can combine booms, transmissions, and engines in a variety of ways to meet a customer's needs. Using a modular bill of materials simplifies the scheduling and control and also makes it easier to forecast the use of different modules. Another benefit in using modular bills is that if the same item is used in a number of products (common parts), then the total inventory investment can be minimized.

A *super* bill of materials includes items with fractional options. (A super bill can specify, for example, 0.3 of a part. What that means is that 30 percent of the units produced contain that part and 70 percent do not.) Modular and super bills of materials are often referred to as planning bills of materials since they simplify the planning process.

Low-Level Coding If all identical parts occur at the same level for each end product, the total number of parts and materials needed for a product can be computed easily. Consider Product L shown in Exhibit 14.6a. Notice that Item N, for example, occurs both as an input to L and as an input to M. Item N, therefore, needs to be lowered to level 2 (Exhibit 14.6b) to bring all Ns to the same level. If all identical items are placed at the same level, it becomes a simple matter for the computer to scan across each level and summarize the number of units of each item required.

EXHIBIT 14.6

Product L Hierarchy in (a) Expanded to the Lowest Level of Each Item in (b)

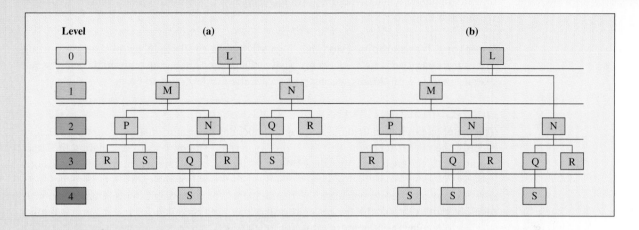

Inventory Records

The inventory records file can be quite lengthy. Exhibit 14.7 shows the variety of information contained in the inventory records. The MRP program accesses the *status* segment of the record according to specific time periods (called *time buckets* in MRP slang). These records are accessed as needed during the program run.

As we will see, the MRP program performs its analysis from the top of the product structure downward, calculating requirements level by level. There are times, however,

EXHIBIT 14.7

The Inventory Status Record for an Item in Inventory

	Part no.	Description		Lead time		Std. cost	Safety stock
Item master data segment	Order quantity		Setup	Cycle	Last year's usage		Class
	Scrap allowance		Cutting data		Pointers	Etc.	

				Period	Totals
	Allocated	Control balance	1 2 3 4 5 6 7 8		Totals
Inventory status segment	Gross requirements				
	Scheduled receipts				
	Projected available balance				
	Planned order releases				
Subsidiary data segment	Order details				
	Pending action				
	Counters				
	Keeping track				

when it is desirable to identify the parent item that caused the material requirement. The MRP program allows the creation of a *peg record* file either separately or as part of the inventory record file. Pegging requirements allows us to retrace a material requirement upward in the product structure through each level, identifying each parent item that created the demand.

Inventory Transactions File The inventory status file is kept up to date by posting inventory transactions as they occur. These changes occur because of stock receipts and disbursements, scrap losses, wrong parts, cancelled orders, and so forth.

MRP Computer Program

The material requirements planning program operates using information from the inventory records, the master schedule, and the bill of materials. The process of calculating the exact requirements for each item managed by the system is often referred to as the "explosion" process. Working from the top level downward in the bill of materials, requirements from parent items are used to calculate the requirements for component items. Consideration is taken of current on-hand balances, and orders that are scheduled for receipt in the future.

The following is a general description of the MRP explosion process:

1. The requirements for level 0 items, typically referred to as "end items," are retrieved from the master schedule. These requirements are referred to as "gross require-ments" by the MRP program. Typically, the gross requirements are scheduled in weekly time buckets.
2. Next, the program uses the current on-hand balance, together with the schedule of orders that will be received in the future to calculate the "net requirements." Net requirements are the amounts that are needed week by week in the future over and above what is currently on hand or committed to through an order already released and scheduled.
3. Using net requirements, the program calculates when orders should be received to meet these requirements. This can be a simple process of just scheduling orders to arrive according to the exact net requirements or a more complicated process where requirements are combined for multiple periods. This schedule of when orders should arrive is referred to as "planned-order receipts."
4. Since there is typically a lead time associated with each order, the next step is to find a schedule for when orders are actually released. Offsetting the "planned-order receipts" by the required lead time does this. This schedule is referred to as the "planned-order release."
5. After these four steps have been completed for all the level zero items, the program moves to level 1 items.
6. The gross requirements for each level 1 item are calculated from the planned-order release schedule for the parents of each level 1 item. Any additional independent demand also needs to be included in the gross requirements.
7. After the gross requirements have been determined, net requirements, planned-order receipts, and planned-order releases are calculated as described in steps 2–4 above.
8. This process is then repeated for each level in the bill of materials.

The process of doing these calculations is much simpler than the description, as you will see in the example that follows. Typically, the explosion calculations are performed each week or whenever changes have been made to the master schedule. Some MRP programs have the option of generating immediate schedules, called *net change* schedules.

Net change systems are "activity" driven and requirements and schedules are updated whenever a transaction is processed that has an impact on the item. Net change enables the system to reflect in "real time" the exact status of each item managed by the system.

AN EXAMPLE USING MRP

Ampere, Inc., produces a line of electric meters installed in residential buildings by electric utility companies to measure power consumption. Meters used on single-family homes are of two basic types for different voltage and amperage ranges. In addition to complete meters, some subassemblies are sold separately for repair or for changeovers to a different voltage or power load. The problem for the MRP system is to determine a production schedule to identify each item, the period it is needed, and the appropriate quantities. The schedule is then checked for feasibility, and the schedule is modified if necessary.

Forecasting Demand

Demand for the meters and components originates from two sources: customers who have placed firm orders and unidentified customers who make the usual random demands for these items. The random requirements were forecast using one of the usual techniques described in Chapter 11 and past demand data. Exhibit 14.8 shows the requirements for meters A and B and Subassembly D for a three-month period (months three through five). There are some "other parts" used to make the meters. In order to keep our example manageable, we are not including them here.

	METER A		METER B		SUBASSEMBLY D	
MONTH	KNOWN	FORECAST	KNOWN	FORECAST	KNOWN	FORECAST
3	1000	250	410	60	200	70
4	600	250	300	60	180	70
5	300	250	500	60	250	70

EXHIBIT 14.8

Future Requirements for Meters A and B and Subassembly D Stemming from Specific Customer Orders (Known) and from Forecast Sources

Developing a Master Production Schedule

For the meter and component requirements specified in Exhibit 14.8, assume that the quantities to satisfy the known and forecast demands must be available during the first week of the month. This assumption is reasonable because management (in our example) prefers to produce meters in a single batch each month rather than a number of batches throughout the month.

Exhibit 14.9 shows the trial master production schedule (MPS) that we use under these conditions, with demand for months 3, 4, and 5 listed in the first week of each month, or as Weeks 9, 13, and 17. For brevity, we will work with demand through Week 9. The schedule we develop should be examined for resource availability, capacity availability, and so on, and then revised and run again. We will stop with our example at the end of this one schedule, however. As shown in Exhibit 14.2, the MPS provides the input for the MRP calculations.

A Master Schedule to Satisfy Demand Requirements as Specified in Exhibit 14.8

	Week								
	9	10	11	12	13	14	15	16	17
Meter A	1250				850				550
Meter B	470				360				560
Subassembly D	270				250				320

Bill of Materials (Product Structure)

The product structure for meters A and B is shown in Exhibit 14.10 in the typical way using low-level coding, in which each item is placed at the lowest level at which it appears in the structure hierarchy. Meters A and B consist of a common subassembly C and some parts that include part D. To keep things simple, we will focus on only one of the parts, part D, which is a transformer.

Product Structure for Meters A and B

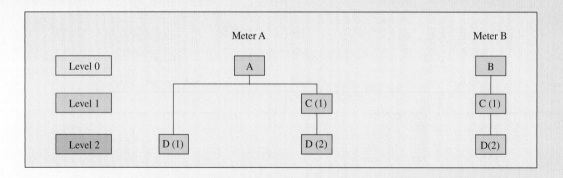

From the product structure, notice that part D (the transformer) is used in subassembly C (which is used in both meters A and B). In the case of meter A, an additional part D (transformer) is needed. The "2" in parentheses next to D, when used to make a C, indicates that two D's are required for every C that is made. The product structure, as well as the indented parts list in Exhibit 14.11, indicates how the meters are actually made. First, subassembly C is made, and potentially these are carried in inventory. In the final step in the process, meters A and B are assembled, and, in the case of meter A, an additional part D is used.

Inventory Records

The inventory records data would be similar to that shown in Exhibit 14.7. As shown earlier in the chapter, additional data such as vendor identity, cost, and lead time would also be included in these data. For this example, the pertinent data include the on-hand

EXHIBIT 14.11

Indented Parts List for Meter A and Meter B, with the Required Number of Items per Unit of Parent Listed in Parentheses

METER A	METER B
A	B
D (1)	
C (1)	C (1)
D (2)	D (2)

EXHIBIT 14.12

Number of Units on Hand and Lead Time Data That Would Appear on the Inventory Record File

ITEM	ON-HAND INVENTORY	LEAD TIME (WEEKS)	SAFETY STOCK	ON ORDER
A	50	2	0	
B	60	2	0	10 (week 5)
C	40	1	5	
D	200	1	20	100 (week 4)

inventory at the start of the program run, safety stock requirements, and the current status of orders that have already been released (see Exhibit 14.12). Safety stock is a minimum amount of inventory that we always want to keep on hand for an item. For example, for subassembly C, we never want the inventory to get below 5 units. We also see that we have an order placed for 10 units of meter B that is scheduled for receipt at the beginning of Week 5. Another order placed for 100 units of part D (the transformer) is scheduled to arrive at the beginning of Week 4.

Performing the MRP Calculations

Conditions are now set to perform the MRP calculations: End-item requirements have been presented in the master production schedule, while the status of inventory and the order lead times are available, and we also have the pertinent product structure data. The MRP calculations (often referred to as an explosion) are done level by level, in conjunction with the inventory data and data from the master schedule.

Exhibit 14.13 shows the details of these calculations. The following analysis explains the logic in detail. We will limit our analysis to the problem of meeting the gross requirements for 1250 units of meter A, 470 units of meter B, and 270 units of transformer D, all in Week 9.

An MRP record is kept for each item managed by the system. The record contains *gross requirements, scheduled receipts, projected available balance, net requirements, planned order receipts,* and *planned order releases* data. *Gross requirements* are the total amount required for a particular item. These requirements can be from external customer demand and also from demand calculated due to manufacturing requirements. *Scheduled receipts* represent orders that have already been released and that are scheduled to arrive as of the beginning of the period. Once the paperwork on an order has been released, what was a "planned" order prior to that event now becomes a *scheduled receipt.*

EXHIBIT 14.13   Material Requirements Planning Schedule for Meters A and B, and Subassemblies C and D

Item		Week					
		4	5	6	7	8	9
A							
LT = 2 weeks	Gross requirements						1250
On hand = 50	Scheduled receipts						
Safety stock = 0	Projected available balance	50	50	50	50	50	50
Order qty = lot-for-lot	Net requirements						1200
	Planned order receipts						1200
	Planned order releases				1200		
B							
LT = 2 weeks	Gross requirements						470
On hand = 60	Scheduled receipts		10				
Safety stock = 0	Projected available balance	60	60	70	70	70	70
Order qty = lot-for-lot	Net requirements						400
	Planned order receipts						400
	Planned order releases				400		
C					400+		
LT = 1 week	Gross requirements				1200		
On hand = 40	Scheduled receipts						
Safety stock = 5	Projected available balance	35	35	35	35	435	435
Order qty = 2000	Net requirements				1565		
	Planned order receipts				2000		
	Planned order releases			2000			
D							
LT = 1 week	Gross requirements			4000	1200		270
On hand = 200	Scheduled receipts	100					
Safety stock = 20	Projected available balance	180	280	280	1280	80	80
Order qty = 5000	Net requirements			3720			190
	Planned order receipts			5000			5000
	Planned order releases		5000			5000	

Projected available balance is the amount of inventory that is expected as of the beginning of a period. This can be calculated as follows:

$$
\begin{aligned}
\text{Projected} \\
\text{available} \\
\text{balance}_t
\end{aligned} =
\begin{aligned}
\text{Projected} \\
\text{available} \\
\text{balance}_{t-1}
\end{aligned} -
\begin{aligned}
\text{Gross} \\
\text{requirements}_{t-1}
\end{aligned} +
\begin{aligned}
\text{Scheduled} \\
\text{receipts}_{t-1}
\end{aligned} +
\begin{aligned}
\text{Planned} \\
\text{order} \\
\text{receipts}_{t-1}
\end{aligned} -
\begin{aligned}
\text{Safety} \\
\text{stock}
\end{aligned}
$$

A *net requirement* is the amount needed when the *projected available* balance plus the *scheduled receipts* in a period are not sufficient to cover the *gross requirement*. The *planned order receipt* is the amount of an order that is required to meet a net requirement in the period. Finally, the *planned order release* is the planned order receipt offset by the lead time.

Beginning with meter A, the projected available balance is 50 units and there are no net requirements until Week 9. In Week 9, an additional 1200 units are needed to cover the demand of 1250 generated from the order scheduled through the master schedule. The order quantity is designated "lot-for-lot," which means that we can order the exact quantity needed to meet net requirements. An order, therefore, is planned for receipt of 1200 units for the beginning of Week 9. Since the lead time is two weeks, this order must be released at the beginning of Week 7.

Meter B is similar to A, although an order for 10 units is scheduled for receipt in period 5. We project that 70 units will be available in week 6. There is a net requirement for 400 additional units to meet the gross requirement of 470 units in Week 9. This requirement is met with an order for 400 units that must be released at the beginning of Week 7.

Item C is the subassembly used in both meters A and B. We only need additional C's when either A or B is being made. Our analysis of A indicates that an order for 1200 will be released in Week 7. An order for 400 B's will also be released in Week 7, so total demand for C is 1600 units in Week 7. The projected available balance is the 40 units on hand minus the safety stock of 5 units that we have specified, or 35 units. In Week 7, the net requirement is 1565 units. The order policy for C indicates an order quantity of 2000 units, so an order receipt for 2000 is planned for Week 7. This order needs to be released in Week 6 due to the one-week lead time. Assuming this order is actually processed in the future, the projected available balance is 435 units in Weeks 8 and 9.

Item D, the transformer, has demand from three different sources. The demand in Week 6 is due to the requirement to put D's into subassembly C. In this case two D's are needed for every C, or 4000 units (the product structure indicates this two-to-one relationship). In the seventh week, 1200 D's are needed for the order for 1200 A's that are scheduled to be released in Week 7. Another 270 units are needed in Week 9 to meet the independent demand that is scheduled through the master schedule. Projected available balance coming into Week 4 is 180 units (200 on hand minus the safety stock of 20 units), 280 units in Weeks 2 and 3. There is a net requirement for an additional 3720 units in Week 6, so we plan to receive an order for 5000 units (the order quantity). This results in a projected balance of 1280 in Week 7, of which 1200 are used to meet demand. Eighty units are projected to be available in Weeks 8 and 9. Due to the demand for 270 in Week 9, a net requirement of 190 units in Week 9 results in planning the receipt of an additional 5000-unit order in Week 9.

LOT SIZING IN MRP SYSTEMS

Determining lot sizes in an MRP system is a complicated and difficult problem. Lot sizes are the part quantities issued in the planned order receipt and planned order release sections of an MRP schedule. For parts produced in-house, lot sizes are the production quantities of batch sizes. For purchased parts, these are the quantities ordered from the supplier. Lot sizes generally meet part requirements for one or more periods.

Most lot-sizing techniques deal with how to balance the set-up or order costs and holding costs associated with meeting the net requirements generated by the MRP planning process. Many MRP systems have options for computing lot sizes based on some of the more commonly used techniques. The use of lot-sizing techniques increases the complexity of running MRP schedules in a plant. In an attempt to save set-up costs, the inventory generated with the larger lot sizes needs to be stored, making the logistics in the plant much more complicated.

Next, we explain two lot-sizing techniques using a common example. The lot-sizing techniques presented are lot-for-lot (L4L) and economic order quantity (EOQ). There are other techniques, such as the Wagner–Whitin algorithm, the Silver-Meal heuristic, least total cost (LTC), and least unit cost (LUC), which are discussed in more advanced textbooks on supply chain management.

Consider the following MRP lot-sizing problem; the net requirements are shown for eight scheduling weeks:

Cost per item					$10.00		
Order or set-up cost					$47.00		
Inventory carrying cost/week					0.5%		
Weekly net requirements:							
1	2	3	4	5	6	7	8
50	60	70	60	95	75	60	55

Lot-for-Lot

Lot-for-lot (L4L)

- Sets planned orders to exactly match the net requirements.
- Produces exactly what is needed each week, with none carried over into future periods.
- Minimizes carrying cost.
- Does not take into account set-up costs or capacity limitations.

Exhibit 14.14 shows the lot-for-lot calculations. The net requirements are given in column 2. Because the logic of lot-for-lot says the production quantity (column 3) will exactly match the required quantity (column 2), there will be no inventory left at the end (column 4). Without any inventory to carry over into the next week, there is zero holding cost (column 5). However, lot-for-lot requires a set-up cost each week (column 6). Incidentally, there is a set-up cost each week because this is a work centre where a variety of items are worked on each week. This is not a case where the work centre is committed to one product and sits idle when it is not working on that product (in which case only one set-up would result). Lot-for-lot causes high set-up costs.

EXHIBIT 14.14　Lot-for-Lot Run Size for an MRP Schedule

(1) WEEK	(2) NET REQUIREMENTS	(3) PRODUCTION QUANTITY	(4) ENDING INVENTORY	(5) HOLDING COST	(6) SET-UP COST	(7) TOTAL COST
1	50	50	0	$0.00	$47.00	$ 47.00
2	60	60	0	0.00	47.00	94.00
3	70	70	0	0.00	47.00	141.00
4	60	60	0	0.00	47.00	188.00
5	95	95	0	0.00	47.00	235.00
6	75	75	0	0.00	47.00	282.00
7	60	60	0	0.00	47.00	329.00
8	55	55	0	0.00	47.00	376.00

Economic Order Quantity

In Chapter 13, we discussed the EOQ model, which explicitly balances set-up and holding costs. In an EOQ model, either fairly constant demand must exist or safety stock must be kept to provide for demand variability. The EOQ model uses an estimate of total annual demand, the set-up or order cost, and the annual holding cost. EOQ was not designed for a system with discrete time periods such as MRP. The lot-sizing techniques used for MRP

	Economic Order Quantity Run Size for an MRP Schedule					**EXHIBIT 14.15**
WEEK	NET REQUIREMENTS	PRODUCTION QUANTITY	ENDING INVENTORY	HOLDING COST	SET-UP COST	TOTAL COST
1	50	351	301	$15.05	$47.00	$ 62.05
2	60	0	241	12.05	0.00	74.10
3	70	0	171	8.55	0.00	82.65
4	60	0	111	5.55	0.00	88.20
5	95	0	16	0.80	0.00	89.00
6	75	351	292	14.60	47.00	150.60
7	60	0	232	11.60	0.00	162.20
8	55	0	177	8.85	0.00	171.05

assume that part requirements are satisfied at the start of the period. Holding costs are then charged only to the ending inventory for the period, not to the average inventory as in the case of the EOQ model. EOQ assumes that parts are used continuously during the period. The lot sizes generated by EOQ do not always cover the entire number of periods. For example, the EOQ might provide the requirements for 4.6 periods. Using the same data as in the lot-for-lot example, the economic order quantity is calculated as follows:

$$\text{Annual demand based on the 8 weeks} = D = \frac{525}{8} \times 52 = 3412.5 \text{ units}$$

$$\text{Annual holding cost} = H = 0.5\% \times \$10 \times 52 \text{ weeks} = \$2.60 \text{ per unit}$$

$$\text{Set-up cost} = S = \$47 \text{ (given)}$$

$$\therefore \text{EOQ} = \sqrt{\frac{2DS}{H}} = \sqrt{\frac{2(3412.5)(\$47)}{\$2.60}} = 351 \text{ units}$$

Exhibit 14.15 shows the MRP schedule using an EOQ of 351 units. The EOQ lot size in Week 1 is enough to meet requirements for Weeks 1 through 5 and a portion of Week 6. Then, in Week 6 another EOQ lot is planned to meet the requirements for Weeks 6 through 8. Notice that the EOQ plan leaves some inventory at the end of Week 8 to carry forward into Week 9.

Choosing the Best Lot Size

Using the lot-for-lot method, the total cost for the eight weeks is $376; the EOQ total cost is $171.05. Though not shown, the least total cost method (LTC) for this problem would yield a cost of $140.50; the least unit cost (LUC), $153.50; and the Silver-Meal heuristic, $131.00. Thus, the lowest cost was obtained using the Silver-Meal heuristic. If there were more than eight weeks, the best method could differ. Note that since demand was not constant, the EOQ does not perform as wall as some of the other techniques.

CAPACITY REQUIREMENTS PLANNING (CRP)

MRP, as described in this chapter, assumes that production can be scheduled when required, i.e., that capacity is unlimited. In practice, of course, capacity is generally constrained. So often the unconstrained MRP schedule may need to be revised based on capacity constraints. This process is called capacity requirements planning.

For example, if it is seen that the unconstrained plan will require more hours than are available in a certain week, one option is to increase the available capacity though additional shifts, overtime, part-time work, or subcontracting. Another option is to shift some of the production to an earlier period with excess capacity or to a later period (in which case the job might be delayed). It is important to do capacity requirements planning as otherwise the MRP plan may be infeasible. We may be making promises to customers that we will not be able to keep, which is not desirable from a customer service perspective.

MANUFACTURING RESOURCE PLANNING (MRP II)

As MRP matured, it was logical to expect that managers would want the material planning system be integrated with other functions in the organization. Initially, this integration started with the purchasing function. Capacity planning and the detailed shop floor aspects of manufacturing planning and control (such as order scheduling) also became integrated with MRP. This expansion of the MRP system became known as **Manufacturing Resource Planning** or **MRP II**. As shown in Exhibit 14.16, the intent was to link all the resources of the firm, including manufacturing, marketing, finance, human resources, purchasing, and engineering, from a planning and control perspective. Further, as seen in Exhibit 14.16, the MRP II functions as a *closed loop system*, where there is feedback. So, for example, if the CRP indicates that capacity is insufficient, the plan is modified. Thus, the MRP II system allows firm wide visibility of its operations. As mentioned in the opening vignette, ERP systems are an evolution of MRP II systems.

EXHIBIT 14.16	Manufacturing Resource Planning

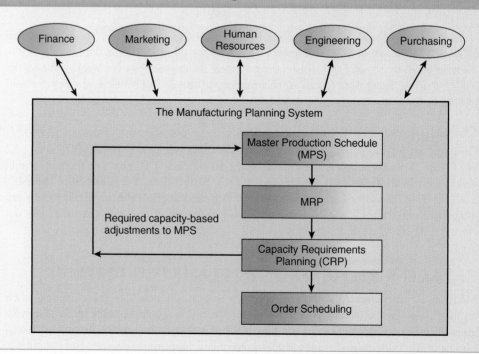

DISTRIBUTION REQUIREMENTS PLANNING (DRP)

The use of MRP logic in the planning of distribution inventories is called **distribution requirements planning (DRP)**. Consider the product structure in Exhibit 14.17. Let A represent the factory, let B and C represent distribution centres (DCs), and let D, E, F, G and H represent retail outlets. If we know the lead times for shipping from the retail outlets to the DCs and from the DCs to the factory, the DRP problem becomes very similar to an MRP problem except in reverse.

Starting from the retail outlets and moving up to the DC and the factory, given the gross requirements, the available inventories, and lot sizes, we can calculate the scheduled receipts, net requirements, and the planned shipping releases just as we would do in MRP. Thus DRP is an MRP-like tool for planning shipments and production in a supply chain. At the factory, the DRP shipping plan would become the input for the gross requirements in the MRP.

Distribution Requirements Planning	EXHIBIT 14.17

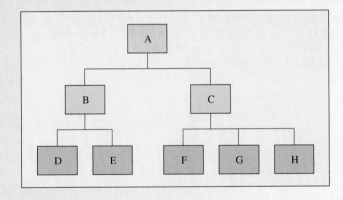

MRP AND JIT

One issue that often comes up is whether MRP and JIT are compatible, since they both address inventory and scheduling, but in different environments. Recall that the JIT scheduling method, kanban, is typically used in stable high-volume low-variety manufacturing, while MRP is useful in medium-volume, higher-variety manufacturing. Pycraft et al.[1] provide a good discussion of how they can be combined. Many factories, while making a variety of products (and thus good candidates for MRP), use many standardized and common components. These components will tend to have high volume and stable demand, since they are needed regardless of various end items scheduled for production. So, while MRP can be used to schedule end-item production based on a forecast or actual customer demand, kanban can be used to schedule the high-volume standardized components. Thus, combining JIT and MRP (and even EOQ) intelligently can be an effective method of managing a factory making customized products.

Summary

Since the 1970s, MRP has grown from its original purpose of determining simple time schedules for production and material procurement to its present use as an integral part of enterprise resource planning, which ties together all the major functions of a firm. MRP has proved to be a flexible platform that has been adapted to many different situations, including repetitive manufacturing using just-in-time systems.

In this chapter, we have covered the basic concepts needed to understand MRP. The MRP engine takes information from a master schedule that is a detailed plan for future production. Depending on the needs of the firm, the master schedule can be stated in terms of individual products, generic products, or modules and subassemblies. Master scheduling is part of the sales and operations planning process that is critical to implementing the firm's operations strategy successfully.

The bill of materials depicts exactly how a firm makes the items in the master schedule. The "structure" of the bill of materials (sometimes referred to as the "product structure") captures how raw materials and purchased parts come together to form subassemblies and how those subassembles are brought together to make the items in the master schedule.

The MRP "explosion" process is the heart of the system. Using the master schedule and bill of materials, together with the current inventory status (amount on-hand and on-order) of each part in the bill of materials, detailed schedules are calculated that show the exact timing of needed parts in the future. In a typical company, this process can require a significant computation effort involving literally thousands of detailed schedules.

This chapter also addressed the important topic of how to consider inventory-related costs. A number of common MRP lot-sizing rules were discussed that consider the fixed cost and variable cost trade-off, which can be significant in minimizing inventory costs.

The evolution of MRP systems includes incorporating capacity constraints (CRP), linking it to other functions in the firm (MRP II), and using the concept in managing distribution inventories (DRP).

Key Terms

Bill of Materials (BOM)   A computer file that contains the complete product description, listing the materials, parts, and components and the sequence in which the product is created.

Capacity Requirements Planning (CRP)   Revising the MRP schedule based on capacity constraints.

Distribution Requirements Planning (DRP)   The use of MRP logic in the planning of distribution inventories.

Manufacturing Resource Planning (MRP II)   MRP linked to the other functions in the firm.

Master Production Schedule (MPS)   A time-phased plan specifying how many and when the firm plans to build each end item.

Material Requirements Planning (MRP)   The logic for determining the number of parts, components, and materials needed to produce a product. MRP also provides the schedule specifying when each of these materials, parts, and components should be ordered or produced.

Net change system   An MRP system that calculates the impact of a change in the MRP data (the inventory status, BOM, or master schedule) immediately. This is a common feature in current systems.

Solved Problems

Solved Problem 1

Product X is made of two units of Y and three of Z. Y is made of one unit of A and two units of B. Z is made of two units of A and four units of C.

Lead time for X is one week; Y, two weeks; Z, three weeks; A, two weeks; B, one week; and C, three weeks.

a. Draw the bill of materials (product structure tree).

b. If 100 units of X are needed in week 10, develop a planning schedule showing when each item should be ordered and in what quantity.

Solved Problem

SOLUTION

a.

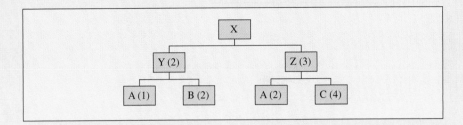

b.

		3	4	5	6	7	8	9	10
X	LT = 1							100	100
Y	LT = 2					200		200	
Z	LT = 3				300			300	
A	LT = 2			600	600	200			
				200					
B	LT = 1				400	400			
C	LT = 3	1200			1200				

Solved Problem 2

Product M is made of two units of N and three of P. N is made of two units of R and four units of S. R is made of one unit of S and three units of T. P is made of two units of T and four units of U.

a. Show the bill of materials (product structure tree).
b. If 100 M are required, how many units of each component are needed?
c. Show both a single-level parts list and an indented parts list.

SOLUTION

a.

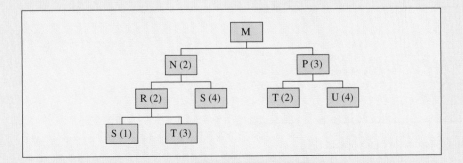

b. M = 100   S = 800 + 400 = 1200
    N = 200   T = 600 + 1200 = 1800
    P = 300   U = 1200
    R = 400

c.

SINGLE-LEVEL PARTS LIST		INDENTED PARTS LIST		
M		M		
	N (2)	N (2)		
	P (3)		R (2)	
N				S (1)
	R (2)			T (3)
	S (4)		S (4)	
R		P (3)		
	S (1)		T (2)	
	T (3)		U (4)	
P				
	T (2)			
	U (4)			

Review and Discussion Questions

1. Discuss the meaning of MRP terms such as *planned order release* and *scheduled order receipt.*
2. Many practitioners currently update MRP weekly or biweekly. Would it be more valuable if it were updated daily? Discuss.
3. What is the role of safety stock in an MRP system?
4. Contrast the significance of the term *lead time* in the traditional EOQ context and in an MRP system.
5. Discuss the importance of the master production schedule in an MRP system.
6. "MRP just prepares shopping lists. It does not do the shopping or cook the dinner." Comment.
7. What are the sources of demand in an MRP system? Are these dependent or independent, and how are they used as inputs to the system?
8. State the types of data that would be carried in the bill of materials file and the inventory record file.

Problems

1. Bodnarchuk is a manufacturer that produces bracket assemblies. Demand for bracket assemblies (X) is 130 units. The following is the BOM in indented form:

ITEM			DESCRIPTION	USAGE
X			Bracket assembly	1
	A		Wall board	4
	B		Hanger subassembly	2
		D	Hanger casting	3
		E	Ceramic knob	1
	C		Rivet head screw	3
		F	Metal tong	4
		G	Plastic cap	2

Below is a table indicating current inventory levels:

Item	X	A	B	C	D	E	F	G
Inventory	25	16	60	20	180	160	1000	100

a. Using Excel, create the MRP using the product tree structure.

b. What are the net requirements of each item in the MPS?

2. In the following MRP planning schedule for Item J, indicate the correct net requirements, planned order receipts, and planned order releases to meet the gross requirements. Lead time is one week.

ITEM J	WEEK NUMBER					
	0	1	2	3	4	5
Gross requirements			75		50	70
On-hand	40					
Net requirements						
Planned order receipt						
Planned order release						

3. Repeat Solved Problem 1 using current on-hand inventories of 20 X, 40 Y, 30 Z, 50 A, 100 B, and 900 C.

4. Assume that Product Z is made of two units of A and four units of B. A is made of three units of C and four D. D is made of two units of E.

   Lead times for purchase or fabrication of each unit to final assembly are: Z takes two weeks; A, B, C, and D take one week each; and E takes three weeks.

   Fifty units are required in Period 10. (Assume that there is currently no inventory on hand of any of these items.)

   a. Show the bill of materials (product structure tree).

   b. Develop an MRP planning schedule showing gross and net requirements and order release and order receipt dates.

5. *Note:* For Problems 5 through 10, the following six-level scheme can be used to simplify data handling to include the receipt of orders that have actually been placed in previous periods. (A number of different techniques are used in practice, but the important issue is to keep track of what is on hand, what is expected to arrive, what is needed, and what size orders should be placed.) One way to calculate the numbers is as follows:

	WEEK
Gross requirements	
Scheduled receipts	
Projected available balance	
Net requirements	
Planned order receipt	
Planned order release	

One unit of A is made of three units of B, one unit of C, and two units of D. B is composed of two units of E and one unit of D. C is made of one unit of B and two units of E. E is made of one unit of F.

   Items B, C, E, and F have one-week lead times; A and D have lead times of two weeks.

   Assume that lot-for-lot (L4L) lot sizing is used for Items A, B, and F; lots of size 50, 50, and 200 are used for Items C, D, and E, respectively. Items C, E, and F have on-hand (beginning) inventories of 10, 50, and 150, respectively; all other items have zero beginning inventory. We are scheduled to receive 10 units of A in Week 2, 50 units of E in Week 1, and also 50 units of F in Week 1. There are no other scheduled receipts. If 30 units of A are required in Week 8, use the low-level-coded bill of materials to find the necessary planned order releases for all components.

6. One unit of A is made of two units of B, three units of C, and two units of D. B is composed of one unit of E and two units of F. C is made of two units of F and one unit of D. E is made of two units of D. Items A, C, D, and F have one-week lead times; B and E have lead times of two weeks. Lot-for-lot (L4L) lot sizing is used for Items A, B, C, and D; lots of size 50 and 180 are used for Items E and F, respectively. Item C has an on-hand (beginning) inventory of 15;

D has an on-hand inventory of 50; all other items have zero beginning inventory. We are scheduled to receive 20 units of Item E in Week 2; there are no other scheduled receipts.

Construct simple and low-level-coded bills of materials (product structure tree) and indented and summarized parts lists.

If 20 units of A are required in Week 8, use the low-level-coded bill of materials to find the necessary planned order releases for all components. (See the note in Problem 5.)

7. One unit of A is made of one unit of B and one unit of C. B is made of four units of C and one unit each of E and F. C is made of two units of D and one unit of E. E is made of three units of F. Item C has a lead time of one week; Items A, B, E, and F have two-week lead times; and Item D has a lead time of three weeks. Lot-for-lot lot sizing is used for Items A, D, and E; lots of size 50, 100, and 50 are used for Items B, C, and F, respectively. Items A, C, D, and E have on-hand (beginning) inventories of 20, 50, 100, and 10, respectively; all other items have zero beginning inventory. We are scheduled to receive 10 units of A in Week 1, 100 units of C in Week 1, and 100 units of D in Week 3; there are no other scheduled receipts. If 50 units of A are required in Week 10, use the low-level-coded bill of materials (product structure tree) to find the necessary planned order releases for all components. (See the note in Problem 5.)

8. One unit of A is made of two units of B and one unit of C. B is made of three units of D and one unit of F. C is composed of three units of B, one unit of D, and four units of E. D is made of one unit of E. Item C has a lead time of one week; Items A, B, E, and F have two-week lead times; and Item D has a lead time of three weeks. Lot-for-lot lot sizing is used for Items C, E, and F; lots of size 20, 40, and 160 are used for Items A, B, and D, respectively. Items A, B, D, and E have on-hand (beginning) inventories of 5, 10, 100, and 100, respectively; all other items have zero beginning inventories. We are scheduled to receive 10 units of A in Week 3, 20 units of B in Week 7, 40 units of F in Week 5, and 60 units of E in Week 2; there are no other scheduled receipts. If 20 units of A are required in Week 10, use the low-level-coded bill of materials (product structure tree) to find the necessary planned order releases for all components. (See the note in Problem 5.)

9. One unit of A is composed of 2 units of B and three units of C. Each B is composed of one unit of F. C is made of one unit of D, one unit of E, and two units of F. Items A, B, C, and D have 20, 50, 60, and 25 units of on-hand inventory. Items A, B, and C use lot-for-lot (L4L) as their lot-sizing technique, while D, E, and F require multiples of 50, 100, and 100, respectively, to be purchased. B has scheduled receipts of 30 units in Period 1. No other scheduled receipts exist. Lead times are one period for Items A, B, and D, and two periods for Items C, E, and F. Gross requirements for A are 20 units in Period 1, 20 units in Period 2, 60 units in Period 6, and 50 units in Period 8. Find the planned order releases for all items.

10. Each unit of A is composed of one unit of B, two units of C, and one unit of D. C is composed of two units of D and three units of E. Items A, C, D, and E have on-hand inventories of 20, 10, 20, and 10 units, respectively. Item B has a scheduled receipt of 10 units in Period 1, and C has a scheduled receipt of 50 units in Period 1. Lot-for-lot (L4L) is used for Items A and B. Item C requires a minimum lot size of 50 units. D and E are required to be purchased in multiples of 100 and 50, respectively. Lead times are one period for Items A, B, and C, and two periods for Items D and E. The gross requirements for A are 30 in Period 2, 30 in Period 5, and 40 in Period 8. Find the planned order releases for all items.

11. The MRP gross requirements for Item A are shown here for the next 10 weeks. Lead time for A is three weeks and set-up cost is $10. There is a carrying cost of $0.01 per unit per week. Beginning inventory is 90 units.

		WEEK								
	1	2	3	4	5	6	7	8	9	10
Gross requirements	30	50	10	20	70	80	20	60	200	50

Use the least total cost or the least unit cost lot-sizing method to determine when and for what quantity the first order should be released.

12. Product A is an end item and is made from two units of B and four of C. B is made of three units of D and two of E. C is made of two units of F and two of E.

    A has a lead time of one week. B, C, and E have lead times of two weeks, and D and F have lead times of three weeks.

    a. Show the bill of materials (product structure tree).

    b. If 100 units of A are required in Week 10, develop the MRP planning schedule, specifying when items are to be ordered and received. There are currently no units of inventory on hand.

13. Product A consists of two units of Subassembly B, three units of C, and one unit of D. B is composed of four units of E and three units of F. C is made of two units of H and three units of D. H is made of five units of E and two units of G.

    a. Construct a simple bill of materials (product structure tree).

    b. Construct a product structure tree using low-level coding.

    c. Construct an indented parts list.

    d. To produce 100 units of A, determine the numbers of units of B, C, D, E, F, G, and H required.

14. The MRP gross requirements for Item ABC are shown here for the next 10 weeks. Lead time for ABC is two weeks, and set-up cost is $9. There is a carrying cost of $0.02 per unit per week. Beginning inventory is 70 units.

	WEEK									
	1	2	3	4	5	6	7	8	9	10
Gross requirements	20	10	15	45	10	30	100	20	40	150

    Use the least total cost or the least unit cost lot-sizing method to determine when and for what quantity the first order should be released.

15. Zhou Audio Products, Inc., produces two AM/FM/CD players for cars. The radio/CD units are identical, but the mounting hardware and finish trim differ. The standard model fits intermediate and full-size cars, and the sports model fits small sports cars.

    Zhou Audio Products handles the production in the following way. The chassis (radio/CD unit) is assembled in Mexico and has a manufacturing lead time of two weeks. The mounting hardware is purchased from a sheet steel company and has a three-week lead time. The finish trim is purchased from a Taiwan electronics company, with offices in Los Angeles, as prepackaged units consisting of knobs and various trim pieces. Trim packages have a two-week lead time. Final assembly time may be disregarded because adding the trim package and mounting are performed by the customer.

    Zhou Audio Products supplies wholesalers and retailers, who place specific orders for both models up to eight weeks in advance. These orders, together with enough additional units to satisfy the small number of individual sales, are summarized in the following demand schedule:

	WEEK							
MODEL	1	2	3	4	5	6	7	8
Standard model				300				400
Standard model					200			100

    There are currently 50 radio/CD units on hand but no trim packages or mounting hardware.

    Prepare a material requirements plan to meet the demand schedule exactly. Specify the gross and net requirements, on-hand amounts, and the planned order release and receipt periods for the radio/CD chassis, the standard trim and sports car model trim, and the standard mounting hardware and the sports car mounting hardware.

CASE 1 | Brunswick Motors, Inc.—An Introductory Case for MRP

Recently, Phil Harris, the production control manager at Brunswick, read an article on time-phased requirements planning. He was curious about how this technique might work in scheduling Brunswick's engine assembly operations and decided to prepare an example to illustrate the use of time-phased requirements planning.

Phil's first step was to prepare a master schedule for one of the engine types produced by Brunswick: the Model 1000 engine. This schedule indicates the number of units of the Model 1000 engine to be assembled each week during the last 12 weeks and is shown below. Next, Phil decided to simplify his requirements planning example by considering only two of the many components that are needed to complete the assembly of the Model 1000 engine. These two components, the gear box and the input shaft, are shown in the product structure diagram shown on the next page. Phil noted that the gear box is assembled by the Subassembly Department and is subsequently sent to the main engine assembly line. The input shaft is one of several component parts manufactured by Brunswick that are needed to produce a gear box subassembly. Thus, levels 0, 1, and 2 are included in the product structure diagram to indicate the three manufacturing stages that are involved in producing an engine: the Engine Assembly Department, the Subassembly Department, and the Machine Shop.

The manufacturing lead times required to produce the gear box and input shaft components are also indicated in the product structure diagram. Note that two weeks are required to produce a batch of gear boxes and that all the gear boxes must be delivered to the assembly line parts stockroom before Monday morning of the week in which they are to be used. Likewise, it takes three weeks to produce a lot of input shafts, and all the shafts that are needed for the production of gear

boxes in a given week must be delivered to the Subassembly Department stockroom before Monday morning of that week.

In preparing the MRP example, Phil planned to use the worksheets shown on the next page and make the following assumptions:

1. Seventeen gear boxes are on hand at the beginning of Week 1, and five gear boxes are currently on order to be delivered at the start of Week 2.
2. Forty input shafts are on hand at the start of Week 1, and 22 are scheduled for delivery at the beginning of Week 2.

Assignment

1. Initially, assume that Phil wants to minimize his inventory requirements. Assume that each order will be only for what is required for a single period. Using the following forms, calculate the net requirements and planned order releases for the gear boxes and input shafts. Assume that lot sizing is done using lot-for-lot.
2. Phil would like to consider the costs that his accountants are currently using for inventory carrying and set-up for the gear boxes and input shafts. These costs are as follows:

PART	COST	
Gear Box	Set-up = $90/order	
	Inventory carrying cost = $2/unit/week	
Input Shaft	Set-up = $45/order	
	Inventory carrying cost = $1/unit/week	

Given the cost structure, evaluate the cost of the schedule from (1). Assume inventory is valued at the end of each week.

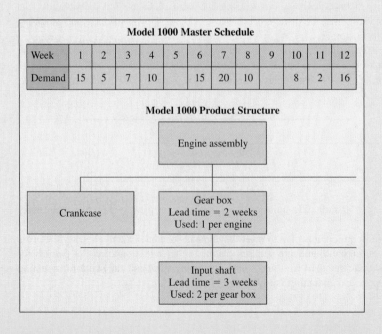

Model 1000 Master Schedule

Week	1	2	3	4	5	6	7	8	9	10	11	12
Demand	15	5	7	10		15	20	10		8	2	16

Model 1000 Product Structure

Engine assembly

Crankcase

Gear box
Lead time = 2 weeks
Used: 1 per engine

Input shaft
Lead time = 3 weeks
Used: 2 per gear box

Engine Assembly Master Schedule

Week	1	2	3	4	5	6	7	8	9	10	11	12
Quantity												

Gear Box Requirements

Week	1	2	3	4	5	6	7	8	9	10	11	12
Gross requirements												
Scheduled receipts												
Projected available balance												
Net requirements												
Planned order release												

Input Shaft Requirements

Week	1	2	3	4	5	6	7	8	9	10	11	12
Gross requirements												
Scheduled receipts												
Projected available balance												
Net requirements												
Planned order release												

CASE 2 Merdeka Gas Grills: Implementing MRP

In the case at the end of Chapter 13 (Case 2), you were introduced to the Merdeka Company. As mentioned, Merdeka manufactures premium gas grills for the North American market. Each of these gas grills requires over 30 separate components. You may also recall that Merdeka used an integrated business system (ERP) software package to manage its purchasing, sales, inventory and production management, and accounting functions. Assume that the ERP software has MRP embedded in it.

Questions:

1. Should every item be controlled using an MRP system? What types of items might you want to manage using the MRP system? Why? What type of items might you not want to manage using the MRP system? Why not?

2. Would you keep safety stock separately for each part? For example, if subassembly C consisted of components A and B, would you have safety stocks for A, B, and C?

3. What characteristics of an item used by Merdeka would make it ideal for a JIT system? For an EOQ system?

This case was written for classroom discussion by Brent Snider and Jaydeep Balakrishnan of the Haskayne School of Business at the University of Calgary. It is based on a real situation.

Footnotes

[1]M. Pycraft, H. Singh, K. Phihlela, N. Slack, S. Chambers, C. Harland, A. Harrison, and R. Johnston, *Operations Management*, Cape Town: Pearson South Africa, 2000, pp.558–560.

Selected Bibliography

Orlicky, J. *Materials Requirements Planning.* 2nd ed. New York: McGraw-Hill, 1994. (This is the classic book on MRP.)

Sheikh, K. *Manufacturing Resource Planning (MRP II) with Introduction to ERP, SCM, and CRM.* New York: McGraw-Hill, 2002.

Vollmann, T. E.; W. L. Berry; D. C. Whybark; and F. R. Jacobs. *Manufacturing Planning and Control Systems for Supply Chain Management.* 5th ed. Burr Ridge, IL: McGraw-Hill, 2004.

PHOTO CREDITS

NAME INDEX

SUBJECT INDEX